COLLINS ESSENTIAL ATLAS

Printed and bound by Wm. Collins Sons & Co. Ltd.
© Copyright Wm. Collins Sons & Co. Ltd. 1975

Wm. Collins Sons & Co. Ltd.
144 Cathedral Street
Glasgow G4 ONB

First published 1975
ISBN 0 00 447064 8

GENERAL MAPS
The symbols used on general maps in this atlas are explained below.

BRITISH ISLES GENERAL MAPS
Additional or variant symbols used on these maps.

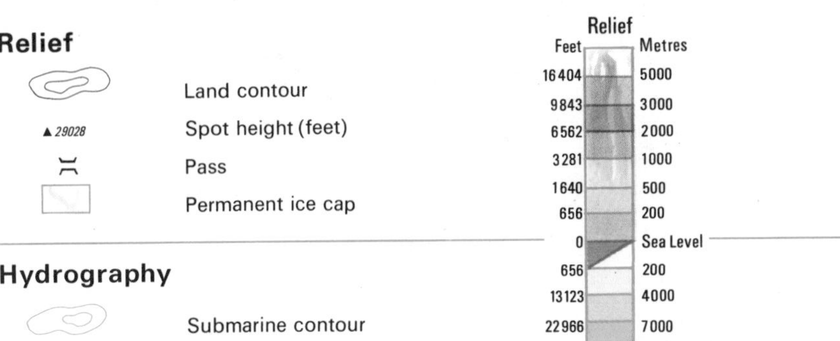

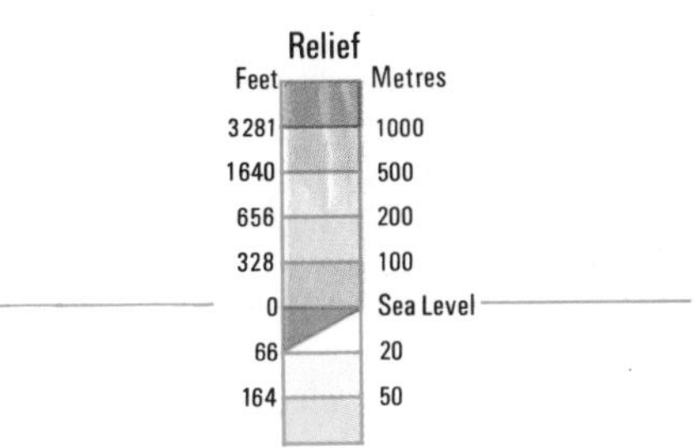

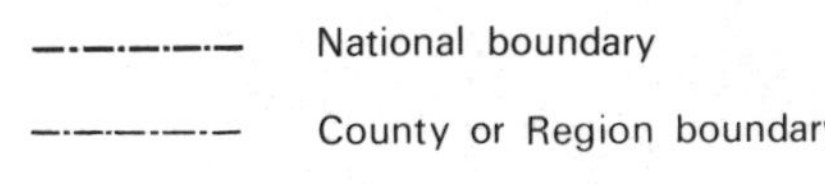

Relief

Land contour	
▲ 29028	Spot height (feet)
	Pass
	Permanent ice cap

Relief

Feet		Metres
16404		5000
9843		3000
6562		2000
3281		1000
1640		500
656		200
0	Sea Level	
656		200
13123		4000
22966		7000

Relief

Feet		Metres
3281		1000
1640		500
656		200
328		100
0	Sea Level	
66		20
164		50

Hydrography

	Submarine contour
• 36200	Ocean depth (feet)
	Reef
	River
	Intermittent river
	Falls/Dam
	Gorge
	Canal
	Lake/Reservoir
	Intermittent lake
	Marsh/Swamp

Communications

Tunnel	Railway
Tunnel	Road
- - - - - - -	Desert track

Access Point	Motorway
	Main road
⊕	International airport
✈	Other airport

Administration

———————	International boundary
– – – – –	Undefined boundary
–·–·–·–	Internal boundary
▨ ◉ ◎ ⊙	National capitals

–·–·–·–	National boundary
–··–··–	County or Region boundary

Settlement

▨	**Calcutta**	Over 1,000,000 inhabitants
◉	**Dortmund**	500,000–1,000,000 inhabitants
◎	Veracruz	100,000–500,000 inhabitants
⊙	Timbuktu	Under 100,000 inhabitants

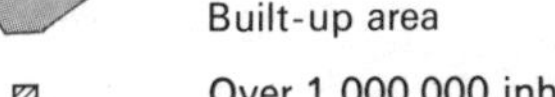

	Built-up area
▨	Over 1 000 000 inhabitants
◉	500 000–1 000 000 inhabitants
◎	100 000–500 000 inhabitants
⊙	25 000–100 000 inhabitants
○	10 000–25 000 inhabitants
•	Under 10 000 inhabitants

Lettering
Various styles of lettering are used in this atlas, each style for a different type of feature.

Physical features	*ALPS*	*Congo Basin*	*Nicobar Islands*	*Mt Cook*
Hydrographic features	*PACIFIC OCEAN*	*Red Sea*	*Lake Erie*	*Amazon*
Country name	CHILE	Internal division	IOWA	Territorial admin.	*(Fr.)*

© Collins ○ Longman Atlases

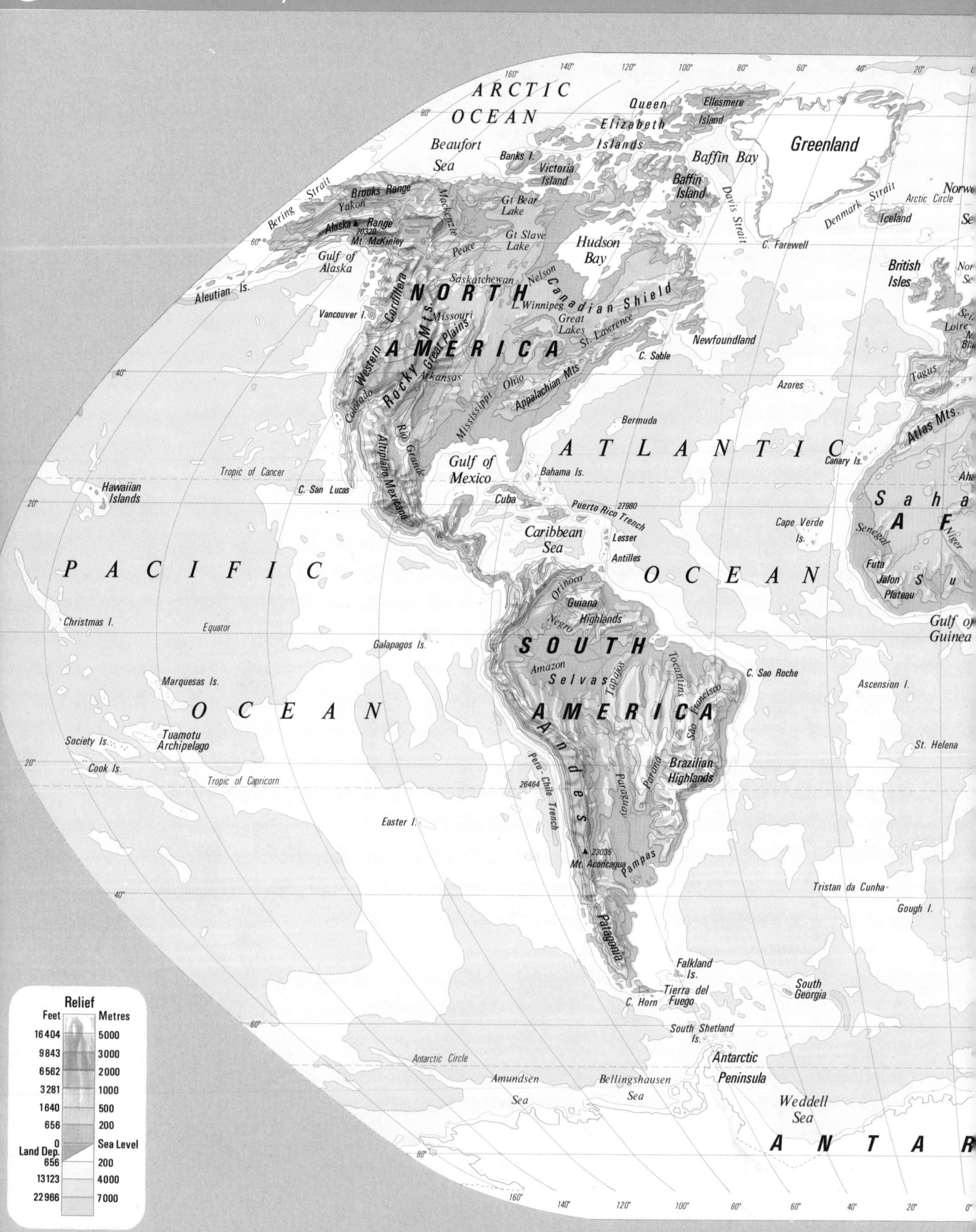

ARCTIC OCEAN

Queen
Elizabeth
Islands

Ellesmere
Island

Greenland

Beaufort
Sea

Banks I.

Victoria
Island

Baffin Bay

Baffin
Island

Norwe

Davis Strait

Denmark Strait

Arctic Circle

Bering Strait

Brooks Range

Yukon

Mackenzie

Gt Bear
Lake

Hudson
Bay

C. Farewell

Iceland

Se

Alaska ▲ Range
20320 Mt. McKinley

Gt Slave
Lake

British
Isles

Nor
Se

Gulf of
Alaska

Peace

Canadian Shield

Sei
Loire
M
Bla

Aleutian Is.

Vancouver I.

Cordillera

Saskatchewan

Nelson

L. Winnipeg

NORTH
AMERICA

Great
Lakes

St. Lawrence

Newfoundland

C. Sable

Azores

Tagus

Western Mts.

Missouri

Rocky Great Plains

Arkansas

Ohio

Appalachian Mts

Atlas Mts.

Colorado

Mississippi

A T L A N T I C

Canary Is.

Rio Grande

Bermuda

Tropic of Cancer

Altiplano Mexicano

C. San Lucas

Gulf of
Mexico

Bahama Is.

Hawaiian
Islands

Cuba

Puerto Rico Trench 27980

Cape Verde
Is.

S a h a
A F
S u

Caribbean
Sea

Lesser
Antilles

O C E A N

Futa
Jalon
Plateau

P A C I F I C

Senegal
Niger

Christmas I.

Equator

Galapagos Is.

Orinoco

Guiana
Highlands

Negro

SOUTH

Gulf of
Guinea

Marquesas Is.

Amazon

Selvas

Tapajos

Tocantins

C. Sao Roche

Ascension I.

O C E A N

Andes

São Francisco

AMERICA

St. Helena

Society Is.

Tuamotu
Archipelago

Peru-Chile Trench

Parana

Brazilian
Highlands

Cook Is.

Tropic of Capricorn

26464

Paraguay

Easter I.

Mt. Aconcagua
▲ 23035

Pampas

Tristan da Cunha

Patagonia

Gough I.

Falkland
Is.

South
Georgia

Tierra del
Fuego

C. Horn

South Shetland
Is.

Antarctic
Peninsula

Antarctic Circle

Amundsen
Sea

Bellingshausen
Sea

Weddell
Sea

80°

A N T A R

Relief

Feet		Metres
16 404		5000
9 843		3000
6 562		2000
3 281		1000
1 640		500
656		200
0		Sea Level
Land Dep.		
656		200
13 123		4000
22 966		7000

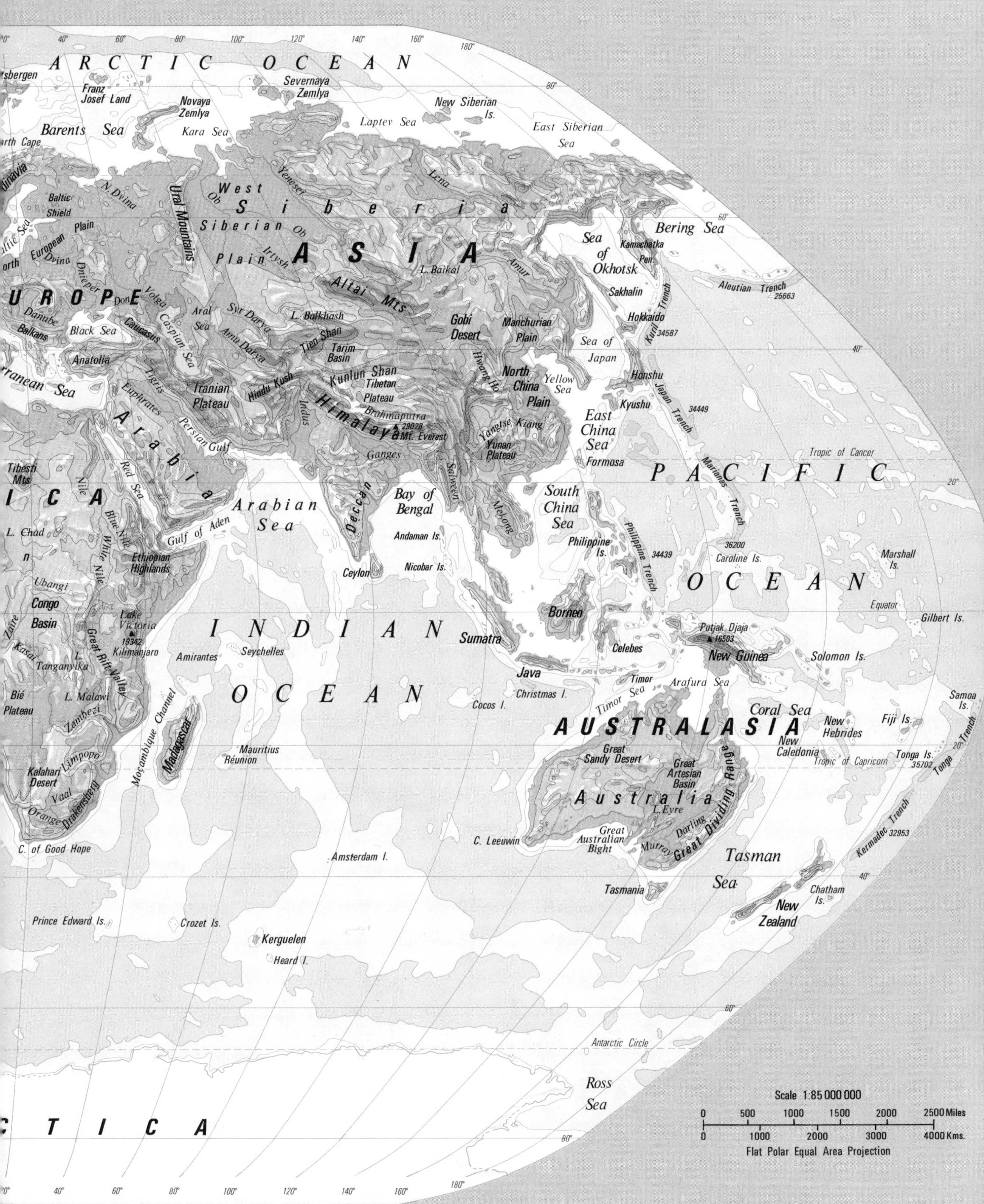

ARCTIC OCEAN

Spitsbergen
Franz
Josef Land
Severnaya
Zemlya
New Siberian
Is.
Novaya
Zemlya
North Cape
Barents Sea
Kara Sea
Laptev Sea
East Siberian
Sea

Scandinavia
Baltic
Shield
N. Dvina
West
Ob
Siberian
Yenesei
Lena
Bering Sea
80°
60°

Baltic
Sea
European
Plain
Ural Mountains
Siberian
Plain
Ob
Irtysh
ASIA
L. Baikal
Amur
Kamchatka
Pen.
Sea
of
Okhotsk
Aleutian Trench
25663

EUROPE
North
Drina
Dnieper
Don
Volga
Caspian Sea
Aral
Sea
L. Balkhash
Altai Mts
Sakhalin
Hokkaido
Kuril Trench
34587
40°

Danube
Balkans
Black Sea
Caucasus
Syr Darya
Amu Darya
Tien Shan
Tarim
Basin
Gobi
Desert
Manchurian
Plain
Sea of
Japan
Honshu
Japan Trench
34449

Mediterranean
Sea
Anatolia
Tigris
Euphrates
Iranian
Plateau
Hindu Kush
Kunlun Shan
Tibetan
Plateau
Hwang Ho
North
China
Plain
Yellow
Sea
East
China
Sea
Kyushu

Arabia
Red Sea
Persian Gulf
Indus
Himalaya
Brahmaputra
29028
▲Mt. Everest
Yangtse Kiang
Yunan
Plateau
Formosa
PACIFIC
Tropic of Cancer
20°

AFRICA
Tibesti
Mts
Nile
Gulf of Aden
Arabian
Sea
Deccan
Ganges
Bay of
Bengal
Salween
Mekong
South
China
Sea
Marianas
Trench
OCEAN

L. Chad
Blue Nile
White Nile
Ethiopian
Highlands
Andaman Is.
Philippine
Is.
Philippine Trench
34439
36200
Caroline Is.
Marshall
Is.

Ubangi
Congo
Basin
Ceylon
Nicobar Is.
Equator
Gilbert Is.

Zaire
Kasai
L.
Tanganyika
Great Victoria
19342
Kilimanjaro
Great Rift Valley
Amirantes
Seychelles
INDIAN
Sumatra
Borneo
Celebes
Putjak Djaja
▲ 16503
New Guinea
Solomon Is.

Bié
Plateau
L. Malawi
Zambezi
Java
Christmas I.
Timor
Sea
Arafura Sea
Coral Sea
New
Hebrides
Samoa
Is.
Fiji Is.

Kalahari
Desert
Vaal
Limpopo
Mozambique Channel
Madagascar
Mauritius
Réunion
OCEAN
Cocos I.
AUSTRALASIA
New
Caledonia
Tropic of Capricorn
Tonga Is.
35702
Tonga Trench

Orange
Drakensberg
C. of Good Hope
Amsterdam I.
C. Leeuwin
Great
Sandy Desert
Australia
Great
Artesian
Basin
L. Eyre
Great Dividing Range
Darling
Murray
Tasman
Sea
Kermadec Trench 32953
40°

Prince Edward Is.
Crozet Is.
Great
Australian
Bight
Tasmania
Chatham
Is.

Kerguelen
New
Zealand

Heard I.

60°

Antarctic Circle

80°
Ross
Sea

ANTARCTICA

Scale 1:85 000 000

0   500   1000   1500   2000   2500 Miles
0   1000   2000   3000   4000 Kms.

Flat Polar Equal Area Projection

40°   60°   80°   100°   120°   140°   160°   180°

© Collins ◇ Longman Atlases

ARCTIC

GREENLAND
(Denmark)

Svalbard
(Norway)

Jan Mayen
(Norway)

N O R W A Y

SWEDEN

Helsi

•Godthaab

ICELAND
Reykjavik □

Faroe Is.
(Den.)

Oslo □

Stockh

U.S.A.
ALASKA

Arctic Circle

•Anchorage

C A N A D A

•Edmonton

Calgary ◎

•Winnipeg

Vancouver ◎
Seattle □

Quebec

Ottawa □
Toronto
Minneapolis ◎◎ St. Paul **Buffalo**
Milwaukee □ **Montreal**
Chicago □ **Detroit** **Boston**
New York
Philadelphia
St. Louis □
Washington

Salt Lake City ◎
Denver □

San Francisco ◎

UNITED STATES
OF AMERICA

Los Angeles ◎

Dallas □

New Orleans
Houston

Halifax

DENMARK
Copenhag
Glasgow ◎
London Bonn EAST
Paris □ GERMANY
Munich
Vienna
Bordeaux ◎ SWITZ Belgrade
FRANCE
Marseille ITALY
Rome □
ANDORRA
PORTUGAL
Madrid □
Lisbon □ SPAIN
Algiers
Tunis
TUNISIA

UNITED
KINGDOM
REPUBLIC
OF
IRELAND

Dublin □

NETH
WEST BELG
L
A

POLA
Pragu
CZECH
H
YUG
ALBANI
GR
Athe

MEDITERRANE

Madeira
(Port.)
Rabat MOROCCO
Canary Is.
(Spain)
El Aaiún
SPANISH
SAHARA

ALGERIA

LIBYA

Tripoli
Ben

Monterrey ◎
Gulf of **Miami** □
Mexico

Bermuda
(Br.)

A T L A N T I C

Azores
(Port.)

O C E A N

Havana □

CUBA

Mexico City □

Revilla Gigedo Is.
(Mex.)

GUATEMALA
Guatemala City ◎
EL SALVADOR

HONDURAS
◎ Tegucigalpa
NICARAGUA
Managua

BELIZE
JAMAICA HAITI

DOMINICAN
REPUBLIC

Caribbean Sea

MAURITANIA

Cape Verde Is.
(Port.)

Nouakchott

MALI

NIGER

CH

Dakar ◎
SENEGAL
GAMBIA
GUINEA BISSAU
Conakry ◎
Freetown
SIERRA LEONE
Monrovia
LIBERIA

Bamako

UPPER
VOLTA Ouagadougou
GUINEA

IVORY
COAST

Abidjan

Niamey

N'Dj

NIGERIA
DAHOMEY
Lagos

Accra

CAMEROON

Yaoundé

Bangui

Tropic of Cancer

M
E
X
I
C
O

San José
COSTA RICA
Panamá City
PANAMA

Caracas □ TRINIDAD

Georgetown
Paramaribo
Cayenne

VENEZUELA

GUYANA
SURINAM
GUIANA (Fr.)

EQUATORIAL
GUINEA
Libreville

GABON

O C E A N

CONGO
Brazzaville

COLOMBIA

Bogotá □

ANGOLA

Kinsh

Equator
Galapagos Is.
(Ecuador)

Quito ◎

ECUADOR

Guayaquil ◎

Manaus

Belém

Luanda

P A C I F I C

P
E
R
U

B R A Z I L

Recife □

Ascension I.
(Br.)

ANGO

Lima □

O C E A N

La Paz

Brasília ◎

St. Helena
(Br.)

BOLIVIA

Belo Horizonte

Tropic of Capricorn

P
A
R
A
G
U
A
Y

Rio de Janeiro
São Paulo

SOUTH
Windhoek
WALVIS BAY
WEST

Asunción

AFRICA

C
H
I
L
E

A
R
G
E
N
T
I
N
A

Pôrto Alegre

Cape Town □

Valparaiso
Santiago □

Rosario
URUGUAY
Montevideo
Buenos Aires

Juan Fernández Is.
(Chile)

Tristan da Cunha
(Br.)

Bahia Blanca

Gough I.
(Br.)

A. : AUSTRIA
BELG. : BELGIUM
CZECH. : CZECHOSLOVAKIA
F. : FR. TERR. OF AFARS AND ISSAS
H. : HUNGARY
L. : LUXEMBOURG
MAL : MALAWI
NETH. : NETHERLANDS
ROM. : ROMANIA
S. : SIKKIM
SWITZ. : SWITZERLAND
YUGO. : YUGOSLAVIA

Falkland Is.
(Br.)

South Georgia
(Br.)

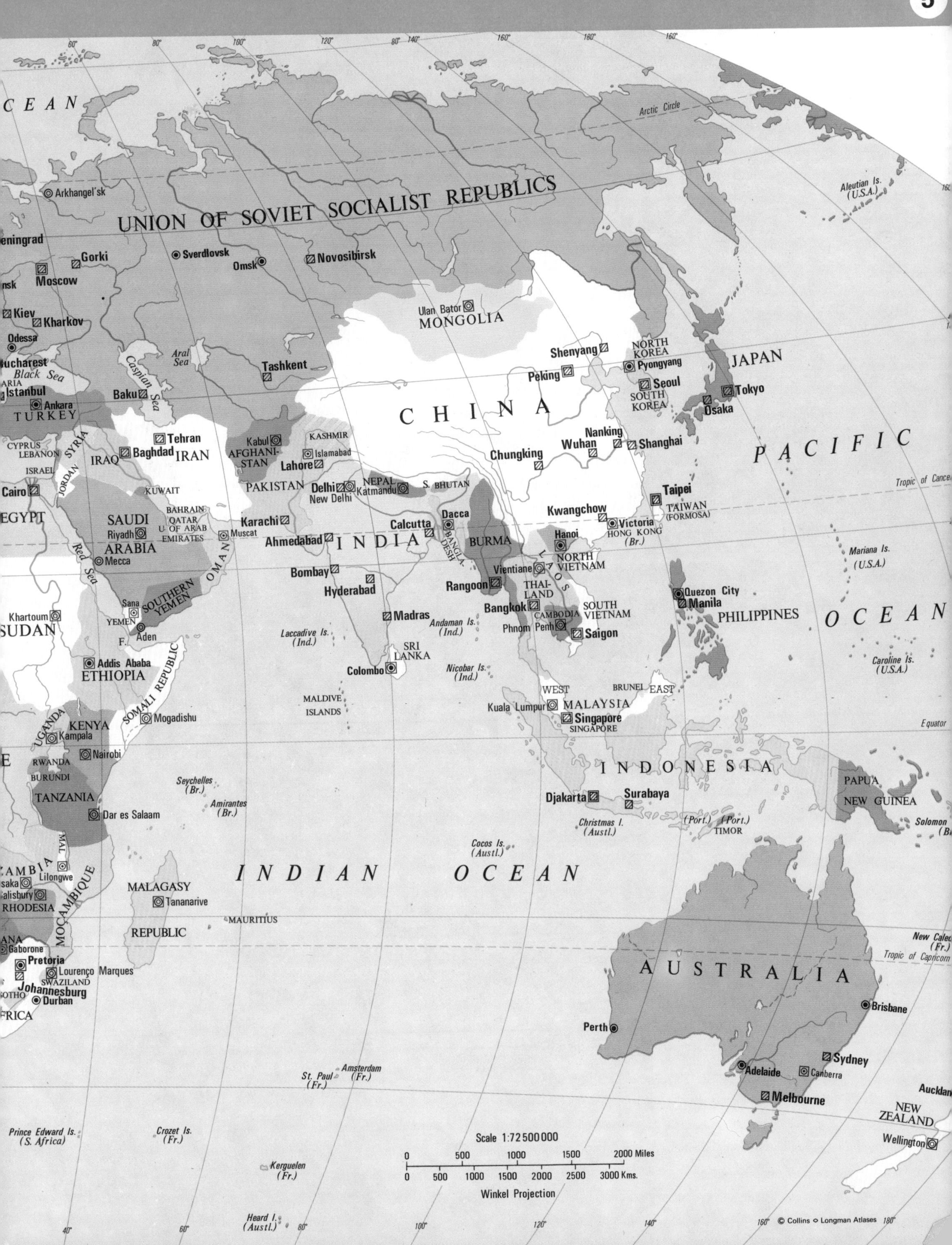

OCEAN

Arctic Circle

○ Arkhangel'sk

UNION OF SOVIET SOCIALIST REPUBLICS

Aleutian Is.
(U.S.A.)

eningrad

Gorki ● Sverdlovsk ● Novosibirsk

nsk
Moscow Omsk ●

● Kiev
● Kharkov Tashkent Ulan Bator ○
MONGOLIA

Odessa
ucharest
Black Sea Aral
Sea Shenyang ☑ NORTH
KOREA JAPAN
stanbul
Ankara Baku ● Caspian
Sea Peking ☑ ● Pyongyang
Seoul ☑ Tokyo
TURKEY Osaka

CYPRUS
LEBANON SYRIA Tehran ☑ KASHMIR
Kabul ○ CHINA Nanking ☑ Shanghai PACIFIC
Baghdad IRAN AFGHANI- ☑ Islamabad Chungking ○ Wuhan
ISRAEL IRAQ STAN Lahore ☑
Cairo PAKISTAN Delhi ☑ NEPAL Tropic of Cancer
EGYPT KUWAIT New Delhi Katmandu S. BHUTAN Kwangchow ○ Taipei ☑
BAHRAIN Karachi ☑ ☑ TAIWAN
SAUDI QATAR Dacca Hanoi ● Victoria ○ (FORMOSA)
Riyadh ○ U. OF ARAB Ahmedabad ☑ BANGLA- BURMA NORTH HONG KONG
ARABIA EMIRATES ○ Muscat INDIA DESH VIETNAM (Br.)
Red ● Mecca OMAN Calcutta ☑ Vientiane ○ Mariana Is.
Sea Bombay ☑ LAOS (U.S.A.)
Khartoum ○ Sana ○ SOUTHERN Hyderabad ☑ Rangoon ☑ THAI- SOUTH Quezon City
SUDAN YEMEN YEMEN LAND VIETNAM ☑ Manila
F. ● Aden Madras ☑ Bangkok ☑ CAMBODIA PHILIPPINES OCEAN
Laccadive Is. Andaman Is. Phnom Penh ○ Saigon ☑ Caroline Is.
● Addis Ababa (Ind.) (Ind.) (U.S.A.)
ETHIOPIA SRI
LANKA WEST BRUNEI EAST
Colombo ☑ Kuala Lumpur ○ MALAYSIA Equator
UGANDA SOMALI REPUBLIC MALDIVE ☑ Singapore
KENYA ● Mogadishu ISLANDS SINGAPORE
Kampala ○
RWANDA ● Nairobi INDONESIA PAPUA
BURUNDI NEW GUINEA
TANZANIA Seychelles Solomon
(Br.) Djakarta ☑ Surabaya (B
● Dar es Salaam Amirantes
(Br.) Christmas I. (Port.) (Port.)
(Austl.) TIMOR

E INDIAN OCEAN
AMBIA Lilongwe MALAGASY
saka ☑ MAURITIUS
alisbury Tananarive ○
RHODESIA REPUBLIC AUSTRALIA
ANA Gaborone New Caled
● Pretoria Lourenço Marques (Fr.)
SWAZILAND Tropic of Capricorn
Johannesburg ● Brisbane
OTHO Durban

Perth ● ● Sydney
Adelaide ● ☑ Canberra

St. Paul Amsterdam
(Fr.) (Fr.) ● Melbourne NEW
Auckland
ZEALAND
Prince Edward Is. Crozet Is. Wellington
(S. Africa) (Fr.)

Scale 1:72 500 000

0 500 1000 1500 2000 Miles
Kerguelen
(Fr.) 0 500 1000 1500 2000 2500 3000 Kms.

Winkel Projection

Heard I. © Collins ○ Longman Atlases
(Austl.)

BEL : BELGIUM
L : LIECHTENSTEIN
LUX : LUXEMBOURG
NETH : NETHERLANDS
SM : SAN MARINO
SWITZ : SWITZERLAND

Scale 1:20 000 000

500 Miles
800 Kms.
400
600
300
400
200
100
200
0
0

Bonne Projection

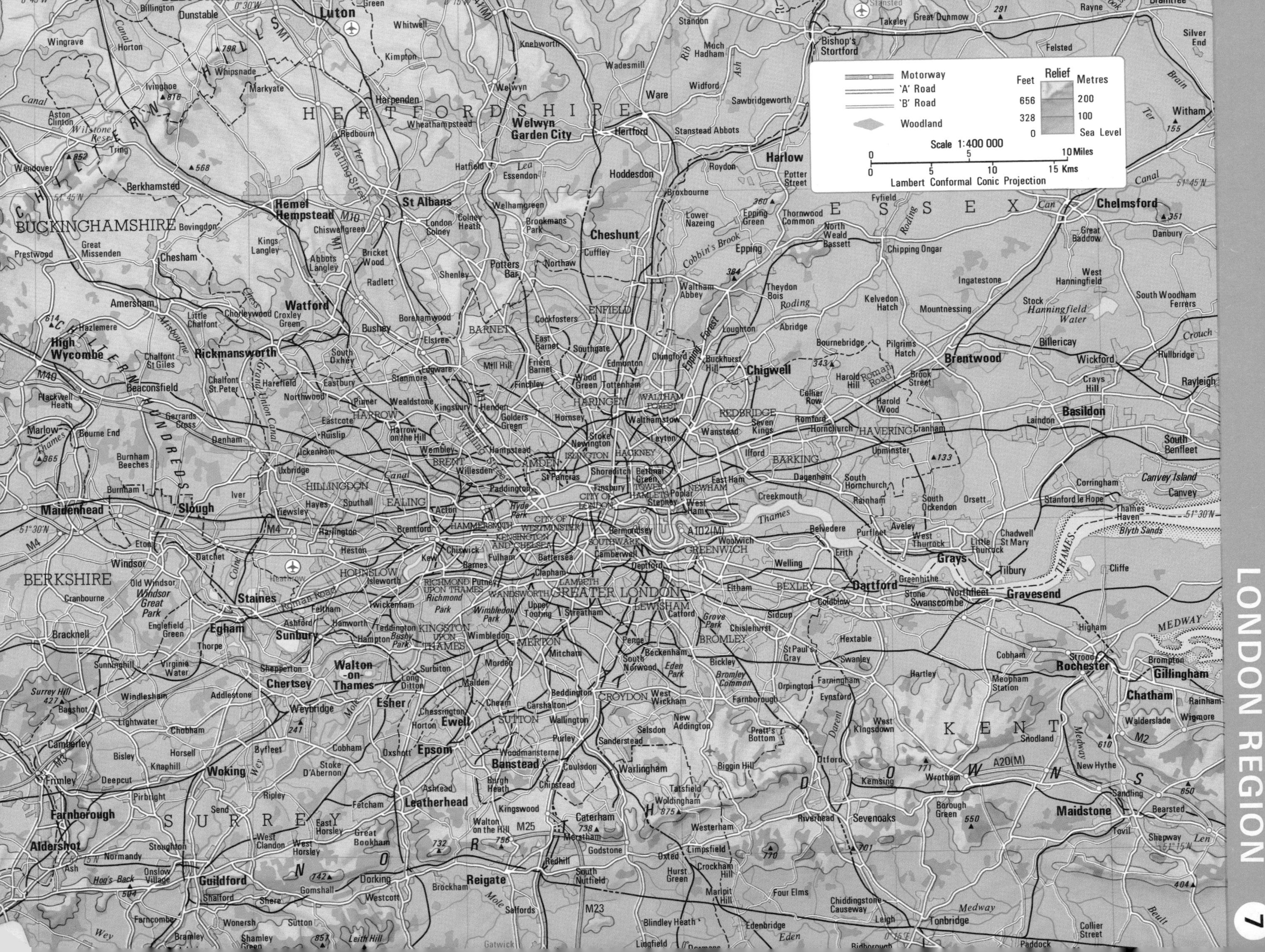
Motorway
'A' Road
'B' Road
Woodland
Relief
Feet
Metres
656
200
328
100
0
Sea Level
Scale 1:400 000
0
5
10 Miles
0
5
10
15 Kms
Lambert Conformal Conic Projection
HERTFORDSHIRE
BUCKINGHAMSHIRE
ESSEX
BERKSHIRE
SURREY
KENT
GREATER LONDON
CHILTERN HUNDREDS
NORTH DOWNS
THAMES
Luton
Welwyn Garden City
Hertford
Harlow
Bishop's Stortford
Chelmsford
St Albans
Hemel Hempstead
Cheshunt
Watford
Rickmansworth
High Wycombe
Chigwell
Brentwood
Basildon
Maidenhead
Slough
Windsor
Staines
Egham
Sunbury
Chertsey
Walton -on- Thames
Esher
Ewell
Epsom
Banstead
Leatherhead
Woking
Guildford
Farnborough
Aldershot
Reigate
Dartford
Gravesend
Grays
Rochester
Chatham
Gillingham
Maidstone
Sevenoaks
Tonbridge

Counties / regions: SALOP, STAFFORDSHIRE, LEICESTERSHIRE, POWYS, WEST MIDLANDS, WARWICKSHIRE, HEREFORD AND WORCESTER, NORTHAMPTONSHIRE, GWENT, GLOUCESTERSHIRE, OXFORDSHIRE, BUCKINGHAMSHIRE, MID GLAMORGAN, SOUTH GLAMORGAN, AVON, WILTSHIRE, BERKSHIRE, SOMERSET, HAMPSHIRE, DORSET, DEVON, SUSSEX, ISLE OF WIGHT

Towns and cities: Shrewsbury, Wellington, Telford, Wolverhampton, Walsall, West Bromwich, Dudley, Warley, Birmingham, Solihull, Coventry, Nuneaton, Bedworth, Rugby, Leicester, Wigston Magna, Hinckley, Market Harborough, Kidderminster, Stourbridge, Halesowen, Bromsgrove, Redditch, Droitwich, Worcester, Royal Leamington Spa, Warwick, Stratford-upon-Avon, Banbury, Northampton, Wellingborough, Ludlow, Leominster, Hereford, Great Malvern, Malvern Hills, Evesham, Vale of Evesham, Broadway, Chipping Norton, Woodstock, Oxford, Aylesbury, Tewkesbury, Gloucester, Cheltenham, Stow on the Wold, Ross-on-Wye, Monmouth, Forest of Dean, Chepstow, Cirencester, Lechlade, Witney, Abingdon, Wantage, Didcot, Wallingford, Henley on Thames, Maidenhead, Reading, Newbury, Cardiff, Penarth, Barry, Newport, Pontypridd, Caerphilly, Cwmbran, Bristol, Avonmouth, Portishead, Clevedon, Weston-super-Mare, Bath, Keynsham, Kingswood, Chippenham, Calne, Swindon, Marlborough, Devizes, Trowbridge, Melksham, Bradford-on-Avon, Frome, Warminster, Basingstoke, Farnborough, Aldershot, Farnham, Andover, Camberley, Wokingham, Bridgwater, Burnham-on-Sea, Minehead, Watchet, Williton, Taunton, Wellington, Glastonbury, Street, Wells, Cheddar, Shepton Mallet, Castle Cary, Somerton, Langport, Yeovil, Sherborne, Salisbury, Winchester, Eastleigh, Southampton, Totton, Romsey, Stockbridge, Alton, Petersfield, Havant, Portsmouth, Gosport, Ryde, Cowes, Newport, Sandown, Shanklin, Ventnor, Bournemouth, Poole, Christchurch, Lymington, Wareham, Dorchester, Weymouth, Bridport, Lyme Regis, Axminster, Honiton, Exmouth, Sidmouth, Crewkerne, Chard, Ilminster, Shaftesbury, Sturminster Newton, Blandford Forum, Wimborne Minster, Ferndown, Ringwood, Chichester, Bognor Regis

Physical features: The Wrekin, The Long Mynd, Clee Hills, Wyre Forest, Clun Forest, Black Mountains, Brecon Beacons, Severn, Wye, Mendip Hills, Quantock Hills, Blackdown Hills, Salisbury Plain, Marlborough Downs, Berkshire Downs, Hampshire Downs, Vale of White Horse, Vale of Berkeley, Bristol Channel, Bridgwater Bay, Chesil Beach, Lyme Bay, Poole Bay, The Needles, The Solent, Spithead, New Forest, Thames, Kennet, Isle of Portland, Isle of Purbeck, St Alban's or St Aldhelm's Hd, St Catherine's Pt, Durlston Hd, Selsey Bill, Bembridge Foreland

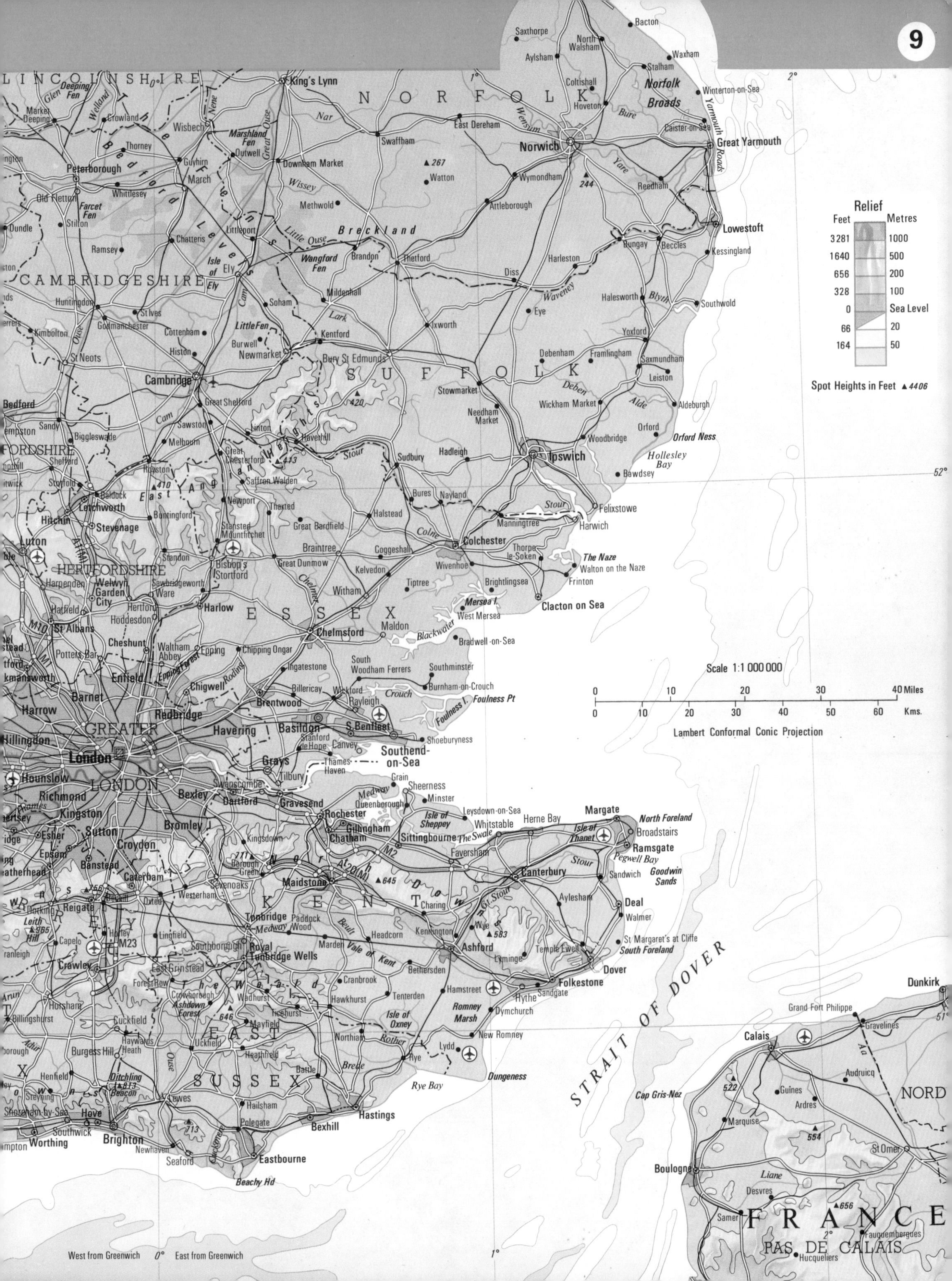
LINCOLNSHIRE
NORFOLK
CAMBRIDGESHIRE
SUFFOLK
HERTFORDSHIRE
ESSEX
GREATER LONDON
KENT
SURREY
EAST SUSSEX
FRANCE
NORD
PAS DE CALAIS
STRAIT OF DOVER
Relief
Feet
Metres
3281
1000
1640
500
656
200
328
100
0
Sea Level
66
20
164
50
Spot Heights in Feet ▲4406
Scale 1:1 000 000
0
10
20
30
40 Miles
0
10
20
30
40
50
60
Kms.
Lambert Conformal Conic Projection
West from Greenwich
0°
East from Greenwich
1°
2°
52°
51°
Saxthorpe
Bacton
North Walsham
Aylsham
Waxham
Stalham
Coltishall
Norfolk Broads
Winterton-on-Sea
Hoveton
Bure
Yarmouth Roads
Caister-on-Sea
Great Yarmouth
King's Lynn
Glen
Deeping Fen
Welland
Market Deeping
Crowland
Wisbech
Nene
Marshland Fen
Outwell
Great Ouse
Nar
Swaffham
East Dereham
Wensum
Norwich
Thorney
Peterborough
Guyhirn
March
Downham Market
▲267
Watton
Wymondham
▲244
Yare
Reedham
Old Fletton
Farcet Fen
Stilton
Whittlesey
Wissey
Methwold
Attleborough
Lowestoft
Bungay
Beccles
Kessingland
Ramsey
Chatteris
Littleport
Little Ouse
Breckland
Brandon
Thetford
Harleston
Isle of Ely
Ely
Wangford Fen
Diss
Waveney
Halesworth
Blyth
Southwold
Huntingdon
St Ives
Godmanchester
Kimbolton
Soham
Mildenhall
Lark
Eye
Cottenham
Little Fen
Ixworth
Yoxford
Kentford
Burwell
Newmarket
Bury St Edmunds
Debenham
Framlingham
Saxmundham
Leiston
St Neots
Histon
Cambridge
Stowmarket
Deben
Alde
Aldeburgh
Bedford
Great Shelford
▲420
Needham Market
Wickham Market
Orford
Orford Ness
Sandy
Biggleswade
Cam
Sawston
Linton
Haverhill
Melbourn
Stour
Sudbury
Hadleigh
Ipswich
Woodbridge
Hollesley Bay
Bawdsey
Shefford
Royston
Great Chesterford
▲413
Saffron Walden
Stotfold
Baldock
▲410
East Anglian Heights
Letchworth
Newport
Thaxted
Bures
Nayland
Felixstowe
Hitchin
Stevenage
Buntingford
Great Bardfield
Halstead
Manningtree
Harwich
Stansted Mountfitchet
Colne
Colchester
Luton
Braintree
Coggeshall
Thorpe le-Soken
The Naze
Walton on the Naze
Standon
Bishop's Stortford
Great Dunmow
Wivenhoe
Frinton
Harpenden
Welwyn Garden City
Sawbridgeworth
Ware
Kelvedon
Tiptree
Brightlingsea
Clacton on Sea
Hatfield
Hertford
Harlow
Chelmer
Witham
Mersea I.
West Mersea
St Albans
Hoddesdon
Maldon
M10
Chelmsford
Blackwater
Bradwell-on-Sea
Cheshunt
Waltham Abbey
Epping
Epping Forest
Chipping Ongar
Potters Bar
South Woodham Ferrers
Southminster
Ingatestone
Enfield
Roding
Chigwell
Billericay
Wickford
Burnham-on-Crouch
Barnet
Brentwood
Rayleigh
Crouch
Foulness I.
Foulness Pt
Harrow
Redbridge
Havering
Basildon
S. Benfleet
Shoeburyness
Hillingdon
Stanford le Hope
Canvey
Southend-on-Sea
London
Grays
Thames Haven
Tilbury
Hounslow
Grain
Swanscombe
Medway
Sheerness
Richmond
Bexley
Dartford
Gravesend
Queenborough
Minster
Kingston
Rochester
Isle of Sheppey
Leysdown-on-Sea
Margate
North Foreland
Whitstable
Herne Bay
Esher
Sutton
Bromley
Gillingham
Chatham
Sittingbourne
The Swale
Isle of Thanet
Broadstairs
Epsom
Croydon
Kingsdown
M2
Faversham
Ramsgate
Pegwell Bay
Banstead
▲771
Borough Green
North Downs
Stour
Caterham
Sevenoaks
Maidstone
A20(M)
▲645
Canterbury
Sandwich
Goodwin Sands
Redhill
Westerham
Oxted
Aylesham
Dorking
Reigate
Charing
Gt. Stour
Deal
Walmer
Leith Hill
▲965
Tonbridge
Paddock Wood
Beult
Kennington
Wye
▲583
Capelo
Horley
M23
Lingfield
Southborough
Royal Tunbridge Wells
Marden
Headcorn
Vale of Kent
Ashford
St Margaret's at Cliffe
South Foreland
Crawley
Temple Ewell
Lyminge
East Grinstead
Bethersden
Dover
Forest Row
Crowborough
Cranbrook
Folkestone
Ashdown Forest
The Weald
Wadhurst
Hawkhurst
Tenterden
Hamstreet
Hythe
Sandgate
Horsham
Ticehurst
Romney Marsh
Dymchurch
Billingshurst
Cuckfield
▲646
Mayfield
Isle of Oxney
Haywards Heath
Uckfield
Northiam
Rother
New Romney
Burgess Hill
Ouse
Heathfield
Rye
Lydd
Adur
Brede
Battle
Rye Bay
Dungeness
Henfield
Ditchling Beacon
▲813
Steyning
Lewes
Hailsham
Hastings
Shoreham-by-Sea
Hove
Polegate
Bexhill
Southwick
Brighton
▲713
Cuckmere
Worthing
Newhaven
Eastbourne
Seaford
Beachy Hd
Cap Gris-Nez
Dunkirk
Grand Fort Philippe
Gravelines
Calais
Aa
▲522
Audruicq
Guînes
Ardres
Marquise
▲554
St Omer
Boulogne
Liane
Desvres
▲656
Samer
Fauquembergues
Hucqueliers

Scale 1:1,000,000

Lambert Conformal Conic Projection

40 Miles

Kms.

IRISH SEA

CARDIGAN BAY

ST GEORGE'S CHANNEL

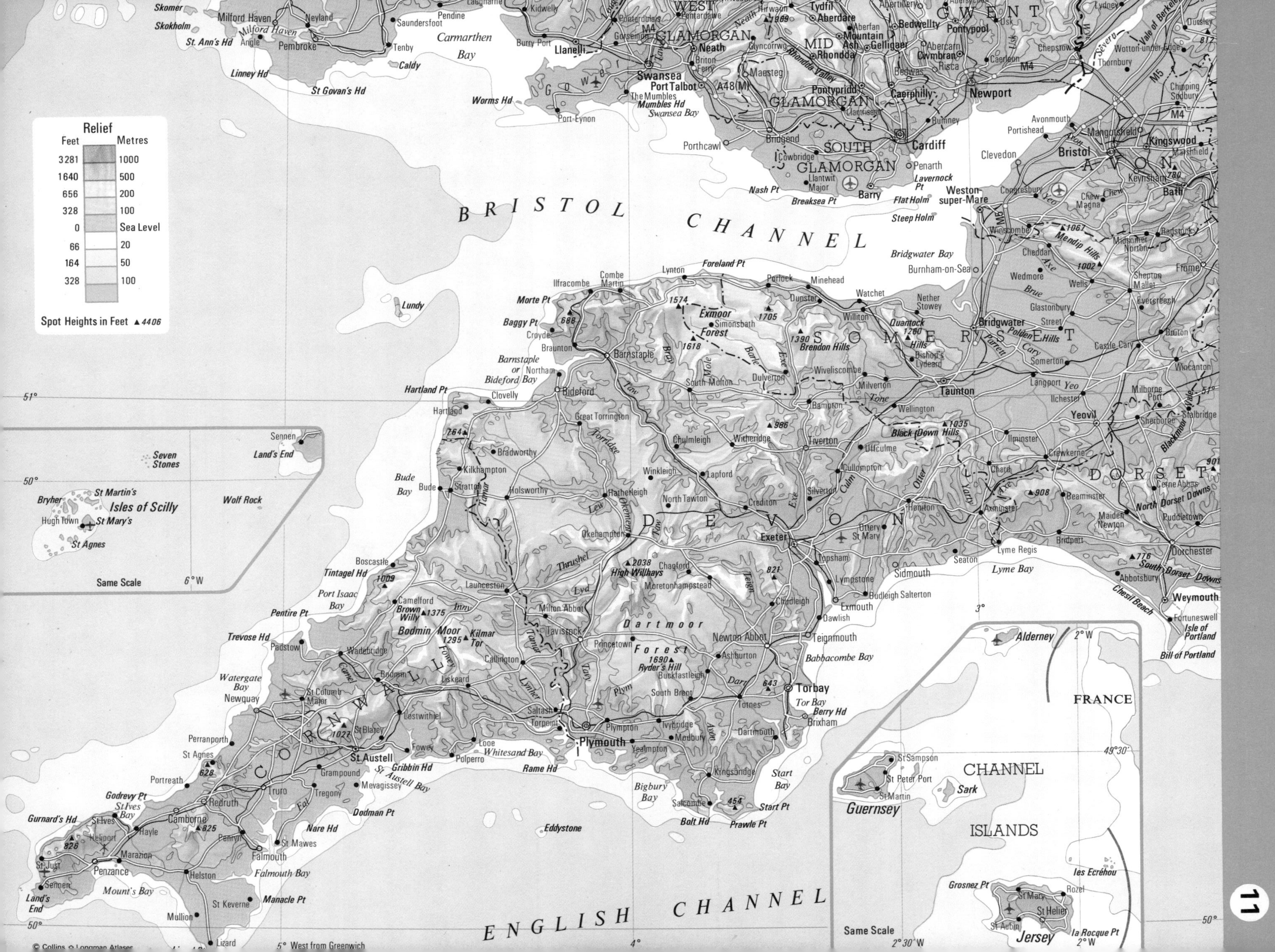
BRISTOL CHANNEL
ENGLISH CHANNEL
CORNWALL
DEVON
SOMERSET
DORSET
AVON
GWENT
SOUTH GLAMORGAN
MID GLAMORGAN
WEST GLAMORGAN
Bristol
Bath
Newport
Cardiff
Swansea
Port Talbot
Neath
Llanelli
Weston super-Mare
Bridgwater
Taunton
Exeter
Torbay
Plymouth
Barnstaple
Bideford
Yeovil
Dorchester
Weymouth
St Austell
Truro
Falmouth
Penzance
Land's End
Lizard
Lundy
Exmoor Forest
Dartmoor Forest
Bodmin Moor
Mendip Hills
Quantock Hills
Brendon Hills
Blackdown Hills
Carmarthen Bay
Swansea Bay
Bridgwater Bay
Barnstaple or Bideford Bay
Lyme Bay
Mount's Bay
Isle of Portland
Bill of Portland
Chesil Beach
Isles of Scilly
St Mary's
St Martin's
St Agnes
Bryher
Hugh Town
Seven Stones
Wolf Rock
Same Scale
FRANCE
CHANNEL ISLANDS
Alderney
Guernsey
Sark
Jersey
St Peter Port
St Helier
Relief
Feet
Metres
3281 1000
1640 500
656 200
328 100
0 Sea Level
66 20
164 50
328 100
Spot Heights in Feet ▲4406
5° West from Greenwich
© Collins-Longman Atlases

DUMFRIES AND GALLOWAY

The Machers

Wigtown Bay
Port William · Whithorn · Garlieston
Isle of Whithorn
Burrow Hd
Kirkcudbright
Kirkcudbright Bay

Silloth · Carlisle · Wetheral
Abbey Town · Wigton · Thursby
SOLWAY FIRTH
Aspatria · Caldbeck
Maryport · Ellen · Kirkoswald
Flimby · Seaton · Keswick
Workington · Cockermouth
Derwent Wr · ▲3053 Skiddaw · Pooley Bridge · Penrith
Whitehaven · Crummock Wr · Keswick · Ullswater
St Bees Hd · Cleator Moor · LAKE · Helvellyn ▲3118
St Bees · Ennerdale Wr · Hawes Water · Shap
Egremont · ▲3210 · Ambleside · Sedbergh
West Water · Scafell Pike · Coniston · Windermere · Kendal
Seascale · DISTRICT · Esk · Broughton in Furness
Bootle · Black Combe ▲1969 · Millom · Grange-over-Sands
CUMBRIA
Barrow-in-Furness · Ulverston · Dalton-in-Furness · Carnforth
Isle of Walney · Morecambe Bay · Morecambe
Hilpsford Pt · Heysham · Lancaster · Ward's Stone ▲1836
Glasson

PENNINES
Alston · Cross Fell ▲2591 · Weardale · Wolsingham
NORTHUMBERLAND · DURHAM
Bishop Auckland · Barnard Castle · Bowes
Middleton in Teesdale · Teesdale · Tees
Brough · Kirkby Stephen · Rogan's Seat ▲2203 · Richmond
Gt Shunner Fell ▲2349 · Swale · Leyburn
Wensleydale · Aysgarth
Whernside ▲2419 · Ingleborough ▲2373 · Pen-y-ghent ▲2231 · Gt Whernside ▲2310
High Bentham · Ingleton · Settle · Hellifield
Clapham · Skipton · Ilkley · Silsden

IRISH SEA

Fleetwood · Rossall Pt · Preesall
Cleveleys · Thornton · Garstang
Blackpool · Great Eccleston · LANCASHIRE
Kirkham · Longridge · Clitheroe · Whalley
Lytham St Anne's · Preston · Gt Harwood · Accrington · Burnley
Southport · Tarleton · Leyland · Chorley · Darwen · Blackburn · Nelson · Colne
Rufford · Adlington · Haslingden · Rawtenstall
Burscough · Horwich · Ramsbottom · Bacup · Todmorden
Ormskirk · Skelmersdale · Wigan · Bolton · Bury · Rochdale
Formby · Maghull · Kirkby · Ashton-in-Makerfield · Farnworth · Radcliffe · Middleton · Oldham
Formby Pt · Crosby · St Helens · Leigh · Atherton · Eccles · MANCHESTER · Ashton-under-Lyne
Liverpool Bay · Bootle · Prescot · Newton-le-Willows · Salford · Hyde
MERSEYSIDE · Wallasey · Liverpool · Warrington · Urmston · Sale · Stockport · Marple
Hoylake · Birkenhead · Widnes · Runcorn · Altrincham · Cheadle · Wilmslow
West Kirby · Bebington · Mersey · Frodsham · Knutsford · Whaley Bridge

GREATER MANCHESTER

The Skerries · Cemaes Bay
Carmel Hd · Amlwch
Holyhead Bay · Llanerchymedd · Red Wharf Bay · Benllech · Puffin I.
Holyhead · ANGLESEY · Gt Ormes Hd · Llandudno · Prestatyn · Rhyl · Flint
Holy I. · Llangefni · Conway Bay · Colwyn Bay · Abergele · Holywell
Rhosneigr · Beaumaris · Conway · Penmaenmawr · Denbigh · Mold · Buckley · Chester
Aberffraw · Menai Bridge · Bangor · Bethesda · Llanrwst · Ruthin · CHESHIRE
Menai Str · Port Dinorwic · Llanfairfechan · Kelsall · Winsford
Caernarfon · Llanberis · Betws-y-Coed · Northwich · Middlewich · Macclesfield
Caernarvon Bay · Snowdon ▲3560 · Tarporley · Sandbach · Buxton
Nefyn · Pen-y-groes · CLWYD · Farndon · Crewe · Congleton · Bakewell
GWYNEDD · Blaenau Ffestiniog · Corwen · Nantwich · Alsager · Biddulph · Leek
Tudweiliog · Ffestiniog · Carnedd y Filiast ▲2194 · Bala · Rhosllanerchrugog · Ruabon · Newcastle-under-Lyme · Stoke-on-Trent
Lleyn Peninsula · Criccieth · Portmadoc · Llangollen · Wrexham · Audlem
Pwllheli · Tremadoc Bay · Harlech · Y Llethr ▲2475 · Overton · Whitchurch · Market Drayton · Trentham · Upper Tean
Abersoch · Aran Fawddwy ▲2970 · Llandrillo · Berwyn ▲2713 · Ellesmere · Wem · Hodnet · Eccleshall · STAFFORDSHIRE
Barmouth · Dolgellau · Lake Vyrnwy · Whittington · West Felton · Harmerhill · Stafford · Burton upon
Fairbourne · Cader Idris ▲2927 · POWYS · Oswestry · SALOP · Newport · Wellington · Stone · Rugeley
Severn · Shrewsbury · Cannock

ISLE OF MAN

Pt of Ayre
Jurby Hd · Andreas · Bride
Ramsey Bay · Ramsey
Kirk Michael · Maughold Hd
Peel · Snaefell ▲2034 · Laxey · Clay Hd
Crosby · ISLE OF MAN
▲1585 · Douglas
South Barrule · Castletown
Port Erin · Langness

West from Greenwich 0° East from Greenwich

Scale 1:1 000 000

| 0 | 10 | 20 | 30 | 40 Miles |

| 0 | 10 | 20 | 30 | 40 | 50 | 60 | Kms. |

Lambert Conformal Conic Projection

Relief

Feet		Metres
3281		1000
1640		500
656		200
328		100
0		Sea Level
66		20
164		50
328		100

Spot Heights in Feet ▲ 4406

N O R T H

S E A

South Shields
TYNE AND
Sunderland
WEAR
Houghton-le-Spring
Seaham
Hetton
le Hole
Easington
Peterlee
Wingate
Sedgefield
Billingham
Hartlepool
Tees Bay
Stockton-on-Tees
Redcar CLEVELAND
Marske-by-the-Sea
Middlesbrough
Saltburn-by-the-Sea
Eston
Brotton
Thornaby-on-Tees
Guisborough
Loftus
Stokesley
Whitby
Broughton
Cleveland Hills
Esk
Sleights
Robin Hood's Bay
▲ 1489
North York Moors
Hambleton Hills
Dove
Fylingdales
Kirkbymoorside
Scalby
Helmsley
Pickering
Scarborough
Thirsk
Vale of Pickering
Derwent
Filey
Hovingham
Easingwold
Malton
Staxton
Norton
Flamborough
Boroughbridge
Flamborough Head
Bridlington
Sledmere
Burton Agnes
Bridlington Bay
Knaresborough
Shipton
Great Driffield
Harrogate
Nidd
Stamford Bridge
Hutton Cranswick
Wetherby
Wharfe
York
Wilberfoss
Pocklington
Middleton on the Wolds
Hornsea
Tadcaster
Ouse
Market Weighton
Leven
Selby
Riccall
Holme upon Spalding Moor
Beverley
Aldbrough
HUMBERSIDE
Cawood
Kingston upon Hull
Hambleton
Howden
South Cave
Cottingham
Hessle
Hedon
Withernsea
Castleford
Snaith
Goole
Ouse
Whitton
New Holland
Keyingham
Patrington
Pontefract
Garthorpe
Barton-upon-Humber
Wakefield
Winterton
Humber
Easington
Askern
Thorne
Immingham
Crowle
Grimsby
Spurn Hd
Doncaster
Scunthorpe
Great Coates
Cleethorpes
Isle of Axholme
Brigg
Rotherham
Bawtry
Caistor
Tetney
▲ 550
North Somercotes
Saltfleet
Gainsborough
Market Rasen
Louth
Worksop
East Retford
Dunholme
Wragby
Mablethorpe
Sutton on Sea
East Markham
▲ 496
Burwell
Chapel St Leonards
Lincoln
Bardney
Horncastle
Lincoln Edge
LINCOLNSHIRE
Spilsby
Burgh le Marsh
Skegness
Mansfield
Woodhall Spa
Newark-on-Trent
Navenby
Metheringham
Coningsby
Wainfleet All Saints
Gibraltar Pt
Southwell
North Kyme
Wrangle
Holland Fen
Holkham Bay
Blakeney Pt
Sheringham
Nottingham
Sleaford
Heckington
Boston
Cromer
West Bridgford
Long Bennington
THE WASH
Hunstanton
Burnham Market
Wells-next-the-Sea
Holt
Grantham
Bottesford
Dennington
Kirton
Heacham
Docking
▲ 293
Mundesley
Bingham
Folkingham
Dersingham
Saxthorpe
North Walsham
Keyworth
Waltham on the Wolds
Bourne
Long Sutton
Sandringham
Fakenham
Aylsham
Melton Mowbray
Colsterworth
Spalding
Holbeach
Sutton Bridge
King's Lynn
East Dereham
Coltishall
Deeping Fen
NORFOLK
LEICESTERSHIRE
Loughborough
Coalville

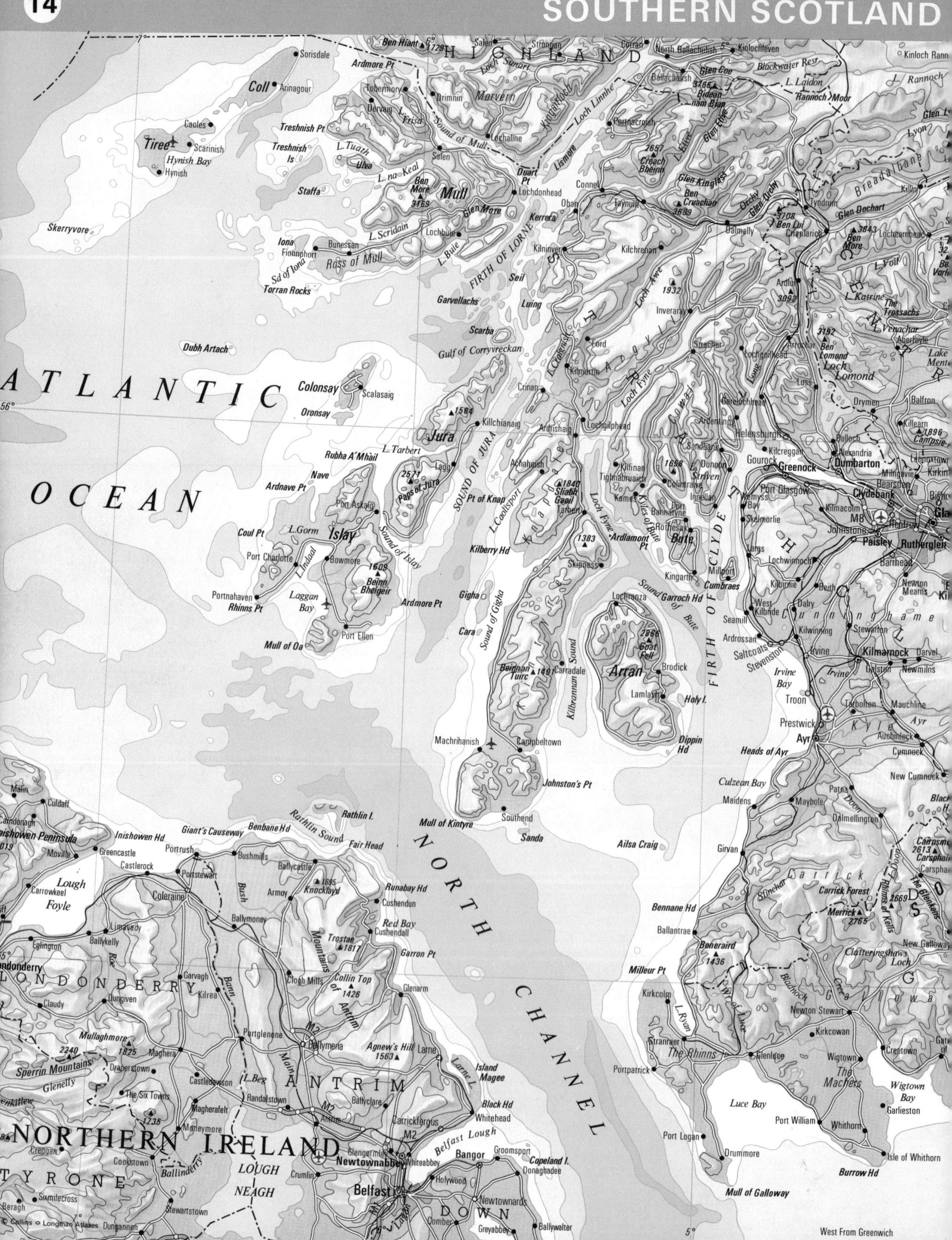

ATLANTIC

OCEAN

NORTH CHANNEL

NORTHERN IRELAND

West From Greenwich

© Collins · Longman Atlases

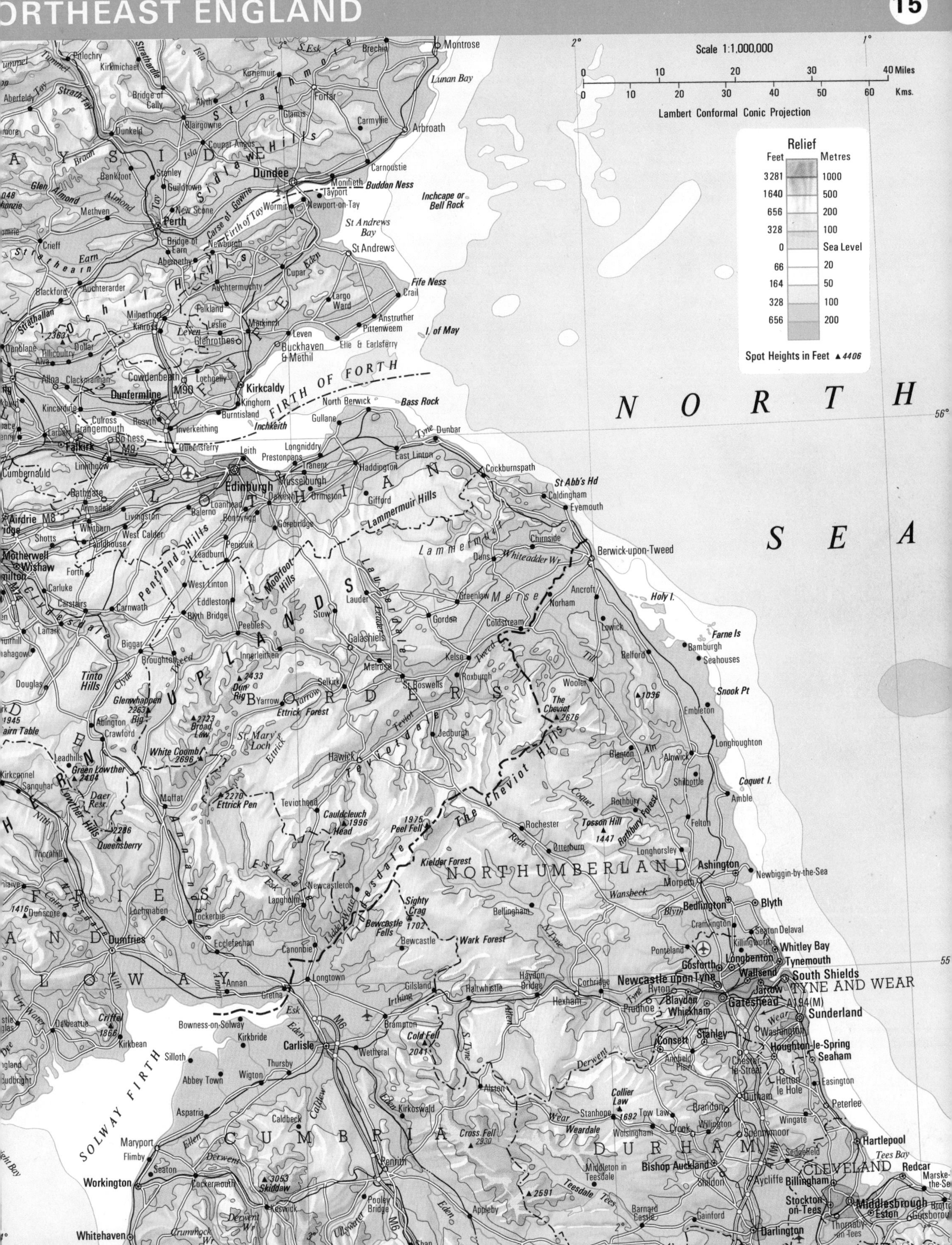
Scale 1:1,000,000
0 10 20 30 40 Miles
0 10 20 30 40 50 60 Kms.
Lambert Conformal Conic Projection
Relief
Feet
Metres
3281 1000
1640 500
656 200
328 100
0 Sea Level
66 20
164 50
328 100
656 200
Spot Heights in Feet ▲4406
NORTH SEA
Montrose
Lunan Bay
Brechin
Pitlochry
Kirkmichael
Kirriemuir
Forfar
Glamis
Alyth
Blairgowrie
Dunkeld
Carmyllie
Arbroath
Coupar Angus
Carnoustie
Dundee
Monifieth
Buddon Ness
Tayport
Newport-on-Tay
Wormit
Inchcape or Bell Rock
St Andrews Bay
St Andrews
Perth
Bridge of Earn
Newburgh
Abernethy
Cupar
Auchtermuchty
Crieff
Auchterarder
Blackford
Fife Ness
Crail
Largo Ward
Anstruther
Pittenweem
I. of May
Milnathort
Kinross
Falkland
Leslie
Glenrothes
Markinch
Leven
Buckhaven & Methil
Elie & Earlsferry
FIRTH OF FORTH
Dollar
Tillicoultry
Alva
Alloa
Clackmannan
Cowdenbeath
Lochgelly
Kirkcaldy
Kinghorn
Burntisland
Dunfermline
Kincardine
Culross
Grangemouth
Rosyth
Inverkeithing
Inchkeith
North Berwick
Bass Rock
Gullane
Falkirk
Bo'ness
Queensferry
Leith
Longniddry
Prestonpans
Tranent
Haddington
East Linton
Dunbar
Linlithgow
Cumbernauld
Edinburgh
Musselburgh
Dalkeith
Ormiston
Gifford
Cockburnspath
St Abb's Hd
Coldingham
Eyemouth
Bathgate
Armadale
Livingston
Balerno
Loanhead
Bonnyrigg
Gorebridge
Lammermuir Hills
Airdrie
Whitburn
West Calder
Shotts
Fauldhouse
Penicuik
Pentland Hills
Leadburn
Chirnside
Berwick-upon-Tweed
Motherwell
Wishaw
Forth
Moorfoot Hills
Duns
Whiteadder Wr.
Carluke
Carstairs
Carnwath
West Linton
Eddleston
Lauder
Greenlaw
Ancroft
Norham
Holy I.
Lanark
Blyth Bridge
Peebles
Stow
Gordon
Coldstream
Lowick
Farne Is
Bamburgh
Seahouses
Biggar
Broughton
Innerleithen
Galashiels
Kelso
Belford
Melrose
Roxburgh
Wooler
Douglas
Tinto Hills
Selkirk
St Boswells
The Cheviot 2676
Snook Pt
Dun Rig
Yarrow
Ettrick Forest
Abington
Crawford
Broad Law 2723
Jedburgh
Embleton
St Mary's Loch
White Coomb 2696
Hawick
Longhoughton
Alnwick
Leadhills
Green Lowther 2404
Sanquhar
Kirkconnel
Daer Resr.
Ettrick Pen
Moffat
Teviothead
Cauldcleuch Head 1996
Peel Fell 1975
Rochester
Rothbury
Shilbottle
Coquet I.
Amble
Felton
Tosson Hill 1447
Otterburn
Longhorsley
Queensberry
Thornhill
Kielder Forest
NORTHUMBERLAND
Ashington
Newbiggin-by-the-Sea
Morpeth
Newcastleton
Langholm
Sighty Crag 1702
Bedlington
Blyth
Lochmaben
Lockerbie
Bellingham
Cramlington
Seaton Delaval
Whitley Bay
Dumfries
Ecclefechan
Canonbie
Bewcastle
Bewcastle Fells
Wark Forest
Ponteland
Killingworth
Longbenton
Tynemouth
Gosforth
Newcastle upon Tyne
Wallsend
South Shields
TYNE AND WEAR
Jarrow
Gateshead
Sunderland
Annan
Gretna
Longtown
Gilsland
Haltwhistle
Haydon Bridge
Hexham
Corbridge
Ryton
Prudhoe
Blaydon
Whickham
Washington
Bowness-on-Solway
Kirkbride
Carlisle
Brampton
Wetheral
Cold Fell 2041
Consett
Stanley
Houghton-le-Spring
Seaham
Criffel 1866
Dalbeattie
Kirkbean
Silloth
Abbey Town
Wigton
Thursby
Annfield Plain
Chester-le-Street
Hetton le Hole
Easington
SOLWAY FIRTH
Alston
Durham
Peterlee
Collier Law 1692
Aspatria
Caldbeck
Kirkoswald
Stanhope
Tow Law
Brandon
Willington
Wingate
Wolsingham
Crook
Spennymoor
Weardale
Maryport
Flimby
CUMBRIA
Cross Fell 2930
DURHAM
Hartlepool
Sedgefield
Tees Bay
Seaton
Workington
Cockermouth
Penrith
Middleton in Teesdale
Bishop Auckland
Shildon
Aycliffe
Billingham
CLEVELAND
Redcar
Skiddaw 3053
Stockton on-Tees
Middlesbrough
Eston
Keswick
Pooley Bridge
Appleby
Barnard Castle
Gainford
Darlington
Thornaby-on-Tees
Whitehaven
Shap
NORTH SEA

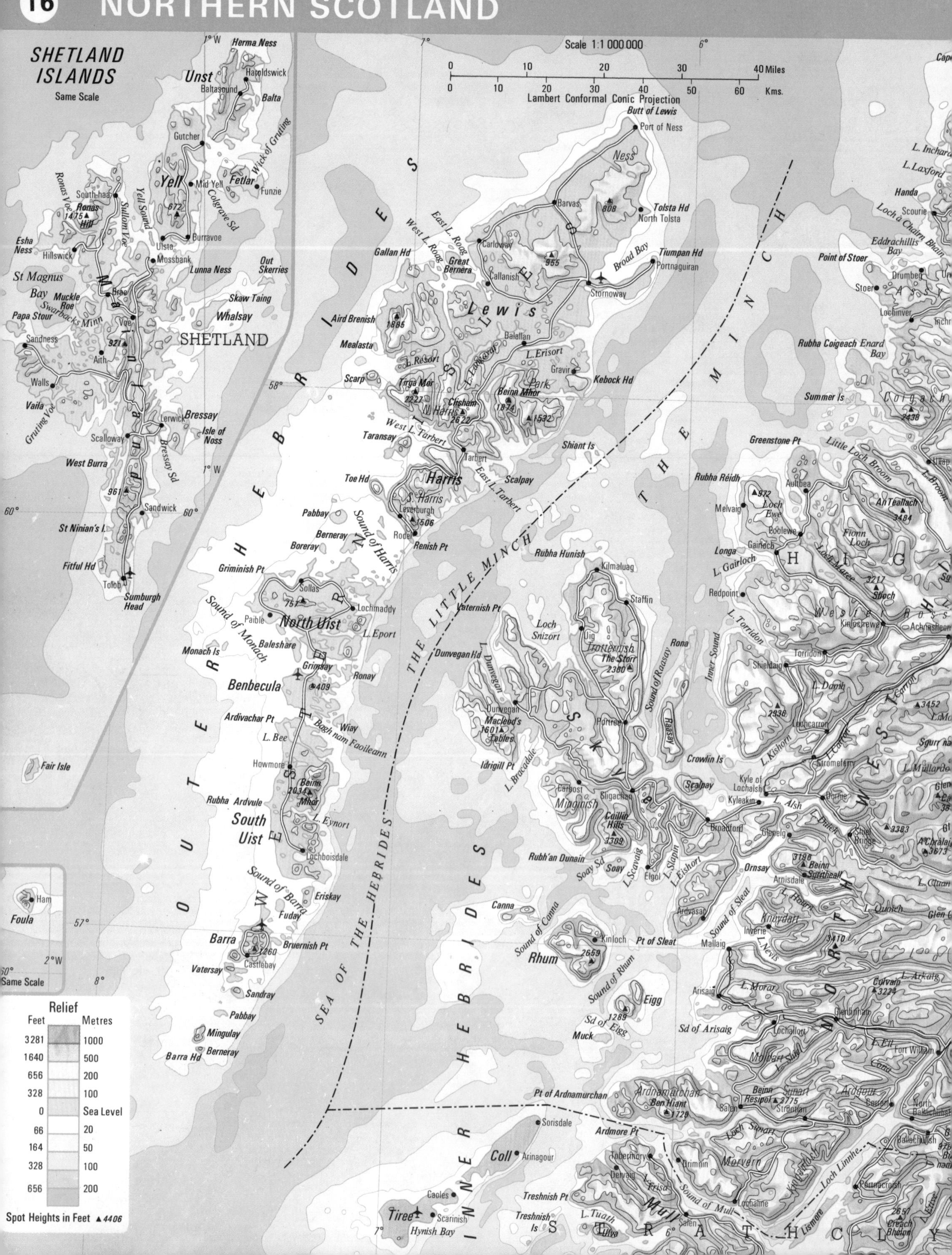

SHETLAND ISLANDS
Same Scale

Herma Ness
Unst
Haroldswick
Baltasound
Balta

Gutcher
Yell
Mid Yell
Fetlar
Funzie
Wick of Gruting
South-haa
Ronas
1475
Hill
Colgrave Sd
Burravoe
Esha
Ness
Ulsta
Mossbank
Lunna Ness
Out
Skerries
St Magnus
Bay
Muckle
Roe
Swarbacks Minn
Brae
Skaw Taing
Papa Stour
Voe
Whalsay
Sandness
Aith
321
SHETLAND
Walls
Vaila
Lerwick
Bressay
Isle of
Noss
Gruting Voe
West Burra
961
Scalloway
Bressay Sd
St Ninian's I.
Sandwick
Fitful Hd
Toloб
Sumburgh
Head

Ham
Foula

Fair Isle

Relief
Feet	Metres
3281	1000
1640	500
656	200
328	100
0	Sea Level
66	20
164	50
328	100
656	200

Spot Heights in Feet ▲ 4406

Scale 1:1 000 000

0 10 20 30 40 Miles

0 10 20 30 40 50 60 Kms.

Lambert Conformal Conic Projection

Butt of Lewis
Port of Ness
Ness
Barvas
808
Tolsta Hd
North Tolsta
955
Carloway
Broad Bay
Tiumpan Hd
Gallan Hd
Great
Bernera
Callanish
Stornoway
Portnaguiran
Aird Brenish
Balallan
3485
Lewis
L. Erisort
Mealasta
L. Resort
Gravir
Scarp
Tirga Mòr
2227
Clisham
2622
Park
Beinn Mhor
1874
Kebock Hd
N. Harris
1532
West L. Tarbert
Taransay
Tarbert
Scalpay
Shiant Is
Harris
East L. Tarbert
Toe Hd
S. Harris
Leverburgh
1506
Renish Pt
Rodel
Pabbay
Berneray
Boreray
Rubha Hunish
Griminish Pt
Kilmaluag
Sollas
Staffin
751
Vaternish Pt
Lochmaddy
Uig
North Uist
L. Eport
Trotternish
The Storr
2360
Paible
Loch
Snizort
Rona
Monach Is
Baleshare
Grimsay
Ronay
Dunvegan Hd
Benbecula
409
Wiay
Dunvegan
Ardivachar Pt
L. Bee
Macleod's
Tables
1601
Idrigill Pt
Howmore
L. Bracadale
Beinn
2034
Mhor
Rubha Ardvule
Carbost
L. Eynort
Mingnish
South Uist
Portree
Lochboisdale
Cuillin
Hills
3309
Sound of Barra
Eriskay
Rubh'an Dunain
Fuday
Soay Sd
Soay
Canna
Barra
1260
Castlebay
Bruernish Pt
Vatersay
Sandray
Sound of Canna
Pabbay
Kinloch
Mingulay
Berneray
Rhum
2659
Barra Hd
Sound of Rhum
Eigg
Sd of Eigg
1289
Muck

Pt of Ardnamurchan
Sorisdale
Ardmore Pt
Coll
Arinagour
Ben Hiant
729
Caoles
Tiree
Treshnish Pt
Treshnish
Is
Scarinish
Hynish Bay
L. Tuath
Ulva

Geographic labels (outer seas / regions)
OUTER HEBRIDES
THE MINCH
THE LITTLE MINCH
SKYE
SEA OF THE HEBRIDES
INNER HEBRIDES
Sound of Harris
Sound of Monach

60°
58°
57°
2°W
1°W
7°
6°

L. Inchard
L. Laxford
Handa
Scourie
Loch à Chairn Bhain
Eddrachillis
Bay
Point of Stoer
Drumbeg
Stoer
Lochinver
Rubha Coigeach Enard
Bay
Summer Is
2438
Greenstone Pt
Little Loch Broom
Rubha Réidh
An Teallach
Melvaig
972
Loch
Ewe
3484
Poolewe
Fionn
Loch
Longa
Gairloch
L. Gairloch
Redpoint
L. Torridon
Slioch
3217
Kinlochewe
Torridon
Achnasheen
Shieldaig
L. Damh
2936
3452
Applecross
Lochcarron
Sgurr a
Crowlin Is
L. Kishorn
Stromeferry
Scalpay
Kyle of
Lochalsh
3383
Kyleakin
A'Chralaig
3673
Broadford
Glenelg
Shiel
Bridge
9190
Beinn
Sgritheall
Elgol
L. Slapin
L. Eishort
Ornsay
Arnisdale
Ardvasar
Sound of Sleat
Knoydart
Inverie
L. Quoich
Pt of Sleat
Mallaig
L. Nevis
3410
Arisaig
L. Morar
Glenfinnan
Culvain
3224
L. Arkaig
Lochailort
L. Eil
Fort William
Moidart
Beinn
Resipol
2775
Strontian
Ardgour
Ardnamurchan
Morvern
Tobermory
Aros
Sound of Mull
Loch Linnhe
Salen
Lochaline
MULL
STRATHCLYDE
HIGHLAND
WESTER ROSS

8°
7°
2°W
60°
Same Scale

PENTLAND FIRTH

Brough Ness
Muckle Skerry
Dunnet Hd
Stroma
John O' Groats
Duncansby Hd
Dunnet Bay
Dunnet

ORKNEY ISLANDS
Same Scale

Mull Hd
Noup Hd
Papa Westray
North Ronaldsay
N. Ronaldsay Firth
Pierowall
The North Sound
Start Point
Westray
Westray Firth
Sanday
Sacquoy Hd
Eday
Sanday Sound
Rousay
Egilsay
Stronsay
Brough Hd
Eynhallow Sd
Wyre
Gairsay
Stronsay Firth
Shapinsay
Mainland
Auskerry
ORKNEY
Shapinsay Sd
Stromness
Ward Hill 881
Kirkwall
Mull Hd
Hoy Sd
Skaill
Ward Hill 1565
Quoyness
St Mary's
Copinsay
Rora Hd
Scapa Flow
Burray
Hoy
Flotta
St Margaret's Hope
Hurliness
S. Walls
South Ronaldsay
59°
58°
PENTLAND FIRTH
Dunnet Hd
Stroma
John O' Groats
Duncansby Hd
Dunnet
3° W

Whiten Hd
Durness
L. Eriboll
Ben Hutig 1338
Strathy Pt
Strathy
Portskerra
Dounreay
Thurso
Dunnet Bay
Dunnet
Kyle of Tongue
Bettyhill
Thurso
Halkirk
L. Watten
Reiss
Sinclair's Bay
Noss Hd
Tongue
L. Hope
Ben Hope 3042
L. Loyal
Ben Loyal 2504
Strathnaver
Beinn nam Bad Mor 952
Strath Halladale
Wick
Wick
Ben Hee 2864
Altnaharra
L. Naver
Ben Klibreck 3154
Ben Griam More 1936
942
Kinbrace
Lybster
Morven 2313
Dunbeath
Strath of Kildonan
Berriedale
Beinn Dhorain 2060
Helmsdale
L. Shin
Ben Horn 1706
Brora
Lairg
Brora
Golspie
Bonar Bridge
Dornoch
Oykel Bridge
Oykel
Dornoch Firth
Tarbat Ness
2302
Carron
Portmahomack
Tain
Beinn Tharsuinn 2270
Hill of Fearn
Easter Ross
MORAY FIRTH
L. Morie
Alness
Ben Wyvis 3429
N. Glass
Invergordon
Cromarty
Garve
Evanton
Cromarty Firth
Loch Luichart
Strathpeffer
Dingwall
Fortrose
Black Isle
Conon
Muir of Ord
Moray Firth
Glen Orrin
Beauly F.
Burghead
Lossiemouth
Spey Bay
Portknockie
Cullen
Portsoy
Banff
Macduff
Troup Hd
Rosehearty
Kinnairds Hd
Fraserburgh
Findhorn
Buckie
Garmouth
Elgin
Fochabers
Knock Hill 1409
New Pitsligo
Strichen
Rattray Hd
Beauly
Nairn
Forres
Rothes
Keith
Turriff
Cuminestown
Mintlaw
Ugie
Peterhead
The Aird
Inverness
Nairn
Lossie
New Deer
Boddam
Buchan Ness
Dores
Ferness
Charlestown of Aberlour
Dufftown
Huntly
Fyvie
Ythan
Cruden Bay
Strathglass
Enrick
Drummadrochit
Findhorn
Càrn na Loine 1799
2755
Ben Rinnes
Strathbogie
Insch
Oldmeldrum
Newburgh
Loch Ness
Tomatin
Grantown-on-Spey
2563
Corryhabbie Hill
The Buck 2368
Garioch
Inverurie
Formartine
Invermoriston
2162
Strathdearn
Carrbridge
Tomintoul
Càrn Mòr 2636
Lumsden
Don
Kintore
Dyce
Don
Fort Augustus
2658
Aviemore
Spey
Avon
Geal Chàrn 2692
Don
Alford
Aberdeen
L. Oich
3087
Kingussie
Cairn Gorm 4084
3843
Ben Avon
Tarland
Hill of Fare 1545
Banchory
Dee
Newtonmore
4300
Ben Macdhui
Cairngorms
Ballater
Aboyne
Dee
L. Treig
Glen Roy
3700
Creag Meagaidh
L. Laggan
Dalwhinnie
Braemar
Dee
Lochnagar
Mt Keen 3077
Glen Dye
Kerloch 1747
1741
Stonehaven
Ben Alder 3765
Loch Ericht
Forest of Atholl
Glen Tilt
3671
Beinn a Ghlo
3786
Glas Maol 3502
Mt Battock 2555
Glen Esk
West Water
Fettercairn
Inverbervie
Glen Clova
Edzell
Laurencekirk
Kinloch Rannoch
L. Rannoch
Blair Atholl
Glen Garry
3546
Schiehallion
Pitlochry
Kirkmichael
Strathardle
Glen Prosen
Brechin
Montrose
Blackwater Resr
L. Laidon
Rannoch Moor
Glen Lyon
Ben Lawers 3984
Kenmore
Aberfeldy
Strath Tay
Isla
Alyth
Kirriemuir
Glamis
Forfar
Lunan Bay
Killin
L. Tay
Dunkeld
Coupar Angus
Blairgowrie
Bridge of Cally
Sidlaw Hills
Carmyllie
Arbroath
Banknoot
Dundee
Monifieth
Buddon Ness

NORTH SEA

West from Greenwich
2° © Collins © Longman Atlases
57°

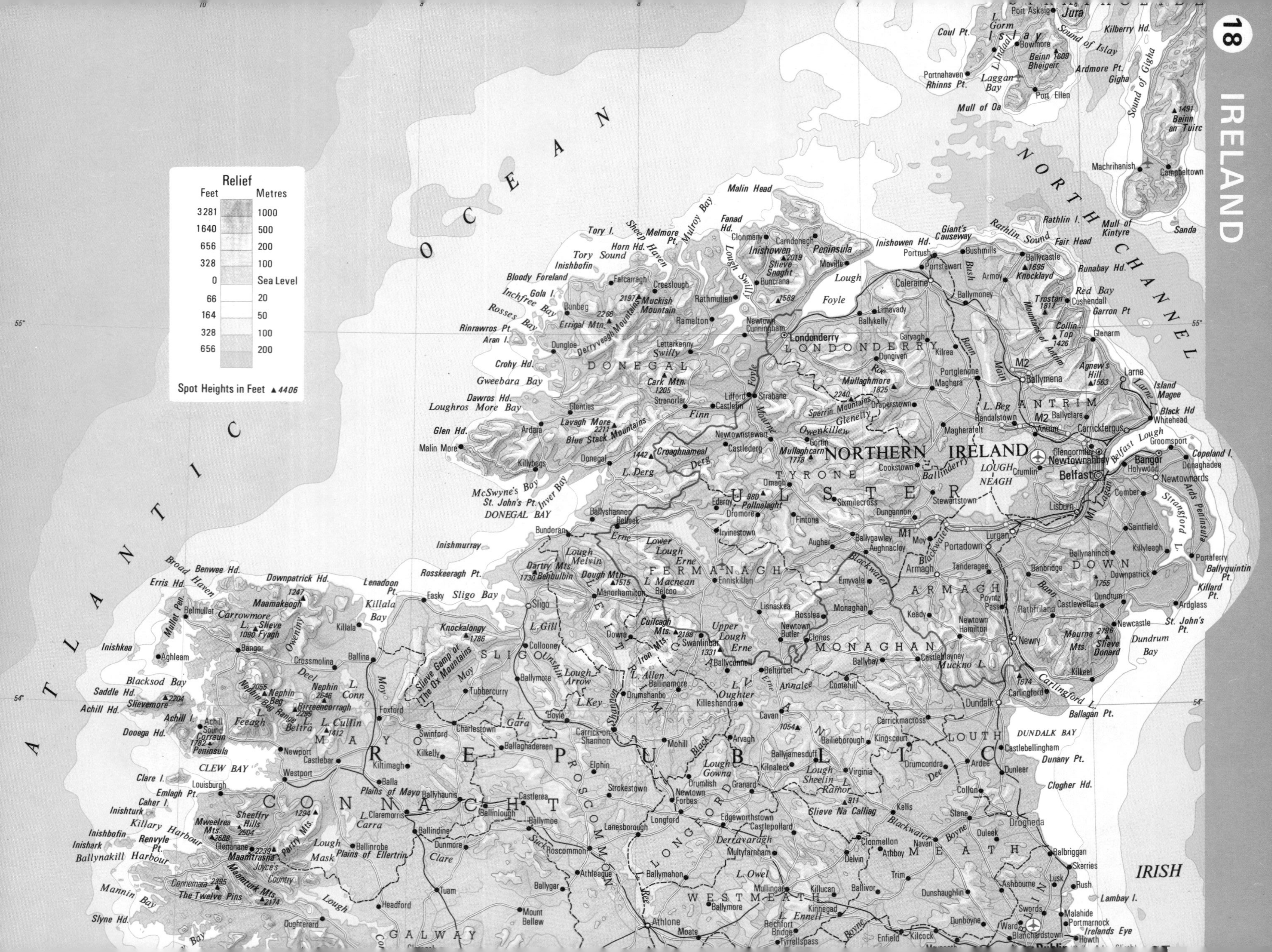

Relief

	Metres		Feet
	1000	3281	
	500	1640	
	200	656	
	100	328	
	Sea Level	0	
	20	66	
	50	164	
	100	328	
	200	656	

Spot Heights in Feet ▲4406

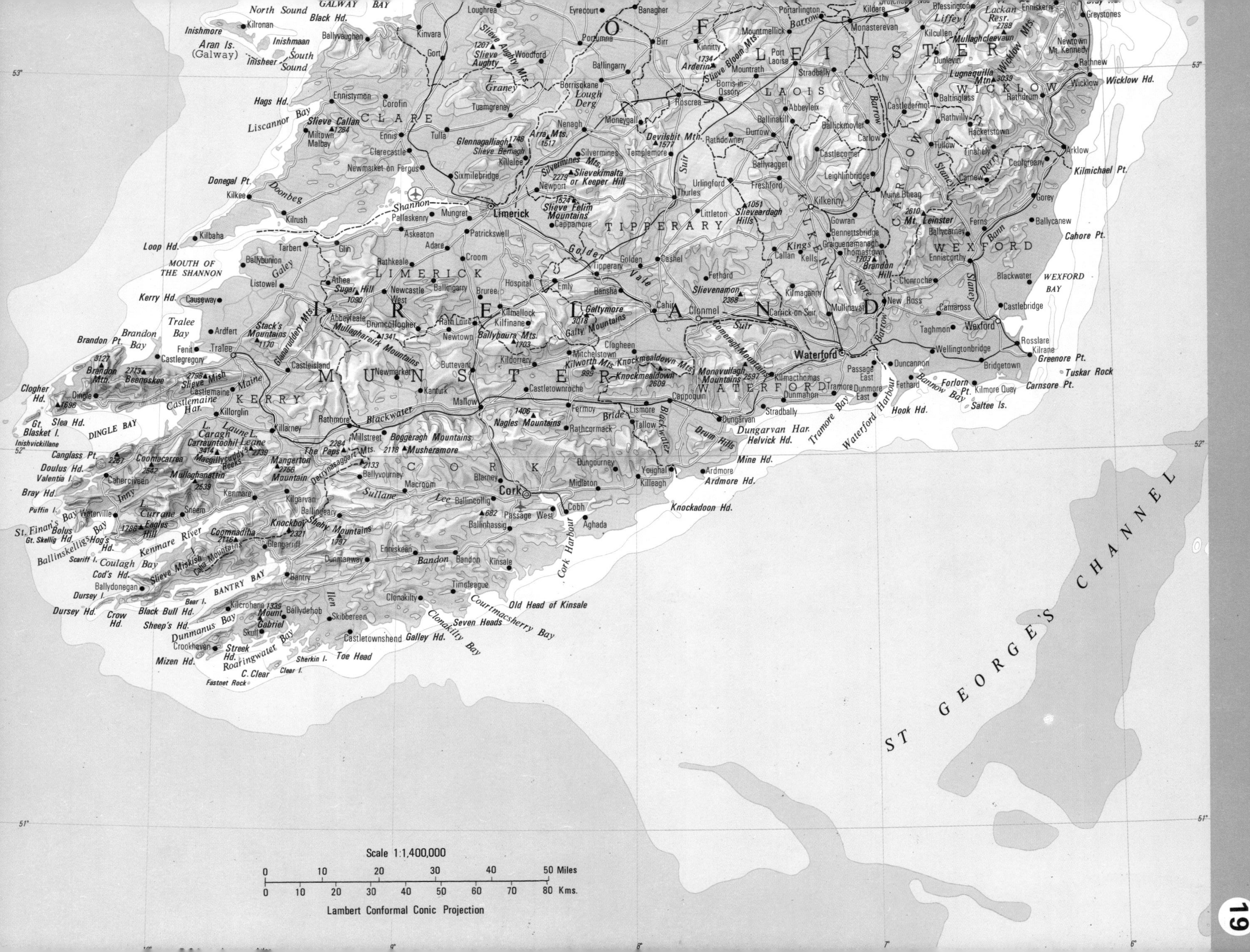

ST GEORGES CHANNEL

Scale 1:1,400,000

Lambert Conformal Conic Projection

| 0 | 10 | 20 | 30 | 40 | 50 Miles |

| 0 | 20 | 40 | 60 | 80 Kms. |

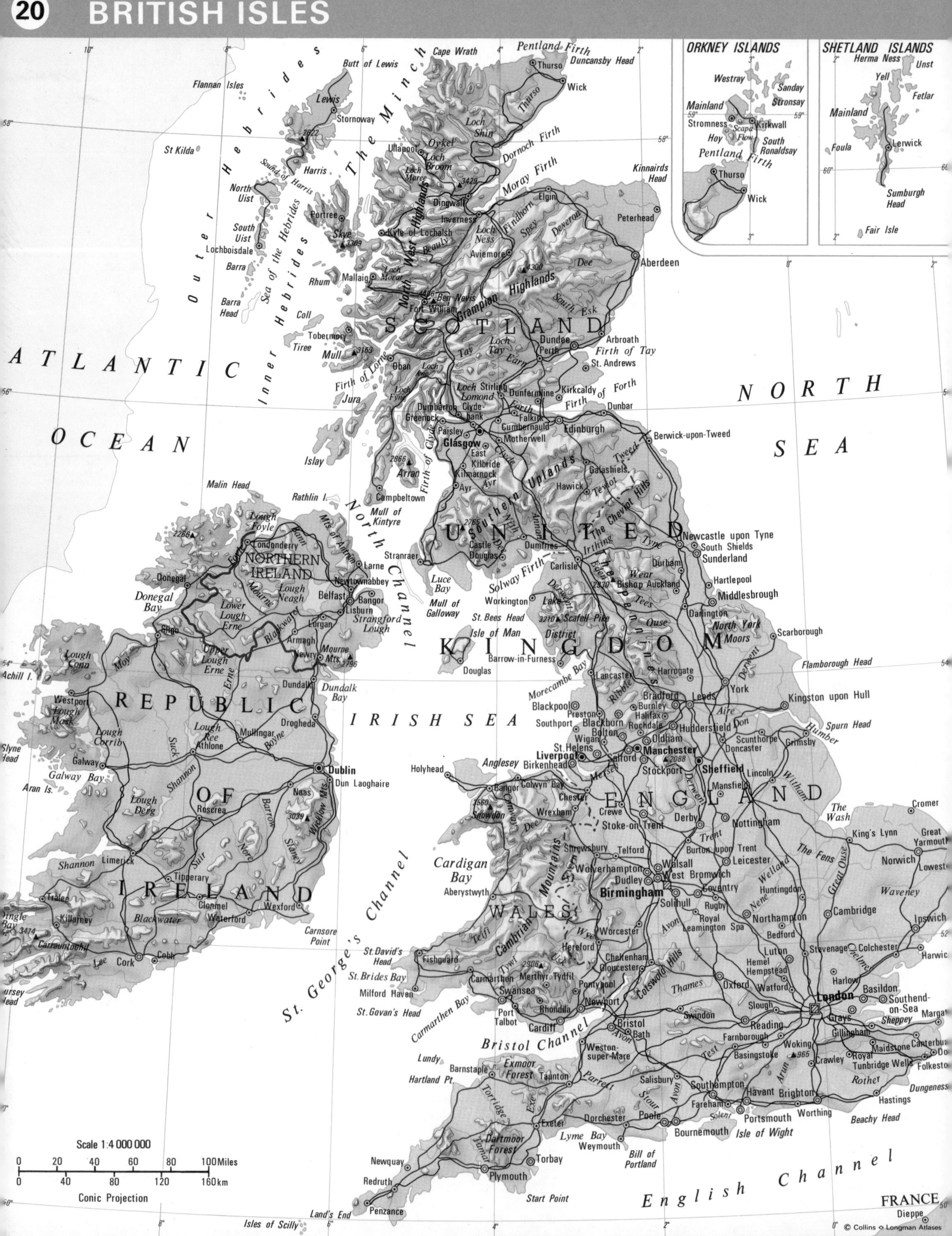

ORKNEY ISLANDS

SHETLAND ISLANDS

ATLANTIC

OCEAN

NORTH

SEA

IRISH SEA

REPUBLIC

OF

IRELAND

NORTHERN IRELAND

UNITED

KINGDOM

SCOTLAND

ENGLAND

WALES

St. George's Channel

Bristol Channel

English Channel

FRANCE

Scale 1:4 000 000

| 0 | 20 | 40 | 60 | 80 | 100 Miles |

| 0 | 40 | 80 | 120 | 160 km |

Conic Projection

© Collins ○ Longman Atlases

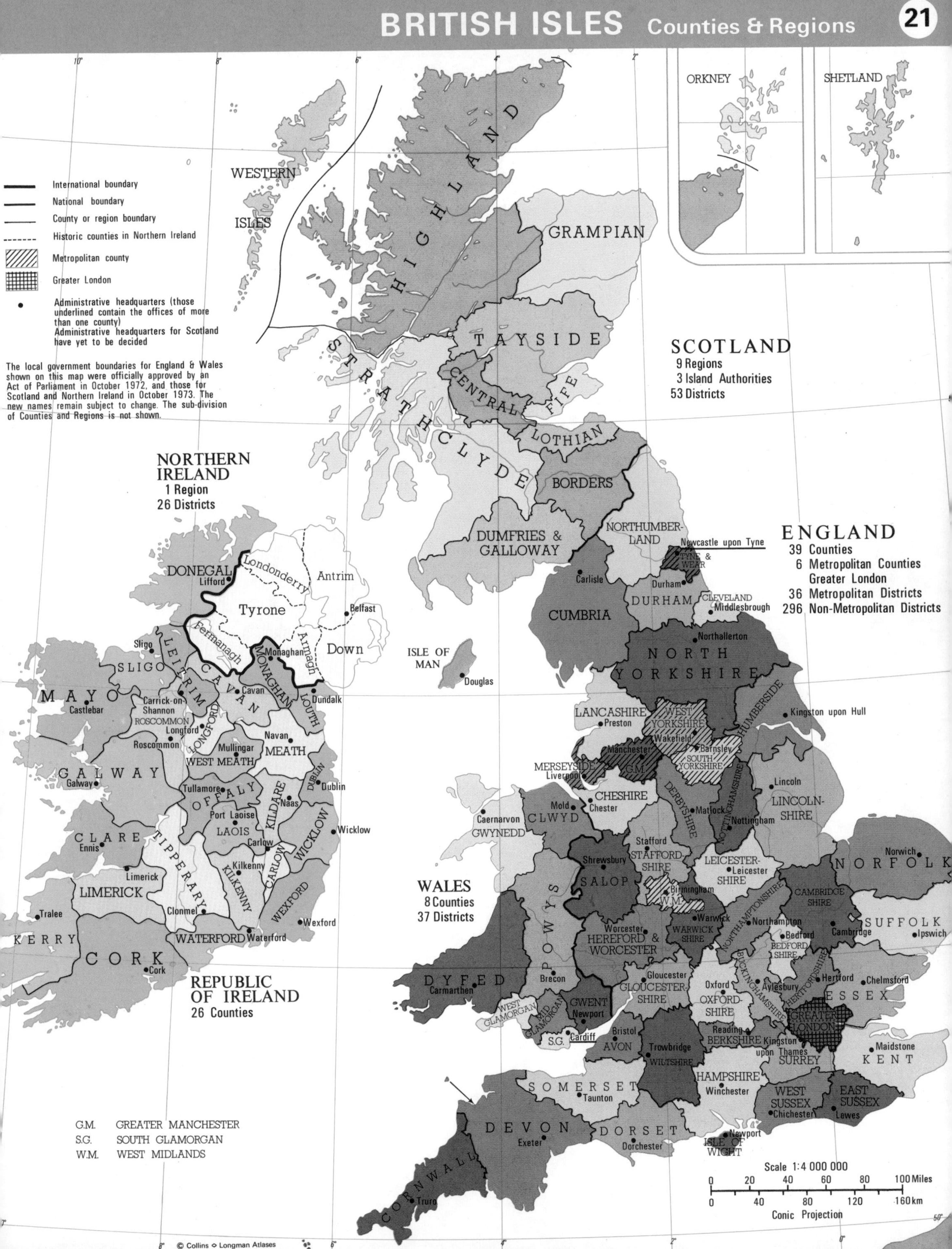

ORKNEY

SHETLAND

WESTERN

ISLES

HIGHLAND

GRAMPIAN

TAYSIDE

CENTRAL FIFE

STRATHCLYDE LOTHIAN

SCOTLAND
9 Regions
3 Island Authorities
53 Districts

BORDERS

DUMFRIES & GALLOWAY

NORTHUMBER-LAND

Newcastle upon Tyne
TYNE & WEAR

Carlisle

Durham

NORTHERN IRELAND
1 Region
26 Districts

DONEGAL
Lifford

Londonderry

Antrim

Tyrone

Belfast

Fermanagh

Armagh

Down

ENGLAND
39 Counties
6 Metropolitan Counties
Greater London
36 Metropolitan Districts
296 Non-Metropolitan Districts

DURHAM

CLEVELAND
Middlesbrough

CUMBRIA

Northallerton

NORTH YORKSHIRE

ISLE OF MAN

Douglas

Kingston upon Hull

LANCASHIRE
Preston

WEST YORKSHIRE
Wakefield

HUMBERSIDE

Sligo

LEITRIM

CAVAN

MONAGHAN

Monaghan

LOUTH

SLIGO

Carrick-on-Shannon
ROSCOMMON
Longford

Cavan

Dundalk

MANCHESTER G.M.

Barnsley

SOUTH YORKSHIRE

Lincoln

MERSEYSIDE
Liverpool

CHESHIRE
Chester

DERBYSHIRE
Matlock

Nottingham

NOTTINGHAMSHIRE

LINCOLN-SHIRE

MAYO
Castlebar

ROSCOMMON
Roscommon

LONGFORD

Mullingar

MEATH
Navan

WEST MEATH

Mold
Caernarvon

CLWYD

GWYNEDD

Stafford
STAFFORD-SHIRE

Shrewsbury

LEICESTER-SHIRE
Leicester

Norwich

NORFOLK

GALWAY
Galway

OFFALY

KILDARE

DUBLIN
Dublin

Tullamore
Port Laoise
LAOIS
Naas
Carlow

WICKLOW
Wicklow

POWYS

SALOP

Birmingham
W.M.

Warwick
WARWICK-SHIRE

NORTHAMPTONSHIRE
Northampton

BEDFORD-SHIRE
Bedford

CAMBRIDGE-SHIRE
Cambridge

SUFFOLK
Ipswich

CLARE
Ennis

TIPPERARY

CARLOW

KILKENNY
Kilkenny

WEXFORD

WALES
8 Counties
37 Districts

DYFED
Carmarthen

Brecon

Worcester
HEREFORD & WORCESTER

Gloucester
GLOUCESTER-SHIRE

Oxford
OXFORD-SHIRE

BUCKINGHAMSHIRE
Aylesbury

HERTFORDSHIRE
Hertford

Chelmsford

ESSEX

LIMERICK
Limerick
Tralee

Clonmel

WATERFORD
Waterford

KERRY

CORK
Cork

REPUBLIC OF IRELAND
26 Counties

WEST GLAMORGAN

MID GLAMORGAN

GWENT
Newport

S.G.
Cardiff

Bristol

AVON

Trowbridge
WILTSHIRE

Reading
BERKSHIRE
Kingston upon Thames

GREATER LONDON

SURREY

Maidstone

KENT

SOMERSET
Taunton

HAMPSHIRE
Winchester

WEST SUSSEX
Chichester

EAST SUSSEX
Lewes

DEVON
Exeter

DORSET
Dorchester

Newport
ISLE OF WIGHT

CORNWALL
Truro

G.M. GREATER MANCHESTER
S.G. SOUTH GLAMORGAN
W.M. WEST MIDLANDS

Scale 1:4 000 000

| 0 | 20 | 40 | 60 | 80 | 100 Miles |

| 0 | 40 | 80 | 120 | 160 km |

Conic Projection

Legend:
— International boundary
— National boundary
— County or region boundary
--- Historic counties in Northern Ireland
▨ Metropolitan county
▦ Greater London
• Administrative headquarters (those underlined contain the offices of more than one county)
Administrative headquarters for Scotland have yet to be decided

The local government boundaries for England & Wales shown on this map were officially approved by an Act of Parliament in October 1972, and those for Scotland and Northern Ireland in October 1973. The new names remain subject to change. The sub-division of Counties and Regions is not shown.

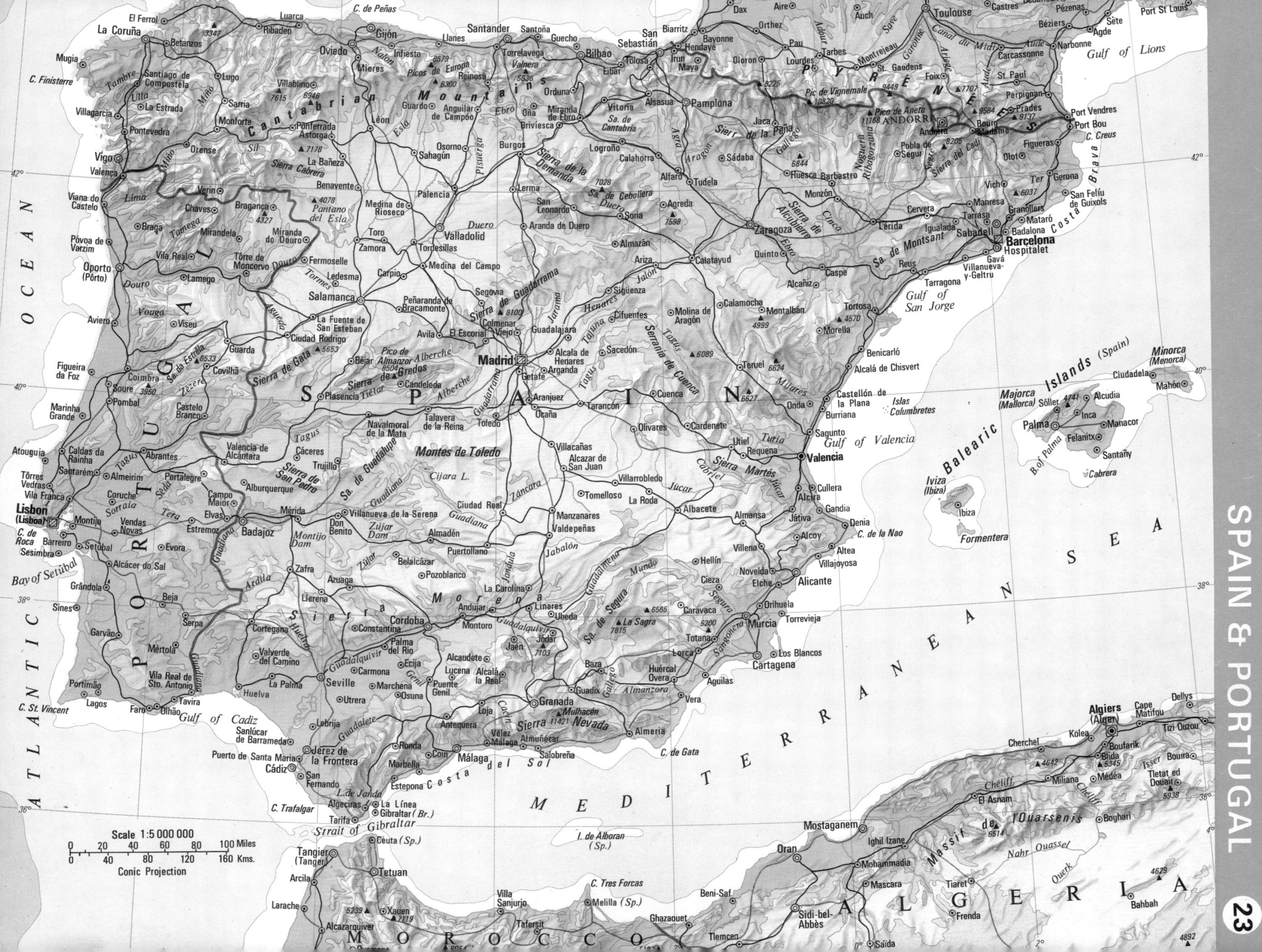
SPAIN
PORTUGAL
MOROCCO
ALGERIA
MEDITERRANEAN SEA
ATLANTIC
OCEAN
Balearic Islands (Spain)
Gulf of Lions
Gulf of Valencia
Gulf of San Jorge
Gulf of Cadiz
Strait of Gibraltar
Bay of Setúbal
Costa del Sol
Costa Brava
Madrid
Lisbon (Lisboa)
Barcelona
Valencia
Seville
Algiers (Alger)
Cantabrian Mountains
Pyrénées
Sierra Morena
Sierra Nevada
Montes de Toledo
Scale 1:5 000 000
Conic Projection

AUSTRIA

Wildspitze 12382

Bremer Pass

Gr. Glockner 12461

Meran

Klagenfurt

Villach

Drau

Celje

Triglav 9396

Gorizia

Ljubljana

Sava

Karlovac

Thiers

Clermont Ferrand

Roanne

Geneva

SWITZ

Simplon Tunnel

Locarno

Bernina 13284

Bolzano

Trento

Dolomites

Catnic Alps

Udine

Trieste

Istra

Rijeka

Lyon

Chamonix

Matterhorn 14688

Mt. Rosa 15203

Traño

Adige

Brent

Bernard Pass

Maggiore

Como

Bergamo

Brescia

Garda

Verona

Vicenza

Treviso

Padua

Venice

Gulf of Venice

Rovinj

Pula

Cres

Krk

Ogulin

Gospić

FRANCE

Mt. Dore 6188

Montbrison

St. Etienne

Villeurbanne

Loire

Annecy

Mont Blanc 15781

Gt. St. Bernard Pass

Aosta

Gran Paradiso 13323

Monza

Milan

Novara

Pavia

Ticino

Adda

Po

Cremona

Mantua

Adige

Ferrara

Po

Reno

Ravenna

Lošinj

Pag

Zadar

Dugi Otok

Le Puy

Grenoble

Romans

Valence

Vienne

Turin

Asti

Vercelli

Voghera

Piacenza

Parma

Modena

Bologna

Faenza

Forlì

Rimini

San Marino

Pésaro

ADRIATIC

Kornat

Plomb du Cantal 6096

Mende

Sérévac

Briançon

Les Ecrins 13462

Gap

Mt. Viso 12603

Cuneo

Mondovi

Acqui

Alessandria

Tanaro

Mt. Cimone 7103

Prato

Florence

Arno

Carrara

Massa

San Marino

Senigallia

Ancona

Macerata

Iesi

Šibenik

Millau

Nîmes

Avignon

Digne

Mt. Pelat 10016

Alps Maritimes

Savona

Genoa

Rapallo

Chiavari

La Spezia

Leghorn

Pisa

Volterra

Siena

Arezzo

Perugia

Frasimeno

Montre

Foligno

Monte Vettore 8130

Ascoli Piceno

Téramo

Marvejols

Alès

Orange

Salon

Duance

Var

San Remo

Imperia

Gulf of Genoa

Cecina

Piombino

Grosseto

Ombrone

Amiata 5689

Bolsena

Viterbo

Terni

Rieti

L'Aquila

Mt. Corno 9560

Mt. Amaro 9170

Pescara

Béziers

Sète

Montpellier

Aix en Provence

Draguignan

Grasse

Menton

Monte Carlo

MONACO

Nice

Cannes

Fréjus

LIGURIAN SEA

C. Corse

Capraia

Elba

Pianosa

Giglio

Montecristo

Civitavecchia

Rome

Avezzano

Sulmona

Chieti

Termoli

Marseille

Toulon

Hyères

Iles d'Hyères

Gulf of Lions

Calvi

Bastia

Corsica (Fr.)

Mt. Cinto 8890

Corte

Aleria

G. of Valinco

Sartène

Ajaccio

7008

Pto. Vecchio

Str. of Bonifacio

Bonifacio

Velletri

Frosinone

Pontine Is.

Gaeta

G. of Gaeta

Caserta

San Severo

Campobasso

Benevento

Ariano

Foggia

Ofanto

Melfi

Bră

42°

Asinara

C. Falcone

G. of Asinara

Caprera

Témpio

Olbia

Porto Torres

Sássari

Alghero

Bosa

Coghinas

Orosei

Macomer

Gulf of Orosei

C. Mte. Santu

Naples

Ischia

G. of Naples

Vesuvius

Capri

Salerno

Potenza

G. of Salerno

Ser

40°

Minorca

Mahón

Sardinia (Italy)

G. of Orisiano

Oristano

Tirso

6019

Arbatax

TYRRHENIAN SEA

Pisciotta

G. of Policastro

38°

Relief

Feet	Metres
16 404	5000
9843	3000
6562	2000
3281	1000
1640	500
656	200
0	Sea Level
Land Dep.	
656	200
13 123	4000
22 966	7000

Iglésias

San Pietro

Tirso

Cágliari

Villaputzu

C. Carbonara

G. of Cágliari

G. of Palmas

C. Spartivento

MEDITERRANEAN

Stromboli 3038

Ustica (Italy)

Lipari Is.

Páola

Nic

Sicily

Palermo

Messina

Reggio

Str. of Messina

Palmi

Spar

Marettimo

Trápani

Cefalù

Barcellona

Favignana

Alcamo

Termini

Nebrodi Mts.

M. Etna 10758

Adrano

Galita

Marsala

Sciacca

Enna

Platani

Caltanissetta

Catánia

C. de Fer

C. Serrat

Bizerta

Béjaïa

Skikda

Annaba

Tabarka

Mateur

Gulf of Tunis

C. Bon

Salso

Agrigento

Licata

Caltagirone

Siracusa

Ragusa

Módica

C. Passero

Akbou

La Calle

Medjerda Mts.

Tunis

Pantelleria (Italy)

Vittória

Constantine Mts.

Constantine

Wadi

Medjerda

Nabeul

Sétif

Souk Ahras

Le Kef

Enfida

ALGERIA

Batna

Aïn Beïda

TUNISIA

Sousse

Malta Channel

Gozo

MALTA

Valletta

Barika

Biskra

el Abiod

Thala

Kairouan

Monastir

Linosa

Malta

el Aieb

Tebessa

Sbeitla

W. el Hatob

Msaken

Mahdia

Lampione

Lampedusa (Italy)

MEDITERRANEAN

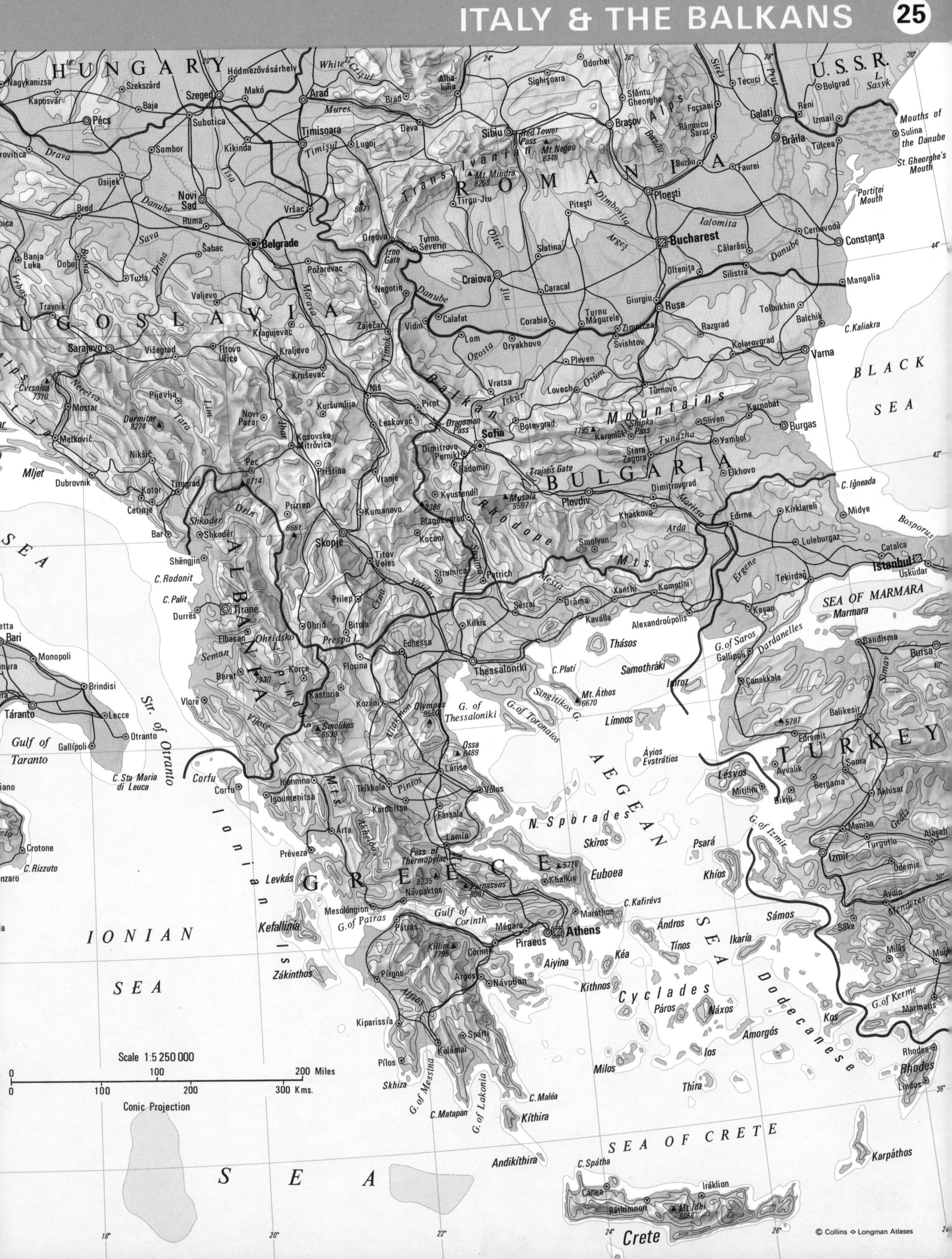

Scale 1:5 250 000

100   200 Miles

0   100   200   300 Kms.

Conic Projection

© Collins ◆ Longman Atlases

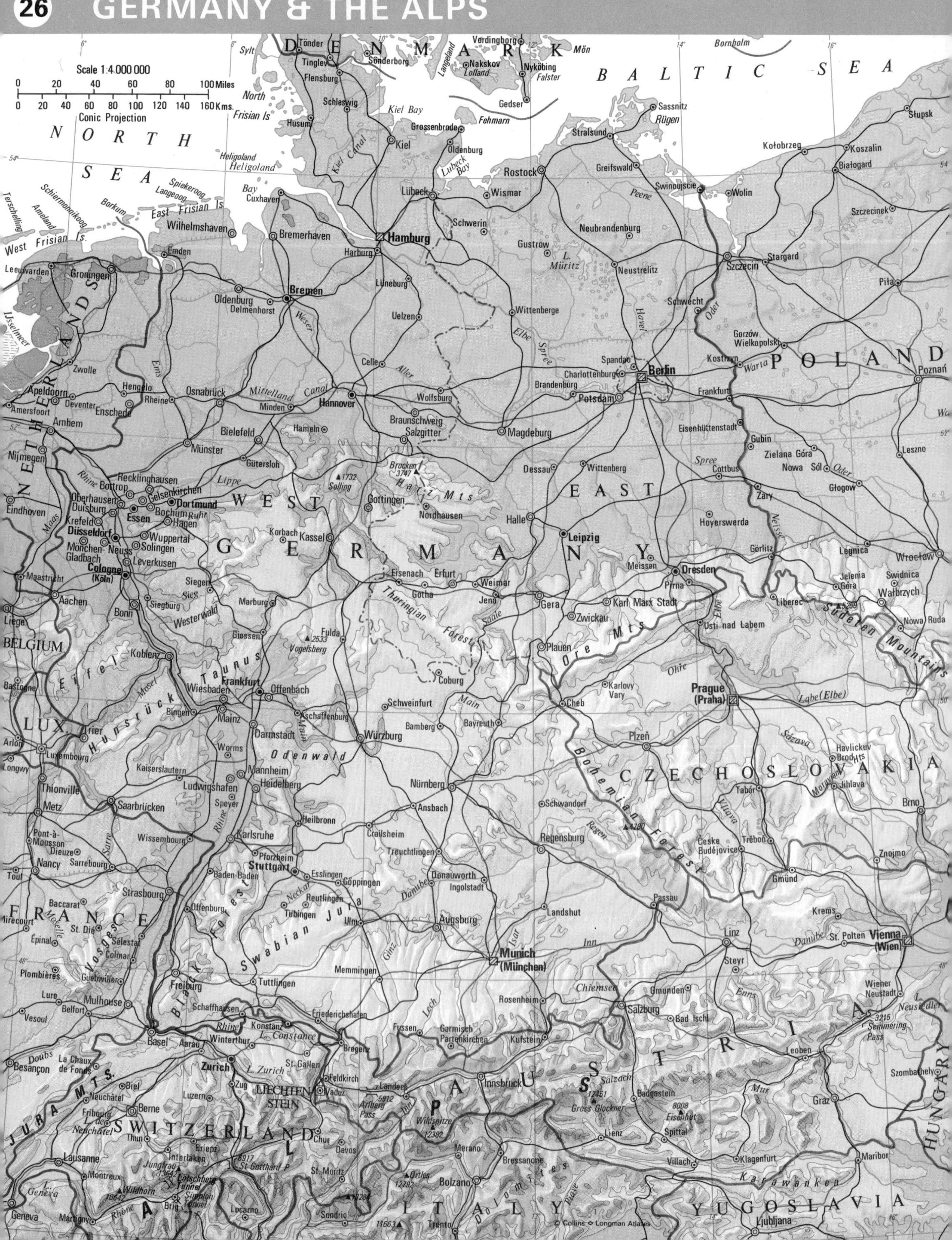

Scale 1:4 000 000
0 20 40 60 80 100 Miles
0 20 40 60 80 100 120 140 160 Kms.
Conic Projection
NORTH SEA
BALTIC SEA
DENMARK
Tönder
Tinglev
Sönderborg
Flensburg
Vordingborg
Nakskov
Lolland
Nykøbing
Falster
Mön
Langeland
Bornholm
Sylt
North Frisian Is
Schleswig
Kiel Bay
Husum
Kiel Canal
Kiel
Grossenbrode
Oldenburg
Fehmarn
Gedser
Heligoland
Heligoland Bay
Cuxhaven
Spiekeroog
Langeoog
Borkum
East Frisian Is
West Frisian Is.
Terschelling
Ameland
Schiermonnikoog
Wilhelmshaven
Emden
Bremerhaven
Lübeck
Lubeck Bay
Wismar
Rostock
Stralsund
Sassnitz
Rügen
Greifswald
Peene
Swinoujscie
Wolin
Kołobrzeg
Koszalin
Słupsk
Białogard
Szczecinek
Schwerin
Hamburg
Harburg
Gustrow
L. Müritz
Neubrandenburg
Neustrelitz
Szczecin
Stargard
Piła
Leeuwarden
Groningen
Oldenburg
Delmenhorst
Bremen
Lüneburg
Uelzen
Wittenberge
Schwecht
Oder
Havel
Elbe
Spree
Weser
IJsselmeer
NETHERLANDS
Gorzów Wielkopolski
Kostrzyn
Warta
POLAND
Poznań
Spandau
Charlottenburg
Berlin
Brandenburg
Potsdam
Frankfurt
Celle
Aller
Wolfsburg
Zwolle
Apeldoorn
Amersfoort
Deventer
Hengelo
Rheine
Enschede
Ems
Osnabrück
Mittelland Canal
Minden
Hannover
Arnhem
Bielefeld
Hameln
Braunschweig
Salzgitter
Magdeburg
Eisenhüttenstadt
Gubin
Zielana Góra
Nowa Sól
Leszno
Nijmegen
Münster
Gütersloh
Brocken 3747
Harz Mts
Dessau
Wittenberg
Spree
Cottbus
Głogow
Żary
Recklinghausen
Bottrop
Gelsenkirchen
Dortmund
Lippe
Oberhausen
Duisburg
Essen
Bochum
Ruhr
Hagen
Krefeld
Düsseldorf
Wuppertal
Solingen
Mönchen-Gladbach
Neuss
Leverkusen
Eindhoven
Maas
Rhine
1732 Solling
Göttingen
Nordhausen
WEST GERMANY
EAST GERMANY
Halle
Leipzig
Hoyerswerda
Neisse
Korbach
Kassel
Cologne (Köln)
Maastricht
Aachen
Liege
Bonn
Siegen
Sieg
Siegburg
Westerwald
Marburg
Eisenach
Erfurt
Gotha
Weimar
Jena
Gera
Meissen
Dresden
Pirna
Görlitz
Legnica
Wrocław
Jelenia Góra
Swidnica
Wałbrzych
Liberec
Karl Marx Stadt
Zwickau
Thuringian Forest
Saale
Usti nad Labem
5259
Sudeten Mountains
Nowa Ruda
BELGIUM
Giessen
Fulda
2533 Vogelsberg
Plauen
Ore Mts
Ohře
Eifel
Koblenz
Taunus
Coburg
Karlovy Vary
Prague (Praha)
Bastogne
Mosel
Wiesbaden
Frankfurt
Offenbach
Main
Cheb
Labe (Elbe)
Hunsrück
Bingen
Mainz
Aschaffenburg
Schweinfurt
LUX
Trier
Arlon
Luxembourg
Darmstadt
Bamberg
Bayreuth
Würzburg
Plzeň
Sázava
Havlickuv Brod
Longwy
Worms
Odenwald
Bohemian Forest
CZECHOSLOVAKIA
Kaiserslautern
Mannheim
Heidelberg
Nürnberg
Moravian Hts
Jihlava
Thionville
Ludwigshafen
Speyer
Tabor
Metz
Saarbrücken
Ansbach
Schwandorf
Vltava
Brno
Pont-à-Mousson
Dieuze
Sarre
Wissembourg
Karlsruhe
Heilbronn
Crailsheim
Regen
4780
Regensburg
České Budějovice
Třeboň
Znojmo
Nancy
Sarrebourg
Pforzheim
Stuttgart
Treuchtlingen
Toul
Baden-Baden
Esslingen
Göppingen
Donauworth
Ingolstadt
Gmünd
Strasbourg
Neckar
Reutlingen
Tübingen
Danube
Black Forest
Passau
Baccarat
Offenburg
Swabian Jura
Landshut
Krems
FRANCE
Moselle
St. Dié
Vosges
Ulm
Augsburg
Épinal
Sélestat
Colmar
Isar
Inn
Linz
Danube
St. Polten
Vienna (Wien)
Plombières
Guebwiller
Memmingen
Munich (München)
Steyr
Freiburg
Tuttlingen
Ginz
Chiemsee
Gmunden
Wiener Neustadt
Lure
Mulhouse
Rosenheim
Enns
Neusiedler
Vesoul
Belfort
Schaffhausen
Friedrichshafen
Lech
Salzburg
Bad Ischl
3215 Semmering Pass
Basel
Konstanz
Rhine
L. Constance
Fussen
Garmisch Partenkirchen
Kufstein
Doubs
Besançon
La Chaux de Fonds
Aarau
Winterthur
Bregenz
AUSTRIA
Leoben
Zurich
L. Zurich
St. Gallen
Feldkirch
Landeck
Innsbruck
Salzach
Szombathely
JURA MTS.
Biel
Zug
LIECHTENSTEIN
Vaduz
5912 Arlberg Pass
Inn
Badgastein
Mur
Neuchâtel
Luzern
12461 Gross Glockner
8008 Eisenhut
Graz
Fribourg
Berne
L. de Neuchâtel
SWITZERLAND
Chur
Davos
Wildspitze 12382
Spittal
Lienz
HUNGARY
Thun
Brienz
Interlaken
Jungfrau 13642
8917 St. Gotthard P.
Merano
Bressanone
Villach
Klagenfurt
Maribor
Lausanne
Lötschberg Tunnel
St. Moritz
Ortles 12792
Karawanken
Montreux
L. Geneva
Wildhorn 10642
Simplon Tunnel
Rhône
Brig
13284
Bolzano
Dolomites
ALPS
Geneva
Martigny
Locarno
Sondrio
11663
Trento
ITALY
Piave
YUGOSLAVIA
Ljubljana
© Collins • Longman Atlases

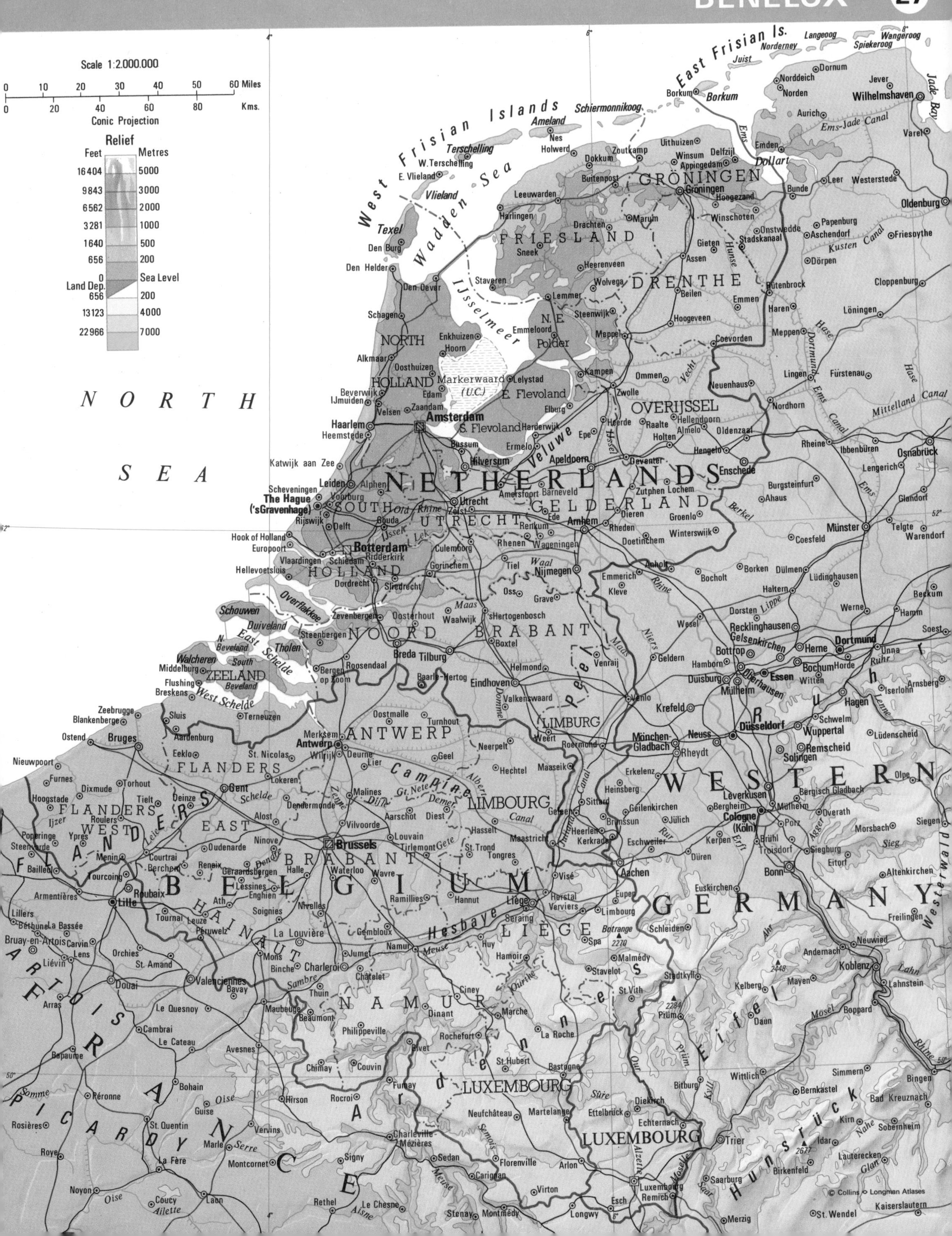
Scale 1:2.000.000
0 10 20 30 40 50 60 Miles
0 20 40 60 80 Kms.
Conic Projection
Relief
Feet Metres
16404 5000
9843 3000
6562 2000
3281 1000
1640 500
656 200
0 Sea Level
Land Dep.
656 200
13123 4000
22966 7000
NORTH SEA
West Frisian Islands
East Frisian Is.
Wadden Sea
IJsselmeer
NETHERLANDS
BELGIUM
GERMANY
LUXEMBOURG
FRANCE
GRONINGEN
FRIESLAND
DRENTHE
OVERIJSSEL
GELDERLAND
UTRECHT
NORTH HOLLAND
SOUTH HOLLAND
ZEELAND
NOORD BRABANT
LIMBURG
ANTWERP
FLANDERS
WEST FLANDERS
EAST FLANDERS
BRABANT
LIMBOURG
HAINAUT
LIÈGE
NAMUR
ARTOIS
PICARDY
Ardennes
Eifel
Hunsrück
Ruhr
WESTERN
Westerwald
Campine
Hesbaye
Veluwe
Peel
Amsterdam
The Hague ('sGravenhage)
Rotterdam
Utrecht
Brussels
Antwerp
Luxembourg
Cologne (Köln)
Düsseldorf
Essen
Dortmund
Lille
Gent
Liège
Aachen
Bonn
Koblenz
Trier
Münster
Osnabrück
Oldenburg
Wilhelmshaven
Emden
Gröningen
Leeuwarden
Arnhem
Nijmegen
Eindhoven
Tilburg
Breda
Maastricht
Namur
Charleroi
Mons
Bruges
Ostend
Markerwaard (U.C.)
E. Flevoland
S. Flevoland
N.E. Polder
Botrange 2270
Rhine
Maas
Meuse
Waal
Mosel
Scheldt
© Collins - Longman Atlases

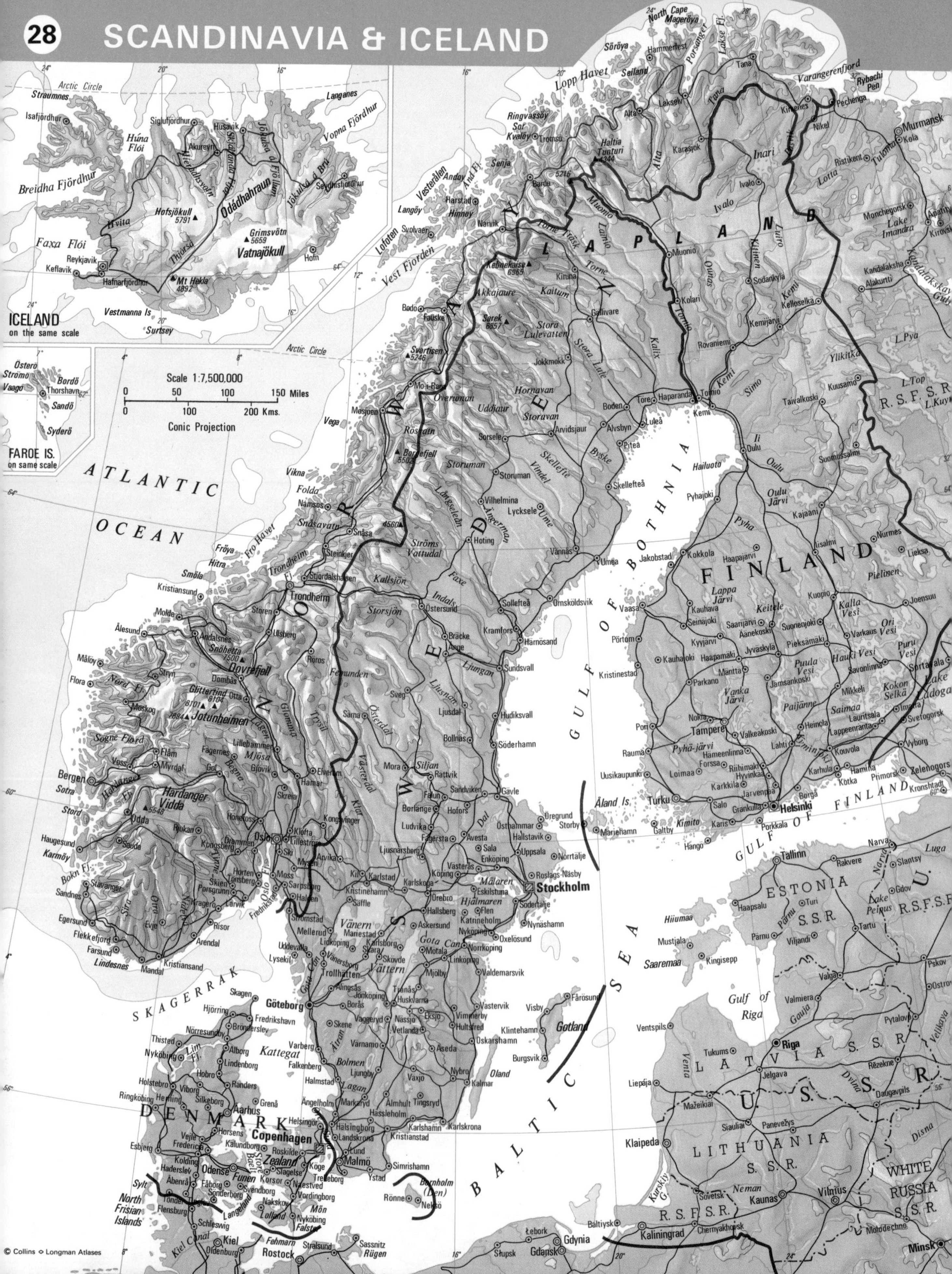

ICELAND
on the same scale

FAROE IS.
on same scale

Scale 1:7,500,000

| 0 | 50 | 100 | 150 Miles |

| 0 | 100 | 200 Kms. |

Conic Projection

© Collins ◇ Longman Atlases

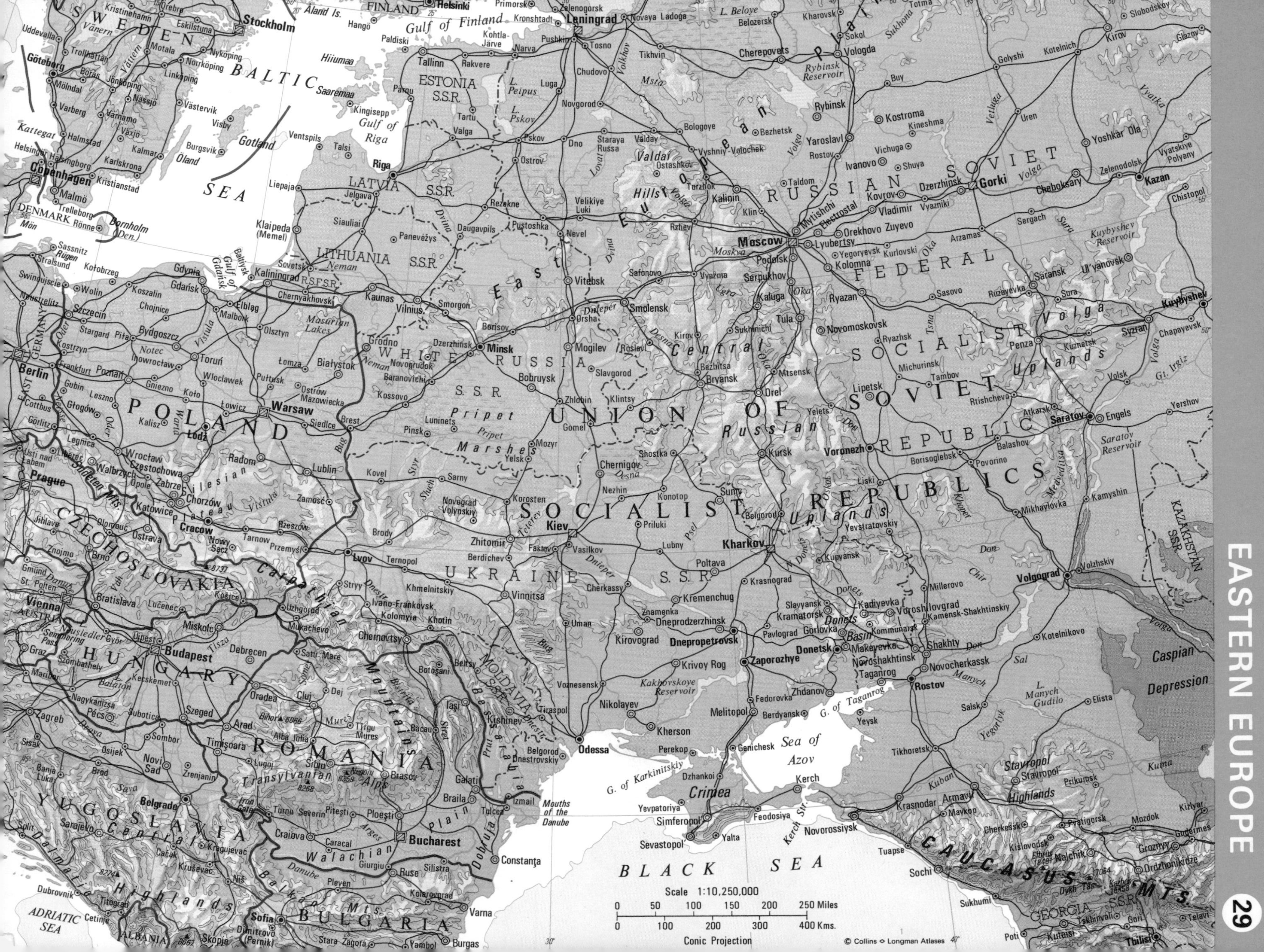
UNION OF SOVIET SOCIALIST REPUBLICS
RUSSIAN SOVIET FEDERAL SOCIALIST REPUBLIC
UKRAINE S.S.R.
WHITE RUSSIA S.S.R.
ESTONIA S.S.R.
LATVIA S.S.R.
LITHUANIA S.S.R.
MOLDAVIA S.S.R.
GEORGIA S.S.R.
KAZAKHSTAN S.S.R.
R.S.F.S.R.
POLAND
CZECHOSLOVAKIA
HUNGARY
ROMANIA
BULGARIA
YUGOSLAVIA
ALBANIA
AUSTRIA
SWEDEN
FINLAND
DENMARK
BALTIC SEA
BLACK SEA
Sea of Azov
ADRIATIC SEA
Caspian Depression
East European Plain
Gulf of Finland
Gulf of Riga
Gulf of Gdańsk
G. of Taganrog
G. of Karkinitskiy
Mouths of the Danube
CAUCASUS MTS.
Stavropol Highlands
Carpathian Mountains
Transylvanian Alps
Balkan Mts.
Dinaric Alps
Central Highlands
Valdai Hills
Central Russian Uplands
Volga Uplands
Donets Basin
Pripet Marshes
Silesian Plateau
Masurian Lakes
Crimea
Bessarabia
Dobruja
Walachian Plain
Moscow
Leningrad
Kiev
Warsaw
Budapest
Bucharest
Sofia
Belgrade
Prague
Berlin
Vienna
Stockholm
Helsinki
Copenhagen
Minsk
Riga
Vilnius
Odessa
Kharkov
Volgograd
Rostov
Gorki
Kazan
Kuybyshev
Saratov
Voronezh
Donetsk
Dnepropetrovsk
Zaporozhye
Lvov
Tbilisi
Scale 1:10,250,000
0 50 100 150 200 250 Miles
0 100 200 300 400 Kms.
Conic Projection
© Collins ◇ Longman Atlases

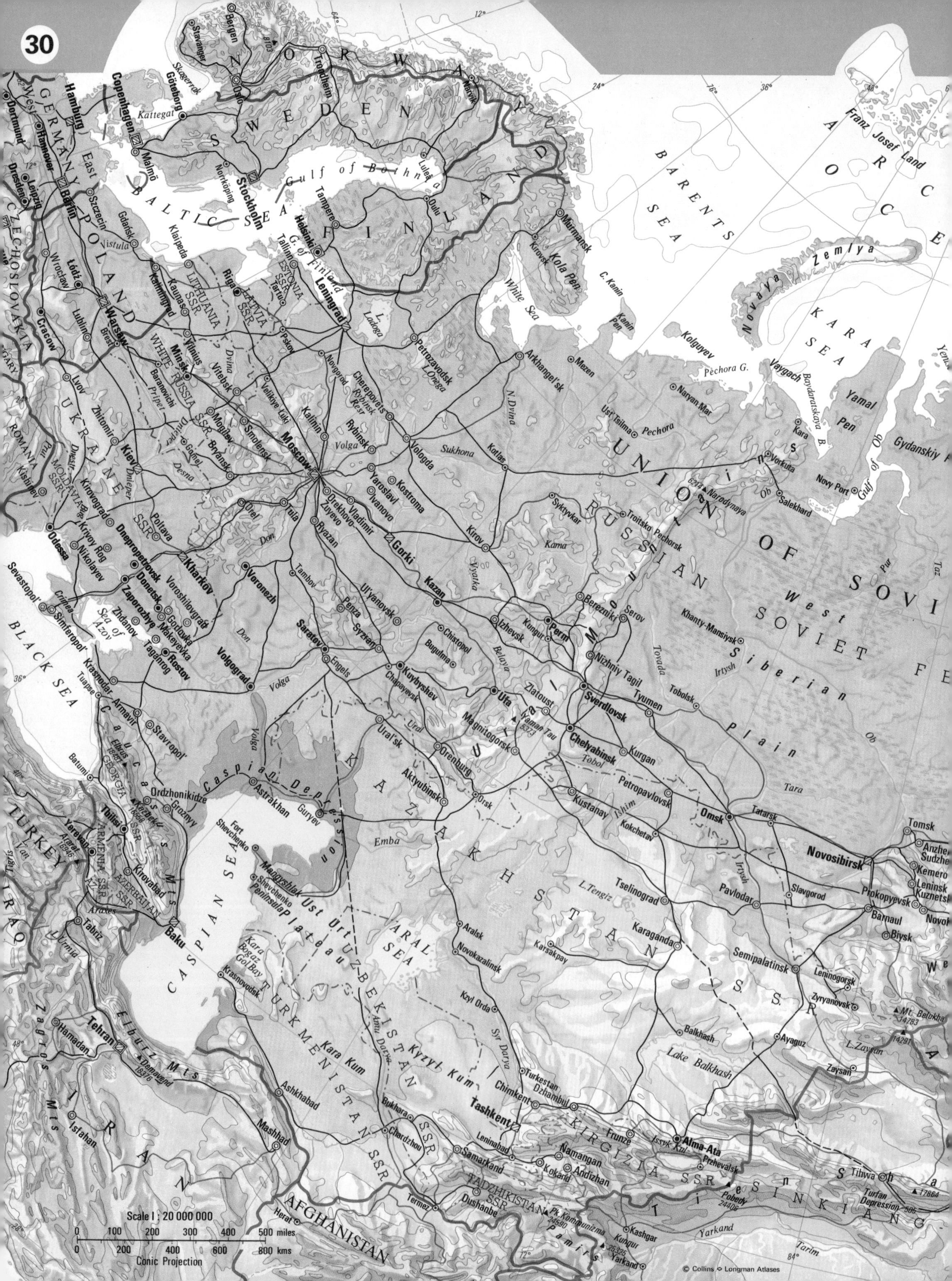
NORWAY
SWEDEN
FINLAND
POLAND
GERMANY
CZECHOSLOVAKIA
ROMANIA
UKRAINE
WHITE RUSSIA
LITHUANIA SSR
LATVIA SSR
ESTONIA SSR
MOLDAVIA SSR
GEORGIA
ARMENIA SSR
AZERBAIJAN SSR
TURKEY
IRAQ
IRAN
AFGHANISTAN
TURKMENISTAN SSR
UZBEKISTAN SSR
TADZHIKISTAN SSR
KIRGIZIA SSR
KAZAKHSTAN SSR
UNION OF SOVI
RUSSIAN
SINKIANG
BALTIC SEA
Gulf of Bothnia
G. of Finland
BARENTS SEA
ARCTIC OCEAN
KARA SEA
White Sea
BLACK SEA
Sea of Azov
CASPIAN SEA
ARAL SEA
Caspian Depression
Ust Urt Plateau
Kara Kum
Kyzyl Kum
Kara Bogaz Gol Bay
West Siberian Plain
Caucasus Mts
Elburz Mts
Zagros Mts
Pamirs
Franz Josef Land
Novaya Zemlya
Kola Pen
Kanin Pen
C. Kanin
Kolguyev
Vaygach
Yamal Pen
Gydanskiy
Pechora G.
Baydaratskaya B.
Gulf of Ob
Mangyshlak Peninsula
Lake Balkhash
L. Ladoga
L. Onega
L. Tengiz
L. Zaysan
Kattegat
Skagerrak
Bergen
Stavanger
Oslo
Trondheim
Narvik
Göteborg
Copenhagen
Malmö
Stockholm
Norrköping
Luleå
Oulu
Tampere
Helsinki
Tallinn
Tartu
Riga
Kaunas
Klaipeda
Kaliningrad
Gdansk
Szczecin
Hamburg
Hannover
Dortmund
Dresden
Leipzig
Berlin
Wroclaw
Lódz
Warsaw
Cracow
Lublin
Brest
Vilnius
Minsk
Baranovichi
Vitebsk
Mogilev
Smolensk
Gomel
Bryansk
Lvov
Zhitomir
Kiev
Kishinev
Kirovograd
Odessa
Nikolayev
Krivoy Rog
Dnepropetrovsk
Zaporozhye
Poltava
Kharkov
Donetsk
Zhdanov
Makeyevka
Gorlovka
Voroshilovgrad
Taganrog
Rostov
Sevastopol'
Simferopol'
Crimea
Krasnodar
Tuapse
Armavir
Stavropol
Batumi
Ordzhonikidze
Groznyy
Tbilisi
Yerevan
Kirovabad
Baku
Tabriz
Urmia
Araxes
Hamadan
Tehran
Damavand 18376
Isfahan
Mashhad
Ashkhabad
Herat
Krasnovodsk
Shevchenko
Fort Shevchenko
Pskov
Leningrad
Novgorod
Velikiye Luki
Kalinin
Moscow
Petrozavodsk
Cherepovets
Rybinsk
Rybinsk Resr
Yaroslavl
Kostroma
Ivanovo
Vologda
Vladimir
Orekhovo Zuyevo
Tula
Orel
Ryazan
Tambov
Voronezh
Gorki
Kirov
Kazan
Ul'yanovsk
Penza
Syzran
Saratov
Engels
Volgograd
Astrakhan
Guryev
Kuybyshev
Chapayevsk
Ural'sk
Orenburg
Aktyubinsk
Orsk
Chistopol
Bugulma
Izhevsk
Perm
Kungur
Berezniki
Ufa
Zlatoust
Magnitogorsk
Yamantau 5373
Chelyabinsk
Sverdlovsk
Nizhniy Tagil
Serov
Tyumen
Tobolsk
Kurgan
Petropavlovsk
Kustanay
Kokchetav
Omsk
Tatarsk
Tselinograd
Karaganda
Pavlodar
Slavgorod
Novosibirsk
Tomsk
Anzhero Sudzhensk
Kemerovo
Leninsk Kuznetskiy
Prokopyevsk
Barnaul
Biysk
Semipalatinsk
Leninogorsk
Zyryanovsk
Mt. Belukha 14783
Ayaguz
Zaysan
Balkhash
Karsakpay
Aralsk
Novokazalinsk
Kzyl Orda
Turkestan
Chimkent
Dzhambul
Tashkent
Frunze
Alma-Ata
Przhevalsk
Issyk Kul
Leninabad
Namangan
Andizhan
Kokand
Samarkand
Bukhara
Chardzhou
Termez
Dushanbe
Pk. Kommunizma 24590
Pobedy 24406
Kashgar
Kungur 25325
Yarkand
Tihwa
Turfan Depression
Khanty-Mansiysk
Salekhard
Novy Port
Vorkuta
Narodnaya
Troitsko Pechorsk
Syktyvkar
Kotlas
Ust' Tsilma
Naryan Mar
Mezen
Arkhangel'sk
Murmansk
Kirovsk
Kara
Volga
Don
Dnieper
Dnestr
Prut
Desna
Pripet
Dvina
N. Dvina
Sukhona
Pechora
Kama
Vyatka
Belaya
Ural
Emba
Tobol
Ishim
Irtysh
Tavda
Ob
Tara
Pur
Amu Darya
Syr Darya
Tarim
Scale 1 : 20 000 000
0 100 200 300 400 500 miles
0 200 400 600 800 kms
Conic Projection
© Collins ◇ Longman Atlases

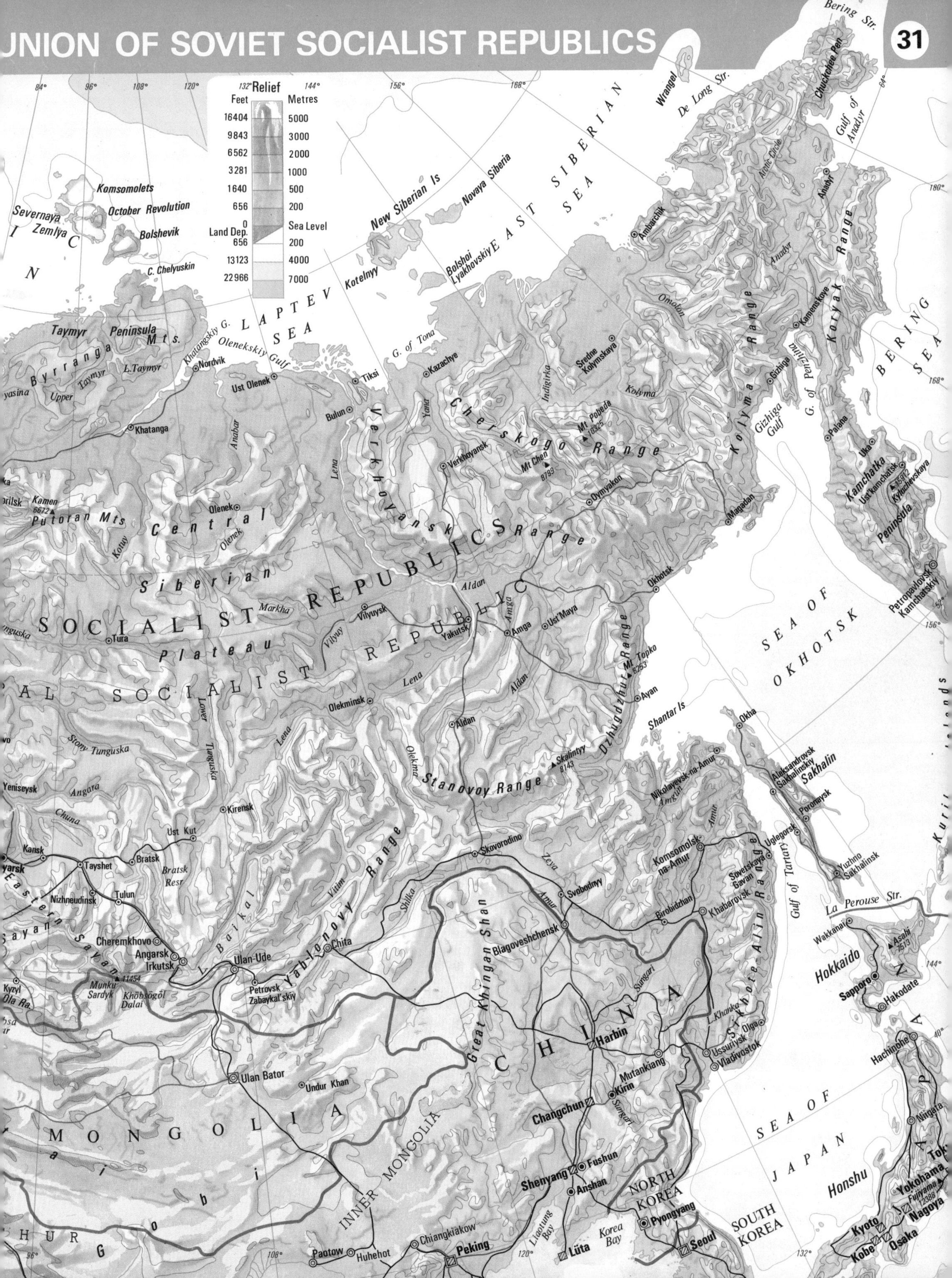

Bering Str.

Relief

Feet	Metres
16404	5000
9843	3000
6562	2000
3281	1000
1640	500
656	200
0	Sea Level
Land Dep.	
656	200
13123	4000
22966	7000

Wrangel

De Long Str.

Arctic Circle

Chuckchee Pen.

Gulf of Anadyr

Anadyr

Severnaya Zemlya

Komsomolets
October Revolution
Bolshevik

C. Chelyuskin

New Siberian Is

Novaya Siberia

Bolshoi Lyakhovskiy

EAST SIBERIAN SEA

Ambarchik

Srednekolymsk

Omolon

Gizhiga

G. of Penzhina

Gizhiga Gulf

Palana

Uka

BERING SEA

Koryak Range

Kolyma Range

Kamenskoye

Taymyr Peninsula

Byrranga Mts.

L. Taymyr

Upper Taymyr

yasina

Nordvik

Ust Olenek

Khatanga

Anabar

Khatangskiy G.

Olenekskiy Gulf

LAPTEV SEA

Tiksi

Bulun

Kotelnyy

G. of Tona

Yana

Kazachye

Indigirka

Srednekolymskaya

Kolyma

Verkhoyansk

Cherskogo Range

Mt Pobeda
3325

Kamchatka

Ust Kamchatsk

Klyuchevskaya

Petropavlovsk Kamchatskiy

Kamen
6672

Putoran Mts.

Konvy

Olenek

Central

Siberian

Plateau

Tura

Markha

Olenek

Vilyuy

Vilyuysk

Yakutsk

Verkhoyansk

Mt Chen
8795

Oymyakon

Aldan

Amga

Ust Maya

Magadan

Okhotsk

Dzhugdzhur Range

Mt Topko
6253

SEA OF OKHOTSK

nguska

SOCIALIST REPUBLIC

AL SOCIALIST REPUBLIC

Stony Tunguska

Olekminsk

Lena

Lena

Aldan

Aldan

Ayan

Shantar Is

Okha

Yeniseysk

Angara

Chuna

Lower Tunguska

Kirensk

Olekma

Skalistyy
8143

Stanovoy Range

Nikolaevsk-na-Amur

Sakhalin

Alexandrovsk Sakhalinskiy

Poronaysk

Kansk

Tayshet

Bratsk

Bratsk Resr

Tulun

Skovorodino

Amur

Zeya

Svobodnyy

Amur

Komsomolsk-na-Amur

Sovetskaya Gavan

Uglegorsk

Gulf of Tartary

La Perouse Str.

Yuzhno Sakhalinsk

yarsk

Nizhneudinsk

Cheremkhovo

Angarsk

Irkutsk

L. Baikal

Ulan-Ude

Petrovsk Zabaykal'skiy

Ula Ra

Munku Sardyk

Khőbsőgől Dalai

Shilka

Chita

Yablonovyy Range

Vitim

Great Khingan Shan

Blagoveshchensk

Birobidzhan

Khabarovsk

Sungari

Sovetskaya

Sikhote Alin Range

Wakkanai

Asahi
2513

Hokkaido

Sapporo

Hakodate

Kyzyl

sa

Eastern Sayan

11454

Ulan Bator

Undur Khan

CHINA

Harbin

Mutankiang

Kirin

Khanka

St Olga

Ussuriysk

Vladivostok

La Perouse Str.

Hachinohe

MONGOLIA

INNER MONGOLIA

Changchun

Shenyang

Fushun

Anshan

NORTH KOREA

SEA OF JAPAN

N

Honshu

Niigata

Tok

Yokohama

Fujiyama
12388

Nagoya

HUR

Gobi

Paotow

Huhehot

Chiangkiakow

Peking

Liaotung Bay

Lüta

Korea Bay

Pyongyang

Seoul

SOUTH KOREA

JAPAN

Kyoto

Kobe

Osaka

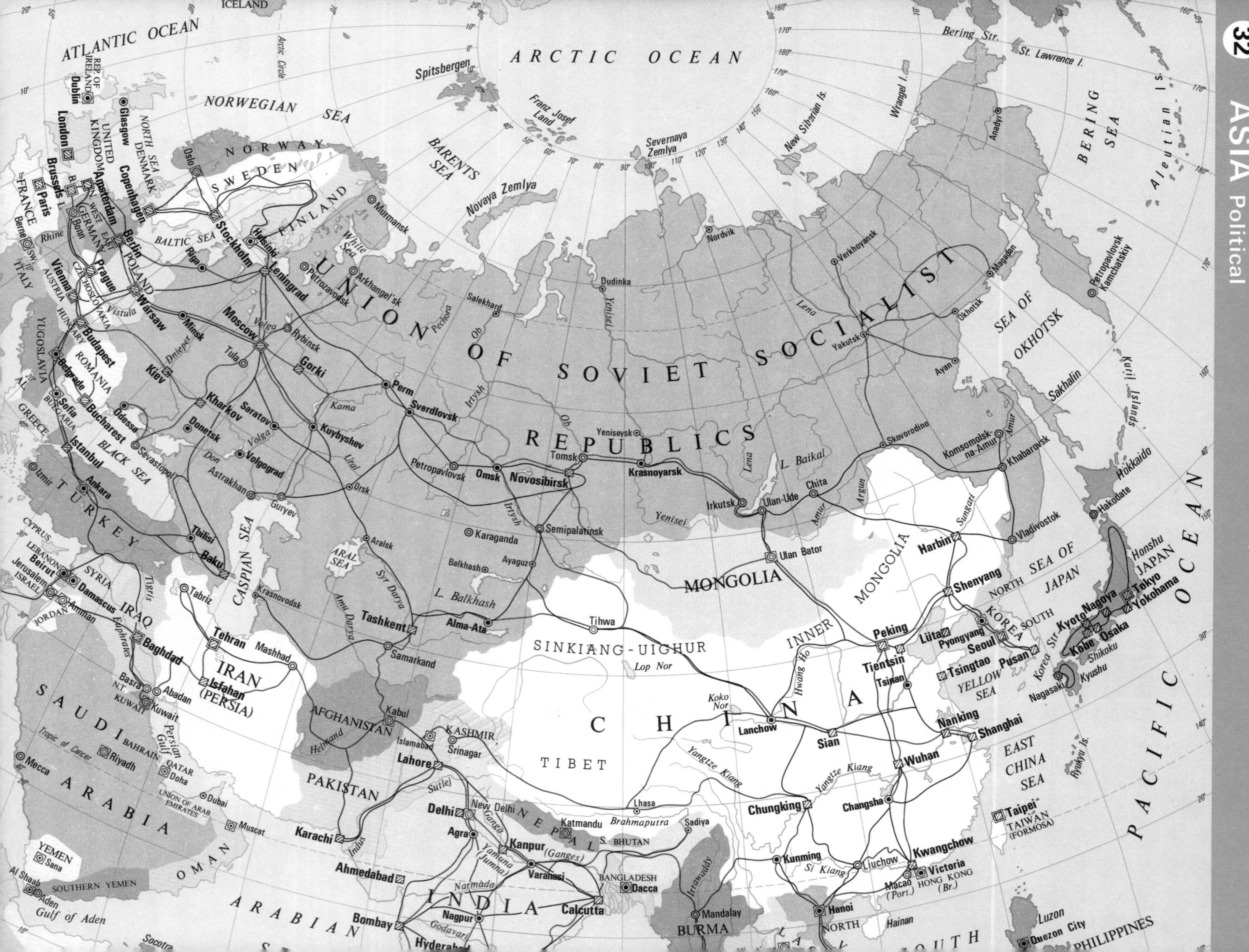

ARCTIC OCEAN
PACIFIC OCEAN
ATLANTIC OCEAN
NORWEGIAN SEA
BARENTS SEA
BERING SEA
SEA OF OKHOTSK
SEA OF JAPAN
YELLOW SEA
EAST CHINA SEA
ARABIAN SEA
CASPIAN SEA
ARAL SEA
BLACK SEA
NORTH SEA
BALTIC SEA
White Sea
Persian Gulf
Gulf of Aden
UNION OF SOVIET SOCIALIST REPUBLICS
MONGOLIA
INNER MONGOLIA
CHINA
SINKIANG-UIGHUR
TIBET
NORTH KOREA
SOUTH KOREA
JAPAN
TAIWAN (FORMOSA)
HONG KONG (Br.)
Macao (Port.)
PHILIPPINES
BURMA
BANGLADESH
BHUTAN
NEPAL
INDIA
KASHMIR
PAKISTAN
AFGHANISTAN
IRAN (PERSIA)
IRAQ
SYRIA
LEBANON
ISRAEL
JORDAN
CYPRUS
TURKEY
SAUDI ARABIA
KUWAIT
BAHRAIN
QATAR
UNION OF ARAB EMIRATES
OMAN
YEMEN
SOUTHERN YEMEN
NORWAY
SWEDEN
FINLAND
DENMARK
ICELAND
UNITED KINGDOM
REP. OF IRELAND
FRANCE
WEST GERMANY
EAST GERMANY
POLAND
CZECHOSLOVAKIA
AUSTRIA
HUNGARY
ROMANIA
YUGOSLAVIA
BULGARIA
GREECE
ITALY
Aleutian Is.
Kuril Islands
Hokkaido
Honshu
Shikoku
Kyushu
Ryukyu Is.
Sakhalin
Wrangel I.
St. Lawrence I.
Bering Str.
New Siberian Is.
Severnaya Zemlya
Franz Josef Land
Novaya Zemlya
Spitsbergen
Arctic Circle
Tropic of Cancer
Luzon
Hainan
Socotra
Korea Str.
Lena
Yenisei
Ob
Irtysh
Amur
Argun
Sungari
Hwang Ho
Yangtze Kiang
Si Kiang
Brahmaputra
Ganga (Ganges)
Yamuna (Jumna)
Narmada
Godavari
Sutlej
Indus
Irrawaddy
Tigris
Euphrates
Syr Darya
Amu Darya
Volga
Don
Dnieper
Kama
Ural
Pechora
Vistula
Rhine
Helmand
L. Baikal
L. Balkhash
Koko Nor
Lop Nor
Tokyo
Yokohama
Nagoya
Kyoto
Osaka
Kobe
Hakodate
Nagasaki
Pusan
Seoul
Pyongyang
Vladivostok
Khabarovsk
Komsomolsk-na-Amur
Petropavlovsk Kamchatskiy
Magadan
Okhotsk
Ayan
Anadyr
Yakutsk
Verkhoyansk
Skovorodino
Chita
Ulan-Ude
Ulan Bator
Irkutsk
Krasnoyarsk
Yeniseysk
Nordvik
Dudinka
Tomsk
Novosibirsk
Semipalatinsk
Ayaguz
Karaganda
Balkhash
Alma-Ata
Omsk
Petropavlovsk
Salekhard
Sverdlovsk
Perm
Murmansk
Arkhangel'sk
Petrozavodsk
Leningrad
Helsinki
Stockholm
Oslo
Copenhagen
Riga
Minsk
Moscow
Rybinsk
Gorki
Kuybyshev
Orsk
Aralsk
Guryev
Saratov
Volgograd
Astrakhan
Tula
Kharkov
Donetsk
Kiev
Odessa
Sevastopol
Tbilisi
Baku
Krasnovodsk
Tashkent
Samarkand
Mashhad
Tehran
Tabriz
Isfahan
Abadan
Basra
Kuwait
Baghdad
Damascus
Beirut
Amman
Jerusalem
Ankara
Istanbul
Izmir
Riyadh
Mecca
Doha
Dubai
Muscat
Sana
Aden
Al Shaab
Kabul
Islamabad
Lahore
Srinagar
Karachi
Ahmedabad
Bombay
Hyderabad
Nagpur
Agra
Delhi
New Delhi
Kanpur
Varanasi
Katmandu
Calcutta
Dacca
Lhasa
Sadiya
Mandalay
Hanoi
Kunming
Chungking
Lanchow
Sian
Tihwa
Changsha
Wuhan
Kwangchow
Liuchow
Victoria
Taipei
Quezon City
Nanking
Shanghai
Tsinan
Tsingtao
Tientsin
Peking
Harbin
Shenyang
Lüta
Glasgow
Dublin
London
Amsterdam
Brussels
Paris
Bonn
Berlin
Prague
Warsaw
Vienna
Budapest
Berne
Belgrade
Bucharest
Sofia

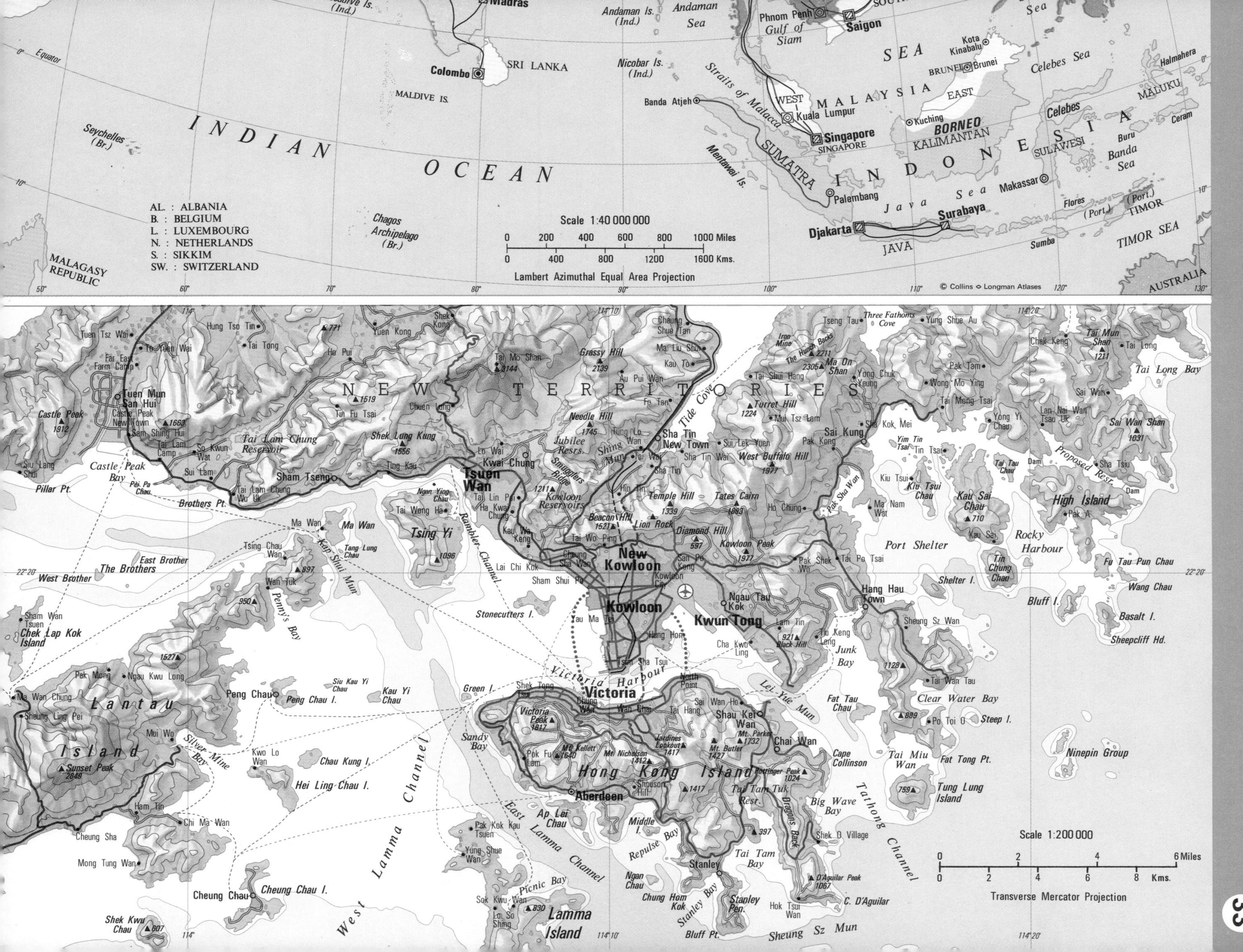

INDIAN OCEAN
SRI LANKA
Colombo
Madras
MALDIVE IS.
Seychelles (Br.)
Chagos Archipelago (Br.)
MALAGASY REPUBLIC
Andaman Is. (Ind.)
Andaman Sea
Nicobar Is. (Ind.)
Banda Atjeh
Straits of Malacca
Mentawai Is.
SUMATRA
Palembang
Phnom Penh
Gulf of Siam
Saigon
SEA
MALAYSIA
WEST
Kuala Lumpur
Singapore
SINGAPORE
Kota Kinabalu
BRUNEI
Brunei
EAST
Kuching
BORNEO
KALIMANTAN
INDONESIA
Celebes Sea
Celebes
SULAWESI
Halmahera
MALUKU
Ceram
Buru
Banda Sea
Makassar
Java Sea
Surabaya
Djakarta
JAVA
Flores
Sumba
(Port.) TIMOR
TIMOR SEA
AUSTRALIA
Equator
AL. : ALBANIA
B. : BELGIUM
L. : LUXEMBOURG
N. : NETHERLANDS
S. : SIKKIM
SW. : SWITZERLAND
Scale 1:40 000 000
0 200 400 600 800 1000 Miles
0 400 800 1200 1600 Kms.
Lambert Azimuthal Equal Area Projection
© Collins ◇ Longman Atlases
NEW TERRITORIES
Tuen Mun
San Hui
Castle Peak
Castle Peak Bay
Tai Lam Chung Reservoir
Sham Tseng
Tsuen Wan
Kwai Chung
Sha Tin
New Town
Tide Cove
Tai Mo Shan
Grassy Hill
Needle Hill
Jubilee Resrs.
Shing Mun
Tsing Yi
Rambler Channel
Kap Shui Mun
Ma Wan
Penny's Bay
The Brothers
East Brother
West Brother
Chek Lap Kok Island
Lantau Island
Sunset Peak
Silver Mine Bay
Peng Chau
Peng Chau I.
Kau Yi Chau
Hei Ling Chau I.
Chau Kung I.
Cheung Chau
Cheung Chau I.
West Lamma Channel
East Lamma Channel
Lamma Island
Picnic Bay
Stonecutters I.
Green I.
New Kowloon
Kowloon
Kwun Tong
Victoria Harbour
Victoria
Victoria Peak
Hong Kong Island
Aberdeen
Ap Lei Chau
Repulse Bay
Stanley
Stanley Bay
Tai Tam Bay
Shau Kei Wan
Chai Wan
Lei Yue Mun
Junk Bay
Clear Water Bay
Tathong Channel
Big Wave Bay
C. D'Aguilar
Sheung Sz Mun
Sai Kung
Port Shelter
Rocky Harbour
High Island
Tai Long Bay
Ninepin Group
Tung Lung Island
Fat Tong Pt.
Tai Miu Wan
Basalt I.
Sheepcliff Hd.
Scale 1:200 000
0 2 4 6 Miles
0 2 4 6 8 Kms.
Transverse Mercator Projection

BLACK SEA

BLACK SEA

GREECE

Thessaloniki
Khalkidhiki
Mt Athos 6670
Alexandroúpolis
Komotiní
Xánthi
Kaválla
Tekirdağ
Istanbul
Bosporus
Üsküdar
İzmit
Adapazarı
Bolu
Ereğli
Zonguldak
Bartın
Sinop
İnebolu
Kastamonu
Bafra
Samsun
Çarşamba
Ünye
Ordu
Tirebolu
Giresun
Trabzon
Rize
Artvin
Batumi
Akhali

Limnos
Thásos
Samothraki
Ímroz
Gallipoli
Çanakkale
Dardanelles
Sea of Marmara
Gemlik
Bursa
Bilecik
Geyve
Sakarya
Kandıra
Gebze
Bandırma
Balıkesir
Eskişehir
Kütahya
Sogut
Porsuk
Sivrihisar
Polatlı
Ankara
Kalecik
Çankırı
Çorum
Amasya
Merzifon
İskilip
Osmancık
Devrek
Yeşil
Kızıl
Pontine Mountains
Gümüşane
Bayburt

AEGEAN SEA
Skíros
Euboea
Athens
Piraeus
Corinth
Andros
Tínos
Cyclades
Páros
Náxos
Milos
Thira
Íkaria
Sámos
Dódecanese
Kos

Mítilíni
Lésvos
Ayvalık
Akhisar
Manisa
Gediz
İzmir
Aydın
Nazilli
Menderes
Milas
Muğla
G. of Kerme

Khíos
Khíos

Uşak
Alaşehir
Kula
Afyon
Eğridir Lake
Isparta
Beyşehir Lake
Konya
Denizli
Burdur
Manistar
Karaman
Ereğli
Nevşehir
Niğde
Ulukışla
Tarsus
Adana
Mersin

TAURUS MOUNTAINS
Kırşehir
Avanos
Mt Erciyas 12848
Kayseri
Pınarbaşı
Sivas
Divriği
Kemaliye
Erzincan
Erzurum
Bingöl D. 11972

ANATOLIA
TURKEY
Kırıkkale
Yozgat
Sungurlu
Zile
Tokat
Zara
Şebinkarahisar
Gürün
Malatya
Elazığ
Bingöl
Muş
Bitlis
Arapkir
Elbistan
Maraş
Adıyaman
Diyarbakır
Ergani
Tatvan
Siirt
Mardin
Cizre
Nusaybin
Tel Kotcher

Gaziantep
Birecik
Urfa
Kilis
Antakya
İskenderun
G. of İskenderun
Feyzipaşa

CRETE
Réthimnon
Iráklion
Khaniá
Kárpathos
Kásos

MEDITERRANEAN SEA

CYPRUS
Nicosia
Kyrenia
Famagusta
Mt Olympus 6403
Larnaca
Limassol
Paphos
C Gata
C Andreas
C Arnauti

Aleppo
Raqqa
Latakia
Hama
Homs
SYRIA
Palmyra
Deir-ez-Zor
Meyadin
Euphrates
Khabur
Al Jazira

Tripoli
LEBANON
Beirut
Sidon
Tyre
Zahle
Ba'albek
Mt Lebanon
Anti-Lebanon
Mt Hermon 9232
Damascus
Jebel ed Druz 5892
Ar Rutba
Ar Rar

Haifa
Nazareth
Tiberias
Safi
Mafraq
Zarqa
Amman
ISRAEL
Tel Aviv
Jaffa
Jerusalem
Jericho
Gaza
Hebron
Beersheba
Karak
Ma'an
JORDAN
Dead Sea
Negev
PETRA
Eilat
Aqaba

Syrian Desert
Ash Sham
Wadi Sirhan
El Azraq
J. Aneiza 3068
W. al Mir
W. Arar
W. al Ghadaf
W. Hauran
Hit

Tobruk
Bardia
Sidi Barrani
Salúm
Buqbuq
Matrúh
El Alamein
Alexandria
Rosetta
Damietta
Port Said
Nile Delta
L. Burullus
L. Manzala
Damanhúr
El Mahalla el Kubra
El Mansúra
Tanta
Zagazig
Ismâ'ilia
El Qantara
El 'Arish
W. el 'Arish

LIBYA
Jaghbub
Siwa Oasis
Siwa
Qara
Qattara Depression
Qattâra
Libyan Plateau

EGYPT
Lower Egypt
Cairo
El Giza
Heliopolis
Memphis
Helwan
Suez
Suez Canal
Bitter Lakes
Wadi el Natrún
Beni Suef
Birket Qarún
El Faiyúm
Galala Plateau
Arabian Plateau or Eastern Desert
W. Tarfa
El Minya
Mallawi
Bawiti
Asyút
Abu Tig
Sohag
Nag' Hammâdi
Qêna
THEBES
Luxor
Isna
Idfu
Aswân
Aswân High Dam
Lake Nasser
Abu Simbel
W. Qena
W. Allaqi

Farafra
Qasr Farafra Oasis
Dakhla Oasis
El Qasr
Kharga Oasis
El Khârga

Libyan Desert

Sinai Peninsula
Plateau of El Tih
Abu Zenima
G. Katherina 8651
Tor
Gulf of Suez
Gulf of Aqaba
Ras Muhammad
Hurghada
Port Safâga
 Qoseir
Al Wajh
Umm Lajj
J. el-Loz 8461
Tebúk
Hail
Taima
Medina
Yanbu

RED SEA

Tropic of Cancer

AN NAFUD (Great Sandy Desert)

Sakaka
Al Jauf
Shaib al Qur
Safâha
Aqlat as Suqur
Nuqra
W. Jizl
W. al Ubaid
W. Hamdh
Hanakiya
J. Radhwa 5906

Ras Banas

SUDAN
Wadi Halfa
Nubian Desert

Scale 1:9 000 000
0 50 100 150 200 250 Miles
0 100 200 300 400 Kms.
Sonic Projection

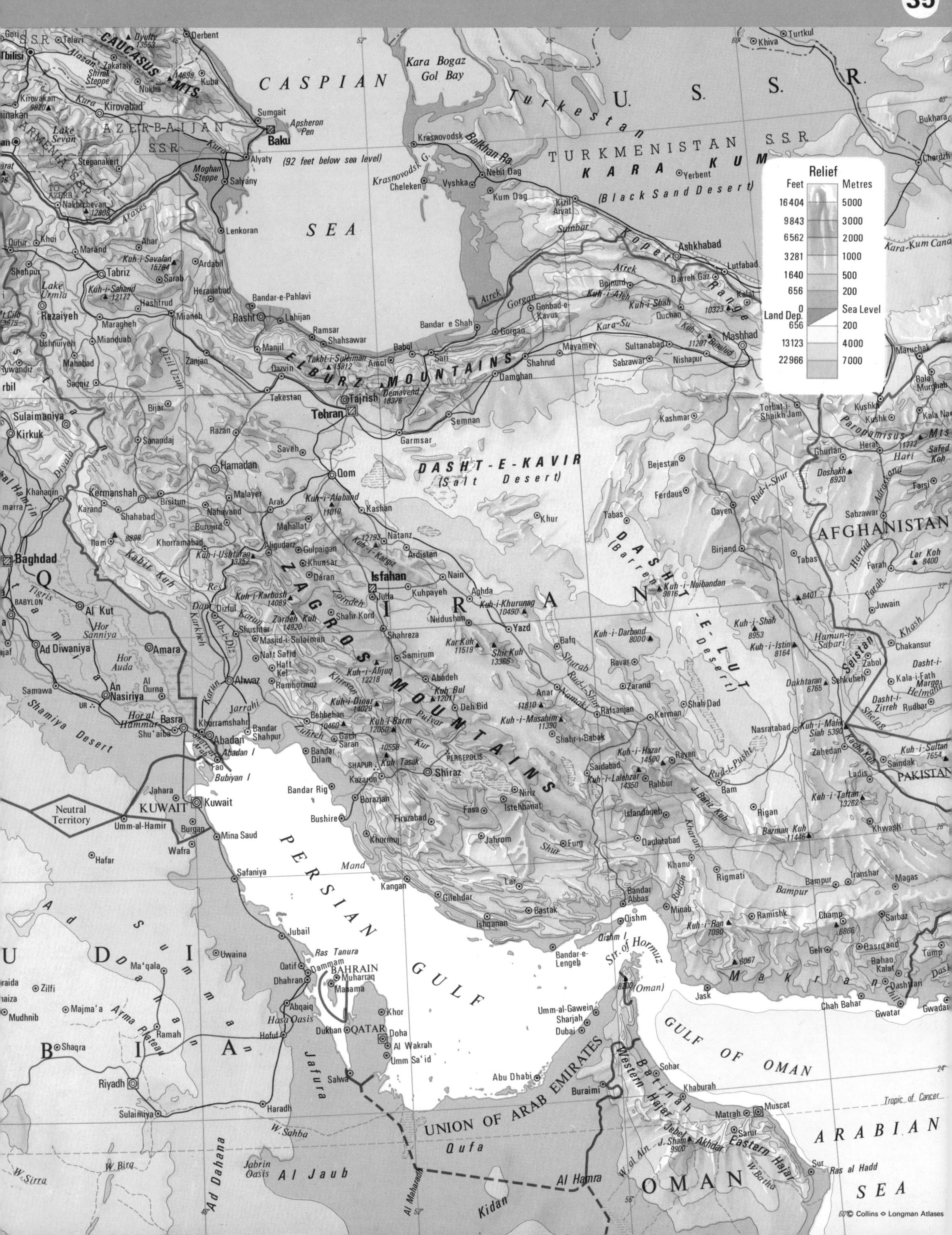

Relief

Feet		Metres
16 404		5000
9843		3000
6562		2000
3281		1000
1640		500
656		200
0		Sea Level
Land Dep.		200
656		
13 123		4000
22 966		7000

60 © Collins ◆ Longman Atlases

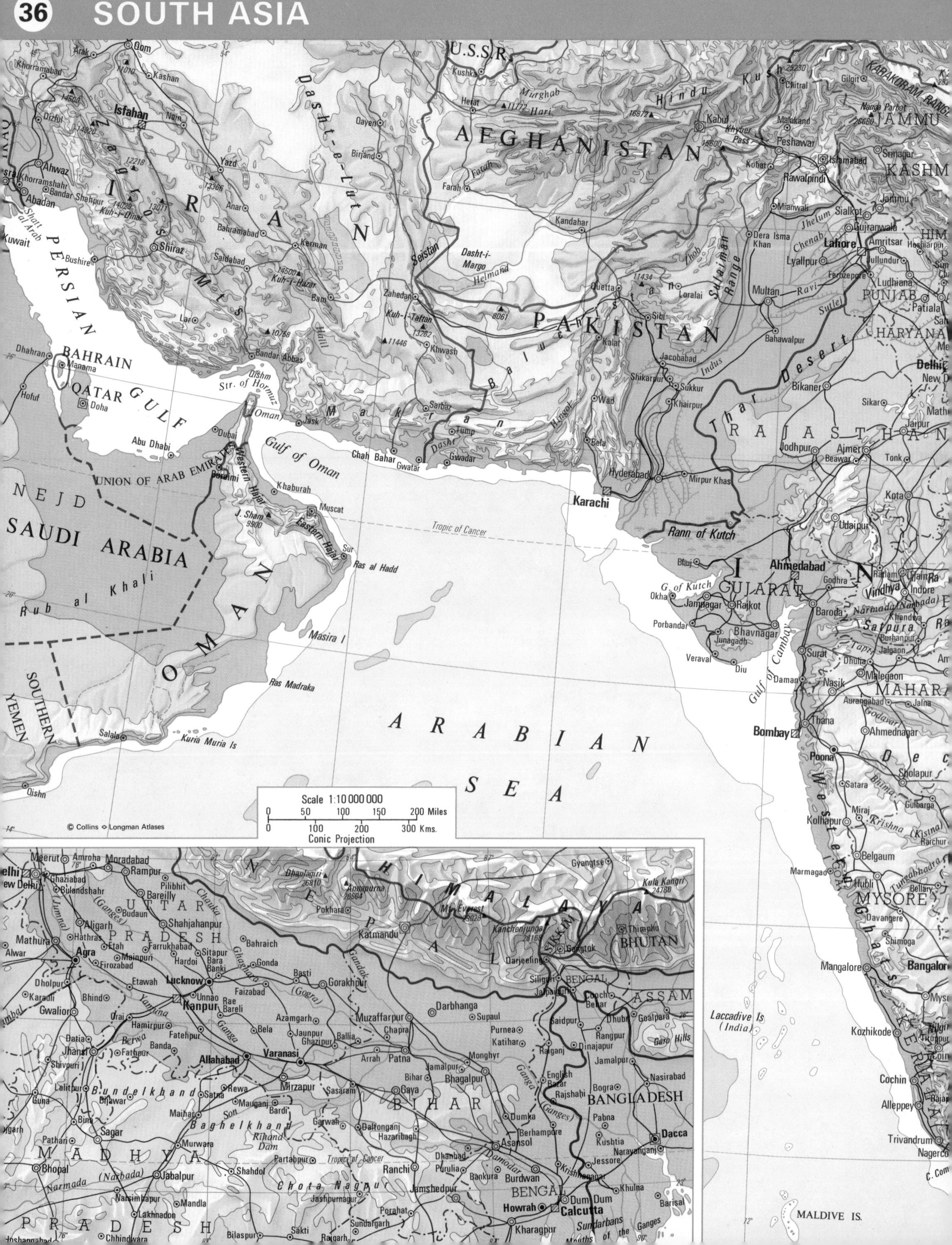

U.S.S.R.
AFGHANISTAN
PAKISTAN
IRAN
Zagros Mts
Dasht-e-Lut
Hindu Kush
KARAKORAM RANGE
JAMMU
KASHMIR
PERSIAN GULF
BAHRAIN
QATAR
UNION OF ARAB EMIRATES
NEJD
SAUDI ARABIA
Rub al Khali
OMAN
SOUTHERN YEMEN
Gulf of Oman
Str. of Hormuz
Tropic of Cancer
ARABIAN SEA
Rann of Kutch
G. of Kutch
Gulf of Cambay
Thar Desert
RAJASTHAN
GUJARAT
PUNJAB
HARYANA
MYSORE
Western Ghats
Laccadive Is (India)
MALDIVE IS.
Qom
Isfahan
Arak
Kashan
Khorramabad
Dizful
Ahwaz
Khorramshahr
Abadan
Bandar Shahpur
Shatt al Arab
Kuwait
Bushire
Shiraz
Yazd
Kerman
Bam
Lar
Bandar Abbas
Qishm
Jask
Dubai
Abu Dhabi
Dhahran
Manama
Hofuf
Doha
Buraimi
Khaburah
Muscat
J. Sham 9900
Western Hajar
Eastern Hajar
Sur
Ras al Hadd
Masira I
Ras Madraka
Kuria Muria Is
Salala
Qishn
Herat
Kushka
Murghab
Hari
Qayen
Birjand
Farah
Kandahar
Seistan
Dasht-i-Margo
Helmand
Zahedan
Kuh-i-Taftan 13262
Khwash
Sarbaz
Chah Bahar
Gwatar
Gwadar
Kabul
Khyber Pass
Peshawar
Chitral
Gilgit
Nanga Parbat 26660
Malakand
Islamabad
Rawalpindi
Srinagar
Jammu
Kohat
Mianwali
Sialkot
Gujranwala
Lahore
Amritsar
Dera Ismail Khan
Lyallpur
Jhelum
Chenab
Ravi
Sutlej
Indus
Quetta
Sibi
Loralai
Sulaiman Range
Multan
Bahawalpur
Kalat
Jacobabad
Shikarpur
Sukkur
Khairpur
Wad
Bela
Hyderabad
Mirpur Khas
Karachi
Ludhiana
Ferozepore
Patiala
Delhi
New Delhi
Bikaner
Sikar
Jaipur
Jodhpur
Ajmer
Beawar
Tonk
Kota
Udaipur
Bhuj
Ahmedabad
Okha
Jamnagar
Rajkot
Porbandar
Bhavnagar
Junagadh
Veraval
Diu
Godhra
Ratlam
Indore
Vindhya
Baroda
Narmada (Narbada)
Satpura
Burhanpur
Jalgaon
Surat
Daman
Dhulia
Malegaon
Nasik
Aurangabad
Jalna
Godavari
Thana
Bombay
Ahmednagar
Poona
Satara
Sholapur
Bhima
Miraj
Kolhapur
Krishna (Kistna)
Gulbarga
Raichur
Belgaum
Marmagao
Hubli
Tungabhadra
Bellary
Davangere
Shimoga
Mangalore
Kozhikode
Cochin
Alleppey
Trivandrum
Scale 1:10 000 000
0 50 100 150 200 Miles
0 100 200 300 Kms.
Conic Projection
© Collins ◇ Longman Atlases
Meerut
Amroha
Moradabad
Rampur
Ghaziabad
Bulandshahr
Bareilly
Pilibhit
Budaun
UTTAR PRADESH
Aligarh
Shahjahanpur
Mathura
Hathras
Etah
Farrukhabad
Agra
Mainpuri
Firozabad
Sitapur
Hardoi
Bara Banki
Gonda
Bahraich
Etawah
Lucknow
Unnao
Kanpur
Rae Bareli
Faizabad
Basti
Gorakhpur
Gogra
Ghaghara
Gandak
Dholpur
Bhind
Gwalior
Orai
Hamirpur
Yamuna
Ganga
Azamgarh
Jaunpur
Ghazipur
Ballia
Bela
Fatehpur
Banda
Datia
Jhansi
Betwa
Shivpuri
Allahabad
Varanasi
Mirzapur
Lalitpur
Bundelkhand
Rewa
Satna
Guna
Bijawar
Mauganj
Maihar
Son
Baghelkhand
Bina
Sagar
Rihand Dam
Murwara
Shahdol
Bhopal
Jabalpur
Narmada (Narbada)
Narsimhapur
Mandla
Lakhnadon
MADHYA PRADESH
Chhindwara
Bilaspur
Raigarh
NEPAL
Dhaulagiri 26810
Annapurna 26504
Pokhara
Katmandu
HIMALAYA
Mt. Everest 29028
Kanchenjunga 28168
SIKKIM
Gangtok
Gyangtse
Kula Kangri 24780
Thimphu
BHUTAN
Darjeeling
Siliguri
Jalpaiguri
BENGAL
Cooch Behar
ASSAM
Dhubri
Goalpara
Garo Hills
Muzaffarpur
Darbhanga
Supaul
Chapra
Purnea
Katihar
Raiganj
Monghyr
Arrah
Patna
Bihar
Jamalpur
Bhagalpur
Saidpur
Rangpur
Dinajpur
Jamalpur
Nasirabad
English Bazar
Rajshahi
Bogra
BANGLADESH
Gaya
Sasaram
BIHAR
Dumka
Garwah
Daltonganj
Hazaribagh
Berhampore
Pabna
Kushtia
Dacca
Narayanganj
Jessore
Asansol
Damodar
Dhanbad
Purulia
Bankura
Burdwan
Ranchi
Tropic of Cancer
Chota Nagpur
Jamshedpur
Jashpurnagar
Krishnagar
Khulna
Barisal
Howrah
Calcutta
Dum Dum
Sundargarh
Kharagpur
Sakti
Sundarbans
Mouths of the Ganges

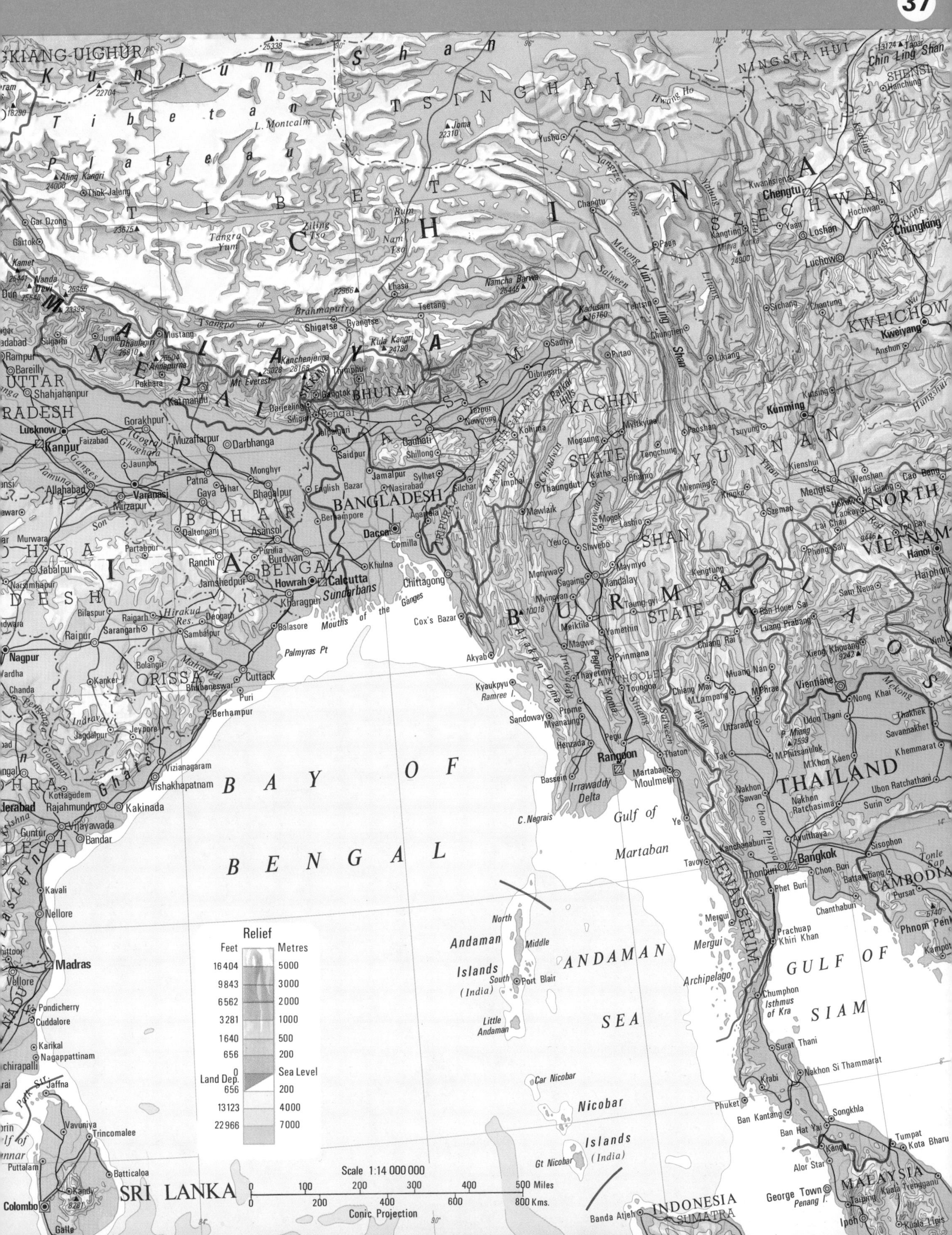

SINKIANG-UIGHUR

Kunlun Shan

Tibetan Plateau

CHINA

TSINGHAI

NINGSTA-HUT

Chin Ling Shan

SHENSI

Hanchung

L. Montcalm

Hwang Ho

Yangtze

Chengtu

SZECHWAN

Hochwan

Chungking

Yushu

Ating Kangri

Thok Jalung

Gar Dzong

Gartok

Tangra Yum

Ziling Tso

Bum Tso

Nam Tso

Joma

Yangtze

Kiang

Kwanhsien

Kiating

Loshan

Luchow

KWEICHOW

Kweiyang

Anshun

Kamet

Wanda Devi

HIMALAYA

Mustang

Dhaulagiri

Annapurna

Pokhara

NEPAL

Kanchenjunga

Mt Everest

Kathmandu

SIKKIM

Darjeeling

Siliguri

Jalpaiguri

N Bengal

Gangtok

Thimphu

BHUTAN

Brahmaputra or Tsangpo

Lhasa

Shigatse

Byangtse

Tsetang

Namcha Barwa

Kula Kangri

Salween

Mekong Yün

Likiang

Sichang

Chaotung

Kunming

Kusing

Hungshui

Sadiya

Kadusam

Teltsin

Chungtien

Yaan

YUNNAN

NORTH

VIETNAM

UTTAR

RADESH

Bareilly

Shahjahanpur

Lucknow

Kanpur

Faizabad

Gorakhpur

Ghaghara

Muzaffarpur

Darbhanga

Ganges

Jaunpur

Patna

Bihar

Monghyr

Bhagalpur

ASSAM

Dibrugarh

Tezpur

Gauhati

Shillong

Jamalpur

Sylhet

Nowgong

Kohima

NAGALAND

MANIPUR

Imphal

Thaungdut

Mogaung

Katha

Bhamo

KACHIN STATE

Myitkyina

Tengchung

Paoshan

Tsuyung

Mienning

Ha Giang

Mengtsz

Laokay

Cao Bang

Phong Saly

Hanoi

Haiphong

Allahabad

Varanasi

Mirzapur

Gaya

Asansol

English Bazar

Nasirabad

Silchar

BANGLADESH

Agartala

Dacca

Comilla

Mewlaik

Yeu

Shwebo

Mogok

Lashio

SHAN STATE

Kengtung

Ban Houei Sai

Luang Prabang

Sam Neua

Murwara

Jabalpur

Narsimhapur

DESH

Nagpur

Wardha

MADHYA

Bilaspur

Partabpur

Daltonganj

Purulia

Burdwan

Ranchi

Jamshedpur

BENGAL

Howrah

Calcutta

Sunderbans

Khulna

Chittagong

Chandpur

BURMA

Monywa

Sagaing

Mandalay

Maymyo

Myingyan

Meiktila

Yamethin

Taung-gyi

Chanda

Raigarh

Deogarh

Sambalpur

Hirakud Res.

Raipur

Sarangarh

Bolangir

Mahanadi

ORISSA

Cuttack

Bhubaneswar

Puri

Mouths of the Ganges

Cox's Bazar

Akyab

Kyaukpyu

Ramree I.

Sandoway

Myanaung

Prome

Magwe

Thayetmyo

Pyinmana

Toungoo

KAWTHOOLEI

Pegu

Chiang Rai

Muang Nan

M. Phrae

Chiang Mai

Lampang

M. Prae

Xieng Khouang

Vientiane

Nong Khai

Udon Thani

Thakhek

Savannakhet

LAOS

Indravati

Jeypore

Jagdalpur

Godavari

Eastern Ghats

Vizianagaram

Vishakhapatnam

Palmyras Pt

Berhampur

Henzada

Bassein

Rangoon

Irrawaddy Delta

Martaban

Moulmein

Pegu

Thaton

Tak

Phitsanulok

Nakhon Sawan

Nakhon Ratchasima

Khemmarat

Ubon Ratchathani

Surin

THAILAND

Kottagudem

Rajahmundry

Kakinada

C. Negrais

Gulf of Martaban

Ye

Tavoy

TENASSERIM

Ayutthaya

Thonburi

Bangkok

Chon Buri

Battambang

CAMBODIA

Pursat

Phet Buri

Chanthaburi

Guntur

Vijayawada

Bandar

Krishna

Kavali

Nellore

B A Y   O F

B E N G A L

North Andaman

Middle Andaman

South Andaman

Port Blair

ANDAMAN

SEA

Mergui

Mergui Archipelago

Prachuap Khiri Khan

Chumphon

Isthmus of Kra

GULF OF

SIAM

Madras

Vellore

Pondicherry

Cuddalore

Karikal

Nagappattinam

chirapalli

rai

Relief

Feet | | Metres
16 404 | | 5000
9843 | | 3000
6562 | | 2000
3281 | | 1000
1640 | | 500
656 | | 200
0 | | Sea Level
Land Dep.
656 | | 200
13123 | | 4000
22966 | | 7000

Little Andaman

Car Nicobar

Nicobar

Islands

(India)

Gt Nicobar

Surat Thani

Krabi

Ban Kantang

Phuket

Nakhon Si Thammarat

Songkhla

Ban Hat Yai

Tumpat

Kota Bharu

MALAYSIA

George Town

Penang I.

Kangar

Alor Star

Taiping

Ipoh

Kuala Trengganu

Jaffna

Vavuniya

Trincomalee

Batticaloa

Kandy

SRI LANKA

Colombo

Galle

Scale 1:14 000 000

0   100   200   300   400   500 Miles

0   200   400   600   800 Kms.

Conic Projection

Banda Atjeh   INDONESIA   SUMATRA

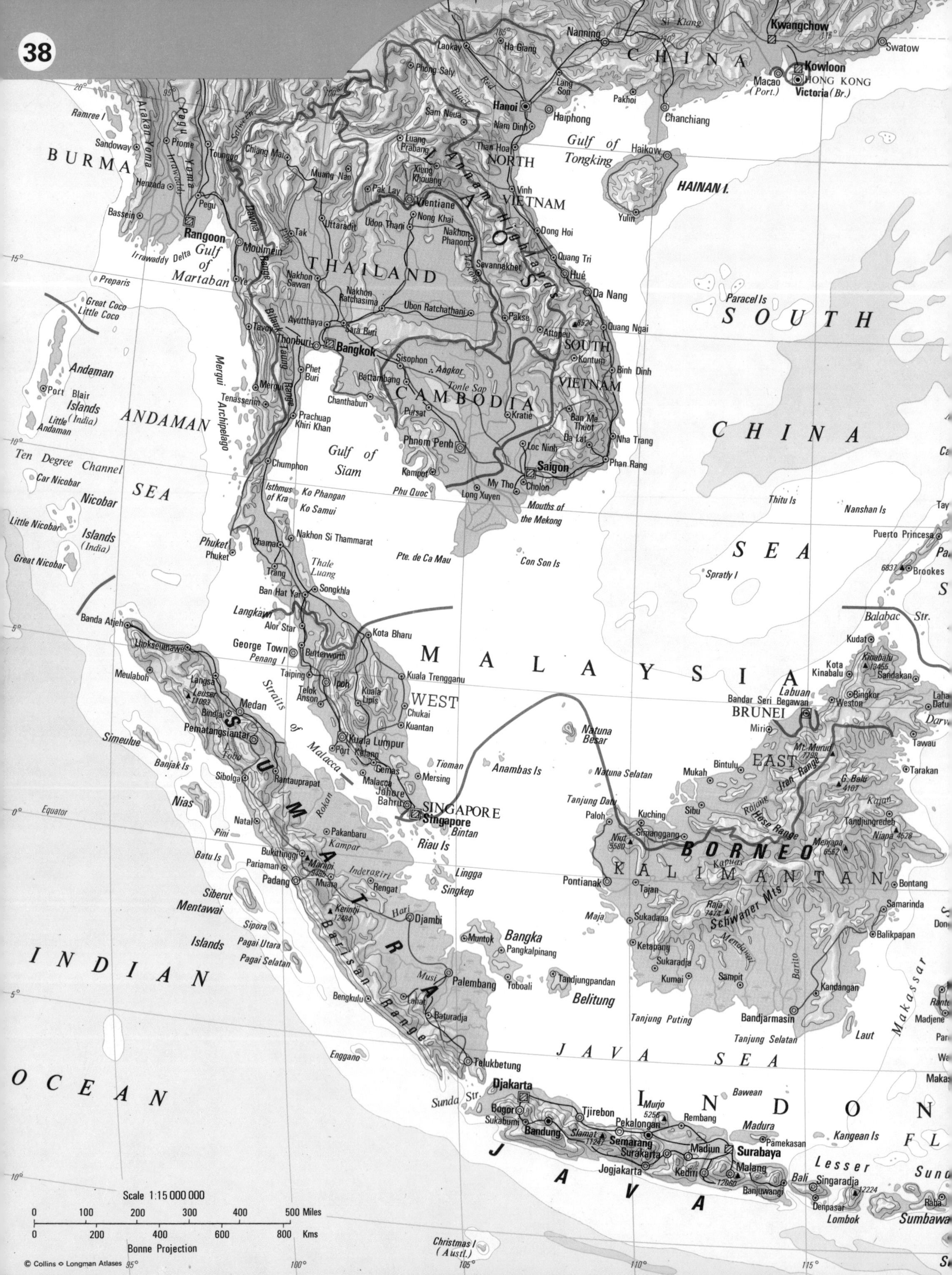

CHINA
Kwangchow
Nanning
Swatow
Kowloon
HONG KONG
Victoria (Br.)
Macao (Port.)
Pakhoi
Chanchiang
Laokay
Ha Giang
Phong Saly
Lang Son
Hanoi
Haiphong
Nam Dinh
Sam Neua
Luang Prabang
Thanh Hoa
NORTH VIETNAM
Vinh
Gulf of Tongking
Haikow
HAINAN I.
Yulin
BURMA
Ramree I
Sandoway
Prome
Toungoo
Henzada
Bassein
Pegu
Rangoon
Gulf of Martaban
Irrawaddy Delta
Moulmein
Arakan Yoma
Pegu Yoma
Chiang Mai
Muang Nan
Xieng Khouang
Pak Lay
Vientiane
Nong Khai
Udon Thani
Uttaradit
Tak
Nakhon Phanom
Dong Hoi
Quang Tri
Savannakhet
Hué
Da Nang
THAILAND
Nakhon Sawan
Nakhon Ratchasima
Ubon Ratchathani
Ayutthaya
Sara Buri
Thonburi
Bangkok
Pakse
Attapeu
Quang Ngai
SOUTH VIETNAM
Kontum
Binh Dinh
Preparis
Great Coco
Little Coco
Tavoy
Ye
Mergui Archipelago
Andaman Islands (India)
Port Blair
Little Andaman
ANDAMAN SEA
Mergui
Tenasserim
Phet Buri
Sisophon
Angkor
Tonle Sap
Battambang
CAMBODIA
Chanthaburi
Pursat
Kratie
Ban Me Thuot
Da Lat
Nha Trang
Phan Rang
Prachuap Khiri Khan
Gulf of Siam
Phnom Penh
Loc Ninh
Saigon
Cholon
My Tho
Kampot
Ten Degree Channel
Car Nicobar
Nicobar Islands (India)
Little Nicobar
Great Nicobar
Chumphon
Isthmus of Kra
Ko Phangan
Ko Samui
Phu Quoc
Long Xuyen
Mouths of the Mekong
Paracel Is
SOUTH CHINA SEA
Thitu Is
Nanshan Is
Puerto Princesa
Brookes
Spratly I
Nakhon Si Thammarat
Phuket
Thale Luang
Pte. de Ca Mau
Con Son Is
Trang
Ban Hat Yai
Songkhla
Langkawi
Alor Star
Kota Bharu
Balabac Str.
Banda Atjeh
Lhokseumawe
George Town
Penang I
Butterworth
MALAYSIA
Kudat
Kinabalu 13455
Kota Kinabalu
Sandakan
Meulaboh
Langsa
Leuser 11093
Medan
Taiping
Ipoh
Kuala Trengganu
Telok Anson
Kuala Lipis
WEST
Labuan
Bandar Seri Begawan
Beaufort
Weston
BRUNEI
Miri
Bindjai
Pematangsiantar
Straits of Malacca
Chukai
Kuantan
Kuala Lumpur
Port Kelang
Natuna Besar
Tawau
Simeulue
Toba
Banjak Is
Sibolga
Rantauprapat
Gemas
Malacca
Tioman
Mersing
Anambas Is
Natuna Selatan
Bintulu
Mukah
EAST
Mt. Murud 7798
Iran Range
Tarakan
G. Balu 4107
Nias
Johore Bahru
SINGAPORE
Singapore
Bintan
Tanjung Datu
Paloh
Kuching
Sibu
Rajang
Hose Range
Kajan
Tandjungredeb
Niapa 4528
Equator
Natal
Pini
Pakanbaru
Kampar
Rokan
Riau Is
Niut 5580
Simanggang
BORNEO
Menjapa 8552
Kapuas
Batu Is
Bukittinggi
Pariaman
Marapi 9485
Padang
Muara
Inderagiri
Rengat
Lingga
Singkep
Pontianak
Tajan
KALIMANTAN
Bontang
Siberut
Mentawai Islands
Sipora
Pagai Utara
Pagai Selatan
Kerintji 12484
Hari
Djambi
Maja
Sukadana
Raja 7474
Schwaner Mts
Samarinda
Balikpapan
SUMATRA
Barisan Range
Muntok
Bangka
Pangkalpinang
Ketapang
Sukaradja
Kumai
Sampit
Mendawai
Barito
INDIAN OCEAN
Musi
Palembang
Toboali
Tandjungpandan
Belitung
Kandangan
Makassar
Bengkulu
Lahat
Baturadja
Tanjung Puting
Bandjarmasin
Tanjung Selatan
Laut
Madjene
Enggano
Telukbetung
JAVA SEA
Djakarta
Sunda Str.
Bogor
Sukabumi
Bandung
Tjirebon
Murjo 5256
Pekalongan
Rembang
Bawean
INDONESIA
Slamat 11247
Semarang
Surakarta
Madiun
Surabaya
Madura
Pamekasan
Kangean Is
Jogjakarta
Kediri
Malang
12060
Lesser Sunda
JAVA
Bali
Singaradja
Banjuwangi
Denpasar
Lombok
12224
Raba
Sumbawa
Christmas I (Austl.)
Scale 1:15 000 000
0 100 200 300 400 500 Miles
0 200 400 600 800 Kms
Bonne Projection
© Collins • Longman Atlases
95°
100°
105°
110°
115°
20°
15°
10°
5°
0°
5°
10°

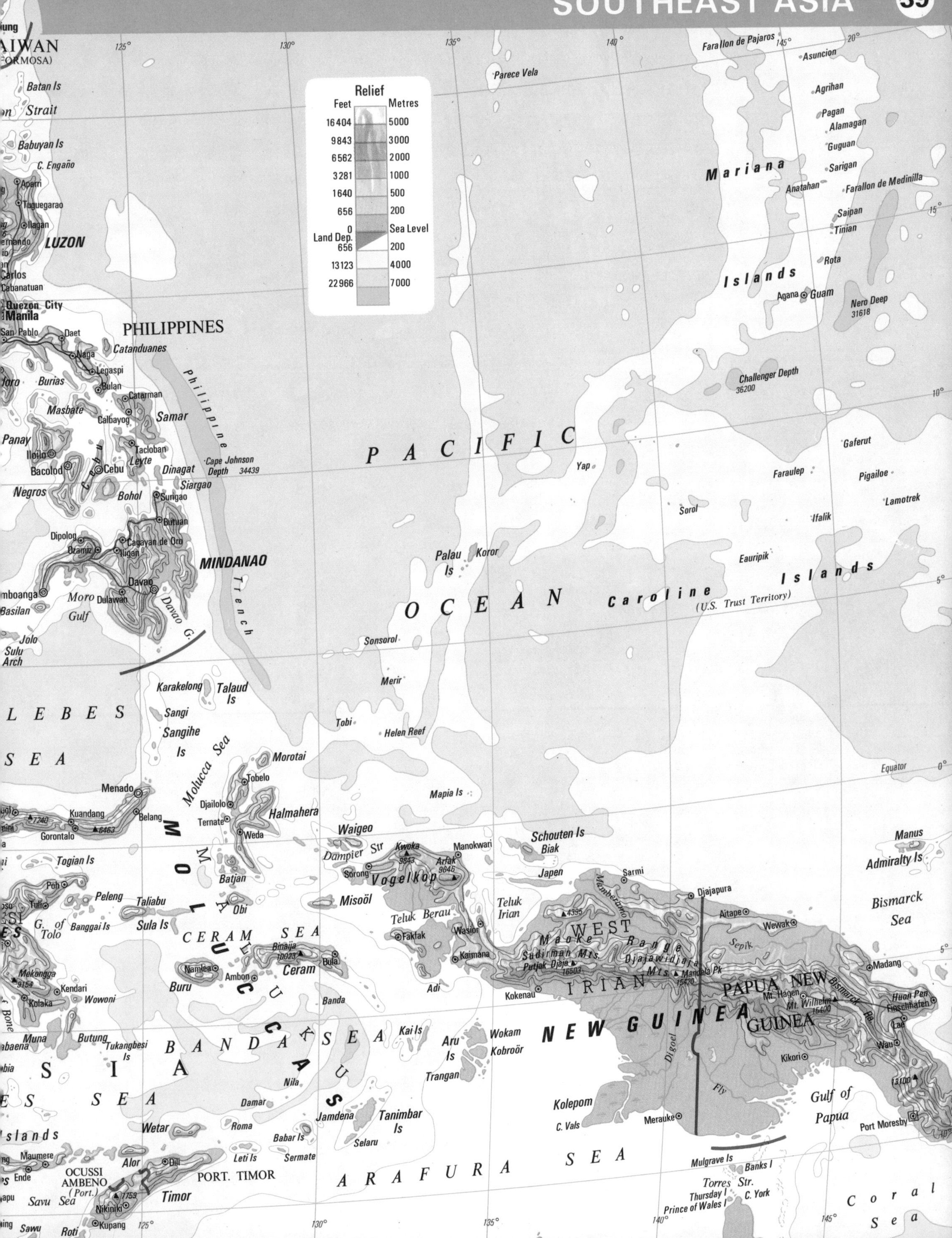

Relief

Feet		Metres
16 404		5000
9843		3000
6562		2000
3281		1000
1640		500
656		200
0		Sea Level
Land Dep.		
656		200
13 123		4000
22 966		7000

TAIWAN (FORMOSA)

Cancer

Batan Is

Strait

Babuyan Is

C. Engaño

Apparri
Taguegarao
Ilagan

LUZON

Fernando
Carlos
Cabanatuan

Quezon City
Manila
San Pablo
Daet

PHILIPPINES

Naga
Legaspi

Catanduanes

Moro
Burias
Bulan
Masbate
Catarman
Calbayog
Samar
Panay
Iloilo
Tacloban
Leyte
Negros
Bacolod
Cebu
Dinagat
Siargao
Bohol
Surigao
Dipolog
Buruan
Oramiz
Cagayan de Oro
Iligan
Zamboanga
Davao
Basilan
Moro
Dulawan
Gulf
Jolo
Sulu
Arch

MINDANAO

Cape Johnson
Depth 34439

Davao G.

Davao Trench

Philippine Trench

Parece Vela

Farallon de Pajaros
Asuncion
Agrihan
Pagan
Alamagan
Guguan

Mariana

Sarigan
Anatahan
Farallon de Medinilla
Saipan
Tinian

Islands

Rota

Agana Guam
Nero Deep 31618

Challenger Depth 36200

PACIFIC

Yap

Gaferut

Faraulep
Pigailoe

Sorol
Ifalik
Lamotrek

OCEAN
Caroline Islands
(U.S. Trust Territory)

Palau Is
Koror

Eauripik

Sonsorol

Merir

Tobi
Helen Reef

Manus
Admiralty Is

Bismarck Sea

CELEBES SEA

Karakelong
Talaud Is

Sangi
Sangihe Is

Molucca Sea

Morotai

Tobelo

Mapia Is

Schouten Is
Biak

Japen

Sarmi

Djapura

Aitape
Wewak

Madang

Menado
7240
Kuandang
6463
Gorontalo
Belang

Ternate
Djailolo
Weda

Halmahera

Waigeo

Manokwari

Mamberamo
4395

WEST
Maoke Range
Sepik

Sudirman Mts.
Djajawidjaja Mts.
Putjak Djaja 16503
Mandala Pk. 15420

PAPUA NEW

Mt. Hagen
Mt. Wilhelm 16400

GUINEA

Finschhafen
Huon Pen
Lae

Togian Is

Poh
Tulli

Peleng

Taliabu

Batjan

Obi

Misool

Sorong

Vogelkop
Arfak 9646
Kwoka 9843

Dampier Str

Teluk Irian

IRIAN

NEW GUINEA

Kikori

13100

Gulf of Papua

MOLUCCA

Banggai Is
Sula Is

Ceram Sea

Namlea
Binaija 10023

Ceram
Bula

Teluk Berau
Fakfak

Wasior

Kaimana

Kokenau

Disoel

Fly

Port Moresby

Mekongga 9154
Kendari
Wowoni

Buru
Ambon

Adi

Banda

BANDA SEA

MOLUCCAS

Kai Is
Aru Is
Kobroör

Wokam

Trangan

Port Moresby

Muna
Butung
Tukangbesi Is

Nila

Damar

Kolepom
C. Vals

Merauke

Mulgrave Is
Banks I
Torres Str.
Thursday I
Prince of Wales I
C. York

Ende

Maumere
Alor
Dili

OCUSSI AMBENO (Port.)

Timor
7755
Nikiniki

Kupang

PORT. TIMOR

Wetar
Roma
Babar Is
Leti Is
Sermata
Selaru

Tanimbar Is

Jamdena

ARAFURA SEA

Coral Sea

Savu Sea
Sawu
Roti

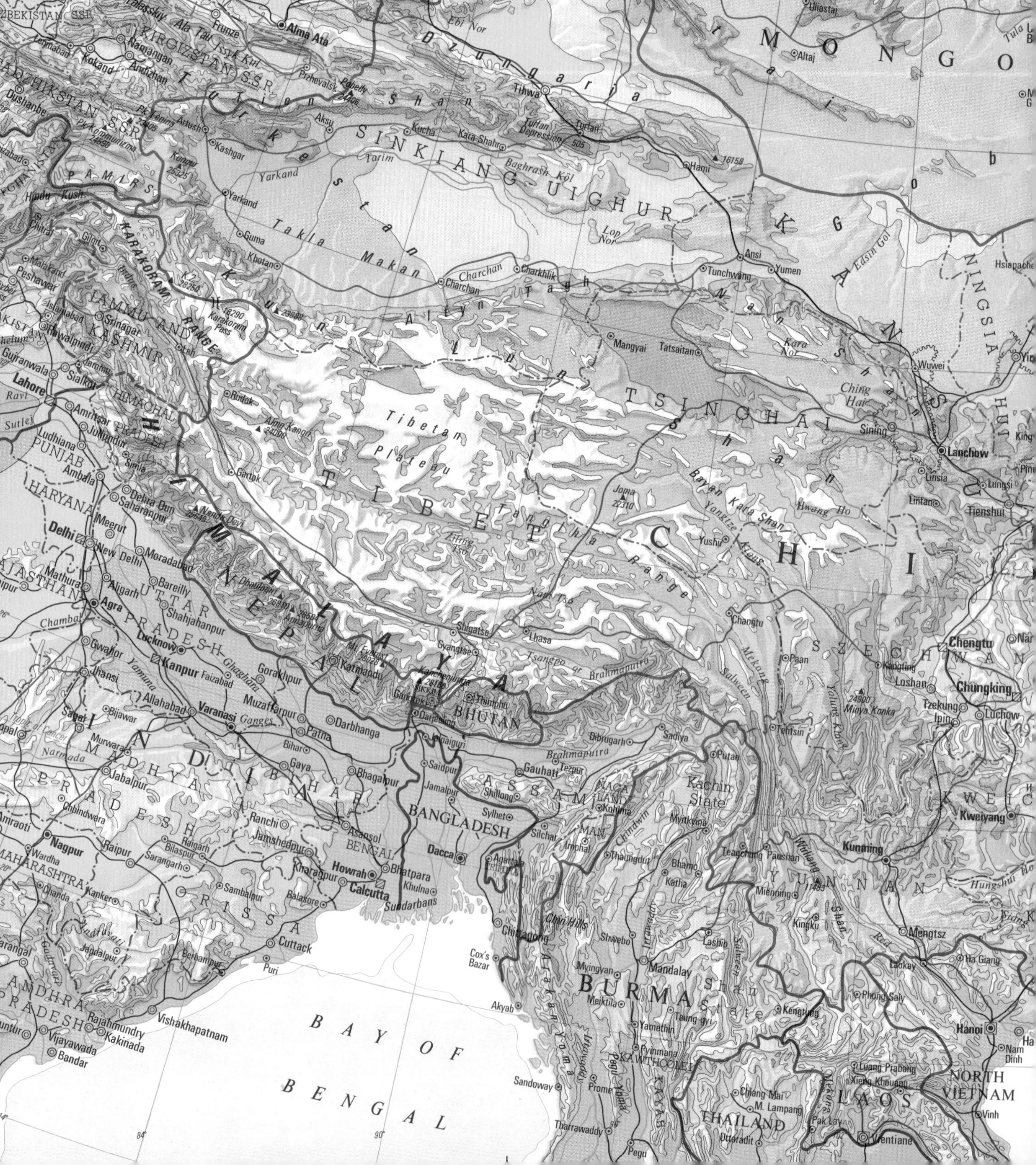

U.S.S.R.

MONGOLIA

KAZAKHSTAN S.S.R.

KIRGIZSTAN S.S.R.

UZBEKISTAN S.S.R.

TADZHIKISTAN S.S.R.

SINKIANG-UIGHUR

KANSU

NINGSIA HUI

TSINGHAI

TIBET

CHINA

SZECHWAN

KWEICHOW

YUNNAN

JAMMU AND KASHMIR

HIMACHAL PRADESH

PUNJAB

HARYANA

RAJASTHAN

UTTAR PRADESH

MADHYA PRADESH

BIHAR

NEPAL

BHUTAN

BANGLADESH

ASSAM

NAGALAND

MANIPUR

WEST BENGAL

ORISSA

MAHARASHTRA

ANDHRA PRADESH

BURMA

THAILAND

LAOS

NORTH VIETNAM

HIMALAYA

KARAKORAM RANGE

PAMIRS

HINDU KUSH

Tien Shan

Dzungaria

Takla Makan

Tarim

Tibetan Plateau

BAY OF BENGAL

Lake Balkhash

Lake Baikal

Tashkent

Alma Ata

Frunze

Delhi

New Delhi

Lahore

Amritsar

Kanpur

Lucknow

Agra

Varanasi

Patna

Calcutta

Howrah

Dacca

Nagpur

Kathmandu

Lhasa

Chengtu

Chungking

Kunming

Kweiyang

Lanchow

Hanoi

Mandalay

Bay of Bengal

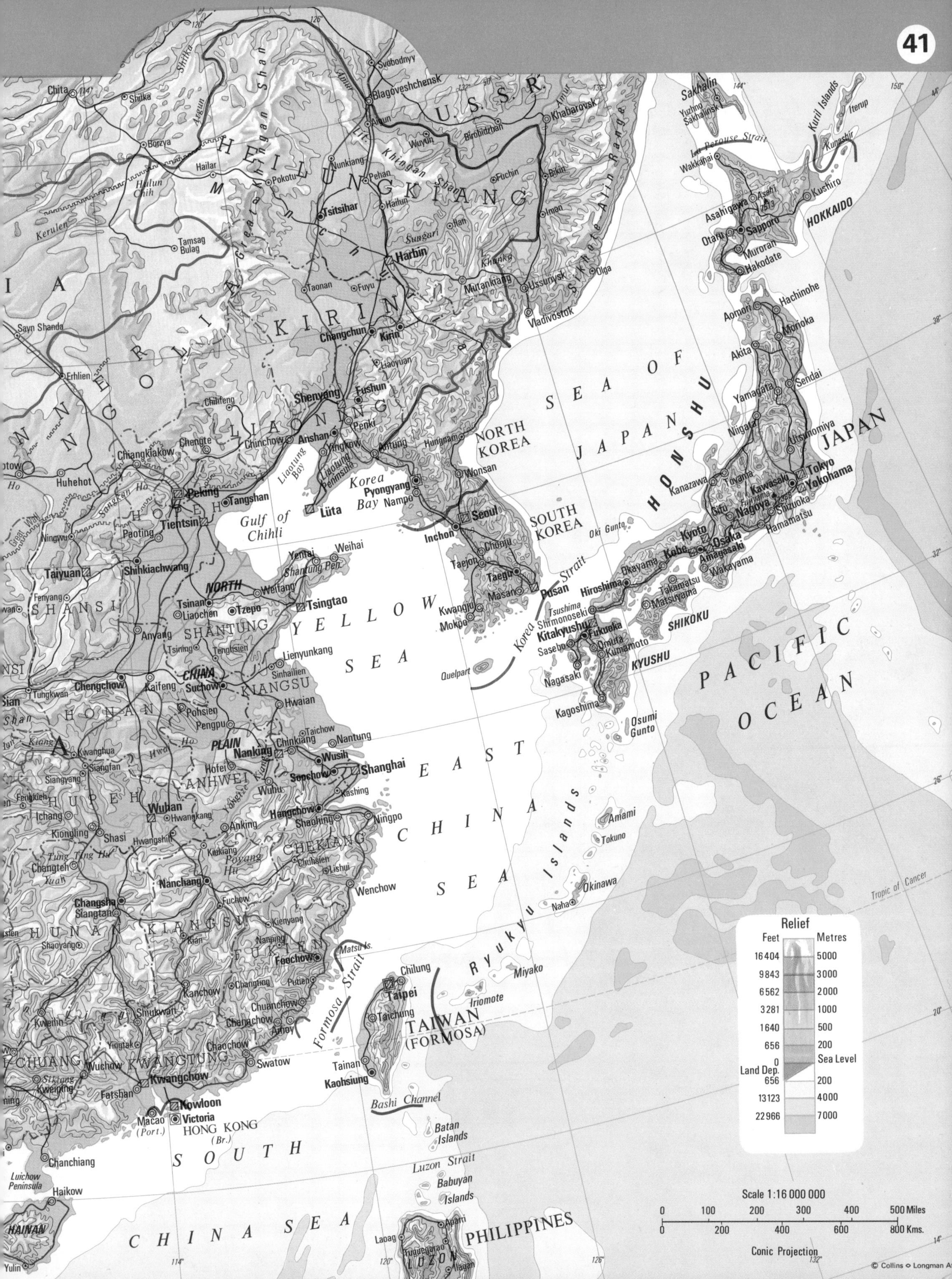
U.S.S.R.
HEILUNGKIANG
KIRIN
LIAONING
MONGOLIA
NORTH KOREA
SOUTH KOREA
JAPAN
HONSHU
HOKKAIDO
SHIKOKU
KYUSHU
SEA OF JAPAN
YELLOW SEA
EAST CHINA SEA
SOUTH CHINA SEA
PACIFIC OCEAN
TAIWAN
(FORMOSA)
PHILIPPINES
LUZON
HAINAN
HOPEH
SHANSI
SHANTUNG
HONAN
KIANGSU
ANHWEI
HUPEH
CHEKIANG
HUNAN
KIANGSI
FUKIEN
KWANGTUNG
CHINA
NORTH
PLAIN
Sakhalin
Kuril Islands
La Perouse Strait
Korea Strait
Tsushima
Formosa Strait
Bashi Channel
Luzon Strait
Ryukyu Islands
Osumi Gunto
Oki Gunto
Quelpart
Amami
Tokuno
Okinawa
Naha
Miyako
Iriomote
Matsu Is.
Batan Islands
Babuyan Islands
Gulf of Chihli
Liaotung Bay
Korea Bay
Liaotung Peninsula
Shantung Pen.
Luichow Peninsula
Tropic of Cancer
Chita
Shilka
Borzya
Hailar
Blagoveshchensk
Svobodnyy
Khabarovsk
Birobidzhan
Tsitsihar
Harbin
Mutankiang
Ussuriysk
Vladivostok
Changchun
Kirin
Shenyang
Fushun
Anshan
Penki
Antung
Peking
Tientsin
Tangshan
Lüta
Pyongyang
Nampo
Wonsan
Seoul
Inchon
Taejon
Taegu
Pusan
Kwangju
Mokpo
Masan
Sapporo
Asahigawa
Otaru
Muroran
Hakodate
Kushiro
Wakkanai
Aomori
Hachinohe
Morioka
Akita
Sendai
Yamagata
Niigata
Utsunomiya
Tokyo
Yokohama
Kawasaki
Kanazawa
Toyama
Nagoya
Gifu
Shizuoka
Hamamatsu
Kyoto
Osaka
Kobe
Amagasaki
Wakayama
Okayama
Hiroshima
Takamatsu
Matsuyama
Shimonoseki
Kitakyushu
Fukuoka
Omuta
Kumamoto
Sasebo
Nagasaki
Kagoshima
Taiyuan
Shihkiachwang
Paoting
Tsinan
Tzepo
Tsingtao
Weifang
Yentai
Weihai
Lienyunkang
Chengchow
Kaifeng
Suchow
Hwaian
Nanking
Shanghai
Wusih
Soochow
Hangchow
Ningpo
Wuhan
Anking
Nanchang
Changsha
Siangtan
Foochow
Wenchow
Amoy
Swatow
Kwangchow
Kowloon
Victoria
HONG KONG
(Br.)
Macao
(Port.)
Chanchiang
Haikow
Taipei
Chilung
Taichung
Tainan
Kaohsiung
Relief
Feet
Metres
16404
5000
9843
3000
6562
2000
3281
1000
1640
500
656
200
0
Sea Level
Land Dep.
656
200
13123
4000
22966
7000
Scale 1:16 000 000
0
100
200
300
400
500 Miles
0
200
400
600
800 Kms.
Conic Projection
© Collins • Longman At

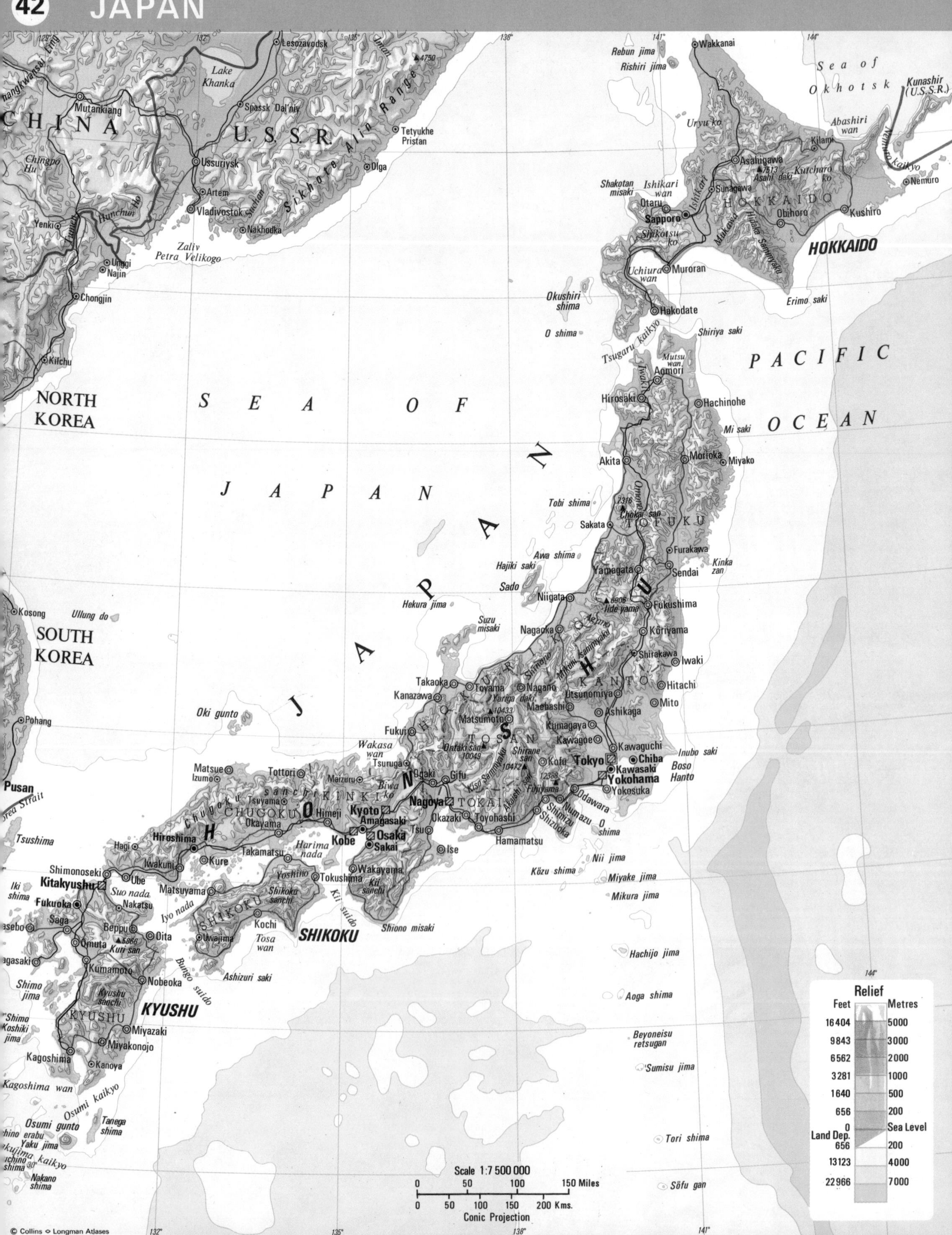

Scale 1:7 500 000

0   50   100   150 Miles

0   50   100   150   200 Kms.

Conic Projection

© Collins ◇ Longman Atlases

Relief

Feet		Metres
16 404		5000
9843		3000
6562		2000
3281		1000
1640		500
656		200
0		Sea Level
Land Dep.		
656		200
13 123		4000
22 966		7000

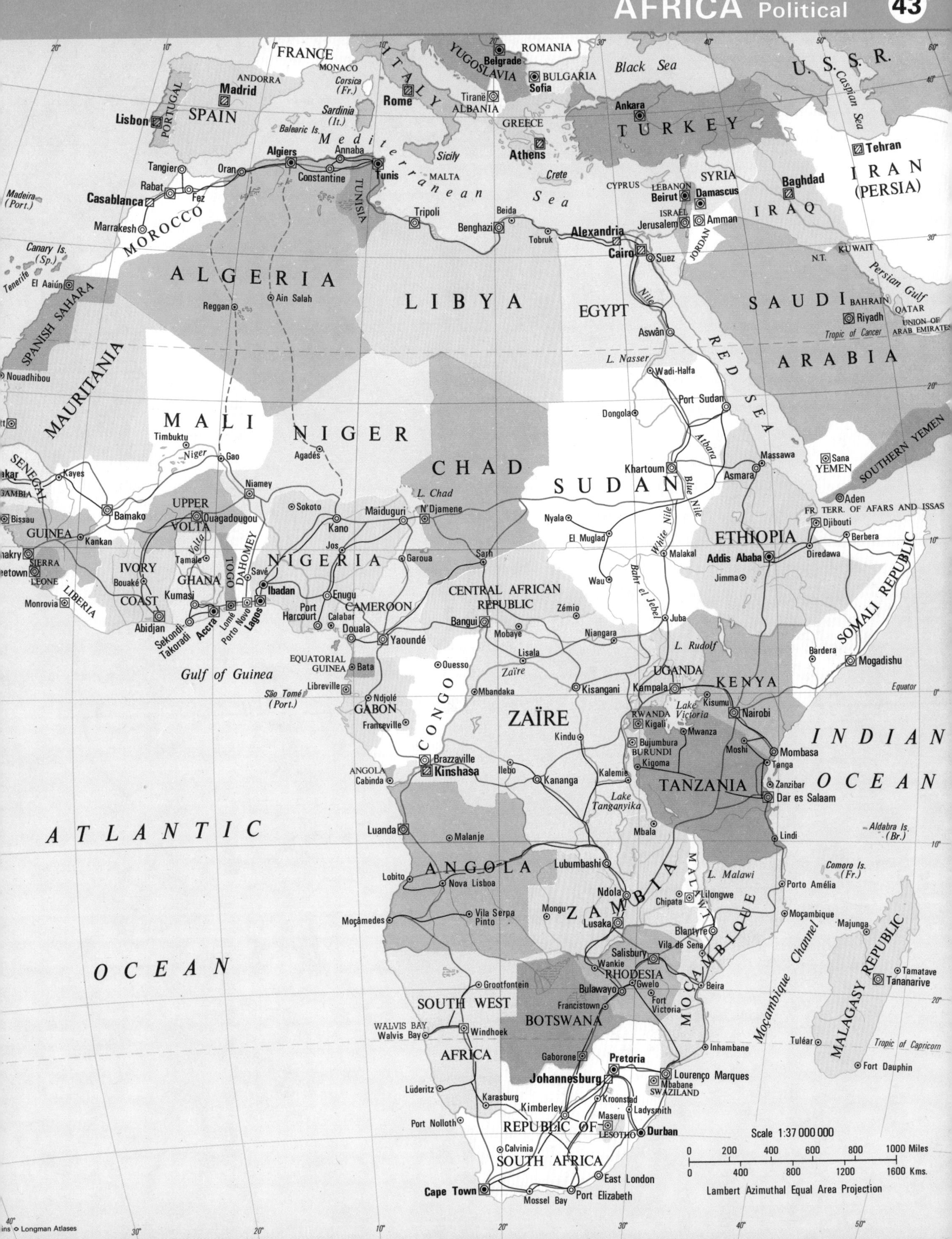

FRANCE
MONACO
ANDORRA
Madrid
SPAIN
PORTUGAL
Lisbon
Corsica
(Fr.)
Balearic Is.
Sardinia
(It.)
ITALY
Rome
MONACO
ALBANIA
Tiranë
Sicily
MALTA
ROMANIA
Belgrade
YUGOSLAVIA
BULGARIA
Sofia
GREECE
Athens
Crete
Black Sea
Caspian Sea
U.S.S.R.
TURKEY
Ankara
CYPRUS
SYRIA
LEBANON
Beirut
Damascus
ISRAEL
Jerusalem
Amman
JORDAN
Tehran
Baghdad
IRAQ
IRAN
(PERSIA)

Madeira
(Port.)
Tangier
Rabat
Casablanca
Fez
Marrakesh
MOROCCO
Oran
Algiers
Constantine
Annaba
TUNISIA
Tunis
Mediterranean Sea
Tripoli
Benghazi
Beida
Tobruk
Alexandria
Cairo
Suez
EGYPT
KUWAIT
N.T.
Persian Gulf
BAHRAIN
QATAR
Riyadh
SAUDI
ARABIA
UNION OF
ARAB EMIRATES

Canary Is.
(Sp.)
Tenerife
El Aaiún
SPANISH SAHARA
Nouadhibou
MAURITANIA
ALGERIA
Reggan
Ain Salah
LIBYA
Tropic of Cancer
Aswân
L. Nasser
Wadi-Halfa
Port Sudan
Dongola
RED SEA
MALI
Timbuktu
Niger
Gao
NIGER
Agadès
L. Chad
CHAD
SUDAN
Khartoum
Atbara
Blue Nile
Massawa
Asmara
Sana
YEMEN
Aden
FR. TERR. OF AFARS AND ISSAS
SOUTHERN YEMEN

SENEGAL
Kayes
GAMBIA
Bissau
GUINEA
Bamako
Kankan
Sokoto
Niamey
Kano
Maiduguri
N'Djamene
Nyala
El Muglad
ETHIOPIA
Addis Ababa
Diredawa
Berbera
Djibouti
SOMALI
REPUBLIC

SIERRA
LEONE
Freetown
LIBERIA
Monrovia
IVORY
COAST
Bouaké
GHANA
Kumasi
Abidjan
UPPER
VOLTA
Ouagadougou
Tamale
Volta
DAHOMEY
TOGO
Jos
NIGERIA
Garoua
Sarh
Wau
Bangui
CENTRAL AFRICAN
REPUBLIC
Zémio
Niangara
Juba
L. Rudolf
Bardera
Mogadishu

Akkra
Lomé
Porto Novo
Lagos
Ibadan
Enugu
Port
Harcourt
Calabar
CAMEROON
Douala
Yaoundé
EQUATORIAL
GUINEA
Bata
Ouesso
Mobaye
Lisala
Zaïre
Mbandaka
Kisangani
UGANDA
Kampala
KENYA
Nairobi
Equator

São Tomé
(Port.)
Gulf of Guinea
Libreville
Ndjolé
GABON
Franceville
CONGO
ZAÏRE
Kindu
RWANDA
Kigali
BURUNDI
Bujumbura
Kigoma
Lake
Victoria
Kisumu
Mwanza
Moshi
Mombasa
Tanga
INDIAN
OCEAN

Brazzaville
Kinshasa
Ilebo
Kananga
Kalemie
Lake
Tanganyika
TANZANIA
Zanzibar
Dar es Salaam
Aldabra Is.
(Br.)

ANGOLA
Cabinda
Luanda
Malanje
Lumbumbashi
Mbala
Lindi

ATLANTIC
OCEAN
Lobito
ANGOLA
Nova Lisboa
Moçâmedes
Vila Serpa
Pinto
Mongu
ZAMBIA
Ndola
Lusaka
MALAWI
Chipata
Lilongwe
L. Malawi
Porto Amélia
Moçambique
Comoro Is.
(Fr.)
Majunga
Blantyre
Vila de Sena
MOÇAMBIQUE
Beira

Grootfontein
SOUTH WEST
WALVIS BAY
Walvis Bay
AFRICA
Windhoek
Salisbury
Wankie
RHODESIA
Bulawayo
Gwelo
Fort
Victoria
Francistown
BOTSWANA
Inhambane
Tuléar
Tropic of Capricorn
Fort Dauphin
MALAGASY REPUBLIC
Tamatave
Tananarive

Lüderitz
Karasburg
Gaborone
Pretoria
Johannesburg
Mbabane
SWAZILAND
Lourenço Marques
Kroonstad
Ladysmith
LESOTHO
Maseru
Durban
Kimberley
Port Nolloth
REPUBLIC OF
Calvinia
SOUTH AFRICA
East London
Cape Town
Mossel Bay
Port Elizabeth

Scale 1:37 000 000
0   200   400   600   800   1000 Miles
0   400   800   1200   1600 Kms.
Lambert Azimuthal Equal Area Projection

Longman Atlases

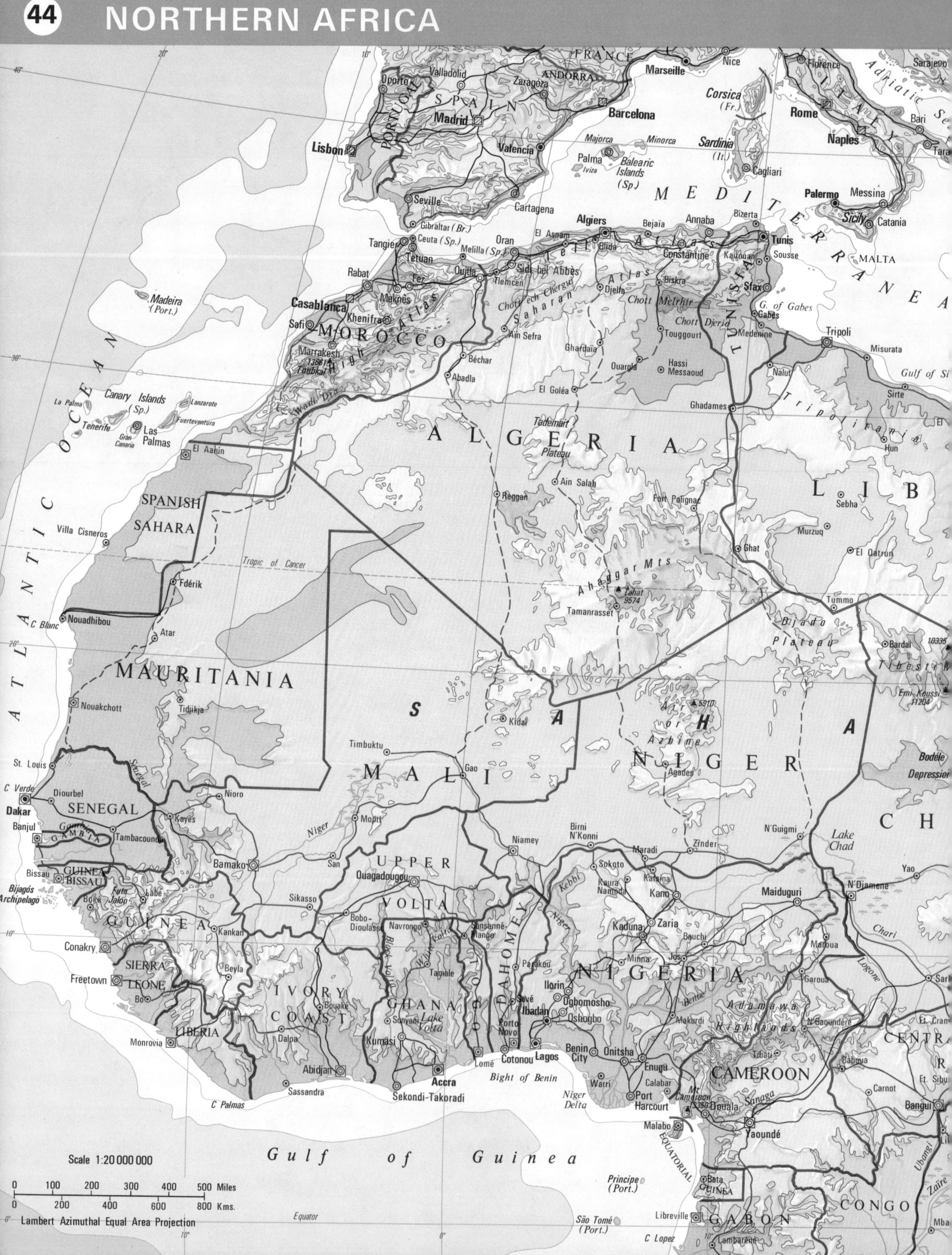

Scale 1:20 000 000

0   100   200   300   400   500 Miles
0   200   400   600   800 Kms.

Lambert Azimuthal Equal Area Projection

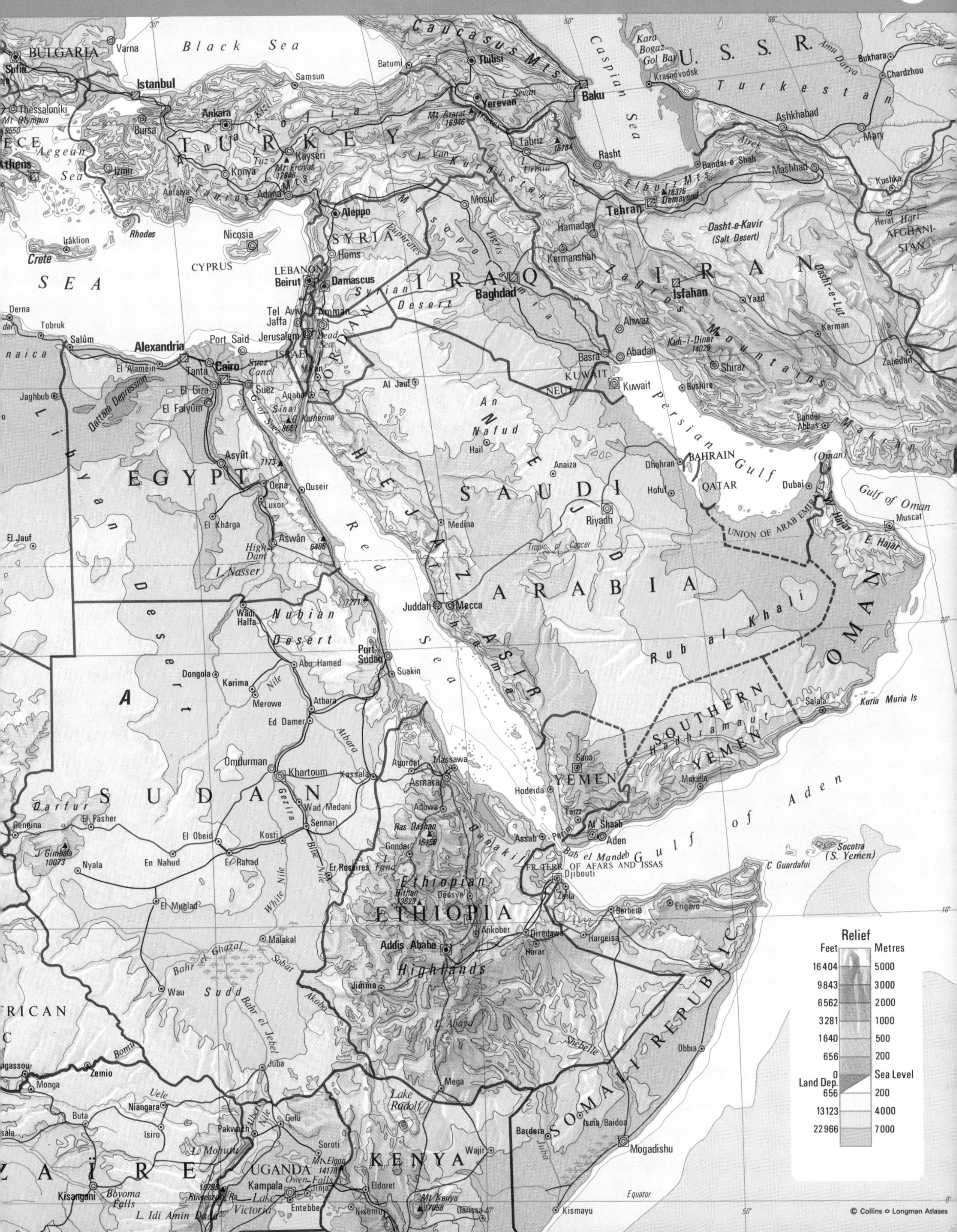

BULGARIA
Varna
Sofia
Black Sea
Istanbul
Thessaloniki
Mt Olympus
9550
ECE
Athens
Aegean
Sea
Crete
SEA
Iráklion
CYPRUS
Nicosia
Rhodes
Derna
dari
Tobruk
Salûm
naica
Jaghbub
Qattara Depression
El 'Alamein
Alexandria
Tanta
Cairo
Port Said
El Giza
Suez
EGYPT
El Faiyûm
Asyût
Jauf
Qena
Luxor
Quseir
El Khârga
Aswân
High
Dam
L. Nasser
Wadi
Halfa
Nubian
Desert
Dongola
Karima
Merowe
Atbara
Ed Damer
Omdurman
Khartoum
SUDAN
Darfur
El Fasher
Geneina
J.Gimbala
10073
Nyala
En Nahud
El Obeid
Kosti
Er Rahad
El Muglad
FRICAN
C
Bahr el Ghazal
Wau
Sudd
agassou
Zemio
Monga
Uele
Buta
Niangara
Isiro
ZAIRE
Kisangani
Boyoma
Falls
L. Mobutu
UGANDA
Kampala
Ruwenzori Ra
Lake
L. Idi Amin Dada
Victoria

Ankara
Bursa
TURKEY
Izmir
Konya
Kayseri
Tuz
Mt Erciyas
12848
Antalya
Adana
Taurus
Caucasus Mts
Batumi
Tbilisi
Yerevan
Mt Ararat
16946
L. Van
Kurdistan
Samsun
Kizil
Aleppo
SYRIA
Homs
Euphrates
Mosul
Tabriz
Urmia
L.
Beirut
LEBANON
Damascus
Syrian
Desert
IRAQ
Baghdad
Tel Aviv
Jaffa
Amman
JORDAN
Jerusalem
ISRAEL
Dead
Sea
Maan
Al Jauf
An
Nafud
Hail
Suez Canal
G of Suez
Sinai
Katherina
8661
Aqaba
HEJAZ
Red
Sea
Juddah
Mecca
Medina
Tropic of Cancer
SAUDI
ARABIA
Riyadh
ASIR
Rub al Khali
Port
Sudan
Suakin
Abu Hamed
Agordat
Massawa
Asmara
Kassala
Adowa
Ras Dashan
15158
Gondar
Lake Tana
Er Roseires
Wad Medani
Sennar
Gezira
Blue Nile
Ethiopian
Highlands
ETHIOPIA
Addis Ababa
Ankober
Harar
Diredawa
Jimma
Akobo
Sobat
White Nile
Malakal
Mega
Lake
Rudolf
Bardera
Wajir
KENYA
Mt Elgon
14178
Owen
Falls
Soroti
Jinja
Eldoret
Mt Kenya
17058
Garissa
Kisumu
Kismayu
Equator

U.S.S.R.
Kara
Bogaz
Gol Bay
Krasnovodsk
Caspian
Sea
Baku
Turkestan
Bukhara
Chardzhou
Amu Darya
Ashkhabad
Mary
Bandar-e Shah
Rasht
Elburz Mts
Mashhad
Kushka
Herat Hari
AFGHANI-
STAN
Tehran
Demavend
18376
Hamadan
Dasht-e-Kavir
(Salt Desert)
Kermanshah
IRAN
Isfahan
Yazd
Zagros
Ahwaz
Kuh-i-Dinar
14029
Kerman
Dasht-e-Lut
Basra
Abadan
Shiraz
Zahedan
NEUT
KUWAIT
Kuwait
Bushire
Persian
Gulf
Bandar
Abbas
Makran
Dhahran
BAHRAIN
Dubai
Hofuf
QATAR
UNION OF ARAB EMIRATES
Gulf of Oman
Muscat
W Hajar
E. Hajar
OMAN
Hadhramaut
SOUTHERN
YEMEN
Salala
Kuria Muria Is
Saua
YEMEN
Hodeida
Mukalla
Taizz
At Shaab
Aden
Gulf of Aden
Socotra
(S. Yemen)
C. Guardafui
Assab
Perim
Bab el Mandeb
FR TERR OF AFARS AND ISSAS
Djibouti
Zeila
Berbera
Erigavo
SOMALI REPUBLIC
Hargeisa
Obbia
Isciá/Baidoa
Mogadishu
Shebelle
Juba

Relief		
Feet		Metres
16404		5000
9843		3000
6562		2000
3281		1000
1640		500
656		200
0		Sea Level
Land Dep.		
656		200
13123		4000
22966		7000

© Collins ◇ Longman Atlases

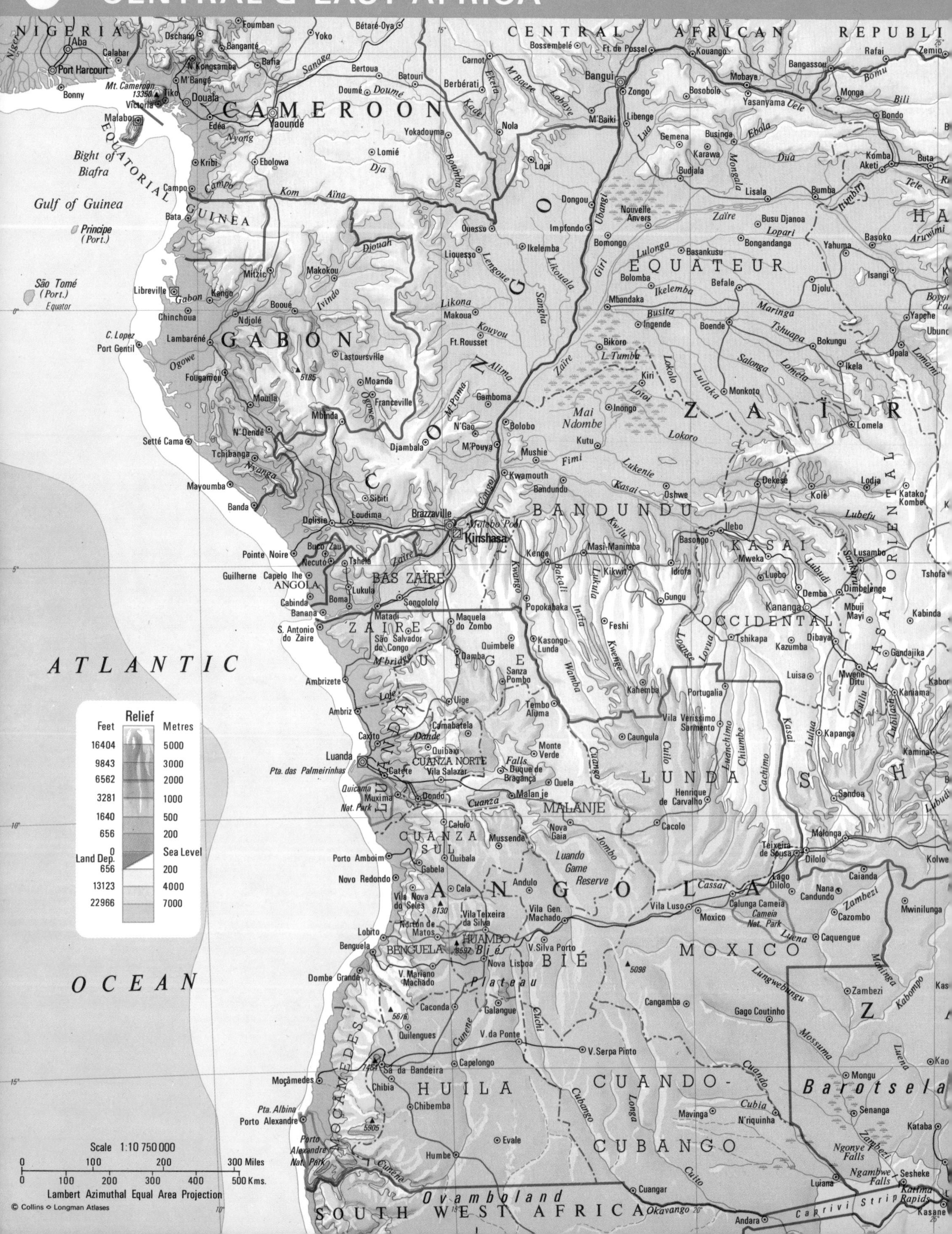

NIGERIA
Aba
Calabar
Port Harcourt
Bonny
Malabo
Bight of
Biafra
Gulf of Guinea
Principe
(Port.)
São Tomé
(Port.)
Equator
C. Lopez
Port Gentil

EQUATORIAL GUINEA
Foumban
Dschang
Bangante
Yoko
Bafia
M'Bange
Tiko
Douala
Edéa
Yaoundé
Kribi
Ebolowa
Campo
Bata
Libreville
Gabon
Kango
Chinchoua
Lambaréné
Fougamou
Mouila

CAMEROON
Betare-Oya
Bertoua
Doumé
Berbérati
Nola
Ouesso
Ikelemba
Liouesso
Mitzic
Makokou
Booué
Ndjolé
Lastoursville
Moanda
Franceville
Mbinda
N'Dendé
Djambala

GABON
5185

CENTRAL AFRICAN REPUBLIC
Bossembélé
Ft. de Possel
Kouango
Rafai
Zemio
Carnot
Bangui
Zongo
Bosobolo
Mobaye
Monga
Bangassou
Bili
Bondo
Libenge
Gemena
Businga
Ebola
Komba
Aketi
Buta
Budjala
Lisala
Bumba
Ichimbiri
Tele
Basoko
Aruwimi
Yahuma
Isangi
Yapehe
Ubunc

EQUATEUR
Mbandaka
Ingende
Boende
Bokungu
Ikela
Opala

Z A I R E

ATLANTIC

OCEAN

Scale 1:10 750 000
0   100   200   300 Miles
0   100   200   300   400   500 Kms.
Lambert Azimuthal Equal Area Projection
© Collins ◇ Longman Atlases

ANGOLA
SOUTH WEST AFRICA
Ovamboland
Caprivi Strip

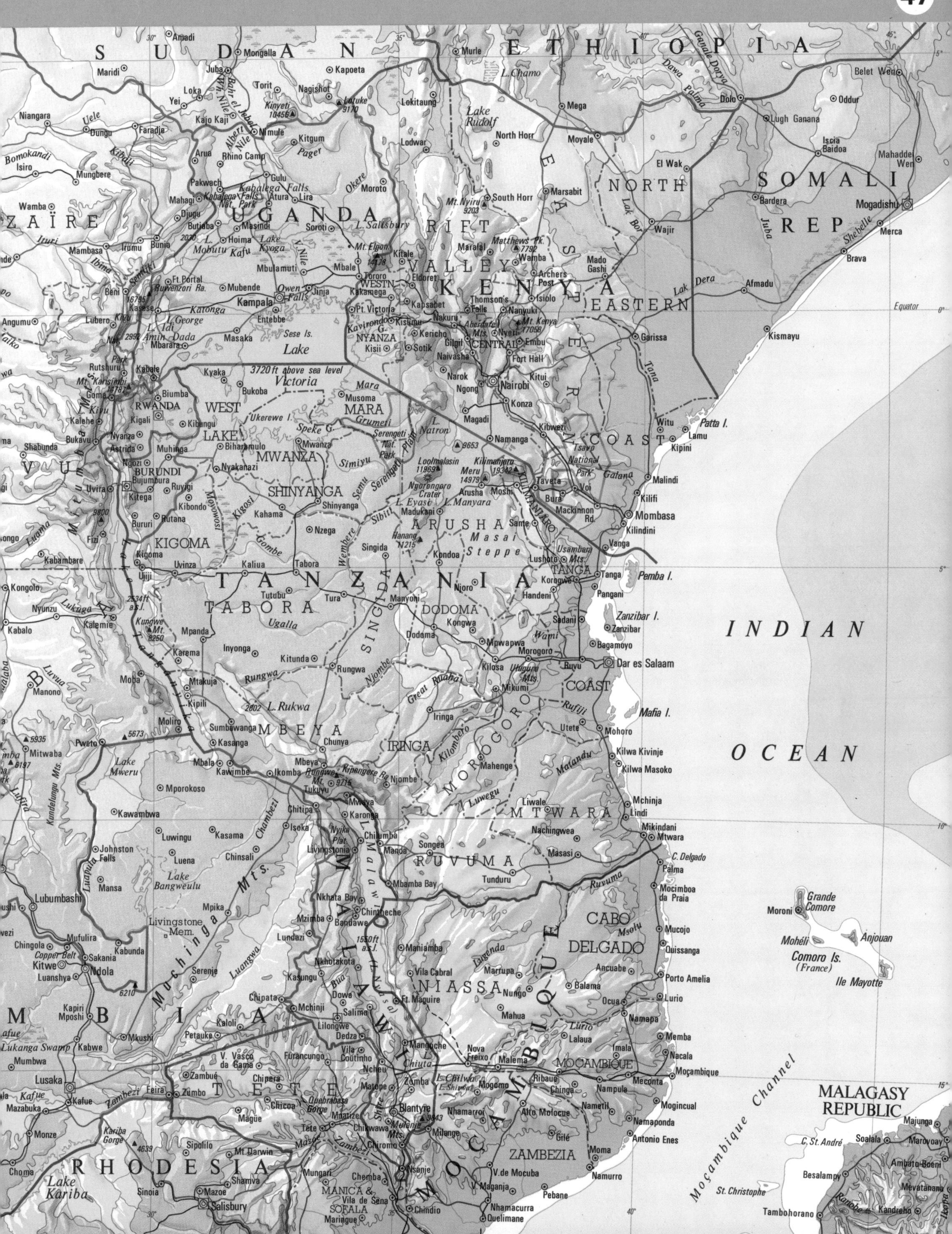

SUDAN
ETHIOPIA
UGANDA
ZAÏRE
KENYA
TANZANIA
SOMALI REP
RWANDA
BURUNDI
MALAWI
MOÇAMBIQUE
RHODESIA
ZAMBIA
MALAGASY REPUBLIC
INDIAN OCEAN
Moçambique Channel
Comoro Is.
(France)
Grande Comore
Mohéli
Anjouan
Ile Mayotte
Moroni
Equator
NORTH EASTERN
RIFT VALLEY
WESTN
NYANZA
CENTRAL
EASTERN
COAST
WEST LAKE
MARA
MWANZA
SHINYANGA
KIGOMA
TABORA
SINGIDA
ARUSHA
KILIMANJARO
TANGA
DODOMA
COAST
MOROGORO
IRINGA
MBEYA
MTWARA
RUVUMA
CABO DELGADO
NIASSA
TETE
ZAMBEZIA
MOÇAMBIQUE
MANICA & SOFALA
Lake Rudolf
L. Chamo
Lake Victoria
3720 ft above sea level
L. Albert
L. Mobutu
L. Kyoga
L. Salisbury
L. George
L. Idi Amin Dada
L. Kivu
L. Tanganyika
2534 ft a.s.l.
L. Rukwa
L. Natron
L. Eyasi
L. Manyara
L. Malawi
1550 ft a.s.l.
L. Chilwa
Lake Mweru
Lake Bangweulu
Lake Kariba
Kariba Gorge
Quebrabasa Gorge
Mt. Kenya 17058
Kilimanjaro 19342
Meru 14979
Mt. Elgon 14178
Ruwenzori Ra.
Mt. Karisimbi 14787
Ngorongoro Crater
Serengeti Nat. Park
Serengeti Plain
Masai Steppe
Usambara Mts.
Uluguru Mts.
Kipengere Ra.
Muchinga Mts.
Mitumba Mts.
Kundelungu Mts.
Livingstone Mem.
Mulanje Mts.
Nairobi
Kampala
Dar es Salaam
Mogadishu
Lusaka
Salisbury
Zomba
Blantyre
Lilongwe
Mombasa
Tanga
Zanzibar
Zanzibar I.
Pemba I.
Mafia I.
Patta I.
Lamu
Malindi
Kilifi
Kilindini
Vanga
Pangani
Bagamoyo
Kilwa Kivinje
Kilwa Masoko
Lindi
Mikindani
Mtwara
C. Delgado
Palma
Mocimboa da Praia
Porto Amelia
Quissanga
Mucojo
Lurio
Memba
Nacala
Moçambique
Quelimane
Kismayu
Brava
Merca
Afmadu
Garissa
Wajir
Mandera
Moyale
Marsabit
Lodwar
Juba
Gulu
Masindi
Jinja
Entebbe
Tororo
Mbale
Kisumu
Nakuru
Eldoret
Kitale
Nyeri
Nanyuki
Arusha
Moshi
Dodoma
Morogoro
Iringa
Mbeya
Tabora
Kigoma
Ujiji
Mwanza
Musoma
Bukoba
Kigali
Bujumbura
Goma
Bukavu
Uvira
Kalemie
Ndola
Kitwe
Mufulira
Lubumbashi
Kabwe
Kafue
Tete
Nampula
Chipata
Mzimba
Karonga
Nkhata Bay
Nkhotakota
Mangoche
Songea
Tunduru
Masasi
Newala
Majunga
Marovoay
Soalala
Besalampy
Maintirano
Tambohorano
C. St. André
St. Christophe
Zambezi
Ruvuma
Rufiji
Great Ruaha
Tana
Galana
Juba
Shebelle
Luangwa
Kafue
Lugenda
Shire
Kagera
Grumeti
Victoria Nile
Albert Nile
Bahr el Jebel

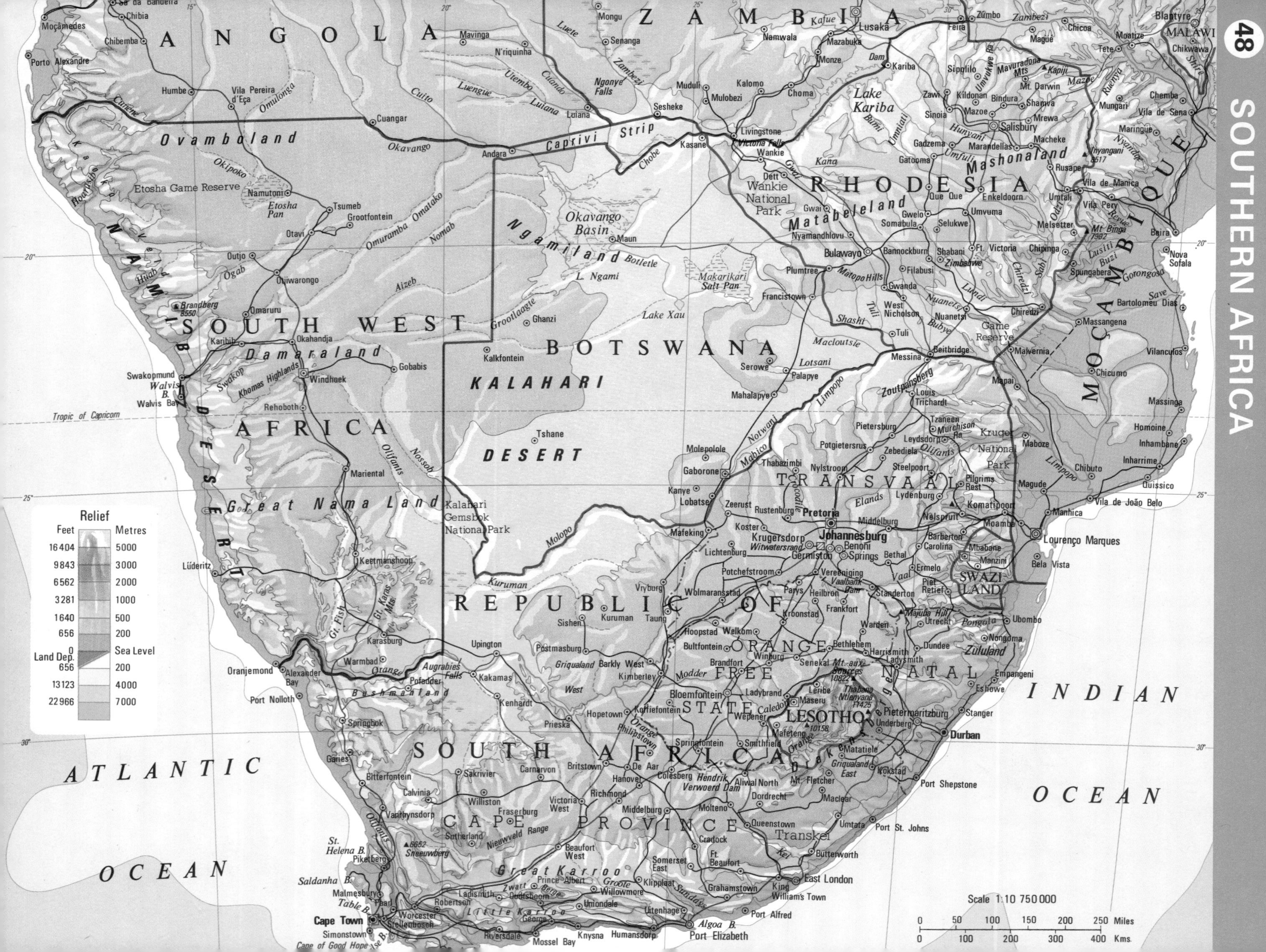

Relief

Feet	Metres
16 404	5000
9843	3000
6562	2000
3281	1000
1640	500
656	200
	Sea Level
Land Dep.	200
656	656
13123	4000
22966	7000

Scale 1:10 750 000

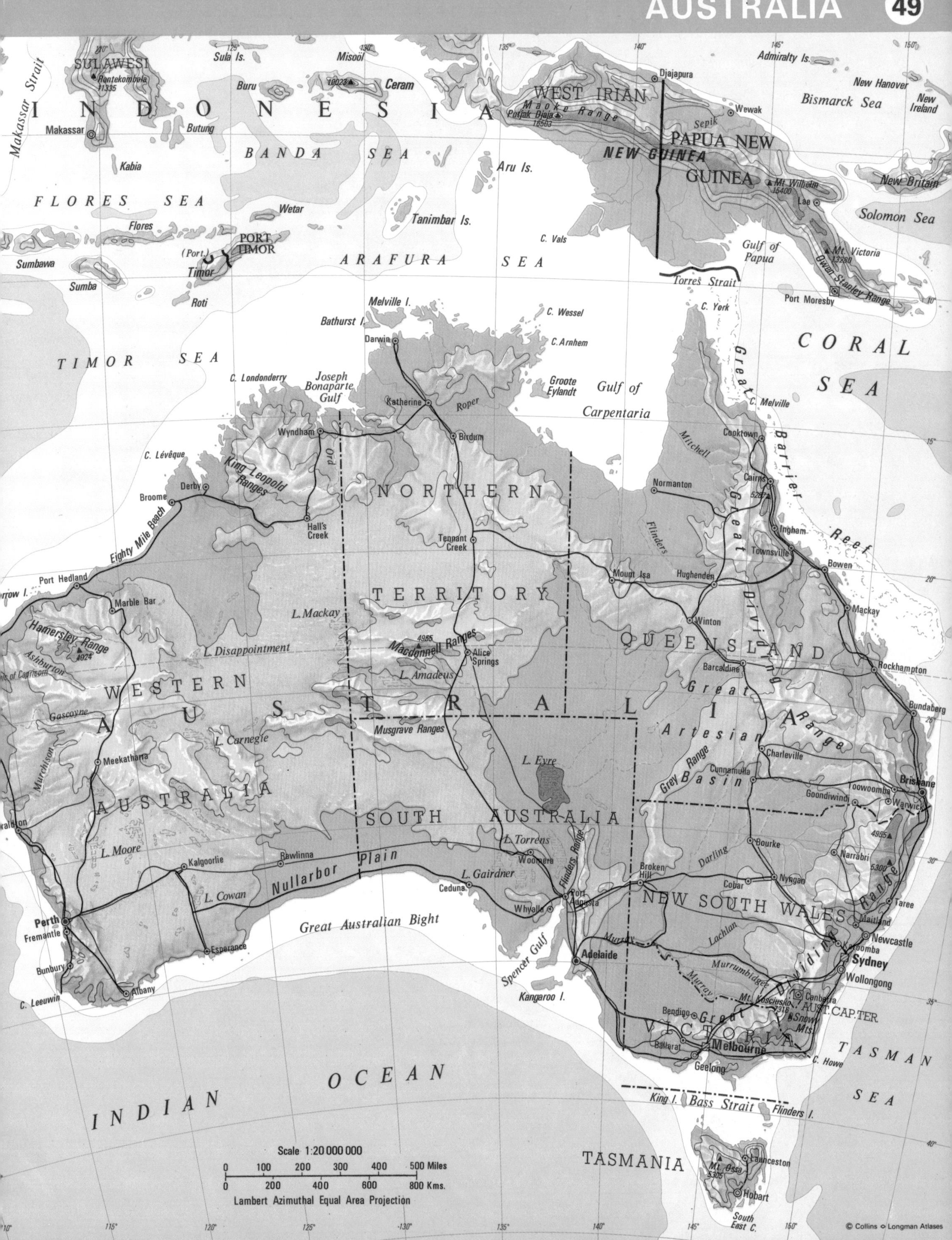

INDONESIA

Makassar Strait

SULAWESI
Rantekombela
11335

Makassar

Butung

Kabia

Sula Is.

BANDA   SEA

FLORES   SEA

Flores

Sumbawa

Sumba

Roti

Buru

Misool

Ceram
10023

Wetar

(Port.)
Timor

PORT
TIMOR
(Port.)

Aru Is.

Tanimbar Is.

ARAFURA   SEA

TIMOR   SEA

WEST IRIAN
Maoke Range
Puntjak Djaja
16503

Djajapura

Wewak

Sepik

PAPUA NEW
GUINEA

NEW GUINEA

Mt Wilhelm
15400

Admiralty Is.

New Hanover

New
Ireland

Bismarck Sea

Lae

New Britain

Solomon Sea

Mt Victoria
13280

Owen Stanley Range

Port Moresby

C. Vals

Gulf of
Papua

Torres Strait

CORAL
SEA

C. Wessel

C. York

C. Arnhem

Gulf of
Carpentaria

Groote
Eylandt

C. Melville

Cooktown

Great   Barrier   Reef

Melville I.

Bathurst I.

Darwin

C. Londonderry

Joseph
Bonaparte
Gulf

Katherine

Roper

Birdum

Wyndham

Ord

King Leopold
Ranges

C. Lévêque

Derby

Broome

Eighty Mile Beach

Hall's
Creek

NORTHERN

TERRITORY

Tennant
Creek

Cairns
5287

Ingham

Townsville

Bowen

Mackay

Normanton

Mitchell

Flinders

Mount Isa

Hughenden

Winton

QUEENSLAND

Port Hedland

Marble Bar

Hamersley Range
4024

Ashburton

of Capricorn

WESTERN

Gascoyne

Murchison

Meekatharra

L. Mackay

L. Disappointment

L. Carnegie

AUSTRALIA

L. Moore

Kalgoorlie

Rawlinna

4985
Macdonnell Ranges

Alice
Springs

L. Amadeus

Musgrave Ranges

SOUTH   AUSTRALIA

L. Eyre

Nullarbor   Plain

L. Cowan

Perth

Fremantle

Esperance

Bunbury

Albany

C. Leeuwin

Great Australian Bight

Ceduna

L. Gairdner

Whyalla

Spencer Gulf

Kangaroo I.

L. Torrens

Woomera

Flinders Range

Port
Augusta

Barcaldine

Rockhampton

Bundaberg

Charleville

Great   Artesian   Basin

Cunnamulla

Grey   Range

Great   Dividing   Range

Toowoomba

Brisbane

Warwick

Goondiwindi

Narrabri
4985
6300

Taree

Bourke

Cobar

Nyngan

Broken
Hill

Darling

Lachlan

NEW   SOUTH   WALES

Murrumbidgee

Murray

Mt Kosciusko
7316

Snowy
Mts

Bendigo

Ballarat

Geelong

VICTORIA

Melbourne

Great

AUST.CAP.TER.

Canberra

Sydney

Wollongong

Newcastle

Maitland

Dividing   Range

AUST.CAP.TER

TASMAN

SEA

C. Howe

King I. Bass Strait Flinders I.

South
East C.

INDIAN   OCEAN

TASMANIA

Launceston

Mt Ossa
5305

Hobart

Scale 1:20 000 000

0   100   200   300   400   500 Miles

0   200   400   600   800 Kms.

Lambert Azimuthal Equal Area Projection

© Collins ○ Longman Atlases

TASMAN SEA

PACIFIC OCEAN

NORTH ISLAND

SOUTH ISLAND

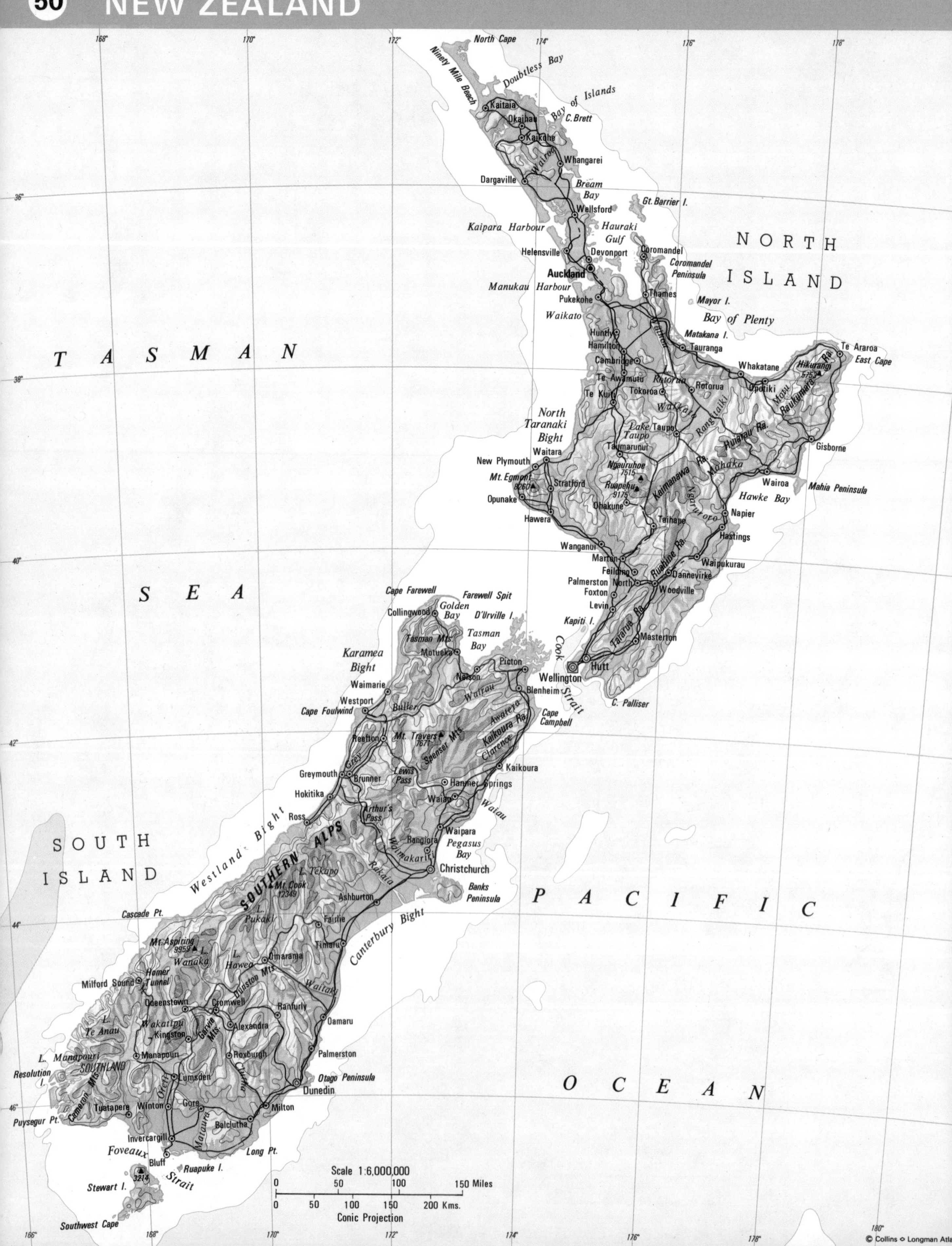

North Cape
Ninety Mile Beach
Doubtless Bay
Bay of Islands
Kaitaia
Okaihau
C. Brett
Kaikohe
Wairoa
Whangarei
Dargaville
Bream Bay
Wellsford
Gt. Barrier I.
Kaipara Harbour
Hauraki Gulf
Helensville
Coromandel
Devonport
Coromandel Peninsula
Auckland
Thames
Manukau Harbour
Pukekohe
Mayor I.
Waikato
Bay of Plenty
Huntly
Matakana I.
Hamilton
Tauranga
Cambridge
Whakatane
Te Araroa
Te Awamutu
Rotorua
Opotiki
East Cape
Te Kuiti
Tokoroa
Rotorua
Hikurangi 1751
Waikato
Raukumara
Mangonui
North Taranaki Bight
Lake Taupo
Rangitaiki Ra.
Waitara
Taumarunui
Huiarau Ra.
Gisborne
New Plymouth
Ngauruhoe 7515
Mohaka
Mt. Egmont 8260
Stratford
Ruapehu 9175
Wairoa
Mahia Peninsula
Opunake
Ohakune
Kaimanawa Mts.
Hawke Bay
Hawera
Ngaruroro
Taihape
Napier
Wanganui
Hastings
Marton
Ruahine Ra.
Waipukurau
Feilding
Dannevirke
Palmerston North
Woodville
Foxton
Levin
Tararua Ra.
Kapiti I.
Masterton
Hutt
Wellington
Cook Strait
C. Palliser

Cape Farewell
Farewell Spit
Collingwood
Golden Bay
D'Urville I.
Karamea Bight
Tasman Mts.
Motueka
Tasman Bay
Picton
Waimarie
Nelson
Westport
Buller
Wairau
Blenheim
Cape Foulwind
Cape Campbell
Reefton
Mt. Travers 7677
Spenser Mts.
Kaikoura Ra.
Awatere
Greymouth
Grey
Lewis Pass
Clarence
Brunner
Hanmer Springs
Kaikoura
Hokitika
Waiau
Ross
Arthur's Pass
Waiau
Waimakariri
Waipara
Rangiora
Pegasus Bay
SOUTHERN ALPS
L. Tekapo
Christchurch
Westland Bight
Mt. Cook 12349
Rakaia
Banks Peninsula
Cascade Pt.
Pukaki
Ashburton
Mt. Aspiring 9959
Fairlie
Wanaka
L. Hawea
Timaru
Canterbury Bight
Milford Sound
Homer Tunnel
Cromwell
Omarama
Hunston Mts.
Waitaki
Queenstown
Ranfurly
Oamaru
L. Te Anau
L. Wakatipu
Kingston
Alexandra
L. Manapouri
Manapouri
Roxburgh
Palmerston
Resolution I.
SOUTHLAND
Lumsden
Otago Peninsula
Puysegur Pt.
Tuatapere
Winton
Gore
Dunedin
Milton
Invercargill
Balclutha
Foveaux
Bluff
Long Pt.
Stewart I.
Ruapuke I.
Southwest Cape

Scale 1:6,000,000
0 50 100 150 Miles
0 50 100 150 200 Kms.
Conic Projection

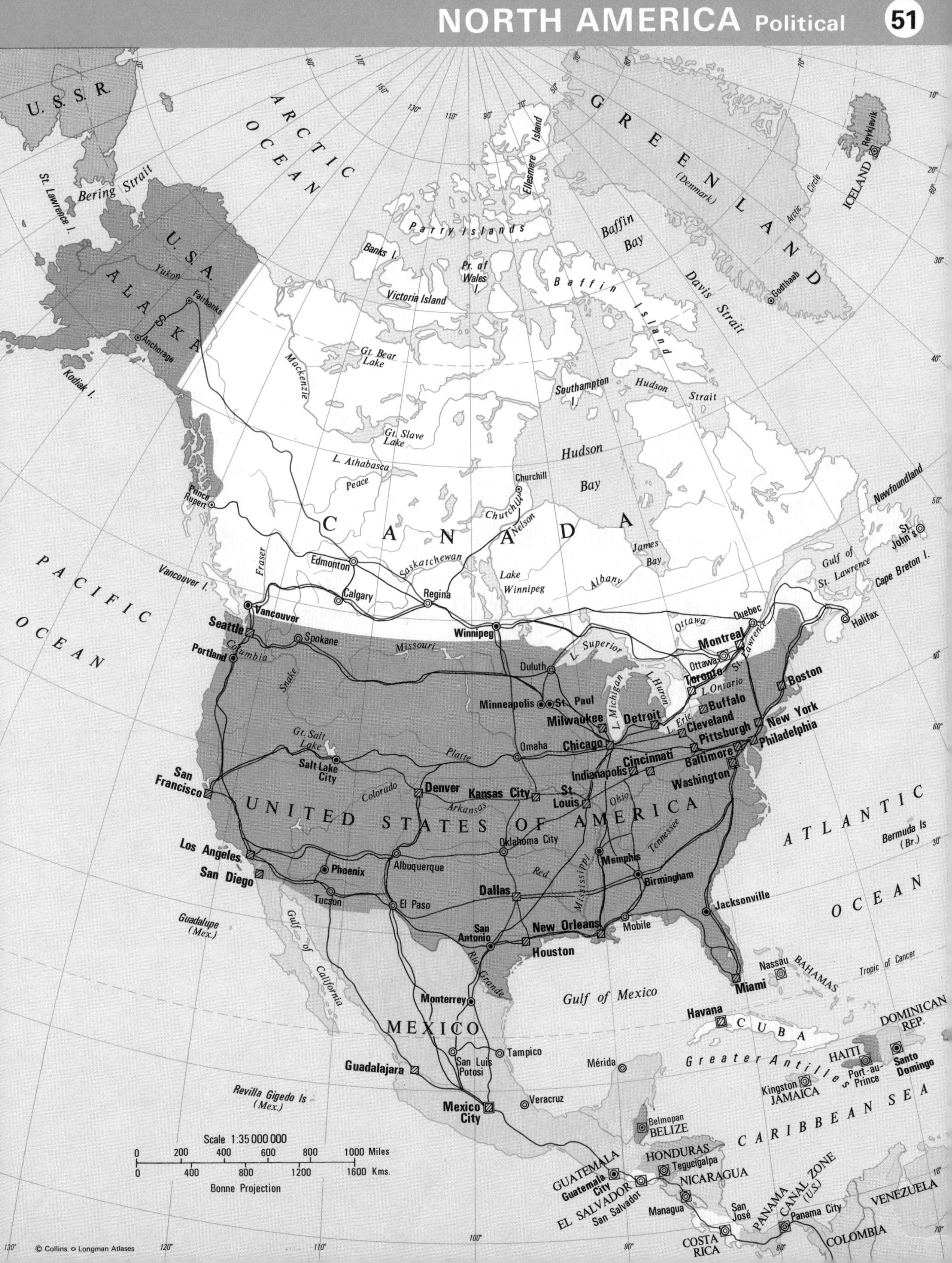

U.S.S.R.

St. Lawrence I.

Bering Strait

ARCTIC OCEAN

GREENLAND
(Denmark)

ICELAND
Reykjavík

Arctic Circle

Ellesmere Island

Parry Islands

Baffin Bay

Banks I.

Pr. of Wales I.

Victoria Island

U.S.A.

ALASKA

Yukon

Fairbanks

Anchorage

Kodiak I.

Baffin Island

Davis Strait

Goothaab

Mackenzie

Gt. Bear Lake

Southampton I.

Hudson Strait

Gt. Slave Lake

L. Athabasca

Peace

Churchill

Churchill

Nelson

Hudson Bay

James Bay

Newfoundland

St. John's

PACIFIC OCEAN

Prince Rupert

Vancouver I.

Fraser

C A N A D A

Edmonton

Calgary

Saskatchewan

Regina

Lake Winnipeg

Albany

Gulf of St. Lawrence

Cape Breton I.

Seattle

Vancouver

Spokane

Portland

Columbia

Snake

Winnipeg

Missouri

Duluth

L. Superior

Ottawa

St. Lawrence

Quebec

Montreal

Halifax

Minneapolis

St. Paul

Milwaukee

L. Michigan

L. Huron

Detroit

L. Ontario

Toronto

Ottawa

L. Erie

Buffalo

Cleveland

Pittsburgh

Boston

New York

Gt. Salt Lake

Salt Lake City

Platte

Omaha

Chicago

Indianapolis

Cincinnati

Baltimore

Philadelphia

San Francisco

U N I T E D   S T A T E S   O F   A M E R I C A

Colorado

Denver

Kansas City

St. Louis

Ohio

Washington

ATLANTIC

Bermuda Is (Br.)

Los Angeles

San Diego

Phoenix

Arkansas

Oklahoma City

Red

Memphis

Tennessee

Birmingham

Mississippi

OCEAN

Tucson

El Paso

Dallas

San Antonio

New Orleans

Mobile

Jacksonville

Houston

Rio Grande

Gulf of Mexico

Miami

Nassau BAHAMAS

Tropic of Cancer

Guadalupe (Mex.)

Gulf of California

Monterrey

M E X I C O

San Luis Potosí

Tampico

Mérida

Havana

C U B A

G r e a t e r   A n t i l l e s

DOMINICAN REP.

HAITI

Port-au-Prince

Santo Domingo

Revilla Gigedo Is (Mex.)

Guadalajara

Veracruz

Mexico City

Kingston

JAMAICA

CARIBBEAN SEA

Belmopan

BELIZE

HONDURAS

Tegucigalpa

NICARAGUA

VENEZUELA

Scale 1:35 000 000

0   200   400   600   800   1000 Miles

0   400   800   1200   1600 Kms.

Bonne Projection

GUATEMALA

Guatemala City

EL SALVADOR

San Salvador

Managua

San José

COSTA RICA

PANAMA CANAL ZONE (U.S.)

Panama City

COLOMBIA

Hawaiian Islands
(U.S.A.)
Tropic of Cancer
PACIFIC OCEAN
Kauai
Lihue
Oahu
Molokai
Honolulu
Maui
Hawaii
13796
Hilo
Pahala
Scale 1:20 000 000

Vancouver Island
Str. of Georgia
C. Flattery
Victoria
Vancouver
Kamloops
Kelowna
Penticton
Revelstoke
Golden
Kicking Horse Pass
Banff
Calgary
Mt. Assiniboine
Drumheller
Red Deer
Sth. Saskatchewan
Saskatoon
Quill Lakes
Yorkton
Melville
Regina
Qu'Appelle
Swan River
L. Winnipegosis
Medicine Hat
Trans Canada Highway
Swift Current
Moose Jaw
Lethbridge
Weyburn
Brandon
Estevan
CANADA
Bellingham
Mt. Baker 10778
Glacier Pk. 10568
Grand Coulee
Franklin D. Roosevelt L.
Port Angeles
Aberdeen
Tacoma
Seattle
Mt. Rainier 14408
Wenatchee
Spokane
Mt. Adams 12307
Yakima
Richland
Snake
Columbia
Astoria
Portland
WASHINGTON
Crowsnest Pass
Cranbrook
Coleman
Selkirk Mts.
Shelby
Kalispell
Flathead L.
Havre
Milk
Missouri
Fort Peck Resr.
Fort Peck Dam
Glasgow
Williston
Minot
Great Falls
Missoula
Helena
Big Snowy Mt. 8730
MONTANA
Garrison Resr.
Glendive
Dickinson
Bismarck
Roundup
Butte
Yellowstone
Baker
Miles City
Billings
Bighorn
Powder
Bozeman
Dillon
Lemmon
Oahe Resr.
NORTH DAKOTA
Albany
Eugene
North Bend
Bend
Blue Mountains
Baker
Salmon
Salmon River Mts.
C. Blanco
Roseburg
OREGON
Harney Basin
Borah Pk. 12654
Hyndman Pk. 12078
Boise
Grants Pass
Crescent City
Klamath Falls
Goose L.
Lakeview
IDAHO
Granite Pk. 12799
Yellowstone
Yellowstone L. Nat. Park
Cloud Pk. 13175
Sheridan
Mobridge
SOUTH DAKOTA
Pierre
Eureka
C. Mendocino
Mt. Shasta 14162
Redding
Red Bluff
Black Rock Desert
Twin Falls
Burley
Pocatello
Idaho Falls
Grand Teton 13766
Gannett Pk. 13785
Worland
Buffalo
WYOMING
Newcastle
Rapid City
White
Casper
Lusk
Point Arena
Ukiah
Chico
Pyramid L.
Great Salt Lake
Elko
Ogden
Rock Springs
Seminoe Resr.
Pathfinder Resr.
Niobrara
Alliance
NEBRASKA
Scottsbluff
North Platte
L. McConaughy
Sacramento
Reno
Carson City
Salt Lake City
Flaming Gorge Resr.
Uinta Mts.
Rawlins
Cheyenne
Laramie
San Francisco
Oakland
San Jose
Stockton
Mt. Lyell 13114
NEVADA
Great Basin
Mt. Jefferson 11807
Hawthorne
Delta
Provo
Green
UTAH
Fort Collins
Longs Pk. 14256
Greeley
Sterling
Kingsley Dam
Platte
Boulder
Denver
McCook
Monterey Bay
Monterey
Merced
Boundary Pk. 13146
White Mt. Pk. 14242
Wheeler Pk. 13058
Fresno
Caliente
Grand Junction
Mt. Elbert 14431
Pikes Pk. 14110
COLORADO
Colorado Springs
Mt. Whitney 14496
Mt. Ellen 11615
Cedar City
Mt. Peale 12721
Montrose
Mt. Wilson 14246
Uncompahgre Pk. 14314
San Juan Mts.
Canon City
Pueblo
Lamar
KANSAS
San Luis Obispo
Coast Ranges
Sierra Nevada
Death Valley
Delano
Las Vegas
Mead
Colorado
Powell
Alamosa
La Junta
Arkansas
Dodge City
Santa Maria
Point Conception
Bakersfield
Santa Barbara
Barstow
Hoover Dam
Grand Canyon
Roof Butte 9808
Wheeler Pk. 13161
Raton
Trinidad
Liberal
Cimarron
Los Angeles
Pasadena
Nelson
Needles
Humphreys Pk. 12670
Flagstaff
Gallup
Rio Grande
Truchas Pk. 13024
Santa Fe
Clayton
N. Canadian
Long Beach
San Bernardino
Palm Springs
Parker Dam
Colorado Plateau
Prescott
Holbrook
Mt. Taylor 11301
Albuquerque
Tucumcari
Canadian
Borger
Pampa
Amarillo
OKLAHOMA
San Diego
Salton Sea
Brawley
Imperial Dam
Gila
Phoenix
ARIZONA
NEW MEXICO
Belen
Vaughn
Clovis
Tijuana
Mexicali
Yuma
Laguna Dam
Theodore Roosevelt L.
Elephant Butte Resr.
Sierra Blanca 12003
Ensenada
Eloy
Silver City
Lubbock
Wichita Falls
Brazos
Tucson
Lordsburg
Las Cruces
C. Colnett
Puerto Penasco
San Felipe
El Paso
Big Spring
Sweetwater
Abilene
Nogales
Ciudad Juárez
Odessa
TEXAS
Pecos
PACIFIC OCEAN
Guadalupe (Mex.)
Pta. San Antonio
Lower California
Gulf of California
Magdalena
Lucero
Mt. Livermore 8382
Alpine
Colorado
Edwards Plateau
Angel de la Guarda
Tiburon
Hermosillo
Sonora
Chinati Pk. 7730
Cedros I.
Sebastian Vizcaino Bay
Punta Eugenia
Conchos
Emory Pk. 7835
Rio Grande
Del Rio
Ciudad Guerrero
Guaymas
Yaqui
MEXICO
Chihuahua
Eagle Pass
Piedras Negras
Santa Rosalia
Ciudad Obregon
Delicias
Ciudad Camargo
Ballenas Bay
Sabinas
Nueces
Fuerte
Parral
Monclova
Nuevo Laredo
Laredo
UNITED STATES OF AMERICA
ROCKY MOUNTAINS

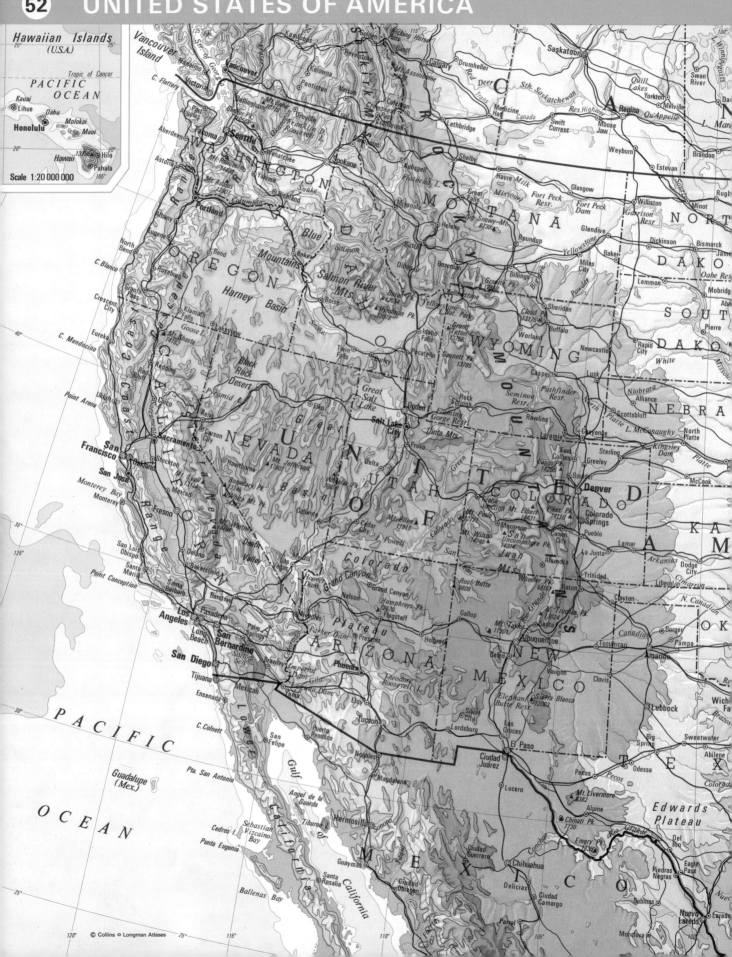

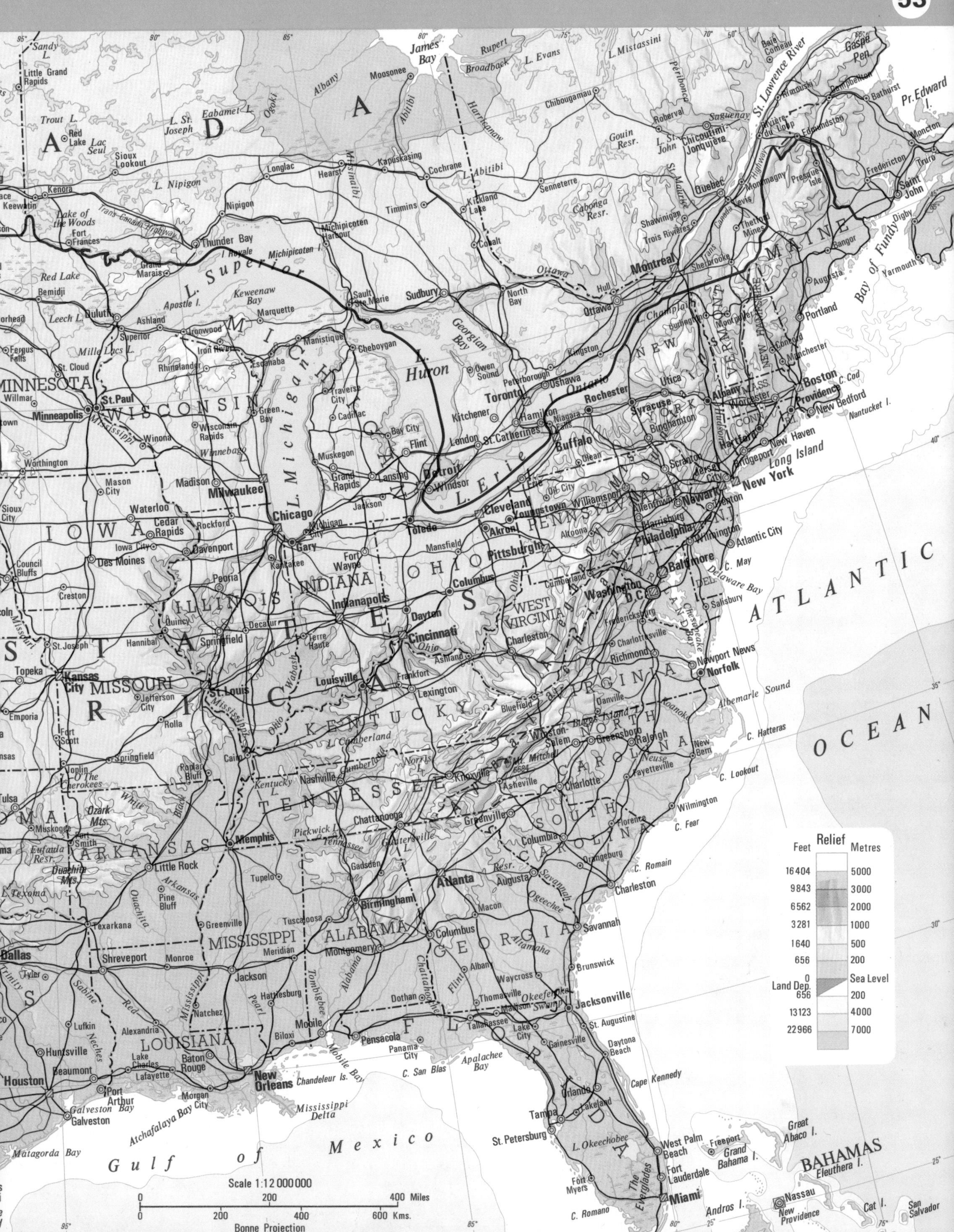

Relief

Feet		Metres
16 404		5000
9843		3000
6562		2000
3281		1000
1640		500
656		200
0		Sea Level
Land Dep.		
656		200
13 123		4000
22 966		7000

Scale 1:12 000 000

0   200   400 Miles

0   200   400   600 Kms.

Bonne Projection

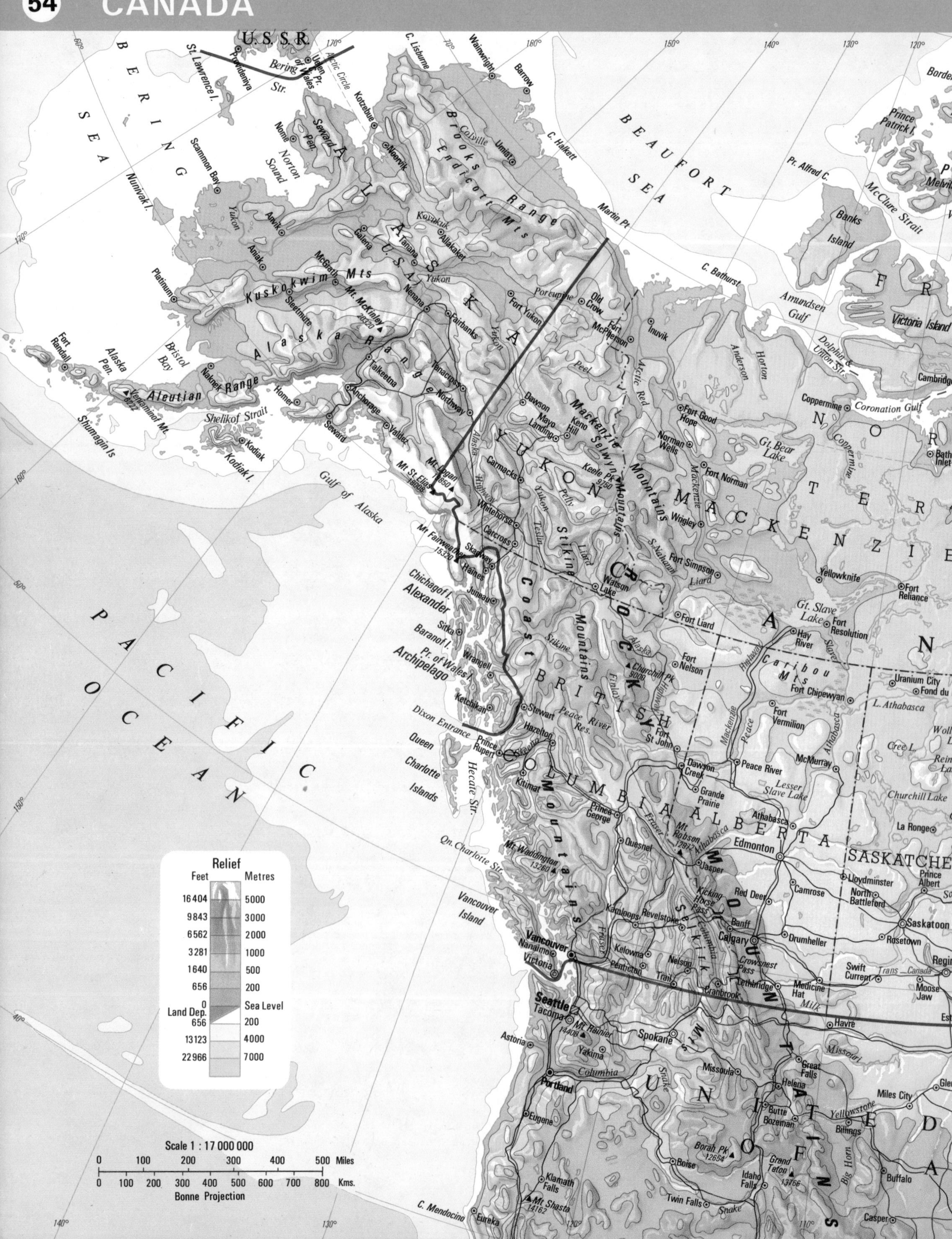

U.S.S.R.

60°   170°   180°   Arctic Circle   170°   160°   150°   140°   130°   120°   Border

St. Lawrence I.
Providéniya
Bering Str.
C. Lisburne
Wainwright
Barrow
C. Halkett
BEAUFORT SEA
Prince Patrick I.
Pt. Alfred C.
Melvil
McClure Strait

BERING SEA
Scammon Bay
Norton Sound
Nome
Kotzebue
Kovukuk
Colville
Umiat
C. Bathurst
Amundsen Gulf
Banks Island
Victoria Island
FR

Nunivak I.
Platinum
Bristol Bay
Naknek
Anvik
Galena
McGrath Mts
Nenana
Fairbanks
Yukon
Fort Yukon
Porcupine
Old Crow
McPherson
Inuvik
Anderson
Horton
Dolphin & Union Str.
Coppermine
Cambridge
Coronation Gulf
Bath Inlet

Alaska Pen.
Fort Randall
Alaska Range
Mt. McKinley
6194
Talkeetna
Anchorage
Northway
Dawson
Mayo
Keno Hill
Fort Good Hope
Norman Wells
Gt. Bear Lake
Coppermine
NOR

Aleutian Range
Veniaminof Mt.
Shelikof Strait
Homer
Seward
Valdez
Mt. Logan
6050
Carmacks
Pelly
Yukon
Fort Norman
Wrigley
Mackenzie
Fort Simpson
Yellowknife
Fort Reliance

Shumagin Is
Kodiak
Kodiak I.
Gulf of Alaska
Mt. St. Elias
5489
Whitehorse
Carcross
Teslin
S. Nahanni
Liard
Gt. Slave Lake
Fort Resolution
Hay River
Fort Liard

PACIFIC OCEAN
Mt. Fairweather
4663
Skagway
Haines
Juneau
Stikine
Watson Lake
Churchill Pk.
9090
Fort Nelson
Liard
Caribou Mts
Fort Reliance
Uranium City
Fond du

Chichagof I.
Alexander Archipelago
Sitka
Baranof I.
Pr. of Wales I.
Wrangell
Ketchikan
Coast Mountains
Stikine
Finlay
Fort Vermilion
Fort Chipewyan
L. Athabasca
Woll
Cree L.
Rein
La Ronge

Dixon Entrance
Queen Charlotte Islands
Hecate Str.
Stewart
Hazelton
Prince Rupert
Kitimat
Peace River Res.
BRITISH
Peace River
McMurray
Lesser Slave Lake
Athabasca
Churchill Lake
La Ronge

Qn. Charlotte Str.
Vancouver Island
Mt. Waddington
3266
Columbia Mountains
Prince George
Quesnel
Dawson Creek
Peace River
Grande Prairie
Athabasca
Mt. Robson
3997
ALBERTA
Edmonton
SASKATCHE

Relief
Feet   Metres
16 404   5000
9843   3000
6562   2000
3281   1000
1640   500
656   200
0   Sea Level
Land Dep.
656   200
13 123   4000
22 966   7000

Vancouver
Nanaimo
Victoria
Jasper
Kicking Horse Pass
Red Deer
Camrose
Lloydminster
North Battleford
Prince Albert
Saskatoon
Rosetown

Seattle
Tacoma
Mt. Rainier
14408
Kamloops
Revelstoke
Banff
Kelowna
Nelson
Calgary
Drumheller
MOUNT
Crowsnest Pass
Lethbridge
Medicine Hat
Swift Current
Moose Jaw
Regi

Astoria
Portland
Columbia
Yakima
Spokane
Penticton
Trail
Cranbrook
Milk
Havre
Trans Canada
Est

Scale 1 : 17 000 000
0   100   200   300   400   500 Miles
0   100 200 300 400 500 600 700 800 Kms.
Bonne Projection

Eugene
Klamath Falls
Mt. Shasta
14162
Eureka
C. Mendocino
Missoula
Helena
Butte
Bozeman
Borah Pk.
12654
Boise
Twin Falls
Snake
Idaho Falls
Grand Teton
13766
Yellowstone
Big Horn
Billings
Miles City
Great Falls
UNITED
STATES
Buffalo
Casper
Gler

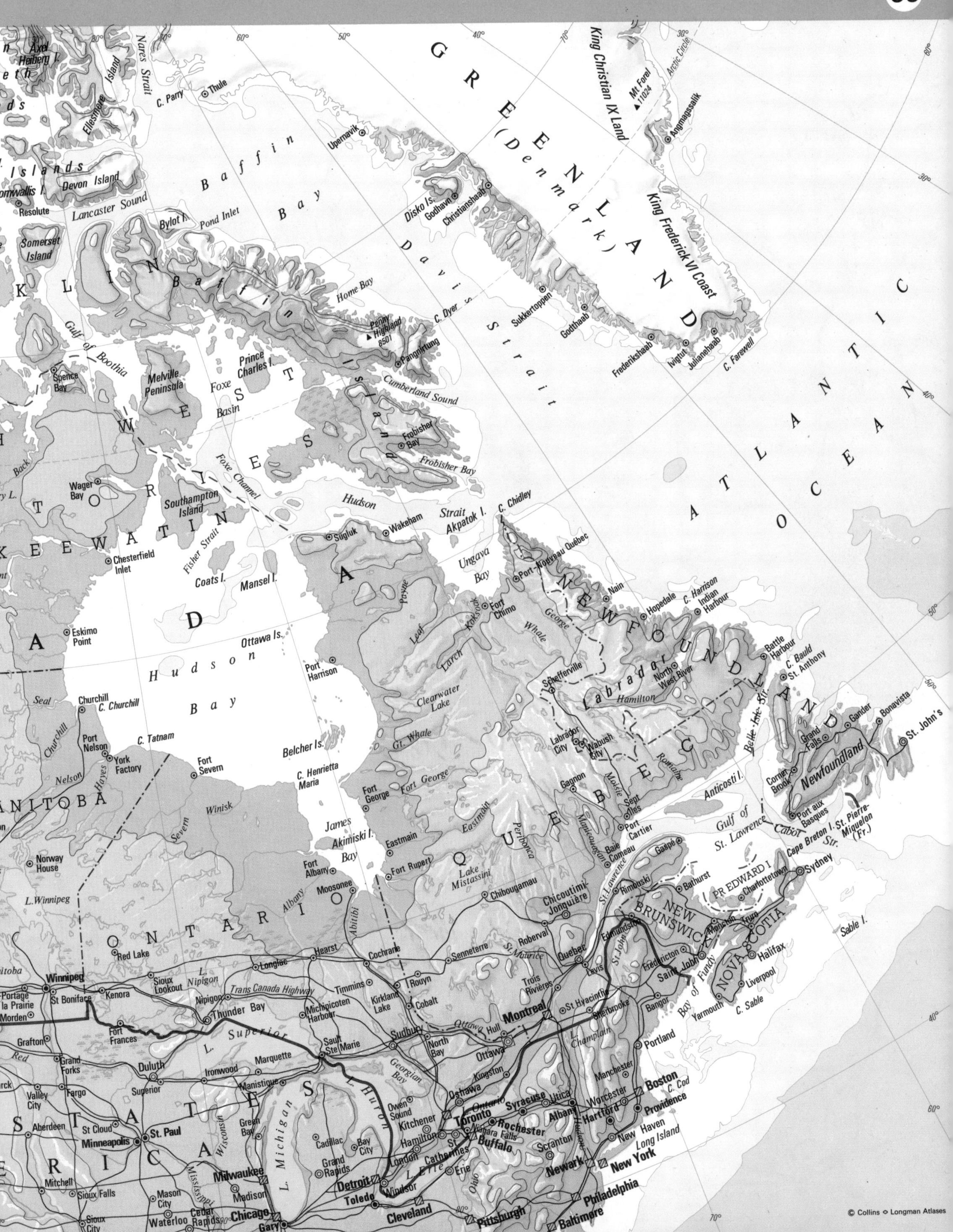
GREENLAND
(Denmark)
King Christian IX Land
King Frederick VI Coast
Mt Forel 11024
Angmagssalik
Arctic Circle
Thule
C. Parry
Nares Strait
Ellesmere Island
Axel Heiberg I.
Devon Island
Resolute
Lancaster Sound
Baffin Bay
Upernavik
Disko Is.
Godhavn
Christianshaab
Bylot I.
Pond Inlet
Somerset Island
Davis Strait
Home Bay
Baffin Island
Sukkertoppen
Godthaab
Penny Highland 8501
C. Dyer
Pangnirtung
Frederikshaab
Ivigtut
Julianehaab
C. Farewell
Gulf of Boothia
Spence Bay
Melville Peninsula
Prince Charles I.
Foxe Basin
Cumberland Sound
Frobisher Bay
Foxe Channel
Wager Bay
Southampton Island
Hudson Strait
Akpatok I.
C. Chidley
Sugluk
Wakeham
Chesterfield Inlet
Fisher Strait
Coats I.
Mansel I.
Ungava Bay
Port-Nouveau Québec
Fort Chimo
Nain
Hopedale
C. Harrison
Indian Harbour
Eskimo Point
Ottawa Is.
Hudson Bay
Port Harrison
Churchill
C. Churchill
Port Nelson
York Factory
C. Tatnam
Fort Severn
Belcher Is.
C. Henrietta Maria
Fort George
James Bay
Akimiski I.
Eastmain
Fort Rupert
Fort Albany
Moosonee
Norway House
L. Winnipeg
Lake Mistassini
Chibougamau
Clearwater Lake
Schefferville
Labrador
North West River
Hamilton
Battle Harbour
C. Bauld
St. Anthony
Labrador City
Wabush City
Gagnon
Sept Îles
Port Cartier
Baie Comeau
Anticosti I.
Gulf of St. Lawrence
Belle Isle Str.
Newfoundland
Grand Falls
Gander
Bonavista
St. John's
Corner Brook
Port aux Basques
Cabot Str.
St. Pierre-Miquelon (Fr.)
Cape Breton I.
Sydney
Gaspé
Rimouski
Bathurst
PR EDWARD I
Charlottetown
NEW BRUNSWICK
NOVA SCOTIA
Moncton
Truro
Halifax
Sable I.
Fredericton
Saint John
Bay of Fundy
Yarmouth
Liverpool
C. Sable
Chicoutimi-Jonquière
Roberval
Quebec
Lévis
Edmundston
Trois Rivières
St Hyacinthe
Sherbrooke
Montreal
Bangor
Portland
L. Champlain
KEEWATIN
DISTRICT OF
NORTHWEST TERRITORIES
CANADA
MANITOBA
ONTARIO
QUEBEC
NEWFOUNDLAND
ATLANTIC OCEAN
UNITED STATES OF AMERICA
Winnipeg
Portage la Prairie
St Boniface
Morden
Kenora
Red Lake
Sioux Lookout
L. Nipigon
Nipigon
Thunder Bay
Trans Canada Highway
Longlac
Hearst
Cochrane
Timmins
Kirkland Lake
Rouyn
Cobalt
Senneterre
Michipicoten Harbour
Fort Frances
L. Superior
Sault Ste Marie
Sudbury
North Bay
Hull
Ottawa
Kingston
Georgian Bay
L. Huron
Grafton
Grand Forks
Duluth
Ironwood
Marquette
Manistique
Superior
Fargo
Valley City
Aberdeen
St Cloud
Minneapolis
St. Paul
Green Bay
L. Michigan
Milwaukee
Madison
Chicago
Gary
Mitchell
Sioux Falls
Sioux City
Mason City
Waterloo
Cedar Rapids
Cadillac
Bay City
Grand Rapids
Owen Sound
Kitchener
Hamilton
London
Detroit
Windsor
Toledo
Cleveland
L. Erie
Erie
Pittsburgh
Oshawa
Toronto
L. Ontario
St Catharines
Niagara Falls
Buffalo
Rochester
Syracuse
Utica
Albany
Scranton
Manchester
Worcester
Boston
C. Cod
Providence
Hartford
New Haven
Long Island
New York
Newark
Philadelphia
Baltimore
Back
Churchill
Nelson
Hayes
Severn
Winisk
Albany
Abitibi
Red
Payne
Leaf
Larch
Koksoak
Whale
George
Gt. Whale
Eastmain
Peribonca
Manicouagan
Moisie
Romaine
St. Maurice
St. Lawrence
St. John
Hudson
Mississippi
Wisconsin
Ohio
© Collins ◇ Longman Atlases

Fort Frances
Rainy L.
International Falls
Atikokan
Lac des Mille Lacs
L. Nipigon
Long L.
Nipigon
Hearst
Kapuskasing
Cochrane
Iroquois Falls
Oba
Franz
Timmins
Dog L.
Thunder Bay
Heron Bay
Pic
Ely
Virginia
Grand Marais
Michipicoten Harbour
Chapleau
Elk Lake
MINNESOTA
Isle Royale
Lake Superior
Michipicoten I.
Duluth
Two Harbors
Apostle Is.
Hancock
Keweenaw Pt.
Sault Ste. Marie
Sudbury
Cloquet
Superior
Ashland
Ontonagon
Keweenaw Bay
Whitefish Pt.
Biskotasi L.
Timaga L.
Mille Lac L.
St. Croix
Ironwood
Marquette
Newberry
Blind River
Capreol
Spooner
Park Falls
Iron River
Iron Mountain
Negaunee
Munising
Sault Ste. Marie
North Channel
Little Current
Minneapolis
St. Paul
Ladysmith
Rhinelander
Escanaba
Manistique
Mackinaw City
Cheboygan
Manitoulin I.
Georgian Bay
Hastings
Chippewa Falls
Antigo
Wolf
Marinette
Green Bay
Beaver I.
Manitou Is.
Rogers City
C. Hurd
Eau Claire
Wausau
Shawano
MICHIGAN
Alpena
North Pt.
Owen Sound
WISCONSIN
Marshfield
Appleton
Green Bay
Traverse City
Au Sable
Grayling
Collingwood
Wisconsin Rapids
L. Winnebago
Manitowoc
Manistee
Cadillac
Au Sable Pt.
Winona
Sparta
La Crosse
Fond du Lac
Sheboygan
Ludington
Clare
Au Sable Bay
Port Austin
Goderich
Austin
Portage
Saginaw Bay
Waterloo
Kitchener
Watertown
Muskegon
Bay City
Stratford
Cedar Falls
Madison
Waukesha
Milwaukee
Grand Rapids
Alma
Saginaw
Flint
Port Huron
London
Waterloo
Dubuque
Janesville
Racine
Muskegon
Owosso
Sarnia
St. Thomas
IOWA
Rockford
Kenosha
Lansing
Pontiac
L. St. Clair
Port Burwell
Cedar Rapids
Clinton
Waukegan
South Haven
Battle Creek
Jackson
Ann Arbor
Detroit
Windsor
Chatham
Iowa City
Elgin
Evanston
Kalamazoo
Adrian
Monroe
Leamington
Rock Island
La Salle
Joliet
Chicago
E. Chicago
Gary
Michigan City
South Bend
Toledo
Pt. Pelee
Davenport
Aurora
Harvey
Hammond
Plymouth
Sandusky
Lorain
Lakewood
Cleveland
Painesville
Ashtabula
Galesburg
Kankakee
Fort Wayne
Maumee
Defiance
Findlay
Elyria
Euclid
Warren
Fort Madison
Peoria
Logansport
Peru
Wabash
Lima
Fostoria
Mansfield
Akron
Canton
Quincy
Bloomington
Lafayette
Kokomo
Marion
Portland
Piqua
Wooster
Aliquippa
Steubenville
Hannibal
ILLINOIS
Danville
Urbana
Anderson
INDIANA
Springfield
Marion
Coshocton
Zanesville
Cambridge
Mexico
Decatur
Champaign
Tuscola
Indianapolis
Richmond
OHIO
Columbus
Wheeling
Missouri
Springfield
Jacksonville
Terre Haute
Franklin
Dayton
Chillicothe
Athens
Clarksburg
Jefferson City
Alton
Effingham
Bloomington
Hamilton
Miami
Ohio
Parkersburg
Fairm
St. Louis
East St. Louis
Lawrenceville
Vincennes
Bedford
Seymour
Cincinnati
Covington
Newport
Portsmouth
WEST VIRGINIA
MISSOURI
Salem
Centralia
Princeton
KENTUCKY

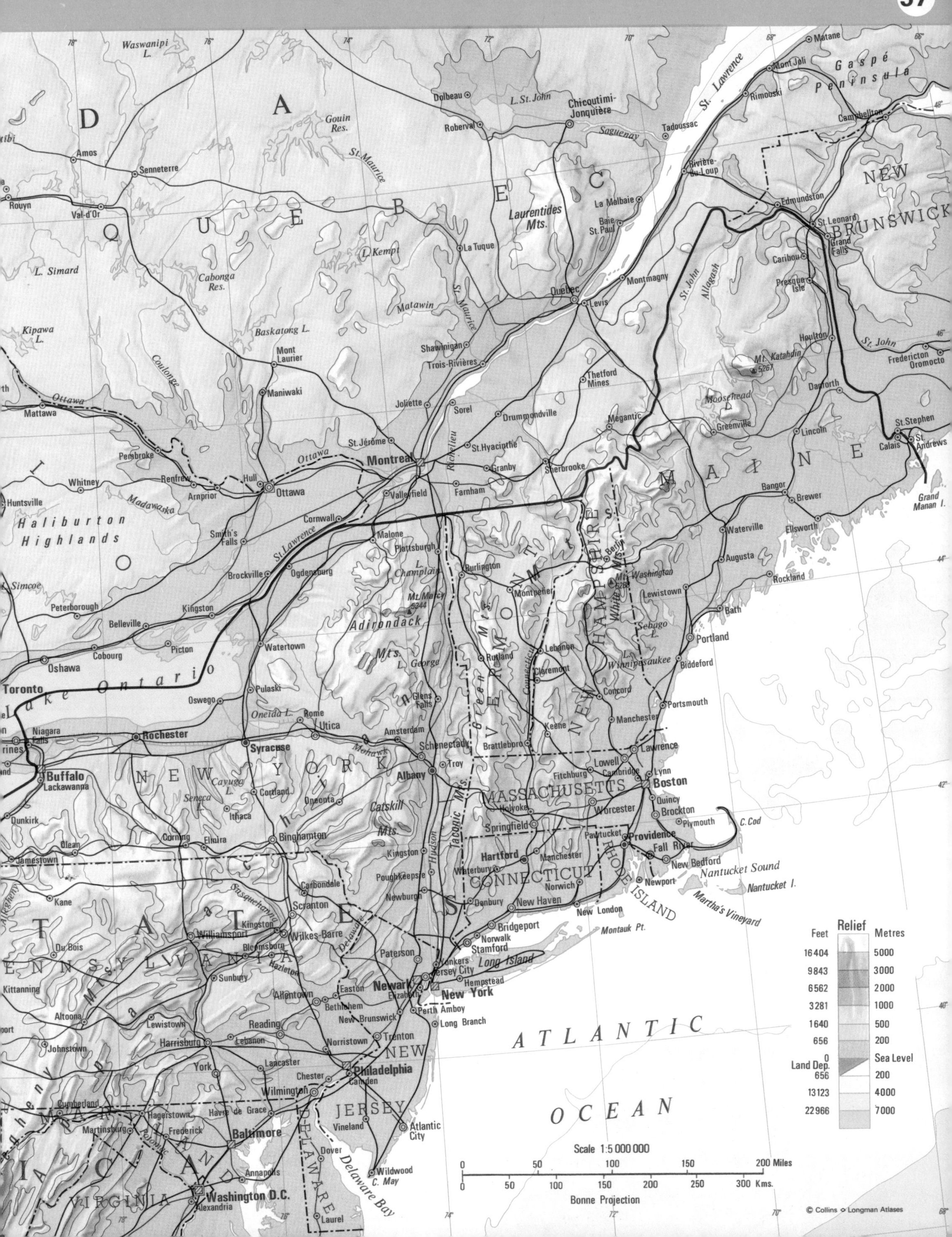

ATLANTIC

OCEAN

Feet	Relief	Metres
16 404		5000
9843		3000
6562		2000
3281		1000
1640		500
656		200
0		Sea Level
Land Dep.		200
656		
13123		4000
22 966		7000

Scale 1:5 000 000

0   50   100   150   200 Miles

0   50   100   150   200   250   300 Kms.

Bonne Projection

© Collins • Longman Atlases

GULF OF MEXICO

PACIFIC OCEAN

Mexican States numbered on map.
1 FEDERAL DISTRICT
2 TLAXCALA
3 AGUASCALIENTES
4 MORELOS

Relief

Feet	Metres
16 404	5000
9843	3000
6562	2000
3281	1000
1640	500
656	200
0	Sea Level
Land Dep.	
656	200
13 123	4000
22 966	7000

Scale 1:12 500 000

0 100 200 300 400 500 Miles
0 100 200 300 400 500 600 700 800 Kms.

Lambert Azimuthal Equal Area Projection

© Collins ◇ Longman Atlases

TEXAS • Houston • San Antonio • Austin • Waco • Corpus Christi • Brownsville • Laredo

LOUISIANA • MISSISSIPPI • ALABAMA • GEORGIA • New Orleans • Baton Rouge • Mobile • Pensacola • Tallahassee • Tampa • St. Petersburg • Key West

COAHUILA • NUEVO LEON • Monterrey • Saltillo • Torreón • Tampico

Edwards Plateau • Padre Island • Madre Lagoon

Sierra Madre Occidental • Sierra Madre Oriental • Sierra Madre del Sur

Guadalajara • San Luis Potosí • León • MICHOACAN • Mexico City • PUEBLA • GUERRERO • Veracruz • Acapulco • OAXACA • CHIAPAS • TABASCO

Campeche Bay • Campeche • YUCATAN • Mérida • Progreso • QUINTANA ROO (Terr.) • Chetumal • Yucatán Peninsula • Yucatán Channel • Cozumel I.

Havana • Marianao • Pinar del Río • Isle of Pines • Gulf of Batabanó

BELIZE • Belmopan • Gulf of Honduras • GUATEMALA • Guatemala City • HONDURAS • Tegucigalpa • San Pedro Sula • La Ceiba • Mosquito Coast • Mosquitia Plain • Caratasca Lagoon

EL SALVADOR • San Salvador • G. of Fonseca • NICARAGUA • Managua • Lake Nicaragua • León • Granada • Bluefields • Rio Grande

COSTA RICA • San José • Nicoya Peninsula • Isthmus of Tehuantepec • Gulf of Tehuantepec

Isthmus of Tehuantepec

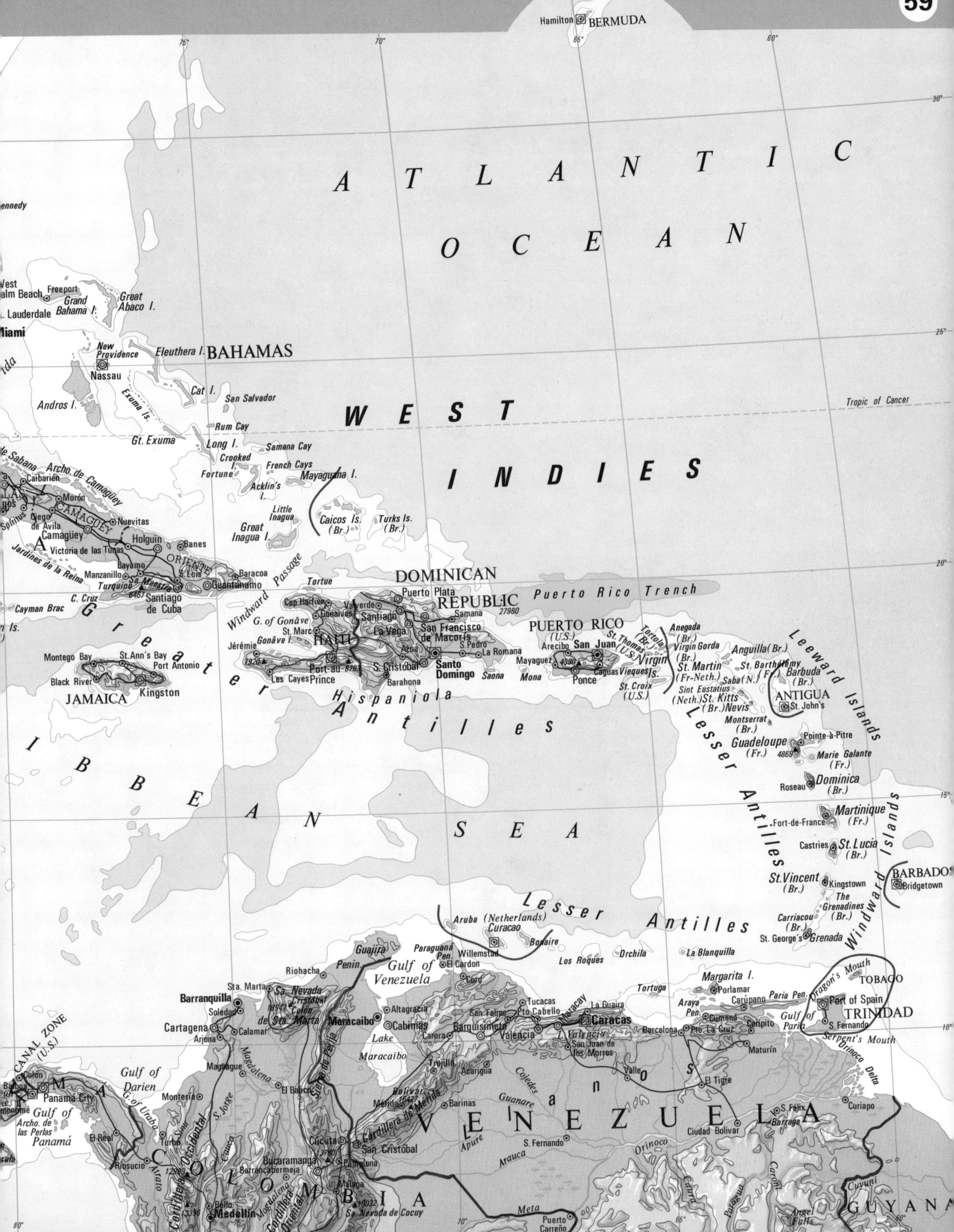
Hamilton
BERMUDA
ATLANTIC
OCEAN
WEST
INDIES
BAHAMAS
Freeport
Grand Bahama I.
Great Abaco I.
New Providence
Nassau
Eleuthera I.
Andros I.
Exuma Is.
Cat I.
San Salvador
Rum Cay
Gt. Exuma
Long I.
Samana Cay
Crooked I.
French Cays
Fortune
Acklin's I.
Mayaguana I.
Little Inagua
Great Inagua I.
Caicos Is. (Br.)
Turks Is. (Br.)
Tropic of Cancer
Caibarién
Archo. de Camagüey
Morón
CAMAGÜEY
Nuevitas
Camagüey
Holguín
Banes
Victoria de las Tunas
ORIENTE
Jardines de la Reina
Manzanillo
Bayamo
S. Luis
Baracoa
Turquino
Guantánamo
Santiago de Cuba
C. Cruz
Cayman Brac
Windward Passage
Tortue
Cap Haïtien
G. of Gonâve
Gonâve I.
Jérémie
St. Marc
HAITI
Port-au-Prince
Les Cayes
Valverde
Santiago
La Vega
Puerto Plata
DOMINICAN REPUBLIC
Samana
San Francisco de Macorís
S. Pedro
La Romana
Santo Domingo
S. Cristóbal
Barahona
Saona
Hispaniola
Puerto Rico Trench
27980
PUERTO RICO (U.S.)
San Juan
Arecibo
Mayaguez
Mona
Ponce
Caguas
Vieques
St. Thomas (U.S.)
Tortola (Br.)
Virgin Is.
St. Croix (U.S.)
Anegada (Br.)
Virgin Gorda (Br.)
St. Martin (Fr-Neth.)
Sint Eustatius (Neth.)
St. Kitts (Br.)
Nevis
Saba (N.)
Anguilla (Br.)
St. Barthélemy (Fr.)
Barbuda (Br.)
ANTIGUA
St. John's
Montserrat (Br.)
Guadeloupe (Fr.)
Pointe-à-Pitre
Marie Galante (Fr.)
Dominica (Br.)
Roseau
Martinique (Fr.)
Fort-de-France
St. Lucia (Br.)
Castries
St. Vincent (Br.)
Kingstown
BARBADOS
Bridgetown
The Grenadines (Br.)
Carriacou (Br.)
St. George's
Grenada
Leeward Islands
Windward Islands
Lesser Antilles
Greater Antilles
JAMAICA
Montego Bay
St. Ann's Bay
Port Antonio
Black River
Kingston
CARIBBEAN SEA
Aruba
(Netherlands)
Curaçao
Bonaire
Los Roques
Orchila
La Blanquilla
Margarita I.
Porlamar
Tortuga
TOBAGO
Dragon's Mouth
Port of Spain
TRINIDAD
S. Fernando
Serpent's Mouth
Orinoco Delta
Guajira Penin.
Paraguaná Pen.
Willemstad
El Cardón
Coro
Riohacha
Gulf of Venezuela
Sta. Marta
Barranquilla
Soledad
Sa. Nevada de Sta. Marta
Cristóbal Colón
Cartagena
Calamar
Arjona
Maracaibo
Altagracia
Cabimas
Lake Maracaibo
Carora
Barquisimeto
San Felipe
Pto. Cabello
Tucacas
Valencia
Maracay
La Guaira
Caracas
San Juan de los Morros
Barcelona
Pto. La Cruz
Cumaná
Carúpano
Paria Pen.
Gulf of Paria
Araya Pen.
Maturín
El Tigre
Valle
Trujillo
Acarigua
Cojedes
Guanare
Barinas
Mérida
Bolívar
Cordillera de Mérida
VENEZUELA
Llanos
Ciudad Bolívar
S. Félix
Curiapo
Apure
Arauca
S. Fernando
Orinoco
Meta
Puerto Carreño
Caura
Caroní
Cuyuni
Angel Falls
GUYANA
El Banco
Magangué
Magdalena
CANAL ZONE (U.S.)
Colón
Balboa
Panamá City
PANAMA
Gulf of Darien
G. of Urabá
Gulf of Panamá
Archo. de las Perlas
Montería
El Real
Turbo
Sinú
S. Jorge
Riosucio
Atrato
Cauca
Cordillera Occidental
COLOMBIA
Cúcuta
San Cristóbal
Pamplona
Bucaramanga
Barrancabermeja
Málaga
Sa. Nevada de Cocuy
Cordillera Oriental
Medellín
Bello
Sierra de Perijá
75°
70°
65°
60°
80°
30°
25°
20°
15°
10°

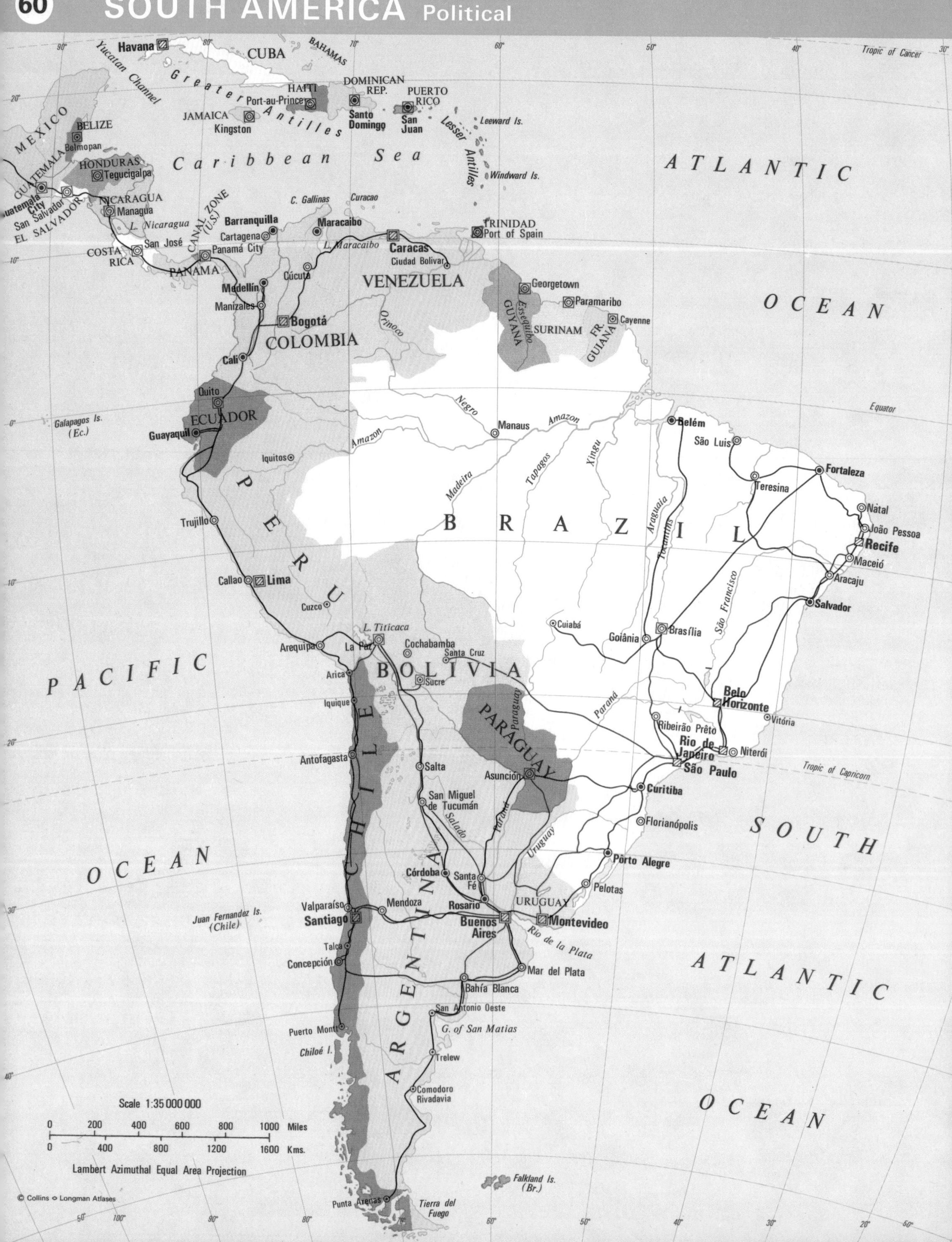

Tropic of Cancer

Havana CUBA BAHAMAS
Yucatan Channel
Greater Antilles
HAITI DOMINICAN REP. PUERTO RICO
Port-au-Prince Santo Domingo San Juan
JAMAICA Leeward Is.
Kingston
Lesser Antilles
Windward Is.

MEXICO BELIZE
Belmopan
GUATEMALA HONDURAS Tegucigalpa
Guatemala City
San Salvador NICARAGUA
EL SALVADOR Managua
L. Nicaragua

Caribbean Sea

ATLANTIC

OCEAN

COSTA RICA San José
PANAMA CANAL ZONE (U.S.)
Panamá City
C. Gallinas Curacao
Barranquilla Maracaibo
Cartagena TRINIDAD Port of Spain
Cúcuta L. Maracaibo Caracas
Medellín Ciudad Bolivar
Manizales VENEZUELA
Georgetown Paramaribo
Bogotá GUYANA Cayenne
COLOMBIA Essequibo SURINAM FR. GUIANA
Cali
Orinoco

Quito
ECUADOR
Guayaquil Negro Amazon Belém
Galapagos Is. (Ec.) São Luis
Equator
Iquitos Manaus Amazon Fortaleza
Madeira Teresina
P Tapajos Xingu Natal
E João Pessoa
Trujillo R Araguaia **Recife**
U B R A Z I L Maceió
Callao **Lima** Tocantins Aracaju
Cuzco São Francisco Salvador
L. Titicaca
Arequipa Cochabamba Cuiabá
La Paz Santa Cruz Goiânia Brasília
Arica BOLIVIA
Sucre Belo Horizonte
Iquique Paraguay Vitória
PARAGUAY Paraná Ribeirão Prêto
Antofagasta Salta Rio de Janeiro
Asunción Niterói
C San Miguel São Paulo Tropic of Capricorn
H de Tucumán Paraná Curitiba
Salado
I Florianópolis SOUTH
L Uruguay Pôrto Alegre
Córdoba Santa Fé Pelotas
Valparaíso Mendoza Rosario URUGUAY
Santiago Buenos **Montevideo**
Aires Rio de la Plata ATLANTIC
Talca Mar del Plata
Concepción Bahía Blanca
A San Antonio Oeste OCEAN
R G. of San Matias
Puerto Montt G
Chiloé I. E Trelew
N Comodoro
T Rivadavia
I
N
A

PACIFIC

OCEAN

Juan Fernandez Is. (Chile)

Scale 1:35 000 000

0   200   400   600   800   1000 Miles
0   400   800   1200   1600 Kms.

Lambert Azimuthal Equal Area Projection

© Collins ◇ Longman Atlases

Falkland Is. (Br.)

Punta Arenas Tierra del Fuego

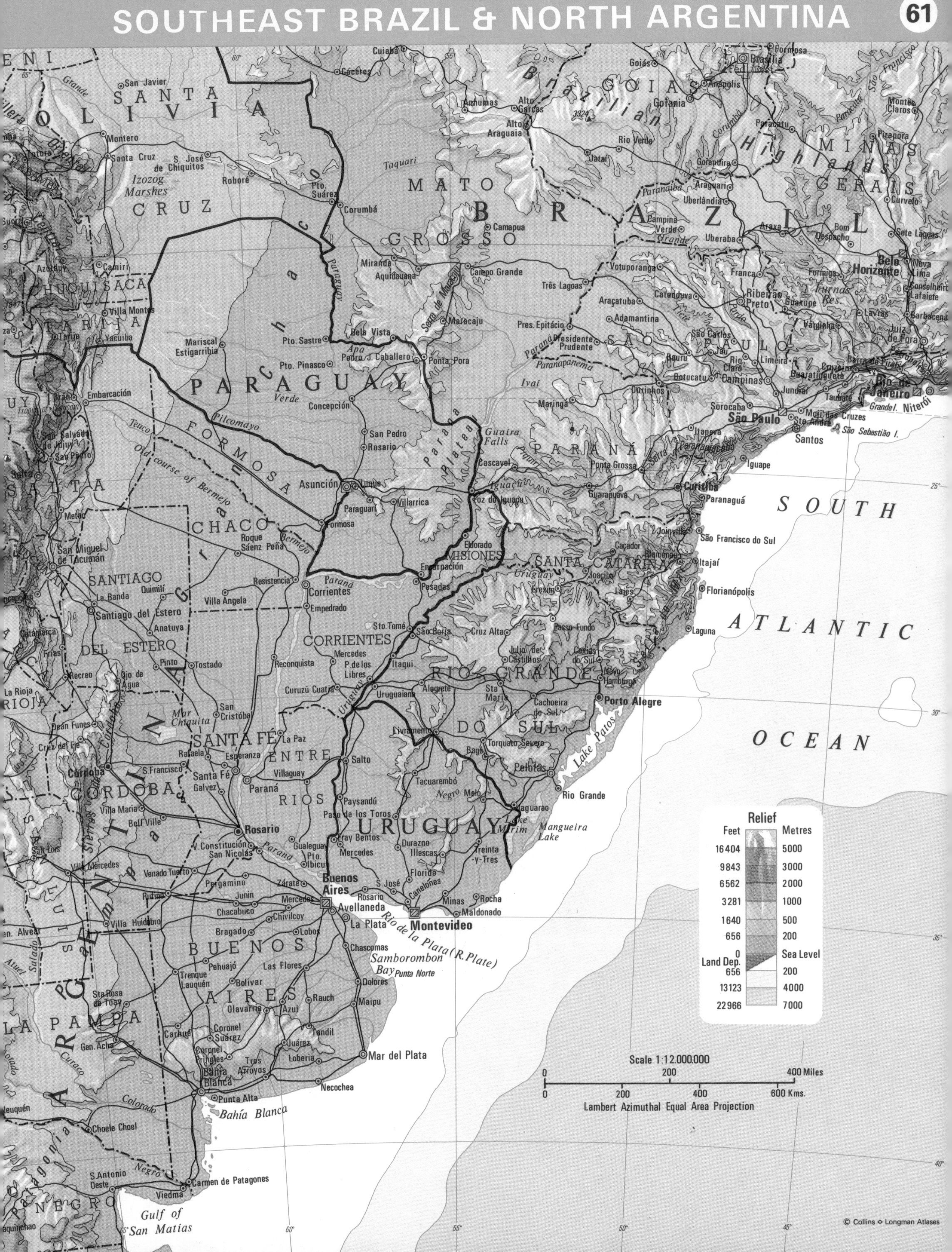

Relief

Feet		Metres
16 404		5000
9843		3000
6562		2000
3281		1000
1640		500
656		200
		Sea Level
Land Dep.	0	
656		200
13 123		4000
22 966		7000

Scale 1:12.000.000

0   200   400 Miles

0   200   400   600 Kms.

Lambert Azimuthal Equal Area Projection

© Collins ◇ Longman Atlases

ATLANTIC OCEAN

Tropic of Cancer

Equator

BRAZIL

Brazilian

Mato Grosso

BOLIVIA

ANDES

Mouths of the Amazon

Marajó I. · Belém

Tocantins

Amazon

Santarém

Manaus

Negro

Branco

Roosevelt

Madeira

Purus

Juruá

Japurá

Putumayo

Marañón

Xingu

Tapajós

Araguaia

Tocantins

Pôrto Velho

Guajará Mirim

Trinidad

Mamore

Río Branco

Cobija

Goiânia

Brasília

Januária

Januária

Cuiabá

Mato Grosso

C. São Roque · Natal · João Pessoa · Recife · Maceió

Mossoró · Campina Grande · Caruaru · Aracaju

Fortaleza · Sobral · Teresina

Salvador · Feira · Itabuna

Vitória · Januária

São Luís

Parnaíba

São Francisco

FRENCH GUIANA · Cayenne · C. Orange

SURINAM · Paramaribo · Amsterdam

GUYANA · Georgetown · Essequibo

GUYANA HIGHLANDS

Roraima 9094

VENEZUELA · Caracas · Barcelona · Cumaná

Maracaibo · Valencia · Barquisimeto

Ciudad Bolívar · San Fernando

Orinoco Delta · Orinoco

El Tigre · Apure · Meta

Cerro Marahuaca 3840

COLOMBIA · Bogotá · Medellín · Cali · Cartagena · Barranquilla

Cúcuta · Bucaramanga · Ibagué · Manizales

Cordillera Occidental · Cordillera Oriental

Buenaventura · Pasto · Popayán

ECUADOR · Quito · Guayaquil · Cuenca · Ambato

Gulf of Guayaquil

Chimborazo 6267

Iquitos

Leticia

São Paulo de Olivença

Catral de Pasco · Callao · Lima

Trujillo · Chimbote · Chiclayo · Sullana

C. San Francisco · C. Negra

Tumaco

Ipiales

PERU

Huancayo

Cuzco

Apurímac

Ucayali

Marañón

Huallaga

Caribbean Sea

Greater Antilles

Lesser Antilles

Windward Islands

Leeward Islands

ANTIGUA · Guadeloupe (Fr.) · Dominica (Br.) · Martinique (Fr.) · BARBADOS

TRINIDAD · Port of Spain

Netherlands Antilles · Curaçao · Aruba

C. Gallinas · G. of Venezuela · Gulf of Darien

BAHAMAS · Nassau · Grand Bahama I. · Gt. Abaco I. · Andros · Gt. Inagua I.

CUBA · Havana · Santiago de Cuba · Camagüey · Holguín · Santa Clara · Cienfuegos

JAMAICA · Kingston

HAITI · Port-au-Prince · Gonaïves

DOMINICAN REP. · Santo Domingo · Santiago · Puerto Plata

PUERTO RICO · San Juan · Ponce

Puerto Rico Trench 27380

U.S.A. · Miami · Tampa · St. Petersburg · West Palm Beach · Fort Lauderdale · Orlando · C. Kennedy · Key West · Florida · Straits of Florida

MEXICO · Yucatan · Yucatan Pen. · Puerto Juárez

BELIZE · Belmopan

HONDURAS · Tegucigalpa

NICARAGUA · Managua

COSTA RICA · San José

PANAMA · Panamá · Colón · Gulf of Panamá · CANAL ZONE

Gulf of Honduras · C. Gracias á Dios · Windward Passage · Yucatan Channel

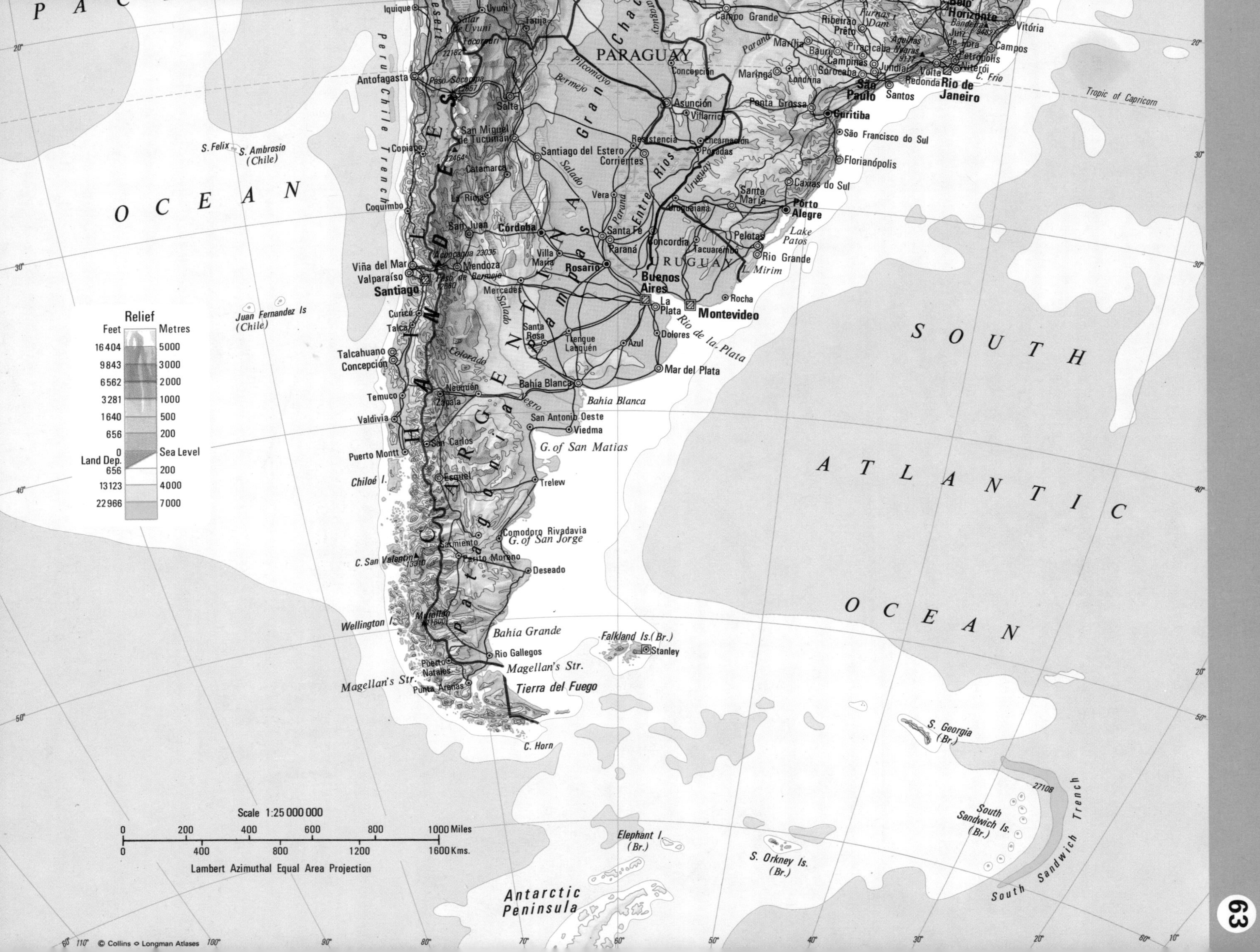

P A C I F I C   O C E A N

S O U T H   A T L A N T I C   O C E A N

Tropic of Capricorn

Vitória
Belo Horizonte
Campos
Rio de Janeiro
Niterói
C. Frio
São Paulo
Santos
Curitiba
São Francisco do Sul
Florianópolis
Porto Alegre
Rio Grande
Lake Patos
Pelotas
Santa Maria
Montevideo
Rocha
Rio de la Plata
Mar del Plata
Dolores
Buenos Aires
La Plata
Azul
Bahía Blanca
Viedma
San Antonio Oeste
G. of San Matías
Trelew
G. of San Jorge
Comodoro Rivadavia
Deseado
Bahía Grande
Río Gallegos
Magellan's Str.
Tierra del Fuego
C. Horn

PARAGUAY
Asunción
Concepción
Resistencia
Corrientes
URUGUAY
Santiago del Estero
Córdoba
Rosario
Santa Fe
Paraná
Villa María
Mendoza
San Juan
La Rioja
Catamarca
San Miguel de Tucumán
Salta
Jujuy

ANDES

Santiago
Valparaíso
Viña del Mar
Talca
Talcahuano
Concepción
Temuco
Valdivia
Puerto Montt
Chiloé I.

Antofagasta
Iquique
Coquimbo

Peru–Chile Trench

S. Félix   S. Ambrosio (Chile)

Juan Fernández Is (Chile)

Falkland Is. (Br.)
Stanley

S. Georgia (Br.)

South Sandwich Is. (Br.)

South Sandwich Trench

S. Orkney Is. (Br.)

Elephant I. (Br.)

Antarctic Peninsula

Scale 1:25 000 000

Lambert Azimuthal Equal Area Projection

1000 Miles
1600 Kms.
0   200   400   600   800   1200

© Collins © Longman Atlases

Relief

Feet	Metres
16404	5000
9843	3000
6562	2000
3281	1000
1640	500
656	200
0	Sea Level
	Land Dep.
656	200
13123	4000
22966	7000

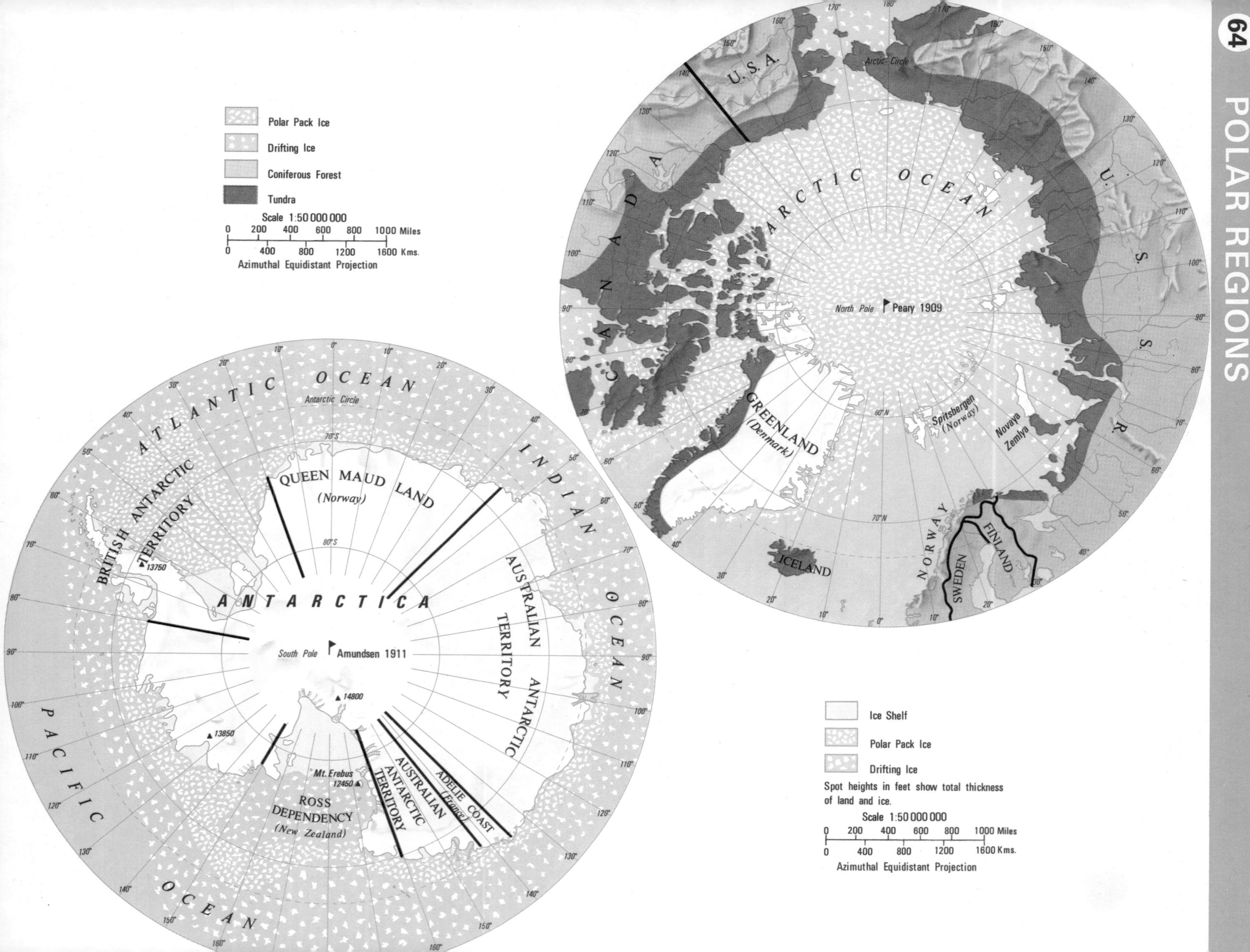

U. S. S. R.

U. S. S. R.

Novaya Zemlya

Spitsbergen (Norway)

FINLAND

SWEDEN

NORWAY

ICELAND

ARCTIC OCEAN

North Pole ▲ Peary 1909

Arctic Circle

GREENLAND (Denmark)

U. S. A.

C A N A D A

Ice Shelf

Polar Pack Ice

Drifting Ice

Spot heights in feet show total thickness of land and ice.

Scale 1:50 000 000

0   200   400   600   800   1000 Miles
0 200 400 600 800 1200 1600 Kms.

Azimuthal Equidistant Projection

INDIAN   OCEAN

AUSTRALIAN   ANTARCTIC

TERRITORY

ADELIE COAST (France)

AUSTRALIAN ANTARCTIC TERRITORY

QUEEN MAUD LAND (Norway)

A N T A R C T I C A

South Pole ▲ Amundsen 1911

▲14800

Mt. Erebus ▲12850

ROSS DEPENDENCY (New Zealand)

ATLANTIC OCEAN

Antarctic Circle

▲13850

BRITISH ANTARCTIC TERRITORY

▲13750

PACIFIC   OCEAN

Polar Pack Ice

Drifting Ice

Coniferous Forest

Tundra

Scale 1:50 000 000

0   200   400   600   800   1000 Miles
0 200 400 600 800 1200 1600 Kms.

Azimuthal Equidistant Projection

The names in the atlas, except for some, mostly on the thematic maps, will be found in this index, printed in bold type. Each entry indicates the country or region of the world in which the name is located. This is followed by the number of the most appropriate page on which the name appears—generally the largest scale map. Lastly the latitude and longitude is given. Where the name applies to a very large area of the map these co-ordinates are sometimes omitted. For names that do apply to an area the reference is to the centre of the feature, which will usually also be the position of the name. In the case of rivers the mouth or confluence is always taken as the point of reference. Therefore it is necessary to follow the river upstream from this point to find its name on the map.

Towns listed in the index are not described as such unless the name could be misleading. Thus Whitley Bay is followed by 'town' in italic. Elsewhere, when the name itself does not indicate clearly what it is, a description is always added in italic immediately after. These descriptions have had to be abbreviated in many cases.

Abbreviations used in the index are explained below.

Abbreviations

Afghan.	Afghanistan
Bangla.	Bangladesh
b., B.	bay, Bay
Beds.	Bedfordshire
Berks.	Berkshire
Bucks.	Buckinghamshire
Cambs.	Cambridgeshire
c., C.	cape, Cape
C.A.R.	Central African Republic
Czech.	Czechoslovakia
d.	internal division eg. county, region, state
Derbys.	Derbyshire
des.	desert
Dom. Rep.	Dominican Republic
D. and G.	Dumfries and Galloway
E. Germany	Eastern Germany
E. Sussex	East Sussex
Equat. Guinea	Equatorial Guinea
est.	estuary
f.	physical feature eg. valley, plain, geographic district or region
F.T.A.I.	French Territory of Afars and Issas
Game Res.	Game Reserve
Glos.	Gloucestershire
G.L.	Greater London
G.M.	Greater Manchester
G.	Gulf
Hants.	Hampshire
H. and W.	Hereford and Worcester
Herts.	Hertfordshire
Humber.	Humberside
i., I., is., Is.	island, Island, islands, Islands
I.o.M.	Isle of Man
I.o.W.	Isle of Wight
l., L.	lake, Lake
Lancs.	Lancashire
Leics.	Leicestershire
Liech.	Liechtenstein
Lincs.	Lincolnshire
Lux.	Luxembourg
Malagasy Rep.	Malagasy Republic
Mersey.	Merseyside
M.G.	Mid Glamorgan
Mt.	Mount
mtn., Mtn.	mountain, Mountain
mts., Mts.	mountains, Mountains
Nat. Park	National Park

Neth.	Netherlands
N. Ireland	Northern Ireland
Northants.	Northamptonshire
Northum.	Northumberland
N. Korea	North Korea
N. Vietnam	North Vietnam
N. Yorks.	North Yorkshire
Notts.	Nottinghamshire
Oxon.	Oxfordshire
P.N.G.	Papua New Guinea
pen., Pen.	peninsula, Peninsula
Phil.	Philippines
Pt.	Point
Port. Timor	Portuguese Timor
r., R.	river, River
Rep. of Ire.	Republic of Ireland
R.S.A.	Republic of South Africa
Resr.	Reservoir
Somali Rep.	Somali Republic
Sd.	Sound
S. Yemen	Southern Yemen
S.G.	South Glamorgan
S. Korea	South Korea
S. Vietnam	South Vietnam
S.W. Africa	South West Africa
S. Yorks.	South Yorkshire
Span. Sahara	Spanish Sahara
Staffs.	Staffordshire
str., Str.	strait, Strait
Strath.	Strathclyde
Switz.	Switzerland
T. and W.	Tyne and Wear
U.A.E.	Union of Arab Emirates
U.S.S.R.	Union of Soviet Socialist Republics
U.K.	United Kingdom
U.S.A.	United States of America
U. Volta	Upper Volta
Warwicks.	Warwickshire
W. Germany	Western Germany
W.G.	West Glamorgan
W. Isles	Western Isles
W. Midlands	West Midlands
W. Sussex	West Sussex
W. Yorks.	West Yorkshire
Wilts.	Wiltshire
Yugo.	Yugoslavia

A

Aa r. France 9 51.00N 2.06E
Aachen W. Germany 27 50.46N 6.06E
Äänekoski Finland 28 62.36N 25.44E
Aarau Switz. 26 47.24N 8.04E
Aardenburg Neth. 27 51.16N 3.26E
Aare r. Switz. 22 47.03N 7.18E
Aarhus Denmark 28 56.10N 10.13E
Aarschot Belgium 27 50.59N 4.50E
Aba Nigeria 46 5.06N 7.21E
Abadan Iran 35 30.21N 48.15E
Abadan I. Iran 35 30.10N 48.30E
Abadeh Iran 35 31.10N 52.40E
Abadla Algeria 44 31.01N 2.45W
Abakan U.S.S.R. 31 53.43N 91.25E
Abashiri wan b. Japan 42 44.02N 144.17E
Abaya, L. Ethiopia 45 6.20N 38.00E
Abbeville France 22 50.06N 1.51E
Abbeyfeale Rep. of Ire. 19 52.23N 9.18W
Abbeyleix Rep. of Ire. 19 52.55N 7.22W
Abbey Town England 12 54.50N 3.18W
Abbotsbury England 8 50.40N 2.36W
Abbots Langley England 7 51.43N 0.25W
Abéché Chad 45 13.49N 20.49E

Åbenrå Denmark 28 55.03N 9.26E
Aberayron Wales 10 52.15N 4.16W
Abercarn Wales 11 51.39N 3.09W
Aberdare Wales 11 51.43N 3.27W
Aberdare Mts. Kenya 47 0.20S 36.40E
Aberdaron Wales 10 52.48N 4.41W
Aberdeen Hong Kong 33 22.15N 114.09E
Aberdeen Scotland 17 57.08N 2.07W
Aberdeen S. Dak. U.S.A. 52 45.28N 98.30W
Aberdeen Wash. U.S.A. 52 46.58N 123.49W
Aberdovey Wales 10 52.33N 4.03W
Aberfan Wales 11 51.42N 3.20W
Aberfeldy Scotland 15 56.37N 3.54W
Aberffraw Wales 10 53.11N 4.28W
Aberfoyle Scotland 14 56.11N 4.23W
Abergavenny Wales 11 51.49N 3.01W
Abergele Wales 10 53.17N 3.34W
Abernethy Scotland 15 56.20N 3.19W
Aberporth Wales 10 52.08N 4.33W
Abersoch Wales 10 52.50N 4.31W
Abersychan Wales 8 51.44N 3.03W
Abertillery Wales 11 51.44N 3.09W
Aberystwyth Wales 10 52.25N 4.06W
Ab-i-Diz r. Iran 35 31.38N 48.54E
Abidjan Ivory Coast 44 5.19N 4.01W

Abilene U.S.A. 52 32.27N 99.45W
Abingdon England 8 51.40N 1.17W
Abington Scotland 15 55.29N 3.42W
Abitibi r. Canada 53 51.15N 81.30W
Abitibi, L. Canada 57 48.40N 79.35W
Aboyne Scotland 17 57.05N 2.48W
Abqaiq Saudi Arabia 35 25.55N 49.40E
Abrantes Portugal 23 39.28N 8.12W
Abridge England 7 51.40N 0.08E
Abu Dhabi U.A.E. 35 24.27N 54.23E
Abu Hamed Sudan 45 19.32N 33.20E
Abu Simbel Egypt 34 22.18N 31.40E
Abu Tig Egypt 34 27.06N 31.17E
Abu Zenima Egypt 34 29.03N 33.06E
Acámbaro Mexico 58 20.01N 101.42W
Acapulco Mexico 58 16.51N 99.56W
Acarigua Venezuela 59 9.35N 69.12W
Acatlán Mexico 58 18.12N 98.02W
Accra Ghana 44 5.33N 0.15W
Accrington England 12 53.46N 2.22W
Achahoish Scotland 14 55.57N 5.30W
à Chairn Bhain, Loch Scotland 16 58.16N 5.05W
Achill Head Rep. of Ire. 18 53.59N 10.15W
Achill I. Rep. of Ire. 18 53.57N 10.00W
Achill Sound town Rep. of Ire. 18 53.56N 9.56W

Achnasheen Scotland 16 57.34N 5.05W
A'Chràlaig mtn. Scotland 16 57.11N 5.09W
Acklin's I. Bahamas 59 22.30N 74.10W
Ackworth Moor Top town England 13 53.39N 1.20W
Aconcagua, Mt. Argentina 63 32.37S 70.00W
Acqui Italy 24 44.41N 8.28E
Acton England 7 51.31N 0.17W
Adamantina Brazil 61 21.41S 51.04W
Adamawa Highlands Nigeria 44 7.05N 12.00E
Adams, Mt. U.S.A. 52 46.13N 121.29W
Adana Turkey 34 37.00N 35.19E
Adapazari Turkey 34 40.45N 30.23E
Adare Rep. of Ire. 19 52.33N 8.48W
Adda r. Italy 22 45.08N 9.55E
Ad Dahana des. Saudi Arabia 35 26.00N 47.00E
Adderbury England 8 52.01N 1.19W
Addis Ababa Ethiopia 45 9.03N 38.42E
Ad Diwaniya Iraq 35 31.59N 44.57E
Addlestone England 7 51.22N 0.31W
Adelaide Australia 49 34.56S 138.36E
Adélie Coast Antarctica 64 80.00S 140.00E
Aden S. Yemen 45 12.50N 45.00E
Aden, G. of Indian Oc. 45 13.00N 50.00E
Adi i. Asia 39 4.10S 133.10E

Adige *r.* Italy **24** 45.10N 12.20E
Adirondack Mts. U.S.A. **57** 44.00N 74.15W
Adiyaman Turkey **34** 37.46N 38.15E
Adlington England **12** 53.37N 2.36W
Admiralty Is. Pacific Oc. **39** 2.30S 147.20E
Adour *r.* France **22** 43.28N 1.35W
Adrano Italy **24** 37.39N 14.49E
Adraskand *r.* Afghan. **35** 33.17N 62.08E
Adrian U.S.A. **56** 41.55N 84.01W
Adriatic Sea Med. Sea **24** 42.30N 16.00E
Adur *r.* England **9** 50.50N 0.16W
Aduwa Ethiopia **45** 14.12N 38.56E
Adwick le Street England **13** 53.35N 1.12W
Aegean Sea Med. Sea **25** 39.00N 25.00E
Aeron *r.* Wales **10** 52.14N 4.16W
Afghanistan Asia **36** 34.00N 65.30E
Afif Saudi Arabia **34** 23.53N 42.59E
Afmadu Somali Rep. **47** 0.27N 42.05E
Africa 43
Afyon Turkey **34** 38.46N 30.32E
Agadès Niger **44** 17.00N 7.56E
Agana Asia **39** 13.28N 144.45E
Agano *r.* Japan **42** 37.58N 139.02E
Agartala India **37** 23.49N 91.15E
Agde France **23** 43.25N 3.30E
Agedabia Libya **44** 30.48N 20.15E
Agen France **22** 44.12N 0.38E
Agger *r.* W. Germany **27** 50.45N 7.06E
Aghada Rep. of Ire. **19** 51.50N 8.13W
Aghda Iran **35** 32.25N 33.38E
Aghleam Rep. of Ire. **18** 54.08N 10.06W
Agnew's Hill N. Ireland **14** 54.51N 5.59W
Agordat Ethiopia **45** 15.35N 37.55E
Agout *r.* France **23** 43.40N 1.40E
Agra India **37** 27.09N 78.00E
Agra *r.* Spain **23** 42.12N 1.43W
Agreda Spain **23** 41.51N 1.55W
Agri *r.* Italy **25** 40.13N 16.45E
Agri Turkey **34** 39.44N 43.04E
Agrigento Italy **24** 37.19N 13.36E
Agrihan *i.* Asia **39** 18.44N 145.39E
Aguascalientes Mexico **58** 21.51N 102.18W
Aguascalientes *d.* Mexico **58** 22.00N 102.00W
Agueda *r.* Spain **23** 41.00N 6.56W
Aguilar de Campóo Spain **22** 42.47N 4.15W
Aguilas Spain **23** 37.25N 1.35W
Agulhas, C. R.S.A. **48** 34.50S 20.00E
Agulhas Negras *mtn.* Brazil **63** 22.20S 44.43W
Ahaggar Mts. Algeria **44** 24.00N 5.50E
Ahar Iran **35** 38.25N 47.07E
Ahaus W. Germany **27** 52.04N 7.01E
Ahmedabad India **36** 23.03N 72.40E
Ahmednagar India **36** 19.08N 74.48E
Ahr *r.* W. Germany **27** 50.34N 7.16E
Ahwaz Iran **35** 31.17N 48.44E
Aigun China **41** 49.40N 127.10E
Ailette *r.* France **27** 49.35N 3.09E
Ailsa Craig *i.* Scotland **14** 55.15N 5.07W
Ain *r.* France **22** 45.47N 5.12E
Aïna *r.* Gabon **46** 0.38N 12.47E
Ain Beida Algeria **24** 35.50N 7.29E
Ain Salah Algeria **44** 27.12N 2.29E
Ain Sefra Algeria **44** 32.45N 0.35W
Aïr *mts.* Niger **44** 18.30N 8.30E
Aird Brenish *c.* Scotland **16** 58.08N 7.08W
Airdrie Scotland **15** 55.52N 3.59W
Aire *r.* England **13** 53.42N 0.54W
Aire France **22** 43.39N 0.15W
Airedale *f.* England **12** 53.56N 1.54W
Aisne *r.* France **27** 49.27N 2.51E
Aitape P.N.G. **39** 3.10S 142.17E
Aith Scotland **16** 60.17N 1.23W
Aix-en-Provence France **22** 43.31N 5.27E
Aiyina *i.* Greece **25** 37.43N 23.30E
Aizeb *r.* Botswana **48** 20.20S 21.10E
Ajaccio France **22** 41.55N 8.43E
Ajmer India **36** 26.29N 74.40E
Akaishi san *mts.* Japan **42** 35.20N 138.05E
Akbou Algeria **24** 36.26N 4.33E
Aketi Zaire **46** 2.46N 23.51E
Akhaltsikhe U.S.S.R. **34** 41.37N 42.59E
Akhdar, Jebel *mts.* Libya **45** 32.10N 22.00E
Akhdar, Jebel *mts.* Oman **35** 23.10N 57.25E
Akhdar, Wadi *r.* Saudi Arabia **34** 28.30N 36.48E
Akhelóös Greece **25** 38.20N 21.04E
Akhisar Turkey **25** 38.54N 27.49E
Akimiski I. Canada **55** 53.00N 81.20W
Akita Japan **42** 39.44N 140.05E
Akkajaure *l.* Sweden **28** 67.40N 17.30E
Akobo *r.* Sudan/Ethiopia **45** 8.30N 33.15E
Akola India **36** 20.40N 77.02E
Akpatok I. Canada **55** 60.30N 68.30W
Akron U.S.A. **56** 41.04N 81.31W
Aksaray Turkey **34** 38.22N 34.02E
Akşehir Turkey **34** 38.22N 31.24E
Aksu China **40** 42.10N 80.00E
Aktogay U.S.S.R. **40** 46.59N 79.42E
Aktyubinsk U.S.S.R. **30** 50.16N 57.13E
Akureyri Iceland **28** 65.41N 18.04W
Akyab Burma **37** 20.09N 92.55E
Alabama *d.* U.S.A. **53** 33.00N 87.00W
Alabama *r.* U.S.A. **53** 31.05N 87.55W
Alagez *mtn.* U.S.S.R. **35** 40.32N 44.11E
Al Ain, Wadi *r.* Oman **35** 22.18N 55.35E
Alakol, L. U.S.S.R. **40** 46.00N 81.40E
Alakurtti U.S.S.R. **28** 67.00N 30.23E
Alamagan *i.* Asia **39** 17.35N 145.50E
Alamosa U.S.A. **52** 37.28N 105.54W
Aland Is. Finland **28** 60.20N 20.00E
Alanya Turkey **34** 36.32N 32.02E
Alaşehir Turkey **25** 38.22N 28.29E
Alaska *d.* U.S.A. **54** 65.00N 153.00W
Alaska, G. of U.S.A. **54** 58.45N 145.00W
Alaska Pen. U.S.A. **54** 56.00N 160.00W
Alaska Range *mts.* U.S.A. **54** 62.10N 152.00W
Alazan *r.* U.S.S.R. **35** 41.06N 46.40E
Albacete Spain **23** 39.00N 1.52W
Alba Iulia Romania **25** 46.04N 23.33E
Albania Europe **25** 41.00N 20.00E
Albany Australia **49** 34.57S 117.54E
Albany *r.* Canada **53** 52.10N 82.00W
Albany Ga. U.S.A. **53** 31.37N 84.10W
Albany N.Y. U.S.A. **57** 42.40N 73.49W
Albany Oreg. U.S.A. **52** 44.38N 123.07W
Albemarle Sd. U.S.A. **53** 36.10N 76.00W
Alberche *r.* Spain **23** 40.00N 4.45W
Albert France **22** 50.00N 2.40E
Alberta *d.* Canada **54** 55.00N 115.00W
Albert Canal Belgium **27** 51.00N 5.15E
Albert Nile *r.* Uganda **47** 3.30N 32.00E
Albi France **22** 43.56N 2.08E
Albina, Punta Angola **46** 15.52S 11.44E
Alboran, Isleta de Spain **23** 35.55N 3.10W
Ålborg Denmark **28** 57.03N 9.56E
Albuquerque U.S.A. **52** 35.05N 106.38W
Alburquerque Spain **23** 39.13N 6.59W
Alcácer do Sal Portugal **23** 38.22N 8.30W
Alcalá de Chisvert Spain **23** 40.19N 0.13E
Alcalá de Henares Spain **23** 40.28N 3.22W
Alcalá la Real Spain **23** 37.28N 3.55W
Alcamo Italy **24** 37.59N 12.58E
Alcañiz Spain **23** 41.03N 0.09W
Alcaudete Spain **23** 37.35N 4.05W
Alcazar de San Juan Spain **23** 39.24N 3.12W
Alcazarquiver Morocco **23** 35.01N 5.54W
Alcester England **8** 52.13N 1.52W
Alcira Spain **23** 39.10N 0.27W
Alcoy Spain **23** 38.42N 0.29W
Alcubierre, Sierra de *mts.* Spain **23** 41.40N 0.20W
Alcudia Spain **23** 39.51N 3.09E
Aldabra Is. Indian Oc. **43** 9.00S 47.00E
Aldan U.S.S.R. **31** 58.44N 125.22E
Aldan *r.* U.S.S.R. **31** 63.30N 130.00E
Aldbourne England **8** 51.28N 1.38W
Aldbrough England **13** 53.50N 0.07W
Alde *r.* England **9** 52.02N 1.28E
Aldeburgh England **9** 52.09N 1.35E
Alderney *i.* Channel Is. **11** 49.42N 2.11W
Aldershot England **7** 51.15N 0.47W
Aldridge England **8** 52.36N 1.55W
Aldsworth England **8** 51.48N 1.46W
Alegrete Brazil **61** 29.45S 55.46W
Aleksandrovsk Sakhalinskiy U.S.S.R. **31** 50.55N 142.12E
Alençon France **22** 48.25N 0.05E
Aleppo Syria **34** 36.14N 37.10E
Aleria France **22** 42.05N 9.30E
Alès France **22** 44.08N 4.05E
Alessandria Italy **22** 44.55N 8.37E
Alesund Norway **28** 62.28N 6.11E
Aleutian Is. U.S.A. **32** 57.00N 180.00
Aleutian Range *mts.* U.S.A. **54** 58.00N 156.00W
Aleutian Trench Pacific Oc. **3** 50.00N 178.00E
Alexander Archipelago *is.* U.S.A. **54** 56.30N 134.30W
Alexander Bay *town* R.S.A. **48** 28.40S 16.30E
Alexandra New Zealand **50** 45.14S 169.26E
Alexandria Egypt **34** 31.13N 29.55E
Alexandria Scotland **14** 55.59N 4.35W
Alexandria La. U.S.A. **53** 31.19N 92.29W
Alexandria Va. U.S.A. **57** 38.49N 77.06W
Alexandroúpolis Greece **25** 40.50N 25.53E
Alfaro Spain **23** 42.11N 1.45W
Alfiós *r.* Greece **25** 37.37N 21.27E
Alford. Scotland **17** 57.14N 2.42W
Alfreton England **13** 53.06N 1.22W
Algeciras Spain **23** 36.08N 5.27W
Alger *see* Algiers Algeria **23**
Algeria Africa **44** 28.00N 2.00E
Al Ghadaf, Wadi *r.* Iraq **34** 32.54N 43.33E
Alghero Italy **24** 40.33N 8.20E
Algiers Algeria **23** 36.50N 3.00E
Algoa B. R.S.A. **48** 33.56S 26.10E
Al Hamra *des.* U.A.E. **35** 22.45N 55.10E
Aliákmon *r.* Greece **25** 40.30N 22.38E
Alicante Spain **23** 38.21N 0.29W
Alice U.S.A. **52** 27.45N 98.06W
Alice Springs *town* Australia **49** 23.42S 133.52E
Aligarh India **37** 27.54N 78.04E
Aligudarz Iran **35** 33.25N 49.38E
Alima *r.* Congo **46** 1.36S 16.35E
Aling Kangri *mtn.* China **37** 32.51N 81.03E
Alingsås Sweden **28** 57.55N 12.30E
Aliquippa U.S.A. **56** 40.38N 80.16W
Aliwal North R.S.A. **48** 30.42S 26.43E
Al Jaub *f.* Saudi Arabia **35** 23.00N 50.00E
Al Jauf Saudi Arabia **34** 29.49N 39.52E
Al Jazi *des.* Iraq **34** 35.00N 41.00E
Al Khurr *r.* Iraq **34** 32.00N 44.15E
Alkmaar Neth. **27** 52.37N 4.44E
Al Kut Iraq **35** 32.30N 45.51E
Allagash *r.* U.S.A. **57** 47.08N 69.10W
Allahabad India **37** 25.57N 81.50E
Allakaket U.S.A. **54** 66.30N 152.45W
Allaqi, Wadi *r.* Egypt **34** 22.55N 33.02E
Allegheny Mts. U.S.A. **57** 40.00N 79.00W
Allegheny *r.* U.S.A. **57** 40.26N 80.00W
Allen *r.* England **15** 54.58N 2.18W
Allen, Lough Rep. of Ire. **18** 54.07N 8.04W
Allentown U.S.A. **57** 40.37N 75.30W
Alleppey India **36** 9.30N 76.22E
Aller *r.* W. Germany **26** 52.43N 9.38E
Alliance U.S.A. **52** 42.08N 103.00W
Allier *r.* France **22** 46.58N 3.04E
Alloa Scotland **15** 56.07N 3.49W
Alma U.S.A. **56** 43.23N 84.40W
Alma-Ata U.S.S.R. **40** 43.19N 76.55E
Almadén Spain **23** 38.47N 4.50W
Al Maharadh *des.* Saudi Arabia **35** 20.00N 52.30E
Almansa Spain **23** 38.52N 1.06W
Almanzor, Pico de *mtn.* Spain **23** 40.20N 5.22W
Almanzora *r.* Spain **23** 37.16N 1.49W
Almazán Spain **23** 41.29N 2.31W
Almeirim Portugal **23** 39.12N 8.37W
Almelo Neth. **27** 52.21N 6.40E
Almeria Spain **23** 36.50N 2.26W
Älmhult Sweden **28** 56.32N 14.10E
Al Mira, Wadi *r.* Iraq **34** 32.27N 41.21E
Almond *r.* Scotland **15** 56.25N 3.28W
Almuñécar Spain **23** 36.44N 3.41W
Aln *r.* England **15** 55.23N 1.36W
Alness Scotland **17** 57.42N 4.15W
Alnwick England **15** 55.25N 1.41W
Alor *i.* Indonesia **39** 8.20S 124.30E
Alor Star Malaysia **38** 6.06N 100.23E
Alost Belgium **27** 50.57N 4.03E
Alpena U.S.A. **56** 45.04N 83.27W
Alpes Maritimes *mts.* France **22** 44.07N 7.08E
Alphen Neth. **27** 52.08N 4.40E
Alpine U.S.A. **52** 30.22N 103.40W
Alps *mts.* Europe **26** 47.00N 10.00E
Al Qurna Iraq **35** 31.00N 47.26E
Alsager England **12** 53.07N 2.20W
Alsásua Spain **23** 42.54N 2.10W
Alsh, Loch Scotland **16** 57.15N 5.36W
Al Shaab S. Yemen **45** 12.50N 44.56E
Alston England **12** 54.48N 2.26W
Alta Norway **28** 69.57N 23.10E
Alta *r.* Norway **28** 70.00N 23.15E
Altagracia Venezuela **59** 10.44N 71.30W
Altai China **40** 47.48N 88.07E
Altai *mts.* Mongolia **40** 46.30N 93.30E
Altaj Mongolia **40** 46.20N 97.00E
Altamaha *r.* U.S.A. **53** 31.15N 81.23W
Altamura Italy **25** 40.50N 16.32E
Altea Spain **23** 38.37N 0.03W
Altenkirchen W. Germany **27** 50.41N 7.40E
Al Tihama *des.* Saudi Arabia **34** 27.50N 35.30E
Altiplano Mexicano *mts.* N. America **2** 24.00N 105.00W
Altnaharra Scotland **17** 58.16N 4.26W
Alto Araguaia Brazil **61** 17.19S 53.10W
Alto Garcas Brazil **61** 16.57S 53.30W
Alto Molocue Moçambique **47** 15.38S 37.42E
Alton England **8** 51.08N 0.59W
Alton U.S.A. **56** 38.55N 90.10W
Altoona U.S.A. **57** 40.32N 78.23W
Altrincham England **12** 53.25N 2.21W
Altyn Tagh *mts.* China **40** 38.10N 87.50E
Al'Ula Saudi Arabia **34** 26.39N 37.58E
Alva Scotland **15** 56.09N 3.49W
Alva U.S.A. **52** 36.48N 98.40W
Alvarado Mexico **58** 18.49N 95.46W
Älvsbyn Sweden **28** 65.41N 21.00E
Al Wajh Saudi Arabia **34** 26.16N 36.28E
Al Wakrah Qatar **35** 25.09N 51.36E
Alyaty U.S.S.R. **35** 39.59N 49.20E
Alyth Scotland **15** 56.38N 3.14W
Alzette *r.* Lux. **27** 49.52N 6.07E
Amadeus, L. Australia **49** 24.50S 131.00E
Amadi Sudan **47** 5.32N 30.20E
Amagasaki Japan **42** 34.43N 135.20E
Amami *i.* Japan **41** 28.20N 129.30E
Amara Iraq **35** 31.52N 47.50E
Amarillo U.S.A. **52** 35.14N 101.50W
Amaro, Monte *mtn.* Italy **24** 42.06N 14.04E
Amasya Turkey **34** 40.37N 35.50E
Amazon *r.* Brazil **62** 2.00S 50.00W
Amazon, Mouths of the Brazil **62** 0.00 50.00W
Ambala India **36** 30.19N 76.49E
Ambarchik U.S.S.R. **31** 69.39N 162.27E
Ambato-Boeni Malagasy Rep. **47** 16.30S 46.33E
Ambergris Cay *i.* Belize **58** 18.00N 87.58W
Amberley England **9** 50.54N 0.33W
Amble England **15** 55.20N 1.34W
Ambleside England **12** 54.26N 2.58W
Ambon Indonesia **39** 4.50S 128.10E
Ambriz Angola **46** 7.54S 13.12E
Ambrizete Angola **46** 7.13S 12.56E
Ameland *i.* Neth. **27** 53.28N 5.48E
Amersfoort Neth. **27** 52.10N 5.23E
Amersham England **7** 51.40N 0.38W
Amesbury England **8** 51.10N 1.46W
Amga U.S.S.R. **31** 60.51N 131.59E
Amga *r.* U.S.S.R. **31** 62.40N 135.20E
Amgun *r.* U.S.S.R. **31** 53.10N 139.47E
Amiata *mtn.* Italy **24** 42.53N 11.37E
Amiens France **22** 49.54N 2.18E
Amirantes *is.* Indian Oc. **5** 6.00S 52.00E
Amlwch Wales **10** 53.24N 4.21W
Amman Jordan **34** 31.57N 35.56E
Ammanford Wales **11** 51.48N 4.00W
Amol Iran **35** 36.26N 52.24E
Amorgós *i.* Greece **25** 36.50N 25.55E
Amos Canada **57** 48.04N 78.08W
Amoy China **41** 24.26N 118.07E
Ampala Honduras **58** 13.16N 87.39W
Ampthill England **9** 52.03N 0.30W
Amraoti India **36** 20.58N 77.50E
Amritsar India **36** 31.35N 74.56E
Amsterdam Neth. **27** 52.22N 4.54E
Amsterdam U.S.A. **57** 42.56N 74.12W
Amsterdam I. Indian Oc. **5** 37.00S 79.00E
Amu Darya *r.* U.S.S.R. **30** 43.50N 59.00E
Amundsen G. Canada **54** 70.30N 122.00W
Amundsen Sea Antarctica **2** 70.00S 116.00W
Amur *r.* U.S.S.R. **31** 53.17N 140.00E
Anabar *r.* U.S.S.R. **31** 72.40N 113.30E
Anadyr U.S.S.R. **31** 64.40N 177.32E
Anadyr *r.* U.S.S.R. **31** 65.00N 176.00E
Anadyr, G. of U.S.S.R. **31** 64.30N 177.50W
Anaiza Saudi Arabia **35** 26.05N 43.57E
Anambas Is. Indonesia **38** 3.00N 106.10E
Anápolis Brazil **61** 16.19S 48.58W
Anar Iran **35** 30.54N 55.18E
Anatahan *i.* Asia **39** 16.22N 145.38E
Anatolia *f.* Turkey **34** 38.00N 35.00E
Anatuya Argentina **61** 28.26S 62.48W
Anchorage U.S.A. **54** 61.10N 150.00W
Ancona Italy **24** 43.37N 13.33E
Ancroft England **15** 55.42N 2.00W
Ancuabe Moçambique **47** 13.00S 39.50E
Andalsnes Norway **28** 62.33N 7.43E
Andaman Is. India **37** 12.00N 93.00E
Andaman Sea Indian Oc. **37** 11.15N 95.30E
Andara S.W. Africa **48** 18.04S 21.29E
Andernach W. Germany **27** 50.25N 7.24E
Anderson *r.* Canada **54** 69.45N 129.00W
Anderson U.S.A. **56** 40.05N 85.41W
Andes *mts.* S. America **62** 15.00S 72.00W
And Fjord *est.* Norway **28** 69.10N 16.20E
Andhra Pradesh *d.* India **37** 17.00N 79.00E
Andikíthira *i.* Greece **25** 35.52N 23.18E
Andizhan U.S.S.R. **40** 40.48N 72.23E
Andorra *town* Andorra **23** 42.29N 1.31E
Andorra Europe **23** 42.30N 1.32E
Andover England **8** 51.13N 1.29W
Andoy *i.* Norway **28** 69.00N 15.30E
Andreas I.o.M. **12** 54.22N 4.26W
Andreas, C. Cyprus **34** 35.40N 34.35E
Andros *i.* Greece **34** 37.50N 24.50E
Andros I. Bahamas **53** 24.30N 78.00W
Andujar Spain **23** 38.02N 4.03W
Andulo Angola **46** 11.28S 16.43E
Anegada *i.* Virgin Is. **59** 18.46N 64.24W
Aneiza, Jebel *mtn.* Asia **34** 32.15N 39.19E
Aneto, Pico de *mtn.* Spain **23** 42.40N 0.19E
Angara *r.* U.S.S.R. **31** 58.00N 93.00E
Angarsk U.S.S.R. **31** 52.31N 103.55E
Ange Sweden **28** 62.31N 15.40E
Angel de la Guarda *i.* Mexico **52** 29.10N 113.20W
Angel Falls *f.* Venezuela **59** 5.55N 62.30W
Ängelholm Sweden **28** 56.15N 12.50E
Ångerman Sweden **28** 62.52N 17.45E
Angers France **22** 47.29N 0.32W
Angkor *ruins* Cambodia **38** 13.26N 103.50E
Angle Wales **11** 51.40N 5.03W
Anglesey *i.* Wales **10** 53.16N 4.25W
Angmagssalik Greenland **55** 65.40N 38.00W
Ango Zaire **46** 4.01N 25.52E
Angola Africa **46** 11.00S 18.00E
Angoulême France **22** 45.40N 0.10E
Anguilar de Campóo Spain **23** 42.55N 4.15W
Anguilla C. America **59** 18.14N 63.05W
Angumu Zaire **47** 0.10S 27.38E
Anholt W. Germany **27** 51.51N 6.26E
Anhumas Brazil **61** 16.58S 54.43W
Anhwei *d.* China **41** 31.30N 116.45E
Aniak U.S.A. **54** 61.32N 159.40W
Anjouan *i.* Comoro Is. **47** 12.12S 44.28E
Ankara Turkey **34** 39.55N 32.50E
Anking China **41** 30.20N 116.50E
Ankober Ethiopia **45** 9.32N 39.43E
Annaba Algeria **24** 36.55N 7.47E
An Nafud *des.* Saudi Arabia **34** 28.40N 41.30E
An Najaf Iraq **35** 31.59N 44.19E
Annalee *r.* Rep. of Ire. **18** 54.02N 7.25W
Annam Highlands *mts.* Asia **38** 17.40N 105.30E
Annan Scotland **15** 54.59N 3.16W
Annan *r.* Scotland **15** 54.58N 3.16W
Annandale *f.* Scotland **15** 55.12N 3.25W
Annapolis U.S.A. **57** 38.59N 76.30W
Annapurna *mtn.* Nepal **37** 28.34N 83.50E
Ann Arbor U.S.A. **56** 42.18N 83.43W
An Nasiriya Iraq **35** 31.04N 46.16E
Annecy France **22** 45.54N 6.07E
Annfield Plain *town* England **12** 54.42N 1.45W
Annonay France **22** 45.15N 4.40E
Ansbach W. Germany **26** 49.18N 10.36E
Anshan China **41** 41.05N 122.58E
Anshun China **37** 26.02N 105.57E
Ansi China **40** 40.32N 95.57E
Anston England **13** 53.22N 1.13W
Anstruther Scotland **15** 56.14N 2.42W
Antakya Turkey **34** 36.12N 36.10E
Antalya Turkey **34** 36.53N 30.42E
Antalya, G. of Turkey **34** 36.38N 31.00E
Antarctica 64
Antarctic Pen. Antarctica **63** 65.00S 64.00W
An Teallach *mtn.* Scotland **16** 57.48N 5.16W
Antequera Spain **23** 37.01N 4.34W
Anticosti I. Canada **55** 49.20N 63.00W
Antigo U.S.A. **56** 45.10N 89.10W
Antigua C. America **59** 17.09N 61.49W
Antigua Guatemala **58** 14.33N 90.42W
Anti-Lebanon *mts.* Lebanon **34** 34.00N 36.25E
Antofagasta Chile **63** 23.40S 70.23W
Antonio Enes Moçambique **47** 16.10S 39.57E
Antrim N. Ireland **14** 54.43N 6.14W
Antrim *d.* N. Ireland **14** 54.58N 6.20W
Antrim, Mts. of N. Ireland **14** 55.00N 6.10W
Antung China **41** 40.06N 124.25E
Antwerp Belgium **27** 51.13N 4.25E
Antwerp *d.* Belgium **27** 51.16N 4.45E
Anvik U.S.A. **54** 62.38N 160.20W
Anyang China **41** 36.04N 114.20E
Anzhero-Sudzhensk U.S.S.R. **30** 56.10N 86.10E
Aoga shima *i.* Japan **42** 32.28N 139.45E
Aomori Japan **42** 40.50N 140.43E
Aosta Italy **22** 45.43N 7.19E
Apa *r.* Paraguay **61** 22.06S 58.00W
Apalachee B. U.S.A. **53** 29.30N 84.00W
Aparri Phil. **39** 18.22N 121.40E
Apatity U.S.S.R. **28** 67.32N 33.21E
Apeldoorn Neth. **27** 52.13N 5.57E
Apennines *mts.* Italy **24** 42.00N 13.30E

Ap Lei Chau *i.* Hong Kong **33** 22.14N 114.09E
Apostle Is. U.S.A. **56** 47.00N 90.30W
Appalachian Mts. U.S.A. **53** 39.30N 78.00W
Appennino Ligure *mts.* Italy **22** 44.33N 8.45E
Appingedam Neth. **27** 53.18N 6.52E
Appleby England **12** 54.35N 2.29W
Appleton U.S.A. **56** 44.17N 88.24W
Apsheron Pen. U.S.S.R. **35** 40.28N 50.00E
Apure *r.* Venezuela **59** 7.44N 66.38W
Aqaba Jordan **34** 29.32N 35.00E
Aqaba, G. of Asia **34** 28.45N 34.45E
Aqlat as Suqur Saudi Arabia **34** 25.50N 42.12E
Aquidauana Brazil **61** 20.27S 55.45W
Aquila Mexico **58** 18.30N 103.50W
Arabia Asia **3** 25.00N 45.00E
Arabian Desert Egypt **34** 28.15N 31.55E
Arabian Sea Asia **36** 16.00N 65.00E
Aracaju Brazil **62** 10.54S 37.07W
Araçatuba Brazil **61** 21.12S 50.24W
Arad Romania **25** 46.12N 21.19E
Arafura Sea Austa. **39** 9.00S 135.00E
Aragon *r.* Spain **23** 42.20N 1.45W
Araguaia *r.* Brazil **62** 5.30S 48.05W
Araguari Brazil **61** 18.38S 48.13W
Arak Iran **35** 34.06N 49.44E
Arakan Yoma *mts.* Burma **37** 20.00N 94.00E
Aral Sea U.S.S.R. **30** 45.00N 60.00E
Aralsk U.S.S.R. **30** 46.56N 61.43E
Aranda de Duero Spain **23** 41.40N 3.41W
Aran Fawddwy *mtn.* Wales **10** 52.48N 3.42W
Aran I. Rep. of Ire. **18** 54.59N 8.27W
Aran Is. Rep. of Ire. **19** 53.07N 9.38W
Aranjuez Spain **23** 40.02N 3.37W
Arapkir Turkey **34** 39.03N 38.29E
Arar, Wadi *r.* Iraq **34** 32.00N 42.30E
Ararat, Mt. Turkey **35** 39.45N 44.15E
Aras *r. see* Araxes Turkey **34**
Arauca *r.* Venezuela **59** 7.20N 66.40W
Araxa Brazil **61** 19.37S 46.50W
Araxes *r.* U.S.S.R. **35** 40.00N 48.28E
Araya Pen. Venezuela **59** 10.30N 64.30W
Arbatax Italy **24** 39.56N 9.41E
Arbroath Scotland **17** 56.34N 2.35W
Arcachon France **22** 44.40N 1.11W
Archers Post Kenya **47** 0.42N 37.40E
Arcila Morocco **23** 35.28N 6.04W
Arctic Ocean **64**
Arctic Red *r.* Canada **54** 67.26N 133.48W
Arda *r.* Greece **25** 41.39N 26.30E
Ardabil Iran **35** 38.15N 48.18E
Ardara Rep. of Ire. **18** 54.46N 8.25W
Ardèche *r.* France **22** 44.31N 4.40E
Ardee Rep. of Ire. **18** 53.51N 6.33W
Ardennes *mts.* Belgium **27** 50.10N 5.30E
Ardentinny Scotland **14** 56.03N 4.55W
Arderin *mtn.* Rep. of Ire. **19** 53.02N 7.40W
Ardfert Rep. of Ire. **19** 52.20N 9.48W
Ardglass N. Ireland **18** 54.16N 5.37W
Ardgour *f.* Scotland **16** 56.45N 5.20W
Ardila Spain **23** 38.10N 7.30W
Ardistan Iran **35** 33.22N 52.25E
Ardivachar Pt. Scotland **16** 57.23N 7.26W
Ardlamont Pt. Scotland **14** 55.49N 5.12W
Ardlui Scotland **14** 56.18N 4.43W
Ardmore Rep. of Ire. **19** 51.58N 7.43W
Ardmore Head Rep. of Ire. **19** 51.56N 7.43W
Ardmore Pt. Strath. Scotland **16** 56.39N 6.08W
Ardmore Pt. Strath. Scotland **14** 55.42N 6.01W
Ardnamurchan *f.* Scotland **16** 56.44N 6.00W
Ardnamurchan, Pt. of Scotland **16** 56.44N 6.14W
Ardnave Pt. Scotland **14** 55.54N 6.20W
Ardres France **9** 50.51N 1.59E
Ardrishaig Scotland **14** 56.00N 5.26W
Ardrossan Scotland **14** 55.38N 4.49W
Ards Pen. N. Ireland **18** 54.30N 5.30W
Ardvasar Scotland **16** 57.03N 5.54W
Arecibo Puerto Rico **59** 18.29N 66.44W
Arena, Pt. U.S.A. **52** 38.58N 123.44W
Arendal Norway **28** 58.27N 8.56E
Arequipa Peru **62** 16.25S 71.32W
Arès France **22** 44.47N 1.08W
Arezzo Italy **24** 43.27N 11.52E
Arfak *mtn.* Asia **39** 1.30S 133.50E
Arga *r.* Spain **22** 42.20N 1.44W
Arganda Spain **23** 40.19N 3.26W
Argens *r.* France **22** 43.10N 6.45E
Argentan France **22** 48.45N 0.01W
Argentina S. America **61** 33.30S 64.00W
Argenton France **22** 46.36N 1.30E
Argeș *r.* Romania **25** 44.13N 26.22E
Argos Greece **25** 37.37N 22.45E
Argun *r.* China **41** 53.30N 121.48E
Argyll *f.* Scotland **14** 56.12N 5.15W
Ariano Italy **24** 41.04N 15.00E
Arica Chile **63** 18.30S 70.20W
Ariege *r.* France **23** 43.02N 1.40E
Arinagour Scotland **14** 56.37N 6.31W
Arisaig Scotland **16** 56.55N 5.51W
Arisaig, Sd. of Scotland **16** 56.51N 5.50W
Ariza Spain **23** 41.19N 2.03W
Arizona *d.* U.S.A. **52** 34.00N 112.00W
Arizpe Mexico **58** 30.20N 110.11W
Arjona Colombia **59** 10.14N 75.22W
Arkaig, Loch Scotland **16** 56.58N 5.08W
Arkansas *d.* U.S.A. **53** 35.00N 92.00W
Arkansas *r.* U.S.A. **53** 33.50N 91.00W
Arkansas City U.S.A. **53** 37.03N 97.02W
Arkhangel'sk U.S.S.R. **30** 64.32N 41.10E
Arklow Rep. of Ire. **19** 52.47N 6.10W
Arlberg Pass Austria **26** 47.00N 10.05E
Arles France **22** 43.41N 4.38E
Arlon Belgium **27** 49.41N 5.49E
Armadale Scotland **15** 55.54N 3.41W
Armagh N. Ireland **18** 54.21N 6.41W
Armagh *d.* N. Ireland **18** 54.16N 6.35W
Arma Plateau Saudi Arabia **35** 25.30N 46.30E
Armavir U.S.S.R. **29** 44.59N 41.10E
Armenia Colombia **62** 4.32N 75.40W
Armenia Soviet Socialist Republic *d.* U.S.S.R. **35** 40.00N 45.00E
Armentières France **27** 50.41N 2.53E
Armoy N. Ireland **14** 55.07N 6.20W
Arnauti, C. Cyprus **34** 35.06N 32.17E
Arnhem Neth. **27** 52.00N 5.55E
Arnhem, C. Australia **49** 12.10S 137.00E
Arnisdale Scotland **16** 57.08N 5.34W
Arno *r.* Italy **24** 43.43N 10.17E
Arnold England **13** 53.00N 1.08W
Arnprior Canada **57** 45.26N 76.24W
Arnsberg W. Germany **27** 51.24N 8.03E
Arnside England **12** 54.12N 2.49W
Ar Ramadi Iraq **34** 33.27N 43.19E
Arra Mts. Rep. of Ire. **19** 52.50N 8.22W
Arran *i.* Scotland **14** 55.35N 5.14W
Arras France **27** 50.17N 2.46E
Arrochar Scotland **14** 56.12N 4.44W
Arrow, Lough Rep. of Ire. **18** 54.03N 8.20W
Ar Rutba Iraq **34** 33.03N 40.18E
Arta Greece **25** 39.10N 20.57E
Artem U.S.S.R. **42** 43.21N 132.09E
Arthur's Pass *f.* New Zealand **50** 42.50S 171.45E
Artois *f.* France **27** 50.16N 2.50E
Artush China **40** 38.27N 77.16E
Artvin Turkey **34** 41.12N 41.48E
Arua Uganda **47** 3.02N 30.56E
Aruba *i.* Neth. Antilles **59** 12.30N 70.00W
Aru Is. Indonesia **39** 6.00S 134.30E
Arun *r.* England **8** 50.48N 0.32W
Arundel England **8** 50.52N 0.32W
Arusha Tanzania **47** 3.21S 36.40E
Arusha *d.* Tanzania **47** 4.00S 37.00E
Aruwimi *r.* Zaire **46** 1.20N 23.36E
Arvagh Rep. of Ire. **18** 53.56N 7.35W
Arvidsjaur Sweden **28** 65.37N 19.10E
Arvika Sweden **28** 59.41N 12.38E
Arzamas U.S.S.R. **29** 55.24N 43.48E
Asahi daki *mtn.* Japan **42** 43.42N 142.54E
Asahigawa Japan **42** 43.46N 142.23E
Asansol India **37** 23.40N 87.00E
Ascension I. Atlantic Oc. **4** 8.00S 14.00W
Aschaffenburg W. Germany **26** 49.58N 9.10E
Aschendorf W. Germany **27** 53.03N 7.20E
Ascoli Piceno Italy **24** 42.52N 13.36E
Aseda Sweden **28** 57.10N 15.20E
Ash England **7** 51.14N 0.44W
Ash *r.* England **7** 51.48N 0.00
Ashbourne England **12** 53.02N 1.44W
Ashbourne Rep. of Ire. **18** 53.31N 6.25W
Ashburton *r.* Australia **49** 21.15S 115.00E
Ashburton England **11** 50.31N 3.45W
Ashburton New Zealand **50** 43.54S 171.46E
Ashby de la Zouch England **8** 52.45N 1.29W
Ashdown Forest England **9** 51.03N 0.05E
Asheville U.S.A. **53** 35.35N 82.35W
Ashford Kent England **9** 51.08N 0.53E
Ashford Surrey England **7** 51.26N 0.27W
Ashikaga Japan **42** 36.21N 139.26E
Ashington England **15** 55.11N 1.34W
Ashizuri saki *c.* Japan **42** 32.45N 133.05E
Ashkhabad U.S.S.R. **35** 37.58N 58.24E
Ashland Wisc. U.S.A. **56** 46.34N 90.45W
Ashland Ky. U.S.A. **53** 38.28N 82.40W
Ash Sham *des.* Saudi Arabia **34** 28.15N 43.05E
Ash Shama *des.* Saudi Arabia **34** 31.20N 38.00E
Ashtabula U.S.A. **56** 41.53N 80.47W
Ashtead England **7** 51.19N 0.18W
Ashton-in-Makerfield England **12** 53.29N 2.39W
Ashton-under-Lyne England **12** 53.30N 2.08W
Asia **32**
Asinara *i.* Italy **24** 41.04N 8.18E
Asinara, G. of Med. Sea **24** 41.00N 8.32E
Asir *f.* Saudi Arabia **45** 19.00N 42.00E
Askeaton Rep. of Ire. **19** 52.36N 9.00W
Askern England **13** 53.37N 1.09W
Askersund Sweden **28** 58.55N 14.55E
Asmara Ethiopia **45** 15.20N 38.58E
Aspatria England **12** 54.45N 3.20W
Aspiring, Mt. New Zealand **50** 44.20S 168.45E
Assab Ethiopia **45** 13.01N 42.47E
Assam *d.* India **37** 26.30N 93.00E
Assen Neth. **27** 53.00N 6.34E
Assiniboine, Mt. Canada **52** 50.51N 115.39W
Assynt *f.* Scotland **16** 58.12N 5.08W
Assynt, L. Scotland **16** 58.11N 5.03W
Asti Italy **22** 44.55N 8.13E
Aston Clinton England **7** 51.54N 0.39W
Astorga Spain **23** 42.30N 6.02W
Astoria U.S.A. **52** 46.12N 123.50W
Astrakhan U.S.S.R. **30** 46.22N 48.00E
Astrida Rwanda **47** 2.34S 29.43E
Asuncion *i.* Asia **39** 19.34N 145.24E
Asunción Paraguay **61** 25.15S 57.40W
Aswân Egypt **34** 24.05N 32.56E
Aswân High Dam Egypt **34** 23.59N 32.54E
Asyût Egypt **34** 27.14N 31.07E
Atacama Desert S. America **63** 20.00S 69.00W
Atar Mauritania **44** 20.32N 13.08W
Atbara Sudan **45** 17.42N 34.00E
Atbara *r.* Sudan **45** 17.47N 34.00E
Atchafalaya B. U.S.A. **53** 29.30N 92.00W
Ath Belgium **27** 50.38N 3.45E
Athabasca Canada **54** 54.44N 113.15W
Athabasca *r.* Canada **54** 58.30N 111.00W
Athabasca, L. Canada **54** 59.30N 109.00W
Athboy Rep. of Ire. **18** 53.38N 6.56W
Athea Rep. of Ire. **19** 52.28N 9.19W
Athenry Rep. of Ire. **18** 53.18N 8.45W
Athens Greece **25** 37.59N 23.42E
Athens U.S.A. **56** 39.20N 82.06W
Atherstone England **8** 52.35N 1.32W
Atherton England **12** 53.32N 2.30W
Athleague Rep. of Ire. **18** 53.34N 8.16W
Athlone Rep. of Ire. **18** 53.26N 7.57W
Athos, Mt. Greece **25** 40.09N 24.19E
Athy Rep. of Ire. **19** 53.00N 7.00W
Atikokan Canada **56** 48.45N 91.38W
Atkarsk U.S.S.R. **29** 51.55N 45.00E
Atlanta U.S.A. **53** 33.45N 84.23W
Atlantic City U.S.A. **57** 39.23N 74.27W
Atlantic Ocean **2**
Atlas Mts. Africa **2** 33.00N 4.00W
Atouguia Portugal **23** 39.20N 9.20W
Atran *r.* Sweden **28** 56.54N 12.30E
Atrato *r.* Colombia **59** 8.15N 76.58W
Atrek *r.* Asia **35** 37.23N 54.00E
Attleborough England **9** 52.31N 1.01E
Attopeu Laos **38** 14.51N 106.56E
Atuel *r.* Argentina **61** 36.15S 66.45W
Atura Uganda **47** 2.09N 32.22E
Aubagne France **22** 43.17N 5.35E
Aube *r.* France **22** 48.30N 3.37E
Aubigny-sur-Nère France **22** 47.29N 2.26E
Aubin France **22** 44.32N 2.14E
Auch France **22** 43.40N 0.36E
Auchinleck Scotland **14** 55.28N 4.17W
Auchterarder Scotland **15** 56.18N 3.43W
Auchtermuchty Scotland **15** 56.17N 3.15W
Auckland New Zealand **50** 36.55S 174.45E
Aude *r.* France **22** 43.13N 2.20E
Audlem England **12** 52.59N 2.31W
Audruicq France **9** 50.52N 2.05E
Augher N. Ireland **18** 54.26N 7.09W
Aughnacloy N. Ireland **18** 54.25N 7.00W
Augrabies Falls *f.* R.S.A. **48** 28.30S 20.16E
Augsburg W. Germany **26** 48.21N 10.54E
Augusta Ga. U.S.A. **53** 33.29N 82.00W
Augusta Maine U.S.A. **57** 44.17N 69.50W
Aulne *r.* France **22** 48.30N 4.11W
Aultbea Scotland **16** 57.50N 5.35W
Aumâle France **22** 49.46N 1.45E
Au Pui Wan Hong Kong **33** 22.24N 114.10E
Aurangabad India **36** 19.52N 75.22E
Aurich W. Germany **27** 53.28N 7.29E
Aurillac France **22** 44.56N 2.26E
Aurora U.S.A. **56** 41.45N 88.20W
Au Sable *r.* U.S.A. **56** 44.25N 83.20W
Au Sable Pt. U.S.A. **56** 44.21N 83.20W
Auskerry *i.* Scotland **17** 59.02N 2.34W
Austin Minn. U.S.A. **56** 43.40N 92.58W
Austin Texas U.S.A. **52** 30.18N 97.47W
Australasia **3**
Australia Austa. **49**
Australian Antarctic Territory Antarctica **64** 73.00S 90.00E
Australian Capital Territory *d.* Australia **49** 35.30S 149.00E
Austria Europe **26** 47.30N 14.00E
Autun France **22** 46.58N 4.18E
Auxerre France **22** 47.48N 3.35E
Auzances France **22** 46.02N 2.29E
Avallon France **22** 47.30N 3.54E
Avanos Turkey **34** 38.44N 34.51E
Aveley England **7** 51.31N 0.15E
Avellaneda Argentina **61** 34.42S 58.20W
Avellino Italy **24** 40.55N 14.46E
Avesnes France **27** 50.08N 3.57E
Avesta Sweden **28** 60.09N 16.10E
Aveyron *r.* France **22** 44.09N 1.10E
Avezzano Italy **24** 42.03N 13.26E
Aviemore Scotland **17** 57.12N 3.50W
Aviero Portugal **23** 40.40N 8.35W
Avignon France **22** 43.56N 4.48E
Avila Spain **23** 40.39N 4.42W
Avon *d.* England **8** 51.35N 2.40W
Avon *r.* Avon England **8** 51.30N 2.43W
Avon *r.* Devon England **11** 50.17N 3.52W
Avon *r.* Dorset England **8** 50.43N 1.45W
Avon *r.* Glos. England **8** 52.00N 2.10W
Avon *r.* Scotland **17** 57.25N 3.23W
Avonmouth England **8** 51.30N 2.42W
Avranches France **22** 48.42N 1.21W
Awa shima *i.* Japan **42** 38.30N 139.20E
Awatera *r.* New Zealand **50** 41.37S 174.09E
Awe, Loch Scotland **14** 56.18N 5.24W
Axe *r.* Devon England **11** 50.42N 3.03W
Axe *r.* Somerset England **8** 51.18N 3.00W
Axel Heiberg I. Canada **55** 79.30N 90.00W
Axminster England **8** 50.47N 3.01W
Ayaguz U.S.S.R. **40** 47.59N 80.27E
Ayan U.S.S.R. **31** 56.29N 138.00E
Aycliffe England **13** 54.36N 1.34W
Aydin Turkey **34** 37.52N 27.50E
Ayios Evstrátios *i.* Greece **25** 39.30N 25.00E
Aylesbury England **8** 51.48N 0.49W
Aylesham England **9** 51.14N 1.12E
Aylsham England **9** 52.48N 1.16E
Ayr Scotland **14** 55.28N 4.37W
Ayr *r.* Scotland **14** 55.28N 4.38W
Ayre, Pt. of I.o.M. **12** 54.25N 4.22W
Aysgarth England **12** 54.18N 2.00W
Ayutthaya Thailand **37** 14.25N 100.30E
Ayvalik Turkey **25** 39.19N 26.42E
Azbine *mts. see* Air Niger **44**
Azerbaijan Soviet Socialist Republic *d.* U.S.S.R. **35** 40.10N 47.50E
Azores *is.* Atlantic Oc. **4** 39.00N 30.00W
Azov, Sea of U.S.S.R. **29** 46.00N 36.30E
Azua Dom. Rep. **59** 18.29N 70.44W
Azuaga Spain **23** 38.16N 5.40W
Azuero Pen. Panamá **59** 7.30N 80.30W
Azul Argentina **61** 36.46S 59.50W
Azurduy Bolivia **61** 20.00S 64.29W

B

Ba'albek Lebanon **34** 34.00N 36.12E
Baarle-Hertog Neth. **27** 51.26N 4.56E
Babar Is. Indonesia **39** 8.00S 129.30E
Babbacombe B. England **11** 50.30N 3.28W
Bab el Mandeb *str.* Asia **45** 13.00N 43.10E
Babol Iran **35** 36.32N 52.42E
Baboua C.A.R. **44** 5.49N 14.51E
Babuyan Is. Phil. **39** 19.20N 121.30E
Babylon *ruins* Iraq **35** 32.33N 44.25E
Bacau Romania **29** 46.32N 26.59E
Baccarat France **26** 48.27N 6.45E
Back *r.* Canada **55** 66.37N 96.00W
Bacolod Phil. **39** 10.38N 122.58E
Bacton England **9** 52.50N 1.29E
Bacup England **12** 53.42N 2.12W
Badajoz Spain **23** 38.53N 6.58W
Badalona Spain **23** 41.27N 2.15E
Baden-Baden W. Germany **26** 48.45N 8.15E
Badenoch *f.* Scotland **17** 57.00N 4.10W
Badgastein Austria **26** 47.07N 13.09E
Bad Ischl Austria **26** 47.43N 13.38E
Bad Kreuznach W. Germany **27** 49.51N 7.52E
Baffin B. Canada **55** 74.00N 70.00W
Baffin I. Canada **55** 68.50N 70.00W
Bafia Cameroon **46** 4.47N 11.14E
Bafq Iran **35** 31.35N 55.21E
Bafra Turkey **34** 41.34N 35.56E
Bafwasende Zaire **47** 1.09N 27.12E
Bagamoyo Tanzania **47** 6.26S 38.55E
Bagé Brazil **61** 31.22S 54.06W
Baggy Pt. England **11** 51.08N 4.15W
Baghdad Iraq **35** 33.20N 44.26E
Bagh nam Faoileann *str.* Scotland **16** 57.23N 7.15W
Baghrash Köl *l.* China **40** 42.00N 87.00E
Bagshot England **7** 51.22N 0.42W
Baguio Phil. **39** 16.25N 120.37E
Bahama Is. C. America **2** 25.00N 77.00W
Bahamas C. America **59** 23.30N 75.00W
Bahao Kalat Iran **35** 25.42N 61.28E
Bahawalpur Pakistan **36** 29.24N 71.47E
Bahbah Algeria **23** 35.04N 3.05E
Bahía Blanca Argentina **61** 38.45S 62.15W
Bahía Grande Argentina **63** 50.45S 68.00W
Bahrain Asia **35** 26.00N 50.35E
Bahramabad Iran **36** 30.24N 56.00E
Bahr el Ghazal *r.* Sudan **45** 9.30N 31.30E
Bahr el Jebel *r.* Sudan **45** 9.30N 30.20E
Baie Comeau Canada **53** 49.12N 68.10W
Baie St. Paul Canada **57** 47.27N 70.30W
Baikal, L. U.S.S.R. **40** 53.30N 108.00E
Bailieborough Rep. of Ire. **18** 53.55N 6.59W
Bailleul France **27** 50.44N 2.44E
Bain *r.* England **13** 53.05N 0.12W
Baing Indonesia **39** 10.15S 120.34E
Baise *r.* France **22** 44.15N 0.20E
Baja Hungary **25** 46.12N 18.58E
Bakali *r.* Zaire **46** 3.58S 17.10E
Baker Mont. U.S.A. **52** 46.23N 104.16W
Baker Oreg. U.S.A. **52** 44.46N 117.50W
Baker, Mt. U.S.A. **52** 48.48N 121.10W
Bakersfield U.S.A. **52** 35.25N 119.00W
Bakewell England **12** 53.13N 1.40W
Baku U.S.S.R. **35** 40.22N 49.53E
Bala Wales **10** 52.54N 3.36W
Balabac Str. Asia **38** 7.30N 117.00E
Balallan Scotland **16** 58.25N 6.36W
Balama Moçambique **47** 13.19S 38.35E
Bala Murghab Afghan. **35** 35.34N 63.20E
Balashov U.S.S.R. **29** 51.30N 43.10E
Balasore India **37** 21.31N 86.59E
Balaton, L. Hungary **29** 46.55N 17.50E
Balboa Panama Canal Zone **59** 8.37N 79.33W
Balbriggan Rep. of Ire. **18** 53.36N 6.12W
Balchik Bulgaria **25** 43.24N 28.10E
Balclutha New Zealand **50** 46.16S 169.46E
Baldock England **9** 51.59N 0.11W
Balearic Is. Spain **23** 39.30N 2.30E
Balerno Scotland **15** 55.53N 3.10W
Baleshare *i.* Scotland **16** 57.32N 7.22W
Balfron Scotland **14** 56.04N 4.20W
Bali *i.* Indonesia **38** 8.30S 115.05E
Balikesir Turkey **25** 39.38N 27.51E
Balikpapan Indonesia **38** 1.15S 116.50E
Balkan Mts. Bulgaria **25** 42.50N 24.30E
Balkhan Range *mts.* U.S.S.R. **35** 39.38N 54.30E
Balkhash U.S.S.R. **40** 46.51N 75.00E
Balkhash, L. U.S.S.R. **40** 46.40N 75.00E
Balla Rep. of Ire. **18** 53.48N 9.08W
Ballachulish Scotland **14** 56.40N 5.08W
Ballagan Pt. Rep. of Ire. **18** 54.00N 6.07W
Ballaghaderreen Rep. of Ire. **18** 53.54N 8.36W
Ballantrae Scotland **14** 55.06N 5.01W
Ballarat Australia **49** 37.36S 143.58E
Ballater Scotland **17** 57.03N 3.03W
Ballenas B. Mexico **52** 26.40N 113.30W
Ballickmoyler Rep. of Ire. **19** 52.52N 7.00W
Ballina Rep. of Ire. **18** 54.08N 9.10W
Ballinakill Rep. of Ire. **19** 52.53N 7.20W
Ballinamore Rep. of Ire. **18** 54.03N 7.50W
Ballinasloe Rep. of Ire. **18** 53.20N 8.15W
Ballincollig Rep. of Ire. **19** 51.53N 8.36W
Ballinderry *r.* N. Ireland **14** 54.40N 6.32W
Ballindine Rep. of Ire. **18** 53.40N 8.58W
Ballingarry Limerick Rep. of Ire. **19** 52.28N 8.51W
Ballingarry Tipperary Rep. of Ire. **19** 53.02N 8.02W
Ballingeary Rep. of Ire. **19** 51.50N 9.15W
Ballinhassig Rep. of Ire. **19** 51.48N 8.32W
Ballinlough Rep. of Ire. **18** 53.44N 8.40W
Ballinrobe Rep. of Ire. **18** 53.38N 9.15W
Ballinskelligs B. Rep. of Ire. **19** 51.48N 10.13W
Ballivor Rep. of Ire. **18** 53.31N 6.57W
Balloch Scotland **14** 56.00N 4.36W

Ballybay Rep. of Ire. **18** 54.08N 6.56W
Ballybunion Rep. of Ire. **19** 52.30N 9.40W
Ballycanew Rep. of Ire. **19** 52.36N 6.19W
Ballycarney Rep. of Ire. **19** 52.34N 6.35W
Ballycastle N. Ireland **14** 55.12N 6.15W
Ballyclare N. Ireland **14** 54.45N 6.00W
Ballyconnell Rep. of Ire. **18** 54.06N 7.37W
Ballydehob Rep. of Ire. **19** 51.34N 9.28W
Ballydonegan Rep. of Ire. **19** 51.38N 10.04W
Ballygar Rep. of Ire. **18** 53.32N 8.20W
Ballygawley N. Ireland **18** 54.28N 7.03W
Ballyhaunis Rep. of Ire. **18** 53.45N 8.47W
Ballyhoura Mts. Rep. of Ire. **19** 52.18N 8.31W
Ballyjamesduff Rep. of Ire. **18** 53.52N 7.47W
Ballykelly N. Ireland **14** 55.03N 7.00W
Ballymahon Rep. of Ire. **18** 53.33N 7.47W
Ballymena N. Ireland **14** 54.52N 6.17W
Ballymoe Rep. of Ire. **18** 53.41N 8.29W
Ballymoney N. Ireland **14** 55.04N 6.31W
Ballymore Rep. of Ire. **18** 53.30N 7.42W
Ballymote Rep. of Ire. **18** 54.06N 8.31W
Ballynahinch N. Ireland **18** 54.24N 5.53W
Ballynakill Harbour *est.* Rep. of Ire. **18** 53.34N 10.20W
Ballyquintin Pt. N. Ireland **18** 54.40N 5.30W
Ballyragget Rep. of Ire. **19** 52.47N 7.21W
Ballyshannon Rep. of Ire. **18** 54.30N 8.11W
Ballyvaughan Rep. of Ire. **19** 53.06N 9.09W
Ballyvourney Rep. of Ire. **19** 51.57N 9.10W
Ballywalter N. Ireland **14** 54.33N 5.30W
Balsas *r.* Mexico **58** 18.10N 102.05W
Balta *i.* Scotland **16** 60.44N 0.46W
Baltasound Scotland **16** 60.45N 0.52W
Baltic Sea Europe **28** 56.30N 19.00E
Baltic Shield *f.* Europe **3** 63.00N 30.00E
Baltimore U.S.A. **57** 39.18N 76.38W
Baltinglass Rep. of Ire. **19** 52.56N 6.43W
Baltiysk U.S.S.R. **28** 54.41N 19.59E
Baluchistan *f.* Pakistan **36** 28.00N 66.00E
Bam Iran **35** 29.07N 58.20E
Bamako Mali **44** 12.40N 7.59W
Bamberg W. Germany **26** 49.54N 10.53E
Bambesa Zaïre **46** 3.27N 25.43E
Bambili Zaïre **46** 3.34N 26.07E
Bamburgh England **15** 55.36N 1.41W
Bampton Devon England **8** 51.00N 3.29W
Bampton Oxon. England **8** 51.44N 1.33W
Bampur Iran **35** 27.13N 60.29E
Bampur *r.* Iran **35** 27.18N 59.02E
Banagher Rep. of Ire. **19** 53.12N 8.00W
Banalia Zaïre **46** 1.33N 25.23E
Banana Zaïre **46** 5.55S 12.27E
Banbridge N. Ireland **18** 54.21N 6.17W
Banbury England **8** 52.04N 1.21W
Banchory Scotland **17** 57.03N 2.30W
Banda Gabon **46** 3.47S 11.04E
Banda *i.* Indonesia **39** 4.30S 129.55E
Banda Atjeh Indonesia **38** 5.35N 95.20E
Bandar India **37** 16.13N 81.12E
Bandar Abbas Iran **35** 27.10N 56.15E
Bandar Dilam Iran **35** 30.05N 50.11E
Bandar-e-Lengeh Iran **35** 26.34N 54.53E
Bandar-e-Pahlavi Iran **35** 37.26N 49.29E
Bandar-e-Shah Iran **35** 36.55N 54.05E
Bandar Rig Iran **35** 29.30N 50.40E
Bandar Seri Begawan Brunei **38** 4.56N 114.58E
Bandar Shahpur Iran **35** 30.26N 49.03E
Banda Sea Indonesia **39** 5.00S 128.00E
Bandawe Malaŵi **47** 11.57S 34.11E
Bandeira *mtn.* Brazil **63** 20.25S 41.45W
Bandirma Turkey **25** 40.22N 28.00E
Bandjarmasin Indonesia **38** 3.22S 114.36E
Bandon Rep. of Ire. **19** 51.45N 8.45W
Bandon *r.* Rep. of Ire. **19** 51.43N 8.38W
Bandundu Zaïre **46** 3.20S 17.24E
Bandundu *d.* Zaïre **46** 4.00S 18.30E
Bandung Indonesia **38** 6.57S 107.34E
Banes Cuba **59** 20.59N 75.24W
Banff Canada **52** 51.10N 115.54W
Banff Scotland **17** 57.40N 2.31W
Bangalore India **36** 12.58N 77.35E
Bangangté Cameroon **46** 5.09N 10.29E
Bangassou C.A.R. **46** 4.41N 22.52E
Banggai Is. Indonesia **39** 1.30S 123.10E
Bangka *i.* Indonesia **38** 2.20S 106.10E
Bangkok Thailand **37** 13.45N 100.35E
Bangladesh Asia **37** 24.00N 90.00E
Bangor N. Ireland **14** 54.40N 5.41W
Bangor Rep. of Ire. **18** 54.09N 9.44W
Bangor U.S.A. **57** 44.49N 68.47W
Bangor Wales **10** 53.13N 4.09W
Bangui C.A.R. **46** 4.27N 18.37E
Bangweulu, L. Zambia **47** 11.15S 29.45E
Ban Hat Yai Thailand **38** 7.00N 100.28E
Ban Houei Sai Laos **37** 20.21N 100.26E
Banjak Is. Indonesia **38** 2.15N 97.10E
Banja Luka Yugo. **25** 44.47N 17.10E
Banjul Gambia **44** 13.28N 16.39W
Banjuwangi Indonesia **38** 8.12S 114.22E
Ban Kantang Thailand **37** 7.25N 99.30E
Bankfoot Scotland **15** 56.30N 3.32W
Banks I. Australia **39** 10.15S 142.15E
Banks I. Canada **54** 73.00N 122.00W
Banks Pen. New Zealand **50** 43.45S 173.10E
Ban Me Thuot S. Vietnam **38** 12.41N 108.02E
Bann *r.* N. Ireland **14** 55.10N 6.46W
Bann *r.* Rep. of Ire. **19** 52.33N 6.33W
Bannockburn Rhodesia **48** 20.16S 29.51E
Bannockburn Scotland **15** 56.06N 3.55W
Bannow B. Rep. of Ire. **19** 52.14N 6.48W
Bansha Rep. of Ire. **19** 52.26N 8.04W
Banstead England **7** 51.19N 0.12W
Bantry Rep. of Ire. **19** 51.41N 9.27W
Bantry B. Rep. of Ire. **19** 51.40N 9.40W
Banwy *r.* Wales **10** 52.41N 3.16W
Bapaume France **27** 50.07N 2.51E
Bar Albania **25** 42.05N 19.06E
Baracoa Cuba **59** 20.23N 74.31W
Barahona Dom. Rep. **59** 18.13N 71.07W
Baranof I. U.S.A. **54** 57.05N 135.00W
Baranovichi U.S.S.R. **29** 53.09N 26.00E
Barbacena Brazil **61** 21.13S 43.47W
Barbados C. America **59** 13.20N 59.40W
Barbastro Spain **23** 42.02N 0.07E
Barberton R.S.A. **48** 25.48S 31.03E
Barbezieux France **22** 45.28N 0.09W
Barbuda C. America **59** 17.41N 61.48W
Barcaldine Australia **49** 23.31S 145.15E
Barcellona Italy **24** 38.10N 15.13E
Barcelona Spain **23** 41.25N 2.10E
Barcelona Venezuela **59** 10.08N 64.43W
Bardai Chad **44** 21.21N 16.56E
Bardera Somali Rep. **47** 2.18N 42.18E
Bardia Libya **34** 31.44N 25.08E
Bardney England **13** 53.13N 0.19W
Bardsey *i.* Wales **10** 52.45N 4.48W
Bardsey Sd. Wales **10** 52.45N 4.48W
Bardu Norway **28** 68.54N 18.20E
Bareilly India **37** 28.20N 79.24E
Barents Sea Arctic Oc. **30** 73.00N 40.00E
Bari Italy **25** 41.08N 16.52E
Barika Algeria **24** 35.25N 5.19E
Barinas Venezuela **59** 8.36N 70.15W
Barisan Range *mts.* Indonesia **38** 3.30S 102.30E
Barito *r.* Indonesia **38** 3.35S 114.35E
Bariz Kuh, Jebel *mts.* Iran **35** 28.40N 58.10E
Barking *d.* England **7** 51.32N 0.05E
Barkly West R.S.A. **48** 28.32S 24.32E
Barle *r.* England **11** 51.00N 3.31W
Bar-le-Duc France **22** 48.46N 5.10E
Barletta Italy **24** 41.20N 16.15E
Barmouth Wales **10** 52.44N 4.03W
Barnard Castle *town* England **12** 54.33N 1.55W
Barnaul U.S.S.R. **30** 53.21N 83.15E
Barnes England **7** 51.28N 0.15W
Barnet England **7** 51.39N 0.11W
Barneveld Neth. **27** 52.10N 5.39E
Barnoldswick England **12** 53.55N 2.11W
Barnsley England **13** 53.33N 1.29W
Barnstaple England **11** 51.05N 4.03W
Barnstaple B. England **11** 51.04N 4.20W
Baroda India **36** 22.19N 73.14E
Barquisimeto Venezuela **59** 10.03N 69.18W
Barra *i.* Scotland **16** 56.59N 7.28W
Barra, Sd. of Scotland **16** 57.04N 7.20W
Barra do Pirai Brazil **61** 22.30S 43.50W
Barra Head Scotland **16** 56.47N 7.36W
Barrancabermeja Colombia **59** 7.06N 73.54W
Barrancas Venezuela **62** 8.55N 62.05W
Barranquilla Colombia **59** 11.00N 74.50W
Barreiro Portugal **23** 38.40N 9.05W
Barrhead Scotland **14** 55.47N 4.24W
Barrie Canada **57** 44.22N 79.42W
Barrow *r.* Rep. of Ire. **19** 52.17N 7.00W
Barrow U.S.A. **54** 71.16N 156.50W
Barrow I. Australia **49** 21.40S 115.27E
Barrow-in-Furness England **12** 54.08N 3.15W
Barry Wales **11** 51.23N 3.19W
Barstow U.S.A. **52** 34.55N 117.01W
Bar-sur-Aube France **22** 48.14N 4.43E
Bartin Turkey **34** 41.37N 32.20E
Bartolomeu Dias Moçambique **48** 21.10S 35.09E
Barton on Sea England **8** 50.44N 1.40W
Barton-upon-Humber England **13** 53.41N 0.27W
Barvas Scotland **16** 58.21N 6.31W
Basalt I. Hong Kong **33** 22.19N 114.21E
Basankusu Zaïre **46** 1.12N 19.50E
Basel Switz. **26** 47.33N 7.36E
Bashi Channel Asia **41** 21.40N 121.20E
Basilan *i.* Phil. **39** 6.40N 122.10E
Basildon England **7** 51.34N 0.25E
Basingstoke England **8** 51.15N 1.05W
Baskatong L. Canada **57** 46.50N 75.46W
Basoko Zaïre **46** 1.20N 23.36E
Basongo Zaïre **46** 4.23S 20.28E
Basra Iraq **35** 30.33N 47.50E
Bassein Burma **37** 16.45N 94.30E
Bass Rock *i.* Scotland **15** 56.05N 2.38W
Bass Str. Australia **49** 39.45S 146.00E
Bastak Iran **35** 27.15N 54.26E
Bastelica France **22** 42.00N 9.03E
Bastia France **22** 42.41N 9.26E
Bastogne Belgium **27** 50.00N 5.43E
Bas Zaïre *d.* Zaïre **46** 5.15S 14.00E
Bata Equat. Guinea **46** 1.51N 9.49E
Batabanó, G. of Cuba **58** 23.15N 82.30W
Batangas Phil. **39** 13.46N 121.01E
Batan Is. Phil. **39** 20.50N 121.55E
Bath England **8** 51.22N 2.22W
Bath U.S.A. **57** 43.56N 69.50W
Batha, Wadi *r.* Oman **35** 20.01N 59.39E
Bathgate Scotland **15** 55.44N 3.38W
Bathurst Canada **53** 47.37N 65.40W
Bathurst, C. Canada **54** 70.30N 128.00W
Bathurst I. Australia **49** 11.45S 130.15E
Bathurst I. Canada **55** 76.00N 100.00W
Bathurst Inlet *town* Canada **54** 66.48N 108.00W
Batinah *f.* Oman **35** 24.25N 56.50E
Batjan *i.* Indonesia **39** 0.30S 127.30E
Batley England **12** 53.43N 1.38W
Batna Algeria **24** 35.35N 6.11E
Baton Rouge U.S.A. **53** 30.30N 91.10W
Batouri Cameroon **46** 4.26N 14.27E
Battambang Cambodia **37** 13.06N 103.13E
Battersea England **7** 51.28N 0.10W
Batticaloa Sri Lanka **37** 7.43N 81.42E
Battle England **9** 50.55N 0.30E
Battle Creek *town* U.S.A. **56** 42.20N 85.10W
Battle Harbour Canada **55** 52.16N 55.36W
Battock, Mt. Scotland **17** 56.57N 2.44W
Batu Is. Indonesia **38** 0.30S 98.20E
Batumi U.S.S.R. **34** 41.37N 41.36E
Baturadja Indonesia **38** 4.10S 104.10E
Bauchi Nigeria **44** 10.16N 9.50E
Baugé France **22** 47.33N 0.06W
Bauld, C. Canada **55** 51.30N 55.45W
Bauru Brazil **61** 22.19S 49.07W
Bavay France **27** 50.18N 3.48E
Bawdsey England **9** 52.01N 1.27E
Bawean *i.* Indonesia **38** 5.50S 112.35E
Bawiti Egypt **34** 28.21N 28.51E
Bawtry England **13** 53.25N 1.01W
Bayamo Cuba **59** 20.23N 76.39W
Bayan Kara Shan *mts.* China **40** 34.00N 97.20E
Bayburt Turkey **34** 40.15N 40.16E
Bay City U.S.A. **56** 43.35N 83.52W
Baydaratskaya B. U.S.S.R. **30** 70.00N 66.00E
Bayeux France **22** 49.16N 0.42W
Bay Is. Honduras **58** 16.10N 86.30W
Bayonne France **22** 43.30N 1.28W
Bayreuth W. Germany **26** 49.56N 11.35E
Baza Spain **23** 37.30N 2.45W
Bazman Kuh *mtn.* Iran **35** 28.06N 60.00E
Beachy Head England **9** 50.43N 0.15E
Beacon Hill England **8** 51.12N 1.42W
Beacon Hill Hong Kong **33** 22.21N 114.10E
Beacon Hill Wales **10** 52.23N 3.14W
Beaconsfield England **7** 51.37N 0.39W
Beaminster England **8** 50.48N 2.44W
Beare Green England **7** 51.10N 0.18W
Bear I. Rep. of Ire. **19** 51.38N 9.52W
Bearsden Scotland **14** 55.56N 4.20W
Bearsted England **7** 51.17N 0.35E
Beaufort Sea N. America **54** 72.00N 141.00W
Beaufort West R.S.A. **48** 32.21S 22.35E
Beauly Scotland **17** 57.29N 4.29W
Beauly *r.* Scotland **17** 57.29N 4.25W
Beauly Firth *est.* Scotland **17** 57.29N 4.20W
Beaumaris Wales **10** 53.16N 4.07W
Beaumont Belgium **27** 50.14N 4.16E
Beaumont U.S.A. **53** 30.04N 94.06W
Beaune France **22** 47.02N 4.50E
Beauvais France **22** 49.26N 2.05E
Beaver I. U.S.A. **56** 45.40N 85.35W
Beawar India **36** 26.02N 74.20E
Bebington England **12** 53.23N 3.01W
Beccles England **9** 52.27N 1.33E
Béchar Algeria **44** 31.35N 2.17W
Beckenham England **7** 51.24N 0.01W
Beckum W. Germany **27** 51.45N 8.02E
Bedale England **13** 54.18N 1.35W
Bédarieux France **22** 43.35N 3.10E
Beddington England **7** 51.22N 0.08W
Bedford England **9** 52.08N 0.29W
Bedford U.S.A. **56** 38.51N 86.30W
Bedford Levels *f.* England **9** 52.35N 0.08E
Bedfordshire *d.* England **9** 52.04N 0.28W
Bedlington England **15** 55.08N 1.34W
Bedwas Wales **11** 51.36N 3.10W
Bedwellty Wales **11** 51.42N 3.13W
Bedworth England **8** 52.28N 1.29W
Bee, Loch Scotland **16** 57.23N 7.22W
Beenoskee *mtn.* Rep. of Ire. **19** 52.47N 10.04W
Beersheba Israel **34** 31.15N 34.47E
Beeston England **13** 52.55N 1.11W
Beeville U.S.A. **52** 28.25N 97.47W
Befale Zaïre **46** 0.27N 21.01E
Beg, Lough N. Ireland **14** 54.47N 6.29W
Begna *r.* Norway **28** 60.06N 10.15E
Behbehan Iran **35** 30.35N 50.17E
Beida Libya **45** 32.50N 21.50E
Beilen Neth. **27** 52.51N 6.31E
Beinn à Ghlò *mtn.* Scotland **17** 56.50N 3.42W
Beinn an Tuirc *mtn.* Scotland **14** 55.24N 5.33W
Beinn Bheigeir *mtn.* Scotland **14** 55.44N 6.08W
Beinn Dearg *mtn.* Scotland **17** 57.47N 4.55W
Beinn Dhorain *mtn.* Scotland **17** 58.07N 3.50W
Beinn Mhor *mtn.* Scotland **16** 57.59N 6.40W
Beinn nam Bad Mor *mtn.* Scotland **17** 58.29N 3.43W
Beinn Resipol *mtn.* Scotland **16** 56.43N 6.38W
Beinn Sgritheall *mtn.* Scotland **16** 57.09N 5.34W
Beinn Tharsuinn *mtn.* Scotland **17** 57.47N 4.21W
Beira Moçambique **48** 19.49S 34.52E
Beirut Lebanon **34** 33.52N 35.30E
Beitbridge Rhodesia **48** 22.10S 30.01E
Beith Scotland **14** 55.45N 4.37W
Béja Tunisia **24** 36.44N 9.12E
Beja Portugal **23** 38.01N 7.52W
Bejaïa Algeria **24** 36.45N 5.05E
Béjar Spain **23** 40.24N 5.45W
Bejestan Iran **35** 34.32N 58.08E
Bela Pakistan **36** 26.12N 66.20E
Belalcázar Spain **23** 38.35N 5.10W
Belang Indonesia **39** 0.58N 124.56E
Bela Vista Brazil **61** 22.05S 56.22W
Bela Vista Moçambique **48** 26.20S 32.40E
Belaya *r.* U.S.S.R. **30** 55.40N 52.30E
Belcher Is. Canada **55** 56.00N 79.00W
Belcoo N. Ireland **18** 54.18N 7.53W
Belém Brazil **62** 1.27S 48.29W
Belen U.S.A. **52** 34.39N 106.48W
Belet Wen Somali Rep. **47** 4.38N 45.12E
Belfast N. Ireland **14** 54.36N 5.57W
Belfast Lough N. Ireland **14** 54.42N 5.45W
Belford England **15** 55.36N 1.48W
Belfort France **26** 47.38N 6.52E
Belgaum India **36** 15.54N 74.36E
Belgium Europe **27** 51.00N 4.30E
Belgorod U.S.S.R. **29** 50.38N 36.36E
Belgorod Dnestrovskiy U.S.S.R. **29** 46.10N 30.19E
Belgrade Yugo. **25** 44.49N 20.28E
Belikh *r.* Syria **34** 35.58N 39.05E
Belitung *i.* Indonesia **38** 3.00S 108.00E
Belize Belize **58** 17.29N 88.20W
Belize C. America **58** 17.00N 88.30W
Bellac France **22** 46.07N 1.04E
Bellary India **36** 15.11N 76.54E
Belleek N. Ireland **18** 54.29N 8.06W
Belle Ile France **22** 47.20N 3.10W
Belle Isle Str. Canada **55** 50.45N 58.00W
Belleville Canada **57** 44.10N 77.22W
Bellingham England **15** 55.09N 2.15W
Bellingham U.S.A. **52** 48.45N 122.29W
Bellingshausen Sea Antarctica **2** 70.00S 84.00W
Bello Colombia **59** 6.20N 75.41W
Bell Rock *i. see* Inchcape Scotland **15**
Bell Ville Argentina **61** 32.35S 62.41W
Belmopan Belize **58** 17.25N 88.46W
Belmullet Rep. of Ire. **18** 54.14N 10.00W
Belo Horizonte Brazil **61** 19.45S 43.54W
Beloye, L. U.S.S.R. **29** 60.12N 37.45E
Belozersk U.S.S.R. **29** 60.00N 37.49E
Belper England **13** 53.02N 1.29W
Beltra, Lough Rep. of Ire. **18** 53.56N 9.26W
Beltsy U.S.S.R. **29** 47.45N 27.59E
Belturbet Rep. of Ire. **18** 54.06N 7.27W
Belukha, Mt. U.S.S.R. **40** 49.46N 86.40E
Belvedere England **7** 51.30N 0.10E
Bembridge England **8** 50.41N 1.04W
Bemidji U.S.A. **53** 47.29N 94.52W
Ben Alder *mtn.* Scotland **17** 56.49N 4.28W
Benavente Spain **23** 42.00N 5.40W
Ben Avon *mtn.* Scotland **17** 57.06N 3.27W
Benbane Head N. Ireland **14** 55.15N 6.29W
Benbecula *i.* Scotland **16** 57.26N 7.18W
Benbulbin *mtn.* Rep. of Ire. **18** 54.22N 8.28W
Ben Chonzie *mtn.* Scotland **15** 56.27N 4.00W
Ben Cruachan *mtn.* Scotland **14** 56.26N 5.18W
Bend U.S.A. **52** 44.04N 121.20W
Bendigo Australia **49** 36.48S 144.21E
Beneraird *mtn.* Scotland **14** 55.04N 4.56W
Benevento Italy **24** 41.07N 14.46E
Bengal *d.* India **37** 23.00N 87.40E
Bengal, B. of Indian Oc. **37** 17.00N 89.00E
Benghazi Libya **44** 32.07N 20.05E
Bengkulu Indonesia **38** 3.46S 102.16E
Ben Griam More *mtn.* Scotland **17** 58.20N 4.02W
Benguela Angola **46** 12.34S 13.24E
Benguela *d.* Angola **46** 12.45S 14.00E
Ben Hee *mtn.* Scotland **17** 58.16N 4.41W
Ben Hiant *mtn.* Scotland **14** 56.42N 6.01W
Ben Hope *mtn.* Scotland **17** 58.24N 4.36W
Ben Horn *mtn.* Scotland **17** 58.07N 4.02W
Ben Hutig *mtn.* Scotland **17** 58.33N 4.31W
Beni *d.* Bolivia **61** 15.50S 65.00W
Beni *r.* Bolivia **62** 10.30S 66.00W
Beni Zaïre **47** 0.29N 29.27E
Benicarló Spain **23** 40.25N 0.25E
Benin, Bight of Africa **44** 5.30N 3.00E
Benin City Nigeria **44** 6.19N 5.41E
Beni-Saf Algeria **23** 35.28N 1.22W
Beni Suef Egypt **34** 29.05N 31.05E
Ben Klibreck *mtn.* Scotland **17** 58.15N 4.22W
Ben Lawers *mtn.* Scotland **14** 56.33N 4.14W
Benllech Wales **10** 53.18N 4.15W
Ben Lomond *mtn.* Scotland **14** 56.12N 4.38W
Ben Loyal *mtn.* Scotland **17** 58.24N 4.26W
Ben Lui *mtn.* Scotland **14** 56.23N 4.49W
Ben Macdhui *mtn.* Scotland **17** 57.04N 3.40W
Ben More *mtn.* Central Scotland **14** 56.23N 4.31W
Ben More *mtn.* Strath. Scotland **14** 56.26N 6.02W
Ben More Assynt *mtn.* Scotland **17** 58.07N 4.52W
Bennane Head Scotland **14** 55.08N 5.00W
Bennettsbridge Rep. of Ire. **19** 52.35N 7.11W
Ben Nevis *mtn.* Scotland **16** 56.48N 5.00W
Benoni R.S.A. **48** 26.12S 28.18E
Ben Rinnes *mtn.* Scotland **17** 57.24N 3.15W
Benton Harbor U.S.A. **56** 42.07N 86.27W
Benue *r.* Nigeria **44** 7.52N 6.45E
Ben Vorlich *mtn.* Scotland **14** 56.21N 4.13W
Benwee Head Rep. of Ire. **18** 54.21N 9.48W
Ben Wyvis *mtn.* Scotland **17** 57.40N 4.35W
Beppu Japan **42** 33.18N 131.30E
Beragh N. Ireland **14** 54.34N 7.10W
Berat Albania **25** 40.42N 19.59E
Berbera Somali Rep. **45** 10.28N 45.02E
Berbérati C.A.R. **46** 4.19N 15.51E
Berchem Belgium **27** 50.48N 3.32E
Berdichev U.S.S.R. **29** 49.54N 28.39E
Berdyansk U.S.S.R. **29** 46.45N 36.47E
Berens *r.* Canada **53** 52.25N 97.00W
Berezniki U.S.S.R. **30** 59.26N 57.00E
Bergama Turkey **25** 39.08N 27.10E
Bergamo Italy **22** 45.42N 9.40E
Bergen Norway **28** 60.23N 5.20E
Bergen op Zoom Neth. **27** 51.30N 4.17E
Bergerac France **22** 44.50N 0.29E
Bergheim W. Germany **27** 50.58N 6.39E
Bergisch Gladbach W. Germany **27** 50.59N 7.10E
Berhampore India **37** 24.06N 88.18E
Berhampur India **37** 19.21N 84.51E
Bering Sea N. America/Asia **54** 65.00N 170.00W
Bering Str. U.S.S.R./U.S.A. **54** 65.00N 170.00W
Berkel *r.* Neth. **27** 52.10N 6.12E
Berkhamsted England **7** 51.46N 0.35W
Berkshire *d.* England **8** 51.25N 1.03W
Berkshire Downs *hills* England **8** 51.32N 1.36W
Berlin E. Germany **26** 52.32N 13.25E
Berlin U.S.A. **57** 44.27N 71.13W
Bermejo *r.* Argentina **61** 26.47S 58.30W
Bermondsey England **7** 51.30N 0.04W
Bermuda Atlantic Oc. **59** 32.18N 64.45W
Berne Switz. **26** 46.57N 7.26E
Berneray *i.* W. Isles Scotland **16** 56.47N 7.38W
Berneray *i.* W. Isles Scotland **16** 57.43N 7.11W
Bernina *mtn.* Italy/Switz. **24** 46.22N 9.57E

Bernkastel W. Germany **27** 49.55N 7.05E
Berriedale Scotland **17** 58.11N 3.30W
Berry Head England **11** 50.24N 3.28W
Bertnaghboy B. Rep. of Ire. **18** 53.23N 9.52W
Bertoua Cameroon **46** 4.34N 13.42E
Berwick-upon-Tweed England **15** 55.46N 2.00W
Berwyn *mts.* Wales **10** 52.55N 3.25W
Besalampy Malagasy Rep. **47** 16.53S 44.29E
Besançon France **26** 47.14N 6.02E
Bessarabia *f.* U.S.S.R. **29** 46.30N 28.40E
Betanzos Spain **23** 43.17N 8.13W
Bétaré Oya Cameroon **46** 5.34N 14.09E
Bethal R.S.A. **48** 26.27S 29.28E
Bethersden England **9** 51.08N 0.46E
Bethesda Wales **10** 53.11N 4.03W
Bethlehem R.S.A. **48** 28.15S 28.19E
Bethlehem U.S.A. **57** 40.36N 75.22W
Bethnal Green England **7** 51.32N 0.03W
Béthune France **27** 50.32N 2.38E
Bettyhill Scotland **17** 58.30N 4.14W
Betws-y-Coed Wales **10** 53.05N 3.48W
Beult *r.* England **7** 51.13N 0.26E
Beverley England **13** 53.52N 0.26W
Beverwijk Neth. **27** 52.29N 4.40E
Bewcastle England **15** 55.03N 2.45W
Bewcastle Fells *hills* England **15** 55.05N 2.50W
Bewdley England **8** 52.23N 2.19W
Bexhill England **9** 50.51N 0.29E
Bexley England **7** 51.26N 0.10E
Beyla Guinea **44** 8.42N 8.39W
Beyoneisu retsugan *i.* Japan **42** 31.53N 139.52E
Beysehir L. Turkey **34** 37.47N 31.30E
Bezhetsk U.S.S.R. **29** 57.49N 36.40E
Bezhitsa U.S.S.R. **29** 53.19N 34.17E
Béziers France **22** 43.21N 3.13E
Bhagalpur India **37** 25.14N 85.59E
Bhamo Burma **37** 24.15N 97.15E
Bhatpara India **40** 22.51N 88.31E
Bhavnagar India **36** 21.46N 72.14E
Bhima *r.* India **36** 16.30N 77.10E
Bhopal India **36** 23.17N 77.28E
Bhubaneswar India **37** 20.15N 85.50E
Bhuj India **36** 23.12N 69.54E
Bhutan Asia **37** 27.25N 89.50E
Biak *i.* Asia **39** 0.55S 136.00E
Białogard Poland **26** 54.00N 16.00E
Białystok Poland **29** 53.09N 23.10E
Biarritz France **22** 43.29N 1.33W
Bicester England **8** 51.53N 1.09W
Bickley England **7** 51.24N 0.03E
Bidborough England **7** 51.11N 0.14E
Biddeford U.S.A. **57** 43.29N 70.27W
Biddulph England **12** 53.08N 2.11W
Bidean nam Bian *mtn.* Scotland **14** 56.39N 5.02W
Bideford England **11** 51.01N 4.13W
Bideford B. England **11** 51.04N 4.20W
Bié *d.* Angola **46** 12.30S 17.30E
Biel Switz. **26** 47.09N 7.16E
Bielefeld W. Germany **26** 52.02N 8.32E
Bié Plateau *f.* Angola **46** 13.00S 16.00E
Bigbury B. England **11** 50.15N 3.56W
Biggar Scotland **15** 55.38N 3.31W
Biggin Hill *town* England **7** 51.19N 0.04E
Biggleswade England **9** 52.06N 0.16W
Big Horn *r.* U.S.A. **52** 46.05N 107.20W
Big Snowy Mtn. U.S.A. **52** 46.46N 109.31W
Big Spring *town* U.S.A. **52** 32.15N 101.30W
Big Wave B. Hong Kong **33** 22.15N 114.15E
Bihać Yugo. **24** 44.49N 15.53E
Bihar India **37** 25.13N 85.31E
Bihar *d.* India **37** 24.15N 86.00E
Biharamulo Tanzania **47** 2.34S 31.20E
Bihor *mtn.* Romania **29** 46.26N 22.43E
Bijagos Archipelago *is.* Guinea Bissau **44** 11.30N 16.00W
Bijar Iran **35** 35.52N 47.39E
Bijawar India **37** 24.36N 79.30E
Bikaner India **36** 28.01N 73.22E
Bikin U.S.S.R. **41** 46.52N 134.15E
Bikoro Zaïre **46** 0.45S 18.09E
Bilaspur India **37** 22.03N 82.12E
Bilauktaung Range *mts.* Asia **38** 13.20N 99.30E
Bilbao Spain **23** 43.15N 2.56W
Bilecik Turkey **34** 40.10N 29.59E
Bili *r.* Zaïre **46** 4.09N 22.25E
Billericay England **7** 51.38N 0.25E
Billingham England **13** 54.36N 1.18W
Billings U.S.A. **52** 45.47N 108.30W
Billingshurst England **9** 51.02N 0.28W
Billinghton England **7** 51.54N 0.39W
Bill of Portland *c.* England **11** 50.32N 2.28W
Biloxi U.S.A. **53** 30.30N 89.00W
Bima *r.* Zaïre **46** 3.24N 25.10E
Binaija *mtn.* Indonesia **39** 3.10S 129.30E
Binche Belgium **27** 50.25N 4.10E
Bindjai Indonesia **38** 3.37N 98.25E
Bindura Rhodesia **48** 17.20S 31.21E
Binga, Mt. Rhodesia **48** 19.47S 33.03E
Bingen W. Germany **27** 49.58N 7.55E
Bingham England **13** 52.57N 0.57W
Binghamton U.S.A. **57** 42.06N 75.55W
Bingkor Malaysia **38** 5.26N 116.15E
Bingley England **12** 53.51N 1.50W
Bingöl Turkey **34** 38.54N 40.29E
Bingol Dağlari *mtn.* Turkey **34** 39.21N 41.22E
Binh Dinh S. Vietnam **38** 13.55N 109.07E
Bintan *i.* Indonesia **38** 1.10N 104.30E
Bintulu Malaysia **38** 3.12N 113.01E
Birdum Australia **49** 15.38S 133.12E
Birecik Turkey **34** 37.03N 37.59E
Birhan *mtn.* Ethiopia **45** 11.00N 37.50E
Birjand Iran **35** 32.54N 59.10E
Birkenfeld W. Germany **27** 49.39N 7.10E
Birkenhead England **12** 53.24N 3.01W
Birket Qârûn *l.* Egypt **34** 29.30N 30.40E
Birmingham England **8** 52.30N 1.55W
Birmingham U.S.A. **53** 33.30N 86.55W
Birni N'Konni Niger **44** 13.49N 5.19E
Birobidzhan U.S.S.R. **41** 48.49N 132.54E
Birq, Wadi *r.* Saudi Arabia **35** 24.08N 47.35E
Birr Rep. of Ire. **19** 53.06N 7.56W
Birreencorragh *mtn.* Rep. of Ire. **18** 53.59N 9.31W
Biscay, B. of France **22** 45.30N 4.00W
Bishop Auckland England **12** 54.40N 1.40W
Bishopbriggs Scotland **14** 55.55N 4.12W
Bishop's Castle England **8** 52.29N 3.00W
Bishop's Lydeard England **8** 51.04N 3.12W
Bishop's Stortford England **7** 51.53N 0.09E
Bishops Waltham England **8** 50.57N 1.13W
Bisitun Iran **35** 34.22N 47.29E
Biskotasi L. Canada **56** 47.15N 82.15W
Biskra Algeria **24** 34.48N 5.40E
Bisley England **7** 51.20N 0.39W
Bismarck U.S.A. **52** 46.50N 100.48W
Bismarck Range *mts.* P.N.G. **39** 6.00S 145.00E
Bismarck Sea Pacific Oc. **39** 4.00S 146.30E
Bissau Guinea Bissau **44** 11.52N 15.39W
Bistrita *r.* Romania **29** 46.30N 26.54E
Bitburg W. Germany **27** 49.58N 6.31E
Bitlis Turkey **34** 38.23N 42.04E
Bitola Yugo. **25** 41.02N 21.21E
Bitterfontein R.S.A. **48** 31.03S 18.16E
Bitter Lakes Egypt **34** 30.20N 32.50E
Biumba Rwanda **47** 1.38S 30.02E
Biwa ko *l.* Japan **42** 35.20N 136.10E
Biysk U.S.S.R. **30** 52.35N 85.16E
Bizerta Tunisia **24** 37.17N 9.51E
Black *r.* N. Vietnam **38** 21.20N 105.45E
Black *r.* Rep. of Ire. **18** 53.50N 7.51W
Black *r.* Ark. U.S.A. **53** 35.30N 91.20W
Black *r.* Wisc. U.S.A. **56** 43.55N 91.20W
Black Bull Head Rep. of Ire. **19** 51.35N 10.03W
Blackburn England **12** 53.44N 2.30W
Black Combe *mtn.* England **12** 54.15N 3.20W
Blackcraig Hill Scotland **14** 55.19N 4.08W
Black Down Hills England **8** 50.55N 3.10W
Blackford Scotland **15** 56.16N 3.48W
Black Forest *f.* W. Germany **26** 48.00N 7.45E
Black Head N. Ireland **14** 54.46N 5.41W
Black Head Rep. of Ire. **19** 53.09N 9.16W
Black Hill Hong Kong **33** 22.18N 114.14E
Black Isle *f.* Scotland **17** 57.35N 4.15W
Blackmoor Vale *f.* England **8** 50.55N 2.25W
Black Mtn. Wales **10** 51.52N 3.50W
Black Mts. Wales **10** 51.52N 3.09W
Blackpool England **12** 53.48N 3.03W
Black River *town* Jamaica **59** 18.02N 77.52W
Blackrock Rep. of Ire. **18** 53.18N 6.13W
Black Rock Desert U.S.A. **52** 41.10N 118.45W
Black Sand Desert U.S.S.R. **35** 37.45N 60.00E
Black Sea Europe **29** 43.00N 35.00E
Blacksod B. Rep. of Ire. **18** 54.04N 10.00W
Black Volta *r.* Ghana **44** 8.14N 2.11W
Blackwater *r.* England **9** 51.43N 0.42E
Blackwater *r.* N. Ireland **18** 54.31N 6.36W
Blackwater Rep. of Ire. **19** 52.26N 6.20W
Blackwater *r.* Meath Rep. of Ire. **18** 53.39N 6.41W
Blackwater *r.* Waterford Rep. of Ire. **19** 51.58N 7.52W
Blackwater Resr. Scotland **14** 56.43N 4.58W
Bladnoch *r.* Scotland **14** 54.52N 4.26W
Blaenau Ffestiniog Wales **10** 53.00N 3.57W
Blaenavon Wales **11** 51.46N 3.05W
Blagoevgrad Bulgaria **25** 42.02N 23.04E
Blagoveshchensk U.S.S.R. **41** 50.19N 127.30E
Blair Atholl Scotland **17** 56.46N 3.51W
Blairgowrie Scotland **15** 56.36N 3.21W
Blakeney Pt. England **13** 52.58N 0.57E
Blanc, Cap Mauritania **44** 20.44N 17.05W
Blanc, Mont Europe **22** 45.50N 6.52E
Blanca, Bahía *b.* Argentina **61** 39.15S 61.00W
Blanchardstown Rep. of Ire. **18** 53.24N 6.23W
Blanco, C. Costa Rica **58** 9.36N 85.06W
Blanco, C. U.S.A. **52** 42.50N 124.29W
Blandford Forum England **8** 50.52N 2.10W
Blankenberge Belgium **27** 51.18N 3.08E
Blantyre Malawi **47** 15.46S 35.00E
Blarney Rep. of Ire. **19** 51.56N 8.34W
Blavet *r.* France **22** 47.43N 3.18W
Blaydon England **12** 54.58N 1.42W
Blaye France **22** 45.08N 0.40W
Bleaklow Hill England **12** 53.27N 1.50W
Blenheim New Zealand **50** 41.32S 173.58E
Blessington Rep. of Ire. **19** 53.11N 6.33W
Bletchley England **8** 51.59N 0.45W
Blida Algeria **23** 36.30N 2.50E
Blidworth England **13** 53.06N 1.07W
Blindley Heath England **7** 51.12N 0.04W
Blind River *town* Canada **56** 46.12N 82.59W
Bloemfontein R.S.A. **48** 29.07S 26.14E
Blois France **22** 47.36N 1.20E
Bloody Foreland *c.* Rep. of Ire. **18** 55.09N 8.17W
Bloomington Ind. U.S.A. **56** 39.10N 86.31W
Bloomington Ill. U.S.A. **56** 40.29N 89.00W
Bloomsburg U.S.A. **57** 41.01N 76.27W
Bluefield U.S.A. **53** 37.14N 81.17W
Bluefields Nicaragua **58** 12.00N 83.49W
Blue Mts. U.S.A. **52** 45.00N 118.00W
Blue Nile *r.* Sudan **45** 15.45N 32.25E
Blue Stack Mts. Rep. of Ire. **18** 54.44N 8.09W
Bluff New Zealand **50** 46.38S 168.21E
Bluff I. Hong Kong **33** 22.19N 114.20E
Bluff Pt. Hong Kong **33** 22.12N 114.12E
Blumenau Brazil **61** 26.55S 49.07W
Blyth England **15** 55.07N 1.29W
Blyth *r.* Northum. England **15** 55.08N 1.29W
Blyth *r.* Suffolk England **9** 52.19N 1.36E
Blyth Bridge *town* Scotland **15** 55.42N 3.23W
Blyth Sands England **7** 51.28N 0.33E
Bo Sierra Leone **44** 7.58N 11.45W
Bobo-Dioulasso U. Volta **44** 11.11N 4.18W
Bobruysk U.S.S.R. **29** 53.08N 29.10E
Bocholt W. Germany **27** 51.49N 6.37E
Bochum W. Germany **27** 51.28N 7.11E
Boddam Scotland **17** 57.28N 1.48W
Bodélé Depression *f.* Chad **44** 16.50N 17.10E
Boden Sweden **28** 65.50N 21.44E
Bodenham England **8** 52.09N 2.41W
Bodmin England **11** 50.28N 4.44W
Bodmin Moor England **11** 50.35N 4.35W
Bodö Norway **28** 67.18N 14.26E
Boende Zaïre **46** 0.15S 20.49E
Bogenfels S.W. Africa **48** 27.23S 15.22E
Boggeragh Mts. Rep. of Ire. **19** 52.03N 8.53W
Boghari Algeria **23** 35.55N 2.47E
Bognor Regis England **8** 50.47N 0.40W
Bog of Allen *f.* Rep. of Ire. **18** 53.17N 7.00W
Bogor Indonesia **38** 6.34S 106.45E
Bogotá Colombia **62** 4.38N 74.05W
Bohain France **27** 49.59N 3.28E
Bohemian Forest *mts.* Czech. **26** 49.20N 13.10E
Bohol *i.* Phil. **39** 9.45N 124.10E
Boise U.S.A. **52** 43.38N 116.12W
Bojeador, C. Phil. **39** 18.30N 120.50E
Bojnurd Iran **35** 37.28N 57.20E
Boké Guinea **44** 10.57N 14.13W
Bokn Fjord *est.* Norway **28** 59.15N 5.50E
Bokungu Zaïre **46** 0.44S 22.28E
Bolangir India **37** 20.41N 83.30E
Bolbec France **22** 49.34N 0.28E
Bolgrad U.S.S.R. **25** 45.42N 28.40E
Bolivar Argentina **61** 36.15S 61.07W
Bolivar *mtn.* Venezuela **59** 7.27N 71.00W
Bolivia S. America **62** 17.00S 65.00W
Bollin *r.* England **12** 53.23N 2.29W
Bollnäs Sweden **28** 61.20N 16.25E
Bolmen *l.* Sweden **28** 57.00N 13.45E
Bolobo Zaïre **46** 2.10S 16.17E
Bologna Italy **24** 44.30N 11.20E
Bologoye U.S.S.R. **29** 57.58N 34.00E
Bolomba Zaïre **46** 0.30N 19.13E
Bolsena, Lago di *l.* Italy **24** 42.36N 11.55E
Bolshevik *i.* U.S.S.R. **31** 78.30N 102.00E
Bolshoi Lyakhovskiy *i.* U.S.S.R. **31** 73.30N 142.00E
Bolsover England **13** 53.14N 1.18W
Bolt Head *c.* England **11** 50.13N 3.48W
Bolton England **12** 53.35N 2.26W
Bolu Turkey **34** 40.45N 31.38E
Bolus Head Rep. of Ire. **19** 51.47N 10.20W
Bolvadin Turkey **34** 38.43N 31.02E
Bolzano Italy **26** 46.30N 11.20E
Boma Zaïre **46** 5.50S 13.03E
Bombay India **36** 18.56N 72.51E
Bom Despacho Brazil **61** 19.46S 45.15W
Bomokandi *r.* Zaïre **47** 3.37N 26.09E
Bomongo Zaïre **46** 1.30N 18.21E
Bomu *r.* C.A.R. **46** 4.08N 22.25E
Bon, C. Tunisia **24** 37.05N 11.02E
Bonaire *i.* Neth. Antilles **59** 12.15N 68.27W
Bonar-Bridge *town* Scotland **17** 57.33N 4.21W
Bonavista Canada **55** 48.38N 53.08W
Bondo Zaïre **46** 3.47N 23.45E
Bone, G. of Indonesia **39** 4.00S 120.50E
Bo'ness Scotland **15** 56.01N 3.36W
Bongandanga Zaïre **46** 1.28N 21.03E
Bonifacio France **24** 41.23N 9.10E
Bonifacio, Str. of Med. Sea **24** 41.18N 9.10E
Bonn W. Germany **27** 50.44N 7.06E
Bonny Nigeria **46** 4.25N 7.15E
Bonny, Bight of Africa **46** 3.00N 8.00E
Bonnyrigg Scotland **15** 55.52N 3.07W
Bontang Indonesia **38** 0.05N 117.31E
Boothia, G. of Canada **55** 70.00N 90.00W
Bootle Cumbria England **12** 54.17N 3.24W
Bootle Mersey. England **12** 53.28N 3.01W
Booué Gabon **46** 0.00 11.58E
Boppard W. Germany **27** 50.13N 7.35E
Borah Peak U.S.A. **52** 44.09N 113.47W
Borås Sweden **28** 57.44N 12.55E
Borazjan Iran **35** 29.14N 51.12E
Bordeaux France **22** 44.50N 0.34W
Borden I. Canada **54** 78.30N 111.00W
Borders *d.* Scotland **15** 55.30N 2.53W
Bordö *i.* Faroe Is. **28** 62.10N 7.13W
Bordon Camp England **8** 51.06N 0.52W
Borehamwood England **7** 51.40N 0.16W
Boreray *i.* Scotland **16** 57.43N 7.17W
Borgå Finland **28** 60.24N 25.40E
Borgefjell *mtn.* Norway **28** 65.15N 13.50E
Borger U.S.A. **52** 35.39N 101.24W
Borisoglebsk U.S.S.R. **29** 51.23N 42.02E
Borisov U.S.S.R. **29** 54.09N 28.30E
Borken W. Germany **27** 51.50N 6.52E
Borkum W. Germany **27** 53.34N 6.41E
Borkum *i.* W. Germany **27** 53.35N 6.45E
Borlänge Sweden **28** 60.29N 15.25E
Bormida *r.* Italy **22** 45.02N 8.43E
Borneo *i.* Asia **38** 1.00N 114.00E
Bornholm *i.* Denmark **28** 55.02N 15.00E
Boroughbridge England **13** 54.06N 1.23W
Borough Green England **7** 51.17N 0.19E
Borris-in-Ossory Rep. of Ire. **19** 52.56N 7.39W
Borrisokane Rep. of Ire. **19** 53.00N 8.08W
Borth Wales **10** 52.29N 4.03W
Borzya U.S.S.R. **41** 50.24N 116.35E
Bosa Italy **24** 40.18N 8.29E
Boscastle England **11** 50.42N 4.42W
Bosna *r.* Yugo. **25** 45.04N 18.27E
Bosobolo Zaïre **46** 4.11N 19.55E
Boso Hanto *b.* Japan **42** 35.40N 140.50E
Bosporus *str.* Turkey **25** 41.07N 29.04E
Bossembelé C.A.R. **46** 5.10N 17.44E
Boston England **13** 52.59N 0.02W
Boston U.S.A. **57** 42.20N 71.05W
Botevgrad Bulgaria **25** 42.55N 23.57E
Bothnia, G. of Europe **28** 63.30N 20.30E
Botletle *r.* Botswana **48** 21.06S 24.47E
Botoşani Romania **29** 47.44N 26.41E
Botrange *mtn.* Belgium **27** 50.30N 6.04E
Botswana Africa **48** 22.00S 24.15E
Bottesford England **13** 52.56N 0.48W
Bottrop W. Germany **27** 51.31N 6.55E
Botucatu Brazil **61** 22.52S 48.30W
Bouaké Ivory Coast **44** 7.42N 5.00W
Boufarik Algeria **23** 36.36N 2.54E
Boughton England **13** 53.13N 0.59W
Bouillon Belgium **22** 49.47N 5.04E
Bouira Algeria **23** 36.22N 3.55E
Boulder U.S.A. **52** 40.02N 105.16W
Boulogne France **22** 50.43N 1.37E
Boumba *r.* Cameroon **46** 2.05N 15.10E
Boundary Peak *mtn.* U.S.A. **52** 37.51N 118.23W
Bourg France **22** 46.12N 5.13E
Bourganeuf France **22** 45.57N 1.44E
Bourges France **22** 47.05N 2.23E
Bourg Madame France **22** 42.26N 1.55E
Bourke Australia **49** 30.09S 145.59E
Bourne England **13** 52.46N 0.23W
Bourne *r.* England **8** 51.04N 1.47W
Bournebridge England **7** 51.37N 0.12E
Bourne End England **7** 51.34N 0.42W
Bournemouth England **8** 50.43N 1.53W
Bovingdon England **7** 51.44N 0.32W
Bowen Australia **49** 20.00S 148.15E
Bowes England **12** 54.31N 2.01W
Bowmore Scotland **14** 55.45N 6.17W
Bowness-on-Solway England **15** 54.57N 3.11W
Boxtel Neth. **27** 51.36N 5.20E
Boyle Rep. of Ire. **18** 53.58N 8.19W
Boyne *r.* Rep. of Ire. **18** 53.43N 6.17W
Boyoma Falls *f.* Zaïre **46** 0.18N 25.32E
Bozeman U.S.A. **52** 45.40N 111.00W
Braan *r.* Scotland **15** 56.34N 3.36W
Brabant *d.* Belgium **27** 50.47N 4.30E
Brac *i.* Yugo. **25** 43.20N 16.38E
Bracadale, Loch Scotland **16** 57.22N 6.30W
Bräcke Sweden **28** 62.44N 15.30E
Bracknell England **7** 51.26N 0.46W
Brad Romania **25** 46.06N 22.48E
Bradano *r.* Italy **25** 40.23N 16.52E
Bradford England **12** 53.47N 1.45W
Bradford-on-Avon England **8** 51.20N 2.15W
Bradwell-on-Sea England **9** 51.44N 0.55E
Bradworthy England **11** 50.54N 4.22W
Brae Scotland **16** 60.24N 1.21W
Braemar Scotland **17** 57.01N 3.24W
Braemar *f.* Scotland **17** 57.02N 3.24W
Braga Portugal **23** 41.32N 8.26W
Bragado Argentina **61** 35.10S 60.29W
Braganca Portugal **23** 41.47N 6.46W
Brahmaputra *r.* Asia **37** 23.50N 89.45E
Brăila Romania **25** 45.18N 27.58E
Brailsford England **12** 52.58N 1.35W
Brain *r.* England **7** 51.47N 0.40E
Braintree England **7** 51.53N 0.32E
Bramley England **7** 51.11N 0.35W
Brampton England **15** 54.56N 2.43W
Branco *r.* Brazil **62** 1.30S 62.00W
Brandberg *mtn.* S.W. Africa **48** 21.10S 14.33E
Brandenburg E. Germany **26** 52.25N 12.34E
Brandfort R.S.A. **48** 28.42S 26.28E
Brandon Canada **52** 49.50N 99.57W
Brandon Suffolk England **9** 52.27N 0.37E
Brandon Durham England **12** 54.46N 1.37W
Brandon B. Rep. of Ire. **19** 52.16N 10.05W
Brandon Hill Rep. of Ire. **19** 52.30N 7.00W
Brandon Mtn. Rep. of Ire. **19** 52.14N 10.15W
Brandon Pt. Rep. of Ire. **19** 52.17N 10.11W
Brantford Canada **56** 43.09N 80.17W
Brasília Brazil **61** 15.54S 47.50W
Braşov Romania **25** 45.40N 25.35E
Bratislava Czech. **29** 48.10N 17.10E
Bratsk U.S.S.R. **31** 56.20N 101.15E
Bratsk Resr. U.S.S.R. **31** 54.40N 103.00E
Brattleboro U.S.A. **57** 42.51N 72.36W
Braunschweig W. Germany **26** 52.15N 10.30E
Braunton England **11** 51.06N 4.09W
Brava Somali Rep. **47** 1.02N 44.02E
Brawley U.S.A. **52** 33.10N 115.30W
Bray *r.* England **11** 50.56N 3.54W
Bray Rep. of Ire. **19** 53.12N 6.07W
Bray Head Kerry Rep. of Ire. **19** 51.53N 10.26W
Bray Head Wicklow Rep. of Ire. **19** 53.11N 6.04W
Brazil S. America **61** 19.00S 50.00W
Brazilian Highlands Brazil **61** 17.02S 50.00W
Brazos *r.* U.S.A. **53** 28.55N 95.20W
Brazzaville Congo **46** 4.14S 15.10E
Breadalbane *f.* Scotland **14** 56.30N 4.20W
Breaksea Pt. Wales **11** 51.24N 3.25W
Bream B. New Zealand **50** 36.00S 174.30E
Brechin Scotland **15** 56.44N 2.40W
Breckland *f.* England **9** 52.28N 0.40E
Brecon Wales **10** 51.57N 3.23W
Brecon Beacons *mts.* Wales **10** 51.53N 3.27W
Breda Neth. **27** 51.35N 4.46E
Bredasdorp R.S.A. **48** 34.32S 20.02E
Brede *r.* England **9** 50.57N 0.44E
Bregenz Austria **26** 47.31N 9.46E
Breidha Fjördhur *est.* Iceland **28** 65.15N 23.00W
Bremen W. Germany **26** 53.05N 8.48E
Bremerhaven W. Germany **26** 53.33N 8.35E
Brendon Hills England **8** 51.05N 3.25W
Brenner Pass Austria/Italy **24** 47.00N 11.30E
Brent *d.* England **7** 51.33N 0.16W
Brenta *r.* Italy **24** 45.25N 12.15E
Brentford England **7** 51.30N 0.18W

Brentwood England **7** 51.38N 0.18E
Brescia Italy **24** 45.33N 10.12E
Breskens Neth. **27** 51.24N 3.34E
Bressanone Italy **26** 46.43N 11.40E
Bressay *i.* Scotland **16** 60.08N 1.05W
Bressay Sd. Scotland **16** 60.08N 1.10W
Bressuire France **22** 46.50N 0.28W
Brest France **22** 48.23N 4.30W
Brest U.S.S.R. **29** 52.08N 23.40E
Brest-Nantes Canal France **22** 47.55N 2.30W
Brett, C. New Zealand **50** 35.15S 174.20E
Brewer U.S.A. **57** 44.48N 68.44W
Briançon France **22** 44.53N 6.39E
Bricket Wood *town* England **7** 51.42N 0.20W
Bride I.o.M. **12** 54.23N 4.24W
Bride *r.* Rep. of Ire. **19** 52.05N 7.52W
Bridgend Wales **11** 51.30N 3.35W
Bridge of Allan *town* Scotland **15** 56.09N 3.58W
Bridge of Cally *town* Scotland **15** 56.39N 3.25W
Bridge of Earn *town* Scotland **15** 56.24N 3.25W
Bridgeport U.S.A. **57** 41.12N 73.12W
Bridgetown Barbados **59** 13.06N 59.37W
Bridgetown Rep. of Ire. **19** 52.14N 6.33W
Bridgnorth England **8** 52.33N 2.25W
Bridgwater England **8** 51.08N 3.00W
Bridgwater B. England **8** 51.15N 3.10W
Bridlington England **13** 54.06N 0.11W
Bridlington B. England **13** 54.03N 0.10W
Bridport England **8** 50.43N 2.45W
Brienne-le-Chât France **22** 48.24N 4.32E
Brienz Switz. **26** 46.46N 8.02E
Brierfield England **12** 53.49N 2.15W
Brig Switz. **22** 46.19N 8.00E
Brigg England **13** 53.33N 0.30W
Brighouse England **12** 53.42N 1.47W
Brightlingsea England **9** 51.49N 1.01E
Brighton England **9** 50.50N 0.09W
Brindisi Italy **25** 40.38N 17.57E
Brisbane Australia **49** 27.30S 153.00E
Bristol England **11** 51.26N 2.35W
Bristol B. U.S.A. **54** 58.00N 158.50W
Bristol Channel England/Wales **11** 51.17N 3.20W
British Antarctic Territory Antarctica **64** 70.00S 50.00W
British Columbia *d.* Canada **54** 55.00N 125.00W
British Isles Europe **2** 54.00N 5.00W
Briton Ferry *town* Wales **11** 51.37N 3.50W
Britstown R.S.A. **48** 30.36S 23.30E
Brive France **22** 45.09N 1.32E
Briviesca Spain **23** 42.33N 3.19W
Brixham England **11** 50.24N 3.31W
Brno Czech. **26** 49.11N 16.39E
Broad B. Scotland **16** 58.15N 6.15W
Broadback *r.* Canada **53** 51.15N 78.55W
Broadford Scotland **16** 57.14N 5.54W
Broad Haven *b.* Rep. of Ire. **18** 54.17N 9.53W
Broad Law *mtn.* Scotland **15** 55.30N 3.21W
Broadstairs England **9** 51.22N 1.27E
Broadstone England **8** 50.45N 2.00W
Broadway England **8** 52.02N 1.51W
Brocken *mtn.* E. Germany **26** 51.50N 10.50E
Brockenhurst England **8** 50.49N 1.34W
Brockham England **7** 51.13N 0.16W
Brockton U.S.A. **57** 42.06N 71.01W
Brockville Canada **57** 44.35N 75.44W
Brod Yugo. **25** 45.09N 18.02E
Brodick Scotland **14** 55.34N 5.09W
Brody U.S.S.R. **29** 50.05N 25.08E
Broken Hill *town* Australia **49** 31.57S 141.30E
Bromley England **7** 51.24N 0.02E
Bromley Common England **7** 51.23N 0.04E
Brompton England **7** 51.24N 0.35E
Bromsgrove England **8** 52.20N 2.03W
Bromyard England **8** 52.12N 2.30W
Brönderslev Denmark **28** 57.16N 9.58E
Brookes Point *town* Phil. **38** 8.50N 117.52E
Brookmans Park *town* England **7** 51.43N 0.10W
Brooks Range *mts.* U.S.A. **54** 68.50N 152.00W
Brook Street England **7** 51.37N 0.17E
Broom, Loch Scotland **16** 57.52N 5.07W
Broome Australia **49** 17.58S 122.15E
Brora Scotland **17** 58.01N 3.52W
Brora *r.* Scotland **17** 58.00N 3.51W
Brosna *r.* Rep. of Ire. **19** 53.13N 7.58W
Brothers Pt. Hong Kong **33** 22.21N 114.00E
Brotton England **13** 54.34N 0.55W
Brough England **12** 54.32N 2.19W
Brough Head Scotland **17** 59.09N 3.19W
Brough Ness *c.* Scotland **17** 58.44N 2.57W
Broughton England **13** 54.26N 1.08W
Broughton Scotland **15** 55.37N 3.25W
Broughton in Furness England **12** 54.17N 3.12W
Brownhills England **8** 52.38N 1.57W
Brownsville U.S.A. **58** 25.54N 97.30W
Brown Willy *hill* England **11** 50.36N 4.36W
Broxbourne England **7** 51.45N 0.01W
Bruay-en-Artois France **27** 50.29N 2.36E
Brue *r.* England **8** 51.13N 3.00W
Bruernish Pt. Scotland **16** 56.59N 7.22W
Bruges Belgium **27** 51.13N 3.14E
Brühl W. Germany **27** 50.50N 6.55E
Brunei Asia **38** 4.56N 114.58E
Brunner New Zealand **50** 42.28S 171.12E
Brunssum Neth. **27** 50.57N 5.59E
Brunswick U.S.A. **53** 31.09N 81.21W
Bruree Rep. of Ire. **19** 52.25N 8.40W
Brussels Belgium **27** 50.50N 4.23E
Bruton England **8** 51.06N 2.28W
Bryansk U.S.S.R. **29** 53.15N 34.09E
Bryher *i.* England **11** 49.57N 6.21W
Bryn Brawd *mtn.* Wales **10** 52.08N 3.54W
Brynmawr Wales **11** 51.48N 3.10W
Bua *r.* Malawi **47** 12.42S 34.15E
Bubiyan I. Kuwait **35** 29.45N 48.15E
Bubye *r.* Rhodesia **48** 22.18S 31.00E
Bucaramanga Colombia **59** 7.08N 73.01W
Buchan *f.* Scotland **17** 57.34N 2.03W
Buchan Ness *c.* Scotland **17** 57.28N 1.47W
Bucharest Romania **25** 44.25N 26.06E
Buckfastleigh England **11** 50.28N 3.47W
Buckhaven and Methil Scotland **15** 56.11N 3.03W
Buckhurst Hill England **7** 51.38N 0.03E
Buckie Scotland **17** 57.40N 2.58W
Buckingham England **8** 52.00N 0.59W
Buckinghamshire *d.* England **8** 51.50N 0.48W
Buckley Wales **10** 53.11N 3.04W
Buco Zau Angola **46** 4.46S 12.34E
Budapest Hungary **29** 47.30N 19.03E
Buddon Ness *c.* Scotland **15** 56.29N 2.42W
Bude England **11** 50.49N 4.33W
Bude B. England **11** 50.50N 4.40W
Budjala Zaïre **46** 2.38N 19.48E
Budleigh Salterton England **8** 50.37N 3.19W
Buenaventura Colombia **62** 3.54N 77.02W
Buenos Aires Argentina **61** 34.40S 58.25W
Buenos Aires *d.* Argentina **61** 35.00S 61.00W
Buffalo N.Y. U.S.A. **57** 42.52N 78.55W
Buffalo Wyo. U.S.A. **52** 44.21N 106.40W
Bug *r.* Poland **29** 52.29N 21.11E
Bug *r.* U.S.S.R. **29** 46.55N 31.59E
Buggs Island *l.* U.S.A. **53** 36.35N 78.20W
Bugulma U.S.S.R. **30** 54.32N 52.46E
Buie, Loch Scotland **14** 56.20N 5.53W
Builth Wells Wales **10** 52.09N 3.24W
Buitenpost Neth. **27** 53.15N 6.09E
Bujumbura Burundi **47** 3.22S 29.21E
Bukama Zaïre **46** 9.16S 25.52E
Bukavu Zaïre **47** 2.30S 28.49E
Bukhara U.S.S.R. **35** 39.47N 64.26E
Bukittinggi Indonesia **38** 0.18S 100.20E
Bukoba Tanzania **47** 1.20S 31.49E
Bula Indonesia **39** 3.07S 130.27E
Bulagan Mongolia **40** 48.34N 103.12E
Bulan Phil. **39** 12.40N 123.53E
Bulawayo Rhodesia **48** 20.10S 28.43E
Bulgaria Europe **25** 42.30N 25.00E
Bulkington England **8** 52.29N 1.25W
Buller *r.* New Zealand **50** 41.45S 171.35E
Bultfontein R.S.A. **48** 28.17S 26.10E
Bulun U.S.S.R. **31** 70.50N 127.20E
Bumba Zaïre **46** 2.15N 22.32E
Bumi *r.* Rhodesia **48** 17.00S 28.20E
Bum Tso *l.* China **37** 31.30N 91.10E
Bunbury Australia **49** 33.20S 115.34E
Buncrana Rep. of Ire. **18** 55.08N 7.27W
Bundaberg Australia **49** 24.50S 152.21E
Bunde W. Germany **27** 53.12N 7.16E
Bundoran Rep. of Ire. **18** 54.28N 8.17W
Bunessan Scotland **14** 56.18N 6.14W
Bungay England **9** 52.27N 1.26E
Bungo suido *str.* Japan **42** 32.52N 132.30E
Bunia Zaïre **47** 1.30N 30.10E
Buntingford England **9** 51.57N 0.01W
Buol Indonesia **39** 1.12N 121.28E
Buqbuq Egypt **34** 31.30N 25.32E
Bura Coast Kenya **47** 3.30S 38.19E
Buraida Saudi Arabia **35** 26.18N 43.58E
Buraimi U.A.E. **35** 24.15N 55.45E
Burdur Turkey **34** 37.44N 30.17E
Burdwan India **37** 23.15N 87.52E
Bure *r.* England **9** 52.36N 1.44E
Bures England **9** 51.59N 0.46E
Burford England **8** 51.48N 1.38W
Burgan Kuwait **35** 29.00N 47.53E
Burgas Bulgaria **25** 42.30N 27.29E
Burgess Hill England **9** 50.57N 0.07W
Burghead Scotland **17** 57.42N 3.30W
Burgh Heath England **7** 51.18N 0.12W
Burgh le Marsh England **13** 53.10N 0.15E
Burgos Spain **23** 42.21N 3.41W
Burgsteinfurt W. Germany **27** 52.09N 7.21E
Burgsvik Sweden **28** 57.03N 18.19E
Burhanpur India **36** 21.18N 76.08E
Burias *i.* Phil. **39** 12.50N 123.10E
Burica, Punta Panamá **58** 8.05N 82.50W
Burley U.S.A. **52** 42.32N 113.48W
Burlington U.S.A. **57** 44.28N 73.14W
Burma Asia **37** 21.00N 96.30E
Burnham England **7** 51.35N 0.39W
Burnham Beeches England **7** 51.33N 0.39W
Burnham Market England **13** 52.57N 0.43E
Burnham-on-Crouch England **9** 51.37N 0.50E
Burnham-on-Sea England **8** 51.15N 3.00W
Burnley England **12** 53.47N 2.15W
Burntisland Scotland **15** 56.03N 3.15W
Burravoe Scotland **16** 60.23N 1.20W
Burray *i.* Scotland **17** 58.51N 2.54W
Burriana Spain **23** 30.54N 0.05W
Burrow Head Scotland **14** 54.41N 4.24W
Burry Port Wales **11** 51.41N 4.17W
Bursa Turkey **25** 40.11N 29.04E
Burscough England **12** 53.37N 2.51W
Burton Agnes England **13** 54.04N 0.18W
Burton Latimer England **8** 52.23N 0.41W
Burton upon Trent England **12** 52.58N 1.39W
Buru *i.* Indonesia **39** 3.30S 126.30E
Burujird Iran **35** 33.54N 48.47E
Burullus, L. Egypt **34** 31.30N 30.45E
Burundi Africa **47** 3.00S 30.00E
Bururi Burundi **47** 3.58S 29.35E
Burwell Cambs. England **9** 52.17N 0.20E
Burwell Lincs. England **13** 53.19N 0.02E
Bury England **12** 53.36N 2.19W
Bury St. Edmunds England **9** 52.15N 0.42E
Bush *r.* N. Ireland **14** 55.13N 6.31W
Bushey England **7** 51.39N 0.22W
Bushire Iran **35** 28.57N 50.52E
Bushmanland *f.* R.S.A. **48** 29.20S 18.45E
Bushmills N. Ireland **14** 55.12N 6.32W
Bushy Park *f.* England **7** 51.25N 0.19W
Businga Zaïre **46** 3.16N 20.55E
Busira *r.* Zaïre **46** 0.05N 18.18E
Bussum Neth. **27** 52.17N 5.10E
Busu Djanoa Zaïre **46** 1.42N 21.23E
Buta Zaïre **46** 2.50N 24.50E
Bute *i.* Scotland **14** 55.51N 5.07W
Bute, Sd. of Scotland **14** 55.44N 5.10W
Butiaba Uganda **47** 1.48N 31.15E
Butler, Mt. Hong Kong **33** 22.16N 114.12E
Butser Hill England **8** 50.58N 0.58W
Butte U.S.A. **52** 46.00N 112.31W
Butterworth Malaysia **38** 5.24N 100.22E
Butterworth R.S.A. **48** 32.20S 28.09E
Buttevant Rep. of Ire. **19** 52.14N 8.41W
Butt of Lewis *c.* Scotland **16** 58.31N 6.15W
Butuan Phil. **39** 8.56N 125.31E
Butung *i.* Indonesia **39** 5.00S 122.50E
Buxton England **12** 53.16N 1.54W
Buy U.S.S.R. **29** 58.23N 41.27E
Buzău Romania **25** 45.10N 26.49E
Buzău *r.* Romania **25** 45.24N 27.48E
Buzi *r.* Moçambique **48** 19.52S 34.00E
Bydgoszcz Poland **29** 53.16N 17.33E
Byfield England **8** 52.10N 1.15W
Byfleet England **7** 51.20N 0.29W
Bylot I. Canada **55** 73.00N 78.30W
Byrranga Mts. U.S.S.R. **31** 74.50N 101.00E
Byske *r.* Sweden **28** 64.58N 21.10E

C

Cabanatuan Phil. **39** 15.30N 120.58E
Cabimas Venezuela **59** 10.26N 71.27W
Cabinda Angola **46** 5.34S 12.12E
Cabo Delgado *d.* Moçambique **47** 12.30S 39.00E
Cabonga Resr. Canada **57** 47.35N 76.40W
Cabora Bassa Dam Moçambique **47** 15.36S 32.41E
Cabot Str. Canada **55** 47.00N 59.00W
Cabrera *i.* Spain **23** 39.08N 2.56E
Cabrera, Sierra *mts.* Spain **23** 42.10N 6.30W
Cabriel *r.* Spain **23** 39.13N 1.07W
Caçador Brazil **61** 26.51S 50.54W
Čačak Yugo. **29** 43.45N 20.22E
Cáceres Brazil **61** 16.05S 57.40W
Cáceres Spain **23** 39.29N 6.23W
Cachimo *r.* Zaïre **46** 7.02S 21.13E
Cachoeira do Sul Brazil **61** 30.03S 52.52W
Cacin *r.* Spain **23** 37.10N 4.01W
Cacolo Angola **46** 10.09S 19.15E
Caconda Angola **46** 13.46S 15.06E
Cader Idris *mtn.* Wales **10** 52.40N 3.55W
Cadi, Sierra del *mts.* Spain **23** 42.12N 1.35E
Cadillac U.S.A. **56** 44.15N 85.23W
Cádiz Spain **23** 36.32N 6.18W
Cádiz, G. of Spain **23** 37.00N 7.10W
Caen France **22** 49.11N 0.22W
Caerleon Wales **11** 51.36N 2.57W
Caernarvon Wales **10** 53.08N 4.17W
Caernarvon B. Wales **10** 53.05N 4.25W
Caerphilly Wales **11** 51.34N 3.13W
Cagayan de Oro Phil. **39** 8.29N 124.40E
Cagliari Italy **24** 39.14N 9.07E
Cagliari, G. of Med. Sea **24** 39.07N 9.15E
Caguas Puerto Rico **59** 18.08N 66.00W
Caha Mts. Rep. of Ire. **19** 51.44N 9.45W
Caherciveen Rep. of Ire. **19** 51.56N 10.13W
Caher I. Rep. of Ire. **18** 53.43N 10.03W
Cahir Rep. of Ire. **19** 52.23N 7.56W
Cahore Pt. Rep. of Ire. **19** 52.34N 6.12W
Cahors France **22** 44.28N 0.26E
Caianda Angola **46** 11.02S 23.29E
Caibarién Cuba **59** 22.31N 79.28W
Caicos Is. C. America **59** 21.30N 72.00W
Cairn *r.* Scotland **15** 55.05N 3.38W
Cairn Gorm *mtn.* Scotland **17** 57.06N 3.39W
Cairngorms *mts.* Scotland **17** 57.04N 3.30W
Cairns Australia **49** 16.51S 145.43E
Cairnsmore of Carsphairn *mtn.* Scotland **14** 55.15N 4.12W
Cairn Table *mtn.* Scotland **15** 55.29N 4.02W
Cairo Egypt **34** 30.03N 31.15E
Cairo U.S.A. **53** 37.02N 89.02W
Caister-on-Sea England **9** 52.38N 1.43E
Caistor England **13** 53.29N 0.20W
Cajamarca Peru **62** 7.09S 78.32W
Calabar Nigeria **46** 4.56N 8.22E
Calafat Romania **25** 43.59N 22.57E
Calahorra Spain **23** 41.19N 1.58W
Calais France **9** 50.57N 1.52E
Calais U.S.A. **57** 45.11N 67.16W
Calamar Colombia **59** 10.16N 74.55W
Calamian Group *is.* Phil. **39** 12.00N 120.05E
Calamocha Spain **23** 40.54N 1.18W
Calapan Phil. **39** 13.23N 121.10E
Călăraşi Romania **25** 44.11N 27.21E
Calatayud Spain **23** 41.21N 1.39W
Calbayog Phil. **39** 12.04N 124.58E
Calcutta India **37** 22.35N 88.21E
Caldas da Rainha Portugal **23** 39.24N 9.08W
Caldbeck England **12** 54.45N 3.03W
Caldew *r.* England **12** 54.54N 2.55W
Caldy *i.* Wales **11** 51.38N 4.43W
Caledon *r.* R.S.A. **48** 30.35S 26.00E
Calgary Canada **52** 51.05N 114.05W
Cali Colombia **62** 3.24N 76.30W
Caliente U.S.A. **52** 37.36N 114.31W
California *d.* U.S.A. **52** 37.00N 120.00W
California, G. of Mexico **52** 28.30N 112.30W
Callan Rep. of Ire. **19** 52.33N 7.25W
Callander Scotland **14** 56.15N 4.13W
Callanish Scotland **16** 58.12N 6.45W
Callao Peru **62** 12.05S 77.08W
Callington England **11** 50.30N 4.19W
Calne England **8** 51.26N 2.00W
Caltagirone Italy **24** 37.14N 14.30E
Caltanissetta Italy **24** 37.30N 14.05E
Calulo Angola **46** 10.05S 14.56E
Calunga Cameia Angola **46** 11.30S 20.47E
Calvi France **22** 42.34N 8.44E
Calvinia R.S.A. **48** 31.25S 19.47E
Cam *r.* England **9** 52.34N 0.21E
Camabatela Angola **46** 8.20S 15.29E
Camagüey Cuba **59** 21.25N 77.55W
Camagüey *d.* Cuba **59** 21.30N 78.00W
Camagüey, Archipelago de Cuba **59** 22.30N 78.00W
Camapua Brazil **61** 18.34S 54.04W
Camarón, C. Honduras **58** 15.59N 85.00W
Camaross Rep. of Ire. **19** 52.22N 6.44W
Ca Mau, Pointe de *c.* S. Vietnam **38** 8.30N 104.35E
Cambay, G. of India **36** 20.30N 72.00E
Camberley England **7** 51.21N 0.45W
Camberwell England **7** 51.28N 0.05W
Cambodia Asia **38** 12.00N 105.00E
Camborne England **11** 50.12N 5.19W
Cambrai France **27** 50.11N 3.14E
Cambrian Mts. Wales **10** 52.33N 3.33W
Cambridge England **9** 52.13N 0.08E
Cambridge New Zealand **50** 37.53S 175.29E
Cambridge Mass. U.S.A. **57** 42.22N 71.06W
Cambridge Ohio U.S.A. **56** 40.02N 81.36W
Cambridge Bay *town* Canada **54** 69.09N 105.00W
Cambridgeshire *d.* England **9** 52.15N 0.05E
Camden *d.* England **7** 51.33N 0.10W
Camden U.S.A. **57** 39.52N 75.07W
Cameia Nat. Park Angola **46** 12.00S 21.30E
Camel *r.* England **11** 50.31N 4.50W
Camelford England **11** 50.37N 4.41W
Cameron Mts. New Zealand **50** 45.50S 167.00E
Cameroon Africa **46** 4.00N 12.00E
Cameroon, Mt. Cameroon **46** 4.14N 9.09E
Camiri Bolivia **61** 20.08S 63.33W
Campbell, C. New Zealand **50** 41.45S 174.15E
Campbellton Canada **57** 48.00N 66.41W
Campbeltown Scotland **14** 55.25N 5.36W
Campeche Mexico **58** 19.50N 90.30W
Campeche *d.* Mexico **58** 19.00N 90.00W
Campeche B. Mexico **58** 19.30N 94.00W
Campina Grande Brazil **62** 7.15S 35.53W
Campinas Brazil **61** 22.54S 47.06W
Campina Verde Brazil **61** 19.36S 49.25W
Campine *f.* Belgium **27** 51.05N 5.00E
Campo Cameroon **46** 2.22N 9.52E
Campo *r.* Cameroon **46** 2.21N 9.51E
Campobasso Italy **24** 41.34N 14.39E
Campo Grande Brazil **61** 20.24S 54.35W
Campo Maior Portugal **23** 39.01N 7.04W
Campos Brazil **63** 21.46S 41.21W
Campsie Fells *hills* Scotland **14** 56.02N 4.15W
Camrose Canada **54** 53.01N 112.48W
Can *r.* England **7** 51.44N 0.28E
Canada N. America **54** 60.00N 105.00W
Canadian *r.* U.S.A. **53** 35.20N 95.40W
Canadian Shield *f.* N. America **2** 50.00N 80.00W
Çanakkale Turkey **25** 40.09N 26.26E
Canal du Midi France **22** 43.18N 2.00E
Canarreos, Archipelago de los Cuba **58** 21.40N 82.30W
Canary Is. Atlantic Oc. **44** 29.00N 15.00W
Canberra Australia **49** 35.18S 149.08E
Candeleda Spain **23** 40.10N 5.14W
Canea Greece **25** 35.30N 24.02E
Canelones Uruguay **61** 34.32S 56.17W
Cangamba Angola **46** 13.40S 19.50E
Canglass Pt. Rep. of Ire. **19** 51.59N 10.15W
Çankiri Turkey **34** 40.35N 33.37E
Canna *i.* Scotland **16** 57.03N 6.30W
Canna, Sd. of Scotland **16** 57.03N 6.27W
Cannes France **22** 43.33N 7.00E
Cannich Scotland **17** 57.20N 4.45W
Cannock England **8** 52.42N 2.02W
Cannock Chase *f.* England **8** 52.45N 2.00W
Canonbie Scotland **15** 55.05N 2.56W
Canon City U.S.A. **52** 38.27N 105.14W
Cantabria, Sierra de *mts.* Spain **23** 42.40N 2.30W
Cantabrian Mts. Spain **23** 42.55N 5.10W
Canterbury England **9** 51.17N 1.05E
Canterbury Bight New Zealand **50** 44.15S 172.00E
Canton U.S.A. **56** 40.48N 81.23W
Canvey England **7** 51.32N 0.35E
Canvey Island England **7** 51.32N 0.34E
Cao Bang N. Vietnam **37** 22.37N 106.18E
Caoles Scotland **14** 56.32N 6.44W
Caolisport, Loch Scotland **14** 55.54N 5.38W
Cape Breton I. Canada **55** 46.00N 61.00W
Cape Johnson Depth Pacific Oc. **39** 10.20N 127.20E
Capel England **9** 51.08N 0.18W
Capelongo Angola **46** 14.55S 15.03E
Cape Matifou *town* Algeria **23** 36.51N 3.15E
Cape Province *d.* R.S.A. **48** 31.00S 22.00E
Cape Town R.S.A. **48** 33.56S 18.28E
Cape Verde Is. Atlantic Oc. **4** 17.00N 25.00W
Cap Haïtien *town* Haiti **59** 19.47N 72.17W
Cappamore Rep. of Ire. **19** 52.37N 8.21W
Cappoquin Rep. of Ire. **19** 52.09N 7.52W
Capraia *i.* Italy **24** 43.03N 9.50E
Capreol Canada **56** 46.43N 80.56W
Caprera *i.* Italy **24** 41.48N 9.27E
Capri *i.* Italy **24** 40.33N 14.13E
Caprivi Strip *f.* S.W. Africa **48** 17.50S 22.50E
Caquengue Angola **46** 12.23S 22.31E
Cara *i.* Scotland **14** 55.58N 5.45W
Caracal Romania **25** 44.08N 24.18E
Caracas Venezuela **59** 10.35N 66.56W

Caragh, Lough Rep. of Ire. **19** 52.05N 9.51W
Caratasca Lagoon Honduras **58** 15.10N 89.00W
Caravaca Spain **23** 38.06N 1.51W
Carbonara, C. Italy **24** 39.06N 9.32E
Carbondale U.S.A. **57** 41.35N 75.31W
Carbost Scotland **16** 57.27N 6.18W
Carcassonne France **22** 43.13N 2.21E
Carcross Canada **54** 60.11N 134.41W
Cardenas Cuba **58** 23.02N 81.12W
Cardenete Spain **23** 39.46N 1.42W
Cardiff Wales **11** 51.28N 3.11W
Cardigan Wales **10** 52.06N 4.41W
Cardigan B. Wales **10** 52.30N 4.30W
Carentan France **22** 49.18N 1.14W
Carhaix France **22** 48.16N 3.35W
Carhué Argentina **61** 37.10S 62.45W
Caribbean Sea **59** 15.00N 75.00W
Caribou U.S.A. **57** 46.52N 68.01W
Caribou Mts. Canada **54** 58.30N 115.00W
Carignan France **27** 49.38N 5.10E
Caripito Venezuela **59** 10.07N 63.07W
Cark Mtn. Rep. of Ire. **18** 54.53N 7.53W
Carlingford Rep. of Ire. **18** 54.03N 6.12W
Carlingford Lough Rep. of Ire. **18** 54.03N 6.09W
Carlisle England **12** 54.54N 2.55W
Carlow Rep. of Ire. **19** 52.50N 6.46W
Carlow *d.* Rep. of Ire. **19** 52.43N 6.50W
Carloway Scotland **16** 58.17N 6.47W
Carlton England **13** 52.58N 1.06W
Carluke Scotland **15** 55.44N 3.51W
Carmacks Canada **54** 62.04N 136.21W
Carmarthen Wales **10** 51.52N 4.20W
Carmarthen B. Wales **11** 51.40N 4.30W
Carmel Head Wales **10** 53.24N 4.35W
Carmen Mexico **58** 18.38N 91.50W
Carmen de Patagones Argentina **61** 40.45S 63.00W
Carmen I. Mexico **58** 18.35N 91.40W
Carmona Spain **23** 37.28N 5.38W
Carmyllie Scotland **15** 56.36N 2.41W
Carnarvon R.S.A. **48** 30.59S 22.08E
Carndonagh Rep. of Ire. **14** 55.15N 7.15W
Carnedd y Filiast *mtn.* Wales **10** 52.56N 3.40W
Carnegie, L. Australia **49** 26.15S 123.00E
Carn Eige *mtn.* Scotland **16** 57.17N 5.07W
Carnew Rep. of Ire. **19** 52.43N 6.31W
Carnforth England **12** 54.08N 2.47W
Carnic Alps *mts.* Austria/Italy **24** 46.40N 12.48E
Car Nicobar *i.* India **38** 9.00N 92.30E
Carn Mòr *mtn.* Scotland **17** 57.14N 3.13W
Càrn na Loine *mtn.* Scotland **17** 57.24N 3.33W
Carnot C.A.R. **46** 4.59N 16.00E
Carnoustie Scotland **15** 56.30N 2.44W
Carnsore Pt. Rep. of Ire. **19** 52.10N 6.21W
Carnwath Scotland **15** 55.43N 3.37W
Carolina R.S.A. **48** 26.05S 30.07E
Caroline Is. Pacific Oc. **39** 7.50N 145.00E
Caroni *r.* Venezuela **59** 8.20N 62.45W
Carora Venezuela **59** 10.12N 70.07W
Carpathian Mts. Europe **29** 48.45N 23.45E
Carpentaria, G. of Australia **49** 14.00S 140.00E
Carpentras France **22** 44.03N 5.03E
Carpio Spain **23** 41.13N 5.07W
Carra, Lough Rep. of Ire. **18** 53.41N 9.15W
Carradale Scotland **14** 55.35N 5.28W
Carrara Italy **24** 44.04N 10.06E
Carrauntoohil *mtn.* Rep. of Ire. **19** 52.00N 9.45W
Carrbridge Scotland **17** 57.17N 3.49W
Carriacou *i.* Grenada **59** 12.30N 61.35W
Carrick *f.* Scotland **14** 55.12N 4.38W
Carrickfergus N. Ireland **14** 54.43N 5.49W
Carrick Forest *hills* Scotland **14** 55.11N 4.29W
Carrickmacross Rep. of Ire. **18** 53.58N 6.43W
Carrick-on-Shannon Rep. of Ire. **18** 53.57N 8.06W
Carrick-on-Suir Rep. of Ire. **19** 52.21N 7.26W
Carron *r.* Highland Scotland **16** 57.25N 5.27W
Carron *r.* Highland Scotland **17** 57.54N 4.23W
Carron, Loch Scotland **16** 57.23N 5.30W
Carrowkeel Rep. of Ire. **14** 55.07N 7.12W
Carrowmore Lough Rep. of Ire. **18** 54.11N 9.47W
Çarşamba Turkey **34** 41.13N 36.43E
Çarşamba *r.* Turkey **34** 37.52N 31.48E
Carse of Gowrie *f.* Scotland **15** 56.25N 3.15W
Carshalton England **7** 51.22N 0.10W
Carson City U.S.A. **52** 39.10N 119.46W
Carsphairn Scotland **14** 55.13N 4.15W
Carstairs Scotland **15** 55.42N 3.41W
Cartagena Colombia **59** 10.24N 75.33W
Cartagena Spain **23** 37.36N 0.59W
Cartago Costa Rica **58** 9.50N 83.52W
Caruaru Brazil **62** 8.15S 35.55W
Carúpano Venezuela **59** 10.39N 63.14W
Carvin France **27** 50.30N 2.58E
Cary *r.* England **8** 51.10N 3.00W
Casablanca Morocco **44** 33.39N 7.35W
Cascade Pt. New Zealand **50** 44.00S 168.20E
Cascade Range *mts.* U.S.A. **52** 44.00N 144.00W
Cascavel Brazil **61** 24.59S 53.29W
Caserta Italy **24** 41.06N 14.21E
Cashel Rep. of Ire. **19** 52.31N 7.54W
Caspe Spain **23** 41.14N 0.03W
Casper U.S.A. **52** 42.50N 106.20W
Caspian Depression *f.* U.S.S.R. **30** 47.00N 48.00E
Caspian Sea U.S.S.R. **30** 42.00N 51.00E
Cassai *r.* Angola **46** 10.38S 22.15E
Cassley *r.* Scotland **17** 57.58N 4.35W
Castaños Mexico **58** 26.48N 101.26W
Casteljaloux France **22** 44.19N 0.06W
Castellón de la Plana Spain **23** 39.59N 0.03W
Castelo Branco Portugal **23** 39.50N 7.30W
Castlebar Rep. of Ire. **18** 53.52N 9.19W
Castlebay *town* Scotland **16** 56.58N 7.30W
Castlebellingham Rep. of Ire. **18** 53.53N 6.24W
Castleblayney Rep. of Ire. **18** 54.08N 6.46W
Castlebridge Rep. of Ire. **19** 52.23N 6.28W
Castle Cary England **8** 51.06N 2.31W
Castlecomer Rep. of Ire. **19** 52.48N 7.14W
Castledawson N. Ireland **14** 54.47N 6.35W
Castlederg N. Ireland **18** 54.42N 7.37W
Castledermot Rep. of Ire. **19** 52.54N 6.52W
Castle Douglas Scotland **15** 54.56N 3.56W
Castlefin Rep. of Ire. **18** 54.48N 7.41W
Castleford England **13** 53.43N 1.21W
Castlegregory Rep. of Ire. **19** 52.16N 10.01W
Castleisland *town* Rep. of Ire. **19** 52.13N 9.28W
Castlemaine Rep. of Ire. **19** 52.10N 9.41W
Castlemaine Harbour *est.* Rep. of Ire. **19** 52.08N 9.50W
Castle Peak Hong Kong **33** 22.23N 113.57E
Castle Peak B. Hong Kong **33** 22.22N 113.58E
Castle Peak New Town Hong Kong **33** 22.23N 113.58E
Castlepollard Rep. of Ire. **18** 53.41N 7.20W
Castlerea Rep. of Ire. **18** 53.45N 8.30W
Castlerock N. Ireland **14** 55.09N 6.47W
Castletown I.o.M. **12** 54.04N 4.38W
Castletownroche Rep. of Ire. **19** 52.10N 8.28W
Castletownshend Rep. of Ire. **19** 51.32N 9.12W
Castlewellan N. Ireland **18** 54.16N 5.57W
Castres France **22** 43.36N 2.14E
Castries St. Lucia **59** 14.01N 60.59W
Catalca Turkey **25** 41.09N 28.29E
Catamarca Argentina **61** 28.28S 65.46W
Catamarca *d.* Argentina **61** 27.40S 67.10W
Catanduanes *i.* Phil. **39** 13.45N 124.20E
Catanduva Brazil **61** 21.03S 49.00W
Catania Italy **24** 37.31N 15.05E
Catanzaro Italy **25** 38.55N 16.35E
Catarman Phil. **39** 12.28N 124.50E
Caterham England **9** 51.17N 0.04W
Catete Angola **46** 9.09S 13.40E
Catford England **7** 51.26N 0.00
Cat I. Bahamas **59** 24.30N 75.30W
Catoche, C. Mexico **58** 21.38N 87.08W
Catskill Mts. U.S.A. **57** 42.15N 74.15W
Catterick England **12** 54.23N 1.38W
Cauca *r.* Colombia **59** 8.57N 74.30W
Caucasus Mts. U.S.S.R. **29** 43.00N 44.00E
Cauldcleuch Head *mtn.* Scotland **15** 55.18N 2.50W
Caungula Angola **46** 8.26S 18.35E
Caura *r.* Venezuela **59** 7.30N 65.00W
Causeway Rep. of Ire. **19** 52.25N 9.46W
Cavan Rep. of Ire. **18** 54.00N 7.22W
Cavan *d.* Rep. of Ire. **18** 53.58N 7.10W
Cavite Phil. **39** 14.30N 120.54E
Cawood England **13** 53.50N 1.07W
Caxias do Sul Brazil **61** 29.14S 51.10W
Caxito Angola **46** 8.32S 13.38E
Cayenne French Guiana **62** 4.55N 52.18W
Cayman Brac *i.* Cayman Is. **59** 19.44N 79.48W
Cayman Is. C. America **59** 19.00N 81.00W
Cayuga L. U.S.A. **57** 42.40N 76.40W
Cazombo Angola **46** 11.54S 22.56E
Cebollera, Sierra de *mts.* Spain **23** 41.58N 2.30W
Cebu Phil. **39** 10.17N 123.56E
Cebu *i.* Phil. **39** 10.15N 123.45E
Cecina Italy **24** 43.18N 10.30E
Cedar *r.* U.S.A. **56** 41.10N 91.25W
Cedar City U.S.A. **52** 37.40N 103.04W
Cedar Falls *town* U.S.A. **56** 42.34N 92.26W
Cedar Rapids *town* U.S.A. **56** 41.59N 91.39W
Cedros I. Mexico **52** 28.15N 115.15W
Ceduna Australia **49** 32.07S 133.42E
Cefalù Italy **24** 38.01N 14.03E
Ceiriog *r.* Wales **10** 52.57N 3.01W
Cela Angola **46** 11.26S 15.05E
Celaya Mexico **58** 20.32N 100.48W
Celebes *i.* Indonesia **39** 2.00S 120.30E
Celebes Sea Indonesia **39** 3.00N 122.00E
Celje Yugo. **24** 46.15N 15.16E
Celle W. Germany **26** 52.37N 10.05E
Cemaes Bay *town* Wales **10** 53.24N 4.27W
Cemaes Head Wales **10** 52.08N 4.42W
Central *d.* Kenya **47** 0.30S 37.00E
Central *d.* Scotland **14** 56.10N 4.20W
Central, Cordillera *mts.* Bolivia **61** 19.00S 65.00W
Central, Cordillera *mts.* Colombia **62** 6.00N 75.00W
Central African Republic Africa **44** 6.30N 20.00E
Centralia U.S.A. **56** 38.32N 89.08W
Central Russian Uplands U.S.S.R. **29** 53.00N 37.00E
Central Siberian Plateau *f.* U.S.S.R. **31** 66.00N 108.00E
Ceram *i.* Indonesia **39** 3.10S 129.30E
Ceram Sea Pacific Oc. **39** 2.50S 128.00E
Cerignola Italy **24** 41.17N 15.53E
Cernavodă Romania **25** 44.20N 28.02E
Cerne Abbas England **8** 50.49N 2.29W
Cerro de Pasco Peru **62** 10.43S 76.15W
Cerro Marahuaca *mtn.* Venezuela **62** 4.20N 65.30W
Çervera Spain **23** 41.40N 1.16W
Česke Budějovice Czech. **26** 49.00N 14.30E
Cetinje Yugo. **25** 42.24N 18.55E
Ceuta Spain **23** 35.53N 5.19W
Cevennes *mts.* France **22** 44.25N 4.05E
Ceyhan *r.* Turkey **34** 36.54N 34.58E
Ceylon *i.* Asia **3** 7.00N 81.00E
Chacabuco Argentina **61** 34.40S 60.27W
Chaco *d.* Argentina **61** 26.30S 61.00W
Chad Africa **44** 13.00N 19.00E
Chad, L. Africa **44** 13.30N 14.00E
Chadwell St. Mary England **7** 51.29N 0.22E
Chagford England **11** 50.40N 3.50W
Chagos Archipelago Indian Oc. **33** 7.00S 72.00E
Chah Bahar Iran **35** 25.17N 60.41E
Chai Wan Hong Kong **33** 22.16N 114.14E
Chakansur Afghan. **35** 31.10N 62.02E
Cha Kwo Ling Hong Kong **33** 22.18N 114.13E
Chalfont St. Giles England **7** 51.39N 0.35W
Chalfont St. Peter England **7** 51.37N 0.33W
Challans France **22** 46.51N 1.52W
Challenger Depth Pacific Oc. **39** 11.19N 142.15E
Châlons-sur-Marne France **22** 48.58N 4.22E
Chalon-sur-Saône France **22** 46.47N 4.51E
Chamai Thailand **38** 8.10N 99.41E
Chambal *r.* India **40** 26.30N 79.20E
Chambéry France **22** 45.34N 5.55E
Chambeshi *r.* Zambia **47** 11.15S 30.37E
Chamo, L. Ethiopia **47** 4.45N 36.53E
Chamonix France **22** 45.55N 6.52E
Champ Iran **35** 26.40N 60.31E
Champaign U.S.A. **56** 40.07N 88.14W
Champlain, L. U.S.A. **57** 44.45N 73.20W
Chanchiang China **41** 21.05N 110.12E
Chanda India **37** 19.58N 79.21E
Chandeleur Is. U.S.A. **53** 29.50N 88.50W
Chandigarh India **36** 30.44N 76.54E
Changchow Fukien China **41** 24.31N 117.40E
Changchun China **41** 43.50N 125.20E
Changkiakow China **41** 41.00N 114.50E
Changkwansai Ling *mts.* China **42** 44.30N 128.00E
Changsha China **41** 28.10N 113.00E
Changteh China **41** 29.03N 111.35E
Changting China **41** 25.47N 116.17E
Changtu China **40** 31.11N 97.18E
Channel Is. U.K. **11** 49.28N 2.13W
Chanthaburi Thailand **37** 12.38N 102.12E
Chaochow China **41** 23.43N 116.35E
Chao Phraya *r.* Thailand **37** 13.30N 100.25E
Chaotung China **37** 27.30N 103.40E
Chapala, Lago de Mexico **58** 20.00N 103.00W
Chapayevsk U.S.S.R. **29** 52.58N 49.44E
Chapel en le Frith England **12** 53.19N 1.54W
Chapel St. Leonards England **13** 53.14N 0.20E
Chapleau Canada **56** 47.50N 83.24W
Charchan China **40** 38.08N 85.33E
Charchan *r.* China **40** 40.56N 86.27E
Chard England **8** 50.52N 2.59W
Chardzhou U.S.S.R. **35** 39.09N 63.34E
Chari *r.* Chad **44** 13.00N 14.30E
Charing England **9** 51.12N 0.49E
Charkhlik China **40** 39.00N 88.00E
Charleroi Belgium **27** 50.25N 4.27E
Charleston S.C. U.S.A. **53** 32.48N 79.58W
Charleston W. Va. U.S.A. **53** 38.23N 81.20W
Charlestown Rep. of Ire. **18** 53.57N 8.48W
Charlestown of Aberlour Scotland **17** 57.27N 3.14W
Charleville Australia **49** 26.25S 146.13E
Charleville-Mézières France **27** 49.46N 4.43E
Charlotte U.S.A. **53** 35.05N 80.50W
Charlottenburg W. Germany **26** 52.32N 13.18E
Charlottesville U.S.A. **53** 38.02N 78.29W
Charlottetown Canada **55** 46.14N 63.09W
Charolles France **22** 46.26N 4.17E
Chartres France **22** 48.27N 1.30E
Chascomas Argentina **61** 35.34S 58.00W
Châteaubriant France **22** 47.43N 1.22W
Château du Loir France **22** 47.42N 0.25E
Châteaudun France **22** 48.04N 1.20E
Châteauroux France **22** 46.49N 1.41E
Château Thierry France **22** 49.03N 3.24E
Châtelet Belgium **27** 50.24N 4.32E
Châtellerault France **22** 46.49N 0.33E
Chatham Canada **56** 42.24N 82.11W
Chatham England **7** 51.23N 0.32E
Chatham Is. Pacific Oc. **3** 43.00S 176.00W
Châtillon-s-Seine France **22** 47.52N 4.35E
Chattahoochee *r.* U.S.A. **53** 29.45N 85.00W
Chattanooga U.S.A. **53** 35.01N 85.18W
Chatteris England **9** 52.27N 0.03E
Chau Kung I. Hong Kong **33** 22.15N 114.02E
Chaumont France **22** 48.07N 5.08E
Chaves Portugal **23** 41.44N 7.28W
Cheadle England **12** 53.24N 2.13W
Cheam England **7** 51.22N 0.13W
Cheb Czech. **26** 50.04N 12.20E
Cheboksary U.S.S.R. **29** 56.08N 47.12E
Cheboygan U.S.A. **56** 45.40N 84.28W
Cheddar England **8** 51.16N 2.47W
Chekiang *d.* China **41** 29.15N 120.00E
Chek Keng Hong Kong **33** 22.25N 114.20E
Chek Lap Kok Is. Hong Kong **33** 22.18N 113.56E
Cheleken U.S.S.R. **35** 39.26N 53.11E
Chéliff *r.* Algeria **23** 36.15N 2.05E
Chelmer *r.* England **9** 51.43N 0.40E
Chelmsford England **7** 51.44N 0.28E
Cheltenham England **8** 51.53N 2.07W
Chelyabinsk U.S.S.R. **30** 55.10N 61.25E
Chelyuskin, C. U.S.S.R. **31** 77.20N 106.00E
Chemba Moçambique **47** 17.11S 34.53E
Chen, Mt. U.S.S.R. **31** 65.30N 141.20E
Chenab *r.* Asia **36** 29.26N 71.09E
Chengchow China **41** 34.35N 113.38E
Chengte China **41** 40.48N 118.06E
Chengtu China **40** 30.37N 104.06E
Chepstow Wales **11** 51.38N 2.40W
Cher *r.* France **22** 47.12N 2.04E
Cherbourg France **22** 49.38N 1.37W
Cherchel Algeria **23** 36.36N 2.11E
Cheremkhovo U.S.S.R. **31** 53.08N 103.01E
Cherepovets U.S.S.R. **29** 59.05N 37.55E
Cherkassy U.S.S.R. **29** 49.27N 32.04E
Cherkessk U.S.S.R. **29** 44.14N 42.05E
Chernigov U.S.S.R. **29** 51.30N 31.18E
Chernovtsy U.S.S.R. **29** 48.19N 25.52E
Chernyakhovsk U.S.S.R. **28** 54.36N 12.48E
Cherskogo Range *mts.* U.S.S.R. **31** 65.50N 143.00E
Chertsey England **7** 51.23N 0.27W
Chesapeake B. U.S.A. **53** 38.00N 76.00W
Chesham England **7** 51.43N 0.38W
Cheshire *d.* England **12** 53.14N 2.30W
Cheshunt England **7** 51.43N 0.02W
Chesil Beach *f.* England **8** 50.37N 2.33W
Chess *r.* England **7** 51.38N 0.28W
Chessington England **7** 51.21N 0.18W
Chester England **12** 53.12N 2.53W
Chester U.S.A. **57** 39.50N 75.23W
Chesterfield England **13** 53.14N 1.26W
Chesterfield Inlet *town* Canada **55** 63.00N 91.00W
Chester-le-Street England **13** 54.53N 1.34W
Chetumal Mexico **58** 18.30N 88.17W
Chetumal B. Mexico **58** 18.30N 88.00W
Cheung Chau Hong Kong **33** 22.12N 114.01E
Cheung Chau I. Hong Kong **33** 22.12N 114.02E
Cheung Sha Hong Kong **33** 22.14N 113.57E
Cheung Sha Wan Hong Kong **33** 22.20N 114.09E
Cheung Shue Tan Hong Kong **33** 22.25N 114.12E
Chew *r.* England **8** 51.25N 2.30W
Chew Magna England **8** 51.21N 2.37W
Cheyenne U.S.A. **52** 41.08N 104.50W
Chhindwara India **37** 22.04N 78.58E
Chiang Mai Thailand **37** 18.48N 98.59E
Chiang Rai Thailand **37** 19.56N 99.51E
Chiapas *d.* Mexico **58** 16.30N 93.00W
Chiavari Italy **22** 44.19N 9.19E
Chiba Japan **42** 35.38N 140.07E
Chibemba Angola **48** 15.43S 14.07E
Chibia Angola **46** 15.10S 13.42E
Chibougamau Canada **53** 49.56N 74.24W
Chibuto Moçambique **48** 24.40S 33.33E
Chicago U.S.A. **56** 41.50N 87.45W
Chichagof I. U.S.A. **54** 57.55N 135.45W
Chichester England **8** 50.50N 0.47W
Chiclayo Peru **62** 6.47S 79.47W
Chico U.S.A. **52** 39.46N 121.50W
Chicoa Moçambique **48** 15.34S 32.22E
Chicoutimi-Jonquière Canada **57** 48.26N 71.06W
Chicumo Moçambique **48** 22.38S 33.18E
Chiddingstone Causeway *town* England **7** 51.12N 0.08E
Chidley, C. Canada **55** 60.30N 65.00W
Chiemsee *l.* W. Germany **26** 47.55N 12.30E
Chieti Italy **24** 42.22N 14.12E
Chigwell England **7** 51.38N 0.05E
Chihfeng China **41** 41.17N 118.56E
Chihli, G. of China **41** 38.30N 119.30E
Chihuahua Mexico **52** 28.40N 106.06W
Chihuahua *d.* Mexico **58** 28.40N 104.58W
Chikwawa Malaŵi **47** 16.00S 34.54E
Chil *r.* Iran **35** 25.12N 61.30E
Chilapa Mexico **58** 17.31N 99.27W
Chile S. America **63** 33.00S 71.00W
Chillicothe U.S.A. **56** 38.20N 83.00W
Chiloé I. Chile **63** 43.00S 73.00W
Chilpancingo Mexico **58** 17.33N 99.30W
Chiltern Hills England **7** 51.40N 0.53W
Chiltern Hundreds *hills* England **7** 51.37N 0.38W
Chilumba Malaŵi **47** 10.25S 34.18E
Chilung Taiwan **41** 25.10N 121.43E
Chilwa, L. Malaŵi **47** 15.15S 35.45E
Chi Ma Wan Hong Kong **33** 22.14N 113.59E
Chimay Belgium **27** 50.03N 4.20E
Chimborazo *mtn.* Ecuador **62** 1.10S 78.50W
Chimbote Peru **62** 8.58S 78.34W
Chimkent U.S.S.R. **40** 42.16N 69.05E
China Asia **40** 33.00N 103.00E
Chinandega Nicaragua **58** 12.35N 87.10W
Chinati Peak U.S.A. **52** 30.05N 104.30W
Chinchoua Gabon **46** 0.00 9.48E
Chinchow China **41** 41.07N 121.06E
Chindio Moçambique **47** 17.46S 35.23E
Chindwin *r.* Burma **40** 21.30N 95.12E
Chinga Moçambique **47** 15.14S 38.40E
Chingford England **7** 51.37N 0.00
Ching Hai *l.* China **40** 36.40N 100.00E
Chingola Zambia **47** 12.29S 27.53E
Chingpo Hu *l.* China **42** 43.55N 128.58E
Chin Hills Burma **40** 22.40N 93.30E
Chinkiang China **41** 32.05N 119.30E
Chin Ling Shan *mts.* China **41** 33.40N 109.00E
Chinsali Zambia **47** 10.33S 32.05E
Chintheche Malaŵi **47** 11.50S 34.13E
Chipata Zambia **47** 13.37S 32.40E
Chipera Moçambique **47** 15.20S 32.35E
Chipinga Rhodesia **48** 20.12S 32.38E
Chippenham England **8** 51.27N 2.07W
Chippewa *r.* U.S.A. **56** 44.23N 92.05W
Chippewa Falls *town* U.S.A. **56** 44.56N 91.25W
Chipping Norton England **8** 51.56N 1.32W
Chipping Ongar England **7** 51.43N 0.15E
Chipping Sodbury England **8** 51.31N 2.23W
Chipstead England **7** 51.18N 0.10W
Chiquita, Mar *l.* Argentina **61** 30.50S 62.30W
Chir *r.* U.S.S.R. **29** 48.34N 42.53E
Chiredzi Rhodesia **48** 21.03S 31.39E
Chiredzi *r.* Rhodesia **48** 21.10S 31.50E
Chiriqui *mtn.* Panamá **58** 8.49N 82.38W
Chiriqui Lagoon Panamá **58** 9.00N 82.00W
Chirnside Scotland **15** 55.48N 2.12W
Chiromo Malaŵi **47** 16.28S 35.10E
Chirripo *mtn.* Costa Rica **58** 9.31N 83.30W
Chislehurst England **7** 51.25N 0.05E
Chistopol U.S.S.R. **29** 55.25N 50.38E
Chiswellgreen England **7** 51.43N 0.24W
Chiswick England **7** 51.29N 0.16W
Chita U.S.S.R. **41** 52.03N 113.35E
Chitipa Malaŵi **47** 9.41S 33.19E
Chitral Pakistan **36** 35.52N 71.58E
Chittagong Bangla. **37** 22.20N 91.48E
Chitterne England **8** 51.12N 2.01W
Chittoor India **37** 13.13N 79.06E
Chiumbe *r.* Zaïre **46** 6.37S 21.04E
Chiuta, L. Malaŵi/Moçambique **47** 14.45S 35.50E
Chivilcoy Argentina **61** 34.55S 60.03W
Chobe *r.* Botswana **48** 17.45S 25.12E
Chobham England **7** 51.21N 0.37W

Choele Choel Argentina **61** 39.16S 65.38W
Chojnice Poland **29** 53.42N 17.32E
Chokai san *mtn.* Japan **42** 39.08N 140.04E
Cholet France **22** 47.04N 0.53W
Cholon S. Vietnam **38** 10.45N 106.39E
Choluteca Honduras **58** 13.16N 87.11W
Choma Zambia **47** 16.51S 27.04E
Chon Buri Thailand **37** 13.21N 101.01E
Chongjin N. Korea **42** 41.55N 129.50E
Chonju S. Korea **41** 35.50N 127.05E
Chorley England **12** 53.39N 2.39W
Chorleywood England **7** 51.40N 0.29W
Chorzów Poland **29** 50.19N 18.56E
Chott Djerid *f.* Tunisia **44** 33.30N 8.30E
Chott ech Chergui *f.* Algeria **44** 34.00N 0.30E
Chott Melrhir *f.* Algeria **44** 34.15N 7.00E
Christchurch England **8** 50.44N 1.47W
Christchurch New Zealand **50** 43.33S 172.40E
Christianshaab Greenland **55** 68.50N 51.00W
Christmas I. Indian Oc. **38** 10.30S 105.40E
Christmas I. Pacific Oc. **2** 2.00N 157.00W
Chu *r.* U.S.S.R. **40** 42.30N 76.10E
Chuanchow China **41** 24.57N 118.36E
Chuckchee Pen. U.S.S.R. **31** 66.00N 174.30W
Chudleigh England **11** 50.35N 3.36W
Chudovo U.S.S.R. **29** 59.10N 31.41E
Chuen Lung Hong Kong **33** 22.23N 114.06E
Chugoku *d.* Japan **42** 35.00N 133.00E
Chugoku sanchi *mts.* Japan **42** 35.30N 133.00E
Chuhsien China **41** 28.57N 118.52E
Chuiquimula Guatemala **58** 15.52N 89.50W
Chukai Malaysia **38** 4.16N 103.24E
Chulmleigh England **11** 50.55N 3.52W
Chumphon Thailand **37** 10.35N 99.14E
Chuna *r.* U.S.S.R. **31** 58.00N 94.00E
Chung Hom Kok *c.* Hong Kong **33** 22.12N 114.11E
Chungking China **40** 29.31N 106.35E
Chungtien China **37** 28.00N 99.30E
Chung Wan Hong Kong **33** 22.17N 114.09E
Chunya Tanzania **47** 8.31S 33.28E
Chuquisaca *d.* Bolivia **61** 21.00S 63.45W
Chur Switz. **26** 46.52N 9.32E
Churchill Canada **55** 58.45N 94.00W
Churchill *r.* Canada **55** 58.20N 94.15W
Churchill, C. Canada **55** 58.50N 93.00W
Churchill L. Canada **54** 56.00N 108.00W
Churchill Peak Canada **54** 58.10N 125.00W
Church Stoke Wales **10** 52.32N 3.04W
Church Stretton England **10** 52.32N 2.49W
Churn *r.* England **8** 51.38N 1.53W
Ciego de Avila Cuba **59** 21.51N 78.47W
Ciénaga Colombia **62** 10.30N 74.15W
Cienfuegos Cuba **59** 22.10N 80.27W
Cieza Spain **23** 38.14N 1.25W
Cifuentes Spain **23** 40.47N 2.37W
Cijara L. Spain **23** 39.20N 4.50W
Cilo, Mt. Turkey **35** 37.30N 44.00E
Cimarron *r.* U.S.A. **53** 36.15N 96.55W
Cimone, Monte *mtn.* Italy **24** 44.12N 10.42E
Cinca *r.* Spain **23** 41.22N 0.20W
Cincinnati U.S.A. **56** 39.10N 84.30W
Cinderford England **8** 51.49N 2.30W
Ciney Belgium **27** 50.17N 5.06E
Cinto, Mont *mtn.* France **22** 42.23N 8.57E
Cirencester England **8** 51.43N 1.59W
City of London England **7** 51.32N 0.06W
City of Westminster England **7** 51.30N 0.09W
Ciudad Bolívar Venezuela **59** 8.06N 63.36W
Ciudad Camargo Mexico **52** 27.41N 105.10W
Ciudadela Spain **23** 40.00N 3.50E
Ciudad Guerrero Mexico **52** 28.33N 107.28W
Ciudad Ixtepec Mexico **58** 16.32N 95.10W
Ciudad Juárez Mexico **52** 31.42N 106.29W
Ciudad Madera Mexico **58** 22.19N 95.50W
Ciudad Obregon Mexico **52** 27.28N 109.55W
Ciudad Real Spain **23** 38.59N 3.55W
Ciudad Rodrigo Spain **23** 40.36N 6.33W
Ciudad Victoria Mexico **58** 23.43N 99.10W
Civitavecchia Italy **24** 42.06N 11.48E
Civray France **22** 46.09N 0.18E
Civril Turkey **34** 38.18N 29.43E
Cizre Turkey **34** 37.21N 42.11E
Clackmannan Scotland **15** 56.06N 3.46W
Clacton on Sea England **9** 51.47N 1.10E
Clane Rep. of Ire. **18** 53.18N 6.42W
Clapham England **7** 51.27N 0.08W
Clara Rep. of Ire. **18** 53.21N 7.37W
Clare *d.* Rep. of Ire. **19** 52.52N 8.55W
Clare *r.* Rep. of Ire. **18** 53.17N 9.04W
Clare U.S.A. **56** 43.49N 84.47W
Clarecastle Rep. of Ire. **19** 52.49N 8.58W
Claregalway Rep. of Ire. **18** 53.21N 8.57W
Clare I. Rep. of Ire. **18** 53.48N 10.00W
Claremont U.S.A. **57** 43.23N 72.21W
Claremorris Rep. of Ire. **18** 53.44N 9.00W
Clarence *r.* New Zealand **50** 42.10S 173.55E
Clarksburg U.S.A. **56** 39.16N 80.22W
Clatteringshaws Loch Scotland **14** 55.30N 4.25W
Claudy N. Ireland **14** 54.54N 7.09W
Clay Cross England **13** 53.11N 1.26W
Clay Head I.o.M. **12** 54.12N 4.23W
Clayton U.S.A. **52** 36.27N 103.12W
Clear, C. Rep. of Ire. **19** 51.25N 9.32W
Clear I. Rep. of Ire. **19** 51.26N 9.30W
Clear Water B. Hong Kong **33** 22.17N 114.17E
Clearwater L. Canada **55** 56.10N 74.30W
Cleator Moor *town* England **12** 54.30N 3.32W
Clee Hills England **8** 52.25N 2.37W
Cleethorpes England **13** 53.33N 0.02W
Cleobury Mortimer England **8** 52.23N 2.28W
Clermont Ferrand France **22** 45.47N 3.05E
Clevedon England **8** 51.26N 2.52W
Cleveland *d.* England **13** 54.37N 1.08W
Cleveland *f.* England **13** 54.30N 0.55W
Cleveland U.S.A. **56** 41.30N 81.41W
Cleveland Hills England **13** 54.25N 1.10W
Cleveleys England **12** 53.52N 3.01W
Clew B. Rep. of Ire. **18** 53.50N 9.47W
Cliffe England **7** 51.28N 0.30E
Clinton U.S.A. **56** 41.51N 90.12W
Clisham *mtn.* Scotland **16** 57.58N 6.50W
Clitheroe England **12** 53.52N 2.23W
Cloghan Rep. of Ire. **19** 53.13N 7.54W
Clogheen Rep. of Ire. **19** 52.16N 8.00W
Clogher Head Kerry Rep. of Ire. **19** 52.09N 10.28W
Clogher Head Louth Rep. of Ire. **18** 53.47N 6.14W
Clogh Mills N. Ireland **14** 55.00N 6.20W
Clonakilty Rep. of Ire. **19** 51.37N 8.54W
Clonakilty B. Rep. of Ire. **19** 51.35N 8.52W
Clones Rep. of Ire. **18** 54.11N 7.16W
Clonmany Rep. of Ire. **18** 55.16N 7.25W
Clonmel Rep. of Ire. **19** 52.21N 7.44W
Clonmellon Rep. of Ire. **18** 53.40N 7.02W
Clonroche Rep. of Ire. **19** 52.27N 6.45W
Cloppenburg W. Germany **27** 52.52N 8.02E
Cloquet U.S.A. **56** 46.40N 92.30W
Cloud Peak *mtn.* U.S.A. **52** 44.23N 107.11W
Cloughton England **13** 54.20N 0.27W
Clovelly England **11** 51.00N 4.25W
Clovis U.S.A. **52** 34.14N 103.13W
Clowne England **13** 53.18N 1.16W
Cluanie, Loch Scotland **16** 57.08N 5.05W
Cluj Romania **29** 46.47N 23.37E
Clun Forest *f.* England **8** 52.28N 3.10W
Clutha *r.* New Zealand **50** 46.18S 169.05E
Clwyd *d.* Wales **10** 53.07N 3.20W
Clwyd *r.* Wales **10** 53.19N 3.30W
Clwydian Range *mts.* Wales **10** 53.08N 3.15W
Clyde *r.* Scotland **14** 55.58N 4.53W
Clydebank Scotland **14** 55.53N 4.23W
Clydesdale *f.* Scotland **15** 55.41N 3.48W
Coahuila *d.* Mexico **58** 27.00N 103.00W
Coalville England **8** 52.43N 1.21W
Coast *d.* Kenya **47** 3.00S 39.30E
Coast *d.* Tanzania **47** 7.00S 39.00E
Coast Mts. Canada **54** 55.30N 128.00W
Coast Range *mts.* U.S.A. **52** 40.00N 123.00W
Coatbridge Scotland **15** 55.52N 4.02W
Coats I. Canada **55** 62.30N 83.00W
Coatzacoalcos Mexico **58** 18.10N 94.25W
Cobalt Canada **57** 47.24N 79.41W
Cobán Guatemala **58** 15.28N 90.20W
Cobar Australia **49** 31.32S 145.51E
Cobbin's Brook *r.* England **7** 51.40N 0.01W
Cobh Rep. of Ire. **19** 51.50N 8.18W
Cobham Kent England **7** 51.24N 0.25E
Cobham Surrey England **7** 51.20N 0.25W
Cobija Bolivia **62** 11.01S 68.45W
Cobourg Canada **57** 43.58N 78.11W
Coburg W. Germany **26** 50.15N 10.58E
Cochabamba Bolivia **61** 17.26S 66.10W
Cochabamba *d.* Bolivia **61** 17.42S 65.00W
Cochin India **36** 9.56N 76.15E
Cochrane Canada **56** 49.04N 81.02W
Cockburnspath Scotland **15** 55.56N 2.22W
Cockermouth England **12** 54.40N 3.22W
Cockernhoe Green England **7** 51.55N 0.20W
Cockfosters England **7** 51.39N 0.09W
Coco *r.* Honduras **58** 14.58N 83.15W
Cocos Is. Indian Oc. **5** 13.00S 96.00E
Cod, C. U.S.A. **57** 42.08N 70.10W
Cod's Head Rep. of Ire. **19** 51.40N 10.06W
Coesfeld W. Germany **27** 51.55N 7.13E
Coevorden Neth. **27** 52.39N 6.45E
Cofre de Perote *mtn.* Mexico **58** 19.30N 97.10W
Coggeshall England **9** 51.53N 0.41E
Coghinas *r.* Italy **24** 40.57N 8.50E
Cognac France **22** 45.42N 0.19W
Coiba I. Panamá **58** 8.30N 81.45W
Coigach *f.* Scotland **16** 58.00N 5.10W
Coimbatore India **36** 11.00N 76.57E
Coimbra Portugal **23** 40.12N 8.25W
Coin Spain **23** 36.40N 4.45W
Cojedes *r.* Venezuela **59** 7.35N 66.30W
Colchester England **9** 51.54N 0.55E
Coldblow England **7** 51.23N 0.11E
Cold Fell *mtn.* England **15** 54.54N 2.37W
Coldingham Scotland **15** 55.53N 2.10W
Coldstream Scotland **15** 55.39N 2.15W
Coleford England **8** 51.46N 2.38W
Coleman Canada **52** 49.38N 114.28W
Coleraine N. Ireland **14** 55.08N 6.40W
Colesberg R.S.A. **48** 30.44S 25.00E
Colgrave Sd. Scotland **16** 60.30N 0.58W
Colima Mexico **58** 18.00N 103.45W
Colima *d.* Mexico **58** 18.00N 103.45W
Colintraive Scotland **14** 55.56N 5.09W
Coll *i.* Scotland **14** 56.38N 6.34W
Collier Law *mtn.* England **12** 54.45N 1.58W
Collier Row England **7** 51.36N 0.09E
Collier Street *town* England **7** 51.11N 0.27E
Collingwood Canada **56** 44.30N 80.14W
Collingwood New Zealand **50** 40.41S 172.41E
Collinson, C. Hong Kong **33** 22.15N 114.15E
Collin Top *mtn.* N. Ireland **14** 54.58N 6.08W
Collon Rep. of Ire. **18** 53.47N 6.30W
Collooney Rep. of Ire. **18** 54.11N 8.29W
Colmar France **26** 48.05N 7.21E
Colmenar Viejo Spain **23** 40.39N 3.46W
Coln *r.* England **8** 51.41N 1.42W
Colne England **12** 53.51N 2.11W
Colne *r.* Bucks. England **7** 51.26N 0.32W
Colne *r.* Essex England **9** 51.50N 0.59E
Colnett, C. Mexico **52** 31.00N 116.20W
Colney Heath *town* England **7** 51.43N 0 14W
Cologne W. Germany **27** 50.56N 6.57E
Colombia S. America **59** 7.00N 74.00W
Colombo Sri Lanka **37** 6.55N 79.52E
Colón Panama Canal Zone **59** 9.21N 79.54W
Colonsay *i.* Scotland **14** 56.04N 6.13W
Colorado *r.* Argentina **61** 39.50S 62.02W
Colorado *r.* N. America **52** 32.00N 114.58W
Colorado *d.* U.S.A. **52** 39.00N 106.00W
Colorado *r.* Texas U.S.A. **53** 28.30N 96.00W
Colorado Plateau *f.* U.S.A. **52** 35.45N 112.00W
Colorado Springs *town* U.S.A. **52** 38.50N 104.40W
Colsterworth England **13** 52.48N 0.37W
Coltishall England **9** 52.44N 1.22E
Columbia U.S.A. **53** 34.00N 81.00W
Columbia *r.* U.S.A. **52** 46.10N 123.30W
Columbretes, Islas Spain **23** 39.50N 0.40E
Columbus Ga. U.S.A. **53** 32.28N 84.59W
Columbus Ohio U.S.A. **56** 39.59N 83.03W
Colville *r.* U.S.A. **54** 70.06N 151.30W
Colwyn Bay *town* Wales **10** 53.18N 3.43W
Comayagua Honduras **58** 14.30N 87.39W
Combe Martin England **11** 51.12N 4.02W
Comber N. Ireland **14** 54.33N 5.45W
Comeragh Mts. Rep. of Ire. **19** 52.17N 7.34W
Comilla Bangla. **37** 23.28N 91.10E
Como Italy **22** 45.48N 9.04E
Como, L. Italy **24** 46.05N 9.17E
Comodoro Rivadavia Argentina **63** 45.50S 67.30W
Comorin, C. India **36** 8.04N 77.35E
Comoro Is. Africa **47** 12.15S 44.00E
Comrie Scotland **15** 56.23N 4.00W
Cona *r.* Scotland **16** 56.46N 5.13W
Conakry Guinea **44** 9.30N 13.43W
Concarneau France **22** 47.53N 3.55W
Concepcion Argentina **61** 27.20S 65.35W
Concepción Chile **63** 36.50S 73.03W
Concepción Paraguay **61** 23.22S 57.26W
Conception, Pt. U.S.A. **52** 34.27N 120.26W
Conchos *r.* Mexico **52** 29.34N 104.30W
Concord U.S.A. **57** 43.13N 71.34W
Concordia Argentina **63** 31.25S 58.00W
Confolens France **22** 46.01N 0.40E
Congleton England **12** 53.10N 2.12W
Congo Africa **46** 1.00S 16.00E
Congo *r. see* ZaireZaire **46**
Congo Basin *f.* Africa **3** 0.30N 22.00E
Congresbury England **8** 51.20N 2.49W
Coningsby England **13** 53.07N 0.09W
Conisbrough England **13** 53.29N 1.12W
Coniston England **12** 54.22N 3.06W
Coniston Water *l.* England **12** 54.20N 3.05W
Conn, Lough Rep. of Ire. **18** 54.01N 9.15W
Connacht *d.* Rep. of Ire. **18** 53.45N 9.05W
Connah's Quay Wales **10** 53.13N 3.03W
Connecticut *d.* U.S.A. **57** 41.30N 72.50W
Connecticut *r.* U.S.A. **57** 41.20N 72.19W
Connel Scotland **14** 56.27N 5.24W
Connemara *f.* Rep. of Ire. **18** 53.32N 9.56W
Conon *r.* Scotland **17** 57.33N 4.33W
Conselheiro Lafaiete Brazil **61** 20.40S 43.48W
Consett England **12** 54.52N 1.50W
Con Son Is. S. Vietnam **38** 8.30N 106.30E
Constance, L. Europe **26** 47.40N 9.30E
Constanța Romania **25** 44.10N 28.31E
Constantina Spain **23** 37.54N 5.36W
Constantine Algeria **24** 36.22N 6.38E
Constantine Mts. Algeria **24** 36.30N 6.35E
Conway Wales **10** 53.17N 3.50W
Conway *r.* Wales **10** 53.17N 3.49W
Conway B. Wales **10** 53.19N 3.55W
Cook, Mt. New Zealand **50** 43.45S 170.12E
Cook Is. Pacific Oc. **2** 20.00S 157.00W
Cookstown N. Ireland **14** 54.39N 6.46W
Cook Str. New Zealand **50** 41.15S 174.30E
Cooktown Australia **49** 15.29S 145.15E
Coolgreany Rep. of Ire. **19** 52.46N 6.15W
Coomacarrea *mtn.* Rep. of Ire. **19** 51.58N 10.02W
Coomnadiha *mtn.* Rep. of Ire. **19** 51.46N 9.40W
Cootehill Rep. of Ire. **18** 54.05N 7.05W
Copán *ruins* Guatemala **58** 14.52N 89.10W
Copeland I. N. Ireland **14** 54.40N 5.22W
Copenhagen Denmark **28** 55.43N 12.34E
Copiapo Chile **63** 27.20S 70.23W
Copinsay *i.* Scotland **17** 58.54N 2.41W
Copper Belt *f.* Zambia **47** 12.40S 28.00E
Coppermine *r.* Canada **54** 67.54N 115.10W
Coppermine *town* Canada **54** 67.49N 115.12W
Coquet *r.* England **15** 55.21N 1.35W
Coquet I. England **15** 55.20N 1.30W
Coquimbo Chile **63** 30.00S 71.25W
Corabia Romania **25** 43.45N 24.29E
Coral Sea Pacific Oc. **49** 13.00S 148.00E
Corbeil France **22** 48.37N 2.29E
Corbridge England **15** 54.58N 2.01W
Corby England **8** 52.29N 0.41W
Córdoba Argentina **61** 31.25S 64.11W
Córdoba *d.* Argentina **61** 32.00S 64.00W
Cordoba Mexico **58** 18.55N 96.55W
Córdoba Spain **23** 37.53N 4.46W
Córdoba, Sierras de *mts.* Argentina **61** 32.00S 64.10W
Corfu Greece **25** 39.37N 19.50E
Corfu *i.* Greece **25** 39.35N 19.50E
Corigliano Italy **25** 39.36N 16.31E
Corinth Greece **25** 37.56N 22.55E
Corinth, G. of Greece **25** 38.15N 22.30E
Corinto Nicaragua **58** 12.29N 87.14W
Cork Rep. of Ire. **19** 51.54N 8.28W
Cork *d.* Rep. of Ire. **19** 52.00N 8.40W
Cork Harbour *est.* Rep. of Ire. **19** 51.50N 8.17W
Corner Brook *town* Canada **55** 48.58N 57.58W
Corning U.S.A. **57** 42.10N 77.04W
Corno, Monte *mtn.* Italy **24** 42.29N 13.33E
Cornwall Canada **57** 45.02N 74.45W
Cornwall *d.* England **11** 50.26N 4.40W
Cornwallis I. Canada **55** 75.00N 95.00W
Coro Venezuela **59** 11.27N 69.41W
Corofin Rep. of Ire. **19** 52.57N 9.04W
Coromandel New Zealand **50** 36.47S 175.32E
Coromandel Pen. New Zealand **50** 36.45S 175.30E
Coronation G. Canada **54** 68.00N 112.00W
Coronel Pringles Argentina **61** 37.56S 61.25W
Coronel Suárez Argentina **61** 37.30S 61.52W
Corozal Belize **58** 18.23N 88.23W
Corpus Christi U.S.A. **53** 27.47N 97.26W
Corran Scotland **14** 56.43N 5.14W
Corraun Pen. Rep. of Ire. **18** 53.45N 9.52W
Corrib, Lough Rep. of Ire. **20** 53.26N 9.14W
Corrientes Argentina **61** 27.30S 58.48W
Corrientes *d.* Argentina **61** 29.00S 57.30W
Corringham England **7** 51.31N 0.28E
Corry U.S.A. **57** 41.56N 79.39W
Corryhabbie Hill Scotland **17** 57.21N 3.12W
Corryvreckan, G. of Scotland **14** 56.09N 5.42W
Corse, Cap France **24** 43.00N 9.21E
Corsham England **8** 51.26N 2.11W
Corsica *i.* France **22** 42.00N 9.10E
Corte France **22** 42.18N 9.08E
Cortegana Spain **23** 37.55N 6.49W
Cortland U.S.A. **57** 42.36N 76.10W
Coruche Portugal **23** 38.58N 8.31W
Çorum Turkey **34** 40.31N 34.57E
Corumbá Brazil **61** 19.00S 57.25W
Corumbá *r.* Brazil **61** 18.15S 48.55W
Corve *r.* England **8** 52.22N 2.42W
Corwen Wales **10** 52.59N 3.23W
Cosenza Italy **24** 39.17N 16.14E
Coshocton U.S.A. **56** 40.16N 81.53W
Cosne France **22** 47.25N 2.55E
Costa Brava *d.* Spain **23** 41.30N 3.00E
Costa del Sol *d.* Spain **23** 36.30N 4.00W
Costa Rica C. America **58** 10.00N 84.00W
Costelloe Rep. of Ire. **18** 53.17N 9.33W
Côte d'Azur *f.* France **22** 43.20N 6.45E
Cothi *r.* Wales **10** 51.51N 4.10W
Cotonou Dahomey **44** 6.24N 2.31E
Cotopaxi *mtn.* Ecuador **62** 0.40S 38.30W
Cotswold Hills England **8** 51.50N 2.00W
Cottbus E. Germany **26** 51.43N 14.21E
Cottenham England **9** 52.18N 0.08E
Cottingham England **13** 53.17N 0.25W
Coucy France **27** 49.32N 3.20E
Coulagh B. Rep. of Ire. **19** 51.42N 10.00W
Coulonge *r.* Canada **57** 45.55N 76.52W
Coul Pt. Scotland **14** 55.47N 6.29W
Coulsdon England **7** 51.19N 0.07W
Council Bluffs U.S.A. **53** 41.14N 95.54W
Coupar Angus Scotland **15** 56.33N 3.17W
Courtmacsherry B. Rep. of Ire. **19** 51.37N 8.40W
Courtrai Belgium **27** 50.49N 3.17E
Coutances France **22** 49.03N 1.29W
Couvin Belgium **27** 50.03N 4.30E
Coventry England **8** 52.25N 1.31W
Cover *r.* England **12** 54.17N 1.47W
Covilhã Portugal **23** 40.17N 7.30W
Covington U.S.A. **56** 40.06N 84.21W
Cowal *f.* Scotland **14** 56.05N 5.05W
Cowan, L. Australia **49** 32.00S 122.00E
Cowbridge Wales **11** 51.28N 3.28W
Cowdenbeath Scotland **15** 56.07N 3.21W
Cowes England **8** 50.45N 1.18W
Cox's Bazar Bangla. **37** 21.25N 91.59E
Cozumel I. Mexico **58** 20.30N 87.00W
Cracow Poland **29** 50.03N 19.55E
Cradock R.S.A. **48** 32.10S 25.37E
Craignish, Loch Scotland **14** 56.10N 5.32W
Crail Scotland **15** 56.16N 2.38W
Crailsheim W. Germany **26** 49.09N 10.06E
Craiova Romania **25** 44.18N 23.46E
Cramlington England **15** 55.06N 1.33W
Cranbourne England **7** 51.27N 0.42W
Cranbrook Canada **52** 49.29N 115.48W
Cranbrook England **9** 51.06N 0.33E
Cranham England **7** 51.33N 0.16E
Cranleigh England **9** 51.08N 0.29W
Crati *r.* Italy **25** 39.43N 16.29E
Craughwell Rep. of Ire. **19** 53.14N 8.44W
Crawford Scotland **15** 55.28N 3.39W
Crawley England **9** 51.07N 0.10W
Crays Hill *town* England **7** 51.36N 0.30E
Creach Bheinn *mtn.* Scotland **14** 56.40N 5.29W
Creag Meagaidh *mtn.* Scotland **17** 56.57N 4.38W
Credenhill England **8** 52.06N 2.49W
Crediton England **11** 50.47N 3.39W
Cree *r.* Scotland **14** 55.03N 4.35W
Creekmouth England **7** 51.32N 0.06E
Cree L. Canada **54** 57.20N 108.30W
Creeslough Rep. of Ire. **18** 55.07N 7.55W
Creetown Scotland **14** 54.54N 4.22W
Creggan N. Ireland **14** 54.45N 7.02W
Creil France **22** 49.16N 2.29E
Cremona Italy **24** 45.08N 10.03E
Cres *i.* Yugo. **24** 44.50N 14.20E
Crescent City U.S.A. **52** 41.46N 124.13W
Crest France **22** 44.44N 5.02E
Creston U.S.A. **53** 41.04N 94.20W
Creswell England **13** 53.16N 1.12W
Crete *i.* Greece **25** 35.15N 25.00E
Crete, Sea of Med. Sea **25** 36.00N 25.00E
Creus, Cabo Spain **23** 42.20N 3.19E
Creuse *r.* France **22** 47.00N 0.35E
Crewe England **12** 53.06N 2.28W
Crewkerne England **8** 50.53N 2.48W
Crianlarich Scotland **14** 56.23N 4.37W
Criccieth Wales **10** 52.55N 4.15W
Crickhowell Wales **10** 51.52N 3.08W
Cricklade England **8** 51.38N 1.50W
Crieff Scotland **15** 56.23N 3.52W
Criffel *mtn.* Scotland **15** 54.57N 3.38W
Crimea *pen.* U.S.S.R. **29** 45.30N 34.00E
Crinan Scotland **14** 56.06N 5.34W

Cristóbal Colón *mtn.* Colombia **59** 10.53N 73.48W
Crna *r.* Yugo. **25** 41.33N 21.58E
Croaghnameal *mtn.* Rep. of Ire. **18** 54.40N 7.57W
Crockham Hill *town* England **7** 51.14N 0.04E
Crocodile *r.* Transvaal R.S.A. **48** 24.11S 26.48E
Crohy Head Rep. of Ire. **18** 54.55N 8.28W
Cromarty Scotland **17** 57.40N 4.02W
Cromarty Firth *est.* Scotland **17** 57.41N 4.10W
Cromer England **13** 52.56N 1.18E
Cromwell New Zealand **50** 45.03S 169.14E
Crook England **12** 54.43N 1.45W
Crooked I. Bahamas **59** 22.45N 74.00W
Crookhaven Rep. of Ire. **19** 51.29N 9.45W
Croom Rep. of Ire. **19** 52.31N 8.43W
Crosby England **12** 53.30N 3.02W
Crosby I.o.M. **12** 54.11N 4.34W
Cross Fell *mtn.* England **12** 54.43N 2.28W
Cross Gates Wales **10** 52.17N 3.20W
Cross Hands Wales **11** 51.48N 4.05W
Crossmolina Rep. of Ire. **18** 54.06N 9.20W
Crotone Italy **25** 39.05N 17.06E
Crouch *r.* England **9** 51.37N 0.34E
Crowborough England **9** 51.03N 0.09E
Crow Head Rep. of Ire. **19** 51.35N 10.10W
Crowland England **9** 52.41N 0.10W
Crowle England **13** 53.36N 0.49W
Crowlin Is. Scotland **16** 57.20N 5.50W
Crowsnest Pass Canada **52** 49.40N 114.41W
Croxley Green England **7** 51.39N 0.27W
Croyde England **11** 51.07N 4.13W
Croydon England **7** 51.23N 0.06W
Crozet Is. Indian Oc. **5** 46.27S 52.00E
Cruden B. Scotland **17** 57.24N 1.51W
Crumlin N. Ireland **14** 54.38N 6.13W
Crummock Water *l.* England **12** 54.33N 3.19W
Cruz, Cabo Cuba **59** 19.52N 77.44W
Cruz Alta Brazil **61** 28.38S 53.38W
Cruz del Eje Argentina **61** 30.43S 64.45W
Cruzeiro Brazil **61** 22.33S 44.59W
Crymmych Arms Wales **10** 51.59N 4.40W
Cuando *r.* Africa **48** 18.30S 23.32E
Cuando-Cubango *d.* Angola **46** 16.00S 20.00E
Cuangar Angola **48** 17.34S 18.39E
Cuango *r. see* Kwango Zaïre **46**
Cuanza *r.* Angola **46** 9.20S 13.09E
Cuanza Norte *d.* Angola **46** 8.45S 15.00E
Cuanza Sul *d.* Angola **46** 11.00S 15.00E
Cuba C. America **59** 22.00N 79.00W
Cubango *r. see* Okavango Angola **46**
Cubia *r.* Angola **46** 16.00S 21.46E
Cuchi *r.* Angola **46** 15.23S 17.12E
Cuckfield England **9** 51.00N 0.08W
Cuckmere *r.* England **9** 50.45N 0.09E
Cúcuta Colombia **59** 7.55N 72.31W
Cuddalore India **37** 11.43N 79.46E
Cuenca Ecuador **62** 2.54S 79.00W
Cuenca Spain **23** 40.04N 2.07W
Cuenca, Serrania de *mts.* Spain **23** 40.25N 2.00W
Cuernavaca Mexico **58** 18.57N 99.15W
Cuffley England **7** 51.42N 0.06W
Cuiabá Brazil **61** 15.32S 56.05W
Cuiabá *r.* Brazil **62** 17.00S 56.35W
Cuilcagh Mtn. Rep. of Ire. **18** 54.12N 7.50W
Cuillin Hills Scotland **16** 57.12N 6.13W
Cuilo *r. see* Kwilu Zaïre **46**
Cuito *r.* Angola **46** 18.01S 20.50E
Culdaff Rep. of Ire. **14** 55.17N 7.10W
Culemborg Neth. **27** 51.57N 5.14E
Cullen Scotland **17** 57.41N 2.50W
Cullera Spain **23** 39.10N 0.15W
Cullin, Lough Rep. of Ire. **18** 53.59N 9.19W
Cullompton England **8** 50.52N 3.23W
Culm *r.* England **8** 50.46N 3.30W
Culross Scotland **15** 56.03N 3.35W
Culvain *mtn.* Scotland **16** 56.57N 5.16W
Culzean B. Scotland **14** 55.21N 4.50W
Cumaná Venezuela **59** 10.29N 64.12W
Cumberland U.S.A. **57** 39.40N 78.47W
Cumberland *r.* U.S.A. **53** 37.16N 88.25W
Cumberland, L. U.S.A. **53** 37.00N 85.00W
Cumberland Sd. Canada **55** 65.00N 65.30W
Cumbernauld Scotland **15** 55.57N 4.00W
Cumbraes *is.* Scotland **14** 55.45N 4.57W
Cumbria *d.* England **12** 54.30N 3.00W
Cumbrian Mts. England **12** 54.32N 3.05W
Cuminestown Scotland **17** 57.32N 2.20W
Cumnock Scotland **14** 55.27N 4.15W
Cunene *r.* Angola **46** 17.15S 11.50E
Cúneo Italy **22** 44.22N 7.32E
Cunnamulla Australia **49** 28.04S 145.40E
Cunninghame *f.* Scotland **14** 55.40N 4.30W
Cupar Scotland **15** 56.19N 3.01W
Curaçao *i.* Neth. Antilles **59** 12.15N 69.00W
Curaco *r.* Argentina **61** 38.45S 65.10W
Curiapo Venezuela **59** 8.33N 61.05W
Curicó Chile **63** 35.00S 71.15W
Curitiba Brazil **61** 25.24S 49.16W
Currane, Lough Rep. of Ire. **19** 51.50N 10.07W
Curuzú Cuatiá Argentina **61** 29.50S 58.05W
Curvelo Brazil **61** 18.45S 44.27W
Cushendall N. Ireland **14** 55.06N 6.05W
Cushendun N. Ireland **14** 55.07N 6.03W
Cuttack India **37** 20.26N 85.56E
Cuxhaven W. Germany **26** 53.52N 8.42E
Cuyuni *r.* Guyana **59** 6.10N 58.50W
Cuzco Peru **62** 13.32S 72.10W
Cvrsnica *mtn.* Yugo. **25** 43.35N 17.33E
Cwmbran Wales **11** 51.39N 3.01W
Cyclades *is.* Greece **25** 37.00N 25.00E
Cyprus Asia **34** 35.00N 33.00E
Cyrenaica *f.* Libya **45** 31.00N 22.10E
Czechoslovakia Europe **26** 49.30N 15.00E
Czestochowa Poland **29** 50.49N 19.07E

D

Dacca Bangla. **37** 23.42N 90.22E
Daer Resr. Scotland **15** 55.21N 3.37W
Daet Phil. **39** 14.07N 122.58E
Dagenham England **7** 51.33N 0.08E
D'Aguilar, C. Hong Kong **33** 22.12N 114.15E
D'Aguilar Peak Hong Kong **33** 22.13N 114.14E
Dagupan Phil. **39** 16.02N 120.21E
Dahomey Africa **44** 9.30N 2.15E
Daingean Rep. of Ire. **19** 53.18N 7.19W
Dakar Senegal **44** 14.38N 17.27W
Dakhla Oasis Egypt **34** 25.30N 29.00E
Dal *r.* Sweden **28** 60.38N 17.05E
Da Lat S. Vietnam **38** 11.56N 108.25E
Dalbeattie Scotland **15** 54.55N 3.49W
Dalkeith Scotland **15** 55.54N 3.04W
Dallas U.S.A. **53** 32.47N 96.48W
Dalmally Scotland **14** 56.25N 4.58W
Dalmatia *f.* Yugo. **25** 43.30N 17.00E
Dalmellington Scotland **14** 55.19N 4.24W
Daloa Ivory Coast **44** 6.56N 6.28W
Dalry D. and G. Scotland **14** 55.07N 4.10W
Dalry Strath. Scotland **14** 55.43N 4.43W
Daltonganj India **37** 24.02N 84.07E
Dalton-in-Furness England **12** 54.10N 3.11W
Dalwhinnie Scotland **17** 56.56N 4.15W
Dama, Wadi *r.* Saudi Arabia **34** 27.04N 35.48E
Daman India **36** 20.25N 72.58E
Damanhûr Egypt **34** 31.03N 30.28E
Damar *i.* Indonesia **39** 7.10S 128.30E
Damascus Syria **34** 33.30N 36.19E
Damba Angola **46** 6.44S 15.17E
Damghan Iran **35** 36.09N 54.22E
Damh, Loch Scotland **16** 57.29N 5.33W
Damietta Egypt **34** 31.26N 31.48E
Dammam Saudi Arabia **35** 26.23N 50.08E
Dampier Str. Pacific Oc. **39** 0.30S 130.50E
Danakil *f.* Ethiopia **45** 13.00N 41.00E
Da Nang S. Vietnam **38** 16.04N 108.14E
Danbury England **7** 51.44N 0.33E
Danbury U.S.A. **57** 41.24N 73.26W
Dande *r.* Angola **46** 8.30S 13.23E
Danforth U.S.A. **57** 45.42N 67.52W
Danli Honduras **58** 14.02N 86.30W
Dannevirke New Zealand **50** 40.12S 176.08E
Danube *r.* Europe **25** 45.26N 29.38E
Danube, Mouths of the *f.* Romania **25** 45.05N 29.45E
Danville Ill. U.S.A. **56** 40.09N 87.37W
Danville Va. U.S.A. **53** 36.34N 79.25W
Daran Iran **35** 33.00N 50.27E
Darbhanga India **37** 26.10N 85.54E
Dardanelles *str.* Turkey **34** 40.15N 26.30E
Darent *r.* England **7** 51.29N 0.13E
Dar es Salaam Tanzania **47** 6.51S 39.18E
Darfur *mts.* Sudan **45** 12.30N 24.00E
Dargaville New Zealand **50** 35.57S 173.53E
Darhan Suma Mongolia **40** 49.34N 106.23E
Darien, G. of Colombia **59** 9.20N 77.00W
Darjeeling India **37** 27.02N 88.20E
Darling *r.* Australia **49** 34.05S 141.57E
Darlington England **13** 54.33N 1.33W
Darmstadt W. Germany **26** 49.52N 8.30E
Darreh Gaz Iran **35** 37.22N 59.08E
Dart *r.* England **11** 50.24N 3.41W
Dartford England **7** 51.27N 0.14E
Dartmoor Forest *hills* England **11** 50.33N 3.55W
Dartmouth England **11** 50.21N 3.35W
Darton England **13** 53.36N 1.32W
Dartry Mts. Rep. of Ire. **18** 54.23N 8.25W
Darvel Scotland **14** 55.37N 4.17W
Darvel B. Malaysia **38** 4.40N 118.30E
Darwen England **12** 53.42N 2.29W
Darwin Australia **49** 12.23S 130.44E
Dasht *r.* Pakistan **35** 25.07N 61.45E
Dasht-e-Kavir *des.* Iran **35** 34.40N 55.00E
Dasht-e-Lut *des.* Iran **35** 31.30N 58.00E
Dashtiari Iran **35** 25.29N 61.15E
Dasht-i-Margo *des.* Afghan. **35** 30.45N 63.00E
Dasht-i-Zirreh *des.* Afghan. **35** 30.00N 62.00E
Datchet England **7** 51.30N 0.35W
Daugavpils U.S.S.R. **28** 55.52N 26.31E
Daulatabad Iran **35** 28.19N 56.40E
Daun W. Germany **27** 50.11N 6.50E
Dauphin Canada **52** 51.09N 100.05W
Dauphiné, Alpes du *mts.* France **22** 44.35N 5.45E
Davangere India **36** 14.30N 75.52E
Davao Phil. **39** 7.05N 125.38E
Davao G. Phil. **39** 6.30N 126.00E
Davenport U.S.A. **56** 41.32N 90.36W
Daventry England **8** 52.16N 1.10W
David Panamá **58** 8.26N 82.26W
Davis Str. N. America **55** 66.00N 58.00W
Davos Switz. **26** 46.47N 9.50E
Dawa Palma *r.* Ethiopia **47** 4.10N 42.05E
Dawley England **8** 52.40N 2.29W
Dawlish England **8** 50.34N 3.28W
Dawna Range *mts.* Asia **38** 16.10N 98.30E
Dawros Head Rep. of Ire. **18** 54.50N 8.35W
Dawson Canada **54** 64.04N 139.24W
Dawson Creek *town* Canada **54** 55.44N 120.15W
Dax France **22** 43.43N 1.03W
Dayton U.S.A. **56** 39.45N 84.10W
Daytona Beach *town* U.S.A. **53** 29.11N 81.01W
De Aar R.S.A. **48** 30.39S 24.00E
Dead Sea Jordan **34** 31.25N 35.30E
Deal England **9** 51.13N 1.25E
Deán Funes Argentina **61** 30.25S 64.22W
Death Valley *f.* U.S.A. **52** 36.00N 116.45W
Deauville France **22** 49.21N 0.04E
Deben *r.* England **9** 52.06N 1.20E
Debenham England **9** 52.14N 1.10E
Debrecen Hungary **29** 47.30N 21.37E
Decatur Ill. U.S.A. **56** 39.51N 88.57W
Decatur Ind. U.S.A. **56** 40.50N 84.57W
Deccan *f.* India **36** 18.30N 77.30E
Dedza Malaŵi **47** 14.20S 34.24E
Dee *r.* Rep. of Ire. **18** 53.52N 6.21W
Dee *r.* D. and G. Scotland **15** 54.50N 4.05W
Dee *r.* Grampian Scotland **17** 57.07N 2.04W
Dee *r.* Wales **10** 53.13N 3.05W
Deel *r.* Mayo Rep. of Ire. **18** 54.06N 9.17W
Deepcut England **7** 51.19N 0.40W
Deeping Fen *f.* England **9** 52.45N 0.15W
Defiance U.S.A. **56** 41.17N 84.21W
Deh Bid Iran **35** 30.38N 53.12E
Dehra Dun India **37** 30.19N 78.00E
Deinze Belgium **27** 50.59N 3.32E
Deir-ez-Zor Syria **34** 35.20N 40.08E
Dej Romania **29** 47.08N 23.55E
Dekese Zaïre **46** 3.25S 21.24E
Delano U.S.A. **52** 35.45N 119.16W
Delaware *d.* U.S.A. **57** 39.00N 75.30W
Delaware *r.* U.S.A. **57** 39.15N 75.20W
Delaware B. U.S.A. **57** 39.00N 75.05W
Delft Neth. **27** 52.01N 4.23E
Delfzijl Neth. **27** 53.20N 6.56E
Delgado, C. Moçambique **47** 10.45S 40.38E
Delhi India **36** 28.40N 77.14E
Delicias Mexico **52** 28.10N 105.30W
Dellys Algeria **23** 36.57N 3.55E
Delmenhorst W. Germany **26** 53.03N 8.37E
De Long Str. U.S.S.R. **31** 70.00N 178.00E
Del Rio U.S.A. **52** 29.23N 100.56W
Delta U.S.A. **52** 39.22N 112.35W
Delvin Rep. of Ire. **18** 53.37N 7.06W
Demavend *mtn.* Iran **35** 35.47N 52.04E
Demba Zaïre **46** 5.28S 22.14E
Demer *r.* Belgium **27** 50.59N 4.42E
Demirkazik *mtn.* Turkey **34** 37.50N 35.08E
Denbigh Wales **10** 53.11N 3.25W
Den Burg Neth. **27** 53.03N 4.47E
Denby Dale *town* England **12** 53.35N 1.40W
Dendermonde Belgium **27** 51.01N 4.07E
Dendre *r.* Belgium **27** 51.01N 4.07E
Denham England **7** 51.35N 0.31W
Den Helder Neth. **27** 52.58N 4.46E
Denia Spain **23** 38.51N 0.07E
Denizli Turkey **34** 37.46N 29.05E
Denmark Europe **28** 56.00N 10.00E
Denmark Str. Greenland/Iceland **2** 66.00N 25.00W
Denny Scotland **15** 56.02N 3.55W
Den Oever Neth. **27** 52.56N 5.01E
Denpasar Indonesia **38** 8.40S 115.14E
Denver U.S.A. **52** 39.45N 104.58W
Deogarh India **37** 21.22N 84.45E
Deptford England **7** 51.29N 0.03W
Dera Ismail Khan Pakistan **36** 31.51N 70.56E
Derbent U.S.S.R. **35** 42.03N 48.18E
Derby Australia **49** 17.19S 123.38E
Derby England **13** 52.55N 1.28W
Derbyshire *d.* England **13** 52.55N 1.28W
Derg *r.* N. Ireland **18** 54.44N 7.27W
Derg, Lough Donegal Rep. of Ire. **18** 54.37N 7.55W
Derg, Lough Tipperary Rep. of Ire. **19** 52.57N 8.18W
Derna Libya **45** 32.45N 22.39E
Derravaragh, Lough Rep. of Ire. **18** 53.39N 7.23W
Derry *r.* Rep. of Ire. **19** 52.41N 6.40W
Derrynasaggart Mts. Rep. of Ire. **19** 51.58N 9.15W
Derryveagh Mts. Rep. of Ire. **18** 55.00N 8.07W
Dersingham England **13** 52.51N 0.30E
Dervaig Scotland **14** 56.35N 6.11W
Derwent *r.* Cumbria England **12** 54.38N 3.34W
Derwent *r.* Derbys. England **13** 52.52N 1.19W
Derwent *r.* N. Yorks. England **13** 53.44N 0.57W
Derwent *r.* T. and W. England **12** 54.58N 1.40W
Derwent Water *l.* England **12** 54.35N 3.09W
Desborough England **8** 52.27N 0.50W
Deseado Argentina **63** 47.44S 65.56W
Des Moines U.S.A. **53** 41.35N 93.35W
Desna *r.* U.S.S.R. **29** 50.32N 30.37E
Dessau E. Germany **26** 51.51N 12.15E
Desvres France **9** 50.40N 1.50E
Detroit U.S.A. **56** 42.23N 83.05W
Dett Rhodesia **48** 18.38S 26.50E
Deurne Belgium **27** 51.13N 4.26E
Deva Romania **25** 45.54N 22.55E
Deventer Neth. **27** 52.15N 6.10E
Deveron *r.* Scotland **17** 57.40N 2.30W
Devilsbit Mtn. Rep. of Ire. **19** 52.50N 7.55W
Devil's Bridge Wales **10** 52.23N 3.50W
Devils Lake *town* U.S.A. **52** 48.08N 98.50W
Devizes England **8** 51.21N 2.00W
Devon *d.* England **11** 50.50N 3.40W
Devon I. Canada **55** 75.00N 86.00W
Devonport New Zealand **50** 36.49S 174.49E
Devrez *r.* Turkey **34** 41.07N 34.25E
Dewsbury England **12** 53.42N 1.38W
Dhahran Saudi Arabia **35** 26.18N 50.08E
Dhaulagiri *mtn.* Nepal **37** 28.39N 83.28E
Dhulia India **36** 20.52N 74.50E
Diamond Hill Hong Kong **33** 22.20N 114.12E
Dibaya Zaïre **46** 6.31S 22.57E
Dibbagh, Jebel *mtn.* Saudi Arabia **34** 27.51N 35.43E
Dibrugarh India **37** 27.29N 94.56E
Dickinson U.S.A. **52** 46.54N 102.48W
Didcot England **8** 51.36N 1.14W
Die France **22** 44.45N 5.23E
Diekirch Lux. **27** 49.52N 6.10E
Dieppe France **22** 49.55N 1.05E
Dieren Neth. **27** 52.03N 6.06E
Diest Belgium **27** 50.59N 5.03E
Dieuze France **26** 48.49N 6.43E
Digby Canada **53** 44.37N 65.47W
Digne France **22** 44.05N 6.14E
Digoel *r.* Indonesia **39** 7.10S 139.08E
Dijle *r.* Belgium **27** 51.02N 4.25E
Dijon France **22** 47.20N 5.02E
Dikili Turkey **25** 39.05N 26.52E
Dili Port. Timor **39** 8.35S 125.35E
Dillon U.S.A. **52** 45.14N 112.38W
Dilolo Zaïre **46** 10.39S 22.20E
Dimbelenge Zaïre **46** 5.32S 23.04E
Dimbovita *r.* Romania **25** 44.13N 26.22E
Dimitrovgrad Bulgaria **25** 42.01N 25.34E
Dimitrovo Bulgaria **25** 42.35N 23.03E
Dinagat *i.* Phil. **39** 10.15N 125.30E
Dinan France **22** 48.27N 2.02W
Dinant Belgium **27** 50.16N 4.55E
Dinaric Alps *mts.* Yugo. **25** 44.00N 16.30E
Dinas Head Wales **10** 52.03N 4.50W
Dinas Mawddwy Wales **10** 52.44N 3.41W
Dingle Rep. of Ire. **19** 52.09N 10.17W
Dingle B. Rep. of Ire. **19** 52.05N 10.12W
Dingwall Scotland **17** 57.35N 4.26W
Diourbel Senegal **44** 14.30N 16.10W
Dipolog Phil. **39** 8.34N 123.28E
Dippin Head Scotland **14** 55.27N 5.05W
Diredawa Ethiopia **45** 9.35N 41.50E
Disappointment, L. Australia **49** 23.30S 122.55E
Disko I. Greenland **55** 69.45N 53.00W
Disna *r.* U.S.S.R. **28** 55.30N 28.20E
Diss England **9** 52.23N 1.06E
District of Columbia *d.* U.S.A. **57** 38.55N 77.00W
Ditchling Beacon *hill* England **9** 50.55N 0.08W
Diu India **36** 20.41N 71.03E
Divrigi Turkey **34** 39.23N 38.06E
Dixmude Belgium **27** 51.01N 2.52E
Dixon Entrance *str.* Canada **54** 54.10N 133.30W
Diyala *r.* Iraq **35** 33.13N 44.33E
Diyarbakir Turkey **34** 37.55N 40.14E
Dizful Iran **35** 32.24N 48.27E
Dja *r.* Cameroon **46** 1.38N 16.03E
Djado Plateau *f.* Niger **44** 22.00N 12.30E
Djailolo Indonesia **39** 1.05N 127.29E
Djajapura Indonesia **39** 2.28S 160.38E
Djajawidjaja Mts. Asia **39** 4.20S 139.10E
Djakarta Indonesia **38** 6.08S 106.45E
Djambala Congo **46** 2.33S 14.38E
Djambi Indonesia **38** 1.36S 103.39E
Djelfa Algeria **44** 34.43N 3.14E
Djibouti F.T.A.I. **45** 11.35N 43.11E
Djolu Zaïre **46** 0.35N 22.28E
Djouah *r.* Gabon **46** 1.16N 13.12E
Djugu Zaïre **47** 1.55N 30.31E
Dneprodzerzhinsk U.S.S.R. **29** 48.30N 34.37E
Dnepropetrovsk U.S.S.R. **29** 48.29N 35.00E
Dnestr *r.* U.S.S.R. **29** 46.21N 30.20E
Dnieper *r.* U.S.S.R. **29** 46.30N 32.25E
Dno U.S.S.R. **29** 57.50N 30.00E
Doboj Yugo. **25** 44.44N 18.02E
Dobruja *f.* Romania **29** 44.30N 28.15E
Docking England **13** 52.55N 0.39E
Dodecanese *is.* Greece **25** 37.00N 27.00E
Dodge City U.S.A. **52** 37.45N 100.02W
Dodman Pt. England **11** 50.13N 4.48W
Dodoma Tanzania **47** 6.10S 35.40E
Dodoma *d.* Tanzania **47** 6.00S 36.00E
Doetinchem Neth. **27** 51.57N 6.17E
Dog L. Canada **56** 48.45N 89.30W
Doha Qatar **35** 25.15N 51.34E
Dokkum Neth. **27** 53.20N 6.00E
Dolbeau Canada **57** 48.52N 72.15W
Dôle France **22** 47.05N 5.30E
Dolgellau Wales **10** 52.44N 3.53W
Dolisie Congo **46** 4.09S 12.40E
Dollar Scotland **15** 56.09N 3.41W
Dollart *b.* W. Germany **27** 53.20N 7.10E
Dolo Ethiopia **47** 4.11N 42.03E
Dolomites *mts.* Italy **26** 46.25N 11.50E
Dolores Argentina **61** 36.23S 57.44W
Dolphin and Union Str. Canada **54** 69.20N 118.00W
Dombås Norway **28** 62.05N 9.07E
Dombe Grande Angola **46** 13.00S 13.06E
Dominica C. America **59** 15.30N 61.30W
Dominican Republic C. America **59** 18.00N 70.00W
Dommel *r.* Neth. **27** 51.44N 5.17E
Don *r.* England **13** 53.41N 0.50W
Don *r.* Scotland **17** 57.10N 2.05W
Don *r.* U.S.S.R. **29** 47.06N 39.16E
Donaghadee N. Ireland **14** 54.39N 5.33W
Donauworth W. Germany **26** 48.44N 10.48E
Don Benito Spain **23** 38.57N 5.52W
Doncaster England **13** 53.31N 1.09W
Dondo Angola **46** 9.40S 14.25E
Donegal Rep. of Ire. **18** 54.39N 8.06W
Donegal *d.* Rep. of Ire. **18** 54.52N 8.00W
Donegal B. Rep. of Ire. **18** 54.32N 8.18W
Donegal Pt. Rep. of Ire. **19** 52.43N 9.38W
Donets *r.* U.S.S.R. **29** 47.35N 40.55E
Donets Basin *f.* U.S.S.R. **29** 48.20N 38.15E
Donetsk U.S.S.R. **29** 48.00N 37.50E
Donggala Indonesia **38** 0.48S 119.45E
Dong Hoi N. Vietnam **38** 17.32N 106.35E
Dongkala Indonesia **39** 0.12N 120.07E
Dongola Sudan **45** 19.10N 30.27E
Dongou Congo **46** 2.05N 18.00E
Donington England **13** 52.55N 0.12W
Dooega Head Rep. of Ire. **18** 53.55N 10.03W
Doon *r.* Scotland **14** 55.26N 4.38W
Doon, Loch Scotland **14** 55.15N 4.23W
Doonbeg *r.* Rep. of Ire. **19** 52.44N 9.32W
Dora Baltea *r.* Italy **22** 45.08N 8.32E
Dora Riparia *r.* Italy **22** 45.07N 7.45E
Dorchester England **8** 50.52N 2.28W
Dordogne *r.* France **22** 45.03N 0.34W
Dordrecht Neth. **27** 51.48N 4.40E
Dordrecht R.S.A. **48** 31.22S 27.03E
Dore, Mont *mtn.* France **22** 45.32N 2.49E
Dores Scotland **17** 57.23N 4.20W
Dorking England **7** 51.14N 0.20W

Ennerdale Water *l.* England 12 54.31N 3.21W
Ennis Rep. of Ire. 19 52.51N 9.00W
Enniscorthy Rep. of Ire. 19 52.30N 6.35W
Enniskean Rep. of Ire. 19 51.45N 8.55W
Enniskerry Rep. of Ire. 19 53.11N 6.12W
Enniskillen N. Ireland 18 54.21N 7.40W
Ennistymon Rep. of Ire. 19 52.56N 9.18W
Enns *r.* Austria 26 48.14N 14.22E
Enrick *r.* Scotland 17 57.20N 4.28W
Enschede Neth. 27 52.13N 6.54E
Ensenada Mexico 52 31.53N 116.35W
Entebbe Uganda 47 0.08N 32.29E
Entre Rios *d.* Argentina 61 31.50S 59.00W
Enugu Nigeria 44 6.20N 7.29E
Epe Neth. 27 52.21N 5.59E
Epernay France 22 49.02N 3.58E
Epinal France 26 48.10N 6.28E
Eport, Loch Scotland 16 57.30N 7.10W
Epping England 7 51.42N 0.07E
Epping Forest *f.* England 7 51.39N 0.03E
Epping Green England 7 51.43N 0.06E
Epsom England 7 51.20N 0.16W
Epworth England 13 53.30N 0.50W
Equateur *d.* Zaïre 46 0.00 21.00E
Equatorial Guinea Africa 46 2.00N 10.00E
Erbil Iraq 35 36.12N 44.01E
Erciyaş, Mt. Turkey 34 38.33N 35.25E
Erdre *r.* France 22 47.27N 1.34W
Erebus, Mt. Antarctica 64 77.40S 167.20E
Ereğli Konya Turkey 34 37.30N 34.02E
Ereğli Zonguldak Turkey 34 41.17N 31.26E
Erexim Brazil 61 27.35S 52.15W
Erft *r.* W. Germany 27 51.12N 6.45E
Erfurt E. Germany 26 50.58N 11.02E
Ergani Turkey 34 38.17N 39.44E
Ergene *r.* Turkey 25 41.02N 26.22E
Erhlien China 41 43.50N 112.00E
Eriboll, Loch Scotland 17 58.28N 4.41W
Ericht, Loch Scotland 17 56.52N 4.20W
Erie U.S.A. 56 42.07N 80.05W
Erie, L. Canada/U.S.A. 56 42.15N 81.00W
Erigavo Somali Rep. 45 10.40N 47.20E
Erimo saki *c.* Japan 42 41.55N 143.13E
Eriskay *i.* Scotland 16 57.04N 7.17W
Erisort, Loch Scotland 16 58.06N 6.30W
Erith England 7 51.29N 0.11E
Erkelenz W. Germany 27 51.05N 6.18E
Ermelo Neth. 27 52.19N 5.38E
Ermelo R.S.A. 48 26.32S 29.59E
Erne *r.* Rep. of Ire. 18 54.30N 8.17W
Er Rahad Sudan 45 12.42N 30.33E
Errigal Mtn. Rep. of Ire. 18 55.02N 8.08W
Erris Head Rep. of Ire. 18 54.19N 10.00W
Er Roseires Sudan 45 11.52N 34.23E
Erzincan Turkey 34 39.44N 39.30E
Erzurum Turkey 34 39.57N 41.17E
Esbjerg Denmark 28 55.28N 8.28E
Escanaba U.S.A. 56 45.47N 87.04W
Esch Lux. 27 49.31N 5.59E
Eschweiler W. Germany 27 50.49N 6.16E
Escondido *r.* Nicaragua 58 11.58N 83.45W
Escuintla Guatemala 58 14.18N 90.47W
Esha Ness *c.* Scotland 16 60.29N 1.37W
Esher England 7 51.23N 0.22W
Eshowe R.S.A. 48 28.54S 31.28E
Esk *r.* Cumbria England 12 54.20N 3.24W
Esk *r.* Cumbria England 15 54.58N 3.02W
Esk *r.* N. Yorks. England 13 54.29N 0.37W
Eskdale *f.* Scotland 15 55.13N 3.08W
Eskilstuna Sweden 28 59.22N 16.31E
Eskimo Point *town* Canada 55 61.10N 94.15W
Eskişehir Turkey 34 39.46N 30.30E
Esla *r.* Spain 23 41.50N 5.48W
Esperance Australia 49 33.49S 121.52E
Esperanza Argentina 61 31.29S 61.00W
Esquel Argentina 63 42.55S 71.20W
Essen W. Germany 27 51.27N 6.57E
Essendon England 7 51.46N 0.09W
Essequibo *r.* Guyana 62 6.48N 58.23W
Essex *d.* England 7 51.46N 0.30E
Esslingen W. Germany 26 48.45N 9.19E
Estats, Pic d' *mtn.* Spain 22 42.40N 1.23E
Estepona Spain 23 36.26N 5.09W
Estevan Canada 52 49.09N 103.00W
Eston England 13 54.34N 1.07W
Estonia Soviet Socialist Republic *d.* U.S.S.R. 28 58.45N 25.30E
Estrêla, Serra da *mts.* Portugal 23 40.20N 7.40W
Estremoz Portugal 23 38.50N 7.35W
Etaples France 22 50.31N 1.39E
Ethiopia Africa 45 10.00N 39.00E
Ethiopian Highlands Ethiopia 45 10.00N 37.00E
Etive, Loch Scotland 14 56.27N 5.15W
Etna, Mt. Italy 24 37.43N 14.59E
Eton England 7 51.31N 0.37W
Etosha Game Res. S.W. Africa 48 18.45S 14.55E
Etosha Pan *f.* S.W. Africa 48 18.50S 16.30E
Ettelbrück Lux. 27 49.51N 6.06E
Ettrick *r.* Scotland 15 55.36N 2.49W
Ettrick Forest *f.* Scotland 15 55.30N 3.00W
Ettrick Pen *mtn.* Scotland 15 55.21N 3.16W
Et Tubeiq, Jebel *mts.* Saudi Arabia 34 29.30N 37.15E
Euboea *i.* Greece 25 38.30N 23.50E
Euclid U.S.A. 56 41.34N 81.33W
Eufaula Resr. U.S.A. 53 35.15N 95.35W
Eugene U.S.A. 52 44.03N 123.07W
Eugenia, Punta *c.* Mexico 52 27.50N 115.50W
Eupen Belgium 27 50.38N 6.04E
Euphrates *r.* Asia 35 31.00N 47.27E
Eureka U.S.A. 52 40.49N 124.10W
Europa, Picos de *mts.* Spain 23 43.10N 4.40W
Europe 6
Europoort Neth. 27 51.56N 4.08E
Euskirchen W. Germany 27 50.40N 6.47E
Evale Angola 46 16.24S 15.50E
Evans, L. Canada 53 50.55N 77.00W
Evanston U.S.A. 56 42.02N 87.41W
Evanton Scotland 17 57.39N 4.21W
Evenlode *r.* England 8 51.46N 1.21W
Evercreech England 8 51.08N 2.30W
Everest, Mt. Asia 37 27.59N 86.56E
Evesham England 8 52.06N 1.57W
Evje Norway 28 58.36N 7.51E
Evora Portugal 23 38.34N 7.54W
Evreux France 22 49.03N 1.11E
Ewe, Loch Scotland 16 57.48N 5.38W
Ewell England 7 51.21N 0.15W
Exe *r.* England 11 50.40N 3.28W
Exeter England 11 50.43N 3.31W
Exmoor Forest *hills* England 11 51.08N 3.45W
Exmouth England 8 50.37N 3.24W
Exuma Is. Bahamas 59 24.00N 76.00W
Eyasi, L. Tanzania 47 3.40S 35.00E
Eye England 9 52.19N 1.09E
Eyemouth Scotland 15 55.52N 2.05W
Eygurande France 22 45.40N 2.26E
Eynhallow Sd. Scotland 17 59.08N 3.05W
Eynort, Loch Scotland 16 57.13N 7.15W
Eynsford England 7 51.22N 0.14E
Eyre, L. Australia 49 28.30S 137.25E
Eyrecourt Rep. of Ire. 19 53.11N 8.08W

F

Fåborg Denmark 28 55.06N 10.15E
Faenza Italy 24 44.17N 11.52E
Fagernes Norway 28 60.59N 9.17E
Fagersta Sweden 28 59.59N 15.49E
Fairbanks U.S.A. 54 64.50N 147.50W
Fairbourne Wales 10 52.42N 4.03W
Fair Head N. Ireland 14 55.13N 6.09W
Fair Isle Scotland 16 59.32N 1.38W
Fairlie New Zealand 50 44.05S 170.50E
Fairmont U.S.A. 56 39.28N 80.08W
Fairweather, Mt. U.S.A. 54 59.00N 137.30W
Faizabad Afghan. 40 36.17N 64.49E
Faizabad India 37 26.46N 82.08E
Fajr, Wadi *r.* Saudi Arabia 34 30.00N 38.25E
Fakenham England 13 52.50N 0.51E
Fakfak Asia 39 2.55S 132.17E
Fal *r.* England 11 50.14N 4.58W
Falaise France 22 48.54N 0.11W
Falcarragh Rep. of Ire. 18 55.08N 8.06W
Falcone, C. Italy 24 40.57N 8.12E
Falcon Resr. U.S.A. 58 26.46N 98.55W
Falkenberg Sweden 28 56.55N 12.30E
Falkirk Scotland 15 56.00N 3.48W
Falkland Scotland 15 56.15N 3.13W
Falkland Is. S. America 63 52.00S 60.00W
Fall River *town* U.S.A. 57 41.42N 71.08W
Falmouth England 11 50.09N 5.05W
Falmouth B. England 11 50.06N 5.05W
False B. R.S.A. 48 34.20S 18.30E
Falster *i.* Denmark 26 54.30N 12.00E
Falun Sweden 28 60.37N 15.40E
Famagusta Cyprus 34 35.07N 33.57E
Fanad Head Rep. of Ire. 18 55.17N 7.38W
Fannich, Loch Scotland 16 57.38N 5.00W
Fao Iraq 35 29.57N 48.30E
Faradje Zaïre 47 3.45N 29.43E
Farafra Oasis Egypt 34 27.00N 28.20E
Farah Afghan. 35 32.23N 62.07E
Farah *r.* Afghan. 35 31.25N 61.30E
Farallon de Medinilla *i.* Asia 39 16.01N 146.04E
Farallon de Pajaros *i.* Asia 39 20.33N 144.59E
Faraulep *is.* Asia 39 8.36N 144.33E
Farcet Fen England 9 52.32N 0.11W
Far East Farm Camp Hong Kong 33 22.24N 113.58E
Fareham England 8 50.52N 1.11W
Farewell, C. Greenland 55 60.00N 44.20W
Farewell, C. New Zealand 50 40.30S 172.35E
Farewell Spit *f.* New Zealand 50 40.30S 173.00E
Fargo U.S.A. 53 46.52N 96.59W
Faringdon England 8 51.39N 1.34W
Farnborough Hants. England 7 51.17N 0.46W
Farnborough Kent England 7 51.22N 0.05E
Farncombe England 7 51.12N 0.37W
Farndon England 12 53.06N 2.53W
Farne Is. England 15 55.38N 1.36W
Farnham Canada 57 45.17N 72.59W
Farnham England 8 51.13N 0.49W
Farningham England 7 51.23N 0.15E
Farnworth England 12 53.33N 2.33W
Faro Portugal 23 37.01N 7.56W
Faroe Is. Europe 28 62.00N 7.00W
Fårösund Sweden 28 57.51N 19.05E
Farrar *r.* Scotland 17 57.25N 4.39W
Fársala Greece 25 39.17N 22.22E
Farsi Afghan. 35 33.47N 63.12E
Farsund Norway 28 58.05N 6.49E
Fasa Iran 35 28.55N 53.38E
Fashven *mtn.* Scotland 17 58.34N 4.54W
Fastnet Rock *i.* Rep. of Ire. 19 51.23N 9.37W
Fastov U.S.S.R. 29 50.08N 29.59E
Fatshan China 41 23.03N 113.08E
Fat Tau Chau *i.* Hong Kong 33 22.17N 114.16E
Fat Tong Pt. Hong Kong 33 22.15N 114.17E
Fauldhouse Scotland 15 55.49N 3.41W
Fauquembergues France 9 50.35N 2.06E
Faurei Romania 25 45.04N 27.15E
Faüske Norway 28 67.17N 15.25E
Faversham England 9 51.18N 0.54E
Favignana *i.* Italy 24 37.57N 12.19E
Fawley England 8 50.49N 1.20W
Faxa Flói *b.* Iceland 28 64.30N 22.50W
Faxe *r.* Sweden 28 63.15N 17.15E
Fayetteville U.S.A. 53 35.03N 78.53W
Fdérik Mauritania 44 22.30N 12.30W
Fear, C. U.S.A. 53 33.51N 77.59W
Fécamp France 22 49.45N 0.23E
Federal District *d.* Brazil 61 15.50S 47.40W
Federal District *d.* Mexico 58 19.20N 99.10W
Fedorovka U.S.S.R. 29 47.07N 35.19E
Feeagh, Lough Rep. of Ire. 18 53.56N 9.35W
Fehmarn *i.* W. Germany 26 54.30N 11.05E
Feilding New Zealand 50 40.10S 175.25E
Feira Brazil 62 12.17S 38.53W
Feira Zambia 47 15.30S 30.27E
Felanitx Spain 23 39.27N 3.08E
Feldkirch Austria 26 47.15N 9.38E
Felixstowe England 9 51.58N 1.20E
Felsted England 7 51.52N 0.25E
Feltham England 7 51.27N 0.25W
Felton England 15 55.18N 1.42W
Femunden *l.* Norway 28 62.05N 11.55E
Fengkieh China 41 31.00N 109.30E
Fenit Rep. of Ire. 19 52.17N 9.51W
Fenyang China 41 37.14N 111.43E
Feodosiya U.S.S.R. 29 45.03N 35.23E
Fer, Cap de Algeria 24 37.07N 7.10E
Ferbane Rep. of Ire. 19 53.16N 7.50W
Ferdaus Iran 35 34.00N 58.10E
Fergus Falls *town* U.S.A. 53 46.18N 96.00W
Fermanagh *d.* N. Ireland 18 54.21N 7.40W
Fermoselle Spain 23 41.19N 6.24W
Fermoy Rep. of Ire. 19 52.08N 8.17W
Ferndown England 8 50.48N 1.55W
Ferness Scotland 17 57.28N 3.45W
Ferns Rep. of Ire. 19 52.35N 6.31W
Ferozepore India 36 30.55N 74.38E
Ferrara Italy 24 44.49N 11.38E
Ferret, Cap France 22 44.42N 1.16W
Feshi Zaïre 46 6.08S 18.12E
Fetcham England 7 51.17N 0.22W
Fethard Tipperary Rep. of Ire. 19 52.28N 7.42W
Fethard Wexford Rep. of Ire. 19 52.12N 6.51W
Fethiye Turkey 34 36.37N 29.06E
Fetlar *i.* Scotland 16 60.37N 0.52W
Fetlar *i.* U.K. 20 60.37N 0.52W
Fettercairn Scotland 17 56.51N 2.35W
Fevzipaşa Turkey 34 37.07N 36.38E
Fez Morocco 44 34.05N 5.00W
Ffestiniog Wales 10 52.58N 3.56W
Ffostrasol Wales 10 52.06N 4.23W
Fife *d.* Scotland 15 56.10N 3.10W
Fife Ness *c.* Scotland 15 56.17N 2.36W
Figeac France 22 44.32N 2.01E
Figueira da Foz Portugal 23 40.09N 8.51W
Figueras Spain 23 42.16N 2.57E
Fiji Is. Pacific Oc. 3 17.00S 178.00E
Filabusi Rhodesia 48 20.34S 29.20E
Filey England 13 54.13N 0.18W
Fimi *r.* Zaïre 46 3.00S 17.00E
Finchley England 7 51.37N 0.11W
Findhorn Scotland 17 57.39N 3.37W
Findhorn *r.* Scotland 17 57.38N 3.37W
Findlay U.S.A. 56 41.02N 83.40W
Finisterre, C. Spain 23 42.54N 9.16W
Finland Europe 28 64.30N 27.00E
Finland, G. of Finland/U.S.S.R. 28 60.00N 26.50E
Finlay *r.* Canada 54 56.30N 124.40W
Finn *r.* Rep. of Ire. 18 54.50N 7.30W
Finsbury England 7 51.32N 0.06W
Finschhafen P.N.G. 39 6.35S 147.51E
Fintona N. Ireland 18 54.31N 7.19W
Fionn Loch Scotland 16 57.45N 5.27W
Fionnphort Scotland 14 56.19N 6.23W
Firth of Clyde *est.* Scotland 14 55.35N 4.53W
Firth of Forth *est.* Scotland 15 56.05N 3.00W
Firth of Lorne *est.* Scotland 14 56.20N 5.40W
Firth of Tay *est.* Scotland 15 56.24N 3.08W
Firuzabad Iran 35 28.50N 52.35E
Fisher Str. Canada 55 63.00N 84.00W
Fishguard Wales 10 51.59N 4.59W
Fishguard B. Wales 10 52.06N 4.44W
Fitchburg U.S.A. 57 42.35N 71.50W
Fitful Head Scotland 16 59.55N 1.23W
Fizi Zaïre 47 4.18S 28.56E
Flackwell Heath England 7 51.36N 0.43W
Flagstaff U.S.A. 52 35.12N 111.38W
Flåm Norway 28 60.51N 7.08E
Flamborough England 13 54.07N 0.07W
Flamborough Head England 13 54.06N 0.05W
Flaming Gorge Resr. U.S.A. 52 41.10N 109.30W
Flanders *f.* Belgium 27 50.52N 3.00E
Flanders East *d.* Belgium 27 51.00N 3.45E
Flanders West *d.* Belgium 27 51.00N 3.00E
Flannan Is. U.K. 20 58.16N 7.40W
Flathead L. U.S.A. 52 47.50N 114.05W
Flat Holm *i.* England 8 51.23N 3.08W
Flattery, C. U.S.A. 52 48.23N 124.43W
Fleet England 8 51.16N 0.50W
Fleet *r.* Scotland 17 57.57N 4.05W
Fleetwood England 12 53.55N 3.01W
Flekkefjord *town* Norway 28 58.17N 6.40E
Flen Sweden 28 59.04N 16.39E
Flensburg W. Germany 26 54.47N 9.27E
Flers France 22 48.45N 0.34W
Flimby England 12 54.42N 3.31W
Flinders *r.* Australia 49 17.30S 140.45E
Flinders I. Australia 49 40.00S 148.00E
Flinders Range *mts.* Australia 49 31.00S 138.30E
Flin Flon Canada 55 54.47N 101.51W
Flint U.S.A. 56 43.03N 83.40W
Flint *r.* U.S.A. 53 30.52N 84.35W
Flint Wales 10 53.15N 3.07W
Flitwick England 9 51.59N 0.30W
Flora Norway 28 61.45N 4.55E
Florence Italy 24 43.46N 11.15E
Florence U.S.A. 53 34.12N 79.44W
Florenville Belgium 27 49.42N 5.19E
Flores *i.* Indonesia 39 8.40S 121.20E
Flores Sea Indonesia 39 7.00S 121.00E
Florianópolis Brazil 61 27.35S 48.31W
Florida Uruguay 61 34.04S 56.14W
Florida *d.* U.S.A. 53 29.00N 82.00W
Florida, Straits of U.S.A. 59 24.00N 81.00W
Florida Keys *is.* U.S.A. 58 24.30N 81.00W
Florina Greece 25 40.48N 21.25E
Flotta *i.* Scotland 17 58.49N 3.07W
Flushing Neth. 27 51.27N 3.35E
Fly *r.* P.N.G. 39 8.22S 142.23E
Fochabers Scotland 17 57.37N 3.07W
Focşani Romania 25 45.40N 27.12E
Foggia Italy 24 41.28N 15.33E
Foinaven *mtn.* Scotland 17 58.24N 4.53W
Foix France 22 42.57N 1.35E
Folda *est.* Norway 28 64.45N 11.20E
Foligno Italy 24 42.56N 12.43E
Folkestone England 9 51.05N 1.11E
Folkingham England 13 52.54N 0.24W
Fond du Lac Canada 54 59.20N 107.09W
Fond du Lac U.S.A. 56 43.48N 88.27W
Fonseca, G. of Honduras 58 13.10N 87.30W
Fontainebleau France 22 48.24N 2.42E
Fontenay France 22 46.28N 0.48W
Foochow China 41 26.01N 119.20E
Ford Scotland 14 56.10N 5.26W
Fordingbridge England 8 50.56N 1.48W
Forel, Mt. Greenland 55 67.00N 37.00W
Foreland *c.* England 8 50.42N 1.06W
Foreland Pt. England 11 51.15N 3.47W
Forest of Atholl *f.* Scotland 17 56.50N 3.58W
Forest of Bowland *hills* England 12 53.57N 2.30W
Forest of Dean *f.* England 8 51.48N 2.32W
Forest of Rossendale *f.* England 12 53.43N 2.15W
Forest Row England 9 51.06N 0.03E
Forfar Scotland 15 56.38N 2.54W
Forli Italy 24 44.13N 12.02E
Forlorn Pt. Rep. of Ire. 19 52.10N 6.35W
Formartine *f.* Scotland 17 57.21N 2.12W
Formby England 12 53.34N 3.04W
Formby Pt. England 12 53.34N 3.07W
Formentera *i.* Spain 23 38.41N 1.30E
Formiga Brazil 61 20.30S 45.27W
Formosa *d.* Argentina 61 25.00S 60.00W
Formosa *town* Argentina 61 26.06S 58.14W
Formosa *i.* Asia 3 23.00N 121.00E
Formosa *see* Taiwan Asia 41
Formosa Brazil 61 15.30S 47.22W
Formosa Str. Asia 41 25.00N 120.00E
Forres Scotland 17 57.37N 3.38W
Forssa Finland 28 60.49N 23.40E
Fort Albany Canada 55 52.15N 81.35W
Fortaleza Brazil 62 3.45S 38.45W
Fort Augustus Scotland 17 57.09N 4.41W
Fort Beaufort R.S.A. 48 32.47S 26.38E
Fort Chimo Canada 55 58.10N 68.15W
Fort Chipewyan Canada 54 58.46N 111.09W
Fort Collins U.S.A. 52 40.35N 105.05W
Fort Crampel C.A.R. 44 7.00N 19.10E
Fort-Dauphin Malagasy Rep. 43 25.01S 47.00E
Fort-de-France Martinique 59 14.36N 61.05W
Fort de Possel C.A.R. 46 5.03N 19.14E
Fort Frances Canada 56 48.37N 93.23W
Fort George Canada 55 53.50N 79.01W
Fort George *r.* Canada 55 53.50N 79.00W
Fort Good Hope Canada 54 66.16N 128.37W
Forth Scotland 15 55.46N 3.42W
Forth *r.* Scotland 15 56.06N 3.48W
Fort Hall Kenya 47 0.43S 37.10E
Fort Lauderdale U.S.A. 53 26.08N 80.08W
Fort Liard Canada 54 60.14N 123.28W
Fort Madison U.S.A. 56 40.38N 91.21W
Fort Maguire Malaŵi 47 13.38S 34.59E
Fort McPherson Canada 54 67.29N 134.50W
Fort Myers U.S.A. 53 26.39N 81.51W
Fort Nelson Canada 54 58.48N 122.44W
Fort Norman Canada 54 64.55N 125.29W
Fort Peck Dam U.S.A. 52 47.55N 106.15W
Fort Peck Resr. U.S.A. 52 47.55N 107.00W
Fort Polignac Algeria 44 26.20N 8.20E
Fort Portal Uganda 47 0.40N 30.17E
Fort Randall U.S.A. 54 55.10N 162.47W
Fort Reliance Canada 54 62.45N 109.08W
Fort Resolution Canada 54 61.10N 113.39W
Fortrose Scotland 17 57.34N 4.09W
Fort Rousset Congo 46 0.30S 15.48E
Fort Rupert Canada 55 51.30N 79.45W
Fort St. John Canada 54 56.14N 120.55W
Fort Scott U.S.A. 53 37.52N 94.43W
Fort Severn Canada 55 56.00N 87.40W
Fort Shevchenko U.S.S.R. 30 44.31N 50.15E
Fort Sibut C.A.R. 44 5.46N 19.06E
Fort Simpson Canada 54 61.46N 121.15W
Fort Smith U.S.A. 53 35.22N 94.27W
Fortune *i.* Bahamas 59 22.30N 74.15W
Fortuneswell England 8 50.33N 2.27W
Fort Vermilion Canada 54 58.22N 115.59W
Fort Victoria Rhodesia 48 20.10S 30.49E
Fort Wayne U.S.A. 56 41.05N 85.08W
Fort William Scotland 16 56.49N 5.07W
Fort Worth U.S.A. 53 32.45N 97.20W
Fort Yukon U.S.A. 54 66.35N 145.20W
Fostoria U.S.A. 56 41.10N 83.25W
Fo Tan Hong Kong 33 22.23N 114.11E
Fougamou Gabon 46 1.10S 10.31E
Fougères France 22 48.21N 1.12W
Foula *i.* Scotland 16 60.08N 2.05W
Foulness I. England 9 51.35N 0.55E
Foulness Pt. England 9 51.37N 1.00E
Foulwind, C. New Zealand 50 41.45S 171.30E
Foumban Cameroon 46 5.43N 10.50E

Four Elms England **7** 51.14N 0.07E
Foveaux Str. New Zealand **50** 46.40S 168.00E
Fowey England **11** 50.20N 4.39W
Fowey *r.* England **11** 50.22N 4.40W
Foxe Basin *b.* Canada **55** 67.30N 79.00W
Foxe Channel Canada **55** 65.00N 80.00W
Foxford Rep. of Ire. **18** 53.58N 9.08W
Foxton New Zealand **50** 40.27S 175.18E
Foyle *r.* N. Ireland **18** 55.00N 7.20W
Foyle, Lough N. Ireland **14** 55.05N 7.10W
Foz do Iguaçu Brazil **61** 25.33S 54.31W
Framlingham England **9** 52.14N 1.20E
Franca Brazil **61** 20.33S 47.27W
France Europe **22** 47.00N 2.00E
Franceville Gabon **46** 1.38S 13.31E
Francistown Botswana **48** 21.11S 27.32E
Frankfort R.S.A. **48** 27.16S 28.30E
Frankfort U.S.A. **53** 38.11N 84.53W
Frankfurt E. Germany **26** 52.20N 14.32E
Frankfurt W. Germany **26** 50.06N 8.41E
Franklin *d.* Canada **55** 73.00N 100.00W
Franklin U.S.A. **56** 39.29N 86.02W
Franklin D. Roosevelt L. U.S.A. **52** 47.55N 118.20W
Frank Saale *r.* W. Germany **22** 50.00N 8.21E
Franz Canada **56** 48.28N 84.25W
Franz Josef Land *is.* U.S.S.R. **30** 81.00N 54.00E
Fraser *r.* Canada **52** 49.05N 123.00W
Fraserburg R.S.A. **48** 31.55S 21.31E
Fraserburgh Scotland **17** 57.42N 2.00W
Fray Bentos Uruguay **61** 33.10S 58.20W
Fredericia Denmark **28** 55.34N 9.47E
Frederick U.S.A. **57** 39.25N 77.25W
Fredericksburg U.S.A. **53** 38.18N 77.30W
Fredericton Canada **57** 45.57N 66.40W
Frederikshaab Greenland **55** 62.05N 49.30W
Fredrikshavn Denmark **28** 57.28N 10.33E
Fredrikstad Norway **28** 59.15N 10.55E
Freeport Bahamas **59** 26.40N 78.30W
Freetown Sierra Leone **44** 8.30N 13.17W
Freiburg W. Germany **26** 48.00N 7.52E
Freilingen W. Germany **27** 50.33N 7.50E
Fréjus France **22** 43.26N 6.44E
Fremantle Australia **49** 32.07S 115.44E
French Cays *is.* Bahamas **59** 21.31N 72.14W
French Guiana S. America **62** 4.00N 53.00W
French Territory of Afars and Issas Africa **45** 12.00N 42.50E
Frenda Algeria **23** 35.04N 1.03E
Freshford Rep. of Ire. **19** 52.44N 7.23W
Fresno U.S.A. **52** 36.41N 119.57W
Frias Argentina **61** 28.35S 65.06W
Fribourg Switz. **26** 46.50N 7.10E
Friedrichshafen W. Germany **26** 47.39N 9.29E
Friern Barnet England **7** 51.37N 0.09W
Friesland *d.* Neth. **27** 53.05N 5.45E
Friesoythe W. Germany **27** 53.02N 7.52E
Frimley England **7** 51.19N 0.44W
Frinton England **9** 51.50N 1.16E
Frio, Cabo *c.* Brazil **63** 22.50S 42.10W
Frisa, Loch Scotland **14** 56.33N 6.05W
Frobisher B. Canada **55** 63.00N 66.45W
Frobisher Bay *town* Canada **55** 63.45N 68.30W
Frodsham England **12** 53.17N 2.45W
Fro Havet *est.* Norway **28** 63.55N 9.05E
Frome England **8** 51.16N 2.17W
Frome *r.* England **8** 50.41N 2.05W
Frosinone Italy **24** 41.36N 13.21E
Fröya *i.* Norway **28** 63.45N 8.30E
Frunze U.S.S.R. **40** 42.53N 74.46E
Fuchin China **41** 47.15N 131.59E
Fuchow China **41** 28.03N 116.15E
Fuday *i.* Scotland **16** 57.03N 7.23W
Fuerte *r.* Mexico **52** 25.42N 109.20W
Fuerteventura *i.* Canary Is. **44** 28.20N 14.10W
Fujiyama *mtn.* Japan **42** 35.23N 138.42E
Fukien *d.* China **41** 26.30N 118.00E
Fukui Japan **42** 36.04N 136.12E
Fukuoka Japan **42** 33.39N 130.21E
Fukushima Japan **42** 37.44N 140.28E
Fulda W. Germany **26** 50.35N 9.41E
Fulham England **7** 51.29N 0.13W
Fumay France **27** 49.59N 4.42E
Fundy, B. of N.America **53** 44.30N 66.30W
Funen *i.* Denmark **28** 55.15N 10.30E
Funzie Scotland **16** 60.35N 0.48W
Furakawa Japan **42** 38.30N 140.50E
Furancungo Moçambique **47** 14.51S 33.38E
Furg Iran **35** 28.19N 55.10E
Furnas Dam Brazil **63** 20.40S 46.22W
Furnas Resr. Brazil **61** 21.00S 46.00W
Furnes Belgium **27** 51.04N 2.40E
Fürstenau W. Germany **27** 52.32N 7.41E
Fushun China **41** 41.51N 123.53E
Fussen W. Germany **26** 47.35N 10.43E
Futa Jalon *f.* Guinea **44** 11.30N 12.30W
Fu Tau Pun Chau *i.* Hong Kong **33** 22.20N 114.21E
Fuyu China **41** 45.12N 124.49E
Fyfield England **7** 51.45N 0.16E
Fyne, Loch Scotland **14** 55.55N 5.23W
Fyvie Scotland **17** 57.26N 2.24W

G

Gabela Angola **46** 10.52S 14.24E
Gabes Tunisia **44** 33.52N 10.06E
Gabes, G. of Tunisia **44** 34.00N 11.00E
Gabon Africa **46** 0.00 12.00E
Gabon *r.* Gabon **46** 0.15N 10.00E
Gaborone Botswana **48** 24.45S 25.55E
Gabriel, Mt. Rep. of Ire. **19** 51.34N 9.34W
Gach Saran Iran **35** 30.13N 50.49E
Gadsden U.S.A. **53** 34.00N 86.00W
Gadzema Rhodesia **48** 18.02S 30.16E
Gaeta Italy **24** 41.13N 13.35E
Gaeta, G. of Med. Sea **24** 41.05N 13.30E
Gaferut *i.* Asia **39** 9.14N 145.23E
Gagnon Canada **55** 51.56N 68.16W
Gago Coutinho Angola **46** 14.02S 21.35E
Gaillac France **22** 43.54N 1.53E
Gainesville U.S.A. **53** 29.37N 82.31W
Gainford England **12** 54.34N 1.44W
Gainsborough England **13** 53.23N 0.46W
Gairdner, L. Australia **49** 31.30S 136.00E
Gairloch Scotland **16** 57.43N 5.40W
Gairloch, Loch Scotland **16** 57.43N 5.43W
Gairsay *i.* Scotland **17** 59.05N 2.58W
Galala Plateau Egypt **34** 29.00N 32.10E
Galana *r.* Kenya **47** 3.12S 40.09E
Galangue Angola **46** 13.40S 16.00E
Galapagos Is. Ecuador **60** 0.20S 91.00W
Galashiels Scotland **15** 55.37N 2.49W
Galati Romania **25** 45.27N 27.59E
Galena U.S.A. **54** 64.43N 157.00W
Galesburg U.S.A. **56** 40.58N 90.22W
Galey *r.* Rep. of Ire. **19** 52.26N 9.37W
Galita *i.* Tunisia **24** 37.31N 8.55E
Gallan Head Scotland **16** 58.14N 7.01W
Galle Sri Lanka **37** 6.01N 80.13E
Gállego *r.* Spain **23** 41.40N 0.55W
Galley Head Rep. of Ire. **19** 51.32N 8.57W
Gallinas, C. Colombia **62** 12.27N 71.44W
Gallipoli Italy **25** 40.02N 18.01E
Gallipoli Turkey **25** 40.25N 26.31E
Gällivare Sweden **28** 67.10N 20.40E
Galloway *f.* Scotland **14** 55.00N 4.28W
Gallup U.S.A. **52** 35.32N 108.46W
Galston Scotland **14** 55.36N 4.23W
Galtby Finland **28** 60.08N 21.33E
Galtymore *mtn.* Rep. of Ire. **19** 52.22N 8.13W
Galty Mts. Rep. of Ire. **19** 52.20N 8.10W
Galveston U.S.A. **53** 29.17N 94.48W
Galveston B. U.S.A. **53** 29.40N 94.40W
Galvez Argentina **61** 32.03S 61.14W
Galway Rep. of Ire. **18** 53.17N 9.04W
Galway *d.* Rep. of Ire. **18** 53.25N 9.00W
Galway B. Rep. of Ire. **19** 53.12N 9.07W
Gambia Africa **44** 13.30N 15.00W
Gambia *r.* Gambia **44** 13.28N 15.55W
Gamboma Congo **46** 1.50S 15.58E
Ganale Dorya *r.* Ethiopia **47** 4.13N 42.04E
Gandajika Zaire **46** 6.46S 23.58E
Gander Canada **55** 48.58N 54.34W
Gandia Spain **23** 38.59N 0.11W
Ganga *r. see* Ganges India **37**
Ganges *r.* India **37** 23.30N 90.25E
Ganges, Mouths of the India/Bangla. **37** 22.00N 89.35E
Gangtok Sikkim **37** 27.20N 88.39E
Gannat France **22** 46.06N 3.11E
Gannett Peak *mtn.* U.S.A. **52** 43.10N 109.38W
Gao Mali **44** 16.19N 0.09W
Gap France **22** 44.33N 6.05E
Gara, Lough Rep. of Ire. **18** 53.57N 8.27W
Gard *r.* France **22** 43.52N 4.40E
Garda, L. Italy **24** 45.40N 10.40E
Gar Dzong China **37** 32.10N 79.59E
Garelochhead Scotland **14** 56.05N 4.49W
Garforth England **13** 53.48N 1.22W
Garies R.S.A. **48** 30.30S 18.00E
Garioch *f.* Scotland **17** 57.18N 2.30W
Garissa Kenya **47** 0.27S 39.49E
Garlieston Scotland **14** 54.46N 4.22W
Garmisch Partenkirchen W. Germany **26** 47.30N 11.05E
Garmouth Scotland **17** 57.40N 3.07W
Garmsar Iran **35** 35.15N 52.21E
Garonne *r.* France **22** 45.00N 0.37W
Garoua Cameroon **44** 9.17N 13.22E
Garrison Resr. U.S.A. **52** 47.30N 102.20W
Garroch Head Scotland **14** 55.43N 5.02W
Garron Pt. N. Ireland **14** 55.03N 5.57W
Garry, Loch Scotland **17** 57.05N 4.55W
Garry L. Canada **55** 66.00N 100.00W
Garstang England **12** 53.53N 2.47W
Garth Wales **10** 52.08N 3.32W
Garthorpe England **13** 53.40N 0.42W
Gartok China **40** 32.00N 80.20E
Garvagh N. Ireland **14** 54.58N 6.42W
Garvão Portugal **23** 37.42N 8.21W
Garve Scotland **17** 57.37N 4.41W
Garvellachs *i.* Scotland **14** 56.15N 5.45W
Garvie Mts. New Zealand **50** 45.15S 169.00E
Gary U.S.A. **56** 41.34N 87.20W
Gascony, G. of France **22** 44.00N 2.40W
Gascoyne *r.* Australia **49** 25.00S 113.40E
Gaspé Canada **55** 48.50N 64.30W
Gaspé Pen. Canada **57** 48.30N 66.45W
Gata, C. Cyprus **34** 34.33N 33.03E
Gata, Cabo de Spain **23** 36.45N 2.11W
Gata, Sierra de *mts.* Spain **23** 40.20N 6.30W
Gatehouse of Fleet Scotland **14** 54.53N 4.12W
Gateshead England **12** 54.57N 1.35W
Gatooma Rhodesia **48** 18.16S 29.55E
Gatun L. Canal Zone **59** 9.20N 80.00W
Gauhati India **37** 26.05N 91.55E
Gauja *r.* U.S.S.R. **28** 57.10N 24.17E
Gavá Spain **23** 41.18N 2.00E
Gävle Sweden **28** 60.41N 17.10E
Gaya India **37** 24.48N 85.00E
Gaydon England **8** 52.11N 1.27W
Gaza Egypt **34** 31.30N 34.28E
Gaziantep Turkey **34** 37.04N 37.21E
Gdańsk Poland **28** 54.22N 18.38E
Gdańsk, G. of Poland **29** 54.45N 19.15E
Gdov U.S.S.R. **28** 58.48N 27.52E
Gdynia Poland **28** 54.31N 18.30E
Geal Chàrn *mtn.* Scotland **17** 57.06N 3.30W
Gebze Turkey **34** 40.48N 29.26E
Gediz *r.* Turkey **25** 38.37N 26.47E
Gedser Denmark **26** 54.35N 11.57E
Geel Belgium **27** 51.10N 5.00E
Geelong Australia **49** 38.10S 144.26E
Geh Iran **35** 26.14N 60.15E
Geilenkirchen W. Germany **27** 50.58N 6.08E
Gelderland *d.* Neth. **27** 52.05N 6.00E
Geldern W. Germany **27** 51.31N 6.19E
Geleen Neth. **27** 50.58N 5.51E
Gelligaer Wales **11** 51.40N 3.18W
Gelsenkirchen W. Germany **27** 51.30N 7.05E
Gemas Malaysia **38** 2.35N 102.35E
Gembloux Belgium **27** 50.34N 4.42E
Gemena Zaire **46** 3.14N 19.48E
Gemlik Turkey **34** 40.26N 29.10E
Geneina Sudan **45** 13.27N 22.30E
General Acha Argentina **61** 37.25S 64.38W
General Alvear Argentina **61** 34.59S 67.40W
Geneva Switz. **26** 46.13N 6.09E
Geneva, L. Switz. **26** 46.30N 6.30E
Genichesk U.S.S.R. **25** 46.10N 34.49E
Genil *r.* Spain **23** 37.42N 5.20W
Genoa Italy **22** 44.24N 8.54E
Genoa, G. of Italy **22** 44.12N 8.55E
Gent Belgium **27** 51.02N 3.42E
George *r.* Canada **55** 58.30N 66.00W
George R.S.A. **48** 33.57S 22.28E
George, L. Uganda **47** 0.00 30.10E
George, L. U.S.A. **57** 43.30N 73.30W
Georgetown Cayman Is. **58** 19.20N 81.23W
Georgetown Guyana **62** 6.46N 58.10W
George Town Malaysia **38** 5.30N 100.16E
Georgia *d.* U.S.A. **53** 33.00N 83.00W
Georgia, Str. of Canada **52** 49.15N 123.45W
Georgian B. Canada **56** 45.15N 80.45W
Georgia Soviet Socialist Republic *d.* U.S.S.R. **34** 42.00N 43.30E
Gera E. Germany **26** 50.51N 12.11E
Geraardsbergen Belgium **27** 50.47N 3.53E
Geraldton Australia **49** 28.49S 114.36E
Germiston R.S.A. **48** 26.15S 28.10E
Gerona Spain **23** 41.59N 2.49E
Gerrards Cross England **7** 51.35N 0.34W
Getafe Spain **23** 40.18N 3.44W
Gete *r.* Belgium **27** 50.58N 5.07E
Geyve Turkey **34** 40.32N 30.18E
Gezira *f.* Sudan **45** 14.30N 33.00E
Ghadames Libya **44** 30.10N 9.30E
Ghaghara *r.* India **37** 25.45N 84.50E
Ghana Africa **44** 8.00N 1.00W
Ghanzi Botswana **48** 21.34S 21.42E
Ghardaïa Algeria **44** 32.20N 3.40E
Ghat Libya **44** 24.59N 10.11E
Ghazaouet Algeria **23** 35.10N 1.50W
Ghurian Afghan. **35** 34.20N 61.25E
Gialo Libya **45** 29.00N 21.30E
Giant's Causeway *f.* N. Ireland **14** 55.14N 6.32W
Gibraltar Europe **23** 36.07N 5.22W
Gibraltar, Str. of Africa/Europe **23** 36.00N 5.25W
Gibraltar Pt. England **13** 53.05N 0.20E
Giessen W. Germany **26** 50.35N 8.42E
Gieten Neth. **27** 53.01N 6.45E
Gifford Scotland **15** 55.55N 2.45W
Gifu Japan **42** 35.27N 136.50E
Gigha *i.* Scotland **14** 55.41N 5.44W
Gigha, Sd. of Scotland **14** 55.40N 5.41W
Giglio *i.* Italy **24** 42.21N 10.53E
Gijón Spain **23** 43.32N 5.40W
Gila *r.* U.S.A. **52** 32.45N 114.30W
Gilbert Is. Pacific Oc. **3** 2.00S 175.00E
Gilé Moçambique **47** 16.10S 38.17E
Gilehdar Iran **35** 27.36N 52.42E
Gilgil Kenya **47** 0.29S 36.19E
Gilgit Jammu and Kashmir **36** 35.54N 74.20E
Gill, Lough Rep. of Ire. **18** 54.15N 8.14W
Gillingham Dorset England **8** 51.02N 2.17W
Gillingham Kent England **7** 51.24N 0.33E
Gilsland England **15** 54.59N 2.34W
Gimbala, Jebel *mtn.* Sudan **45** 13.00N 24.20E
Ginz *r.* W. Germany **26** 48.28N 10.18E
Giresun Turkey **34** 40.55N 38.25E
Giri *r.* Zaïre **46** 0.30N 17.58E
Gironde *r.* France **22** 45.35N 1.00W
Girvan Scotland **14** 55.15N 4.51W
Gisborne New Zealand **50** 38.41S 178.02E
Giurgiu Romania **25** 43.52N 25.58E
Givet France **27** 50.08N 4.49E
Gizhiga U.S.S.R. **31** 62.00N 160.34E
Gizhiga G. U.S.S.R. **31** 61.00N 158.00E
Gjövik Norway **28** 60.47N 10.41E
Glacier Peak *mtn.* U.S.A. **52** 48.07N 121.06W
Glamis Scotland **15** 56.37N 3.01W
Glan *r.* W. Germany **27** 49.46N 7.43E
Glanamman Wales **11** 51.49N 3.54W
Glanaruddery Mts. Rep. of Ire. **19** 52.19N 9.27W
Glandorf W. Germany **27** 52.05N 8.00E
Glanton England **15** 55.25N 1.53W
Glasgow Scotland **14** 55.52N 4.15W
Glasgow U.S.A. **52** 48.12N 106.37W
Glas Maol *mtn.* Scotland **17** 56.52N 3.22W
Glass, Loch Scotland **17** 57.43N 4.30W
Glasson England **12** 54.00N 2.49W
Glastonbury England **8** 51.09N 2.42W
Glazov U.S.S.R. **29** 58.09N 52.42E
Glen *r.* England **9** 52.50N 0.06W
Glen Affric *f.* Scotland **16** 57.15N 5.03W
Glen Almond *f.* Scotland **15** 56.28N 3.48W
Glenanane Rep. of Ire. **18** 53.37N 9.40W
Glénans, Iles de France **22** 47.43N 3.57W
Glenarm N. Ireland **14** 54.57N 5.58W
Glen Cannich *f.* Scotland **16** 57.19N 5.03W
Glen Clova *f.* Scotland **17** 56.48N 3.01W
Glen Coe *f.* Scotland **14** 56.40N 5.03W
Glendive U.S.A. **52** 47.08N 104.42W
Glen Dochart *f.* Scotland **14** 56.25N 4.30W
Glen Dye *f.* Scotland **17** 56.58N 2.34W
Glenelg Scotland **16** 57.13N 5.37W
Glenelly *r.* N. Ireland **14** 54.45N 7.19W
Glen Esk *f.* Scotland **17** 56.53N 2.46W
Glen Etive *f.* Scotland **14** 56.37N 5.01W
Glenfinnan Scotland **16** 56.53N 5.27W
Glengarriff Rep. of Ire. **19** 51.45N 9.33W
Glen Garry *f.* Highland Scotland **16** 57.03N 5.04W
Glen Garry *f.* Tayside Scotland **17** 56.47N 4.02W
Glengormley N. Ireland **14** 54.40N 5.59W
Glen Head Rep. of Ire. **18** 54.44N 8.46W
Glen Kinglass *f.* Scotland **14** 56.29N 5.03W
Glenluce Scotland **14** 54.53N 4.48W
Glen Lyon *f.* Scotland **14** 56.36N 4.15W
Glen Mòr *f.* Scotland **17** 57.15N 4.30W
Glen More *f.* Scotland **14** 56.25N 5.48W
Glennagalliagh *mtn.* Rep. of Ire. **19** 52.49N 8.32W
Glen Orchy *f.* Scotland **14** 56.28N 4.50W
Glen Orrin *f.* Scotland **17** 57.30N 4.45W
Glen Prosen *f.* Scotland **17** 56.45N 3.05W
Glenrothes Scotland **15** 56.12N 3.10W
Glen Roy *f.* Scotland **17** 56.58N 4.47W
Glens Falls *town* U.S.A. **57** 43.17N 73.41W
Glenshee *f.* Scotland **17** 56.45N 3.25W
Glen Spean *f.* Scotland **17** 56.53N 4.40W
Glenties Rep. of Ire. **18** 54.47N 8.17W
Glen Tilt *f.* Scotland **17** 56.50N 3.45W
Glenwhappen Rig *mtn.* Scotland **15** 55.33N 3.30W
Glin Rep. of Ire. **19** 52.34N 9.17W
Glittertind *mtn.* Norway **28** 61.30N 8.20E
Głogów Poland **26** 51.40N 16.06E
Glomma *r.* Norway **28** 59.15N 10.55E
Glossop England **12** 53.27N 1.56W
Gloucester England **8** 51.52N 2.15W
Gloucestershire *d.* England **8** 51.45N 2.00W
Glyncorrwg Wales **11** 51.40N 3.39W
Glyn Neath Wales **11** 51.45N 3.37W
Gmünd Austria **26** 48.47N 14.59E
Gmunden Austria **26** 47.56N 13.48E
Gniezno Poland **29** 52.32N 17.32E
Goa *d.* India **36** 15.30N 74.00E
Goat Fell *mtn.* Scotland **14** 55.37N 5.12W
Gobabis S.W. Africa **48** 22.30S 18.58E
Gobi *des.* Asia **40** 43.30N 103.30E
Godalming England **7** 51.11N 0.37W
Godavari *r.* India **37** 16.40N 82.15E
Goderich Canada **56** 43.43N 81.43W
Godhavn Greenland **55** 69.20N 53.30W
Godhra India **36** 22.49N 73.40E
Godmanchester England **9** 52.19N 0.11W
Godrevy Pt. England **11** 50.15N 5.25W
Godstone England **7** 51.15N 0.04W
Godthaab Greenland **55** 64.10N 51.40W
Gogra *r. see* Ghaghara India **37**
Goiandira Brazil **61** 18.06S 48.07W
Goiânia Brazil **61** 16.43S 49.18W
Goiás Brazil **61** 15.57S 50.07W
Goiás *d.* Brazil **61** 16.00S 50.10W
Göksun Turkey **34** 38.03N 36.30E
Gol Norway **28** 60.43N 8.55E
Gola I. Rep. of Ire. **18** 55.05N 8.21W
Golden Canada **52** 51.19N 116.58W
Golden Rep. of Ire. **19** 52.30N 7.59W
Golden B. New Zealand **50** 40.45S 172.50E
Golden Vale *f.* Rep. of Ire. **19** 52.30N 8.07W
Golders Green England **7** 51.35N 0.12W
Golfito Costa Rica **58** 8.42N 83.10W
Golspie Scotland **17** 57.58N 3.58W
Golyshi U.S.S.R. **29** 58.26N 45.28E
Goma Zaïre **47** 1.37S 29.10E
Gombe *r.* Tanzania **47** 4.43S 31.30E
Gomel U.S.S.R. **29** 52.25N 31.00E
Gómez Palacio Mexico **58** 25.39N 103.30W
Gomshall England **7** 51.13N 0.25W
Gonaives Haiti **59** 19.29N 72.42W
Gonâve, G. of Haiti **59** 19.20N 73.00W
Gonâve I. Haiti **59** 18.50N 73.00W
Gonbad-e-Kavus Iran **35** 37.15N 55.11E
Gondar Ethiopia **45** 12.39N 37.29E
Good Hope, C. of R.S.A. **48** 34.20S 18.25E
Goodwin Sands *f.* England **9** 51.16N 1.31E
Goole England **13** 53.42N 0.52W
Goondiwindi Australia **49** 28.30S 150.17E
Goose L. U.S.A. **52** 41.55N 120.25W
Göppingen W. Germany **26** 48.43N 9.39E
Gorakhpur India **37** 26.45N 83.23E
Gordon Scotland **15** 55.41N 2.34W
Gore New Zealand **50** 46.06S 168.58E
Gorebridge Scotland **15** 55.51N 3.02W
Gorey Rep. of Ire. **19** 52.40N 6.19W
Gorgan Iran **35** 36.50N 54.29E
Gorgan *r.* Iran **35** 37.00N 54.00E
Gori U.S.S.R. **35** 41.59N 44.05E
Gorinchem Neth. **27** 51.50N 4.59E
Goring England **8** 51.32N 1.08W
Gorizia Italy **24** 45.58N 13.37E
Gorki U.S.S.R. **29** 56.20N 44.00E
Görlitz E. Germany **26** 51.09N 15.00E
Gorlovka U.S.S.R. **29** 48.17N 38.05E
Gorm, Loch Scotland **14** 55.48N 6.25W
Gorongosa *r.* Moçambique **48** 20.29S 34.36E
Gorontalo Indonesia **39** 0.33N 123.05E
Gorseinon Wales **11** 51.40N 4.03W
Gort Rep. of Ire. **19** 53.04N 8.49W
Gortin N. Ireland **18** 54.43N 7.15W
Gorzów Wielkopolski Poland **26** 52.42N 15.12E
Gosforth England **15** 55.02N 1.35W
Gospić Yugo. **24** 4.34N 15.23E
Gosport England **8** 50.48N 1.08W
Göta Canal Sweden **28** 57.50N 11.50E

Göteborg Sweden **28** 57.45N 12.00E
Gotha E. Germany **26** 50.57N 10.43E
Gotland *i.* Sweden **28** 57.30N 18.30E
Gottingen W. Germany **26** 51.32N 9.57E
Gouda Neth. **27** 52.01N 4.43E
Gough I. Atlantic Oc. **4** 41.00S 10.00W
Gouin Resr. Canada **57** 48.40N 74.45W
Gourdon France **22** 44.45N 1.22E
Gournay France **22** 49.29N 1.44E
Gourock Scotland **14** 55.58N 4.49W
Governador Valadares Brazil **63** 18.51S 42.00W
Gower *pen.* Wales **11** 51.37N 4.10W
Gowna, Lough Rep. of Ire. **18** 53.50N 7.34W
Gowran Rep. of Ire. **19** 52.38N 7.04W
Gozo *i.* Malta **24** 36.03N 14.16E
Gracias á Dios, Cabo *c.* Honduras/Nicaragua **58** 15.00N 83.10W
Grafton U.S.A. **53** 48.28N 97.25W
Grahamstown R.S.A. **48** 33.19S 26.32E
Graiguenamanagh Rep. of Ire. **19** 52.33N 6.57W
Grain England **9** 51.28N 0.43E
Grampian *d.* Scotland **17** 57.22N 2.35W
Grampian Highlands Scotland **17** 56.55N 4.00W
Grampound England **11** 50.18N 4.54W
Granada Nicaragua **58** 11.58N 85.59W
Granada Spain **23** 37.10N 3.35W
Granard Rep. of Ire. **18** 53.47N 7.30W
Granby Canada **57** 45.23N 72.44W
Gran Canaria *i.* Canary Is. **44** 28.00N 15.30W
Gran Chaco *f.* S. America **61** 23.20S 60.00W
Grand *r.* Canada **56** 42.53N 79.35W
Grand Bahama I. Bahamas **59** 26.35N 78.00W
Grand Canal Rep. of Ire. **18** 53.21N 6.14W
Grand Canyon *f.* U.S.A. **52** 36.15N 113.00W
Grand Canyon *town* U.S.A. **52** 36.04N 112.07W
Grand Cayman *i.* Cayman Is. **58** 19.20N 81.30W
Grande *r.* Brazil **61** 20.00S 51.00W
Grande Comore *i.* Comoro Is. **47** 11.35S 43.20E
Grande I. Brazil **61** 23.15S 44.30W
Grande Prairie *town* Canada **54** 55.10N 118.52W
Grand Falls *town* New Brunswick Canada **57** 47.02N 67.46W
Grand Falls *town* Newfoundland Canada **55** 48.57N 55.40W
Grand Forks U.S.A. **53** 47.57N 97.05W
Grand Fort Philippe France **9** 51.00N 2.06E
Grand Island *town* U.S.A. **52** 40.56N 98.21W
Grand Junction U.S.A. **52** 39.04N 108.33W
Grand Manan I. Canada **57** 44.45N 66.45W
Grand Marais U.S.A. **56** 47.45N 90.20W
Grândola Portugal **23** 38.10N 8.34W
Grand Rapids *town* Mich. U.S.A. **56** 42.57N 85.40W
Grand Rapids *town* Minn. U.S.A. **56** 47.13N 93.31W
Grand Teton *mtn.* U.S.A. **52** 43.45N 110.50W
Grand Union Canal England **7** 52.37N 0.30W
Graney, Lough Rep. of Ire. **19** 52.59N 8.40W
Grangemouth Scotland **15** 56.01N 3.44W
Grange-over-Sands England **12** 54.12N 2.55W
Granite Peak *mtn.* U.S.A. **52** 45.10N 109.50W
Grankulla Finland **28** 60.12N 24.45E
Granóllers Spain **23** 41.37N 2.18E
Gran Paradiso *mtn.* Italy **24** 45.31N 7.15E
Grantham England **13** 52.55N 0.39W
Grantown-on-Spey Scotland **17** 57.20N 3.38W
Grants Pass *town* U.S.A. **52** 42.26N 123.20W
Granville France **22** 48.50N 1.35W
Grasse France **22** 43.40N 6.56E
Grassy Hill Hong Kong **33** 22.24N 114.09E
Grave Neth. **27** 51.45N 5.45E
Grave, Pointe de France **22** 45.35N 1.04W
Gravelines France **9** 50.59N 2.08E
Gravesend England **7** 51.27N 0.24E
Gravir Scotland **16** 58.03N 6.26W
Gray France **22** 47.27N 5.35E
Grayling U.S.A. **56** 44.40N 84.43W
Grays England **7** 51.29N 0.20E
Graz Austria **26** 47.05N 15.22E
Great Abaco I. Bahamas **59** 26.30N 77.00W
Great Artesian Basin *f.* Australia **49** 26.30S 143.02E
Great Australian Bight Australia **49** 33.20S 130.00E
Great Baddow England **7** 51.43N 0.29E
Great Bardfield England **9** 51.57N 0.26E
Great Barrier I. New Zealand **50** 36.15S 175.30E
Great Barrier Reef *f.* Australia **49** 16.30S 146.30E
Great Basin *f.* U.S.A. **52** 39.00N 115.30W
Great Bear L. Canada **54** 66.00N 120.00W
Great Bend *town* U.S.A. **52** 38.22N 98.47W
Great Bernera *i.* Scotland **16** 58.13N 6.50W
Great Blasket I. Rep. of Ire. **19** 52.05N 10.32W
Great Bookham England **7** 51.16N 0.20W
Great Chesterford England **9** 52.04N 0.11E
Great Coates England **13** 53.34N 0.05W
Great Coco *i.* Burma **38** 14.10N 93.25E
Great Dividing Range *mts.* Australia **49** 29.00S 152.00E
Great Driffield England **13** 54.01N 0.26W
Great Dunmow England **7** 51.53N 0.22E
Great Eccleston England **12** 53.51N 2.52W
Greater Antilles *is.* C. America **59** 17.00N 70.00W
Greater London *d.* England **7** 51.31N 0.06W
Greater Manchester *d.* England **12** 53.30N 2.18W
Great Exuma I. Bahamas **59** 23.00N 76.00W
Great Falls *town* U.S.A. **52** 47.30N 111.16W
Great Fish *r.* S.W. Africa **48** 28.07S 17.10E
Great Harwood England **12** 53.48N 2.24W
Great Inagua I. Bahamas **59** 21.00N 73.20W
Great Irgiz *r.* U.S.S.R. **29** 52.00N 47.20E
Great Karas Mts. S.W. Africa **48** 27.30S 18.45E
Great Karroo *f.* R.S.A. **48** 32.50S 22.30E
Great Khingan Shan *mts.* China **41** 50.00N 122.10E
Great Lakes N. America **2** 47.00N 83.00W
Great Malvern England **8** 52.07N 2.19W
Great Missenden England **7** 51.43N 0.43W
Great Nama Land *f.* S.W. Africa **48** 25.30S 17.30E
Great Nicobar *i.* India **37** 7.00N 93.50E
Great Ormes Head Wales **10** 53.20N 3.52W
Great Ouse *r.* England **13** 52.47N 0.23E
Great Plains *f.* N. America **2** 45.00N 107.00W
Great Rift Valley *f.* Africa **3** 7.00S 33.00E
Great Ruaha *r.* Tanzania **47** 7.55S 37.52E
Great St. Bernard Pass Italy/Switz. **22** 45.52N 7.11E
Great Salt L. U.S.A. **52** 41.10N 112.40W
Great Sandy Desert Australia **3** 22.00S 125.00E
Great Sandy Desert Saudi Arabia **34** 28.40N 41.30E
Great Shelford England **9** 52.09N 0.08E
Great Shunner Fell *mtn.* England **12** 54.22N 2.12W
Great Skellig *i.* Rep. of Ire. **19** 51.46N 10.33W
Great Slave L. Canada **54** 61.30N 114.20W
Great Stour *r.* England **9** 51.19N 1.15E
Great Torrington England **11** 50.57N 4.09W
Great Whale *r.* Canada **55** 55.28N 77.45W
Great Whernside *mtn.* England **12** 54.09N 1.59W
Great Yarmouth England **9** 52.40N 1.45E
Great Zab *r.* Iraq **35** 35.37N 43.20E
Gredos, Sierra de *mts.* Spain **23** 40.18N 5.20W
Greece Europe **25** 39.00N 22.00E
Greeley U.S.A. **52** 40.26N 104.43W
Green *r.* U.S.A. **52** 38.20N 109.53W
Green B. U.S.A. **56** 45.00N 87.30W
Green Bay *town* U.S.A. **56** 44.32N 88.00W
Greencastle Rep. of Ire. **14** 55.12N 6.59W
Greenhithe England **7** 51.28N 0.17E
Green I. Hong Kong **33** 22.17N 114.06E
Greenland N. America **55** 68.00N 45.00W
Greenlaw Scotland **15** 55.43N 2.28W
Green Lowther *mtn.* Scotland **15** 55.23N 3.45W
Green Mts. U.S.A. **57** 43.30N 73.00W
Greenock Scotland **14** 55.57N 4.45W
Greenore Pt. Rep. of Ire. **19** 52.14N 6.19W
Greensboro U.S.A. **53** 36.03N 79.50W
Greenstone Pt. Scotland **16** 57.55N 5.37W
Greenville Maine U.S.A. **57** 45.28N 69.36W
Greenville Miss. U.S.A. **53** 33.23N 91.03W
Greenville S.C. U.S.A. **53** 34.52N 82.25W
Greenwich *d.* England **7** 51.28N 0.00
Greifswald E. Germany **26** 54.06N 13.24E
Grenå Denmark **28** 56.25N 10.53E
Grenada C. America **59** 12.15N 61.45W
Grenade France **22** 43.47N 1.10E
Grenoble France **22** 45.11N 5.43E
Greta *r.* England **12** 54.09N 2.37W
Gretna Scotland **15** 55.00N 3.04W
Grey *r.* New Zealand **50** 42.28S 171.13E
Greyabbey N. Ireland **14** 54.32N 5.35W
Greymouth New Zealand **50** 42.28S 171.12E
Grey Range *mts.* Australia **49** 28.30S 142.15E
Greystones Rep. of Ire. **19** 53.09N 6.04W
Gribbin Head England **11** 50.19N 4.41W
Griminish Pt. Scotland **16** 57.40N 7.29W
Grimsay *i.* Scotland **16** 57.29N 7.14W
Grimsby England **13** 53.35N 0.05W
Grimsvötn *mtn.* Iceland **28** 64.30N 17.10W
Griqualand East *f.* R.S.A. **48** 30.30S 29.00E
Griqualand West *f.* R.S.A. **48** 28.55S 22.50E
Gris Nez, Cap France **9** 50.52N 1.35E
Grodno U.S.S.R. **29** 53.40N 23.50E
Groenlo Neth. **27** 52.02N 6.36E
Groix, Ile de France **22** 47.38N 3.26N
Gröningen Neth. **27** 53.13N 6.35E
Gröningen *d.* Neth. **27** 53.15N 6.45E
Groomsport N. Ireland **14** 54.41N 5.37W
Groot *r.* Cape Province R.S.A. **48** 33.57S 25.00E
Groote Eylandt *i.* Australia **49** 14.00S 136.30E
Grootfontein S.W. Africa **48** 19.32S 18.05E
Grootlaagte *r.* Botswana **48** 20.50S 22.05E
Grosnez Pt. Channel Is. **11** 49.15N 2.15W
Grossenbrode W. Germany **26** 54.23N 11.07E
Grosseto Italy **24** 42.46N 11.08E
Gross Glockner *mtn.* Austria **26** 47.05N 12.50E
Grote Nete *r.* Belgium **27** 51.07N 4.20E
Groundhog *r.* Canada **56** 48.45N 82.00W
Grove Park England **7** 51.24N 0.03E
Groznyy U.S.S.R. **29** 43.21N 45.42E
Grumeti *r.* Tanzania **47** 2.05S 33.45E
Gruting Voe *b.* Scotland **16** 60.12N 1.32W
Guadalajara Mexico **58** 20.30N 103.20W
Guadalajara Spain **23** 40.37N 3.10W
Guadalete *r.* Spain **23** 36.37N 6.15W
Guadalmena *r.* Spain **23** 38.00N 3.50W
Guadalquivir *r.* Spain **23** 36.50N 6.20W
Guadalupe Mexico **58** 25.41N 100.15W
Guadalupe, Sierra de *mts.* Spain **23** 39.30N 5.25W
Guadalupe I. Mexico **52** 29.00N 118.25W
Guadarrama *r.* Spain **23** 39.55N 4.10W
Guadarrama, Sierra de *mts.* Spain **23** 41.00N 3.50W
Guadeloupe C. America **59** 16.20N 61.40W
Guadiana *r.* Spain **23** 37.10N 8.36W
Guadix Spain **23** 37.19N 3.08W
Guaira Falls *f.* Brazil **61** 24.00S 54.10W
Guajará Mirim Brazil **62** 10.50S 65.21W
Guajira Pen. Colombia **59** 12.00N 72.00W
Gualeguay Argentina **61** 33.10S 59.14W
Guam *i.* Pacific Oc. **39** 13.30N 144.40E
Guanajuato Mexico **58** 21.00N 101.16W
Guanajuato *d.* Mexico **58** 21.01N 101.00W
Guanare *r.* Venezuela **59** 8.20N 67.50W
Guane Cuba **58** 22.13N 84.07W
Guantánamo Cuba **59** 20.09N 75.14W
Guaporé *r.* Brazil **62** 12.00S 65.15W
Guarapuava Brazil **61** 25.22S 51.28W
Guaratingueta Brazil **61** 22.49S 45.09W
Guarda Portugal **23** 40.32N 7.17W
Guardafui, C. Somali Rep. **45** 12.00N 51.30E
Guardo Spain **23** 42.47N 4.50W
Guatemala C. America **58** 15.40N 90.00W
Guatemala City Guatemala **58** 14.38N 90.22W
Guaviare *r.* Venezuela **62** 4.30N 77.40W
Guaxupe Brazil **61** 21.17S 46.44W
Guayaquil Ecuador **62** 2.13S 79.54W
Guayaquil, G. of Ecuador **62** 2.30S 80.00W
Guaymas Mexico **52** 27.59N 110.54W
Gubin Poland **26** 51.59N 14.42E
Gudermes U.S.S.R. **29** 43.22N 46.06E
Guebwiller France **26** 47.55N 7.13E
Guecho Spain **23** 43.21N 3.01W
Guelph Canada **56** 43.34N 80.16W
Guéret France **22** 46.10N 1.52E
Guernsey *i.* Channel Is. **11** 49.27N 2.35W
Guerrero *d.* Mexico **58** 18.00N 100.00W
Guguan *i.* Asia **39** 17.20N 145.51E
Guiana Highlands S. America **62** 4.00N 60.00W
Guildford England **7** 51.14N 0.35W
Guildtown Scotland **15** 56.28N 3.25W
Guilherne Capelo Ihe Angola **46** 5.11S 12.10E
Guinea Africa **44** 10.30N 10.30W
Guinea, G. of Africa **44** 2.00N 1.00W
Guinea Bissau Africa **44** 12.00N 15.30W
Güines Cuba **58** 22.50N 82.02W
Guînes France **9** 50.51N 1.52E
Guingamp France **22** 48.34N 3.09W
Güiria Venezuela **62** 10.37N 62.21W
Guisborough England **13** 54.32N 1.02W
Guise France **27** 49.54N 3.39E
Guiseley England **12** 53.53N 1.42W
Gujarat *d.* India **36** 22.45N 71.30E
Gujranwala Pakistan **36** 32.06N 74.11E
Gulbarga India **36** 17.22N 76.47E
Gullane Scotland **15** 56.02N 2.49W
Gulpaigan Iran **35** 33.23N 50.18E
Gulu Uganda **47** 2.46N 32.21E
Guma China **40** 37.30N 78.20E
Gümüşane Turkey **34** 40.26N 39.26E
Gungu Zaïre **46** 5.43S 19.20E
Guntersville L. U.S.A. **53** 34.35N 86.00W
Guntur India **37** 16.20N 80.27E
Gunung Balu *mtn.* Indonesia **38** 3.00N 116.00E
Gurnard's Head *c.* England **11** 50.12N 5.35W
Gürün Turkey **34** 38.44N 37.15E
Guryev U.S.S.R. **30** 47.00N 52.00E
Güstrow E. Germany **26** 53.48N 12.11E
Gutcher Scotland **16** 60.40N 1.00W
Gütersloh W. Germany **26** 51.54N 8.22E
Guyana S. America **59** 6.00N 60.00W
Guyhirn England **9** 52.37N 0.05E
Gwadar Pakistan **35** 25.09N 62.21E
Gwai Rhodesia **48** 19.15S 27.42E
Gwai *r.* Rhodesia **48** 18.00S 26.47E
Gwalior India **37** 26.12N 78.09E
Gwanda Rhodesia **48** 20.59S 29.00E
Gwatar Iran **35** 25.10N 61.31E
Gweebarra B. Rep. of Ire. **18** 54.52N 8.28W
Gwelo Rhodesia **48** 19.25S 29.50E
Gwent *d.* Wales **11** 51.44N 3.00W
Gwynedd *d.* Wales **10** 53.00N 4.00W
Gyangtse China **37** 29.00N 89.40E
Gydanskiy Pen. U.S.S.R. **30** 70.00N 78.30E
Györ Hungary **29** 47.41N 17.40E

H

Haapajärvi Finland **28** 63.45N 25.20E
Haapamäki Finland **28** 62.15N 24.25E
Haapsalu U.S.S.R. **28** 58.58N 23.32E
Haarlem Neth. **27** 52.22N 4.38E
Habbaniya Iraq **34** 33.22N 43.35E
Hachijo jima *i.* Japan **42** 33.06N 139.50E
Hachinohe Japan **42** 40.30N 141.30E
Hacketstown Rep. of Ire. **19** 52.52N 6.35W
Hackney *d.* England **7** 51.33N 0.03W
Haddington Scotland **15** 55.57N 2.47W
Haderslev Denmark **28** 55.15N 9.30E
Hadfield England **12** 53.28N 1.59W
Hadhramaut *d.* S. Yemen **45** 16.30N 49.30E
Hadleigh England **9** 52.03N 0.58E
Hafar Saudi Arabia **35** 28.28N 46.00E
Hafnarfjördhur Iceland **28** 64.04N 21.58W
Haft Kel Iran **35** 31.28N 49.35E
Hagen W. Germany **27** 51.22N 7.27E
Hagerstown U.S.A. **57** 39.39N 77.44W
Hagi Japan **42** 34.25N 131.22E
Ha Giang N. Vietnam **37** 22.50N 104.58E
Hags Head Rep. of Ire. **19** 52.56N 9.29W
Haifa Israel **34** 32.49N 34.59E
Haikow China **41** 20.05N 110.25E
Hail Saudi Arabia **34** 27.31N 41.45E
Hailar China **41** 49.15N 119.41E
Hailsham England **9** 50.52N 0.17E
Hailun China **41** 47.29N 126.58E
Hailuoto *i.* Finland **28** 65.00N 24.50E
Hainan *i.* China **38** 18.30N 109.40E
Hainaut *d.* Belgium **27** 50.30N 3.45E
Haines U.S.A. **54** 59.11N 135.23W
Haiphong N. Vietnam **37** 20.50N 106.41E
Haiti C. America **59** 19.00N 73.00W
Hajiki saki *c.* Japan **42** 38.25N 138.32E
Hakari Turkey **35** 37.36N 43.45E
Hakodate Japan **42** 41.46N 140.44E
Ha Kwai Chung Hong Kong **33** 22.21N 114.07E
Halden Norway **28** 59.08N 11.13E
Halesowen England **8** 52.27N 2.02W
Halesworth England **9** 52.21N 1.30E
Haliburton Highlands Canada **57** 45.10N 78.30W
Halifax Canada **55** 44.38N 63.35W
Halifax England **12** 53.43N 1.51W
Halil *r.* Iran **36** 27.35N 58.44E
Halkett, C. U.S.A. **54** 71.00N 152.00W
Halkirk Scotland **17** 58.30N 3.30W
Halladale *r.* Scotland **17** 58.34N 3.54W
Halle Belgium **27** 50.45N 4.14E
Halle E. Germany **26** 51.28N 11.58E
Hallow England **8** 52.14N 2.15W
Hallsberg Sweden **28** 59.05N 15.07E
Hall's Creek *town* Australia **49** 18.17S 127.44E
Hallstavik Sweden **28** 60.06N 18.42E
Halmahera *i.* Indonesia **39** 0.45N 128.00E
Halmstad Sweden **28** 56.41N 12.55E
Hälsingborg Sweden **28** 56.05N 12.45E
Halstead England **9** 51.57N 0.39E
Haltern W. Germany **27** 51.45N 7.10E
Haltia Tunturi *mtn.* Norway **28** 69.20N 21.10E
Haltwhistle England **15** 54.58N 2.27W
Ham Scotland **16** 6.08N 2.04W
Hama Syria **34** 35.09N 36.44E
Hamadān Iran **35** 34.47N 48.33E
Hamamatsu Japan **42** 34.42N 137.42E
Hamar Norway **28** 60.47N 10.55E
Hamata, Gebel *mtn.* Egypt **34** 24.11N 35.01E
Hamble England **8** 50.52N 1.19W
Hambleton England **13** 53.46N 1.11W
Hambleton Hills England **13** 54.15N 1.11W
Hamborn W. Germany **27** 51.29N 6.46E
Hamburg W. Germany **26** 53.33N 10.00E
Hamdh, Wadi *r.* Saudi Arabia **34** 25.49N 36.37E
Hämeenlinna Finland **28** 61.00N 24.25E
Hameln W. Germany **26** 52.06N 9.21E
Hamersley Range *mts.* Australia **49** 22.00S 118.00E
Hami China **40** 42.40N 93.30E
Hamilton Bermuda **59** 32.18N 64.48W
Hamilton Canada **56** 43.15N 79.50W
Hamilton *r.* Canada **55** 53.20N 60.00W
Hamilton New Zealand **50** 37.46S 175.18E
Hamilton Scotland **15** 55.46N 4.10W
Hamilton U.S.A. **56** 39.23N 84.33W
Hamina Finland **28** 60.33N 27.15E
Hamm W. Germany **27** 51.40N 7.49E
Hammerfest Norway **28** 70.40N 23.44E
Hammersmith *d.* England **7** 51.30N 0.14W
Hammond U.S.A. **56** 39.48N 88.37W
Hamoir Belgium **27** 50.25N 5.32E
Hampshire *d.* England **8** 51.03N 1.20W
Hampshire Downs *hills* England **8** 51.18N 1.25W
Hampstead England **7** 51.33N 0.11W
Hampton England **7** 51.25N 0.22W
Hamrin, Jabal *mts.* Iraq **35** 34.40N 44.10E
Hamstreet England **9** 51.03N 0.52E
Ham Tin Hong Kong **33** 22.14N 113.58E
Hamun-i-Sabari *l.* Iran **35** 31.24N 61.16E
Hanakiya Saudi Arabia **34** 24.53N 40.30E
Hanang *mtn.* Tanzania **47** 4.30S 35.21E
Hanchung China **37** 33.10N 107.02E
Hancock U.S.A. **56** 47.08N 88.34W
Handa *i.* Scotland **16** 58.23N 5.12W
Handeni Tanzania **47** 5.25S 38.04E
Hangchow China **41** 30.10N 120.07E
Hang Hau Town Hong Kong **33** 22.19N 114.16E
Hangö Finland **28** 59.50N 23.00E
Han Kiang *r.* China **41** 30.45N 114.24E
Hanmer Springs *town* New Zealand **50** 42.34S 172.46E
Hannibal U.S.A. **56** 39.41N 91.20W
Hanningfield Water England **7** 51.38N 0.28E
Hannover W. Germany **26** 52.23N 9.44E
Hannut Belgium **27** 50.40N 5.05E
Hanoi N. Vietnam **37** 21.01N 105.52E
Hanover R.S.A. **48** 31.05S 24.27E
Hanworth England **7** 51.26N 0.23W
Haparanda Sweden **28** 65.50N 24.10E
Haradh Saudi Arabia **35** 24.12N 49.08E
Harar Ethiopia **45** 9.20N 42.10E
Harbin China **41** 45.45N 126.41E
Harburg W. Germany **26** 53.27N 9.58E
Hardanger Fjord *est.* Norway **28** 60.15N 6.25E
Hardanger Vidda *f.* Norway **28** 60.20N 8.00E
Harderwijk Neth. **27** 52.21N 5.37E
Harefield England **7** 51.36N 0.28W
Haren W. Germany **27** 52.48N 7.15E
Hargeisa Somali Rep. **45** 9.31N 44.02E
Hari *r.* Afghan. **35** 35.42N 61.12E
Hari *r.* Indonesia **38** 1.00S 104.15E
Harima nada *str.* Japan **42** 34.30N 134.30E
Haringey *d.* England **7** 51.36N 0.06W
Harlech Wales **10** 52.52N 4.08W
Harleston England **9** 52.25N 1.18E
Harlingen Neth. **27** 53.10N 5.25E
Harlington England **7** 51.29N 0.25W
Harlow England **7** 51.47N 0.08E
Harmerhill England **12** 52.48N 2.45W
Harney Basin *f.* U.S.A. **52** 43.20N 119.00W
Härnösand Sweden **28** 62.37N 17.55E
Harold Hill England **7** 51.36N 0.12E
Haroldswick Scotland **16** 60.47N 0.50W
Harold Wood England **7** 51.35N 0.12E
Harpenden England **7** 51.49N 0.22W
Harricanaw *r.* Canada **53** 51.05N 79.45W
Harris *i.* Scotland **16** 57.50N 6.55W
Harris, Sd. of Scotland **16** 57.43N 7.05W
Harrisburg U.S.A. **57** 40.17N 76.54W
Harrismith R.S.A. **48** 28.16S 29.08E
Harrison, C. Canada **55** 55.00N 58.00W
Harrogate England **13** 53.59N 1.32W
Harrow England **7** 51.35N 0.21W
Harrow on the Hill England **7** 51.34N 0.21W
Harstad Norway **28** 68.48N 16.30E
Hartford U.S.A. **57** 41.45N 72.42W
Hartington England **12** 53.08N 1.49W
Hartland England **11** 50.59N 4.29W
Hartland Pt. England **11** 51.01N 4.32W
Hartlepool England **13** 54.42N 1.11W
Hartley England **7** 51.23N 0.18E
Harud *r.* Afghan. **35** 31.36N 61.12E
Harvey U.S.A. **56** 41.38N 87.40W
Harwich England **9** 51.56N 1.18E
Haryana *d.* India **36** 29.15N 76.00E

Ijzer *r.* Belgium **27** 51.09N 2.44E
Ikaría *i.* Greece **25** 37.35N 26.10E
Ikela Zaïre **46** 1.06S 23.04E
Ikelemba Congo **46** 1.15N 16.38E
Ikelemba *r.* Zaïre **46** 0.08N 18.19E
Iki shima *i.* Japan **42** 33.47N 129.43E
Ikomba Tanzania **47** 9.09S 32.20E
Ikopa *r.* Malagasy Rep. **47** 16.00S 46.22E
Ilagan Phil. **39** 17.07N 121.53E
Ilam Iran **35** 33.27N 46.27E
Ilan China **41** 46.22N 129.31E
Ilchester England **8** 51.00N 2.41W
Ilebo Zaïre **46** 4.20S 20.35E
Ilen *r.* Rep. of Ire. **19** 51.53N 9.20W
Ilford England **7** 51.33N 0.06E
Ilfracombe England **11** 51.13N 4.08W
Ili *r.* U.S.S.R. **40** 45.00N 74.20E
Iligan Phil. **39** 8.12N 124.13E
Ilkeston England **13** 52.59N 1.19W
Ilkley England **12** 53.56N 1.49W
Iller *r.* W. Germany **22** 48.29N 10.03E
Illescas Uruguay **61** 33.34S 55.20W
Illinois *d.* U.S.A. **56** 40.15N 89.15W
Illinois *r.* U.S.A. **56** 38.56N 90.27W
Ilminster England **8** 50.55N 2.56W
Iloilo Phil. **39** 10.45N 122.33E
Ilorin Nigeria **44** 8.32N 4.34E
Imala Moçambique **47** 14.39S 39.34E
Iman U.S.S.R. **41** 45.55N 133.45E
Imandra, L. U.S.S.R. **28** 67.30N 32.45E
Imatra Finland **28** 61.14N 28.50E
Immingham England **13** 53.37N 0.12W
Imperia Italy **22** 43.53N 8.00E
Imperial Dam U.S.A. **52** 33.01N 114.25W
Impfondo Congo **46** 1.36N 17.58E
Imphal India **37** 24.47N 93.55E
Imroz *i.* Turkey **25** 40.10N 25.51E
Inari *l.* Finland **28** 69.00N 28.00E
Inca Spain **23** 39.43N 2.54E
Incesu Turkey **34** 38.39N 35.12E
Inchard, Loch Scotland **16** 58.27N 5.05W
Inchcape *i.* Scotland **15** 56.27N 2.24W
Inchfree B. Rep. of Ire. **18** 55.03N 8.23W
Inchkeith *i.* Scotland **15** 56.02N 3.08W
Inchnadamph Scotland **16** 58.08N 4.58W
Inchon S. Korea **41** 37.30N 126.38E
Indaal, Loch Scotland **14** 55.45N 6.20W
Indals *r.* Sweden **28** 62.30N 17.20E
Inderagiri *r.* Indonesia **38** 0.30S 103.08E
India Asia **37** 23.00N 78.30E
Indiana *d.* U.S.A. **56** 40.00N 86.05W
Indianapolis U.S.A. **56** 39.45N 86.10W
Indian Harbour Canada **55** 54.25N 57.20W
Indian Ocean 3
Indigirka *r.* U.S.S.R. **31** 71.00N 148.45E
Indonesia Asia **38** 6.00S 118.00E
Indore India **36** 22.42N 75.54E
Indravati *r.* India **37** 18.45N 80.16E
Indre *r.* France **22** 47.16N 0.06W
Indus *r.* Pakistan **36** 24.00N 67.33E
Inebolu Turkey **34** 41.57N 33.45E
Infiesto Spain **23** 43.21N 5.21W
Ingatestone England **7** 51.41N 0.22E
Ingende Zaïre **46** 0.17S 18.58E
Ingham Australia **49** 18.35S 146.12E
Ingleborough *mtn.* England **12** 54.10N 2.23W
Ingleton England **12** 54.09N 2.29W
Ingolstadt W. Germany **26** 48.46N 11.27E
Inhambane Moçambique **48** 23.51S 35.29E
Inharrime Moçambique **48** 24.29S 35.01E
Inishark *i.* Rep. of Ire. **18** 53.37N 10.18W
Inishbofin *i.* Donegal Rep. of Ire. **18** 55.10N 8.10W
Inishbofin *i.* Galway Rep. of Ire. **18** 53.38N 10.14W
Inisheer *i.* Rep. of Ire. **19** 53.04N 9.32W
Inishkea *i.* Rep. of Ire. **18** 54.08N 10.13W
Inishmaan *i.* Rep. of Ire. **19** 53.06N 9.36W
Inishmore *i.* Rep. of Ire. **19** 53.08N 9.43W
Inishmurray *i.* Rep. of Ire. **18** 54.26N 8.40W
Inishowen Head Rep. of Ire. **14** 55.09N 6.56W
Inishowen Pen. Rep. of Ire. **14** 55.08N 7.20W
Inishturk *i.* Rep. of Ire. **18** 53.43N 10.08W
Inishvickillane *i.* Rep. of Ire. **19** 52.02N 10.36W
Inn *r.* Europe **26** 48.33N 13.26E
Innellan Scotland **14** 55.54N 4.58W
Inner Hebrides *is.* Scotland **16** 56.50N 6.45W
Innerleithen Scotland **15** 55.37N 3.04W
Inner Mongolia *d.* China **41** 41.30N 112.00E
Inner Sd. Scotland **16** 57.30N 5.55W
Innsbruck Austria **26** 46.17N 11.25E
Inny *r.* England **11** 50.35N 4.17W
Inny *r.* Rep. of Ire. **19** 51.51N 10.10W
Inongo Zaïre **46** 1.55S 18.20E
Inowrocław Poland **29** 52.49N 18.12E
Insch Scotland **17** 57.21N 2.36W
Interlaken Switz. **26** 46.42N 7.52E
International Falls *town* U.S.A. **56** 48.38N 93.26W
Inubo saki *c.* Japan **42** 35.41N 140.52E
Inuvik Canada **54** 68.16N 133.40W
Inveraray Scotland **14** 56.24N 5.05W
Inver B. Rep. of Ire. **18** 54.36N 8.20W
Inverbervie Scotland **17** 56.51N 2.17W
Invercargill New Zealand **50** 46.26S 168.21E
Invergordon Scotland **17** 57.42N 4.10W
Inverie Scotland **16** 57.03N 5.41W
Inverkeithing Scotland **15** 56.02N 3.25W
Invermoriston Scotland **17** 57.13N 4.38W
Inverness Scotland **17** 57.27N 4.15W
Inverurie Scotland **17** 57.17N 2.23W
Inyangani *mtn.* Rhodesia **48** 18.18S 32.54E
Inyonga Tanzania **47** 6.43S 32.02E
Inzia *r.* Zaïre **46** 3.47S 17.57E
Ioánnina Greece **25** 39.39N 20.49E
Iona *i.* Scotland **14** 56.20N 6.25W
Iona, Sd. of Scotland **14** 56.19N 6.24W
Ionian Is. Greece **25** 38.45N 20.00E
Ionian Sea Med. Sea **25** 38.30N 18.45E
Ios *i.* Greece **25** 36.42N 25.20E
Iowa *d.* U.S.A. **53** 42.00N 93.00W
Iowa City U.S.A. **56** 41.39N 91.31W
Iping China **40** 28.50N 104.35E
Ipoh Malaysia **38** 4.36N 101.02E
Ipswich England **9** 52.04N 1.09E
Iquique Chile **63** 20.15S 70.08W
Iquitos Peru **62** 3.51S 73.13W
Iráklion Greece **25** 35.20N 25.08E
Iran Asia **35** 32.00N 54.30E
Iranian Plateau *f.* Asia **3** 33.00N 55.00E
Iran Range *mts.* Malaysia **38** 3.20N 115.00E
Iranshar Iran **35** 27.14N 60.42E
Irapuato Mexico **58** 20.40N 101.40W
Iraq Asia **34** 33.00N 44.00E
Irazu *mtn.* Costa Rica **58** 9.59N 83.52W
Ireland's Eye *i.* Rep. of Ire. **18** 53.25N 6.05W
Iringa Tanzania **47** 7.49S 35.39E
Iringa *d.* Tanzania **47** 8.30S 35.00E
Iriomote *i.* Japan **41** 24.30N 124.00E
Irish Sea U.K./Rep. of Ire. **20** 53.40N 4.30W
Irkutsk U.S.S.R. **40** 52.18N 104.15E
Iron-Bridge England **8** 52.38N 2.30W
Iron Gate *f.* Romania/Yugo. **25** 44.40N 22.30E
Iron Mountain *town* U.S.A. **56** 45.51N 88.05W
Iron Mts. Rep. of Ire. **18** 54.10N 7.56W
Iron River *town* U.S.A. **56** 46.05N 88.38W
Ironwood U.S.A. **56** 46.25N 90.08W
Iroquois Falls *town* Canada **56** 48.47N 80.41W
Irrawaddy *r.* Burma **37** 17.45N 95.25E
Irrawaddy Delta Burma **37** 16.30N 95.20E
Irthing *r.* England **15** 54.55N 2.50W
Irthlingborough England **8** 52.20N 0.37W
Irtysh *r.* U.S.S.R. **30** 61.00N 68.40E
Irumu Zaïre **47** 1.29N 29.48E
Irun Spain **23** 43.20N 1.48W
Irvine Scotland **14** 55.37N 4.40W
Irvine *r.* Scotland **14** 55.37N 4.41W
Irvine B. Scotland **14** 55.36N 4.42W
Irvinestown N. Ireland **18** 54.29N 7.40W
Isabelia, Cordillera *mts.* Nicaragua **58** 13.30N 85.00W
Isafjördhur Iceland **28** 66.05N 23.06W
Isangi Zaïre **46** 0.48N 24.03E
Isar *r.* W. Germany **26** 48.48N 12.57E
Ischia *i.* Italy **24** 40.43N 13.54E
Iscia Baidoa Somali Rep. **47** 3.08N 43.34E
Ise Japan **42** 34.29N 136.41E
Isère *r.* France **22** 45.02N 4.54E
Iserlohn W. Germany **27** 51.23N 7.42E
Isfahan Iran **35** 32.42N 51.40E
Isfandaqeh Iran **35** 28.39N 57.13E
Ishikari *r.* Japan **42** 43.15N 141.21E
Ishikari wan *b.* Japan **42** 43.15N 141.20E
Ishim *r.* U.S.S.R. **30** 57.50N 71.00E
Ishqanan Iran **35** 27.10N 53.38E
Isiolo Kenya **47** 0.20N 37.36E
Isiro Zaïre **47** 2.50N 27.40E
Iskenderun Turkey **34** 36.37N 36.08E
Iskenderun, G. of Turkey **34** 36.40N 35.50E
Iskilip Turkey **34** 40.45N 34.28E
Iskŭr *r.* Bulgaria **25** 43.42N 24.27E
Isla *r.* Scotland **17** 56.32N 3.22W
Islamabad Pakistan **36** 33.40N 73.08E
Island Magee *pen.* N. Ireland **14** 54.48N 5.44W
Islands, B. of New Zealand **50** 35.15S 174.15E
Islay *i.* Scotland **14** 55.45N 6.20W
Islay, Sd. of Scotland **14** 55.50N 6.06W
Isle *r.* France **22** 45.02N 0.08W
Isle of Axholme *f.* England **13** 53.32N 0.50W
Isle of Ely *f.* England **9** 52.25N 0.11E
Isle of Man U.K. **12** 54.15N 4.30W
Isle of Oxney *f.* England **9** 51.02N 0.44E
Isle of Portland *f.* England **8** 50.32N 2.25W
Isle of Purbeck *f.* England **8** 50.40N 2.05W
Isle of Thanet *f.* England **9** 51.22N 1.20E
Isle of Whithorn *town* Scotland **14** 54.43N 4.22W
Isle of Wight *d.* England **8** 50.40N 1.17W
Isleworth England **7** 51.28N 0.20W
Islington *d.* England **7** 51.33N 0.06W
Ismâ'ilîa Egypt **34** 30.36N 32.15E
Isna Egypt **34** 25.16N 32.30E
Isoka Zambia **47** 10.06S 32.39E
Isparta Turkey **34** 37.46N 30.32E
Israel Asia **34** 32.00N 34.50E
Isser *r.* Algeria **23** 36.20N 3.28E
Issoire France **22** 45.33N 3.15E
Is-sur-Tille France **22** 47.30N 5.10E
Issyk Kul *l.* U.S.S.R. **40** 43.30N 77.20E
Istanbul Turkey **25** 41.02N 28.58E
Istehbanat Iran **35** 29.05N 54.03E
Isthmus of Kra Thailand **37** 10.10N 99.00E
Istra *pen.* Yugo. **24** 45.12N 13.55E
Itabuna Brazil **62** 14.48S 39.18W
Itajaí Brazil **61** 26.50S 48.39W
Italy Europe **24** 43.00N 12.00E
Itapeva Brazil **61** 23.59S 48.59W
Itaqui Brazil **61** 29.07S 56.33W
Itchen *r.* England **8** 50.55N 1.23W
Iterup *i.* U.S.S.R. **41** 44.00N 147.30E
Ithaca U.S.A. **57** 42.26N 76.30W
Ithon *r.* Wales **10** 52.12N 3.26W
Itimbiri *r.* Zaïre **46** 2.02N 22.47E
Ituri *r.* Zaïre **47** 1.45N 27.06E
Ivai *r.* Brazil **61** 23.20S 53.40W
Ivalo Finland **28** 68.41N 27.30E
Ivalo *r.* Finland **28** 68.45N 27.36E
Ivano-Frankovsk U.S.S.R. **29** 48.55N 24.42E
Ivanovo U.S.S.R. **29** 57.00N 41.00E
Iver England **7** 51.31N 0.30W
Ivigtut Greenland **55** 61.10N 48.00W
Ivindo Gabon **46** 0.02S 12.13E
Ivinghoe England **7** 51.51N 0.39W
Iviza *i.* Spain **23** 39.00N 1.23E
Ivory Coast Africa **44** 7.00N 5.30W
Ivrea Italy **22** 45.28N 7.52E
Ivybridge England **11** 50.24N 3.56W
Iwaki Japan **42** 36.58N 140.58E
Iwaki *r.* Japan **42** 41.20N 140.00E
Iwakuni Japan **42** 34.10N 132.09E
Ixworth England **9** 52.18N 0.50E
Iyo nada *str.* Japan **42** 33.40N 132.20E
Izabal, L. Guatemala **58** 15.30N 89.00W
Izhevsk U.S.S.R. **30** 56.49N 53.11E
Izmail U.S.S.R. **25** 45.20N 28.50E
Izmir Turkey **25** 38.24N 27.09E
Izmir, G. of Med. Sea **25** 38.30N 26.45E
Izmit Turkey **34** 40.48N 29.55E
Izozog Marshes *f.* Bolivia **61** 18.30S 62.05W
Izumo Japan **42** 35.33N 132.50E

J

Jabalón *r.* Spain **23** 38.55N 4.07W
Jabalpur India **37** 23.10N 79.59E
Jabrin Oasis Saudi Arabia **35** 23.15N 49.15E
Jaca Spain **23** 42.34N 0.33W
Jackson Mich. U.S.A. **56** 42.15N 84.24W
Jackson Miss. U.S.A. **53** 32.20N 90.11W
Jacksonville Fla. U.S.A. **53** 30.20N 81.40W
Jacksonville Ill. U.S.A. **56** 39.44N 90.14W
Jacobabad Pakistan **36** 28.16N 68.30E
Jade B. W. Germany **27** 53.30N 8.12E
Jaén Spain **23** 37.46N 3.48W
Jaffna Sri Lanka **37** 9.38N 80.02E
Jafura *des.* Saudi Arabia **35** 24.40N 50.20E
Jagdalpur India **37** 19.04N 82.05E
Jaghbub Libya **34** 29.42N 24.38E
Jaguarao Brazil **61** 32.30S 53.25W
Jahara Kuwait **35** 29.20N 47.41E
Jahrom Iran **35** 28.30N 53.30E
Jaipur India **36** 26.53N 75.50E
Jakobstad Finland **28** 63.41N 22.40E
Jalapa Mexico **58** 19.45N 96.48W
Jalgaon India **36** 21.01N 75.39E
Jalisco *d.* Mexico **58** 21.00N 103.00W
Jalna India **36** 19.50N 75.58E
Jalón *r.* Spain **23** 41.47N 1.02W
Jalpaiguri India **37** 26.30N 88.50E
Jamaica C. America **59** 18.00N 77.00W
Jamalpur Bangla. **37** 24.54N 89.57E
Jamdena *i.* Asia **39** 7.30S 131.00E
James *r.* U.S.A. **53** 42.50N 97.15W
James B. Canada **53** 52.00N 80.00W
Jamestown N. Dak. U.S.A. **52** 46.54N 98.42W
Jamestown N.Y. U.S.A. **57** 42.05N 79.15W
Jammu and Kashmir *d.* Pakistan **36** 36.00N 75.00W
Jammu and Kashmir *d.* India **36** 33.30N 76.00W
Jamnagar India **36** 22.28N 70.06E
Jämsänkoski Finland **28** 61.54N 25.10E
Jamshedpur India **37** 22.47N 86.12E
Janda, Lago de Spain **23** 36.15N 5.50W
Jandula *r.* Spain **23** 38.08N 4.08W
Janesville U.S.A. **56** 42.42N 89.02W
Jan Mayen *i.* Arctic Oc. **4** 71.00N 9.00W
Januária Brazil **62** 15.28S 44.23W
Japan Asia **42** 36.00N 138.00E
Japan, Sea of Asia **42** 40.00N 135.00E
Japan Trench Pacific Oc. **42** 32.00N 142.30E
Japen *i.* Indonesia **39** 1.45S 136.10E
Japura *r.* Brazil **62** 3.00S 64.30W
Jarama *r.* Spain **23** 40.27N 3.32W
Jardines de la Reina *is.* Cuba **59** 20.30N 79.00W
Jardines Lookout *mtn.* Hong Kong **33** 22.16N 114.11E
Jarrahi *r.* Iran **35** 30.40N 48.23E
Jarrow England **13** 54.59N 1.28W
Järvenpää Finland **28** 60.29N 25.06E
Jask Iran **35** 25.40N 57.45E
Jasper Canada **54** 52.55N 118.05W
Jataí Brazil **61** 17.58S 51.45W
Játiva Spain **23** 39.00N 0.32W
Jau Brazil **61** 22.11S 48.35W
Jaunpur India **37** 25.44N 82.41E
Java *i.* Indonesia **38** 7.30S 110.00E
Javari *r.* Peru **62** 4.30S 70.00W
Java Sea Indonesia **38** 5.00S 111.00E
Jedburgh Scotland **15** 55.29N 2.33W
Jefferson, Mt. U.S.A. **52** 38.47N 116.58W
Jefferson City U.S.A. **56** 38.33N 92.10W
Jelenia Góra Poland **26** 50.55N 15.45E
Jelgava U.S.S.R. **28** 56.39N 23.40E
Jena E. Germany **26** 50.56N 11.35E
Jérémie Haiti **59** 18.40N 74.09W
Jerez de la Frontera Spain **23** 36.41N 6.08W
Jericho Jordan **34** 31.51N 35.27E
Jersey *i.* Channel Is. **11** 49.13N 2.08W
Jersey City U.S.A. **57** 40.44N 74.04W
Jerusalem Israel/Jordan **34** 31.47N 35.13E
Jever W. Germany **27** 53.34N 7.54E
Jeypore India **37** 18.51N 82.41E
Jhansi India **37** 25.27N 73.34E
Jhelum *r.* Pakistan **36** 31.04N 72.10E
Jihlava Czech. **26** 49.24N 15.35E
Jimma Ethiopia **45** 7.39N 36.47E
Jinja Uganda **47** 0.27N 33.10E
Jinotepe Nicaragua **58** 11.50N 86.10W
Jiu *r.* Romania **25** 43.44N 23.52E
Jizl, Wadi *r.* Saudi Arabia **34** 25.37N 38.20E
Joaçiba Brazil **61** 27.05S 51.31W
João Pessoa Brazil **62** 7.06S 34.53W
Jódar Spain **23** 37.50N 3.21W
Jodhpur India **36** 26.18N 73.08E
Joensuu Finland **28** 62.35N 29.46E
Jogjakarta Indonesia **38** 7.48S 110.24E
Johannesburg R.S.A. **48** 26.10S 28.02E
John O'Groats Scotland **17** 58.39N 3.02W
Johnstone Scotland **14** 55.50N 4.30W
Johnston's Pt. Scotland **14** 55.22N 5.31W
Johnstown U.S.A. **57** 40.20N 78.56W
Johore Bahru Malaysia **38** 1.29N 103.40E
Joinville Brazil **61** 26.20S 48.49W
Jokkmokk Sweden **28** 66.37N 19.50E
Jökulsá á Brú *r.* Iceland **28** 65.33N 14.23W
Jökulsá á Fjöllum *r.* Iceland **28** 66.05N 16.32W
Joliet U.S.A. **56** 41.32N 88.05W
Joliette Canada **57** 46.02N 73.27W
Jolo *i.* Phil. **39** 5.55N 121.20E
Joma *mtn.* China **37** 33.45N 93.08E
Jombo *r.* Angola **46** 10.20S 16.37E
Jönköping Sweden **28** 57.45N 14.10E
Joplin U.S.A. **53** 37.04N 94.31W
Jordan Asia **34** 31.00N 36.00E
Jordan *r.* Asia **34** 31.47N 35.31E
Jos Nigeria **44** 9.54N 8.53E
Joseph Bonaparte G. Australia **49** 14.00S 128.30E
Jotunheimen *mts.* Norway **28** 61.30N 9.00E
Joyce's Country *f.* Rep. of Ire. **18** 53.33N 9.36W
Juan Fernandez Is. Chile **63** 34.20S 80.00W
Juárez Argentina **61** 37.40S 59.48W
Juba *r.* Somali Rep. **47** 0.20S 42.40E
Juba Sudan **47** 4.50N 31.35E
Jubail Saudi Arabia **35** 27.59N 49.40E
Jubilee Resr. Hong Kong **33** 22.23N 114.08E
Júcar *r.* Spain **23** 39.10N 0.15W
Juchitán Mexico **58** 20.04N 104.06W
Juddah Saudi Arabia **45** 21.30N 39.10E
Juist *i.* W. Germany **27** 53.43N 7.00E
Juiz de Fora Brazil **61** 21.47S 43.23W
Jujuy *d.* Argentina **61** 23.00S 66.00W
Julfa Iran **35** 32.40N 51.39E
Juliana Canal Neth. **27** 51.00N 5.48E
Julianehaab Greenland **55** 60.45N 46.00W
Jülich W. Germany **27** 50.55N 6.21E
Julio de Castilhos Brazil **61** 29.13S 53.40W
Jullundur India **36** 31.18N 75.40E
Jumet Belgium **27** 50.27N 4.27E
Jumla Nepal **37** 29.17N 82.10E
Jumna *r. see* Yamuna India **36**
Junagadh India **36** 21.32N 70.32E
Junction City U.S.A **53** 39.02N 96.51W
Jundiaí Brazil **61** 23.10S 46.54W
Juneau U.S.A. **54** 58.20N 134.20W
Jungfrau *mtn.* Switz. **26** 46.30N 8.00E
Junin Argentina **61** 34.34S 60.55W
Junk B. Hong Kong **33** 22.18N 114.15E
Jura *i.* Scotland **14** 55.58N 5.55W
Jura, Sd. of Scotland **14** 56.00N 5.45W
Jura Mts. Europe **26** 46.55N 6.45E
Jurby Head I.o.M. **12** 54.22N 4.33W
Juruá *r.* Brazil **62** 2.30S 65.40W
Juticalpa Honduras **58** 14.45N 86.12W
Juwain Afghan. **35** 31.43N 61.39E
Jyväskylä Finland **28** 62.16N 25.50E

K

K2 *mtn.* Asia **40** 35.53N 76.32E
Kabaena *i.* Indonesia **39** 5.25S 122.00E
Kabale Uganda **47** 1.13S 30.00E
Kabalega Falls *f.* Uganda **47** 2.17N 31.46E
Kabalega Falls Nat. Park Uganda **47** 2.15N 31.45E
Kabalo Zaïre **47** 6.02S 27.00E
Kabambare Zaïre **47** 4.40S 27.41E
Kabia *i.* Indonesia **39** 6.07S 120.28E
Kabinda Zaïre **46** 6.10S 24.29E
Kabir Kuh *mts.* Iran **35** 33.00N 47.00E
Kabompo *r.* Zambia **46** 14.17S 23.15E
Kabongo Zaïre **46** 7.22S 25.34E
Kabul Afghan. **36** 34.30N 69.10E
Kabunda Zaïre **47** 12.27S 29.15E
Kabwe Zambia **47** 14.27S 28.25E
Kacha Kuh *mts.* Iran **35** 29.30N 61.20E
Kachin State *d.* Burma **37** 25.30N 96.30E
Kadei *r.* C.A.R. **46** 3.29N 16.07E
Kadiyevka U.S.S.R. **29** 48.34N 38.40E
Kaduna Nigeria **44** 10.28N 7.25E
Kadusam *mtn.* China **37** 28.30N 96.45E
Kafirévs, C. Greece **25** 38.11N 24.30E
Kafo *r.* Uganda **47** 1.40N 32.07E
Kafue Zambia **47** 15.40S 28.13E
Kafue *r.* Zambia **47** 15.53S 28.55E
Kafue Nat. Park Zambia **46** 15.30S 25.35E
Kağizman Turkey **34** 40.08N 43.07E
Kagoshima Japan **42** 31.37N 130.32E
Kagoshima wan *b.* Japan **42** 31.00N 131.00E
Kahama Tanzania **47** 3.48S 32.38E
Kahemba Zaïre **46** 7.20S 19.00E
Kaifeng China **41** 34.47N 114.20E
Kai Is. Indonesia **39** 5.45S 132.55E
Kaikohe New Zealand **50** 35.25S 173.49E
Kaikoura New Zealand **50** 42.24S 173.41E
Kaikoura Range *mts.* New Zealand **50** 42.00S 173.40E
Kaimana Asia **39** 3.39S 133.44E
Kaimanawa Range *mts.* New Zealand **50** 37.10S 176.15E
Kaipara Harbour New Zealand **50** 36.30S 174.00E
Kairouan Tunisia **24** 35.40N 10.04E
Kaiserslautern W. Germany **27** 49.27N 7.47E
Kaitaia New Zealand **50** 35.08S 173.18E
Kaitum *r.* Sweden **28** 67.30N 21.00E
Kajaani Finland **28** 64.14N 27.37E
Kajan *r.* Indonesia **38** 2.47N 117.46E

Kajo Kaji Sudan **47** 3.56N 31.40E
Kakamas R.S.A. **48** 28.45S 20.33E
Kakamega Kenya **47** 0.21N 34.47E
Kakhovskoye Resr. U.S.S.R. **29** 47.30N 34.00E
Kakinada India **37** 16.59N 82.20E
Kalahari Desert Botswana **48** 23.30S 22.00E
Kalahari Gemsbok Nat. Park R.S.A. **48** 25.30S 20.30E
Kala-i-Fath Afghan. **35** 30.32N 61.52E
Kalámai Greece **25** 37.02N 22.05E
Kalamazoo U.S.A. **56** 42.17N 85.36W
Kala Nao Afghan. **35** 34.58N 63.04E
Kalat Iran **35** 37.02N 59.46E
Kalat Pakistan **36** 29.01N 66.38E
Kalecik Turkey **34** 40.06N 33.22E
Kalehe Zaïre **47** 2.05S 28.53E
Kalemie Zaïre **47** 5.57S 29.10E
Kalgoorlie Australia **49** 30.49S 121.29E
Kaliakra, C. Bulgaria **25** 43.23N 28.29E
Kalima Zaïre **47** 2.35S 26.34E
Kalimantan *d.* Indonesia **38** 1.00S 113.00E
Kalinin U.S.S.R. **29** 56.47N 35.57E
Kaliningrad U.S.S.R. **28** 54.40N 20.30E
Kalispell U.S.A. **52** 48.12N 114.19W
Kalisz Poland **29** 51.46N 18.02E
Kaliua Tanzania **47** 5.08S 31.50E
Kalix *r.* Sweden **28** 65.50N 23.10E
Kalkfontein Botswana **48** 22.08S 20.53E
Kalla Vesi *l.* Finland **28** 62.45N 28.00E
Kallsjön *l.* Sweden **28** 63.30N 13.00E
Kalmar Sweden **28** 56.39N 16.20E
Kaloli Zambia **47** 14.08S 31.50E
Kalomo Zambia **47** 16.55S 26.29E
Kaluga U.S.S.R. **29** 54.31N 36.16E
Kalundborg Denmark **28** 55.42N 11.06E
Kama *r.* U.S.S.R. **30** 55.30N 52.00E
Kamchatka Pen. U.S.S.R. **31** 56.00N 160.00E
Kamen *mtn.* U.S.S.R. **31** 68.40N 94.20E
Kamenskoye U.S.S.R. **31** 62.31N 165.15E
Kamensk-Shakhtinskiy U.S.S.R. **29** 48.20N 40.16E
Kames Scotland **14** 55.54N 5.15W
Kamet *mtn.* China **37** 31.03N 79.25E
Kamina Zaïre **46** 8.46S 24.58E
Kamloops Canada **52** 50.39N 120.24W
Kampala Uganda **47** 0.19N 32.35E
Kampar *r.* Indonesia **38** 0.20N 102.55E
Kampen Neth. **27** 52.33N 5.55E
Kampot Cambodia **37** 10.37N 104.11E
Kamyshin U.S.S.R. **29** 50.05N 45.24E
Kana *r.* Rhodesia **48** 18.28S 27.03E
Kananga Zaïre **46** 5.53S 22.26E
Kanazawa Japan **42** 36.35N 136.40E
Kanchanaburi Thailand **37** 14.08N 99.31E
Kanchenjunga *mtn.* Asia **37** 27.44N 88.11E
Kanchow China **41** 25.52N 114.51E
Kandahar Afghan. **36** 31.36N 65.47E
Kandalaksha U.S.S.R. **28** 67.09N 32.31E
Kandalakskaya G. U.S.S.R. **28** 66.30N 34.00E
Kandangan Indonesia **38** 2.50S 115.15E
Kandira Turkey **34** 41.05N 30.08E
Kandreho Malagasy Rep. **47** 17.33S 46.00E
Kandy Sri Lanka **37** 7.18N 80.43E
Kane U.S.A. **57** 41.40N 78.48W
Kangan Iran **35** 27.50N 52.07E
Kangar Malaysia **37** 6.27N 100.12E
Kangaroo I. Australia **49** 35.45S 137.30E
Kangean Is. Indonesia **38** 7.00S 115.45E
Kango Gabon **46** 0.15N 10.14E
Kangting China **37** 30.05N 102.04E
Kaniama Zaïre **46** 7.32S 24.11E
Kanin, C. U.S.S.R. **30** 68.50N 43.30E
Kanin Pen. U.S.S.R. **30** 68.00N 45.00E
Kankakee U.S.A. **56** 41.08N 87.52W
Kankan Guinea **44** 10.22N 9.11W
Kanker India **37** 20.17N 81.30E
Kano Nigeria **44** 12.00N 8.31E
Kanoya Japan **42** 31.22N 130.50E
Kanpur India **37** 26.27N 80.14E
Kansas *d.* U.S.A. **52** 38.00N 99.00W
Kansas City U.S.A. **53** 39.02N 94.33W
Kansk U.S.S.R. **31** 56.11N 95.20E
Kanto *d.* Japan **42** 37.00N 140.00E
Kanturk Rep. of Ire. **19** 52.10N 8.54W
Kanye Botswana **48** 24.59S 25.19E
Kaohsiung Taiwan **39** 22.36N 120.17E
Kaoko Veld *f.* S.W. Africa **48** 18.30S 13.30E
Kaoma Zambia **46** 14.55S 24.58E
Kapanga Zaïre **46** 8.22S 22.37E
Kapiji *mtn.* Rhodesia **48** 16.30S 31.50E
Kapiri Mposhi Zambia **47** 13.59S 28.40E
Kapiti I. New Zealand **50** 40.50S 174.50E
Kapoeta Sudan **47** 4.50N 33.35E
Kaposvár Hungary **25** 46.22N 17.47E
Kapsabet Kenya **47** 0.12N 35.05E
Kap Shui Mun *str.* Hong Kong **33** 22.20N 114.03E
Kapuas *r.* Indonesia **38** 0.05N 111.25E
Kapuskasing Canada **56** 49.25N 82.26W
Kara U.S.S.R. **30** 69.12N 65.00E
Kara Bogaz Gol B. U.S.S.R. **35** 41.20N 53.40E
Karabuk Turkey **34** 41.12N 32.36E
Karachi Pakistan **36** 24.51N 67.02E
Karaganda U.S.S.R. **30** 49.53N 73.07E
Kara Irtysh *r.* U.S.S.R. **40** 48.00N 84.20E
Karak Jordan **34** 31.11N 35.42E
Karakelong *i.* Indonesia **39** 4.20N 126.50E
Karakoram Pass Asia **37** 35.53N 77.51E
Karakoram Range *mts.* Jammu and Kashmir **36** 35.30N 76.30E
Kara Kum *des.* U.S.S.R. **35** 37.45N 60.00E
Kara-Kum Canal U.S.S.R. **35** 37.30N 65.48E
Karaman Turkey **34** 37.11N 33.13E
Karamea Bight *b.* New Zealand **50** 41.15S 171.30E
Karamürsel Turkey **34** 40.42N 29.37E
Karand Iran **35** 34.16N 46.15E
Kara Nor *l.* China **40** 38.20N 97.40E
Kara Nur *l.* Mongolia **40** 48.10N 93.20E
Karasburg S.W. Africa **48** 28.00S 18.43E
Kara Sea U.S.S.R. **30** 73.00N 65.00E
Kara-Shahr China **40** 42.00N 86.30E
Karasjok Norway **28** 69.27N 25.30E
Kara-Su *r.* Iran **35** 35.58N 56.25E
Kara Usa Nor *l.* Mongolia **40** 48.10N 92.10E
Karawa Zaïre **46** 3.12N 20.20E
Karawanken *mts.* Austria **26** 46.20N 14.50E
Karbala Iraq **35** 32.37N 44.03E
Kardhítsa Greece **25** 39.22N 21.59E
Karema Tanzania **47** 6.50S 30.25E
Karhula Finland **28** 60.31N 26.50E
Kariba Rhodesia **48** 16.32S 28.50E
Kariba, L. Rhodesia/Zambia **48** 16.50S 28.00E
Kariba Gorge *f.* Rhodesia/Zambia **47** 16.15S 28.55E
Karibib S.W. Africa **48** 21.59S 15.51E
Karikal India **37** 10.58N 79.50E
Karima Sudan **45** 18.32N 31.48E
Karis Finland **28** 60.05N 23.40E
Karisimbi, Mt. Zaïre/Rwanda **47** 1.31S 29.25E
Karkheh *r.* Iran **35** 31.45N 47.52E
Karkinitskiy, G. of U.S.S.R. **29** 45.50N 32.45E
Karkkila Finland **28** 60.32N 24.10E
Kar Kuh *mtn.* Iran **35** 31.37N 53.47E
Karl Marx Stadt E. Germany **26** 50.50N 12.55E
Karlovac Yugo. **24** 45.30N 15.34E
Karlovy Vary Czech. **26** 50.14N 12.53E
Karlsborg Sweden **28** 58.32N 14.32E
Karlshamn Sweden **28** 56.10N 14.50E
Karlskoga Sweden **28** 59.19N 14.33E
Karlskrona Sweden **28** 56.10N 15.35E
Karlsruhe W. Germany **26** 49.00N 8.24E
Karlstad Sweden **28** 59.24N 13.32E
Karmöy *i.* Norway **28** 59.15N 5.05E
Karnobat Bulgaria **25** 42.40N 27.00E
Karonga Malaŵi **47** 9.54S 33.55E
Karpáthos *i.* Greece **25** 35.35N 27.08E
Kars Turkey **34** 40.35N 43.05E
Karsakpay U.S.S.R. **30** 47.47N 66.43E
Karun *r.* Iran **35** 30.25N 48.12E
Kasai *r.* Zaïre **46** 3.10S 16.13E
Kasai Occidental *d.* Zaïre **46** 5.00S 21.30E
Kasai Oriental *d.* Zaïre **46** 5.00S 24.00E
Kasama Zambia **47** 10.10S 31.11E
Kasane Botswana **48** 17.50S 25.05E
Kasanga Tanzania **47** 8.27S 31.10E
Kasempa Zambia **46** 13.28S 25.48E
Kasese Uganda **47** 0.07N 30.06E
Kashan Iran **35** 33.59N 51.31E
Kashgar China **40** 39.29N 76.02E
Kashing China **41** 30.40N 120.50E
Kashmar Iran **35** 35.12N 58.26E
Kaskaskia U.S.A. **56** 38.30N 89.15W
Kasongo Zaïre **47** 4.32S 26.33E
Kasongo-Lunda Zaïre **46** 6.30S 16.47E
Kásos *i.* Greece **34** 35.22N 26.57E
Kassala Sudan **45** 15.24N 36.30E
Kassel W. Germany **26** 51.18N 9.30E
Kasserine Tunisia **24** 35.15N 8.44E
Kastamonu Turkey **34** 41.22N 33.47E
Kastellorizon *i.* Greece **34** 36.08N 29.32E
Kastoria Greece **25** 40.32N 21.15E
Kasungu Malaŵi **47** 13.04S 33.29E
Kataba Zambia **46** 16.12S 25.05E
Katahdin, Mt. U.S.A. **57** 45.55N 68.57W
Katako Kombe Zaïre **46** 3.27S 24.21E
Katha Burma **37** 24.11N 96.20E
Katherina, Gebel *mtn.* Egypt **34** 28.30N 33.57E
Katherine Australia **49** 14.29S 132.20E
Katima Rapids *f.* Zambia **46** 17.15S 24.20E
Katmandu Nepal **37** 27.42N 85.19E
Katonga *r.* Uganda **47** 0.03N 30.15E
Katoomba Australia **49** 33.42S 150.23E
Katowice Poland **29** 50.15N 18.59E
Katrine, Loch Scotland **14** 56.15N 4.30W
Katrineholm Sweden **28** 58.59N 16.15E
Katsina Nigeria **44** 13.00N 7.32E
Kattegat *str.* Denmark/Sweden **28** 57.00N 11.20E
Katwijk aan Zee Neth. **27** 52.13N 4.27E
Kauai *i.* Hawaii U.S.A. **52** 22.05N 159.30W
Kauhajoki Finland **28** 62.26N 21.10E
Kauhava Finland **28** 63.06N 23.05E
Kaunas U.S.S.R. **28** 54.52N 23.55E
Kaura Namoda Nigeria **44** 12.39N 6.38E
Kau Sai Hong Kong **33** 22.20N 114.19E
Kau Sai Chau *i.* Hong Kong **33** 22.21N 114.18E
Kau To Hong Kong **33** 22.24N 114.12E
Kau Wa Keng Hong Kong **33** 22.20N 114.08E
Kau Yi Chau *i.* Hong Kong **33** 22.17N 114.04E
Kavali India **37** 14.55N 80.01E
Kaválla Greece **25** 40.56N 24.24E
Kavirondo G. Kenya **47** 0.15S 34.30E
Kawagoe Japan **42** 35.58N 139.30E
Kawaguchi Japan **42** 35.55N 139.50E
Kawambwa Zambia **47** 9.47S 29.10E
Kawasaki Japan **42** 35.30N 139.45E
Kawimbe Zambia **47** 8.50S 31.31E
Kawthoolei *d.* Burma **37** 19.00N 96.30E
Kayah Burma **40** 18.20N 97.00E
Kayes Mali **44** 14.26N 11.28W
Kayseri Turkey **34** 38.42N 35.28E
Kazachye U.S.S.R. **31** 70.46N 136.15E
Kazakhstan Soviet Socialist Republic *d.* U.S.S.R. **29** 48.00N 48.00E
Kazan U.S.S.R. **29** 55.45N 49.10E
Kazanlŭk Bulgaria **25** 42.38N 25.26E
Kazarun Iran **35** 29.35N 51.39E
Kazbek *mtn.* U.S.S.R. **29** 42.42N 44.30E
Kazumba Zaïre **46** 6.30S 22.02E
Kéa *i.* Greece **25** 37.36N 24.20E
Keady N. Ireland **18** 54.15N 6.43W
Keal, Loch na Scotland **14** 56.28N 6.04W
Kearney U.S.A. **52** 40.42N 99.04W
Kebbi *r.* Nigeria **44** 11.22N 4.10E
Kebnekaise *mtn.* Sweden **28** 67.55N 18.30E
Kebock Head Scotland **16** 58.02N 6.22W
Kecskemet Hungary **29** 46.56N 19.43E
Kediri Indonesia **38** 7.55S 112.01E
Keele Peak *mtn.* Canada **54** 63.15N 129.50W
Keen, Mt. Scotland **17** 56.58N 2.56W
Keene U.S.A. **57** 42.55N 72.17W
Keeper Hill Rep. of Ire. **19** 52.45N 8.17W
Keetmanshoop S.W. Africa **48** 26.36S 18.08E
Keewatin Canada **53** 49.46N 94.30W
Keewatin *d.* Canada **55** 67.00N 90.00W
Kefallinía *i.* Greece **25** 38.15N 20.33E
Keflavik Iceland **28** 64.01N 22.35W
Kei *r.* R.S.A. **48** 32.40S 28.22E
Keighley England **12** 53.52N 1.54W
Keitele *l.* Finland **28** 62.59N 26.00E
Keith Scotland **17** 57.32N 2.57W
Kelberg W. Germany **27** 50.17N 6.56E
Kelkit *r.* Turkey **34** 40.46N 36.32E
Kellett, Mt. Hong Kong **33** 22.15N 114.08E
Kelloselkä Finland **28** 66.55N 28.50E
Kells Kilkenny Rep. of Ire. **19** 52.32N 7.18W
Kells Meath Rep. of Ire. **18** 53.44N 6.53W
Kelowna Canada **52** 49.50N 119.29W
Kelsall England **12** 53.14N 2.44W
Kelso Scotland **15** 55.36N 2.26W
Kelvedon England **9** 51.50N 0.43E
Kelvedon Hatch England **7** 51.40N 0.16E
Kemaliye Turkey **34** 39.16N 38.29E
Kemerovo U.S.S.R. **30** 55.25N 86.10E
Kemi Finland **28** 65.45N 24.12E
Kemi *r.* Finland **28** 55.47N 24.28E
Kemijärvi Finland **28** 66.40N 27.21E
Kempston England **9** 52.07N 0.30W
Kempt, L. Canada **57** 47.30N 74.15W
Kemsing England **7** 51.18N 0.14E
Ken, Loch Scotland **15** 55.02N 4.04W
Kendal England **12** 54.19N 2.44W
Kendari Indonesia **39** 3.57S 122.36E
Kenge Zaïre **46** 4.56S 17.04E
Kengtung Burma **37** 21.16N 99.39E
Kenhardt R.S.A. **48** 29.19S 21.08E
Kenilworth England **8** 52.22N 1.35W
Kenmare Rep. of Ire. **19** 51.53N 9.36W
Kenmare *r.* Rep. of Ire. **19** 51.47N 9.52W
Kenmore Scotland **15** 56.35N 4.00W
Kennedy, C. U.S.A. **53** 28.28N 80.28W
Kennet *r.* England **8** 51.28N 0.57W
Kennington England **9** 51.10N 0.54E
Keno Hill *town* Canada **54** 63.58N 135.22W
Kenora Canada **53** 49.47N 94.26W
Kenosha U.S.A. **56** 42.34N 87.50W
Kensington and Chelsea *d.* England **7** 51.29N 0.12W
Kent *d.* England **9** 51.12N 0.40E
Kentford England **9** 52.16N 0.30E
Kentucky *d.* U.S.A. **53** 38.00N 85.00W
Kentucky L. U.S.A. **53** 36.15N 88.00W
Kenya Africa **47** 1.00N 38.00E
Kenya, Mt. Kenya **47** 0.10S 37.19E
Kerala *d.* India **36** 10.30N 76.30E
Kerch U.S.S.R. **29** 45.22N 36.27E
Kerch Str. U.S.S.R. **29** 45.15N 36.35E
Kerguelen *i.* Indian Oc. **5** 49.30S 69.30E
Kericho Kenya **47** 0.22S 35.19E
Kerintji *mtn.* Indonesia **38** 1.45S 101.20E
Kerkrade Neth. **27** 50.52N 6.02E
Kerloch *mtn.* Scotland **17** 56.59N 2.30W
Kermadec Trench Pacific Oc. **3** 33.00S 176.00W
Kermān Iran **35** 30.18N 57.05E
Kermānshāh Iran **35** 34.19N 47.04E
Kerme, G. of Turkey **25** 36.52N 27.53E
Kerpen W. Germany **27** 50.52N 6.42E
Kerrera *i.* Scotland **14** 56.24N 5.33W
Kerry *d.* Rep. of Ire. **19** 52.07N 9.35W
Kerry Head Rep. of Ire. **19** 52.24N 9.56W
Kerulen *r.* Mongolia **41** 48.45N 117.00E
Keşan Turkey **25** 40.50N 26.39E
Kessingland England **9** 52.25N 1.41E
Keswick England **12** 54.35N 3.09W
Ketapang Indonesia **38** 1.50S 110.02E
Ketchikan U.S.A. **54** 55.25N 131.40W
Kettering England **8** 52.24N 0.44W
Kew England **7** 51.29N 0.18W
Keweenaw B. U.S.A. **56** 47.00N 88.15W
Keweenaw Pt. U.S.A. **56** 47.23N 87.42W
Key, Lough Rep. of Ire. **18** 54.00N 8.15W
Keyingham England **13** 53.42N 0.07W
Keynsham England **8** 51.25N 2.30W
Key West U.S.A. **58** 24.34N 81.48W
Keyworth England **13** 52.52N 1.08W
Khabarovsk U.S.S.R. **41** 48.32N 135.08E
Khabur *r.* Syria **34** 35.07N 40.30E
Khaburah Oman **35** 23.58N 57.10E
Khairpur Pakistan **36** 27.30N 68.50E
Khalkidhiki *pen.* Greece **34** 40.30N 23.25E
Khalkis Greece **25** 38.27N 23.36E
Khanaqin Iraq **35** 34.22N 45.22E
Khandwa India **36** 21.49N 76.23E
Khanka, L. U.S.S.R. **42** 45.00N 132.30E
Khanty-Mansiysk U.S.S.R. **30** 61.00N 69.00E
Khanu Iran **35** 27.55N 57.45E
Kharagpur India **37** 22.23N 87.22E
Kharan *r.* Iran **35** 27.37N 58.48E
Kharga Oasis Egypt **34** 25.00N 30.40E
Kharkov U.S.S.R. **29** 50.00N 36.15E
Kharovsk U.S.S.R. **29** 59.67N 40.07E
Khartoum Sudan **45** 15.33N 32.35E
Khash *r.* Afghan. **35** 31.12N 62.00E
Khaskovo Bulgaria **25** 41.57N 25.33E
Khatanga U.S.S.R. **31** 71.50N 102.31E
Khatangskiy G. U.S.S.R. **31** 75.00N 112.10E
Khemmarat Thailand **37** 16.04N 105.10E
Khenifra Morocco **44** 33.00N 5.40W
Kherson U.S.S.R. **29** 46.39N 32.38E
Khíos Greece **34** 38.23N 26.07E
Khíos *i.* Greece **25** 38.23N 26.04E
Khirsan *r.* Iran **35** 31.29N 48.53E
Khiva U.S.S.R. **35** 41.25N 60.49E
Khmelnitskiy U.S.S.R. **29** 49.25N 26.49E
Khöbsögöl Dalai *l.* Mongolia **40** 51.00N 100.30E
Khoi Iran **35** 38.32N 45.02E
Khomas Highlands S.W. Africa **48** 22.45S 16.20E
Khoper *r.* U.S.S.R. **29** 49.35N 42.17E
Khor Qatar **35** 25.39N 51.32E
Khorramabad Iran **35** 33.29N 48.21E
Khorramshahr Iran **35** 30.26N 48.09E
Khotan China **40** 37.07N 79.57E
Khotin U.S.S.R. **29** 48.30N 26.31E
Khulna Bangla. **37** 22.49N 89.34E
Khunsar Iran **35** 33.12N 50.20E
Khur Iran **35** 33.47N 55.06E
Khurmuj Iran **35** 28.40N 51.20E
Khwash Iran **35** 28.14N 61.15E
Khyber Pass Asia **36** 34.06N 71.05E
Kialing Kiang *r.* China **37** 29.33N 106.30E
Kian China **41** 27.08N 115.00E
Kiangling China **41** 30.20N 112.20E
Kiangsi *d.* China **41** 27.25N 115.20E
Kiangsu *d.* China **41** 34.00N 119.00E
Kibali *r.* Zaïre **47** 3.37N 28.38E
Kibombo Zaïre **46** 3.58S 25.57E
Kibondo Tanzania **47** 3.35S 30.41E
Kibungu Rwanda **47** 2.10S 30.31E
Kibwezi Kenya **47** 2.28S 37.57E
Kicking Horse Pass Canada **52** 51.28N 116.23W
Kidal Mali **44** 18.27N 1.25E
Kidan *des.* Saudi Arabia **35** 22.20N 54.20E
Kidderminster England **8** 52.24N 2.13W
Kidsgrove England **12** 53.06N 2.15W
Kidwelly Wales **11** 51.44N 4.20W
Kiel W. Germany **26** 54.20N 10.08E
Kiel B. W. Germany **26** 54.30N 10.30E
Kiel Canal W. Germany **26** 53.54N 9.12E
Kielder Forest *hills* England **15** 55.15N 2.30W
Kienshui China **37** 23.57N 102.45E
Kienyang Fukien China **41** 27.20N 117.50E
Kiev U.S.S.R. **29** 50.28N 30.29E
Kigali Rwanda **47** 1.59S 30.05E
Kigoma Tanzania **47** 4.52S 29.36E
Kigoma *d.* Tanzania **47** 4.45S 30.00E
Kigosi *r.* Tanzania **47** 4.37S 31.29E
Kii sanchi *mts.* Japan **42** 34.00N 135.20E
Kii suido *str.* Japan **42** 34.00N 135.00E
Kikinda Yugo. **25** 45.51N 20.30E
Kikori P.N.G. **39** 7.25S 144.13E
Kikwit Zaïre **46** 5.02S 18.51E
Kil Sweden **28** 59.30N 13.20E
Kilami Japan **42** 43.57N 143.58E
Kilbaha Rep. of Ire. **19** 52.35N 9.52W
Kilbeggan Rep. of Ire. **18** 53.22N 7.31W
Kilberry Head Scotland **14** 55.47N 5.38W
Kilbirnie Scotland **14** 55.45N 4.41W
Kilbrannan Sd. Scotland **14** 55.37N 5.25W
Kilchrenan Scotland **14** 56.21N 5.11W
Kilchu N. Korea **42** 40.58N 129.21E
Kilcock Rep. of Ire. **18** 53.25N 6.43W
Kilcreggan Scotland **14** 55.59N 4.50W
Kilcrohane Rep. of Ire. **19** 51.35N 9.42W
Kilcullen Rep. of Ire. **19** 53.08N 6.46W
Kildare Rep. of Ire. **19** 53.10N 6.55W
Kildare *d.* Rep. of Ire. **19** 53.10N 6.50W
Kildonan Rhodesia **48** 17.15S 30.44E
Kildorrery Rep. of Ire. **19** 52.14N 8.26W
Kilfinan Scotland **14** 55.58N 5.18W
Kilfinane Rep. of Ire. **19** 52.21N 8.28W
Kilgarvan Rep. of Ire. **19** 51.54N 9.28W
Kilifi Kenya **47** 3.30S 39.50E
Kilimanjaro *d.* Tanzania **47** 3.45S 37.40E
Kilimanjaro *mtn.* Tanzania **47** 3.02S 37.20E
Kilindini Kenya **47** 4.10S 39.37E
Kilis Turkey **34** 36.43N 37.07E
Kilkee Rep. of Ire. **19** 52.41N 9.40W
Kilkeel N. Ireland **18** 54.04N 6.00W
Kilkelly Rep. of Ire. **18** 53.52N 8.52W
Kilkenny Rep. of Ire. **19** 52.39N 7.16W
Kilkenny *d.* Rep. of Ire. **19** 52.35N 7.15W
Kilkhampton England **11** 50.53N 4.29W
Kilkieran B. Rep. of Ire. **18** 53.20N 9.42W
Kilkis Greece **25** 40.59N 22.51E
Killala Rep. of Ire. **18** 54.13N 9.14W
Killala B. Rep. of Ire. **18** 54.15N 9.10W
Killaloe Rep. of Ire. **19** 52.47N 8.28W
Killamarsh England **13** 53.19N 1.19W
Killard Pt. N. Ireland **18** 54.41N 5.31W
Killarney Rep. of Ire. **19** 52.04N 9.32W
Killary Harbour *est.* Rep. of Ire. **18** 53.38N 9.56W
Killchianaig Scotland **14** 56.01N 5.47W
Killeagh Rep. of Ire. **19** 51.56N 8.00W
Killearn Scotland **14** 56.03N 4.22W
Killeshandra Rep. of Ire. **18** 54.01N 7.33W
Killin Scotland **14** 56.29N 4.19W
Killingworth England **15** 55.02N 1.32W
Killíni *mtn.* Greece **25** 37.56N 22.22E
Killorglin Rep. of Ire. **19** 52.07N 9.45W
Killucan Rep. of Ire. **18** 53.30N 7.09W
Killybegs Rep. of Ire. **18** 54.38N 8.27W
Killyleagh N. Ireland **18** 54.24N 5.39W
Kilmacolm Scotland **14** 55.55N 4.38W
Kilmacthomas Rep. of Ire. **19** 52.12N 7.26W
Kilmaganny Rep. of Ire. **19** 52.26N 7.21W
Kilmallock Rep. of Ire. **19** 52.24N 8.35W
Kilmaluag Scotland **16** 57.41N 6.19W
Kilmarnock Scotland **14** 55.37N 4.30W
Kilmartin Scotland **14** 56.18N 5.28W
Kilmar Tor *hill* England **11** 50.34N 4.29W
Kilmichael Pt. Rep. of Ire. **19** 52.44N 6.09W

Kilmore Quay Rep. of Ire. **19** 52.11N 6.34W
Kilnaleck Rep. of Ire. **18** 53.51N 7.20W
Kilninver Scotland **14** 56.21N 5.30W
Kilombero *r.* Tanzania **47** 8.30S 37.28E
Kilosa Tanzania **47** 6.49S 37.00E
Kilrane Rep. of Ire. **19** 52.15N 6.21W
Kilrea N. Ireland **14** 54.57N 6.35W
Kilronan Rep. of Ire. **19** 53.08N 9.41W
Kilrush Rep. of Ire. **19** 52.39N 9.30W
Kilsyth Scotland **15** 55.59N 4.04W
Kiltimagh Rep. of Ire. **18** 53.51N 9.00W
Kilwa Kivinje Tanzania **47** 8.45S 39.21E
Kilwa Masoko Tanzania **47** 8.55S 39.31E
Kilwinning Scotland **14** 55.40N 4.41W
Kilworth Mts. Rep. of Ire. **19** 52.14N 8.12W
Kimberley R.S.A. **48** 28.45S 24.46E
Kimbolton England **9** 52.17N 0.23W
Kimito *i.* Finland **28** 60.05N 22.30E
Kimpton England **7** 51.52N 0.18W
Kinabalu *mtn.* Malaysia **38** 6.10N 116.40E
Kinbrace Scotland **17** 58.15N 3.56W
Kincardine Scotland **15** 56.04N 3.44W
Kinder Scout *hill* England **12** 53.23N 1.53W
Kindu Zaïre **46** 3.00S 25.56E
Kineshma U.S.S.R. **29** 57.28N 42.08E
Kingairloch *f.* Scotland **14** 56.36N 5.35W
Kingarth Scotland **14** 55.46N 5.03W
King Christian Ninth Land *f.* Greenland **55** 68.20N 37.00W
King Frederik Sixth Coast *f.* Greenland **55** 63.00N 44.00W
Kinghorn Scotland **15** 56.04N 3.11W
King I. Australia **49** 39.50S 144.00E
Kingisepp U.S.S.R. **28** 58.12N 22.30E
Kingku China **40** 23.29N 100.19E
King Leopold Ranges *mts.* Australia **49** 17.00S 125.30E
Kings *r.* Rep. of Ire. **19** 52.32N 7.12W
Kingsbridge England **11** 50.17N 3.46W
Kingsbury England **7** 51.35N 0.16W
Kingsclere England **8** 51.20N 1.14W
Kingscourt Rep. of Ire. **18** 53.54N 6.49W
Kingsdown England **9** 51.21N 0.17E
Kings Langley England **7** 51.43N 0.28W
Kingsley Dam U.S.A. **52** 41.15N 101.30W
King's Lynn England **9** 52.45N 0.25E
King's Thorn England **8** 51.59N 2.43W
Kingston Canada **57** 44.14N 76.30W
Kingston Jamaica **59** 17.58N 76.48W
Kingston New Zealand **50** 45.21S 168.44E
Kingston N.Y. U.S.A. **57** 41.55N 74.00W
Kingston Penn. U.S.A. **57** 41.15N 75.52W
Kingston upon Hull England **13** 53.45N 0.20W
Kingston-upon-Thames England **7** 51.25N 0.17W
Kingstown St. Vincent **59** 13.12N 61.14W
Kingswood Avon England **8** 51.27N 2.29W
Kingswood Surrey England **7** 51.17N 0.12W
Kings Worthy England **8** 51.06N 1.18W
Kington England **8** 52.12N 3.02W
Kingussie Scotland **17** 57.05N 4.04W
King William's Town R.S.A. **48** 32.53S 27.24E
Kingyang China **40** 36.06N 107.49E
Kinka zan *c.* Japan **42** 38.20N 141.32E
Kinki *d.* Japan **42** 35.10N 135.00E
Kinloch Scotland **16** 57.00N 6.17W
Kinlochewe Scotland **16** 57.36N 5.18W
Kinlochleven Scotland **14** 56.43N 4.58W
Kinloch Rannoch Scotland **14** 56.42N 4.11W
Kinnairds Head Scotland **17** 57.42N 2.00W
Kinnegad Rep. of Ire. **18** 53.28N 7.08W
Kinnitty Rep. of Ire. **19** 53.06N 7.45W
Kinross Scotland **15** 56.13N 3.27W
Kinsale Rep. of Ire. **19** 51.42N 8.32W
Kinshasa Zaïre **46** 4.18S 15.18E
Kintore Scotland **17** 57.14N 2.21W
Kintyre *pen.* Scotland **14** 55.35N 5.35W
Kinvara Rep. of Ire. **19** 53.08N 8.56W
Kinyeti *mtn.* Sudan **47** 3.56N 32.52E
Kiparissia Greece **25** 37.15N 21.40E
Kipawa L. Canada **57** 46.55N 79.00W
Kipengere Range *mts.* Tanzania **47** 9.15S 34.15E
Kipili Tanzania **47** 7.30S 30.39E
Kipini Kenya **47** 2.31S 40.32E
Kippen Scotland **14** 56.08N 4.11W
Kippure *mtn.* Rep. of Ire. **19** 53.11N 6.20W
Kipushi Zaïre **47** 11.46S 27.15E
Kirensk U.S.S.R. **31** 57.45N 108.00E
Kirgizstan Soviet Socialist Republic *d.* U.S.S.R. **40** 41.30N 75.00E
Kiri Zaïre **46** 1.23S 19.00E
Kirikkale Turkey **34** 39.51N 33.32E
Kirin China **41** 43.53N 126.35E
Kirin *d.* China **41** 43.00N 127.30E
Kirkbean Scotland **15** 54.55N 3.36W
Kirkbride England **15** 54.54N 3.12W
Kirkburton England **12** 53.36N 1.42W
Kirkby England **12** 53.29N 2.54W
Kirkby in Ashfield England **13** 53.06N 1.15W
Kirkby Lonsdale England **12** 54.13N 2.36W
Kirkbymoorside *town* England **13** 54.16N 0.56W
Kirkby Stephen England **12** 54.27N 2.23W
Kirkcaldy Scotland **15** 56.07N 3.10W
Kirkcolm Scotland **14** 54.58N 5.05W
Kirkconnel Scotland **15** 55.23N 4.01W
Kirkcowan Scotland **14** 54.55N 4.36W
Kirkcudbright Scotland **15** 54.50N 4.03W
Kirkcudbright B. Scotland **15** 54.47N 4.05W
Kirkenes Norway **28** 69.44N 30.05E
Kirkham England **12** 53.47N 2.52W
Kirkintilloch Scotland **14** 55.57N 4.10W
Kirkland Lake *town* Canada **56** 48.10N 80.02W
Kirklareli Turkey **25** 41.44N 27.12E
Kirk Michael I.o.M. **12** 54.17N 4.35W
Kirkmichael Scotland **15** 56.44N 3.31W
Kirkmuirhill Scotland **15** 55.40N 3.55W
Kirkoswald England **12** 54.46N 2.41W
Kirkuk Iraq **35** 35.28N 44.26E
Kirkwall Scotland **17** 58.59N 2.58W
Kirn W. Germany **27** 49.47N 7.28E
Kirov R.S.F.S.R. U.S.S.R. **29** 58.38N 49.38E
Kirov R.S.F.S.R. U.S.S.R. **29** 53.59N 34.20E
Kirovabad U.S.S.R. **35** 40.39N 46.20E
Kirovakan U.S.S.R. **35** 40.49N 44.30E
Kirovograd U.S.S.R. **29** 48.31N 32.15E
Kirovsk U.S.S.R. **28** 67.37N 33.39E
Kirriemuir Scotland **15** 56.41N 3.01W
Kirşehir Turkey **34** 39.09N 34.08E
Kirton England **13** 52.56N 0.03W
Kiruna Sweden **28** 67.53N 20.15E
Kisangani Zaïre **46** 0.33N 25.14E
Kishinev U.S.S.R. **29** 47.00N 28.50E
Kishorn, Loch Scotland **16** 57.21N 5.40W
Kisii Kenya **47** 0.40S 34.44E
Kislovodsk U.S.S.R. **29** 43.56N 42.44E
Kismayu Somali Rep. **47** 0.25S 42.31E
Kiso Sammyaku *mts.* Japan **42** 35.30N 137.30E
Kistna *r.* see Krishna India **36**
Kisumu Kenya **47** 0.07S 34.47E
Kitakyushu Japan **42** 33.50N 130.50E
Kitale Kenya **47** 1.01N 35.01E
Kitchener Canada **56** 43.27N 80.30W
Kitega Burundi **47** 3.25S 29.58E
Kitgum Uganda **47** 3.17N 32.54E
Kithira *i.* Greece **25** 36.15N 23.00E
Kithnos *i.* Greece **25** 37.25N 24.25E
Kitimat Canada **54** 54.05N 128.38W
Kitinen *r.* Finland **28** 67.16N 27.30E
Kittanning U.S.A. **57** 40.49N 79.31W
Kitui Kenya **47** 1.22S 38.01E
Kitunda Tanzania **47** 6.48S 33.17E
Kitwe Zambia **47** 12.50S 28.04E
Kiukiang China **41** 29.41N 116.03E
Kiu Tsui Hong Kong **33** 22.22N 114.17E
Kiu Tsui Chau *i.* Hong Kong **33** 22.22N 114.17E
Kivu *d.* Zaïre **47** 3.00S 27.00E
Kivu, L. Rwanda/Zaïre **47** 2.00S 29.10E
Kizil *r.* Turkey **34** 41.45N 35.57E
Kizil Arvat U.S.S.R. **35** 39.00N 56.23E
Kizlyar U.S.S.R. **29** 43.51N 46.43E
Klagenfurt Austria **26** 46.38N 14.20E
Klaipeda U.S.S.R. **28** 55.43N 21.07E
Klamath Falls *town* U.S.A. **52** 42.14N 121.47W
Klar *r.* Sweden **28** 59.25N 13.25E
Kleve W. Germany **27** 51.47N 6.11E
Klin U.S.S.R. **29** 56.20N 36.45E
Klintehamn Sweden **28** 57.24N 18.14E
Klintsy U.S.S.R. **29** 52.45N 32.15E
Klipplaat R.S.A. **48** 33.02S 24.20E
Klöfta Norway **28** 60.04N 11.06E
Knap, Pt. of Scotland **14** 55.53N 5.41W
Knapdale *f.* Scotland **14** 55.53N 5.32W
Knaphill *town* England **7** 51.19N 0.37W
Knaresborough England **13** 54.01N 1.29W
Knebworth England **7** 51.52N 0.12W
Knighton Wales **10** 52.21N 3.02W
Knin Yugo. **24** 44.02N 16.10E
Knockadoon Head Rep. of Ire. **19** 51.52N 7.52W
Knockalongy *mtn.* Rep. of Ire. **18** 54.12N 8.45W
Knockboy *mtn.* Rep. of Ire. **19** 51.48N 9.27W
Knock Hill Scotland **17** 57.35N 2.47W
Knocklayd *mtn.* N. Ireland **14** 55.09N 6.15W
Knockmealdown *mtn.* Rep. of Ire. **19** 52.13N 7.53W
Knockmealdown Mts. Rep. of Ire. **19** 52.15N 7.55W
Knottingley England **13** 53.42N 1.15W
Knoxville U.S.A. **53** 36.00N 83.57W
Knoydart *f.* Scotland **16** 57.03N 5.38W
Knutsford England **12** 53.18N 2.22W
Knysna R.S.A. **48** 34.03S 23.03E
Kobe Japan **42** 34.42N 135.15E
Koblenz W. Germany **27** 50.21N 7.36E
Kobroör *i.* Indonesia **39** 6.10S 134.30E
Kočani Yugo. **25** 41.55N 22.24E
Kochi Japan **42** 33.33N 133.52E
Kodiak U.S.A. **54** 57.49N 152.30W
Kodiak I. U.S.A. **54** 57.00N 153.50W
Koffiefontein R.S.A. **48** 29.22S 24.58E
Kofu Japan **42** 35.44N 138.34E
Köge Denmark **28** 55.28N 12.12E
Kohat Pakistan **36** 33.37N 71.30E
Kohima India **37** 25.40N 84.08E
Kohtla-Järve U.S.S.R. **29** 59.28N 27.20E
Kokand U.S.S.R. **40** 40.33N 70.55E
Kokchetav U.S.S.R. **30** 53.18N 69.25E
Kokenau Asia **39** 4.42S 136.25E
Kokkola Finland **28** 63.50N 23.10E
Kokomo U.S.A. **56** 40.30N 86.09W
Kokon Selka Finland **28** 61.30N 29.30E
Kokpekty U.S.S.R. **40** 48.45N 82.25E
Koksoak *r.* Canada **55** 58.30N 68.15W
Kokstad R.S.A. **48** 30.32S 29.25E
Kola U.S.S.R. **28** 68.53N 33.01E
Kolaka Indonesia **39** 4.04S 121.38E
Kola Pen. U.S.S.R. **30** 67.00N 38.00E
Kolar India **37** 13.10N 78.10E
Kolari Finland **28** 67.22N 23.50E
Kolarovgrad Bulgaria **25** 43.15N 26.55E
Kolding Denmark **28** 55.29N 9.30E
Kole Zaïre **46** 3.28S 22.29E
Kolea Algeria **23** 36.42N 2.46E
Kolepom *i.* Indonesia **39** 8.00S 138.30E
Kolguyev *i.* U.S.S.R. **30** 69.00N 49.00E
Kolhapur India **36** 16.43N 74.15E
Köln see Cologne W. Germany **27**
Koło Poland **29** 52.12N 18.37E
Kołobrzeg Poland **26** 54.10N 15.35E
Kolomna U.S.S.R. **29** 55.05N 38.45E
Kolomyia U.S.S.R. **29** 48.31N 25.00E
Kolwezi Zaïre **46** 10.44S 25.28E
Kolyma *r.* U.S.S.R. **31** 68.50N 161.00E
Kolyma Range *mts.* U.S.S.R. **31** 63.00N 160.00E
Kom *r.* Cameroon **46** 2.20N 10.38E
Komatipoort R.S.A. **48** 25.25S 31.55E
Komba Zaïre **46** 2.52N 24.03E
Kommunarsk U.S.S.R. **29** 48.30N 38.47E
Kommunizma, Peak *mtn.* U.S.S.R. **40** 38.39N 72.01E
Komotini Greece **25** 41.07N 25.26E
Komsomolets *i.* U.S.S.R. **31** 80.20N 96.00E
Komsomolsk-na-Amur U.S.S.R. **31** 50.32N 136.59E
Kondoa Tanzania **47** 4.54S 35.49E
Kongolo Zaïre **47** 5.20S 27.00E
Kongsberg Norway **28** 59.42N 9.39E
Kongsvinger Norway **28** 60.13N 11.59E
Kongwa Tanzania **47** 6.13S 36.28E
Konotop U.S.S.R. **29** 51.15N 33.14E
Konstanz W. Germany **26** 47.40N 9.10E
Kontum S. Vietnam **38** 14.23N 108.00E
Konya Turkey **34** 37.51N 32.30E
Konza Kenya **47** 1.45S 37.07E
Kopet Range *mts.* Asia **35** 38.00N 58.00E
Ko Phangan *i.* Thailand **38** 9.50N 100.00E
Köping Sweden **28** 59.31N 16.01E
Korbach W. Germany **26** 51.16N 8.53E
Korçe Albania **25** 40.37N 20.45E
Korčula *i.* Yugo. **25** 42.56N 16.53E
Korea B. Asia **41** 39.00N 124.00E
Korea Str. Asia **41** 35.00N 129.20E
Köriyama Japan **42** 37.23N 140.22E
Kornat *i.* Yugo. **24** 43.48N 15.20E
Korogwe Tanzania **47** 5.10S 38.35E
Koror *i.* Asia **39** 7.30N 134.30E
Korosten U.S.S.R. **29** 51.00N 28.30E
Korsor Denmark **28** 55.19N 11.09E
Koryak Range *mts.* U.S.S.R. **31** 62.20N 171.00E
Kos *i.* Greece **25** 36.48N 27.10E
Ko Samui *i.* Thailand **38** 9.30N 100.00E
Kosciusko, Mt. Australia **49** 36.28S 148.17E
Košice Czech. **29** 48.44N 21.15E
Kosong S. Korea **42** 37.46N 129.15E
Kosovska-Mitrŏvica Yugo. **25** 42.54N 20.51E
Kossovo U.S.S.R. **29** 52.40N 25.18E
Koster R.S.A. **48** 25.52S 26.54E
Kosti Sudan **45** 13.11N 32.38E
Kostroma U.S.S.R. **29** 57.46N 40.59E
Kostrzyn Poland **26** 52.24N 17.11E
Koszalin Poland **26** 54.10N 16.10E
Kota India **36** 25.11N 75.58E
Kota Bharu Malaysia **38** 6.07N 102.15E
Kota Kinabalu Malaysia **38** 5.59N 116.04E
Kotelnich U.S.S.R. **29** 58.20N 48.10E
Kotelnikovo U.S.S.R. **29** 47.39N 43.08E
Kotelnyy *i.* U.S.S.R. **31** 75.30N 141.00E
Kotka Finland **28** 60.26N 26.55E
Kotlas U.S.S.R. **30** 61.15N 46.28E
Kotor Yugo. **25** 42.28N 18.47E
Kottagudem India **37** 17.32N 80.39E
Kotuy *r.* U.S.S.R. **31** 71.40N 103.00E
Kotzebue U.S.A. **54** 66.51N 162.40W
Kouango C.A.R. **46** 5.00N 20.04E
Kouvola Finland **28** 60.54N 26.45E
Kouyou *r.* Congo **46** 0.40S 16.37E
Kovel U.S.S.R. **29** 51.12N 24.48E
Kovrov U.S.S.R. **29** 56.23N 41.21E
Kowloon Hong Kong **33** 22.19N 114.10E
Kowloon City Hong Kong **33** 22.19N 114.11E
Kowloon Peak Hong Kong **33** 22.20N 114.13E
Kowloon Reservoirs Hong Kong **33** 22.21N 114.09E
Koyukuk *r.* U.S.A. **54** 64.50N 157.30W
Kozan Turkey **34** 37.27N 35.47E
Kozáni Greece **25** 40.18N 21.48E
Kozhikode India **36** 11.15N 75.45E
Kōzu shima *i.* Japan **42** 34.10N 139.08E
Krabi Thailand **37** 8.04N 98.52E
Kragero Norway **28** 58.54N 9.25E
Kragujevac Yugo. **25** 44.01N 20.55E
Kraljevo Yugo. **25** 43.44N 20.41E
Kramatorsk U.S.S.R. **29** 48.43N 37.33E
Kramfors Sweden **28** 62.55N 17.50E
Krasnodar U.S.S.R. **29** 45.02N 39.00E
Krasnograd U.S.S.R. **29** 49.22N 35.28E
Krasnovodsk U.S.S.R. **35** 40.01N 53.00E
Krasnovodsk G. U.S.S.R. **35** 39.50N 53.15E
Krasnoyarsk U.S.S.R. **31** 56.05N 92.46E
Kratie Cambodia **38** 12.30N 106.03E
Krefeld W. Germany **27** 51.20N 6.32E
Kremenchug U.S.S.R. **29** 49.00N 33.25E
Krems Austria **26** 48.25N 15.36E
Kribi Cameroon **46** 2.56N 9.56E
Krishna *r.* India **37** 16.00N 81.00E
Kristiansand Norway **28** 58.08N 7.59E
Kristianstad Sweden **28** 56.02N 14.10E
Kristiansund Norway **28** 63.15N 7.55E
Kristinehamn Sweden **28** 59.17N 14.09E
Kristinestad Finland **28** 62.16N 21.20E
Krivoy Rog U.S.S.R. **29** 47.55N 33.24E
Krk *i.* Yugo. **24** 45.04N 14.36E
Kronshtadt U.S.S.R. **28** 60.00N 29.40E
Kroonstad R.S.A. **48** 27.40S 27.15E
Kruger Nat. Park R.S.A. **48** 24.10S 31.36E
Krugersdorp R.S.A. **48** 26.06S 27.46E
Kruševac Yugo. **25** 43.34N 21.20E
Kuala Lipis Malaysia **38** 4.11N 102.00E
Kuala Lumpur Malaysia **38** 3.08N 101.42E
Kuala Trengganu Malaysia **38** 5.10N 103.10E
Kuandang Indonesia **39** 0.53N 122.58E
Kuantan Malaysia **38** 3.50N 103.19E
Kuba U.S.S.R. **35** 41.23N 48.33E
Kuban *r.* U.S.S.R. **29** 45.20N 37.17E
Kucha China **40** 41.43N 82.58E
Kuching Malaysia **38** 1.32N 110.20E
Kuchino erabu *i.* Japan **42** 30.30N 130.20E
Kuchino shima *i.* Japan **42** 30.00N 129.55E
Kudat Malaysia **38** 6.45N 116.47E
Kufstein Austria **26** 47.36N 12.11E
Kuh Bul *mtn.* Iran **35** 30.48N 52.45E
Kuh-i-Alaband *mtn.* Iran **35** 34.09N 50.48E
Kuh-i-Aleh *mts.* Iran **35** 37.15N 57.30E
Kuh-i-Alijuq *mtn.* Iran **35** 31.27N 51.43E
Kuh-i-Barm *mtn.* Iran **35** 30.21N 52.00E
Kuh-i-Binalud *mts.* Iran **35** 36.15N 59.00E
Kuh-i-Darband *mtn.* Iran **35** 31.33N 57.08E
Kuh-i-Dinar *mtn.* Iran **35** 30.45N 51.39E
Kuh-i-Hazar *mtn.* Iran **35** 29.30N 57.18E
Kuh-i-Istin *mtn.* Iran **35** 31.18N 60.03E
Kuh-i-Karbush *mtn.* Iran **35** 32.36N 50.02E
Kuh-i-Kargiz *mts.* Iran **35** 33.25N 51.40E
Kuh-i-Khurunag *mtn.* Iran **35** 32.10N 54.38E
Kuh-i-Lalehzar *mtn.* Iran **35** 29.26N 56.48E
Kuh-i-Malik Siah *mtn.* Iran **35** 29.52N 60.55E
Kuh-i-Masahim *mtn.* Iran **35** 30.26N 55.08E
Kuh-i-Naibandan *mtn.* Iran **35** 32.25N 57.30E
Kuh-i-Ran *mtn.* Iran **35** 26.46N 58.15E
Kuh-i-Sahand *mtn.* Iran **35** 37.37N 46.27E
Kuh-i-Savalan *mtn.* Iran **35** 38.15N 47.50E
Kuh-i-Shah *mtn.* Iran **35** 31.38N 59.16E
Kuh-i-Shah *mts.* Iran **35** 37.00N 58.00E
Kuh-i-Sultan *mtn.* Pakistan **35** 29.10N 62.48E
Kuh-i-Taftan *mtn.* Iran **35** 28.38N 61.08E
Kuh-i-Ushtaran *mtn.* Iran **35** 33.18N 49.15E
Kuhpayeh Iran **35** 32.42N 52.25E
Kuh Tasak *mtn.* Iran **35** 29.51N 51.52E
Kula Turkey **34** 38.33N 28.38E
Kula Kangri *mtn.* China **37** 28.15N 90.34E
Kuma *r.* U.S.S.R. **29** 44.50N 46.55E
Kumagaya Japan **42** 36.09N 139.22E
Kumai Indonesia **38** 2.45S 111.44E
Kumamoto Japan **42** 32.50N 130.42E
Kumanovo Yugo. **25** 42.08N 21.40E
Kumasi Ghana **44** 6.45N 1.35W
Kum Dag U.S.S.R. **35** 39.14N 54.33E
Kunashir *i.* U.S.S.R. **42** 44.00N 146.00E
Kundelungu Mts. Zaïre **47** 9.30S 27.50E
Kungur *mtn.* China **40** 38.40N 75.30E
Kungur U.S.S.R. **30** 57.27N 56.50E
Kungwe Mt. Tanzania **47** 6.15S 29.54E
Kunlun Shan *mts.* China **40** 36.40N 88.00E
Kunming China **37** 25.04N 102.41E
Kuopio Finland **28** 62.51N 27.30E
Kupa *r.* Yugo. **24** 45.30N 16.20E
Kupang Indonesia **39** 10.13S 123.38E
Kupyansk U.S.S.R. **29** 49.41N 37.37E
Kur *r.* Iran **35** 29.40N 53.17E
Kura *r.* U.S.S.R. **35** 39.18N 49.22E
Kurdistan *f.* Asia **35** 37.00N 43.30E
Kure Japan **42** 34.20N 132.40E
Kurgan U.S.S.R. **30** 55.20N 65.20E
Kuria Muria Is. Oman **36** 17.30N 56.00E
Kuril Is. U.S.S.R. **41** 46.00N 150.30E
Kuril Trench Pacific Oc. **3** 46.00N 150.00E
Kuri san *mtn.* Japan **42** 33.08N 131.10E
Kurlovski U.S.S.R. **29** 55.26N 40.40E
Kurnool India **37** 15.51N 78.01E
Kursk U.S.S.R. **29** 51.45N 36.14E
Kurskiy G. U.S.S.R. **28** 55.00N 21.00E
Kuršumlija Yugo. **25** 43.09N 21.16E
Kuruman R.S.A. **48** 27.28S 23.27E
Kuruman *r.* R.S.A. **48** 27.00S 20.40E
Kushiro Japan **42** 42.58N 144.24E
Kushk Afghan. **35** 34.52N 62.29E
Kushka U.S.S.R. **35** 35.14N 62.15E
Kuskokwim Mts. U.S.A. **54** 62.50N 156.00W
Kustanay U.S.S.R. **30** 53.15N 63.40E
Kusten Canal W. Germany **27** 53.05N 7.46E
Kütahya Turkey **34** 39.25N 29.56E
Kutaisi U.S.S.R. **29** 42.15N 42.44E
Kutch, G. of India **36** 22.30N 69.30E
Kutcharo ko *l.* Japan **42** 43.40N 144.20E
Kutsing China **37** 25.32N 103.47E
Kutu Zaïre **46** 2.42S 18.09E
Kuusamo Finland **28** 65.57N 29.15E
Kuwait Asia **35** 29.20N 47.40E
Kuwait *town* Kuwait **35** 29.20N 48.00E
Kuybyshev U.S.S.R. **29** 53.10N 50.15E
Kuybyshev Resr. U.S.S.R. **29** 55.00N 49.00E
Kuyto, L. U.S.S.R. **28** 65.10N 31.00E
Kuznetsk U.S.S.R. **29** 53.08N 46.36E
Kwai Chung Hong Kong **33** 22.22N 114.08E
Kwamouth Zaïre **46** 3.11S 16.16E
Kwangchow China **38** 23.20N 113.30E
Kwanghua China **41** 32.30N 111.50E
Kwangju S. Korea **41** 35.07N 126.52E
Kwango *r.* Zaïre **46** 3.20S 17.23E
Kwangsi-Chuang *d.* China **41** 23.50N 109.00E
Kwangtung China **41** 23.30N 114.30E
Kwanhsien China **37** 30.59N 103.40E
Kweichow *d.* China **37** 27.00N 106.00E
Kweilin China **41** 25.21N 110.11E
Kweiping China **41** 23.20N 110.04E
Kweiyang China **37** 26.35N 106.40E
Kwenge *r.* Zaïre **46** 4.53S 18.47E
Kwilu *r.* Zaïre **46** 3.18S 17.22E
Kwoka *mtn.* Indonesia **39** 1.30S 132.30E
Kwo Lo Wan Hong Kong **33** 22.19N 114.01E
Kwun Tong Hong Kong **33** 22.19N 114.13E
Kyaka Tanzania **47** 1.16S 31.27E
Kyakhta U.S.S.R. **40** 50.22N 106.30E
Kyaukpyu Burma **37** 19.28N 93.30E
Kyle *f.* Scotland **14** 55.33N 4.28W
Kyleakin Scotland **16** 57.16N 5.44W
Kyle of Durness *est.* Scotland **17** 58.32N 4.50W
Kyle of Lochalsh *town* Scotland **16** 57.17N 5.43W
Kyle of Tongue *est.* Scotland **17** 58.27N 4.26W
Kyles of Bute *str.* Scotland **14** 55.55N 5.12W
Kyll *r.* W. Germany **27** 49.48N 6.42E
Kyluchevskaya *mtn.* U.S.S.R. **31** 56.00N 160.30E
Kyminjoki *r.* Finland **28** 60.30N 27.00E

Kyoga, L. Uganda 47 1.30N 33.00E
Kyoto Japan 42 35.04N 135.50E
Kyrenia Cyprus 34 35.20N 33.20E
Kyushu d. Japan 42 32.00N 130.00E
Kyushu i. Japan 42 32.00N 130.00E
Kyushu sanchi mts. Japan 42 32.20N 131.20E
Kyustendil Bulgaria 25 42.18N 22.39E
Kyyjärvi Finland 28 63.02N 24.34E
Kyzyl U.S.S.R. 40 51.42N 94.28E
Kyzyl Kum des. U.S.S.R. 30 42.00N 64.30E
Kzyl Orda U.S.S.R. 30 44.52N 65.28E

L

La Banda Argentina 61 27.44S 64.14W
La Bañeza Spain 23 42.17N 5.55W
La Barca Mexico 58 20.20N 102.33W
La Bassée France 27 50.32N 2.49E
Labe r. see Elbe Czech. 26
Labé Guinea 44 11.17N 12.11W
La Blanquilla i. Venezuela 59 11.53N 64.38W
Labouheyre France 22 44.13N 0.55W
Labrador f. Canada 55 54.00N 61.30W
Labrador City Canada 55 52.54N 66.50W
Labuan i. Malaysia 38 5.20N 115.15E
La Calle Algeria 24 36.54N 8.25E
La Carolina Spain 23 38.16N 3.36W
Lacaune France 22 43.42N 2.41E
Laccadive Is. Indian Oc. 36 11.00N 72.00E
La Ceiba Honduras 58 15.45N 86.45W
La Charité France 22 47.11N 3.01E
La Chaux de Fonds Switz. 26 47.07N 6.51E
Lachlan r. Australia 49 34.21S 143.58E
Lackan Resr. Rep. of Ire. 19 53.09N 6.31W
Lackawanna U.S.A. 57 42.49N 78.49W
La Coruña Spain 23 43.22N 8.24W
La Crosse U.S.A. 56 43.48N 91.04W
La Demanda, Sierra de mts. Spain 23 42.10N 3.20W
Ladis Iran 35 28.57N 61.18E
Ladismith R.S.A. 48 33.30S 21.15E
Ladoga, L. U.S.S.R. 28 61.00N 32.00E
Ladybrand R.S.A. 48 29.12S 27.27E
Ladysmith R.S.A. 48 28.34S 29.47E
Ladysmith U.S.A. 56 45.27N 91.07W
Lae P.N.G. 39 6.45S 146.30E
La Estrada Spain 23 42.40N 8.30W
Lafayette Ind. U.S.A. 56 40.25N 86.54W
Lafayette La. U.S.A. 53 30.12N 92.18W
La Fère France 27 49.40N 3.22E
La Fuente de San Esteban Spain 23 40.48N 6.15W
Lagan r. N. Ireland 14 54.37N 5.44W
Lagan r. Sweden 28 56.35N 12.55E
Lågen r. Norway 28 60.10N 11.28E
Lagg Scotland 14 55.57N 5.50W
Laggan, Loch Scotland 17 56.57N 4.30W
Laggan B. Scotland 14 55.41N 6.18W
Lago Dilolo town Angola 46 11.27S 22.03E
Lagos Mexico 58 21.21N 101.55W
Lagos Nigeria 44 6.27N 3.28E
Lagos Portugal 23 37.05N 8.40W
La Guaira Venezuela 59 10.38N 66.55W
Laguna Brazil 61 28.29S 48.45W
Laguna Dam U.S.A. 52 32.55N 114.25W
Lahad Datu Malaysia 38 5.05N 118.20E
La Hague, Cap de France 22 49.44N 1.56W
Lahat Indonesia 38 3.46S 103.32E
Lahijan Iran 35 37.12N 50.00E
Lahn r. W. Germany 27 50.18N 7.36E
Lahnstein W. Germany 27 50.17N 7.38E
Lahore Pakistan 36 31.34N 74.22E
Lahti Finland 28 61.00N 25.40E
Lai Chau N. Vietnam 37 22.05N 103.03E
Lai Chi Kok Hong Kong 33 22.20N 114.08E
Laidon England 7 51.34N 0.26E
Laidon, Loch Scotland 14 56.39N 4.38W
Lainio r. Sweden 28 67.26N 22.37E
Lairg Scotland 17 58.01N 4.25W
Lajes Brazil 61 27.48S 50.20W
La Junta U.S.A. 52 37.59N 103.34W
Lak Bor r. Somali Rep. 47 0.32N 42.05E
Lak Dera r. Somali Rep. 47 0.01S 42.45E
Lake Charles town U.S.A. 53 30.13N 93.13W
Lake City U.S.A. 53 30.05N 82.40W
Lake District f. England 12 54.30N 3.10W
Lakeland town U.S.A. 53 28.02N 81.59W
Lakeview U.S.A. 52 42.13N 120.21W
Lakewood U.S.A. 56 41.29N 81.50W
Lakonia, G. of Med. Sea 25 36.35N 22.42E
Lakse Fjord est. Norway 28 70.40N 26.50E
Lakselv Norway 28 70.03N 25.06E
Lalaua Moçambique 47 14.20S 38.30E
La Libertad El Salvador 58 13.28N 89.20W
La Línea Spain 23 36.10N 5.21W
La Louvière Belgium 27 50.29N 4.11E
La Malbaie Canada 57 47.39N 70.11W
Lamar U.S.A. 52 38.04N 102.37W
Lambaréné Gabon 46 0.40S 10.15E
Lambay I. Rep. of Ire. 18 53.29N 6.01W
Lambeth d. England 7 51.27N 0.07W
Lambourn England 8 51.31N 1.31W
Lamego Portugal 23 41.05N 7.49W
Lamía Greece 25 38.53N 22.25E
Lamlash Scotland 14 55.32N 5.08W
Lamma I. Hong Kong 33 22.12N 114.08E
Lammermuir f. Scotland 15 55.50N 2.25W
Lammermuir Hills Scotland 15 55.51N 2.40W
Lamotrek i. Asia 39 7.28N 146.23E
Lampedusa i. Italy 24 35.30N 12.35E
Lampeter Wales 10 52.06N 4.06W
Lampione i. Italy 24 35.33N 12.18E
Lamu Kenya 47 2.20S 40.54E
La Nao, Cabo de Spain 23 38.42N 0.15E
Lanark Scotland 15 55.41N 3.47W
Lancashire d. England 12 53.53N 2.30W
Lancaster England 12 54.03N 2.48W
Lancaster U.S.A. 57 40.01N 76.19W
Lancaster Sd. Canada 55 74.00N 85.00W
Lanchow China 40 36.01N 103.45E
Landeck Austria 26 47.09N 10.35E
Land's End c. England 11 50.03N 5.45W
Landshut W. Germany 26 48.31N 12.10E
Landskrona Sweden 28 55.53N 12.50E
Lanesborough Rep. of Ire. 18 53.40N 8.00W
Langanes c. Iceland 28 66.30N 14.30W
Langavat, Loch Scotland 16 58.04N 6.45W
Langeland i. Denmark 26 54.50N 10.50E
Langeoog i. W. Germany 27 53.46N 7.30E
Langholm Scotland 15 55.09N 3.00W
Langkawi i. Malaysia 38 6.20N 99.30E
Langness c. I.o.M. 12 54.03N 4.37W
Langon France 22 44.33N 0.14W
Langöy i. Norway 28 68.50N 15.00E
Langport England 8 51.02N 2.51W
Langres France 22 47.53N 5.20E
Langsa Indonesia 38 4.28N 97.59E
Långseleån r. Sweden 28 63.30N 16.53E
Lang Son N. Vietnam 38 21.50N 106.55E
Langstrothdale Chase hills England 12 54.13N 2.15W
Lan Nai Wan Tsau Uk Hong Kong 33 22.23N 114.20E
Lannion France 22 48.44N 3.27W
Lansing U.S.A. 56 42.44N 84.34W
Lantau I. Hong Kong 33 22.16N 113.57E
Lanzarote i. Canary Is. 44 29.00N 13.55W
Laoag Phil. 39 18.14N 120.36E
Laois d. Rep. of Ire. 19 53.00N 7.20W
Laokay N. Vietnam 37 22.30N 104.00E
Laon France 27 49.34N 3.37E
La Oroya Peru 62 11.36S 75.54W
Laos Asia 38 19.00N 104.00E
La Palma i. Canary Is. 44 28.50N 18.00W
La Palma Spain 23 37.23N 6.33W
La Pampa d. Argentina 61 37.30S 65.50W
La Paz Argentina 61 30.45S 59.36W
La Paz Bolivia 62 16.30S 68.10W
La Peña, Sierra de mts. Spain 23 42.30N 0.50W
La Perouse Str. U.S.S.R. 31 45.50N 142.30E
Lapford England 11 50.52N 3.49W
Lapland f. Sweden/Finland 28 68.10N 24.00E
La Plata Argentina 61 34.58S 57.55W
La Plata, Rio de est. S. America 61 35.15S 56.45W
Lappa Järvi l. Finland 28 63.05N 23.30E
Lappeenranta Finland 28 61.04N 28.05E
Laptev Sea U.S.S.R. 31 74.30N 125.00E
L'Aquila Italy 24 42.22N 13.25E
Lar Iran 35 27.37N 54.16E
Larache Morocco 23 35.12N 6.10W
Laramie U.S.A. 52 41.20N 105.38W
Larbert Scotland 15 56.02N 3.51W
Larch r. Canada 55 57.40N 69.30W
Laredo U.S.A. 52 27.32N 99.22W
Largo Ward Scotland 15 56.15N 2.52W
Largs Scotland 14 55.48N 4.52W
La Rioja Argentina 61 29.26S 66.50W
La Rioja d. Argentina 61 29.40S 67.00W
Lárisa Greece 25 39.36N 22.24E
Lark r. England 9 52.26N 0.20E
Larkhall Scotland 15 55.45N 3.59W
Lar Koh mtn. Afghan. 35 32.25N 62.36E
Larnaca Cyprus 34 34.54N 33.39E
Larne N. Ireland 14 54.51N 5.49W
Larne Lough N. Ireland 14 54.50N 5.47W
La Roche Belgium 27 50.11N 5.35E
La Rochelle France 22 46.10N 1.10W
La Roche-sur-Yon France 22 46.40N 1.25W
La Rocque Pt. Channel Is. 11 49.09N 2.05W
La Roda Spain 23 39.13N 2.10W
La Romana Dom. Rep. 59 18.27N 68.57W
La Ronge Canada 54 55.07N 105.18W
Larvik Norway 28 59.04N 10.02E
La Sagra mtn. Spain 23 37.58N 2.35W
La Salle U.S.A. 56 41.20N 89.06W
Las Cruces U.S.A. 52 32.18N 106.47W
La Seine, Baie de France 22 49.40N 0.30W
Las Flores Argentina 61 36.03S 59.08W
Lashio Burma 37 22.58N 97.48E
Las Palmas Canary Is. 44 28.08N 15.27W
Las Perlas, Archipelago de Panamá 59 8.45N 79.30W
La Spezia Italy 22 44.07N 9.49E
Lastoursville Gabon 46 0.50S 12.47E
Lastovo i. Yugo. 25 42.45N 16.52E
Las Vegas U.S.A. 52 36.10N 115.10W
Las Villas d. Cuba 59 22.00N 80.00W
Latakia Syria 34 35.31N 35.47E
La Tuque Canada 57 47.26N 72.47W
Latvia Soviet Socialist Republic d. U.S.S.R. 28 57.00N 25.00E
Lauder Scotland 15 55.43N 2.45W
Lauderdale f. Scotland 15 55.43N 2.42W
Laugharne Wales 11 51.45N 4.28W
Launceston Australia 49 41.25S 147.07E
Launceston England 11 50.38N 4.21W
Laune r. Rep. of Ire. 19 52.08N 9.45W
Laurel U.S.A. 57 38.22N 75.34W
Laurencekirk Scotland 17 56.50N 2.29W
Laurencetown Rep. of Ire. 19 53.15N 8.12W
Laurentides Mts. Canada 57 47.40N 71.40W
Lauritsala Finland 28 61.05N 28.20E
Lausanne Switz. 26 46.32N 6.39E
Laut i. Indonesia 38 3.45S 116.20E
Lauterecken W. Germany 27 49.39N 7.36E
Lavagh More mtn. Rep. of Ire. 18 54.45N 8.07W
Laval France 22 48.04N 0.45W
La Vega Dom. Rep. 59 19.15N 70.33W
Lavernock Pt. Wales 11 51.25N 3.10W
Lavras Brazil 61 21.15S 44.59W
Lawers Scotland 14 56.32N 4.10W
Lawrence U.S.A. 57 42.41N 71.12W
Lawrenceville U.S.A. 56 38.44N 87.42W
Laxey I.o.M. 12 54.14N 4.24W
Laxford, Loch Scotland 16 58.25N 5.06W
Lea r. England 7 51.30N 0.00
Leach r. England 8 51.41N 1.39W
Leadburn Scotland 15 55.47N 3.14W
Leader r. Scotland 15 55.37N 2.40W
Leadhills Scotland 15 55.25N 3.46W
Leaf r. Canada 55 58.47N 70.06W
Leamington Canada 56 42.03N 82.35W
Leane, Lough Rep. of Ire. 19 52.03N 9.35W
Leatherhead England 7 51.18N 0.20W
Lebanon Asia 34 34.00N 36.00E
Lebanon N.H. U.S.A. 57 43.39N 72.17W
Lebanon Penn. U.S.A. 57 40.21N 76.25W
Lebork Poland 28 54.32N 17.43E
Lebrija Spain 23 36.55N 6.10W
Le Cateau France 27 50.07N 3.33E
Lecce Italy 25 40.21N 18.11E
Lech r. W. Germany 26 48.45N 10.51E
Le Chesne France 27 49.31N 4.46E
Lechlade England 8 51.42N 1.40W
Le Creusot France 22 46.48N 4.27E
Lectoure France 22 43.56N 0.38E
Ledbury England 8 52.03N 2.25W
Ledesma Spain 23 41.05N 6.00W
Lee r. Rep. of Ire. 19 51.53N 8.25W
Leech L. U.S.A. 53 47.10N 94.30W
Leeds England 13 53.48N 1.34W
Leek England 12 53.07N 2.02W
Leer W. Germany 27 53.14N 7.27E
Leeuwarden Neth. 27 53.12N 5.48E
Leeuwin, C. Australia 49 34.00S 115.00E
Leeward Is. C. America 59 18.00N 61.00W
Legaspi Phil. 39 13.10N 123.45E
Leghorn Italy 24 43.33N 10.18E
Leipzig E. Germany 30 51.20N 12.20E
Legnica Poland 26 51.12N 16.10E
Leh Jammu and Kashmir 36 34.09N 77.35E
Le Havre France 22 49.30N 0.06E
Leicester England 8 52.39N 1.09W
Leicestershire d. England 8 52.29N 1.10W
Leiden Neth. 27 52.10N 4.30E
Leie r. Belgium 27 51.03N 3.44E
Leigh G.M. England 12 53.30N 2.33W
Leigh Kent England 7 51.12N 0.13E
Leighlinbridge Rep. of Ire. 19 52.44N 6.59W
Leighton Buzzard England 8 51.55N 0.39W
Leinster d. Rep. of Ire. 19 53.05N 7.00W
Leinster, Mt. Rep. of Ire. 19 52.38N 6.47W
Leipzig E. Germany 26 51.20N 12.20E
Leiston England 9 52.13N 1.35E
Leith Scotland 15 55.59N 2.09W
Leith Hill England 7 51.11N 0.21W
Leitrim d. Rep. of Ire. 18 54.08N 8.00W
Leixlip Rep. of Ire. 18 53.22N 6.31W
Lei Yue Mun str. Hong Kong 33 22.17N 114.14E
Lek r. Neth. 27 51.55N 4.29E
Le Kef Algeria 24 36.10N 8.40E
Lelystad Neth. 27 52.32N 5.29E
Le Mans France 22 48.01N 0.10E
Lemmer Neth. 27 52.50N 5.43E
Lemmon U.S.A. 52 45.56N 102.00W
Len r. England 7 51.16N 0.31E
Lena r. U.S.S.R. 31 72.00N 127.10E
Lenadoon Pt. Rep. of Ire. 18 54.18N 9.04W
Lengerich W. Germany 27 52.12N 7.52E
Lengoue r. Congo 46 1.15S 16.42E
Lenina, Peak mtn. U.S.S.R. 40 40.14N 69.40E
Leninabad U.S.S.R. 40 40.14N 69.40E
Leninakan U.S.S.R. 35 40.47N 43.49E
Leningrad U.S.S.R. 29 59.55N 30.25E
Leninogorsk U.S.S.R. 30 50.23N 83.32E
Leninsk Kuznetskiy U.S.S.R. 30 54.44N 86.13E
Lenkoran U.S.S.R. 35 38.45N 48.50E
Lenne r. W. Germany 27 51.24N 7.30E
Lennoxtown Scotland 14 55.59N 4.12W
Lens France 27 50.26N 2.50E
Leoben Austria 26 47.23N 15.06E
Leominster England 8 52.15N 2.43W
León Mexico 58 21.10N 101.42W
León Nicaragua 58 12.24N 86.52W
Léon Spain 23 42.35N 5.34W
Le Puy France 22 45.03N 3.54E
Le Quesnoy France 27 50.15N 3.39E
Leribe Lesotho 48 28.52S 28.03E
Lérida Spain 23 41.37N 0.38E
Lerma Spain 23 42.02N 3.46W
Lerwick Scotland 16 60.09N 1.09W
Les Cayes Haiti 59 18.15N 73.46W
Les Ecréhou is. Channel Is. 11 49.17N 1.56W
Les Ecrins mtn. France 22 44.50N 6.20E
Leskovac Yugo. 25 43.00N 21.56E
Leslie Scotland 15 56.13N 3.13W
Lesmahagow Scotland 15 55.38N 3.54W
Lesotho Africa 48 29.00S 28.00E
Lesozavodsk U.S.S.R. 42 45.30N 133.29E
Les Sables d'Olonne France 22 46.30N 1.47W
Lesser Antilles is. C. America 59 13.00N 65.00W
Lesser Slave L. Canada 54 55.30N 115.00W
Lesser Sunda Is. Indonesia 38 8.30S 118.00E
Lessines Belgium 27 50.43N 3.50E
Lésvos i. Greece 25 39.10N 26.16E
Leszno Poland 26 51.51N 16.35E
Letchworth England 9 51.58N 0.13W
Lethbridge Canada 52 49.43N 112.48W
Leticia Colombia 62 4.09S 69.57W
Leti Is. Indonesia 39 8.20S 128.00E
Le Tréport France 22 50.04N 1.22E
Letterkenny Rep. of Ire. 18 54.56N 7.45W
Leuser mtn. Indonesia 38 3.50N 97.10E
Leuze Belgium 27 50.36N 3.37E
Leven England 13 53.54N 0.18W
Leven Scotland 15 56.12N 3.00W
Leven, Loch Scotland 15 56.13N 3.23W
Lévêque, C. Australia 49 16.25S 123.00E
Leverburgh Scotland 16 57.46N 7.00W
Le Verdon France 22 45.33N 1.04W
Leverkusen W. Germany 27 51.02N 6.59E
Levin New Zealand 50 40.37S 175.18E
Levis Canada 57 46.47N 71.12W
Levkás i. Greece 25 38.44N 20.37E
Lew r. England 11 50.50N 4.05W
Lewes England 9 50.53N 0.02E
Lewis i. Scotland 16 58.10N 6.40W
Lewisham d. England 7 51.27N 0.01W
Lewis Pass f. New Zealand 50 42.30S 172.15E
Lewistown Maine U.S.A. 57 44.05N 70.15W
Lewistown Penn. U.S.A. 57 40.37N 77.36W
Lexington U.S.A. 53 38.02N 84.30W
Leyburn England 12 54.19N 1.50W
Leydsdorp R.S.A. 48 23.59S 30.30E
Leyland England 12 53.41N 2.42W
Leysdown-on-Sea England 9 51.23N 0.57E
Leyte i. Phil. 39 10.40N 124.50E
Leyton England 7 51.34N 0.01W
Lezignan France 22 43.12N 2.46E
Lhasa China 37 29.41N 91.10E
Lhokseumawe Indonesia 38 5.09N 97.09E
Liane r. France 9 50.43N 1.35E
Liaocheng China 41 36.29N 115.55E
Liaoning d. China 41 41.30N 123.00E
Liaotung B. China 41 40.20N 121.00E
Liaotung Pen. China 41 40.00N 122.50E
Liaoyuan China 41 42.53N 125.10E
Liard r. Canada 54 61.56N 120.35W
Libenge Zaïre 46 3.39N 18.39E
Liberal U.S.A. 52 37.03N 100.56W
Liberec Czech. 26 50.48N 15.05E
Liberia Africa 44 6.30N 9.30W
Liberia Costa Rica 58 10.39N 85.28W
Libourne France 22 44.55N 0.14W
Libreville Gabon 46 0.25N 9.30E
Libya Africa 44 26.30N 17.00E
Libyan Desert Africa 45 25.00N 26.10E
Libyan Plateau Africa 34 30.45N 26.00E
Licata Italy 24 37.07N 13.58E
Lichfield England 8 52.40N 1.50W
Lichtenburg R.S.A. 48 26.09S 26.11E
Liddel Water r. England 15 54.58N 3.00W
Liddesdale f. Scotland 15 55.10N 2.50W
Lidköping Sweden 28 58.30N 13.10E
Liechtenstein Europe 26 47.08N 9.35E
Liège Belgium 27 50.38N 5.35E
Liège d. Belgium 27 50.32N 5.35E
Lieksa Finland 28 63.13N 30.01E
Lienyunkang China 41 34.42N 119.28E
Lienz Austria 26 46.51N 12.50E
Liepája U.S.S.R. 28 56.30N 21.00E
Lier Belgium 27 51.08N 4.35E
Liévin France 27 50.27N 2.49E
Liffey r. Rep. of Ire. 18 53.21N 6.14W
Lifford Rep. of Ire. 18 54.50N 7.31W
Lightwater England 7 51.21N 0.37W
Ligurian Sea Med. Sea 24 43.30N 9.00E
Lihue Hawaii U.S.A. 52 21.59N 159.23W
Likasi Zaïre 47 10.58S 26.50E
Likiang China 37 26.50N 100.15E
Likona r. Congo 46 0.11N 16.25E
Likouala r. Congo 46 0.51S 17.17E
Lille France 27 50.39N 3.05E
Lillehammer Norway 28 61.06N 10.27E
Lillers France 27 50.34N 2.29E
Lilleström Norway 28 59.58N 11.05E
Lilongwe Malaŵi 47 13.58S 33.49E
Lim r. Yugo. 25 43.45N 19.13E
Lima Peru 62 12.40S 76.40W
Lima r. Portugal 23 41.40N 8.50W
Lima U.S.A. 56 40.43N 84.06W
Limassol Cyprus 34 34.40N 33.03E
Limavady N. Ireland 14 55.03N 6.57W
Limbourg Belgium 27 50.36N 5.57E
Limbourg d. Belgium 27 51.00N 5.30E
Limburg d. Neth. 27 51.15N 5.45E
Limeira Brazil 61 22.34S 47.25W
Limerick Rep. of Ire. 19 52.40N 8.37W
Limerick d. Rep. of Ire. 19 52.40N 8.37W
Lim Fjord est. Denmark 28 56.55N 9.10E
Límnos i. Greece 25 39.55N 25.14E
Limoges France 22 45.50N 1.15E
Limón Costa Rica 58 10.00N 83.01W
Limpopo r. Moçambique 48 25.14S 33.33E
Limpsfield England 7 51.16N 0.02E
Lina Saudi Arabia 35 28.48N 43.45E
Linares Mexico 58 24.54N 99.38W
Linares Spain 23 38.05N 3.38W
Lincoln England 13 53.14N 0.32W
Lincoln Maine U.S.A. 57 45.23N 68.30W
Lincoln Nebr. U.S.A. 53 40.49N 96.41W
Lincoln Edge hills England 13 53.13N 0.31W
Lincolnshire d. England 13 53.14N 0.32W
Lincoln Wolds hills England 13 53.22N 0.08W
Lindenborg Denmark 28 55.56N 10.03E
Lindesnes c. Norway 28 58.00N 7.05E
Lindi Tanzania 47 10.00S 39.41E
Lindi r. Zaïre 46 0.30N 25.06E
Lindos Greece 25 36.05N 28.02E
Lingen W. Germany 27 52.32N 7.19E
Lingfield England 7 51.11N 0.01W
Lingga i. Indonesia 38 0.20S 104.30E
Linköping Sweden 28 58.25N 15.35E
Linlithgow Scotland 15 55.58N 3.36W
Linney Head Wales 11 51.37N 5.05W
Linnhe, Loch Scotland 14 56.35N 5.25W

Linosa *i.* Italy **24** 35.52N 12.50E
Linsia China **40** 35.31N 103.08E
Linslade England **8** 51.55N 0.40W
Lintan China **40** 34.39N 103.40E
Linton England **9** 52.06N 0.19E
Linxe France **22** 43.56N 1.10W
Linz Austria **26** 48.19N 14.18E
Lion Rock *mtn.* Hong Kong **33** 22.21N 114.11E
Lions, G. of France **22** 43.12N 4.15E
Liouesso Congo **46** 1.12N 15.47E
Lipari Is. Italy **24** 38.35N 14.45E
Lipetsk U.S.S.R. **29** 52.37N 39.36E
Liphook England **8** 51.05N 0.49W
Lippe *r.* W. Germany **27** 51.38N 6.37E
Lira Uganda **47** 2.15N 32.55E
Lisala Zaïre **46** 2.13N 21.37E
Lisboa *see* Lisbon Portugal **23**
Lisbon Portugal **23** 38.44N 9.08W
Lisburn U.K. **20** 54.30N 6.03W
Lisburne, C. U.S.A. **54** 69.00N 165.50W
Liscannor B. Rep. of Ire. **19** 52.55N 9.24W
Lishui China **41** 28.30N 119.59E
Liskeard England **11** 50.27N 4.29W
Liski U.S.S.R. **29** 51.00N 39.30E
Lismore Rep. of Ire. **19** 52.08N 7.57W
Lismore *i.* Scotland **14** 56.31N 5.30W
Lisnaskea N. Ireland **18** 54.16N 7.28W
Liss England **8** 51.03N 0.53W
Listowel Rep. of Ire. **19** 52.27N 9.30W
Litang *r.* China **37** 28.09N 101.30E
Lithuania Soviet Socialist Republic *d.* U.S.S.R. **28** 55.00N 23.50E
Little Andaman *i.* India **37** 10.50N 92.38E
Little Cayman *i.* Cayman Is. **59** 19.40N 80.00W
Little Chalfont England **7** 51.39N 0.33W
Little Coco *i.* Burma **38** 13.50N 93.10E
Little Current *town* Canada **56** 45.57N 81.56W
Little Fen *f.* England **9** 52.18N 0.30E
Little Grand Rapids *town* Canada **53** 52.00N 95.01W
Littlehampton England **9** 50.48N 0.32W
Little Inagua *i.* Bahamas **59** 21.30N 73.00W
Little Karroo *f.* R.S.A. **48** 33.40S 21.30E
Little Khingan Shan *mts.* China **41** 48.40N 128.30E
Little Loch Broom *l.* Scotland **16** 57.53N 5.20W
Little Nicobar *i.* Asia **38** 8.00N 93.30E
Little Ouse *r.* England **9** 52.34N 0.20E
Littleport England **9** 52.27N 0.18E
Little Rock *town* U.S.A. **53** 34.42N 92.17W
Little St. Bernard Pass France/Italy **24** 45.40N 6.53E
Little Thurrock England **7** 51.28N 0.20E
Littleton Rep. of Ire. **19** 52.39N 7.44W
Little Zab *r.* Iraq **35** 35.15N 43.27E
Liuchow China **41** 24.17N 109.15E
Livermore, Mt. U.S.A. **52** 30.39N 104.11W
Liverpool Canada **55** 44.03N 64.43W
Liverpool England **12** 53.25N 3.00W
Liverpool B. England **12** 53.30N 3.10W
Livingston Scotland **15** 55.54N 3.31W
Livingstone Zambia **46** 17.40S 25.50E
Livingstonia Malawi **47** 10.35S 34.10E
Livramento Brazil **61** 30.52S 55.30W
Liwale Tanzania **47** 9.47S 38.00E
Lizard England **11** 49.58N 5.12W
Lizard Pt. England **11** 49.57N 5.15W
Ljubljana Yugo. **26** 46.04N 14.28E
Ljungan *r.* Sweden **28** 62.20N 17.19E
Ljungby Sweden **28** 56.49N 13.55E
Ljusdal Sweden **28** 61.49N 16.09E
Ljusnan *r.* Sweden **28** 61.15N 17.08E
Ljusnarsberg Sweden **28** 59.48N 14.57E
Llanbedr Wales **10** 52.40N 4.07W
Llanberis Wales **10** 53.07N 4.07W
Llanbister Wales **10** 52.22N 3.19W
Llandeilo Wales **10** 51.54N 4.00W
Llandovery Wales **10** 51.59N 3.49W
Llandrillo Wales **10** 52.55N 3.25W
Llandrindod Wells Wales **10** 52.15N 3.23W
Llandudno Wales **10** 53.19N 3.49W
Llandyssul Wales **10** 52.03N 4.20W
Llanelli Wales **11** 51.41N 4.11W
Llanerchymedd Wales **10** 53.20N 4.22W
Llanes Spain **23** 43.25N 4.45W
Llanfair-ar-y-bryn Wales **10** 52.04N 3.43W
Llanfair Caereinion Wales **10** 52.39N 3.20W
Llanfairfechan Wales **10** 53.15N 3.58W
Llanfihangel-Ystrad Wales **10** 52.11N 4.11W
Llanfyllin Wales **10** 52.47N 3.17W
Llangadfan Wales **10** 52.41N 3.28W
Llangadog Wales **10** 51.56N 3.53W
Llangefni Wales **10** 53.15N 4.20W
Llangollen Wales **10** 52.58N 3.10W
Llangynog Wales **10** 52.50N 3.24W
Llanidloes Wales **10** 52.28N 3.31W
Llanos *f.* Venezuela **59** 8.30N 67.00W
Llanrhystyd Wales **10** 52.19N 4.09W
Llanrwst Wales **10** 53.08N 3.48W
Llantrisant Wales **11** 51.33N 3.23W
Llantwit Major Wales **11** 51.24N 3.29W
Llanuwchllyn Wales **10** 52.52N 3.41W
Llanwrtyd Wells Wales **10** 52.06N 3.39W
Llanybyther Wales **10** 52.04N 4.10W
Llerena Spain **23** 38.14N 6.00W
Lleyn Pen. Wales **10** 52.50N 4.35W
Lloydminster Canada **54** 53.18N 110.00W
Loange *r.* Zaïre **46** 4.18S 20.05E
Loanhead Scotland **15** 55.53N 3.09W
Lobatse Botswana **48** 25.11S 25.40E
Lobaye *r.* C.A.R. **46** 3.44N 18.35E
Loberia Argentina **61** 38.08S 58.48W
Lobito Angola **46** 12.20S 13.34E
Lobos Argentina **61** 35.11S 59.08W
Locarno Switz. **26** 46.10N 8.48E
Lochaber *f.* Scotland **17** 56.55N 4.55W
Lochailort Scotland **16** 56.50N 5.40W
Lochaline Scotland **14** 56.32N 5.47W
Lochboisdale *town* Scotland **16** 57.09N 7.19W
Lochbuie Scotland **14** 56.22N 5.52W
Lochcarron Scotland **16** 57.25N 5.36W
Lochdonhead Scotland **14** 56.26N 5.41W
Lochearnhead Scotland **14** 56.23N 4.17W
Lochem Neth. **27** 52.10N 6.25E
Loches France **22** 47.08N 1.00E
Lochgelly Scotland **15** 56.08N 3.19W
Lochgilphead Scotland **14** 56.02N 5.26W
Lochgoilhead Scotland **14** 56.10N 4.54W
Lochinver Scotland **16** 58.09N 5.15W
Lochmaben Scotland **15** 55.08N 3.27W
Lochmaddy *town* Scotland **16** 57.36N 7.10W
Lochnagar *mtn.* Scotland **17** 56.57N 3.15W
Lochranza Scotland **14** 55.42N 5.18W
Lochwinnoch Scotland **14** 55.48N 4.38W
Lochy *r.* Scotland **16** 56.50N 5.05W
Lochy, Loch Scotland **17** 56.58N 4.55W
Lockerbie Scotland **15** 55.07N 3.21W
Loc Ninh S. Vietnam **38** 11.55N 106.35E
Loddon *r.* England **8** 51.30N 0.53W
Lodja Zaïre **46** 3.29S 23.33E
Lodwar Kenya **47** 3.06N 35.38E
Łódź Poland **29** 51.49N 19.28E
Lofoten *is.* Norway **28** 68.15N 13.50E
Loftus England **13** 54.33N 0.52W
Logan, Mt. Canada **54** 60.45N 140.00W
Logansport U.S.A. **56** 40.45N 86.25W
Logone *r.* Cameroon/Chad **44** 12.10N 15.00E
Logroño Spain **23** 42.28N 2.26W
Loimaa Finland **28** 60.50N 23.05E
Loir *r.* France **22** 47.29N 0.32E
Loire *r.* France **22** 47.18N 2.00W
Loja Ecuador **62** 3.59S 79.16W
Loja Spain **23** 37.10N 4.09W
Loje *r.* Angola **46** 7.52S 13.08E
Loka Sudan **47** 4.18N 31.00E
Lokeren Belgium **27** 51.06N 3.59E
Lokitaung Kenya **47** 4.15N 35.45E
Lokolo *r.* Zaïre **46** 0.45S 19.36E
Lokoro *r.* Zaïre **46** 1.40S 18.29E
Lolland *i.* Denmark **26** 54.50N 11.30E
Lom Bulgaria **25** 43.49N 23.13E
Lomami *r.* Zaïre **46** 0.45N 24.10E
Lombok *i.* Indonesia **38** 8.30S 116.20E
Lomé Togo **44** 6.10N 1.21E
Lomela Zaïre **46** 2.15S 23.15E
Lomela *r.* Zaïre **46** 0.14S 20.45E
Lomié Cameroon **46** 3.09N 13.35E
Lomond, Loch Scotland **14** 56.07N 4.36W
Łomża Poland **29** 53.11N 22.04E
London Canada **56** 42.58N 81.15W
London England **7** 51.32N 0.06W
London Colney England **7** 51.44N 0.18W
Londonderry N. Ireland **14** 55.00N 7.21W
Londonderry *d.* N. Ireland **14** 55.00N 7.00W
Londonderry, C. Australia **49** 13.58S 126.55E
Londrina Brazil **63** 23.30S 51.13W
Long, Loch Scotland **14** 56.05N 4.52W
Longa *r.* Angola **46** 16.15S 19.07E
Longa *i.* Scotland **16** 57.44N 5.48W
Long Beach *town* U.S.A. **52** 33.57N 118.15W
Long Bennington England **13** 52.59N 0.45W
Longbenton England **15** 55.02N 1.33W
Long Branch U.S.A. **57** 40.17N 73.59W
Long Ditton England **7** 51.23N 0.20W
Long Eaton England **13** 52.54N 1.16W
Longford Rep. of Ire. **18** 53.44N 7.48W
Longford *d.* Rep. of Ire. **18** 53.42N 7.45W
Longhorsley England **15** 55.15N 1.46W
Longhoughton England **15** 55.26N 1.36W
Long I. Bahamas **59** 23.00N 75.00W
Long I. U.S.A. **57** 40.50N 73.20W
Long L. Canada **56** 49.40N 86.45W
Longlac *town* Canada **53** 49.47N 86.34W
Long Mtn. England **8** 52.40N 3.05W
Longniddry Scotland **15** 55.58N 2.53W
Long Pt. Canada **56** 42.33N 80.04W
Long Pt. New Zealand **50** 46.35S 169.35E
Longridge England **12** 53.50N 2.37W
Longs Peak U.S.A. **52** 40.16N 105.37W
Long Sutton England **13** 52.47N 0.09E
Longtown England **15** 55.01N 2.58W
Longwy France **27** 49.32N 5.46E
Long Xuyen S. Vietnam **38** 10.23N 105.25E
Löningen W. Germany **27** 52.44N 7.46E
Looe England **11** 50.51N 4.26W
Lookout, C. U.S.A. **53** 34.34N 76.34W
Loolmalasin *mtn.* Tanzania **47** 3.00S 35.45E
Loop Head Rep. of Ire. **19** 52.33N 9.56W
Lopari *r.* Zaïre **46** 1.20N 20.22E
Lopez, C. Gabon **46** 0.36S 8.40E
Lopi Congo **46** 2.57N 2.47E
Lop Nor *l.* China **40** 40.30N 90.30E
Lopp Havet *est.* Norway **28** 70.30N 21.00E
Lorain U.S.A. **56** 41.28N 82.11W
Loralai Pakistan **36** 30.20N 68.41E
Lorca Spain **23** 37.40N 1.41W
Lordsburg U.S.A. **52** 32.22N 108.43W
Lorient France **22** 47.45N 3.21W
Los Angeles U.S.A. **52** 34.00N 118.17W
Los Blancos Spain **23** 37.37N 0.48W
Loshan China **37** 29.34N 103.42E
Lošinj *i.* Yugo. **24** 44.36N 14.20E
Los Libres, Punta de *c.* Argentina **61** 29.40S 57.06W
Lo So Shing Hong Kong **33** 22.12N 114.07E
Los Roques *i.* Venezuela **59** 12.00N 67.00W
Lossie *r.* Scotland **17** 57.43N 3.18W
Lossiemouth Scotland **17** 57.43N 3.18W
Lostwithiel England **11** 50.24N 4.41W
Lot *r.* France **22** 44.17N 0.22E
Lothian *d.* Scotland **15** 55.50N 3.00W
Lotoi *r.* Zaïre **46** 1.30S 18.30E
Lotsani *r.* Botswana **48** 22.41S 28.06E
Lötschberg Tunnel Switz. **26** 46.25N 7.53E
Lotta *r.* U.S.S.R. **28** 68.36N 31.06E
Lotuke *mtn.* Sudan **47** 4.10N 33.46E
Loudéac France **22** 48.11N 2.45W
Loudima Congo **46** 4.06S 13.05E
Loughborough England **13** 52.47N 1.11W
Loughor *r.* Wales **11** 51.41N 4.04W
Loughrea Rep. of Ire. **19** 53.12N 8.35W
Loughros More B. Rep. of Ire. **18** 54.48N 8.32W
Loughton England **7** 51.39N 0.03E
Louisburgh Rep. of Ire. **18** 53.46N 9.49W
Louisiana *d.* U.S.A. **53** 31.00N 92.30W
Louis Trichardt R.S.A. **48** 23.01S 29.43E
Louisville U.S.A. **53** 38.13N 85.45W
Lourdes France **22** 43.06N 0.02W
Lourenço Marques Moçambique **48** 25.58S 32.35E
Louth England **13** 53.23N 0.00
Louth *d.* Rep. of Ire. **18** 53.55N 6.30W
Louvain Belgium **27** 50.53N 4.45E
Lovat *r.* U.S.S.R. **29** 58.06N 31.37E
Lovech Bulgaria **25** 43.08N 24.44E
Lovoi *r.* Zaïre **47** 8.14S 26.40E
Lovua *r.* Zaïre **46** 6.08S 20.35E
Lowa *r.* Kivu Zaïre **46** 1.25S 25.55E
Lo Wai Hong Kong **33** 22.22N 114.07E
Lowell U.S.A. **57** 42.38N 71.19W
Lower California *pen.* Mexico **52** 30.00N 115.00W
Lower Egypt *f.* Egypt **34** 30.30N 31.00E
Lower Lough Erne N. Ireland **18** 54.28N 7.48W
Lower Nazeing England **7** 51.43N 0.03E
Lower Tunguska *r.* U.S.S.R. **31** 65.50N 88.00E
Lowestoft England **9** 52.29N 1.44E
Lowick England **15** 55.39N 1.58W
Łowicz Poland **29** 52.06N 19.55E
Lowther Hills Scotland **15** 55.20N 3.40W
Loyal, Loch Scotland **17** 58.23N 4.21W
Lua *r.* Zaïre **46** 2.45N 18.28E
Lualaba *r.* Zaïre **46** 0.18N 25.32E
Luama *r.* Zaïre **47** 4.45S 26.55E
Luanchimo *r.* Zaïre **46** 6.32S 20.57E
Luanda Angola **46** 8.50S 13.20E
Luanda *d.* Angola **46** 9.00S 13.30E
Luando Game Res. Angola **46** 11.00S 17.45E
Luang Prabang Laos **38** 19.53N 102.10E
Luangwa *r.* Central Zambia **47** 15.32S 30.28E
Luanshya Zambia **47** 13.09S 28.24E
Luapula *r.* Zambia **47** 9.25S 28.36E
Luarca Spain **23** 43.33N 6.31W
Lubbock U.S.A. **52** 33.35N 101.53W
Lübeck W. Germany **26** 53.52N 10.40E
Lübeck B. W. Germany **26** 54.05N 11.00E
Lubefu *r.* Zaïre **46** 4.05S 23.00E
Lubero Zaïre **47** 0.12S 29.15E
Lubilash *r.* Zaïre **46** 4.59S 23.25E
Lublin Poland **29** 51.18N 22.31E
Lubny U.S.S.R. **29** 50.01N 33.00E
Lubudi Zaïre **46** 9.57S 25.59E
Lubudi *r.* Kasai Occidental Zaïre **46** 4.00S 21.23E
Lubudi *r.* Shaba Zaïre **46** 9.13S 25.40E
Lubumbashi Zaïre **47** 11.44S 27.29E
Lubutu Zaïre **47** 0.48S 26.19E
Lucan Rep. of Ire. **18** 53.21N 6.27W
Luce, Water of *r.* Scotland **14** 54.52N 4.49W
Luce B. Scotland **14** 54.45N 4.47W
Lucena Spain **23** 37.25N 4.29W
Lučenec Czech. **29** 48.20N 19.40E
Lucero Mexico **52** 30.50N 106.30W
Luchow China **37** 28.25N 105.20E
Lucknow India **37** 26.50N 80.54E
Lüdenscheid W. Germany **27** 51.13N 7.36E
Lüderitz S.W. Africa **48** 26.38S 15.10E
Ludgate Canada **56** 45.54N 80.32W
Ludgershall England **8** 51.15N 1.38W
Ludhiana India **36** 30.56N 75.52E
Lüdinghausen W. Germany **27** 51.46N 7.27E
Ludington U.S.A. **56** 43.58N 86.27W
Ludlow England **8** 52.23N 2.42W
Ludvika Sweden **28** 60.08N 15.14E
Ludwigshafen W. Germany **26** 49.29N 8.27E
Luebo Zaïre **46** 5.16S 21.27E
Luena *r.* Angola **46** 12.30S 22.37E
Luena Zambia **47** 10.40S 30.21E
Luena *r.* Western Zambia **46** 14.47S 23.05E
Luengue *r.* Angola **48** 16.58S 21.15E
Luete *r.* Zambia **48** 16.13S 23.15E
Lufira *r.* Zaïre **47** 8.15S 26.30E
Lufkin U.S.A. **53** 31.21N 94.47W
Luga U.S.S.R. **29** 58.42N 29.49E
Luga *r.* U.S.S.R. **28** 59.40N 28.15E
Lugano Switz. **22** 46.01N 8.57E
Lugenda *r.* Moçambique **47** 11.23S 38.30E
Lugg *r.* England **8** 52.01N 2.38W
Lugh Ganana Somali Rep. **47** 3.49N 42.34E
Lugnaquilla Mtn. Rep. of Ire. **19** 52.58N 6.28W
Lugo Spain **23** 43.00N 7.33W
Lugoj Romania **25** 45.42N 21.56E
Luiana Angola **46** 17.08S 22.59E
Luiana *r.* Angola **48** 17.28S 23.02E
Luichart, Loch Scotland **17** 57.36N 4.45W
Luichow Pen. China **41** 20.40N 109.30E
Luilaka *r.* Zaïre **46** 0.15S 19.00E
Luilu *r.* Zaïre **46** 6.22S 23.53E
Luing *i.* Scotland **14** 56.14N 5.38W
Luiro *r.* Finland **28** 67.22N 27.30E
Luisa Zaïre **46** 7.15S 22.27E
Lukala Zaïre **46** 5.23S 13.02E
Lukanga Swamp *f.* Zambia **47** 14.15S 27.30E
Lukenie *r.* Zaïre **46** 2.43S 18.12E
Lukuga *r.* Zaïre **47** 5.37S 26.58E
Lukula *r.* Zaïre **46** 4.15S 17.59E
Luleå Sweden **28** 65.35N 22.10E
Luleburgaz Turkey **25** 41.25N 27.23E
Lulonga *r.* Zaïre **46** 0.42N 18.26E
Lulua *r.* Zaïre **46** 5.03S 21.07E
Lumsden New Zealand **50** 45.45S 168.27E
Lumsden Scotland **17** 57.17N 2.53W
Lunan B. Scotland **15** 56.38N 2.30W
Lund Sweden **28** 55.42N 13.10E
Lunda *d.* Angola **46** 9.30S 20.00E
Lundazi Zambia **47** 12.19S 33.11E
Lundi *r.* Rhodesia **48** 21.16S 32.20E
Lundy *i.* England **11** 51.10N 4.41W
Lune *r.* England **12** 54.03N 2.49W
Lüneburg W. Germany **26** 53.15N 10.24E
Lunga *r.* Zambia **47** 14.28S 26.27E
Lungsi China **40** 35.00N 105.00E
Lungwebungu *r.* Zambia **46** 14.20S 23.15E
Luninets U.S.S.R. **29** 52.18N 26.50E
Lunna Ness *c.* Scotland **16** 60.27N 1.03W
Luque Paraguay **61** 25.15S 57.32W
Lure France **26** 47.42N 6.30E
Lurgan N. Ireland **18** 54.28N 6.21W
Lurio Moçambique **47** 13.30S 40.30E
Lurio *r.* Moçambique **47** 13.32S 40.31E
Lusaka Zambia **47** 15.20S 28.14E
Lusambo Zaïre **46** 4.59S 23.26E
Lushoto Tanzania **47** 4.48S 38.20E
Lusiti *r.* Moçambique **48** 20.00S 33.51E
Lusk Rep. of Ire. **18** 53.32N 6.12W
Lusk U.S.A. **52** 42.47N 104.26W
Luss Scotland **14** 56.06N 4.38W
Lüta China **41** 38.53N 121.37E
Lutfabad U.S.S.R. **35** 37.32N 59.17E
Luton England **7** 51.53N 0.25W
Lutterworth England **8** 52.28N 1.12W
Luvua *r.* Zaïre **47** 6.45S 27.00E
Luwegu *r.* Tanzania **47** 8.30S 37.28E
Luwingu Zambia **47** 10.13S 30.05E
Luxembourg *d.* Belgium **27** 49.58N 5.30E
Luxembourg Europe **27** 49.50N 6.15E
Luxembourg *town* Lux. **27** 49.37N 6.08E
Luxor Egypt **34** 24.41N 32.24E
Luzern Switz. **26** 47.03N 8.17E
Luzon *i.* Phil. **39** 17.50N 121.00E
Luzon Str. Pacific Oc. **39** 20.20N 122.00E
Lvov U.S.S.R. **29** 49.50N 24.00E
Lyallpur Pakistan **36** 31.25N 73.09E
Lybster Scotland **17** 58.18N 3.18W
Lycksele Sweden **28** 64.34N 18.40E
Lyd *r.* England **11** 50.38N 4.18W
Lydd England **9** 50.57N 0.56E
Lydda Israel **34** 31.57N 34.54E
Lydenburg R.S.A. **48** 25.10S 30.29E
Lydney England **8** 51.43N 2.32W
Lyell, Mt. U.S.A. **52** 37.45N 119.18W
Lyme B. England **8** 50.40N 2.55W
Lyme Regis England **8** 50.44N 2.57W
Lyminge England **9** 51.07N 1.06E
Lymington England **8** 50.46N 1.32W
Lympstone England **8** 50.39N 3.25W
Lyndhurst England **8** 50.53N 1.33W
Lynher *r.* England **11** 50.23N 4.18W
Lynn U.S.A. **57** 42.29N 70.57W
Lynn Lake *town* Canada **55** 56.51N 101.01W
Lynton England **11** 51.14N 3.50W
Lyon France **22** 45.46N 4.50E
Lyon *r.* Scotland **15** 56.37N 3.59W
Lysekil Sweden **28** 58.16N 11.26E
Lytham St. Anne's England **12** 53.45N 3.01W
Lyubertsy U.S.S.R. **29** 55.38N 37.58E

M

Maamakeogh *mtn.* Rep. of Ire. **18** 54.17N 9.29W
Maamtrasna *mtn.* Rep. of Ire. **18** 53.37N 9.35W
Maamturk Mts. Rep. of Ire. **18** 53.32N 9.42W
Ma'an Jordan **34** 30.11N 35.43E
Maas *r.* Neth. **27** 51.44N 4.42E
Maaseik Belgium **27** 51.08N 5.48E
Maastricht Neth. **27** 50.51N 5.42E
Mabico *r.* Botswana **48** 24.15S 26.48E
Mablethorpe England **13** 53.21N 0.14E
Maboze Moçambique **48** 23.49S 32.09E
Macao Asia **38** 22.13N 113.36E
Macapá Brazil **62** 0.01N 51.01W
Macclesfield England **12** 53.16N 2.09W
Macdonnell Ranges *mts.* Australia **49** 23.30S 132.00E
Macduff Scotland **17** 57.40N 2.29W
Maceió Brazil **62** 9.34S 35.47W
Macerata Italy **24** 43.18N 13.30E
Macgillycuddy's Reeks *mts.* Rep. of Ire. **19** 52.00N 9.43W
Macheke Rhodesia **48** 18.05S 31.51E
Machrihanish Scotland **14** 55.25N 5.44W
Machynlleth Wales **10** 52.35N 3.51W
Mackay Australia **49** 21.10S 149.10E
Mackay, L. Australia **49** 22.30S 128.58E
Mackenzie *d.* Canada **54** 65.00N 115.00W
Mackenzie *r.* Canada **54** 69.20N 134.00W
Mackenzie King I. Canada **54** 77.30N 112.00W
Mackenzie Mts. Canada **54** 64.00N 130.00W
Mackinaw City U.S.A. **56** 45.47N 84.43W
Mackinnon Road *town* Kenya **47** 3.50S 39.03E
Maclear R.S.A. **48** 31.05S 28.22E
Macleod's Tables *mtn.* Scotland **16** 57.25N 6.45W
Macloutsie *r.* Botswana **48** 22.15S 29.00E
Macnean, Lough N. Ireland **18** 54.19N 7.56W
Macomer Italy **24** 40.16N 8.45E
Mâcon France **22** 46.18N 4.50E
Macon U.S.A. **53** 32.47N 83.37W
Macroom Rep. of Ire. **19** 51.54N 8.58W
Madagascar *i.* Africa **3** 20.00S 45.00E

Madang P.N.G. **39** 5.14S 145.45E
Madawaska *r.* Canada **57** 45.35N 76.25W
Madeira *i.* Atlantic Oc. **44** 32.45N 17.00W
Madeira *r.* Brazil **62** 3.50S 58.30W
Madhya Pradesh *d.* India **37** 23.00N 79.30E
Madison Fla. U.S.A. **53** 30.29N 83.39W
Madison Wisc. U.S.A. **56** 43.04N 89.22W
Madiun Indonesia **38** 7.37S 111.33E
Madjene Indonesia **38** 3.33S 118.59E
Mado Gashi Kenya **47** 0.40N 39.11E
Madras India **37** 13.05N 80.18E
Madre, Sierra *mts.* Mexico **58** 16.00N 93.00W
Madre de Dios *r.* Bolivia **62** 11.00S 66.30W
Madre del Sur, Sierra *mts.* Mexico **58** 17.00N 100.00W
Madre Lagoon Mexico **58** 25.00N 97.30W
Madre Occidental, Sierra *mts.* Mexico **58** 24.00N 103.00W
Madre Oriental, Sierra *mts.* Mexico **58** 24.00N 99.00W
Madrid Spain **23** 40.25N 3.43W
Madukani Tanzania **47** 3.57S 35.49E
Madura *i.* Indonesia **38** 7.00S 113.30E
Madurai India **37** 9.55N 78.07E
Maebashi Japan **42** 36.30N 139.04E
Maesteg Wales **11** 51.36N 3.40W
Maestra, Sierra *mts.* Cuba **59** 20.10N 76.30W
Mafeking R.S.A. **48** 25.53S 25.39E
Mafeteng Lesotho **48** 29.49S 27.14E
Mafia I. Tanzania **47** 7.50S 39.50E
Mafraq Jordan **34** 32.20N 36.12E
Magadan U.S.S.R. **31** 59.38N 150.50E
Magadi Kenya **47** 1.53S 36.18E
Magangue Colombia **59** 9.14N 74.46W
Magas Iran **35** 27.08N 61.36E
Magdalena *r.* Colombia **59** 10.56N 74.58W
Magdalena Mexico **52** 30.38N 110.59W
Magdeburg E. Germany **26** 52.08N 11.36E
Magellan's Str. Chile **63** 53.00S 71.00W
Mageröya *i.* Norway **28** 71.00N 25.50E
Maggiore, L. Italy **22** 45.57N 8.37E
Maghera N. Ireland **14** 54.51N 6.41W
Magherafelt N. Ireland **14** 54.45N 6.38W
Maghull England **12** 53.31N 2.56W
Magnitogorsk U.S.S.R. **30** 53.28N 59.06E
Magude Moçambique **48** 25.02S 32.40E
Magué Moçambique **47** 15.46S 31.42E
Magwe Burma **37** 20.10N 95.00E
Mahabad Iran **35** 36.44N 45.44E
Mahaddei Wen Somali Rep. **47** 2.58N 45.32E
Mahagi Zaire **47** 2.16N 30.59E
Mahalapye Botswana **48** 23.05S 26.51E
Mahallat Iran **35** 33.54N 50.28E
Mahanadi *r.* India **37** 20.17N 86.43E
Maharashtra *d.* India **36** 20.00N 77.00E
Mahdia Tunisia **24** 35.28N 11.01E
Mahenge Tanzania **47** 8.46S 36.38E
Mahia Pen. New Zealand **50** 37.10S 178.30E
Mahón Spain **23** 39.55N 4.18E
Mahua Moçambique **47** 13.43S 37.10E
Maidenhead England **7** 51.32N 0.44W
Maiden Newton England **8** 50.46N 2.35W
Maidens Scotland **14** 55.20N 4.49W
Maidstone England **7** 51.17N 0.32E
Maiduguri Nigeria **44** 11.53N 13.16E
Maiko *r.* Zaire **46** 0.15N 25.35E
Main *r.* N. Ireland **14** 54.43N 6.19W
Main *r.* W. Germany **26** 50.00N 8.19E
Mai Ndombe *l.* Zaire **46** 2.00S 18.20E
Maine *r.* Rep. of Ire. **19** 52.09N 9.44W
Maine *d.* U.S.A. **57** 45.00N 69.00W
Mainland *i.* Orkney Is. Scotland **17** 59.00N 3.10W
Mainland *i.* Shetland Is. Scotland **17** 60.15N 1.22W
Mainz W. Germany **26** 50.00N 8.16E
Maipu Argentina **61** 36.52S 57.52W
Maitland Australia **49** 32.33S 151.33E
Maizuru Japan **42** 35.30N 135.20E
Maja *i.* Indonesia **38** 1.05S 109.25E
Majma'a Saudi Arabia **35** 25.52N 45.25E
Majorca *i.* Spain **23** 39.35N 3.00E
Majuba Hill R.S.A. **48** 27.30S 29.50E
Majunga Malagasy Rep. **47** 15.50S 46.20E
Makarikari Salt Pan *f.* Botswana **48** 20.50S 25.45E
Makassar Indonesia **38** 5.09S 119.30E
Makassar Str. Indonesia **38** 3.00S 118.00E
Makeyevka U.S.S.R. **29** 48.01N 38.00E
Makó Hungary **25** 46.13N 20.30E
Makokou Gabon **46** 0.38N 12.47E
Makoua Congo **46** 0.01S 15.40E
Makran *f.* Asia **35** 26.30N 61.20E
Makurdi Nigeria **44** 7.44N 8.35E
Malabo Equat. Guinea **46** 3.45N 8.48E
Malacca Malaysia **38** 2.14N 102.14E
Malacca, Straits of Indian Oc. **38** 3.00N 100.30E
Málaga Colombia **59** 6.44N 72.45W
Málaga Spain **23** 36.43N 4.25W
Malagasy Republic Africa **47** 17.00S 46.00E
Malahide Rep. of Ire. **18** 53.27N 6.10W
Malakal Sudan **45** 9.31N 31.40E
Malakand Pakistan **36** 34.34N 71.57E
Malang Indonesia **38** 7.59S 112.45E
Malanje Angola **46** 9.36S 16.21E
Malanje *d.* Angola **46** 9.00S 17.00E
Mälaren *l.* Sweden **28** 59.30N 17.00E
Malatya Turkey **34** 38.22N 38.18E
Malaŵi Africa **47** 12.00S 34.00E
Malaŵi, L. Africa **47** 12.00S 34.30E
Malayer Iran **35** 34.19N 48.51E
Malaysia Asia **38** 5.00N 110.00E
Malbork Poland **29** 54.02N 19.01E
Malden England **7** 51.23N 0.15W
Maldive Is. Indian Oc. **36** 6.20N 73.00E
Maldon England **9** 51.43N 0.41E
Maldonado Uruguay **61** 34.57S 54.59W
Maléa, C. Greece **25** 36.27N 23.11E
Malebo Pool *f.* Zaire **46** 4.15S 15.25E
Malegaon India **36** 20.32N 74.38E
Malema Moçambique **47** 14.55S 37.09E
Mali Africa **44** 16.00N 3.00W
Malili Indonesia **39** 2.38S 121.06E
Malin Rep. of Ire. **14** 55.18N 7.15W
Malindi Kenya **47** 3.14S 40.08E
Malines Belgium **27** 51.01N 4.28E
Malin Head Rep. of Ire. **18** 55.23N 7.24W
Malin More Rep. of Ire. **18** 54.42N 8.48W
Ma Liu Shui Hong Kong **33** 22.25N 114.12E
Mallaig Scotland **16** 57.00N 5.50W
Mallawi Egypt **34** 27.44N 30.50E
Mallorca *i. see* MajorcaSpain **23**
Mallow Rep. of Ire. **19** 52.08N 8.39W
Malmédy Belgium **27** 50.25N 6.02E
Malmesbury England **8** 51.35N 2.05W
Malmesbury R.S.A. **48** 33.28S 18.43E
Malmö Sweden **28** 55.35N 13.00E
Malone U.S.A. **57** 44.52N 74.19W
Malonga Zaire **46** 10.26S 23.10E
Målöy Norway **28** 61.57N 5.06E
Malta Europe **24** 35.55N 14.25E
Malta *i.* Malta **24** 35.55N 14.25E
Malta Channel Med. Sea **24** 36.20N 14.45E
Maltby England **13** 53.25N 1.12W
Malton England **13** 54.09N 0.48W
Maluku *d.* Indonesia **39** 4.00S 129.00E
Malvern Hills England **8** 52.05N 2.16W
Malvernia Moçambique **48** 22.06S 31.42E
Mambasa Zaire **47** 1.20N 29.05E
Mamberamo *r.* Asia **39** 1.45S 137.25E
Mambilima Falls *town* Zambia **47** 10.32S 28.45E
Mamore *r.* Bolivia **62** 12.00S 65.15W
Mamudju Indonesia **38** 2.41S 118.55E
Man, Isle of U.K. **20** 54.15N 4.30W
Manacle Pt. England **11** 50.04N 5.05W
Manacor Spain **23** 39.32N 3.12E
Manado Indonesia **39** 1.30N 124.58E
Managua Nicaragua **58** 12.06N 86.18W
Managua, L. Nicaragua **58** 12.10N 86.30W
Manama Bahrain **35** 26.12N 50.36E
Ma Nam Wat Hong Kong **33** 22.21N 114.16E
Manapouri New Zealand **50** 45.35S 167.38E
Manapouri, L. New Zealand **50** 45.30S 167.00E
Manastir Turkey **34** 37.33N 31.37E
Manaus Brazil **62** 3.06S 60.00W
Manchester England **12** 53.30N 2.15W
Manchester Conn. U.S.A. **57** 41.47N 72.31W
Manchester N.H. U.S.A. **57** 42.59N 71.28W
Manchuria *f.* China **41** 46.00N 125.00E
Manchurian Plain *f.* Asia **3** 42.00N 122.00E
Mand *r.* Iran **35** 28.09N 51.16E
Manda Iringa Tanzania **47** 10.30S 34.37E
Mandal Norway **28** 58.02N 7.30E
Mandala Peak Asia **39** 4.45S 140.15E
Mandalay Burma **37** 21.57N 96.04E
Mandal Gobi Mongolia **40** 45.40N 106.10E
Manfredonia Italy **24** 41.38N 15.54E
Mangalia Romania **25** 43.48N 28.30E
Mangalore India **36** 12.54N 74.51E
Mangerton Mtn. Rep. of Ire. **19** 51.58N 9.30W
Mangochi Malaŵi **47** 14.29S 35.15E
Mangotsfield England **8** 51.29N 2.29W
Mangueira L. Brazil **61** 33.15S 52.50W
Mangyai China **40** 37.52N 91.26E
Mangyshlak Pen. U.S.S.R. **30** 44.00N 52.30E
Manhiça Moçambique **48** 25.23S 32.49E
Maniamba Moçambique **47** 12.30S 35.05E
Manica e Sofala *d.* Moçambique **47** 17.30S 34.00E
Manicouagan *r.* Canada **55** 49.00N 68.13W
Manila Phil. **39** 14.36N 120.59E
Maninga *r.* Zambia **46** 13.28S 24.25E
Manipur *d.* India **37** 25.00N 93.40E
Manisa Turkey **25** 38.37N 27.28E
Manistee *r.* U.S.A. **56** 44.17N 85.45W
Manistique U.S.A. **56** 45.58N 86.17W
Manitoba *d.* Canada **55** 54.00N 96.00W
Manitoba, L. Canada **52** 51.35N 99.00W
Manitou Is. U.S.A. **56** 45.05N 86.05W
Manitoulin I. Canada **56** 45.50N 82.15W
Manitowoc U.S.A. **56** 44.04N 87.40W
Maniwaki Canada **57** 46.22N 75.58W
Manizales Colombia **62** 5.03N 75.32W
Manjil Iran **35** 36.44N 49.29E
Mannar, G. of India/Sri Lanka **37** 8.20N 79.00E
Mannheim W. Germany **26** 49.30N 8.28E
Mannin B. Rep. of Ire. **18** 53.28N 10.06W
Manningtree England **9** 51.56N 1.03E
Mannu *r.* Italy **24** 39.16N 9.00E
Manokwari Asia **39** 0.53S 134.05E
Manono Zaire **47** 7.18S 27.24E
Manorhamilton Rep. of Ire. **18** 54.18N 8.10W
Manosque France **22** 43.50N 5.47E
Manresa Spain **23** 41.43N 1.50E
Mansa Zambia **47** 11.10S 28.52E
Mansel I. Canada **55** 62.00N 80.00W
Mansfield England **13** 53.08N 1.12W
Mansfield U.S.A. **56** 40.46N 82.31W
Mänttä Finland **28** 62.00N 24.40E
Mantua Italy **24** 45.09N 10.47E
Manukau Harbour New Zealand **50** 37.10S 174.00E
Manus *i.* Pacific Oc. **39** 2.00S 147.00E
Manyara, L. Tanzania **47** 3.40S 35.50E
Manych *r.* U.S.S.R. **29** 47.14N 40.20E
Manych Gudilo, L. U.S.S.R. **29** 46.20N 42.45E
Manyoni Tanzania **47** 5.46S 34.50E
Manzala, L. Egypt **34** 31.20N 32.00E
Manzanares Spain **23** 39.00N 3.23W
Manzanillo Cuba **59** 20.21N 77.21W
Manzini Swaziland **48** 26.30S 31.22E
Maoke Range *mts.* Indonesia **39** 4.00S 137.30E
Ma On Shan *mtn.* Hong Kong **33** 22.24N 114.15E
Mapai Moçambique **48** 22.51S 32.00E
Mapia Is. Asia **39** 1.00N 134.15E
Ma'qala Saudi Arabia **35** 26.29N 47.20E
Maquela do Zombo Angola **46** 6.06S 15.12E
Maquinchao Argentina **61** 41.19S 68.47W
Mar *f.* Scotland **17** 57.07N 3.03W
Mar, Serra do *mts.* Brazil **61** 28.00S 49.30W
Mara *d.* Tanzania **47** 1.45S 34.30E
Mara *r.* Tanzania **47** 1.30S 33.52E
Maracaibo Venezuela **59** 10.44N 71.37W
Maracaibo, L. Venezuela **59** 10.00N 71.30W
Maracaju Brazil **61** 21.38S 55.10W
Maracaju, Serra de *mts.* Brazil **61** 21.00S 55.05W
Maracay Venezuela **59** 10.20N 67.28W
Maradi Niger **44** 13.29N 7.10E
Maragheh Iran **35** 37.25N 46.13E
Marajó I. Brazil **62** 1.00S 49.30W
Maralal Kenya **47** 1.15N 36.48E
Marand Iran **35** 38.25N 45.50E
Marandellas Rhodesia **48** 18.05S 31.42E
Marañon *r.* Peru **62** 4.00S 73.30W
Marapi *mtn.* Indonesia **38** 0.20S 100.45E
Maraş Turkey **34** 37.34N 36.54E
Marathon Greece **25** 38.10N 23.59E
Marazion England **11** 50.08N 5.29W
Marbella Spain **23** 36.31N 4.53W
Marble Bar Australia **49** 21.16S 119.45E
Marburg W. Germany **26** 50.49N 8.36E
March England **9** 52.33N 0.05E
Marche Belgium **27** 50.13N 5.21E
Marchena Spain **23** 37.20N 5.24W
Marcy, Mt. U.S.A. **57** 44.07N 73.56W
Mar del Plata Argentina **61** 38.00S 57.32W
Marden England **7** 51.11N 0.30E
Mardin Turkey **34** 37.19N 40.43E
Maree, Loch Scotland **16** 57.41N 5.28W
Marettimo *i.* Italy **24** 37.58N 12.05E
Margarita I. Venezuela **59** 11.00N 64.00W
Margate England **9** 51.23N 1.24E
Mariana Is. Asia **39** 15.00N 145.00E
Marianao Cuba **58** 23.03N 82.29W
Marianas Trench Pacific Oc. **3** 19.00N 146.00E
Maribor Yugo. **26** 46.35N 15.40E
Maridi Sudan **47** 4.55N 29.30E
Marie Galante *i.* Guadeloupe **59** 16.00N 61.15W
Mariehamn Finland **28** 60.05N 19.55E
Mariental S.W. Africa **48** 24.36S 17.59E
Mariestad Sweden **28** 58.44N 13.50E
Marília Brazil **63** 22.13S 50.20W
Marinette U.S.A. **56** 45.06N 87.38W
Maringá Brazil **61** 23.36S 52.02W
Maringa *r.* Zaire **46** 1.13N 19.50E
Maringue Moçambique **48** 17.55S 34.24E
Marinha Grande Portugal **23** 39.45N 8.55W
Marion Ind. U.S.A. **56** 40.33N 85.40W
Marion Ohio U.S.A. **56** 40.35N 83.08W
Mariscal Estigarribia Paraguay **61** 22.03S 60.35W
Maritsa *r.* Turkey **25** 41.00N 26.15E
Markaryd Sweden **28** 56.26N 13.35E
Markerwaard *f.* Neth. **27** 52.30N 5.15E
Market Deeping England **9** 52.40N 0.20W
Market Drayton England **12** 52.55N 2.30W
Market Harborough England **8** 52.29N 0.55W
Market Rasen England **13** 53.24N 0.20W
Market Weighton England **13** 53.52N 0.04W
Markha *r.* U.S.S.R. **31** 63.37N 119.00E
Markinch Scotland **15** 56.12N 3.09W
Markyate England **7** 51.51N 0.28W
Marlborough England **8** 51.26N 1.44W
Marlborough Downs *hills* England **8** 51.28N 1.48W
Marle France **27** 49.44N 3.47E
Marlow England **7** 51.35N 0.48W
Marlpit Hill *town* England **7** 51.13N 0.04E
Marmagao India **36** 15.26N 73.50E
Marmara *i.* Turkey **25** 40.38N 27.37E
Marmara, Sea of Turkey **25** 40.45N 28.15E
Marmaris Turkey **25** 36.50N 28.17E
Marne *r.* France **22** 48.50N 2.25E
Maroua Cameroon **44** 10.35N 14.20E
Marovoay Malagasy Rep. **47** 16.05S 46.35E
Marple England **12** 53.23N 2.05W
Marquesas Is. Pacific Oc. **2** 9.00S 139.00W
Marquette U.S.A. **56** 46.33N 87.23W
Marquise France **9** 50.48N 1.42E
Marrakesh Morocco **44** 31.49N 8.00W
Marrupa Moçambique **47** 13.10S 37.30E
Marsabit Kenya **47** 2.20N 37.59E
Marsala Italy **24** 37.48N 12.27E
Marsden England **12** 53.36N 1.55W
Marseille France **22** 43.18N 5.22E
Marshall Is. Pacific Oc. **3** 8.00N 172.00E
Marshfield England **8** 51.28N 2.19W
Marshfield U.S.A. **56** 44.40N 90.11W
Marshland Fen *f.* England **9** 52.40N 0.18E
Marske-by-the-Sea England **13** 54.35N 1.00W
Martaban, G. of Burma **37** 15.10N 96.30E
Martelange Belgium **27** 49.50N 5.44E
Martés, Sierra *mts.* Spain **23** 39.10N 1.00W
Martha's Vineyard *i.* U.S.A. **57** 41.25N 70.35W
Martigny Switz. **26** 46.07N 7.05E
Martinique C. America **59** 14.40N 61.00W
Martin Pt. U.S.A. **54** 70.10N 143.50W
Martinsburg U.S.A. **57** 39.28N 77.59W
Marton New Zealand **50** 40.04S 175.25E
Maruchak Afghan. **35** 35.50N 63.08E
Marum Neth. **27** 53.06N 6.16E
Marvejols France **22** 44.33N 3.18E
Mary U.S.S.R. **45** 37.42N 61.54E
Maryland *d.* U.S.A. **53** 39.00N 76.30W
Maryport England **12** 54.43N 3.30W
Masai Steppe *f.* Tanzania **47** 4.30S 37.00E
Masaka Uganda **47** 0.20S 31.46E
Masan S. Korea **41** 35.10N 128.35E
Masasi Tanzania **47** 10.43S 38.48E
Masbate *i.* Phil. **39** 12.00N 123.30E
Mascara Algeria **23** 35.20N 0.09E
Maseru Lesotho **48** 29.19S 27.29E
Masham England **12** 54.15N 1.40W
Mashhad Iran **35** 36.16N 59.34E
Mashonaland *f.* Rhodesia **48** 18.20S 32.00E
Masi-Manimba Zaire **46** 4.47S 17.54E
Masindi Uganda **47** 1.41N 31.45E
Masira I. Oman **36** 20.30N 58.50E
Masjid-i-Sulaiman Iran **35** 31.59N 49.18E
Mask, Lough Rep. of Ire. **18** 53.38N 9.22W
Mason City U.S.A. **53** 43.10N 93.10W
Massa Italy **24** 44.02N 10.09E
Massachusetts *d.* U.S.A. **57** 43.00N 72.25W
Massangena Moçambique **48** 21.31S 33.03E
Massawa Ethiopia **45** 15.36N 39.29E
Massif Central *mts.* France **22** 45.00N 3.30E
Massif de l'Ouarsenis *mts.* Algeria **23** 35.55N 1.40E
Massinga Moçambique **48** 23.20S 35.25E
Masterton New Zealand **50** 40.57S 175.39E
Masurian Lakes Poland **29** 54.00N 21.45E
Matabeleland *f.* Rhodesia **48** 19.30S 28.15E
Matadi Zaire **46** 5.50S 13.36E
Matagorda B. U.S.A. **53** 28.30N 96.20W
Matakana I. New Zealand **50** 37.35S 176.15E
Matamoros Mexico **58** 25.33N 103.15W
Matandu *r.* Tanzania **47** 8.44S 39.22E
Matane Canada **57** 48.50N 67.13W
Matanzas Cuba **58** 23.04N 81.35W
Matanzas *d.* Cuba **58** 23.04N 81.35W
Matapan, C. Greece **25** 36.22N 22.28E
Mataró Spain **23** 41.32N 2.72E
Matatiele R.S.A. **48** 30.20S 28.49E
Mataura *r.* New Zealand **50** 46.34S 168.45E
Matawin *r.* Canada **57** 46.56N 72.55W
Matehuala Mexico **58** 23.40N 100.40W
Matera Italy **25** 40.41N 16.36E
Mateur Tunisia **24** 37.02N 9.39E
Mathews Peak *mtn.* Kenya **47** 1.18N 37.20E
Mathura India **36** 27.30N 77.42E
Matlock England **13** 53.08N 1.32W
Mato Grosso Brazil **62** 15.05S 59.57W
Mato Grosso *d.* Brazil **61** 19.00S 55.00W
Mato Grosso *f.* Brazil **62** 15.00S 55.00W
Matope Malaŵi **47** 15.20S 34.57E
Matopo Hills Rhodesia **48** 20.45S 28.30E
Matrah Oman **35** 23.37N 58.33E
Matruh Egypt **34** 31.21N 27.15E
Matsue Japan **42** 35.29N 133.00E
Matsu Is. Taiwan **41** 26.12N 120.00E
Matsumoto Japan **42** 36.18N 137.58E
Matsuyama Japan **42** 33.50N 132.47E
Mattawa Canada **57** 46.19N 58.42W
Matterhorn *mtn.* Switz. **22** 45.58N 7.38E
Maturín Venezuela **59** 9.45N 61.16W
Maubeuge France **27** 50.17N 3.58E
Mauchline Scotland **14** 55.31N 4.23W
Maughold Head I.o.M. **12** 54.18N 4.19W
Maui *i.* Hawaii U.S.A. **52** 20.45N 156.15W
Maumee *r.* U.S.A. **56** 41.34N 83.41W
Maumere Indonesia **39** 8.35S 122.13E
Maun Botswana **48** 19.52S 23.40E
Mauritania Africa **44** 20.00N 10.00W
Mauritius Indian Oc. **5** 20.10S 58.00E
Mavinga Angola **46** 15.47S 20.21E
Mavuradonha Mts. Rhodesia **48** 16.30S 31.30E
Ma Wan Hong Kong **33** 22.21N 114.03E
Ma Wan *i.* Hong Kong **33** 22.21N 114.03E
Ma Wan Chung Hong Kong **33** 22.17N 113.55E
Mawlaik Burma **37** 23.40N 94.26E
May, C. U.S.A. **57** 38.55N 74.55W
May, Isle of Scotland **15** 56.12N 2.32W
Maya Spain **23** 43.12N 1.29W
Mayaguana I. Bahamas **59** 22.30N 73.00W
Mayaguez Puerto Rico **59** 18.13N 67.09W
Mayamey Iran **35** 36.27N 55.40E
Maya Mts. Belize **58** 16.30N 89.00W
Maybole Scotland **14** 55.21N 4.41W
Mayen W. Germany **27** 50.19N 7.14E
Mayenne France **22** 48.18N 0.37W
Mayenne *r.* France **22** 48.18N 0.37W
Mayfield England **9** 51.01N 0.17E
Maykop U.S.S.R. **29** 44.37N 40.48E
Maymyo Burma **37** 22.05N 96.33E
Maynooth Rep. of Ire. **18** 53.23N 6.37W
Mayo *d.* Rep. of Ire. **18** 53.47N 9.07W
Mayo Landing Canada **54** 63.45N 135.45W
Mayor I. New Zealand **50** 37.15S 176.15E
Mayotte, Ile *i.* Comoro Is. **47** 12.50S 45.10E
Mayoumba Gabon **46** 3.23S 10.38E
Mazabuka Zambia **47** 15.50S 27.47E
Mazatenango Guatemala **58** 14.31N 91.30W
Mažeikiai U.S.S.R. **28** 56.06N 23.06E
Mazoe *r.* Moçambique **47** 16.22S 33.38E
Mazoe Rhodesia **48** 17.30S 31.03E
Mbabane Swaziland **48** 26.20S 31.08E
M'Baere *r.* C.A.R. **46** 3.45N 17.35E
M'Baiki C.A.R. **46** 3.53N 18.01E
Mbala Zambia **47** 8.50S 31.24E
Mbale Uganda **47** 1.04N 34.12E
Mbamba Bay *town* Tanzania **47** 11.18S 34.50E
Mbandaka Zaire **46** 0.03N 18.21E
M'Bangé Cameroon **46** 4.32N 9.31E
Mbarara Uganda **47** 0.36S 30.40E
Mbeya Tanzania **47** 8.54S 33.29E
Mbeya *d.* Tanzania **47** 8.00S 32.30E
Mbinda Congo **46** 2.11S 12.55E
M'bridge *r.* Angola **46** 7.12S 12.55E
Mbuji Mayi Zaire **46** 6.08S 23.39E
Mbulamuti Uganda **47** 0.50N 33.05E
McClintock Channel Canada **55** 71.20N 102.00W
McClure Str. Canada **54** 74.30N 116.00W
McConaughy, L. U.S.A. **52** 41.20N 102.00W
McCook U.S.A **52** 40.15N 100.45W

McGrath U.S.A. **54** 62.58N 155.40W
Mchinja Tanzania **47** 9.44S 39.45E
Mchinji Malawi **47** 13.48S 32.55E
McKeesport U.S.A. **56** 40.21N 79.52W
McKinley, Mt. U.S.A. **54** 63.00N 151.00W
McMurray Canada **54** 56.45N 111.27W
McSwyne's B. Rep. of Ire. **18** 54.36N 8.26W
Mead, L. U.S.A. **52** 36.10N 114.25W
Mealasta *i.* Scotland **16** 58.05N 7.07W
Meath *d.* Rep. of Ire. **18** 53.32N 6.40W
Meaux France **22** 48.58N 2.54E
Mecca Saudi Arabia **45** 21.26N 39.49E
Meconta Moçambique **47** 15.00S 39.50E
Medan Indonesia **38** 3.35N 98.39E
Médéa Algeria **23** 36.15N 2.48E
Mededsiz *mtn.* Turkey **34** 37.33N 34.38E
Medellín Colombia **59** 6.15N 75.36W
Medenine Tunisia **44** 33.24N 10.25E
Medicine Hat Canada **52** 50.03N 110.41W
Medina Saudi Arabia **34** 24.30N 39.35E
Medina del Campo Spain **23** 41.20N 4.55W
Medina de Rioseco Spain **23** 41.53N 5.03W
Mediterranean Sea **44** 37.00N 15.00E
Medjerda, Wadi *r.* Algeria **24** 37.07N 10.12E
Medjerda Mts. Algeria **24** 36.35N 8.20E
Medveditsa *r.* U.S.S.R. **29** 49.35N 42.45E
Medway *r.* England **7** 51.24N 0.31E
Meekatharra Australia **49** 26.35S 118.30E
Meerut India **36** 29.00N 77.42E
Mega Ethiopia **45** 4.02N 38.19E
Megantic Canada **57** 45.34N 70.53W
Mégara Greece **25** 38.00N 23.21E
Meiktila Burma **37** 20.53N 95.54E
Meissen E. Germany **26** 51.10N 13.28E
Meknès Morocco **44** 33.53N 5.37W
Mekong *r.* Asia **38** 10.00N 106.20E
Mekong Delta S. Vietnam **38** 10.00N 106.20E
Mekongga *mtn.* Indonesia **39** 3.39S 121.15E
Melbourn England **9** 52.05N 0.01E
Melbourne Australia **49** 37.45S 144.58E
Melbourne England **13** 52.50N 1.25W
Melfi Italy **24** 40.59N 15.39E
Melilla Spain **23** 35.17N 2.57W
Melitopol U.S.S.R. **29** 46.51N 35.22E
Melksham England **8** 51.22N 2.09W
Mellerud Sweden **28** 58.42N 12.27E
Melmore Pt. Rep. of Ire. **18** 55.15N 7.49W
Melo Uruguay **61** 32.22S 54.10W
Melrose Scotland **15** 55.36N 2.43W
Melsetter Rhodesia **48** 19.48S 32.50E
Meltham England **12** 53.36N 1.52W
Melton Mowbray England **8** 52.46N 0.53W
Melun France **22** 48.32N 2.40E
Melvaig Scotland **16** 57.48N 5.49W
Melville Canada **52** 50.57N 102.49W
Melville, C. Australia **49** 14.02S 144.30E
Melville I. Australia **49** 11.30S 131.00E
Melville I. Canada **54** 75.30N 110.00W
Melville Pen. Canada **55** 68.00N 84.00W
Melvin, Lough N. Ireland **18** 54.26N 8.12W
Memba Moçambique **47** 14.16S 40.30E
Memel *see* Klaipeda U.S.S.R. **29**
Memmingen W. Germany **26** 47.59N 10.11E
Memphis U.S.A. **53** 35.05N 90.00W
Memphis ruins Egypt **34** 29.52N 31.12E
Menai Bridge *town* Wales **10** 53.14N 4.11W
Menai Str. Wales **10** 53.17N 4.20W
Mendawai *r.* Indonesia **38** 3.17S 113.20E
Mende France **22** 44.32N 3.30E
Menderes *r.* Turkey **25** 37.30N 27.05E
Mendip Hills England **8** 51.15N 2.40W
Mendocino, C. U.S.A. **52** 40.26N 124.24W
Mendoza Argentina **63** 33.00S 68.52W
Mendoza *d.* Argentina **61** 34.00S 67.40W
Mengtsz China **37** 23.20N 103.21E
Menin Belgium **27** 50.48N 3.07E
Menjapa *mtn.* Indonesia **38** 1.00N 116.20E
Menorca *i. see* MinorcaSpain **23**
Mentawai Is. Indonesia **38** 2.50S 99.00E
Menteith, L. of Scotland **14** 56.10N 4.18W
Menton France **22** 43.47N 7.30E
Meon *r.* England **8** 50.49N 1.15W
Meopham Station England **7** 51.23N 0.22E
Meppel Neth. **27** 52.42N 6.12E
Meppen W. Germany **27** 52.42N 7.17E
Merano Italy **26** 46.41N 11.10E
Merauke Indonesia **39** 8.30S 140.22E
Merca Somali Rep. **47** 1.42N 44.47E
Merced U.S.A. **52** 37.17N 120.29W
Mercedes Buenos Aires Argentina **61** 34.42S 59.30W
Mercedes Corrientes Argentina **61** 29.15S 58.05W
Mercedes San Luis Argentina **61** 33.43S 65.29W
Mercedes Uruguay **61** 33.16S 58.05W
Mere England **8** 51.05N 2.16W
Mergui Burma **37** 12.26N 98.34E
Mergui Archipelago *is.* Burma **37** 11.30N 98.15E
Mérida Mexico **58** 20.59N 89.39W
Mérida Spain **23** 38.55N 6.20W
Mérida Venezuela **59** 8.24N 71.08W
Mérida, Cordillera de *mts.* Venezuela **59** 8.00N 71.30W
Meridian U.S.A. **53** 32.21N 88.42W
Merir *i.* Asia **39** 4.19N 132.18E
Merksem Belgium **27** 51.14N 4.25E
Merowe Sudan **45** 18.30N 31.49E
Merrick *mtn.* Scotland **14** 55.08N 4.29W
Merse *f.* Scotland **15** 55.45N 2.15W
Mersea I. England **9** 51.47N 0.58E
Mersey *r.* England **12** 53.22N 2.37W
Merseyside *d.* England **12** 53.28N 3.00W
Mersin Turkey **34** 36.47N 34.37E
Mersing Malaysia **38** 2.25N 103.50E
Merstham England **7** 51.16N 0.09W
Merthyr Tydfil Wales **11** 51.45N 3.23W
Mértola Portugal **23** 37.38N 7.40W
Merton *d.* England **7** 51.25N 0.12W
Meru *mtn.* Tanzania **47** 3.15S 36.44E
Merzifon Turkey **34** 40.52N 35.28E
Merzig W. Germany **27** 49.26N 6.39E
Mesolóngion Greece **25** 38.23N 21.23E
Mesopotamia *f.* Iraq **35** 33.30N 44.30E
Messina Italy **24** 38.13N 15.34E
Messina R.S.A. **48** 22.23S 30.00E
Messina, G. of Med. Sea **25** 36.50N 22.05E
Messina, Str. of Med. Sea **24** 38.10N 15.35E
Mesta *r.* Greece **25** 40.51N 24.48E
Meta *r.* Venezuela **59** 6.10N 67.30W
Metan Argentina **61** 25.30S 64.50W
Metheringham England **13** 53.09N 0.22W
Methven Scotland **15** 56.25N 3.37W
Methwold England **9** 52.30N 0.33E
Metković Yugo. **25** 43.03N 17.38E
Metz France **22** 49.07N 6.11E
Meulaboh Indonesia **38** 4.10N 96.09E
Meuse *r. see* Maas Belgium **27**
Mevagissey England **11** 50.16N 4.48W
Mevatanana Malagasy Rep. **47** 17.06S 46.45E
Mexborough England **13** 53.29N 1.18W
Mexicali Mexico **52** 32.26N 115.30W
Mexico C. America **51** 20.00N 100.00W
Mexico *d.* Mexico **58** 19.45N 99.30W
Mexico U.S.A. **56** 39.10N 91.53W
Mexico, G. of N. America **58** 25.00N 90.00W
Mexico City Mexico **58** 19.25N 99.10W
Meyadin Syria **34** 35.01N 40.28E
Mezen U.S.S.R. **30** 65.50N 44.20E
Mezenc, Mt. France **22** 44.54N 4.11E
Miami U.S.A. **53** 25.45N 80.10W
Miami *r.* U.S.A. **56** 39.07N 84.43W
Mianduab Iran **35** 36.57N 46.06E
Mianeh Iran **35** 37.23N 47.45E
Mianwali Pakistan **36** 32.32N 71.33E
Michigan *d.* U.S.A. **56** 44.50N 85.20W
Michigan, L. U.S.A. **56** 44.00N 87.00W
Michigan City U.S.A. **56** 41.43N 86.54W
Michipicoten Harbour *town* Canada **56** 47.57N 84.55W
Michipicoten I. Canada **56** 47.45N 85.45W
Michoacan *d.* Mexico **58** 19.20N 101.00W
Michurinsk U.S.S.R. **29** 52.54N 40.30E
Middelburg Neth. **27** 51.30N 3.36E
Middelburg Cape Province R.S.A. **48** 31.30S 25.00E
Middelburg Transvaal R.S.A. **48** 25.47S 29.28E
Middle I. Hong Kong **33** 22.14N 114.11E
Middlesbrough England **13** 54.34N 1.13W
Middleton England **12** 53.33N 2.12W
Middleton in Teesdale England **12** 54.38N 2.05W
Middleton on the Wolds England **13** 53.56N 0.35W
Middlewich England **12** 53.12N 2.28W
Mid Glamorgan *d.* Wales **11** 51.38N 3.25W
Midhurst England **8** 50.59N 0.44W
Midi, Canal du France **23** 43.18N 2.00W
Midland Canada **56** 44.45N 79.53W
Midleton Rep. of Ire. **19** 51.55N 8.10W
Midsomer Norton England **8** 51.17N 2.29W
Midye Turkey **25** 41.37N 28.07E
Mid Yell Scotland **16** 60.31N 1.03W
Mienning China **37** 24.00N 100.10E
Mieres Spain **23** 43.15N 5.46W
Mijares *r.* Spain **23** 39.58N 0.01W
Mikhaylovka U.S.S.R. **29** 50.05N 43.15E
Mikindani Tanzania **47** 10.16S 40.05E
Mikkeli Finland **28** 61.44N 27.15E
Mikumi Tanzania **47** 7.22S 37.00E
Mikuni sammyaku *mts.* Japan **42** 37.00N 139.20E
Mikura jima *i.* Japan **42** 33.50N 139.35E
Milan Italy **22** 45.28N 9.10E
Milange Moçambique **47** 16.09S 35.44E
Milâs Turkey **25** 37.18N 27.48E
Milborne Port England **8** 50.58N 2.28W
Mildenhall England **9** 52.20N 0.30E
Miles City U.S.A. **52** 46.24N 105.48W
Milford England **7** 51.10N 0.40W
Milford Haven *b.* Wales **11** 51.42N 5.05W
Milford Haven *town* Wales **11** 51.43N 5.02W
Milford on Sea England **8** 50.44N 1.36W
Milford Sound *town* New Zealand **50** 44.41S 167.56E
Miliana Algeria **23** 36.20N 2.15E
Milk *r.* U.S.A. **52** 47.55N 106.15W
Millau France **22** 44.06N 3.05E
Mille Lacs, Lac des Canada **56** 48.50N 90.30W
Mille Lacs L. U.S.A. **53** 46.15N 93.40W
Millerovo U.S.S.R. **29** 48.55N 40.25E
Milleur Pt. Scotland **14** 55.01N 5.07W
Mill Hill *town* England **7** 51.37N 0.14W
Millom England **12** 54.13N 3.16W
Millport Scotland **14** 55.45N 4.56W
Millstreet Rep. of Ire. **19** 52.04N 9.05W
Milnathort Scotland **15** 56.14N 3.26W
Milngavie Scotland **14** 55.57N 4.19W
Milnthorpe England **12** 54.14N 2.47W
Milos *i.* Greece **25** 36.40N 24.26E
Milton New Zealand **50** 46.08S 169.59E
Milton Abbot England **11** 50.35N 4.16W
Milton Keynes England **8** 52.03N 0.42W
Miltown Malbay Rep. of Ire. **19** 52.51N 9.25W
Milverton England **8** 51.02N 3.15W
Milwaukee U.S.A. **56** 43.03N 87.56W
Minab Iran **35** 27.07N 57.05E
Minas Uruguay **61** 34.20S 55.15W
Mina Saud Kuwait **35** 28.48N 48.24E
Minas Gerais Brazil **61** 18.00S 45.00W
Minatitlán Mexico **58** 17.59N 94.32W
Mindanao *i.* Phil. **39** 7.30N 125.00E
Minden W. Germany **26** 52.18N 8.54E
Mindoro *i.* Phil. **39** 13.00N 121.00E
Mindoro Str. Pacific Oc. **39** 12.30N 120.10E
Mindra, Mt. Romania **25** 45.20N 23.32E
Minehead England **8** 51.12N 3.29W
Mine Head Rep. of Ire. **19** 51.59N 7.35W
Minginish *f.* Scotland **16** 57.15N 6.20W
Mingulay *i.* Scotland **16** 56.48N 7.37W
Minna Nigeria **44** 9.39N 6.32E
Minneapolis U.S.A. **56** 45.00N 93.15W
Minnesota *d.* U.S.A. **53** 46.00N 95.00W
Miño *r.* Spain **23** 42.50N 8.52W
Minorca *i.* Spain **23** 40.00N 4.00E
Minot U.S.A. **52** 48.16N 101.19W
Minsk U.S.S.R. **28** 53.51N 27.30E
Minster England **9** 51.25N 0.50E
Minsterley England **8** 52.38N 2.56W
Mintlaw Scotland **17** 57.31N 2.00W
Minya Konka *mtn.* China **37** 29.30N 101.30E
Miraj India **36** 16.51N 74.42E
Miranda Brazil **61** 20.10S 56.19W
Miranda de Ebro Spain **23** 42.41N 2.57W
Miranda do Douro Portugal **23** 41.30N 6.16W
Mirande France **22** 43.31N 0.25E
Mirandela Portugal **23** 41.28N 7.10W
Mirecourt France **26** 48.18N 6.08E
Miri Malaysia **38** 4.28N 114.00E
Mirim, L. Brazil **61** 33.10S 53.30W
Mirpur Khas Pakistan **36** 25.33N 69.05E
Mirzapur India **37** 25.09N 82.34E
Mi saki *c.* Japan **42** 40.09N 141.52E
Misbourne *r.* England **7** 51.33N 0.29W
Misiones *d.* Argentina **61** 27.00S 54.30W
Miskolc Hungary **29** 48.07N 20.47E
Misoöl *i.* Indonesia **39** 1.50S 130.10E
Missinaibi *r.* Canada **53** 50.50N 81.12W
Mississippi *d.* U.S.A. **53** 33.00N 90.00W
Mississippi *r.* U.S.A. **56** 28.55N 89.05W
Mississippi Delta U.S.A. **53** 29.00N 89.10W
Missoula U.S.A. **52** 46.52N 114.00W
Missouri *d.* U.S.A. **56** 39.45N 91.30W
Missouri *r.* U.S.A. **56** 38.40N 90.20W
Mistassini, L. Canada **53** 50.45N 73.40W
Misurata Libya **44** 32.24N 15.04E
Mitcham England **7** 51.24N 0.09W
Mitchell *r.* Australia **49** 15.12S 141.40E
Mitchell U.S.A. **52** 43.40N 98.01W
Mitchell, Mt. U.S.A. **53** 35.57N 82.16W
Mitchelstown Rep. of Ire. **19** 52.16N 8.17W
Mitilíni Greece **25** 39.06N 26.34E
Mito Japan **42** 36.30N 140.29E
Mittelland Canal W. Germany **27** 52.24N 7.52E
Mitumba Mts. Zaire **47** 3.00S 28.30E
Mitwaba Zaire **47** 8.32S 27.20E
Mitzic Gabon **46** 0.48N 11.30E
Miyake jima *i.* Japan **42** 34.04N 139.31E
Miyako Japan **42** 39.40N 141.59E
Miyako *i.* Japan **41** 24.45N 125.25E
Miyakonojo Japan **42** 31.43N 131.02E
Miyazaki Japan **42** 31.58N 131.50E
Mizen Head Rep. of Ire. **19** 51.27N 9.50W
Mjölby Sweden **28** 58.19N 15.10E
Mjösa *l.* Norway **28** 60.50N 10.50E
Mkushi Zambia **47** 13.40S 29.26E
Mljet *i.* Yugo. **25** 42.45N 17.30E
Moamba Moçambique **48** 25.35S 32.13E
Moanda Gabon **46** 1.25S 13.18E
Moate Rep. of Ire. **18** 53.24N 7.45W
Moatize Moçambique **47** 16.04S 33.40E
Moba Zaire **47** 7.03S 29.42E
Mobaye C.A.R. **46** 4.21N 21.10E
Mobile U.S.A. **53** 30.40N 88.05W
Mobile B. U.S.A. **53** 30.30N 87.50W
Mobridge U.S.A. **52** 45.31N 100.25W
Mobutu, L. Uganda/Zaire **47** 1.45N 31.00E
Moçambique Africa **48** 21.00S 34.00E
Moçambique *d.* Moçambique **47** 15.00S 39.00E
Moçambique *town* Moçambique **47** 15.00S 40.47E
Moçambique Channel Indian Oc. **47** 16.00S 42.30E
Moçâmedes Angola **46** 15.10S 12.10E
Moçâmedes *d.* Angola **46** 15.00S 12.30E
Mocimboa da Praia Moçambique **47** 11.19S 40.19E
Modane France **22** 45.12N 6.40E
Modbury England **11** 50.21N 3.53W
Modder *r.* R.S.A. **48** 29.03S 23.56E
Modena Italy **24** 44.39N 10.55E
Módica Italy **24** 36.51N 14.51E
Moffat Scotland **15** 55.20N 3.27W
Mogadishu Somali Rep. **47** 2.02N 45.21E
Mogaung Burma **37** 25.20N 97.00E
Moghan Steppe *f.* U.S.S.R. **35** 39.40N 48.30E
Mogilev U.S.S.R. **29** 53.54N 30.20E
Mogincual Moçambique **47** 15.33S 40.29E
Mogok Burma **37** 23.00N 96.40E
Mogomo Moçambique **47** 15.25S 36.45E
Mohaka *r.* New Zealand **50** 39.07S 177.10E
Mohammadia Algeria **23** 35.35N 0.05E
Mohawk *r.* U.S.A. **57** 42.50N 73.40W
Mohéli *i.* Comoro Is. **47** 12.22S 43.45E
Mohill Rep. of Ire. **18** 53.55N 7.53W
Mohoro Tanzania **47** 8.09S 39.07E
Moidart *f.* Scotland **16** 56.48N 5.40W
Mo-i-Rana Norway **28** 66.20N 14.12E
Moisie *r.* Canada **55** 50.15N 66.00W
Moissac France **22** 44.07N 1.05E
Moji das Cruzes Brazil **61** 23.33S 46.14W
Mokpo S. Korea **41** 34.50N 126.25E
Mold Wales **10** 53.10N 3.08W
Moldavia Soviet Socialist Republic *d.* U.S.S.R. **29** 47.30N 28.30E
Molde Norway **28** 62.44N 7.08E
Mole *r.* Devon England **11** 50.59N 3.53W
Mole *r.* Surrey England **7** 51.24N 0.20W
Molepolole Botswana **48** 24.25S 25.30E
Molfetta Italy **25** 41.12N 16.36E
Molina de Aragón Spain **23** 40.50N 1.54W
Moliro Zaire **47** 8.11S 30.29E
Mollendo Peru **62** 17.20S 72.10W
Mölndal Sweden **29** 57.40N 12.00E
Molodechno U.S.S.R. **28** 54.16N 26.50E
Molokai *i.* Hawaii U.S.A. **52** 21.20N 157.00W
Molopo *r.* R.S.A. **48** 28.30S 20.07E
Molteno R.S.A. **48** 31.24S 26.22E
Moluccas *is.* Indonesia **39** 4.00S 128.00E
Molucca Sea Pacific Oc. **39** 2.00N 126.30E
Moma Moçambique **47** 16.40S 39.10E
Mombasa Kenya **47** 4.04S 39.40E
Mön *i.* Denmark **26** 54.58N 12.20E
Mona *i.* Puerto Rico **59** 18.06N 67.54W
Monach, Sd. of *str.* Scotland **16** 57.34N 7.35W
Monach Is. Scotland **16** 57.32N 7.38W
Monaco Europe **22** 43.40N 7.25E
Monadhliath Mts. Scotland **17** 57.09N 4.08W
Monaghan Rep. of Ire. **18** 54.15N 6.58W
Monaghan *d.* Rep. of Ire. **18** 54.10N 7.00W
Monar, Loch Scotland **16** 57.25N 5.05W
Monasterevan Rep. of Ire. **19** 53.09N 7.05W
Monastir Tunisia **24** 35.35N 10.50E
Monavullagh Mts. Rep. of Ire. **19** 52.14N 7.37W
Monchegorsk U.S.S.R. **28** 67.55N 33.01E
Mönchen-Gladbach W. Germany **27** 51.12N 6.25E
Monclova Mexico **52** 26.55N 101.20W
Moncton Canada **53** 46.10N 64.50W
Mondovi Italy **22** 44.24N 7.48E
Moneygall Rep. of Ire. **19** 52.53N 7.58W
Moneymore N. Ireland **14** 54.42N 6.40W
Monforte Spain **23** 42.32N 7.30W
Monga Zaire **46** 4.10N 23.00E
Mongala *r.* Zaire **46** 1.58N 19.55E
Mongalla Sudan **47** 5.12N 31.42E
Monghyr India **37** 25.24N 86.29E
Mongolia Asia **40** 46.30N 104.00E
Mong Tung Wan Hong Kong **33** 22.13N 113.58E
Mongu Zambia **46** 15.10S 23.09E
Moniaive Scotland **15** 55.12N 3.55W
Monifieth Scotland **15** 56.29N 2.50W
Monkoto Zaire **46** 1.39S 20.41E
Monmouth Wales **11** 51.48N 2.43W
Monnow *r.* England **8** 51.49N 2.42W
Monongahela *r.* U.S.A. **56** 40.26N 80.00W
Monopoli Italy **25** 40.56N 17.19E
Monroe Mich. U.S.A. **56** 41.56N 83.21W
Monroe La. U.S.A. **53** 32.31N 92.06W
Monrovia Liberia **44** 6.20N 10.46W
Mons Belgium **27** 50.27N 3.57E
Montalbán Spain **23** 40.50N 0.48W
Montana *d.* U.S.A. **52** 47.00N 110.00W
Montargis France **22** 48.00N 2.44E
Montauban France **22** 44.01N 1.20E
Montauk Pt. U.S.A. **57** 41.04N 71.51W
Mont-aux-Sources *mtn.* Lesotho **48** 28.50S 28.50E
Montbrison France **22** 45.37N 4.04E
Montcalm, L. China **37** 34.30N 89.00E
Mont Cenis Pass France **22** 45.15N 6.55E
Montcornet France **27** 49.41N 4.01E
Mont de Marsan *town* France **22** 43.54N 0.30W
Monte Carlo Monaco **22** 43.44N 7.25E
Montecristo *i.* Italy **24** 42.20N 10.19E
Montego Bay *town* Jamaica **59** 18.27N 77.56W
Montélimar France **22** 44.33N 4.45E
Monterey U.S.A. **52** 36.35N 121.55W
Monterey B. U.S.A. **52** 36.45N 122.00W
Montería Colombia **59** 8.45N 75.54W
Montero Bolivia **61** 17.20S 63.15W
Monterrey Mexico **58** 25.40N 100.20W
Monte Santu, C. Italy **24** 40.05N 9.44E
Montes Claros Brazil **61** 16.45S 43.52W
Monte Verde Angola **46** 8.45S 16.50E
Montevideo Uruguay **61** 34.55S 56.10W
Montfort-sur-Meu France **22** 48.08N 1.57W
Montgomery U.S.A. **53** 32.22N 86.20W
Montgomery Wales **10** 52.34N 3.09W
Montijo Portugal **23** 38.42N 8.59W
Montijo Dam Spain **23** 38.52N 6.20W
Mont Joli Canada **57** 48.34N 68.05W
Mont Laurier *town* Canada **57** 46.33N 75.31W
Montluçon France **22** 46.20N 2.36E
Montmagny Canada **57** 46.58N 70.34W
Montmédy France **27** 49.31N 5.21E
Montmorillon France **22** 46.26N 0.52E
Montoro Spain **23** 38.02N 4.23W
Montpelier U.S.A. **57** 44.16N 72.34W
Montpellier France **22** 43.36N 3.53E
Montreal Canada **57** 45.30N 73.36W
Montrejeau France **22** 43.05N 0.33E
Montreuil France **22** 50.28N 1.46E
Montreux Switz. **26** 46.27N 6.55E
Montrose Scotland **15** 56.43N 2.29W
Montrose U.S.A. **52** 38.29N 107.53W
Montsant, Sierra de *mts.* Spain **23** 41.20N 1.00E
Montserrat *i.* C. America **59** 16.45N 62.14W
Monywa Burma **37** 22.07N 95.11E
Monza Italy **22** 45.35N 9.16E
Monze Zambia **47** 16.16S 27.28E
Monzón Spain **23** 41.52N 0.10E
Moore, L. Australia **49** 29.30S 117.30E
Moorfoot Hills Scotland **15** 55.43N 3.03W
Moorhead U.S.A. **53** 46.51N 96.44W
Moosehead L. U.S.A. **57** 45.45N 69.45W
Moose Jaw Canada **52** 50.23N 105.35W
Moosonee Canada **53** 51.18N 80.40W
Mopti Mali **44** 14.29N 4.10W
Mora Sweden **28** 61.00N 14.30E
Moradabad India **37** 28.50N 78.45E
Morar, Loch Scotland **16** 56.56N 5.40W
Morava *r.* Yugo. **25** 44.43N 21.02E
Moravian Heights *mts.* Czech. **26** 49.30N 15.45E
Moray Firth *est.* Scotland **17** 57.35N 4.00W
Morcenx France **22** 44.02N 0.55W
Morden Canada **55** 49.15N 98.10W

Morden England 7 51.23N 0.12W
More, Loch Scotland 17 58.23N 4.51W
Morecambe England 12 54.03N 2.52W
Morecambe B. England 12 54.05N 3.00W
Morelia Mexico 58 19.40N 101.11W
Morella Spain 23 40.37N 0.06W
Morelos d. Mexico 58 18.40N 99.00W
Morena, Sierra mts. Spain 23 38.10N 5.00W
Moretonhampstead England 11 50.39N 3.45W
Morez France 22 46.31N 6.02E
Morgan City U.S.A. 53 29.41N 91.13W
Morie, Loch Scotland 17 57.44N 4.27W
Morioka Japan 42 39.43N 141.10E
Morlaix France 22 48.35N 3.50W
Morley England 13 53.45N 1.36W
Morocco Africa 44 31.00N 5.00W
Moro G. Phil. 39 6.30N 123.20E
Morogoro Tanzania 47 6.47S 37.40E
Morogoro d. Tanzania 47 8.30S 37.00E
Morón Cuba 59 22.08N 78.39W
Mörön Mongolia 40 49.36N 100.08E
Moroni Comoro Is. 47 11.40S 43.19E
Morotai i. Indonesia 39 2.10N 128.30E
Moroto Uganda 47 2.32N 34.41E
Morpeth England 15 55.10N 1.40W
Morsbach W. Germany 27 50.52N 7.44E
Mortagne France 22 48.32N 0.33E
Morte Pt. England 11 51.12N 4.13W
Mortimer Common England 8 51.22N 1.05W
Morven mtn. Scotland 17 58.13N 3.42W
Morvern f. Scotland 16 56.37N 5.45W
Moscow U.S.S.R. 29 55.45N 37.42E
Mosel r. W. Germany 27 50.23N 7.37E
Moselle r. see Mosel France/Lux. 27
Moshi Tanzania 47 3.20S 37.21E
Mosjöen Norway 28 65.50N 13.10E
Moskog Norway 28 61.30N 5.59E
Moskva r. U.S.S.R. 29 55.08N 38.50E
Mosquitia Plain Honduras 58 15.00N 89.00W
Mosquito Coast f. Nicaragua 58 13.00N 84.00W
Mosquitos, G. of Panamá 58 9.00N 81.00W
Moss Norway 28 59.26N 10.41E
Mossbank Scotland 16 60.27N 1.10W
Mossel Bay town R.S.A. 48 34.12S 22.08E
Mossoro Brazil 62 5.10S 37.20W
Mossuma r. Zambia 46 15.11S 23.05E
Mostaganem Algeria 23 35.54N 0.05E
Mostar Yugo. 25 43.20N 17.50E
Mosul Iraq 34 36.21N 43.08E
Motagua r. Guatemala 58 15.56N 87.45W
Motala Sweden 28 58.34N 15.05E
Motherwell Scotland 15 55.48N 4.00W
Motu r. New Zealand 50 37.52S 177.37E
Motueka New Zealand 50 41.08S 173.01E
Mouila Gabon 46 1.50S 11.02E
Moulins France 22 46.34N 3.20E
Moulmein Burma 37 16.30N 97.40E
Mountain Ash Wales 11 51.42N 3.22W
Mount Bellew town Rep. of Ire. 18 53.28N 8.30W
Mount Darwin town Rhodesia 48 16.45S 31.39E
Mount Fletcher town R.S.A. 48 30.41S 28.30E
Mount Hagen town P.N.G. 39 5.54S 144.13E
Mount Isa town Australia 49 20.50S 139.29E
Mountmellick Rep. of Ire. 19 53.08N 7.21W
Mountnessing England 7 51.40N 0.21E
Mountrath Rep. of Ire. 19 53.00N 7.30W
Mount's B. England 11 50.05N 5.25W
Mourne r. N. Ireland 18 54.50N 7.29W
Mourne Mts. N. Ireland 18 54.10N 6.02W
Moville Rep. of Ire. 14 55.11N 7.03W
Moxico Angola 46 11.50S 20.05E
Moxico d. Angola 46 13.00S 21.00E
Moy N. Ireland 18 54.27N 6.43W
Moy r. Rep. of Ire. 18 54.10N 9.09W
Moyale Kenya 47 3.31N 39.04E
Moyowosi r. Tanzania 47 4.59S 30.58E
Mozdok U.S.S.R. 29 43.45N 44.43E
Mozyr U.S.S.R. 29 52.02N 29.10E
M'Pama r. Congo 46 0.59S 15.40E
Mpanda Tanzania 47 6.21S 31.01E
Mpika Zambia 47 11.52S 31.30E
Mporokoso Zambia 47 9.22S 30.06E
M'Pouya Congo 46 2.38S 16.08E
Mpwapwa Tanzania 47 6.23S 36.38E
Mrewa Rhodesia 48 17.35S 31.45E
Msaken Tunisia 24 35.42N 10.33E
Msolu r. Moçambique 47 11.40S 40.28E
Msta r. U.S.S.R. 29 58.28N 31.20E
Mtakuja Tanzania 47 7.21S 30.37E
Mtsensk U.S.S.R. 29 53.18N 36.35E
Mtwara Tanzania 47 10.17S 40.11E
Mtwara d. Tanzania 47 10.00S 38.30E
Muang Khon Kaen Thailand 37 16.25N 102.50E
Muang Lampang Thailand 37 18.16N 99.30E
Muang Nan Thailand 37 18.52N 100.42E
Muang Phitsanulok Thailand 37 16.50N 100.15E
Muang Phrae Thailand 37 18.07N 100.09E
Muara Indonesia 38 0.32S 101.20E
Mubende Uganda 47 0.30N 31.24E
Much Hadham England 7 51.52N 0.04E
Muchinga Mts. Zambia 47 12.15S 31.00E
Much Wenlock England 8 52.36N 2.34W
Muck i. Scotland 16 56.50N 6.14W
Muckish Mtn. Rep. of Ire. 18 55.06N 7.59W
Muckle Roe i. Scotland 16 60.22N 1.26W
Muckle Skerry i. Scotland 17 58.41N 2.53W
Muckno Lough Rep. of Ire. 18 54.07N 6.43W
Mucojo Moçambique 47 12.05S 40.26E
Mudhnib Saudi Arabia 35 25.52N 44.15E
Muduli Zambia 48 16.45S 25.15E
Muff Rep. of Ire. 14 55.04N 7.16W
Mufulira Zambia 47 12.30S 28.12E
Mugia Spain 23 43.06N 9.14W
Muğla Turkey 25 37.12N 28.22E
Muharraq Bahrain 35 26.16N 50.38E
Muhinga Burundi 47 2.48S 30.21E
Muine Bheag town Rep. of Ire. 19 52.42N 6.58W
Muirkirk Scotland 15 55.31N 4.04W
Muir of Ord f. Scotland 17 57.31N 4.28W
Mui Tsz Lam Hong Kong 33 22.23N 114.13E
Mui Wo Hong Kong 33 22.16N 113.59E
Mukachevo U.S.S.R. 29 48.26N 22.45E
Mukah Malaysia 38 2.56N 112.02E
Mukalla S. Yemen 45 14.34N 49.09E
Mukawa r. Japan 42 42.30N 142.20E
Mulanje Mts. Malawi 47 15.57S 35.33E
Mulgrave Is. Australia 39 10.05S 142.00E
Mulhacén mtn. Spain 23 37.04N 3.22W
Mülheim Nordrhein-Westfalen W. Germany 27 51.25N 6.50E
Mülheim Nordrhein-Westfalen W. Germany 27 50.58N 7.00E
Mulhouse France 26 47.45N 7.21E
Mull i. Scotland 14 56.28N 5.56W
Mull, Sd. of str. Scotland 14 56.32N 5.55W
Mullaghanattin mtn. Rep. of Ire. 19 51.56N 9.51W
Mullaghareirk Mts. Rep. of Ire. 19 52.19N 9.06W
Mullaghcarn mtn. N. Ireland 18 54.40N 7.14W
Mullaghcleevaun mtn. Rep. of Ire. 19 53.06N 6.25W
Mullaghmore mtn. N. Ireland 14 54.51N 6.51W
Mullardoch, Loch Scotland 16 57.19N 5.04W
Mullet Pen. Rep. of Ire. 18 54.12N 10.04W
Mull Head Orkney Is. Scotland 17 59.23N 2.53W
Mull Head Orkney Is. Scotland 17 58.58N 2.42W
Mullinavat Rep. of Ire. 19 52.22N 7.11W
Mullingar Rep. of Ire. 18 53.31N 7.21W
Mullion England 11 50.01N 5.15W
Mull of Galloway c. Scotland 14 54.39N 4.52W
Mull of Kintyre c. Scotland 14 55.17N 5.45W
Mull of Oa c. Scotland 14 55.36N 6.20W
Mulobezi Zambia 46 16.45S 25.11E
Mulroy B. Rep. of Ire. 18 55.15N 7.46W
Multan Pakistan 36 30.10N 71.36E
Multyfarnham Rep. of Ire. 18 53.37N 7.25W
Mumbles Head Wales 11 51.35N 3.58W
Mumbwa Zambia 47 14.57S 27.01E
Muna i. Indonesia 39 5.00S 122.30E
München see Munich W. Germany 26
Mundesley England 13 52.53N 1.24E
Mundo r. Spain 23 38.20N 1.50W
Mungari Moçambique 47 17.12S 33.35E
Mungbere Zaïre 47 2.40N 28.25E
Mungret Rep. of Ire. 19 52.38N 8.42W
Munich W. Germany 26 48.08N 11.35E
Munising U.S.A. 56 46.24N 86.40W
Munku Sardyk mtn. Mongolia 31 51.45N 100.30E
Munster d. Rep. of Ire. 19 52.10N 8.25W
Münster W. Germany 27 51.58N 7.37E
Muntok Indonesia 38 2.04S 105.12E
Muonio Finland 28 67.52N 23.45E
Muonio r. Sweden/Finland 28 67.13N 23.30E
Mur r. Austria 26 46.40N 16.03E
Murallón mtn. Argentina 63 49.48S 73.26W
Murchison r. Australia 49 27.30S 114.10E
Murchison Range mts. R.S.A. 48 23.50S 30.30E
Murcia Spain 23 37.59N 1.08W
Mures r. Romania 25 46.16N 20.10E
Muret France 22 43.28N 1.19E
Murghab r. Afghan. 36 36.50N 63.00E
Müritz, L. E. Germany 26 52.25N 12.45E
Murjo mtn. Indonesia 38 6.30S 110.55E
Murle Ethiopia 47 5.11N 36.09E
Murmansk U.S.S.R. 28 68.59N 33.08E
Muroran Japan 42 42.21N 140.59E
Murray r. Australia 49 35.23S 139.20E
Murrumbidgee r. Australia 49 34.38S 143.10E
Murud, Mt. Malaysia 38 3.45N 115.30E
Murwara India 37 23.49N 80.28E
Murzuq Libya 44 25.56N 13.57E
Muş Turkey 34 38.45N 41.30E
Musala mtn. Bulgaria 25 42.11N 23.35E
Muscat Oman 35 23.36N 58.37E
Musgrave Ranges mts. Australia 49 26.30S 131.10E
Musheramore mtn. Rep. of Ire. 19 52.01N 8.58W
Mushie Zaïre 46 2.59S 16.55E
Musi r. Indonesia 38 2.20S 104.57E
Muskegon U.S.A. 56 43.13N 86.15W
Muskegon r. U.S.A. 56 43.13N 86.20W
Muskingum r. U.S.A. 56 39.25N 81.25W
Muskogee U.S.A. 53 35.45N 95.21W
Musoma Tanzania 47 1.31S 33.48E
Musselburgh Scotland 15 55.57N 3.04W
Mussende Angola 46 10.33S 16.02E
Mustang Nepal 37 29.10N 83.55E
Mustjala U.S.S.R. 28 58.30N 22.10E
Mut Turkey 34 36.38N 33.27E
Mutankiang China 41 44.36N 129.42E
Mutsu wan b. Japan 42 41.10N 141.05E
Muwai Hakran Saudi Arabia 34 22.41N 41.37E
Muxima Angola 46 9.33S 13.58E
Muzaffarnagar India 36 29.28N 77.42E
Muzaffarpur India 37 26.07N 85.23E
Mwanza Tanzania 47 2.30S 32.54E
Mwanza d. Tanzania 47 3.00S 32.30E
Mwanza Zaïre 47 7.51S 26.43E
Mwaya Mbeya Tanzania 47 9.33S 33.56E
Mweeirea Mts. Rep. of Ire. 18 53.40N 9.52W
Mweka Zaïre 46 4.51S 21.34E
Mwene Ditu Zaïre 46 7.04S 23.27E
Mweru, L. Zaïre/Zambia 47 9.00S 28.40E
Mwinilunga Zambia 46 11.44S 24.24E
Myanaung Burma 37 18.25N 95.10E
Myingyan Burma 37 21.25N 95.20E
Myitkyina Burma 37 25.24N 97.25E
Mynydd Bach mts. Wales 10 52.18N 4.03W
Mynydd Eppynt mts. Wales 10 52.06N 3.30W
Mynydd Prescelly mts. Wales 10 51.58N 4.47W
Myrdal Norway 28 60.44N 7.08E
Mysen Norway 28 59.33N 11.20E
Mysore India 36 12.18N 76.37E
Mysore d. India 36 14.45N 76.00E
My Tho S. Vietnam 38 10.21N 106.21E
Mytishchi U.S.S.R. 29 55.54N 37.47E
Mzimba Malawi 47 12.00S 33.39E

N

Naas Rep. of Ire. 19 53.13N 6.41W
Nabeul Tunisia 24 36.28N 10.44E
Nacala Moçambique 47 14.30S 40.37E
Nachingwea Tanzania 47 10.21S 38.46E
Nadder r. England 8 51.05N 1.52W
Naestved Denmark 28 55.14N 11.47E
Naft Safid Iran 35 31.38N 49.20E
Naga Phil. 39 13.36N 123.12E
Nagaland d. India 37 26.10N 94.30E
Nagano Japan 42 36.39N 138.10E
Nagaoka Japan 42 37.30N 138.50E
Nagappattinam India 37 10.45N 79.50E
Nagasaki Japan 42 32.45N 129.52E
Nagercoil India 36 8.11N 77.30E
Nag' Hammadi Egypt 34 26.04N 32.13E
Nagishot Sudan 47 4.18N 33.32E
Nagles Mts. Rep. of Ire. 19 52.06N 8.26W
Nagoya Japan 42 35.08N 136.53E
Nagpur India 37 21.10N 79.12E
Nagykanizsa Hungary 25 46.27N 17.01E
Naha Japan 41 26.10N 127.40E
Nahavand Iran 35 34.13N 48.23E
Nahe r. W. Germany 27 49.58N 7.54E
Nahr Ouassel r. Algeria 23 35.30N 2.03E
Nailsworth England 8 51.41N 2.12W
Nain Canada 55 56.30N 61.45W
Nain Iran 35 32.52N 53.05E
Nairn Scotland 17 57.35N 3.52W
Nairn r. Scotland 17 57.35N 3.51W
Nairobi Kenya 47 1.17S 36.50E
Naivasha Kenya 47 0.44S 36.26E
Najin N. Korea 42 42.10N 130.20E
Nakano shima i. Japan 42 29.55N 129.55E
Nakatsu Japan 42 33.37N 131.11E
Nakhichevan U.S.S.R. 35 39.12N 45.24E
Nakhodka U.S.S.R. 42 42.53N 132.54E
Nakhon Phanom Thailand 38 17.22N 104.45E
Nakhon Ratchasima Thailand 37 14.59N 102.12E
Nakhon Sawan Thailand 37 15.35N 100.10E
Nakhon Si Thammarat Thailand 37 8.29N 100.00E
Naknek U.S.A. 54 58.45N 157.00W
Nakskov Denmark 26 54.50N 11.10E
Nakuru Kenya 47 0.16S 36.04E
Nalchik U.S.S.R. 29 43.31N 43.38E
Nalon r. Spain 23 43.35N 6.06W
Nalut Libya 44 31.53N 10.59E
Namaki r. Iran 35 31.02N 55.20E
Namanga Kenya 47 2.33S 36.48E
Namangan U.S.S.R. 40 40.59N 71.41E
Namapa Moçambique 47 13.48S 39.44E
Namaponda Moçambique 47 15.51S 39.52E
Namcha Barwa mtn. China 37 29.30N 95.10E
Nam Dinh N. Vietnam 38 20.25N 106.12E
Nametil Moçambique 47 15.41S 39.30E
Namib Desert S.W. Africa 48 23.30S 15.00E
Namlea Indonesia 39 3.15S 127.07E
Nampo N. Korea 41 38.40N 125.30E
Nampula Moçambique 47 15.09S 39.14E
Namsos Norway 28 64.28N 11.30E
Nam Tso l. China 37 30.40N 90.30E
Namur Belgium 27 50.28N 4.52E
Namur d. Belgium 27 50.20N 4.45E
Namurro Moçambique 47 16.57S 39.06E
Namutoni S.W. Africa 48 18.49S 16.55E
Namwala Zambia 47 15.44S 26.25E
Nana Candundo Angola 46 11.28S 23.01E
Nanaimo Canada 52 49.08N 123.58W
Nanchang China 41 28.38N 115.56E
Nanchung China 40 30.54N 106.06E
Nancy France 26 48.42N 6.12E
Nanda Devi mtn. India 37 30.21N 79.50E
Nander India 36 19.11N 77.21E
Nanga Parbat mtn. Kashmir 36 35.10N 74.35E
Nanking China 41 32.00N 118.40E
Nan Ling mts. China 41 25.20N 110.30E
Nanning China 38 22.50N 108.19E
Nanping China 41 26.40N 118.07E
Nan Shan mts. China 40 38.30N 99.20E
Nanshan Is. Asia 38 10.30N 116.00E
Nantaise r. France 22 47.12N 1.35W
Nantes France 22 47.14N 1.35W
Nantucket I. U.S.A. 57 41.16N 70.00W
Nantucket Sd. U.S.A. 57 41.30N 70.15W
Nantung China 41 32.05N 120.59E
Nantwich England 12 53.05N 2.31W
Nanyuki Kenya 47 0.01N 37.03E
Napier New Zealand 50 39.29S 176.58E
Naples Italy 24 40.50N 14.14E
Naples, G. of Med. Sea 24 40.42N 14.15E
Nar r. England 9 52.45N 0.24E
Narbada r. see Narmada India 36
Narberth Wales 11 51.48N 4.45W
Narbonne France 22 43.11N 3.00E
Nare Head England 11 50.12N 4.55W
Nares Str. Canada 55 78.30N 75.00W
Narmada r. India 36 21.40N 73.00E
Narodnaya mtn. U.S.S.R. 30 65.00N 61.00E
Narok Kenya 47 1.04S 35.54E
Narrabri Australia 49 30.20S 149.49E
Narsimhapur India 37 22.58N 79.15E
Narva U.S.S.R. 28 59.22N 28.17E
Narva r. U.S.S.R. 28 59.30N 28.00E
Narvik Norway 28 68.26N 17.25E
Naryan Mar U.S.S.R. 30 67.37N 53.02E
Nash Pt. Wales 11 51.25N 3.35W
Nashville U.S.A. 53 36.10N 86.50W
Nasik India 36 20.00N 73.52E
Nasirabad Bangla. 37 24.45N 90.23E
Nasratabad Iran 35 29.54N 59.58E
Nassau Bahamas 59 25.03N 77.20W
Nasser, L. Egypt 34 22.40N 32.00E
Nässjö Sweden 28 57.39N 14.40E
Natal Brazil 62 5.46S 35.15W
Natal Indonesia 38 0.35N 99.07E
Natal d. R.S.A. 48 28.30S 31.00E
Natanz Iran 35 33.30N 51.57E
Natchez U.S.A. 53 31.22N 91.24W
Natron, L. Tanzania 47 2.18S 36.05E
Natuna Besar i. Indonesia 38 4.00N 108.20E
Natuna Selatan i. Indonesia 38 3.00N 108.50E
Nava r. Zaïre 47 1.45N 27.06E
Navalmoral de la Mata Spain 23 39.54N 5.33W
Navan Rep. of Ire. 18 53.39N 6.42W
Nave i. Scotland 14 55.55N 6.20W
Navenby England 13 53.07N 0.32W
Naver r. Scotland 17 58.32N 4.14W
Naver, Loch Scotland 17 58.17N 4.20W
Návpaktos Greece 25 38.24N 21.49E
Návplion Greece 25 37.33N 22.47E
Navrongo Ghana 44 10.51N 1.03W
Náxos i. Greece 25 37.03N 25.30E
Nayarit d. Mexico 58 21.30N 104.00W
Nayland England 9 51.59N 0.52E
Nazareth Israel 34 32.41N 35.16E
Nazas r. Mexico 58 25.34N 103.25W
Nazilli Turkey 34 37.55N 28.20E
N'Dendé Gabon 46 2.20S 11.23E
N'Djamene Chad 44 12.10N 14.59E
Ndjolé Gabon 46 0.07S 10.45E
Ndola Zambia 47 13.00S 28.35E
Neagh, Lough N. Ireland 14 54.36N 6.25W
Neath Wales 11 51.39N 3.49W
Neath r. Wales 11 51.39N 3.50W
Nebit Dag U.S.S.R. 35 39.31N 54.24E
Nebraska d. U.S.A. 52 41.30N 100.00W
Nebrodi Mts. Italy 24 37.53N 14.32E
Neches r. U.S.A. 53 29.55N 93.50W
Neckar r. W. Germany 26 49.32N 8.26E
Necochea Argentina 61 38.31S 58.46W
Necuto Angola 46 4.55S 12.38E
Needham Market England 9 52.09N 1.02E
Needle Hill Hong Kong 33 22.23N 114.09E
Needles U.S.A. 52 34.51N 114.36W
Neerpelt Belgium 27 51.13N 5.28E
Nefyn Wales 10 52.55N 4.31W
Negaunee U.S.A. 56 46.31N 87.37W
Negev des. Israel 34 30.42N 34.55E
Negoiu mtn. Romania 25 45.36N 24.32E
Negotin Yugo. 25 44.14N 22.33E
Negra, C. Peru 62 6.06S 81.09W
Negrais, C. Burma 37 16.00N 94.30E
Negro r. Argentina 61 41.00S 62.48W
Negro r. Brazil 62 3.30S 60.00W
Negro r. Uruguay 61 33.27S 58.20W
Negros i. Phil. 39 10.00N 123.00E
Neisse r. Poland/E. Germany 26 52.05N 14.42E
Neiva Colombia 62 2.58N 75.15W
Nejd d. Saudi Arabia 34 25.00N 45.00E
Neksö Denmark 28 55.04N 15.09E
Nellore India 37 14.29N 80.00E
Nelson Canada 52 49.29N 117.17W
Nelson England 12 53.50N 2.14W
Nelson r. Canada 55 57.00N 93.20W
Nelson New Zealand 50 41.18S 173.17E
Nelson U.S.A. 52 35.30N 113.16W
Nelspruit R.S.A. 48 25.30S 30.58E
Neman r. U.S.S.R. 28 55.23N 21.15E
Nemours France 22 48.16N 2.41E
Nemuro Japan 42 43.22N 145.36E
Nemuro kaikyo str. Japan 42 44.00N 145.50E
Nenagh Rep. of Ire. 19 52.52N 8.13W
Nenana U.S.A. 54 64.35N 149.20W
Nene r. England 13 52.49N 0.12E
Nepal Asia 37 28.00N 84.30E
Nephin mtn. Rep. of Ire. 18 54.01N 9.23W
Nephin Beg mtn. Rep. of Ire. 18 54.02N 9.38W
Nephin Beg Range mts. Rep. of Ire. 18 54.00N 9.37W
Nera r. Italy 24 42.33N 12.43E
Neretva r. Yugo. 25 43.02N 17.28E
Nero Deep Pacific Oc. 39 12.40N 145.50E
Nes Neth. 27 53.27N 5.46E
Ness f. Scotland 16 58.26N 6.15W
Ness, Loch Scotland 17 57.16N 4.30W
Neston England 10 53.17N 3.03W
Netherlands Europe 27 52.00N 5.30E
Nether Stowey England 8 51.10N 3.10W
Neto r. Italy 25 39.12N 17.08E
Neubrandenburg E. Germany 26 53.33N 13.16E
Neuchâtel Switz. 26 47.00N 6.56E
Neuchâtel, Lac de Switz. 26 46.55N 6.55E
Neuenhaus W. Germany 27 52.30N 6.58E
Neufchâteau Belgium 27 49.51N 5.26E
Neufchâtel France 22 49.44N 1.26E
Neuquén Argentina 61 38.55S 68.55W
Neuse r. U.S.A. 53 35.04N 77.04W
Neusiedler, L. Austria 26 47.52N 16.45E
Neuss W. Germany 27 51.12N 6.42E
Neustrelitz E. Germany 26 53.22N 13.05E
Neutral Territory Asia 35 29.05N 45.40E
Neuwied W. Germany 27 50.26N 7.28E
Nevada d. U.S.A. 52 39.00N 117.00W
Nevada, Sierra mts. Spain 23 37.04N 3.20W
Nevada, Sierra mts. U.S.A. 52 37.30N 119.00W
Nevada de Cocuy, Sierra mts. Colombia 59 6.15N 72.00W

Nevada de Santa Marta, Sierra *mts.* Colombia **59** 11.00N 73.30W
Nevel U.S.S.R. **29** 56.00N 29.59E
Nevers France **22** 47.00N 3.09E
Nevis *i.* C. America **59** 17.11N 62.35W
Nevis, Loch Scotland **16** 56.59N 5.40W
Nevşehir Turkey **34** 38.38N 34.43E
New Addington England **7** 51.21N 0.00
New Alresford England **8** 51.06N 1.10W
New Amsterdam Guyana **62** 6.18N 57.00W
Newark U.S.A. **57** 40.44N 74.11W
Newark-on-Trent England **13** 53.06N 0.48W
New Bedford U.S.A. **57** 41.38N 70.55W
New Bern U.S.A. **53** 35.05N 77.04W
Newberry U.S.A. **56** 46.22N 85.30W
Newbiggin-by-the-Sea England **15** 55.11N 1.30W
Newbridge on Wye Wales **10** 52.13N 3.27W
New Britain *i.* P.N.G. **49** 6.00S 150.00E
New Brunswick *d.* Canada **55** 47.00N 66.00W
New Brunswick U.S.A. **57** 40.29N 74.27W
Newburgh Fife Scotland **15** 56.21N 3.15W
Newburgh Grampian Scotland **17** 57.19N 2.01W
Newburgh U.S.A. **57** 41.30N 74.00W
Newbury England **8** 51.24N 1.19W
New Caledonia *i.* Pacific Oc. **3** 22.00S 165.00E
Newcastle Australia **49** 32.55S 151.46E
Newcastle N. Ireland **18** 54.13N 5.53W
Newcastle U.S.A. **52** 43.52N 104.14W
Newcastle Emlyn Wales **10** 52.02N 4.29W
Newcastleton Scotland **15** 55.21N 2.49W
Newcastle-under-Lyme England **12** 53.02N 2.15W
Newcastle upon Tyne England **15** 54.58N 1.36W
Newcastle West Rep. of Ire. **19** 52.26N 9.04W
New Cumnock Scotland **14** 55.24N 4.11W
New Deer Scotland **17** 57.31N 2.11W
New Delhi India **36** 28.37N 77.13E
Newent England **8** 51.56N 2.24W
New Forest *f.* England **8** 50.50N 1.35W
Newfoundland *d.* Canada **55** 55.00N 60.00W
Newfoundland *i.* Canada **55** 48.30N 56.00W
New Galloway Scotland **14** 55.05N 4.09W
New Guinea *i.* Austa. **39** 5.00S 140.00E
Newham *d.* England **7** 51.32N 0.03E
New Hampshire *d.* U.S.A. **57** 43.50N 71.45W
New Hanover *i.* Pacific Oc. **49** 2.00S 150.00E
Newhaven England **9** 50.47N 0.04E
New Haven U.S.A. **57** 41.18N 72.55W
New Hebrides *is.* Pacific Oc. **3** 16.00S 167.00E
New Holland England **13** 53.42N 0.22W
New Hythe England **7** 51.18N 0.27E
New Ireland *i.* P.N.G. **49** 2.30S 151.30E
New Jersey *d.* U.S.A. **57** 39.50N 74.45W
New Kowloon Hong Kong **33** 22.20N 114.10E
New London U.S.A. **57** 41.21N 72.06W
Newmarket England **9** 52.15N 0.23E
Newmarket Rep. of Ire. **19** 52.13N 9.00W
Newmarket-on-Fergus Rep. of Ire. **19** 52.46N 8.55W
New Mexico *d.* U.S.A **52** 34.00N 106.00W
New Mills England **12** 53.23N 2.00W
Newmilns Scotland **14** 55.37N 4.20W
Newnham England **8** 51.48N 2.27W
New Orleans U.S.A. **53** 30.00N 90.03W
New Pitsligo Scotland **17** 57.35N 2.12W
New Plymouth New Zealand **50** 39.03S 174.04E
Newport Essex England **9** 51.58N 0.13E
Newport Hants. England **8** 50.43N 1.18W
Newport Salop England **10** 52.47N 2.22W
Newport Mayo Rep. of Ire. **18** 53.53N 9.34W
Newport Tipperary Rep. of Ire. **19** 52.42N 8.25W
Newport Ky. U.S.A. **56** 39.05N 84.27W
Newport R.I. U.S.A. **57** 41.30N 71.19W
Newport Dyfed Wales **10** 52.01N 4.51W
Newport Gwent Wales **11** 51.34N 2.59W
Newport News U.S.A. **53** 36.59N 76.26W
Newport-on-Tay Scotland **15** 56.27N 2.56W
Newport Pagnell England **8** 52.05N 0.42W
New Providence *i.* Bahamas **59** 25.03N 77.25W
Newquay England **11** 50.24N 5.06W
New Quay Wales **10** 52.13N 4.22W
New Radnor Wales **10** 52.15N 3.10W
New Romney England **9** 50.59N 0.58E
New Ross Rep. of Ire. **19** 52.24N 6.57W
Newry N. Ireland **18** 54.11N 6.21W
New Scone Scotland **15** 56.25N 3.25W
New Siberian Is. U.S.S.R. **31** 76.00N 144.00E
New South Wales *d.* Australia **49** 32.30S 146.00E
New Territories *d.* Hong Kong **33** 22.25N 114.10E
Newton Abbot England **11** 50.32N 3.37W
Newton-le-Willows England **12** 53.28N 2.38W
Newton Mearns Scotland **14** 55.46N 4.18W
Newtonmore Scotland **17** 57.04N 4.08W
Newton Stewart Scotland **14** 54.57N 4.29W
Newtown Rep. of Ire. **19** 52.20N 8.48W
Newtown Wales **10** 52.31N 3.19W
Newtownabbey N. Ireland **14** 54.39N 5.57W
Newtownards N. Ireland **14** 54.35N 5.41W
Newtown Butler N. Ireland **18** 54.12N 7.22W
Newtown Cunningham Rep. of Ire. **18** 54.59N 7.31W
Newtown Forbes Rep. of Ire. **18** 53.45N 7.50W
Newtown Hamilton N. Ireland **18** 54.12N 6.36W
Newtown Mount Kennedy Rep. of Ire. **19** 53.06N 6.07W
Newtownstewart N. Ireland **18** 54.43N 7.25W
New York U.S.A. **57** 40.40N 73.50W
New York *d.* U.S.A. **57** 42.50N 75.50W
New Zealand Austa. **50** 41.00S 175.00E
Neyland Wales **11** 51.43N 4.58W
Nezhin U.S.S.R. **29** 51.03N 31.54E
Ngambwe Rapids *f.* Zambia **46** 17.08S 24.10E
Ngami, L. Botswana **48** 20.25S 23.00E
Ngamiland *f.* Botswana **48** 20.00S 22.30E
Ngan Chau *i.* Hong Kong **33** 22.13N 114.11E
Ngan Ying Chau *i.* Hong Kong **33** 22.21N 114.06E
N'Gao Congo **46** 2.28S 15.40E
Ngaoundéré Cameroon **44** 7.20N 13.35E
Ngaruroro *r.* New Zealand **50** 39.34S 176.54E
Ngau Kwu Long Hong Kong **33** 22.17N 113.58E
Ngauruhoe *mtn.* New Zealand **50** 37.10S 175.35E
Ngau Tau Kok Hong Kong **33** 22.19N 114.12E
Ngong Kenya **47** 1.22S 36.40E
Ngonye Falls *f.* Zambia **46** 16.35S 23.39E
Ngorongoro Crater *f.* Tanzania **47** 3.13S 35.32E
Ngozi Burundi **47** 2.52S 29.50E
Nguigmi Niger **44** 14.00N 13.06E
Nhamacurra Moçambique **47** 17.35S 37.00E
Nhamarroi Moçambique **47** 15.58S 36.55E
Nha Trang S. Vietnam **38** 12.15N 109.10E
Niagara Falls *town* U.S.A. **57** 43.06N 79.04W
Niamey Niger **44** 13.32N 2.05E
Niangara Zaïre **47** 3.47N 27.54E
Niapa *mtn.* Indonesia **38** 2.45N 117.30E
Nias *i.* Indonesia **38** 1.05N 97.30E
Niassa *d.* Moçambique **47** 13.00S 36.30E
Nicaragua C. America **58** 13.00N 85.00W
Nicaragua, L. Nicaragua **58** 11.30N 85.30W
Nicastro Italy **24** 38.58N 16.16E
Nice France **22** 43.42N 7.16E
Nicholson, Mt. Hong Kong **33** 22.15N 114.10E
Nicobar Is. India **37** 8.00N 94.00E
Nicosia Cyprus **34** 35.11N 33.23E
Nicoya, G. of Costa Rica **58** 9.30N 85.00W
Nicoya Pen. Costa Rica **58** 10.30N 85.30W
Nidd *r.* England **13** 54.01N 1.12W
Nidderdale *f.* England **12** 54.07N 1.50W
Nidelva *r.* Norway **28** 58.26N 8.44E
Niers *r.* Neth. **27** 51.43N 5.56E
Nieuwpoort Belgium **27** 51.08N 2.45E
Nieuwveld Range *mts.* R.S.A. **48** 32.00S 21.50E
Niğde Turkey **34** 37.58N 34.42E
Niger Africa **44** 17.00N 9.30E
Niger *r.* Nigeria **44** 4.15N 6.05E
Niger Delta Nigeria **44** 5.30N 6.30E
Nigeria Africa **44** 9.00N 7.30E
Niigata Japan **42** 37.58N 139.02E
Nii jima *i.* Japan **42** 34.21N 139.16E
Nijmegen Neth. **27** 51.50N 5.52E
Nikel U.S.S.R. **28** 69.20N 29.44E
Nikiniki Indonesia **39** 9.49S 124.29E
Nikolayev U.S.S.R. **29** 46.57N 32.00E
Nikolayevsk-na-Amur U.S.S.R. **31** 53.20N 140.44E
Niksar Turkey **34** 40.35N 36.59E
Nikšić Yugo. **25** 42.48N 18.56E
Nila *i.* Indonesia **39** 6.45S 129.30E
Nile *r.* Egypt **34** 31.30N 30.25E
Nile Delta Egypt **34** 31.00N 31.00E
Nilgiri Hills India **36** 11.30N 77.30E
Nîmes France **24** 43.50N 4.21E
Nimule Sudan **47** 3.35N 32.04E
Ninepin Group *is.* Hong Kong **33** 22.16N 114.20E
Ninety Mile Beach *f.* New Zealand **50** 34.45S 173.00E
Nineveh *ruins* Iraq **34** 36.24N 43.08E
Ningpo China **41** 29.54N 121.33E
Ningsia Hui *d.* China **37** 34.00N 104.30E
Ningwu China **41** 39.00N 112.19E
Ninove Belgium **27** 50.50N 4.02E
Niobrara *r.* U.S.A. **52** 42.45N 98.10W
Nioro Mali **44** 15.12N 9.35W
Niort France **22** 46.19N 0.27W
Nipigon Canada **56** 49.02N 88.26W
Nipigon, L. Canada **56** 48.40N 88.30W
Nipissing, L. Canada **56** 46.15N 79.45W
Niriz Iran **35** 29.12N 54.17E
Niš Yugo. **25** 43.20N 21.54E
Nishapur Iran **35** 36.13N 58.49E
Niterói Brazil **61** 22.54S 43.06W
Nith *r.* Scotland **15** 55.00N 3.35W
Nithsdale *f.* Scotland **15** 55.15N 3.48W
Niut *mtn.* Indonesia **38** 1.00N 110.00E
Nivelles Belgium **27** 50.36N 4.20E
Nizamabad India **37** 18.40N 78.05E
Nizhneudinsk U.S.S.R. **31** 54.55N 99.00E
Nizhniy Tagil U.S.S.R. **30** 58.00N 60.00E
Njombe Tanzania **47** 9.20S 34.47E
Njombe *r.* Tanzania **47** 7.02S 35.55E
Njoro Tanzania **47** 5.16S 36.30E
Nkhata Bay *town* Malaŵi **47** 11.37S 34.20E
Nkhotakota Malaŵi **47** 12.55S 34.19E
Nkongsamba Cameroon **46** 4.57N 9.53E
Nobeoka Japan **42** 32.36N 131.40E
Nogales Mexico **52** 31.20N 111.00W
Nogent le Rotrou France **22** 48.19N 0.50E
Noguera Ribagorzana *r.* Spain **23** 41.27N 0.25E
Noirmoutier, Ile de *i.* France **22** 47.00N 2.15W
Nokia Finland **28** 61.29N 23.31E
Nola C.A.R. **46** 3.28N 16.08E
Nomab *r.* Botswana **48** 19.20S 22.05E
Nome U.S.A. **54** 64.30N 165.30W
Nong Khai Thailand **37** 17.50N 102.46E
Nongoma R.S.A. **48** 27.54S 31.40E
Noord Brabant *d.* Neth. **27** 51.37N 5.00E
Noorvik U.S.A. **54** 66.50N 161.14W
Noranda Canada **57** 48.16N 79.03W
Nord *d.* France **9** 50.49N 2.21E
Norddeich W. Germany **27** 53.35N 7.10E
Norden W. Germany **27** 53.34N 7.13E
Norderney *i.* W. Germany **27** 53.45N 7.15E
Nord Fjord *est.* Norway **28** 61.50N 6.00E
Nordhausen E. Germany **26** 51.31N 10.48E
Nordhorn W. Germany **27** 52.27N 7.05E
Nordvik U.S.S.R. **31** 73.40N 110.50E
Nore *r.* Rep. of Ire. **19** 52.25N 6.58W
Norfolk *d.* England **9** 52.39N 1.00E
Norfolk U.S.A. **53** 36.54N 76.18W
Norfolk Broads *f.* England **9** 52.43N 1.35E
Norham England **15** 55.43N 2.10W
Norilsk U.S.S.R. **31** 69.21N 88.02E
Normandie, Collines de *hills* France **22** 48.50N 0.40W
Normandy England **7** 51.15N 0.38W
Normanton Australia **49** 17.40S 141.05E
Normanton England **13** 53.41N 1.26W
Norman Wells Canada **54** 65.19N 126.46W
Nörresundby Denmark **28** 57.05N 9.52E
Norris L. U.S.A. **53** 36.20N 83.55W
Norristown U.S.A. **57** 40.07N 75.20W
Norrköping Sweden **28** 58.35N 16.10E
Norrtälje Sweden **28** 59.46N 18.43E
Norte, Punta *c.* Argentina **61** 36.08S 56.50W
Northallerton England **13** 54.20N 1.26W
Northam England **11** 51.02N 4.13W
North America **51**
Northampton England **8** 52.14N 0.54W
Northamptonshire *d.* England **8** 52.18N 0.55W
Northaw England **7** 51.43N 0.09W
North Ballachulish Scotland **16** 56.42N 5.11W
North Battleford Canada **54** 52.47N 108.19W
North Bay *town* Canada **57** 46.20N 79.28W
North Bend U.S.A. **52** 43.26N 124.14W
North Berwick Scotland **15** 56.04N 2.43W
North Beveland *f.* Neth. **27** 51.35N 3.45E
North C. New Zealand **50** 34.28S 173.00E
North C. Norway **28** 71.10N 25.45E
North Canadian *r.* U.S.A. **53** 35.30N 95.45W
North Carolina *d.* U.S.A. **53** 35.30N 79.00W
North Channel Canada **56** 46.05N 83.00W
North Channel U.K. **14** 55.15N 5.52W
North China Plain *f.* China **41** 34.30N 117.00E
North Dakota *d.* U.S.A. **52** 47.00N 100.00W
North Donets *r.* U.S.S.R. **29** 49.08N 37.28E
North Dorset Downs *hills* England **8** 50.46N 2.25W
North Downs *hills* England **9** 51.18N 0.40E
North Dvina *r.* U.S.S.R. **30** 64.40N 40.50E
North Eastern *d.* Kenya **47** 1.00N 40.00E
North East Polder *f.* Neth. **27** 52.45N 5.45E
Northern Ireland U.K. **18** 54.40N 6.45W
Northern Territory *d.* Australia **49** 20.00S 133.00E
North Esk *r.* Scotland **17** 56.45N 2.25W
North European Plain *f.* Europe **3** 56.00N 27.00E
Northfleet England **7** 51.27N 0.20E
North Foreland *c.* England **9** 51.23N 1.26E
North Frisian Is. W. Germany **26** 54.30N 8.00E
North Harris *f.* Scotland **16** 57.58N 6.52W
North Holland *d.* Neth. **27** 52.37N 4.50E
North Horr Kenya **47** 3.19N 37.00E
North I. New Zealand **50** 39.00S 175.00E
Northiam England **9** 50.59N 0.39E
North Korea Asia **41** 40.00N 128.00E
North Kyme England **13** 53.04N 0.17W
Northleach England **8** 51.49N 1.50W
North Platte U.S.A. **52** 41.09N 100.45W
North Platte *r.* U.S.A. **52** 41.09N 100.55W
North Point *town* Hong Kong **33** 22.17N 114.11E
North Pt. U.S.A. **56** 45.02N 83.17W
North Ronaldsay *i.* Scotland **17** 59.23N 2.26W
North Ronaldsay Firth *est.* Scotland **17** 59.20N 2.25W
North Sd. Rep. of Ire. **19** 53.11N 9.34W
North Sea Europe **6** 56.00N 5.00E
North Somercotes England **13** 53.28N 0.08E
North Sporades *is.* Greece **25** 39.00N 24.00E
North Taranaki Bight *b.* New Zealand **50** 38.45S 174.15E
North Tawton England **11** 50.48N 3.55W
North Tidworth England **8** 51.14N 1.40W
North Tolsta Scotland **16** 58.20N 6.13W
North Truchas Peak *mtn.* U.S.A. **52** 35.58N 105.48W
North Tyne *r.* England **15** 54.59N 2.08W
North Uist *i.* Scotland **16** 57.35N 7.20W
Northumberland *d.* England **15** 55.12N 2.00W
North Vietnam Asia **38** 20.00N 105.00E
North Walsham England **9** 52.49N 1.22E
Northway U.S.A. **54** 62.58N 142.00W
North Weald Bassett England **7** 51.42N 0.12E
North West Highlands Scotland **16** 57.30N 5.15W
North West River *town* Canada **55** 53.30N 60.10W
Northwest Territories *d.* Canada **55** 66.00N 95.00W
Northwich England **12** 53.16N 2.30W
Northwood England **7** 51.36N 0.25W
North York Moors *hills* England **13** 54.21N 0.50W
North Yorkshire *d.* England **13** 54.14N 1.14W
Norton England **13** 54.08N 0.47W
Norton de Matos Angola **46** 12.20S 14.45E
Norton Sound *b.* U.S.A. **54** 63.50N 164.00W
Norwalk U.S.A. **57** 41.07N 73.25W
Norway Europe **28** 65.00N 13.00E
Norway House *town* Canada **55** 53.59N 97.50W
Norwegian Sea Europe **32** 65.00N 5.00E
Norwich England **9** 52.38N 1.17E
Norwich U.S.A. **57** 41.32N 72.05W
Noss, I. of Scotland **16** 60.08N 1.01W
Noss Head Scotland **17** 58.28N 3.03W
Nossob *r.* R.S.A./Botswana **48** 26.54S 20.39E
Notec *r.* Poland **29** 52.35N 14.35E
Nottingham England **13** 52.57N 1.10W
Nottinghamshire *d.* England **13** 53.10N 1.00W
Notwani *r.* Botswana **48** 23.14S 27.30E
Nouadhibou Mauritania **44** 20.54N 17.01W
Nouakchott Mauritania **44** 18.09N 15.58W
Noup Head Scotland **17** 59.20N 3.04W
Nouvelle Anvers Zaïre **46** 1.38N 19.10E
Nova Freixo Moçambique **47** 14.48S 36.32E
Nova Gaia Angola **46** 10.09S 17.35E
Nova Lima Brazil **61** 20.00S 43.51W
Nova Lisboa Angola **46** 12.47S 15.44E
Novara Italy **22** 45.27N 8.37E
Nova Scotia *d.* Canada **55** 45.00N 64.00W
Nova Sofala Moçambique **48** 20.09S 34.42E
Novaya Ladoga U.S.S.R. **29** 60.09N 32.15E
Novaya Siberia *i.* U.S.S.R. **31** 75.20N 148.00E
Novaya Zemlya *i.* U.S.S.R. **30** 74.00N 56.00E
Novelda Spain **23** 38.24N 0.45W
Novgorod U.S.S.R. **29** 58.30N 31.20E
Novi-Ligure Italy **22** 44.46N 8.47E
Novi Pazar Yugo. **25** 43.08N 20.28E
Novi Sad Yugo. **25** 45.16N 19.52E
Novocherkassk U.S.S.R. **29** 47.25N 40.05E
Novograd Volynskiy U.S.S.R. **29** 50.34N 27.32E
Novogrudok U.S.S.R. **29** 53.35N 25.50E
Novo Hamburgo Brazil **61** 29.37S 51.07W
Novokazalinsk U.S.S.R. **30** 45.48N 62.06E
Novokuznetsk U.S.S.R. **30** 53.45N 87.12E
Novomoskovsk U.S.S.R. **29** 54.06N 38.15E
Novo Redondo Angola **46** 11.11S 13.52E
Novorossiysk U.S.S.R. **29** 44.44N 37.46E
Novoshakhtinsk U.S.S.R. **29** 47.46N 39.55E
Novosibirsk U.S.S.R. **30** 55.04N 82.55E
Novy Port U.S.S.R. **30** 67.38N 72.33E
Nowa Ruda Poland **26** 50.34N 16.30E
Nowa Sól Poland **26** 51.49N 15.41E
Nowgong India **37** 26.20N 92.41E
Nowy Sącz Poland **29** 49.39N 20.40E
Noyon France **27** 49.35N 3.00E
N'riquinha Angola **46** 15.50S 21.40E
Nsanje Malaŵi **47** 16.55S 35.12E
Ntcheu Malaŵi **47** 14.50S 34.45E
Nuanetsi *r.* Moçambique **48** 22.42S 31.45E
Nuanetsi Rhodesia **48** 21.22S 30.45E
Nubian Desert Sudan **45** 21.00N 34.00E
Nudushan Iran **35** 32.03N 53.33E
Nueces *r.* U.S.A. **53** 27.55N 97.30W
Nueva Gerona Cuba **58** 21.53N 82.49W
Nuevitas Cuba **59** 21.34N 77.18W
Nuevo Laredo Mexico **52** 27.30N 99.30W
Nuevo Leon *d.* Mexico **58** 26.00N 99.00W
Nukha U.S.S.R. **35** 41.12N 47.10E
Nullarbor Plain *f.* Australia **49** 31.30S 128.00E
Numazu Japan **42** 35.08N 138.50E
Nuneaton England **8** 52.32N 1.29W
Nungo Moçambique **47** 13.25S 37.45E
Nunivak I. U.S.A. **54** 60.00N 166.30W
Nunkiang China **41** 49.10N 125.15E
Nuqra Saudi Arabia **34** 25.35N 41.28E
Nure *r.* Italy **22** 45.06N 9.50E
Nurmes Finland **28** 63.32N 29.10E
Nürnberg W. Germany **26** 49.27N 11.05E
Nusaybin Turkey **34** 37.05N 41.11E
Nyakanazi Tanzania **47** 3.05S 31.16E
Nyala Sudan **45** 12.01N 24.50E
Nyamandhlovu Rhodesia **48** 19.50S 28.15E
Nyandqe *r.* Moçambique **48** 19.45S 34.40E
Nyanga *r.* Gabon **46** 3.00S 10.17E
Nyanza *d.* Kenya **47** 0.30S 34.30E
Nyanza Rwanda **47** 2.20S 29.42E
Nyasa, L. *see* Malaŵi, L. Africa **47**
Nybro Sweden **28** 56.44N 15.55E
Nyeri Kenya **47** 0.22S 36.56E
Nyika Plateau *f.* Malaŵi **47** 10.25S 33.50E
Nyiru, Mt. Kenya **47** 2.06N 36.44E
Nyköbing Falster Denmark **26** 54.47N 11.53E
Nyköbing Thystad Denmark **28** 56.49N 8.50E
Nyköping Sweden **28** 58.45N 17.03E
Nylstroom R.S.A. **48** 24.42S 28.20E
Nynäshamn Sweden **28** 58.54N 17.55E
Nyngan Australia **49** 31.34S 147.14E
Nyong *r.* Cameroon **46** 3.15N 9.55E
Nyons France **22** 44.22N 5.08E
Nyunzu Zaïre **47** 5.55S 28.00E
Nzega Tanzania **47** 4.13S 33.09E

O

Oadby England **8** 52.37N 1.07W
Oahe Resr. U.S.A. **52** 45.45N 100.20W
Oahu *i.* Hawaii U.S.A. **52** 21.30N 158.00W
Oakengates England **8** 52.42N 2.29W
Oakham England **8** 52.40N 0.43W
Oakland U.S.A. **52** 37.50N 122.15W
Oakville Canada **57** 43.27N 79.41W
Oamaru New Zealand **50** 45.07S 170.58E
Oaxaca Mexico **58** 17.05N 96.41W
Oaxaca *d.* Mexico **58** 17.30N 97.00W
Ob *r.* U.S.S.R. **30** 66.50N 69.00E
Ob, G. of U.S.S.R. **30** 68.30N 74.00E
Oba Canada **56** 49.04N 84.07W
Oban Scotland **14** 56.26N 5.28W
Obbia Somali Rep. **45** 5.20N 48.30E
Oberhausen W. Germany **27** 51.28N 6.51E
Obi *i.* Indonesia **39** 1.45S 127.30E
Obihoro Japan **42** 42.55N 143.00E
Obo C.A.R. **47** 5.18N 26.28E
Ocaña Spain **23** 39.57N 3.30W
Occidental, Cordillera *mts.* Colombia **62** 6.00N 76.15W
Ochil Hills Scotland **15** 56.16N 3.25W
Ock *r.* England **8** 51.40N 1.18W
Ocotlán Mexico **58** 20.21N 102.42W
October Revolution *i.* U.S.S.R. **31** 79.30N 96.00E
Ocua Moçambique **47** 13.37S 39.42E
Ocussi Ambeno *d.* Port. Timor **39** 9.15S 124.15E
Odádhahraun *mts.* Iceland **28** 65.00N 17.30W
Odawara Japan **42** 35.20N 139.08E
Odda Norway **28** 60.03N 6.45E
Oddur Somali Rep. **47** 4.11N 43.52E
Ödemis Turkey **25** 38.12N 28.00E
Odense Denmark **28** 55.24N 10.25E
Odenwald *mts.* W. Germany **26** 49.40N 9.20E
Oder *r.* Europe **26** 53.30N 14.36E
Odessa U.S.A. **52** 31.50N 102.23W
Odessa U.S.S.R. **29** 46.30N 30.46E
Odorhei Romania **25** 46.18N 25.18E

Odzi *r.* Rhodesia **48** 19.49S 32.15E
Ofanto *r.* Italy **24** 41.22N 16.12E
Offaly *d.* Rep. of Ire. **19** 53.15N 7.30W
Offenbach W. Germany **26** 50.06N 8.46E
Offenburg W. Germany **26** 48.29N 7.57E
Ogab *r.* S.W. Africa **48** 21.10S 13.40E
Ogaki Japan **42** 35.25N 136.36E
Ogbomosho Nigeria **44** 8.05N 4.11E
Ogden U.S.A. **52** 41.14N 111.59W
Ogdensburg U.S.A. **57** 44.42N 75.31W
Ogeechee *r.* U.S.A. **53** 32.54N 81.05W
Ognon *r.* France **22** 47.20N 5.37E
Ogoki *r.* Canada **53** 51.00N 84.30W
Ogosta *r.* Bulgaria **25** 43.44N 23.51E
Ogowe *r.* Gabon **46** 1.00S 9.05E
Ogulin Yugo. **24** 45.17N 15.14E
Ohakune New Zealand **50** 39.24S 175.25E
Ohio *d.* U.S.A. **56** 40.10N 82.20W
Ohio *r.* U.S.A. **56** 37.07N 89.10W
Ohře *r.* Czech. **26** 50.32N 14.08E
Ohrid Yugo. **25** 41.06N 20.48E
Ohridsko, L. Albania/Yugo. **25** 41.00N 20.43E
Oich *r.* Scotland **17** 57.04N 4.46W
Oich, Loch Scotland **17** 57.04N 4.46W
Oil City U.S.A. **57** 41.26N 79.44W
Oise *r.* France **22** 49.00N 2.10E
Oita Japan **42** 33.15N 131.40E
Ojocaliente Mexico **58** 22.35N 102.18W
Ojo de Agua Argentina **61** 29.30S 63.44W
Oka *r.* U.S.S.R. **29** 56.09N 43.00E
Okahandja S.W. Africa **48** 21.59S 16.58E
Okaihau New Zealand **50** 35.18S 173.47E
Okanogan *r.* U.S.A. **52** 47.45N 120.05W
Okavango *r.* Botswana **48** 18.30S 22.04E
Okavango Basin *f.* Botswana **48** 19.30S 23.00E
Okayama Japan **42** 34.40N 133.54E
Okazaki Japan **42** 34.58N 137.10E
Okeechobee, L. U.S.A. **53** 27.00N 80.45W
Okeefenoke Swamp *f.* U.S.A. **53** 30.40N 82.40W
Okehampton England **11** 50.44N 4.01W
Okement *r.* England **11** 50.50N 4.04W
Okere *r.* Uganda **47** 1.37N 33.53E
Okha India **36** 22.29N 69.09E
Okha U.S.S.R. **31** 53.35N 142.50E
Okhotsk U.S.S.R. **31** 59.20N 143.15E
Okhotsk, Sea of U.S.S.R. **31** 55.00N 150.00E
Oki gunto *is.* Japan **42** 36.10N 133.10E
Okinawa *i.* Japan **41** 26.30N 128.00E
Okipoko *r.* S.W. Africa **48** 18.40S 16.03E
Oklahoma *d.* U.S.A. **53** 35.00N 97.00W
Oklahoma City U.S.A. **53** 35.28N 97.33W
Okushiri shima *i.* Japan **42** 42.00N 139.50E
Oland *i.* Sweden **28** 56.50N 16.50E
Olavarria Argentina **61** 36.57S 60.20W
Olbia Italy **24** 40.55N 9.29E
Old Crow Canada **54** 67.34N 139.43W
Oldenburg Niedersachsen West W. Germany **27** 53.08N 8.13E
Oldenburg Schleswig Holstein W. Germany **26** 54.17N 10.52E
Oldenzaal Neth. **27** 52.19N 6.55E
Old Fletton England **9** 52.34N 0.14W
Oldham England **12** 53.33N 2.08W
Old Head of Kinsale *c.* Rep. of Ire. **19** 51.37N 8.33W
Oldmeldrum Scotland **17** 57.20N 2.20W
Old Rhine *r.* Neth. **27** 52.14N 4.26E
Old Windsor England **7** 51.28N 0.35W
Olean U.S.A. **57** 42.05N 78.26W
Olekma *r.* U.S.S.R. **31** 60.20N 120.30E
Olekminsk U.S.S.R. **31** 60.25N 120.00E
Olenek U.S.S.R. **31** 68.38N 112.15E
Olenek *r.* U.S.S.R. **31** 73.00N 120.00E
Olenekskiy G. U.S.S.R. **31** 74.00N 120.00E
Oléron, Ile d' *i.* France **22** 45.55N 1.16W
Olga U.S.S.R. **42** 43.48N 135.17E
Olhão Portugal **23** 37.01N 7.50W
Olifants *r.* Cape Province R.S.A. **48** 31.43S 18.10E
Olifants *r.* Transvaal R.S.A. **48** 24.08S 32.40E
Olifants *r.* S.W. Africa **48** 25.28S 19.23E
Olivares Spain **23** 39.45N 2.21W
Olney England **8** 52.09N 0.42W
Ölögey Mongolia **40** 48.54N 90.00E
Olomouc Czech. **29** 49.38N 17.15E
Oloron France **22** 43.12N 0.35W
Olot Spain **23** 42.11N 2.30E
Olpe W. Germany **27** 51.02N 7.52E
Olsztyn Poland **29** 53.48N 20.29E
Oltenița Romania **25** 44.05N 26.31E
Oltet *r.* Romania **25** 44.13N 24.28E
Olympus, Mt. Cyprus **34** 34.55N 32.52E
Olympus, Mt. Greece **25** 40.04N 22.20E
Omagh N. Ireland **18** 54.36N 7.20W
Omaha U.S.A. **53** 41.15N 96.00W
Oman Asia **36** 22.30N 57.30E
Oman, G. of Asia **35** 25.00N 58.00E
Omarama New Zealand **50** 44.29S 169.59E
Omaruru S.W. Africa **48** 21.28S 15.56E
Ombrone *r.* Italy **24** 42.40N 11.00E
Omdurman Sudan **45** 15.37N 32.59E
Ommen Neth. **27** 52.32N 6.25E
Omolon *r.* U.S.S.R. **31** 68.50N 158.30E
Omono *r.* Japan **42** 39.44N 140.05E
Omsk U.S.S.R. **30** 55.00N 73.22E
Omulonga *r.* S.W. Africa **48** 18.30S 16.15E
Omuramba Omatako *r.* S.W. Africa **48** 17.59S 20.32E
Omuta Japan **42** 33.02N 130.26E
Oña Spain **23** 42.44N 3.25W
Onda Spain **23** 39.58N 0.16W
Onega, L. U.S.S.R. **30** 62.00N 35.30E
Oneida L. U.S.A. **57** 43.13N 75.55W
Oneonta U.S.A. **57** 42.28N 75.04W
Onitsha Nigeria **44** 6.10N 6.47E
Onslow Village England **7** 51.14N 0.36W
Onstwedde Neth. **27** 53.04N 7.02E
Ontaki san *mtn.* Japan **42** 35.55N 137.29E
Ontario *d.* Canada **56** 47.00N 80.40W
Ontario, L. N. America **57** 43.40N 78.00W
Ontonagon U.S.A. **56** 46.52N 89.18W
Oosterhout Neth. **27** 51.38N 4.50E
Oosthuizen Neth. **27** 52.33N 5.00E
Oostmalle Belgium **27** 51.18N 4.45E
Opala Zaire **46** 0.42S 24.15E
Opole Poland **29** 50.40N 17.56E
Oporto Portugal **23** 41.09N 8.37W
Opotiki New Zealand **50** 38.00S 177.18E
Opunake New Zealand **50** 39.27S 173.52E
Oradea Romania **29** 47.03N 21.55E
Oran Algeria **23** 35.45N 0.38W
Orán Argentina **61** 23.07S 64.16W
Orange France **22** 44.08N 4.48E
Orange *r.* R.S.A. **48** 28.43S 16.30E
Orange, Cabo *c.* Brazil **62** 4.25N 51.32W
Orangeburg U.S.A. **53** 33.28N 80.53W
Orange Free State *d.* R.S.A. **48** 29.00S 26.30E
Oranjemond S.W. Africa **48** 28.38S 16.24E
Oranmore Rep. of Ire. **19** 53.17N 8.52W
Orchies France **27** 50.28N 3.15E
Orchila *i.* Venezuela **59** 11.52N 66.10W
Orchy *r.* Scotland **14** 56.25N 5.02W
Ord *r.* Australia **49** 15.30S 128.30E
Ordu Turkey **34** 41.00N 37.52E
Orduna Spain **23** 43.00N 3.00W
Ordzhonikidze U.S.S.R. **29** 43.02N 44.43E
Orebro Sweden **28** 59.17N 15.13E
Oregon *d.* U.S.A. **52** 44.00N 120.00W
Oregrund Sweden **28** 60.20N 18.30E
Orekhovo Zuyevo U.S.S.R. **29** 55.47N 39.00E
Orel U.S.S.R. **29** 52.58N 36.04E
Ore Mts. E. Germany **26** 50.30N 12.50E
Orenburg U.S.S.R. **30** 51.50N 55.00E
Orense Spain **23** 42.20N 7.52W
Ore Sund *str.* Denmark **28** 56.00N 12.30E
Oreti *r.* New Zealand **50** 46.27S 168.14E
Orford England **9** 52.06N 1.31E
Orford Ness *c.* England **9** 52.05N 1.36E
Oriental, Cordillera *mts.* Bolivia **61** 17.00S 65.00W
Oriental, Cordillera *mts.* Colombia **62** 6.00N 74.00W
Oriente *d.* Cuba **59** 20.30N 75.30W
Orihuela Spain **23** 38.05N 0.56W
Orinoco *r.* Venezuela **59** 9.00N 61.30W
Orinoco Delta *f.* Venezuela **59** 9.00N 61.30W
Orissa *d.* India **37** 20.15N 84.00E
Oristano Italy **24** 39.53N 8.36E
Oristano, G. of Med. Sea **24** 39.50N 8.30E
Ori Vesi *l.* Finland **28** 62.20N 29.30E
Orizaba Mexico **58** 18.51N 97.08W
Orkney Is. *d.* Scotland **17** 59.00N 3.00W
Orlando U.S.A. **53** 28.33N 81.21W
Orléans France **22** 47.54N 1.54E
Ormiston Scotland **15** 55.55N 2.56W
Ormskirk England **12** 53.35N 2.53W
Orne *r.* France **22** 49.17N 0.10W
Ornsay *i.* Scotland **16** 57.08N 5.49W
Ornsköldsvik Sweden **28** 63.19N 18.45E
Oromocto Canada **57** 45.50N 66.28W
Oronsay *i.* Scotland **14** 56.01N 6.14W
Orosei Italy **24** 40.23N 9.40E
Orosei, G. of Med. Sea **24** 40.15N 9.45E
Oroville U.S.A. **52** 48.57N 119.27W
Orpington England **7** 51.23N 0.06E
Orrin *r.* Scotland **17** 57.33N 4.29W
Orsett England **7** 51.31N 0.23E
Orsha U.S.S.R. **29** 54.30N 30.23E
Orsk U.S.S.R. **30** 51.13N 58.35E
Orşova Romania **25** 44.42N 22.22E
Orthez France **22** 43.29N 0.46W
Ortles *mtn.* Italy **26** 46.30N 10.30E
Oruro Bolivia **62** 18.05S 67.00W
Oryakhovo Bulgaria **25** 43.42N 23.58E
Osaka Japan **42** 34.40N 135.30E
Osa Pen. Costa Rica **58** 8.20N 83.30W
Oshawa Canada **57** 43.53N 78.51W
O shima *i.* Tosan Japan **42** 34.40N 139.28E
O shima *i.* Hokkaido Japan **42** 41.40N 139.40E
Oshogbo Nigeria **44** 7.50N 4.35E
Oshwe Zaire **46** 3.27S 19.32E
Osijek Yugo. **25** 45.35N 18.43E
Oskarshamn Sweden **28** 57.16N 16.25E
Oskol *r.* U.S.S.R. **29** 49.08N 37.10E
Oslo Norway **28** 59.56N 10.45E
Oslo Fjord *est.* Norway **28** 59.30N 10.30E
Osmancik Turkey **34** 40.58N 34.50E
Osmaniye Turkey **34** 37.04N 36.15E
Osnabrück W. Germany **27** 52.17N 8.03E
Osorno Spain **23** 42.24N 4.22W
Oss Neth. **27** 51.46N 5.31E
Ossa *mtn.* Greece **25** 39.47N 22.41E
Ossa, Mt. Australia **49** 41.52S 146.04E
Ossett England **13** 53.40N 1.35W
Ostashkov U.S.S.R. **29** 57.09N 33.10E
Ostend Belgium **27** 51.13N 2.55E
Osterdal *r.* Sweden **28** 61.03N 14.30E
Osterö *i.* Faroe Is. **28** 62.10N 7.00W
Ostersund Sweden **28** 63.10N 14.40E
Osthammar Sweden **28** 60.15N 18.25E
Ostrava Czech. **29** 49.50N 18.15E
Ostrov U.S.S.R. **28** 57.22N 28.22E
Ostrów Mazowiecka Poland **29** 52.50N 21.51E
Osũm *r.* Bulgaria **25** 43.41N 24.51E
Osumi gunto *is.* Japan **42** 30.30N 131.00E
Osumi kaikyo *str.* Japan **42** 31.30N 131.00E
Osuna Spain **23** 37.14N 5.06W
Oswego U.S.A. **57** 43.27N 76.31W
Oswestry England **10** 52.52N 3.03W
Otago Pen. New Zealand **50** 45.48S 170.45E
Otaru Japan **42** 43.14N 140.59E
Otavi S.W. Africa **48** 19.39S 17.20E
Otford England **7** 51.19N 0.12E
Otjiwarongo S.W. Africa **48** 20.29S 16.36E
Otley England **12** 53.54N 1.41W
Otra *r.* Norway **28** 58.10N 8.00E
Otranto Italy **25** 40.09N 18.30E
Otranto, Str. of Med. Sea **25** 40.10N 19.00E
Otta Norway **28** 61.46N 9.33E
Ottawa Canada **57** 45.25N 75.43W
Ottawa *r.* Canada **57** 45.23N 73.55W
Ottawa Is. Canada **55** 59.50N 80.00W
Otter *r.* England **11** 50.38N 3.19W
Otterburn England **15** 55.14N 2.10W
Ottery St. Mary England **11** 50.45N 3.16W
Ouachita *r.* U.S.A. **53** 33.10N 92.10W
Ouachita Mts. U.S.A. **53** 34.40N 94.30W
Ouagadougou U. Volta **44** 12.20N 1.40W
Ouargla Algeria **44** 32.00N 5.16E
Oudenarde Belgium **27** 50.50N 3.37E
Oudtshoorn R.S.A. **48** 33.35S 22.12E
Ouerk *r.* Algeria **23** 35.15N 2.15E
Ouessant, Ile d' *i.* France **22** 48.28N 5.05W
Ouesso Congo **46** 1.38N 16.03E
Ouezzane Morocco **23** 34.52N 5.35W
Oughter, Lough Rep. of Ire. **18** 54.01N 7.28W
Oughterard Rep. of Ire. **18** 53.27N 9.22W
Oujda Morocco **44** 34.41N 1.45W
Oulu Finland **28** 65.02N 25.27E
Oulu *r.* Finland **28** 65.04N 25.23E
Oulu Järvi *l.* Finland **28** 64.30N 27.00E
Ounas *r.* Finland **28** 66.33N 25.37E
Oundle England **9** 52.28N 0.28W
Our *r.* Lux. **27** 49.53N 6.16E
Ourinhos Brazil **61** 23.00S 49.54W
Ourthe *r.* Belgium **27** 50.38N 5.36E
Ouse *r.* E. Sussex England **9** 50.46N 0.03E
Ouse *r.* Humber. England **13** 53.41N 0.42W
Outer Hebrides *is.* Scotland **16** 57.40N 7.35W
Outjo S.W. Africa **48** 20.08S 16.08E
Out Skerries *is.* Scotland **16** 60.20N 0.45W
Outwell England **9** 52.36N 0.15E
Ovamboland *f.* S.W. Africa **48** 17.45S 16.00E
Overath W. Germany **27** 50.56N 7.18E
Overflakkee *i.* Neth. **27** 51.45N 4.08E
Overijssel *d.* Neth. **27** 52.25N 6.30E
Overton England **8** 51.15N 1.15W
Overton Wales **10** 52.58N 2.56W
Overuman *l.* Sweden **28** 66.06N 14.40E
Oviedo Spain **23** 43.21N 5.50W
Owel, Lough Rep. of Ire. **18** 53.34N 7.24W
Owen Falls Dam Uganda **47** 0.30N 33.07E
Oweniny *r.* Rep. of Ire. **18** 54.08N 9.51W
Owenkillew *r.* N. Ireland **14** 54.43N 7.23W
Owen Sound *town* Canada **56** 44.34N 80.56W
Owen Stanley Range *mts.* P.N.G. **49** 9.30S 148.00E
Owosso U.S.A. **56** 43.00N 84.11W
Oxelösund Sweden **28** 58.40N 17.10E
Oxford England **8** 51.45N 1.15W
Oxfordshire *d.* England **8** 51.46N 1.10W
Oxshott England **7** 51.19N 0.20W
Oxted England **7** 51.16N 0.01E
Oykel *r.* Scotland **17** 57.53N 4.21W
Oykel Bridge *town* Scotland **17** 57.57N 4.44W
Oymyakon U.S.S.R. **31** 63.30N 142.44E
Ozamiz Phil. **39** 8.09N 123.59E
Ozark Plateau U.S.A. **53** 36.00N 93.35W

P

Paan China **37** 30.02N 99.01E
Paarl R.S.A. **48** 33.45S 18.58E
Pabbay *i.* W. Isles Scotland **16** 57.46N 7.14W
Pabbay *i.* W. Isles Scotland **16** 56.51N 7.35W
Pachuca Mexico **58** 20.10N 98.44W
Pacific Ocean 2
Padang Indonesia **38** 0.55S 100.21E
Paddington England **7** 51.31N 0.12W
Paddock Wood England **9** 51.11N 0.23E
Padre I. U.S.A. **53** 27.00N 97.20W
Padstow England **11** 50.33N 4.57W
Padua Italy **24** 45.27N 11.52E
Pag *i.* Yugo. **24** 44.28N 15.00E
Pagai Selatan *i.* Indonesia **38** 3.00S 100.30E
Pagai Utara *i.* Indonesia **38** 2.40S 100.10E
Pagan *i.* Asia **39** 18.08N 145.46E
Pager *r.* Uganda **47** 3.05N 32.28E
Pahala Hawaii U.S.A. **52** 19.12N 155.28W
Paible Scotland **16** 57.35N 7.27W
Paijänne *l.* Finland **28** 61.30N 25.30E
Paimboeuf France **22** 47.14N 2.01W
Painesville U.S.A. **56** 41.43N 81.15W
Painswick England **8** 51.47N 2.11W
Paisley Scotland **14** 55.50N 4.26W
Pak A Hong Kong **33** 22.21N 114.20E
Pakanbaru Indonesia **38** 0.33N 101.20E
Pakhoi China **38** 21.39N 109.10E
Pakistan Asia **36** 30.00N 70.00E
Pak Kok Kau Tsuen Hong Kong **33** 22.14N 114.06E
Pak Kong Hong Kong **33** 22.22N 114.15E
Pak Lay Laos **38** 18.10N 101.24E
Pak Mong Hong Kong **33** 22.17N 113.58E
Pakse Laos **38** 15.05N 105.50E
Pak Sha Wan *b.* Hong Kong **33** 22.21N 114.15E
Pak Shek Wo Hong Kong **33** 22.20N 114.14E
Pak Tam Hong Kong **33** 22.24N 114.19E
Pakwach Uganda **47** 2.27N 31.18E
Palana U.S.S.R. **31** 59.05N 159.59E
Palapye Botswana **48** 22.37S 27.06E
Palau Is. Asia **39** 7.00N 134.25E
Palawan *i.* Phil. **38** 9.30N 118.30E
Paldiski U.S.S.R. **29** 59.22N 24.08E
Palembang Indonesia **38** 2.59S 104.50E
Palencia Spain **23** 42.01N 4.34W
Palenque Mexico **58** 17.32N 91.59W
Palermo Italy **24** 38.09N 13.22E
Palit, C. Albania **25** 41.24N 19.23E
Palk Str. India/Sri Lanka **37** 10.00N 79.40E
Pallaskenry Rep. of Ire. **19** 52.39N 8.52W
Palliser, C. New Zealand **50** 41.35S 175.15E
Palma Moçambique **47** 10.48S 40.25E
Palma Spain **23** 39.36N 2.39E
Palma, B. of Spain **23** 39.30N 2.40E
Palma del Rio Spain **23** 37.43N 5.17W
Palmas, C. Liberia **44** 4.30N 7.55W
Palmas, G. of Med. Sea **24** 39.00N 8.30E
Palmeirinhas, Punta das Angola **46** 9.09S 12.58E
Palmerston New Zealand **50** 45.30S 170.42E
Palmerston North New Zealand **50** 40.20S 175.39E
Palmi Italy **24** 38.22N 15.50E
Palmira Colombia **62** 3.33N 76.17W
Palm Springs *town* U.S.A. **52** 33.49N 116.34W
Palmyra Syria **34** 34.36N 38.15E
Palmyras Pt. India **37** 20.40N 87.00E
Paloh Indonesia **38** 1.46N 109.17E
Palopo Indonesia **39** 3.01S 120.12E
Pamekasan Indonesia **38** 7.11S 113.50E
Pamiers France **22** 43.07N 1.36E
Pamirs *mts.* U.S.S.R. **40** 37.50N 73.30E
Pampa U.S.A. **52** 35.32N 100.58W
Pampas *f.* Argentina **61** 34.00S 64.00W
Pamplona Colombia **59** 7.24N 72.38W
Pamplona Spain **23** 42.49N 1.39W
Panama C. America **59** 9.00N 80.00W
Panamá, G. of Panama **59** 8.30N 79.00W
Panama Canal Zone C. America **59** 9.10N 79.55W
Panamá City Panama **59** 8.57N 79.30W
Panama City U.S.A. **53** 30.10N 85.41W
Panay *i.* Phil. **39** 11.10N 122.30E
Panevežys U.S.S.R. **28** 55.44N 24.24E
Pangani Tanga Tanzania **47** 5.21S 39.00E
Pangi Zaïre **47** 3.10S 26.38E
Pangkalpinang Indonesia **38** 2.05S 106.09E
Pangnirtung Canada **55** 66.05N 65.45W
Pantano del Esla *l.* Spain **23** 41.40N 5.50W
Pantelleria *i.* Italy **24** 36.48N 12.00E
Paoki China **40** 34.23N 107.16E
Páola Italy **24** 39.21N 16.03E
Paoshan China **37** 25.07N 99.08E
Paoting China **41** 38.54N 115.26E
Paotow China **41** 40.38N 109.59E
Papa Stour *i.* Scotland **16** 60.20N 1.42W
Papa Westray *i.* Scotland **17** 59.22N 2.54W
Papenburg W. Germany **27** 53.05N 7.25E
Paphos Cyprus **34** 34.45N 32.25E
Paps of Jura *mts.* Scotland **14** 55.55N 6.00W
Papua, G. of P.N.G. **39** 8.50S 145.00E
Papua New Guinea Austa. **39** 6.00S 143.00E
Paracatu Brazil **61** 17.14S 46.52W
Paracatu *r.* Brazil **61** 16.30S 45.10W
Paracel Is. Asia **38** 16.20N 112.00E
Paragua *r.* Venezuela **59** 6.45N 63.00W
Paraguaná Pen. Venezuela **59** 12.00N 70.00W
Paraguarí Paraguay **61** 25.36S 57.06W
Paraguay *r.* Argentina **61** 27.30S 58.50W
Paraguay S. America **61** 23.00S 57.00W
Parakou Dahomey **44** 9.23N 2.40E
Paramaribo Surinam **62** 5.50N 55.14W
Paraná Argentina **61** 31.45S 60.30W
Paraná *r.* Argentina **61** 34.00S 58.30W
Paraná *d.* Brazil **61** 24.30S 52.00W
Paranaguá Brazil **61** 25.32S 48.36W
Paranaiba *r.* Brazil **61** 20.00S 51.00W
Paranapanema *r.* Brazil **61** 22.30S 53.03W
Paranapiacaba, Serra *mts.* Brazil **61** 24.30S 49.15W
Parana Plateau Paraguay **61** 24.32S 55.00W
Pardo *r.* Brazil **61** 20.10S 48.30W
Parece Vela *i.* Asia **39** 20.24N 136.02E
Parepare Indonesia **38** 4.03S 119.40E
Paria, G. of Venezuela **59** 10.30N 62.00W
Pariaman Indonesia **38** 0.36S 100.09E
Paria Pen. Venezuela **59** 10.45N 62.30W
Paris France **22** 48.52N 2.20E
Park *f.* Scotland **16** 58.05N 6.32W
Parkano Finland **28** 62.03N 23.00E
Parker, Mt. Hong Kong **33** 22.16N 114.13E
Parker Dam U.S.A. **52** 34.25N 114.05W
Parkersburg U.S.A. **56** 39.17N 81.33W
Park Falls *town* U.S.A. **56** 45.57N 90.28W
Parma Italy **24** 44.48N 10.18E
Parnaíba *r.* Brazil **62** 3.00S 42.00W
Parnassos *mtn.* Greece **25** 38.33N 22.35E
Pärnu U.S.S.R. **28** 58.28N 24.30E
Pärnu *r.* U.S.S.R. **28** 58.23N 24.32E
Paropamisus Mts. Afghan. **35** 34.30N 63.30E
Páros *i.* Greece **25** 37.04N 25.11E
Parral Mexico **52** 26.58N 105.40W
Parrett *r.* England **8** 51.10N 3.00W
Parry, C. Greenland **55** 76.50N 71.00W
Parry Is. Canada **55** 76.00N 102.00W
Parry Sound *town* Canada **56** 45.21N 80.03W
Partabpur India **37** 23.28N 83.15E
Parthenay France **22** 46.39N 0.14W
Partry Mts. Rep. of Ire. **18** 53.40N 9.30W
Parys R.S.A. **48** 26.55S 27.28E
Pasadena U.S.A. **52** 34.10N 118.09W
Pas de Calais *d.* France **9** 50.30N 2.30E
Paso de Bermejo *f.* Argentina **63** 32.50S 70.00W
Paso de los Toros *town* Uruguay **61** 32.45S 56.47W
Paso Socompa *f.* Chile **63** 24.27S 68.18W
Passage East *town* Rep. of Ire. **19** 52.14N 7.00W
Passage West *town* Rep. of Ire. **19** 51.52N 8.20W
Passau W. Germany **26** 48.35N 13.28E
Passero, C. Italy **24** 36.40N 15.08E
Pass of Thermopylae Greece **25** 38.47N 22.34E
Passo Fundo Brazil **61** 28.16S 52.20W
Pasto Colombia **62** 1.12N 77.17W
Pasvik *r.* Norway **28** 69.45N 30.00E

Patagonia *f.* Argentina **61** 40.20S 67.00W
Pate I. Kenya **47** 2.08S 41.02E
Pateley Bridge *town* England **12** 54.05N 1.45W
Paterson U.S.A. **57** 40.55N 74.10W
Pathfinder Resr. U.S.A. **52** 42.25N 106.55W
Patiala India **36** 30.21N 76.27E
Patkai Hills Burma **37** 26.30N 95.40E
Patna India **37** 25.37N 85.12E
Patna Scotland **14** 55.22N 4.30W
Patos, L. Brazil **61** 31.00S 51.10W
Patras Greece **25** 38.15N 21.45E
Patras, G. of Med. Sea **25** 38.15N 21.35E
Patrickswell Rep. of Ire. **19** 52.36N 8.43W
Patrington England **13** 53.41N 0.02W
Patuca *r.* Honduras **58** 30.48N 84.25W
Pau France **22** 43.18N 0.22W
Pauillac France **22** 45.12N 0.44W
Pavia Italy **22** 45.12N 9.09E
Pavlodar U.S.S.R. **30** 52.21N 76.59E
Pavlograd U.S.S.R. **29** 48.34N 35.50E
Pawtucket U.S.A. **57** 41.53N 71.23W
Payne *r.* Canada **55** 60.00N 69.45W
Paysandú Uruguay **61** 32.21S 58.05W
Peace *r.* Canada **54** 59.00N 111.26W
Peace River *town* Canada **54** 56.15N 117.18W
Peace River Resr. Canada **54** 55.00N 126.00W
Peale, Mt. U.S.A. **52** 38.26N 109.14W
Pearl *r.* U.S.A. **53** 30.15N 89.25W
Pebane Moçambique **47** 17.14S 38.10E
Pec Yugo. **25** 42.40N 20.17E
Pechenga U.S.S.R. **28** 69.28N 31.04E
Pechora *r.* U.S.S.R. **30** 68.10N 54.00E
Pechora G. U.S.S.R. **30** 69.00N 56.00E
Pecos U.S.A. **58** 31.25N 103.30W
Pecos *r.* U.S.A. **52** 29.45N 101.25W
Pécs Hungary **25** 46.05N 18.14E
Pedro J. Caballero Paraguay **61** 22.30S 55.44W
Peebles Scotland **15** 55.39N 3.12W
Peel *r.* Canada **54** 68.13N 135.00W
Peel I.o.M. **12** 54.14N 4.42W
Peel *f.* Neth. **27** 51.30N 5.50E
Peel Fell *mtn.* England/Scotland **15** 55.17N 2.35W
Peene *r.* E. Germany **26** 53.53N 13.49E
Pegasus B. New Zealand **50** 43.15S 173.00E
Pegu Burma **37** 17.18N 96.31E
Pegu Yoma *mts.* Burma **37** 18.40N 96.00E
Pegwell B. England **9** 51.18N 1.25E
Pehan China **41** 48.17N 126.33E
Pehuajó Argentina **61** 35.50S 61.50W
Pei Pa Chau *i.* Hong Kong **33** 22.22N 113.59E
Peipus, L. U.S.S.R. **28** 58.30N 27.30E
Pekalongan Indonesia **38** 6.54S 109.37E
Peking China **41** 39.55N 116.25E
Pelat, Mont *mtn.* France **22** 44.17N 6.41E
Pelee, Pt. Canada **56** 41.45N 82.09W
Peleng *i.* Indonesia **39** 1.30S 123.10E
Pelly *r.* Canada **54** 62.50N 137.35W
Pelotas Brazil **61** 31.45S 52.20W
Pematangsiantar Indonesia **38** 2.59N 99.01E
Pemba I. Tanzania **47** 5.10S 39.45E
Pembridge England **8** 52.13N 2.54W
Pembroke Canada **57** 45.49N 77.08W
Pembroke Wales **11** 51.41N 4.57W
Penang I. Malaysia **38** 5.30N 100.10E
Peñaranda de Bracamonte Spain **23** 40.54N 5.13W
Penarth Wales **11** 51.26N 3.11W
Peñas, Cabo de Spain **23** 43.42N 5.52W
Pendine Wales **11** 51.44N 4.33W
Pendle Hill England **12** 53.52N 2.18W
Penganga *r.* India **37** 18.52N 79.56E
Peng Chau Hong Kong **33** 22.17N 114.02E
Peng Chau I. Hong Kong **33** 22.17N 114.02E
Penge England **7** 51.25N 0.04W
Pengpu China **41** 32.56N 117.27E
Penicuik Scotland **15** 55.49N 3.13W
Penistone England **12** 53.31N 1.38W
Penki China **41** 41.21N 123.45E
Penmaenmawr Wales **10** 53.16N 3.54W
Pennsylvania *d.* U.S.A. **57** 41.00N 75.45W
Penny Highland Canada **55** 67.10N 66.50W
Penny's B. Hong Kong **33** 22.19N 114.02E
Penonomé Panamá **59** 8.30N 80.20W
Penrhyndeudraeth Wales **10** 52.56N 4.04W
Penrith England **12** 54.40N 2.45W
Penryn England **11** 50.10N 5.07W
Pensacola U.S.A. **53** 30.30N 87.12W
Penticton Canada **52** 49.29N 119.38W
Pentire Pt. England **11** 50.35N 4.55W
Pentland Firth *str.* Scotland **17** 58.40N 3.00W
Pentland Hills Scotland **15** 55.50N 3.20W
Pen-y-ghent *mtn.* England **12** 54.10N 2.14W
Pen-y-groes Wales **10** 53.03N 4.18W
Penza U.S.S.R. **29** 53.11N 45.00E
Penzance England **11** 50.07N 5.32W
Penzhina, G. of U.S.S.R. **31** 61.00N 163.00E
Peoria U.S.A. **56** 40.43N 89.38W
Pereira Colombia **62** 4.47N 75.46W
Perekop U.S.S.R. **29** 46.10N 33.42E
Pergamino Argentina **61** 33.55S 60.32W
Peribonca *r.* Canada **53** 48.50N 72.00W
Périgueux France **22** 45.12N 0.44E
Perija, Sierra de *mts.* Venezuela **59** 9.00N 73.00W
Perim *i.* Asia **45** 12.40N 43.24E
Perito Moreno Argentina **63** 46.35S 71.00W
Perm U.S.S.R. **30** 58.01N 56.10E
Pernik *see* Dimitrovo Bulgaria **25**
Péronne France **27** 49.56N 2.57E
Perpignan France **22** 42.42N 2.54E
Perranporth England **11** 50.21N 5.09W
Persepolis *ruins* Iran **35** 29.55N 53.00E
Pershore England **8** 52.07N 2.04W
Persian G. Asia **35** 27.00N 50.00E
Perth Australia **49** 31.58S 115.49E
Perth Scotland **15** 56.24N 3.28W
Perth Amboy U.S.A. **57** 40.32N 74.17W
Peru S. America **62** 10.00S 75.00W
Peru U.S.A. **56** 40.45N 86.04W
Peru-Chile Trench Pacific Oc. **63** 23.00S 71.30W
Perugia Italy **24** 43.06N 12.24E
Péruwelz Belgium **27** 50.32N 3.36E
Pésaro Italy **24** 43.54N 12.54E
Pescara Italy **24** 42.27N 14.13E
Pescara *r.* Italy **24** 42.28N 14.13E
Peshawar Pakistan **36** 34.01N 71.40E
Petatlán Mexico **58** 17.31N 101.16W
Petauke Zambia **47** 14.16S 31.21E
Peterborough Canada **57** 44.19N 78.20W
Peterborough England **9** 52.35N 0.14W
Peterhead Scotland **17** 57.30N 1.46W
Peterlee England **15** 54.45N 1.18W
Petersfield England **8** 51.00N 0.56W
Petra *ruins* Jordan **34** 30.19N 35.26E
Petrich Bulgaria **25** 41.25N 23.13E
Petropavlovsk U.S.S.R. **30** 54.53N 69.13E
Petropavlovsk Kamchatskiy U.S.S.R. **31** 53.03N 158.43E
Petrópolis Brazil **61** 22.30S 43.06W
Petrovsk Zabaykal'skiy U.S.S.R. **31** 51.20N 108.55E
Petrozavodsk U.S.S.R. **30** 61.46N 34.19E
Petworth England **8** 50.59N 0.37W
Pewsey England **8** 51.20N 1.46W
Pézenas France **22** 43.28N 3.25E
Pforzheim W. Germany **26** 48.53N 8.41E
Phan Rang S. Vietnam **38** 11.35N 109.00E
Phet Buri Thailand **37** 13.01N 99.55E
Philadelphia U.S.A. **57** 40.00N 75.10W
Philippeville Belgium **27** 50.12N 4.32E
Philippine Is. Asia **3** 10.00N 124.00E
Philippines Asia **39** 13.00N 123.00E
Philippine Trench Pacific Oc. **39** 8.45N 127.20E
Philipstown R.S.A. **48** 30.26S 24.28E
Phnom Penh Cambodia **37** 11.35N 104.55E
Phoenix U.S.A. **52** 33.30N 111.55W
Phong Saly Laos **38** 21.40N 102.06E
Phukao Miang *mtn.* Thailand **37** 16.50N 101.00E
Phuket Thailand **37** 8.00N 98.28E
Phuket *i.* Thailand **38** 8.10N 98.20E
Phu Quoc *i.* Cambodia **38** 10.10N 104.00E
Piacenza Italy **24** 45.03N 9.42E
Pianosa *i.* Italy **24** 42.35N 10.05E
Piave *r.* Italy **24** 45.33N 12.45E
Pic *r.* Canada **56** 48.35N 86.17W
Picardy *f.* France **27** 49.47N 2.45E
Pickering England **13** 54.15N 0.46W
Pickwick L. U.S.A. **53** 35.00N 88.10W
Picnic B. Hong Kong **33** 22.12N 114.07E
Picton Canada **57** 44.01N 77.09W
Picton New Zealand **50** 41.17S 174.02E
Piedras Negras Mexico **52** 28.40N 100.32W
Pieksämäki Finland **28** 62.18N 27.10E
Pielinen *l.* Finland **28** 63.20N 29.50E
Pierowall Scotland **17** 59.19N 3.00W
Pierre U.S.A. **52** 44.23N 100.20W
Pietermaritzburg R.S.A. **48** 29.36S 30.24E
Pietersburg R.S.A. **48** 23.54S 29.23E
Piet Retief R.S.A. **48** 27.00S 30.49E
Pigailoe *i.* Asia **39** 8.08N 146.40E
Pikes Peak U.S.A. **52** 38.50N 105.03W
Piketberg R.S.A. **48** 32.55S 18.45E
Piła Poland **26** 53.09N 16.44E
Pilcomayo *r.* Argentina/Paraguay **61** 25.15S 57.43W
Pilgrim's Hatch England **7** 51.37N 0.16E
Pilgrims Rest R.S.A. **48** 24.55S 30.44E
Pillar Pt. Hong Kong **33** 22.22N 113.56E
Pílos Greece **25** 36.55N 21.40E
Pinarbaşi Turkey **34** 38.43N 36.23E
Pinar del Rio Cuba **58** 22.24N 83.42W
Pinar del Rio *d.* Cuba **58** 22.30N 83.30W
Pindus Mts. Albania/Greece **25** 39.40N 21.00E
Pine Bluff U.S.A. **53** 34.13N 92.00W
Pines, I. of Cuba **58** 21.40N 82.40W
Ping *r.* Thailand **37** 15.45N 100.10E
Pingliang China **40** 35.25N 107.14E
Pini *i.* Indonesia **38** 0.10N 98.30E
Pinios *r.* Greece **25** 37.51N 22.37E
Pinner England **7** 51.36N 0.23W
Pinsk U.S.S.R. **29** 52.08N 26.01E
Pinto Argentina **61** 29.09S 62.38W
Piombino Italy **24** 42.56N 10.30E
Piqua U.S.A. **56** 40.08N 84.14W
Piquiri *r.* Brazil **61** 24.00S 54.00W
Piracicaba Brazil **63** 22.20S 47.40W
Piraeus Greece **25** 37.56N 23.38E
Pirapora Brazil **61** 17.20S 44.54W
Pirbright England **7** 51.18N 0.39W
Pírgos Greece **25** 37.42N 21.27E
Pirna E. Germany **26** 50.58N 13.58E
Pirot Yugo. **25** 43.10N 22.32E
Pisa Italy **24** 43.43N 10.24E
Pisciotta Italy **24** 40.08N 15.12E
Pisuerga *r.* Spain **23** 41.35N 5.40W
Pitea Sweden **28** 65.19N 21.30E
Piteşti Romania **25** 44.52N 24.51E
Pitlochry Scotland **17** 56.43N 3.45W
Pittenweem Scotland **15** 56.13N 2.44W
Pittsburgh U.S.A. **56** 40.26N 80.00W
Plains of Ellertrin *f.* Rep. of Ire. **18** 53.37N 9.11W
Plains of Mayo *f.* Rep. of Ire. **18** 53.46N 9.05W
Plasencia Spain **23** 40.02N 6.05W
Platani *r.* Italy **24** 37.24N 13.15E
Plate, R. *see* la Plata, Rio de Argentina **61**
Platí, C. Greece **25** 40.26N 23.59E
Platinum U.S.A. **54** 59.00N 161.50W
Platte *r.* U.S.A. **53** 41.05N 96.50W
Plattsburgh U.S.A. **57** 44.42N 73.29W
Plauen E. Germany **26** 50.29N 12.08E
Plenty, B. of New Zealand **50** 37.40S 176.50E
Pleven Bulgaria **25** 43.25N 24.39E
Pljevlja Yugo. **25** 43.22N 19.22E
Ploeşti Romania **25** 44.57N 26.02E
Plomb du Cantal *mtn.* France **22** 45.04N 2.45E
Plombières France **26** 47.58N 6.28E
Ploudalmézeau France **22** 48.33N 4.39W
Plovdiv Bulgaria **25** 42.09N 24.45E
Plumtree Rhodesia **48** 20.30S 27.50E
Plym *r.* England **11** 50.21N 4.06W
Plymouth England **11** 50.23N 4.09W
Plymouth Ind. U.S.A. **56** 41.20N 86.19W
Plymouth Mass. U.S.A. **57** 41.58N 70.40W
Plympton England **11** 50.24N 4.02W
Plzeň Czech. **26** 49.45N 13.22E
Po *r.* Italy **24** 44.51N 12.30E
Pobeda, Mt. U.S.S.R. **31** 65.20N 145.50E
Pobedy *mtn.* China **40** 42.09N 80.12E
Pobla de Segur Spain **23** 42.15N 0.58E
Pocatello U.S.A. **52** 42.53N 112.26W
Pocklington England **13** 53.56N 0.48W
Podolsk U.S.S.R. **29** 55.23N 37.32E
Pods Brook *r.* England **7** 51.52N 0.33E
Pofadder R.S.A. **48** 29.09S 19.25E
Poh Indonesia **39** 1.00S 122.50E
Pohang S. Korea **42** 36.10N 129.26E
Pohsien China **41** 33.40N 115.50E
Pointe-à-Pitre Guadeloupe **59** 16.14N 61.32W
Pointe Noire *town* Congo **46** 4.46S 11.53E
Poitiers France **22** 46.35N 0.20E
Pok Fu Lam Hong Kong **33** 22.15N 114.08E
Pokhara Nepal **37** 28.14N 83.58E
Poko Zaïre **47** 3.08N 26.51E
Pokotu China **41** 48.45N 121.58E
Poland Europe **29** 52.30N 19.00E
Polatli Turkey **34** 39.34N 32.08E
Polden Hills England **8** 51.07N 2.50W
Polegate England **9** 50.49N 0.15E
Policastro, G. of Med. Sea **24** 40.00N 15.35E
Poligny France **22** 46.50N 4.42E
Pollina *mtn.* Italy **24** 39.53N 16.11E
Pollnalaght *mtn.* N. Ireland **18** 54.34N 7.27W
Polperro England **11** 50.19N 4.31W
Poltava U.S.S.R. **29** 49.35N 34.35E
Pombal Portugal **23** 39.55N 8.38W
Ponce Puerto Rico **59** 18.00N 66.40W
Pondicherry India **37** 11.59N 79.50E
Pond Inlet *str.* Canada **55** 72.30N 75.00W
Ponferrada Spain **23** 42.32N 6.31W
Pongola *r.* Moçambique **48** 26.13S 32.38E
Ponta Grossa Brazil **61** 25.00S 50.09W
Pont-à-Mousson France **26** 48.55N 6.03E
Ponta Pora Brazil **61** 22.27S 55.39W
Pontardawe Wales **11** 51.44N 3.51W
Pontardulais Wales **11** 51.42N 4.03W
Pontchartrain, L. U.S.A. **58** 30.50N 90.00W
Pontefract England **13** 53.42N 1.19W
Ponteland England **15** 55.03N 1.43W
Ponterwyd Wales **10** 52.25N 3.50W
Pontevedra Spain **23** 42.25N 8.39W
Pontiac U.S.A. **56** 42.39N 83.18W
Pontianak Indonesia **38** 0.05S 109.16E
Pontine Is. Italy **24** 40.56N 12.58E
Pontine Mts. Turkey **34** 40.32N 38.00E
Pontoise France **22** 49.03N 2.05E
Pontrilas England **8** 51.56N 2.53W
Pontypool Wales **11** 51.42N 3.01W
Pontypridd Wales **8** 51.36N 3.21W
Poole England **8** 50.42N 2.02W
Poole B. England **8** 50.40N 1.55W
Poolewe Scotland **16** 57.45N 5.37W
Pooley Bridge *town* England **12** 54.37N 2.49W
Poona India **36** 18.34N 73.58E
Poopó, L. Bolivia **63** 19.00S 67.00W
Poperinge Belgium **27** 50.51N 2.44E
Poplar England **7** 51.31N 0.01E
Poplar Bluff U.S.A. **53** 36.40N 90.25W
Popocatépetl *mtn.* Mexico **58** 19.02N 98.38W
Popokabaka Zaïre **46** 5.41S 16.40E
Porbandar India **36** 21.40N 69.40E
Porcupine *r.* U.S.A. **54** 66.25N 145.20W
Pori Finland **28** 61.28N 21.45E
Porkkala Finland **28** 60.00N 24.25E
Porlamar Venezuela **59** 11.01N 63.54W
Porlock England **11** 51.14N 3.36W
Pornic France **22** 47.07N 2.05W
Pornivir Colombia **62** 4.45N 71.24W
Poronaysk U.S.S.R. **31** 49.13N 142.55E
Porsanger *est.* Norway **28** 70.30N 25.45E
Porsgrunn Norway **28** 59.10N 9.40E
Porsuk *r.* Turkey **34** 39.41N 31.56E
Portadown N. Ireland **18** 54.25N 6.27W
Portaferry N. Ireland **18** 54.23N 5.33W
Portage U.S.A. **56** 43.33N 89.29W
Portage la Prairie *town* Canada **52** 50.01N 98.20W
Portalegre Portugal **23** 39.17N 7.25W
Port Alfred R.S.A. **48** 33.36S 26.54E
Port Angeles U.S.A. **52** 48.06N 123.26W
Port Antonio Jamaica **59** 18.10N 76.27W
Portarlington Rep. of Ire. **19** 53.10N 7.12W
Port Arthur U.S.A. **53** 29.55N 93.56W
Port Askaig Scotland **14** 55.51N 6.07W
Port Augusta Australia **49** 32.30S 137.46E
Port-au-Prince Haiti **59** 18.33N 72.20W
Port Austin U.S.A. **56** 44.04N 82.59W
Port aux Basques Canada **55** 47.35N 59.10W
Port Bannatyne Scotland **14** 55.52N 5.04W
Port Blair India **37** 11.40N 92.30E
Port Bou Spain **23** 42.25N 3.09E
Port Burwell Canada **56** 42.39N 80.47W
Port Cartier Canada **55** 50.03N 66.46W
Port Charlotte Scotland **14** 55.45N 6.23W
Port Dinorwic Wales **10** 53.11N 4.12W
Port Elizabeth R.S.A. **48** 33.58S 25.36E
Port Ellen Scotland **14** 55.38N 6.12W
Port Erin I.o.M. **12** 54.05N 4.45W
Port-Eynon Wales **11** 51.33N 4.13W
Port Gentil Gabon **46** 0.40S 8.46E
Port Glasgow Scotland **14** 55.56N 4.40W
Portglenone N. Ireland **14** 54.52N 6.30W
Port Harcourt Nigeria **44** 4.43N 7.05E
Port Harrison Canada **55** 58.25N 78.18W
Porthcawl Wales **11** 51.28N 3.42W
Port Hedland Australia **49** 20.24S 118.36E
Port Huron U.S.A. **56** 42.59N 82.28W
Portimão Portugal **23** 37.08N 8.32W
Port Isaac B. England **11** 50.36N 4.50W
Portishead England **8** 51.29N 2.46W
Portiţei Mouth *f.* Romania **25** 44.40N 29.00E
Port Kelang Malaysia **38** 2.57N 101.24E
Portknockie Scotland **17** 57.42N 2.52W
Portland Ind. U.S.A. **56** 40.25N 84.58W
Portland Maine U.S.A. **57** 43.41N 70.18W
Portland Oreg. U.S.A. **52** 45.32N 122.40W
Portland, I. of England **11** 50.32N 2.25W
Port Laoise Rep. of Ire. **19** 53.03N 7.20W
Port Logan Scotland **14** 54.43N 4.57W
Portmadoc Wales **10** 52.55N 4.08W
Portmahomack Scotland **17** 57.49N 3.50W
Portmarnock Rep. of Ire. **18** 53.25N 6.09W
Port Moresby P.N.G. **39** 9.30S 147.07E
Portnacroish Scotland **16** 56.25N 5.22W
Portnaguiran Scotland **16** 58.15N 6.10W
Portnahaven Scotland **14** 55.41N 6.31W
Port Nelson Canada **55** 57.10N 92.35W
Port Nolloth R.S.A. **48** 29.17S 16.51E
Port-Nouveau Québec Canada **55** 58.35N 65.59W
Pôrto *see* Oporto Portugal **23**
Pôrto Alegre Brazil **61** 30.03S 51.10W
Porto Alexandre Angola **46** 15.55S 11.51E
Porto Alexandre Nat. Park Angola **46** 16.40S 12.00E
Porto Amboim Angola **46** 10.45S 13.43E
Porto Amelia Moçambique **47** 13.02S 40.30E
Port of Ness Scotland **16** 58.30N 6.13W
Port of Spain Trinidad **59** 10.38N 61.31W
Pörtom Finland **28** 62.44N 21.35E
Porton England **8** 51.08N 1.44W
Porto-Novo Dahomey **44** 6.30N 2.47E
Porto Torres Italy **24** 40.49N 8.24E
Porto Vecchio France **22** 41.35N 9.16E
Pôrto Velho Brazil **62** 8.45S 63.54W
Portpatrick Scotland **14** 54.51N 5.07W
Portreath England **11** 50.15N 5.17W
Portree Scotland **16** 57.24N 6.12W
Portrush N. Ireland **14** 55.12N 6.40W
Port Safâga Egypt **34** 26.45N 33.55E
Port Said Egypt **34** 31.17N 32.18E
Port St. Johns R.S.A. **48** 31.37S 29.32E
Port St. Louis France **22** 43.25N 4.40E
Port Shelter *b.* Hong Kong **33** 22.20N 114.17E
Port Shepstone R.S.A. **48** 30.44S 30.28E
Portskerra Scotland **17** 58.33N 3.55W
Portsmouth England **8** 50.48N 1.06W
Portsmouth N.H. U.S.A. **57** 43.03N 70.47W
Portsmouth Ohio U.S.A. **56** 38.45N 82.59W
Portsoy Scotland **17** 57.41N 2.41W
Portstewart N. Ireland **14** 55.11N 6.43W
Port Sudan Sudan **45** 19.39N 37.01E
Port Talbot Wales **11** 51.35N 3.48W
Portugal Europe **23** 39.30N 8.05W
Portugalia Angola **46** 7.25S 20.43E
Portuguese Timor Austa. **39** 9.00S 126.00E
Portumna Rep. of Ire. **19** 53.06N 8.14W
Port Vendres France **22** 42.31N 3.06E
Port Victoria Kenya **47** 0.07N 34.00E
Port William Scotland **14** 54.46N 4.35W
Porz W. Germany **27** 50.53N 7.05E
Posadas Argentina **61** 27.25S 55.48W
Poso Indonesia **39** 1.23S 120.45E
Postmasburg R.S.A. **48** 28.20S 23.05E
Potchefstroom R.S.A. **48** 26.42S 27.06E
Potenza Italy **24** 40.40N 15.47E
Potgietersrus R.S.A. **48** 24.15S 28.55E
Poti U.S.S.R. **29** 42.11N 41.41E
Po Toi O Hong Kong **33** 22.16N 114.17E
Potomac *r.* U.S.A. **57** 38.35N 77.00W
Potosí Bolivia **61** 19.34S 65.45W
Potosí *d.* Bolivia **61** 21.50S 66.00W
Potsdam E. Germany **26** 52.24N 13.04E
Potters Bar England **7** 51.42N 0.11W
Potter Street England **7** 51.46N 0.08E
Pottinger Peak Hong Kong **33** 22.15N 114.14E
Poughkeepsie U.S.A. **57** 41.43N 73.56W
Póvoa de Varzim Portugal **23** 41.22N 8.46W
Povorino U.S.S.R. **29** 51.12N 42.15E
Powder *r.* U.S.A. **52** 46.40N 105.15W
Powell, L. U.S.A. **52** 37.30N 110.45W
Powys *d.* Wales **10** 52.26N 3.26W
Poyang Hu *l.* China **41** 29.05N 116.20E
Poyntzpass N. Ireland **18** 54.16N 6.23W
Požarevac Yugo. **25** 44.38N 21.12E
Poza Rica Mexico **58** 20.34N 97.26W
Poznań Poland **26** 52.25N 16.53E
Pozoblanco Spain **23** 38.23N 4.51W
Prachuap Khiri Khan Thailand **37** 11.50N 99.49E
Prades France **22** 42.38N 2.25E
Prague Czech. **26** 50.05N 14.25E
Praha *see* Prague Czech. **26**
Prato Italy **24** 43.52N 10.50E
Pratt's Bottom England **7** 51.21N 0.06E
Prawle Pt. England **11** 50.12N 3.43W
Preesall England **12** 53.55N 2.58W
Preparis *i.* Burma **38** 14.40N 93.40E
Prescot England **12** 53.27N 2.49W
Prescott U.S.A. **52** 34.34N 112.28W
Presidente Epitácio Brazil **61** 21.56S 52.07W
Presidente Prudente Brazil **61** 22.09S 51.24W

Prespa, L. Albania/Greece/Yugo. **25** 40.53N 21.02E
Presque Isle *town* U.S.A. **57** 46.42N 68.01W
Prestatyn Wales **10** 53.20N 3.24W
Presteigne Wales **10** 52.17N 3.00W
Preston England **12** 53.46N 2.42W
Prestonpans Scotland **15** 55.57N 3.00W
Prestwick Scotland **14** 55.30N 4.36W
Prestwood England **7** 51.42N 0.43W
Pretoria R.S.A. **48** 25.45S 28.12E
Préveza Greece **25** 38.58N 20.43E
Prieska R.S.A. **48** 29.40S 22.45E
Prikumsk U.S.S.R. **29** 44.46N 44.10E
Prilep Yugo. **25** 41.20N 21.32E
Priluki U.S.S.R. **29** 50.35N 32.24E
Primorsk U.S.S.R. **28** 60.18N 28.35E
Prince Albert Canada **54** 53.13N 105.45W
Prince Albert R.S.A. **48** 33.15S 22.03E
Prince Alfred C. Canada **54** 74.30N 125.00W
Prince Charles I. Canada **55** 67.50N 76.00W
Prince Edward I. Canada **53** 46.15N 64.00W
Prince Edward Is. Indian Oc. **3** 47.00S 37.00E
Prince Edward Island *d.* Canada **55** 46.15N 63.10W
Prince George Canada **54** 53.55N 122.49W
Prince of Wales, C. U.S.A. **54** 66.00N 168.30W
Prince of Wales I. Australia **39** 10.55S 142.05E
Prince of Wales I. Canada **55** 73.00N 99.00W
Prince of Wales I. U.S.A. **54** 55.00N 132.30W
Prince Patrick I. Canada **54** 77.00N 120.00W
Prince Rupert Canada **54** 54.09N 130.20W
Princes Risborough England **8** 51.43N 0.50W
Princeton U.S.A. **56** 38.21N 87.33W
Princetown England **11** 50.33N 4.00W
Principe *i.* Africa **46** 1.37N 7.27E
Prinzapolca Nicaragua **58** 13.19N 83.35W
Pripet *r.* U.S.S.R. **29** 51.08N 30.30E
Pripet Marshes *f.* U.S.S.R. **29** 52.15N 28.00E
Priština Yugo. **25** 42.39N 21.10E
Prizren Yugo. **25** 42.13N 20.42E
Progreso Mexico **58** 21.20N 89.40W
Prokopyevsk U.S.S.R. **30** 53.55N 86.45E
Prome Burma **37** 18.50N 95.14E
Providence U.S.A. **57** 41.50N 71.25W
Provideniya U.S.S.R. **54** 64.30N 173.11W
Provins France **22** 48.34N 3.18E
Provo U.S.A. **52** 40.15N 111.40W
Prudhoe England **15** 54.58N 1.51W
Prüm W. Germany **27** 50.12N 6.25E
Prüm *r.* W. Germany **27** 49.50N 6.29E
Prut *r.* Romania/U.S.S.R. **25** 45.29N 28.14E
Przemyśl Poland **29** 49.48N 22.48E
Przhevalsk U.S.S.R. **40** 42.31N 78.22E
Psará *i.* Greece **25** 38.34N 25.35E
Psel *r.* U.S.S.R. **29** 49.03N 33.26E
Pskov U.S.S.R. **28** 57.48N 28.00E
Pskov, L. U.S.S.R. **29** 58.00N 28.00E
Puddletown England **8** 50.45N 2.21W
Pudsey England **12** 53.47N 1.40W
Puebla Mexico **58** 19.03N 98.10W
Puebla *d.* Mexico **58** 18.30N 98.00W
Pueblo U.S.A. **52** 38.17N 104.38W
Puente Genil Spain **23** 37.24N 4.46W
Puerto Armuelles Panamá **58** 8.19N 82.15W
Puerto Barrios Guatemala **58** 15.41N 88.32W
Puerto Cabello Venezuela **59** 10.29N 68.02W
Puerto Cabezas Nicaragua **58** 14.02N 83.24W
Puerto Carreño Colombia **59** 6.00N 67.35W
Puerto Cortes Honduras **58** 15.50N 87.55W
Puerto de Santa Maria Spain **23** 36.36N 6.14W
Puerto Ibicuy Argentina **61** 33.44S 59.10W
Puerto Juárez Mexico **58** 21.26N 86.51W
Puerto la Cruz Venezuela **59** 10.14N 64.40W
Puertollano Spain **23** 38.41N 4.07W
Puerto Montt Chile **63** 41.28S 73.00W
Puerto Natales Chile **63** 51.41S 72.15W
Puerto Penasco Mexico **52** 31.20N 113.35W
Puerto Pinasco Paraguay **61** 22.36S 57.53W
Puerto Plata Dom. Rep. **59** 19.48N 70.41W
Puerto Princesa Phil. **38** 9.46N 118.45E
Puerto Quepos Costa Rica **58** 9.28N 84.10W
Puerto Rico C. America **59** 18.20N 66.30W
Puerto Rico Trench Atlantic Oc. **59** 19.50N 66.00W
Puerto Sastre Paraguay **61** 22.02S 58.00W
Puerto Suárez Bolivia **61** 18.59S 57.46W
Puffin I. Rep. of Ire. **19** 51.50N 10.25W
Puffin I. Wales **10** 53.18N 4.04W
Pukaki, L. New Zealand **50** 44.00S 170.10E
Pukekohe New Zealand **50** 37.12S 174.56E
Pula Yugo. **24** 44.52N 13.53E
Pulaski U.S.A. **57** 43.34N 76.06W
Pulborough England **9** 50.58N 0.30W
Pulog, Mt. Phil. **39** 16.50N 120.50E
Pułtusk Poland **29** 52.42N 21.02E
Pulvar *r.* Iran **35** 29.50N 52.47E
Pumlumon Fawr *mtn.* Wales **10** 52.28N 3.47W
Pumpsaint Wales **10** 52.03N 3.58W
Punjab *d.* India **36** 30.30N 75.15E
Puno Peru **62** 15.53S 70.03W
Punta Alta *town* Argentina **61** 38.50S 62.00W
Punta Arenas *town* Chile **63** 53.10S 70.56W
Punta Gorda *town* Belize **58** 16.10N 88.45W
Puntarenas Costa Rica **58** 10.00N 84.50W
Pur *r.* U.S.S.R. **30** 67.30N 75.30E
Purfleet England **7** 51.29N 0.15E
Puri India **37** 19.49N 85.54E
Purley England **7** 51.21N 0.07W
Pursat Cambodia **37** 12.33N 105.55E
Purulia India **37** 23.20N 86.24E
Purus *r.* Brazil **62** 3.15S 61.30W
Puru Vesi *l.* Finland **28** 62.00N 29.50E
Pusan S. Korea **41** 35.05N 129.02E
Pushkin U.S.S.R. **29** 59.43N 30.22E
Pustoshka U.S.S.R. **29** 56.20N 29.20E
Putao Burma **37** 27.22N 97.27E
Putien China **41** 25.32N 119.02E
Putjak Djaja *mtn.* Indonesia **39** 4.00S 137.15E
Putney England **7** 51.28N 0.14W
Putoran Mts. U.S.S.R. **31** 68.30N 96.00E
Puttalam Sri Lanka **37** 8.02N 79.50E
Putumayo *r.* Brazil **62** 3.00S 67.30W
Puula Vesi *l.* Finland **28** 63.45N 25.25E
Puy de Dôme *mtn.* France **22** 45.46N 2.56E
Puysegur Pt. New Zealand **50** 46.10S 166.35E
Pweto Zaïre **47** 8.27S 28.52E
Pwllheli Wales **10** 52.53N 4.25W
Pya, L. U.S.S.R. **28** 66.00N 31.00E
Pyasina *r.* U.S.S.R. **31** 73.10N 84.55E
Pyatigorsk U.S.S.R. **29** 44.04N 43.06E
Pyha *r.* Finland **28** 64.30N 24.20E
Pyhä-järvi *l.* Finland **28** 61.00N 22.10E
Pyhajoki Finland **28** 64.28N 24.15E
Pyinmana Burma **37** 19.45N 96.12E
Pyongyang N. Korea **41** 39.00N 125.47E
Pyramid L. U.S.A. **52** 40.00N 119.35W
Pyrénées *mts.* France/Spain **22** 42.40N 0.30E
Pytalovo U.S.S.R. **28** 57.30N 27.57E

Q

Qara Egypt **34** 29.38N 26.30E
Qasr Farafra Egypt **34** 27.05N 28.00E
Qasrqand Iran **35** 26.13N 60.37E
Qatar Asia **35** 25.20N 51.10E
Qatif Saudi Arabia **35** 26.31N 5.00E
Qattara Depression *f.* Egypt **34** 29.40N 27.30E
Qayen Iran **35** 33.44N 59.07E
Qazvin Iran **35** 36.16N 50.00E
Qena Egypt **34** 26.08N 32.42E
Qena, Wadi *r.* Egypt **34** 26.07N 32.42E
Qishm Iran **35** 26.58N 57.17E
Qishm *i.* Iran **35** 26.48N 55.48E
Qishn S. Yemen **36** 15.25N 51.40E
Qizil Uzun *r.* Iran **35** 36.44N 49.27E
Qom Iran **35** 34.40N 50.57E
Quang Ngai S. Vietnam **38** 15.09N 108.50E
Quang Tri S. Vietnam **38** 16.46N 107.11E
Quantock Hills England **8** 51.06N 3.12W
Qu'Appelle *r.* Canada **52** 49.40N 99.40W
Quchan Iran **35** 37.04N 58.29E
Quebec Canada **57** 46.50N 71.15W
Quebec *d.* Canada **55** 51.00N 70.00W
Quebrabasa Gorge *f.* Moçambique **47** 15.34S 33.00E
Queenborough England **9** 51.24N 0.46E
Queen Charlotte Is. Canada **54** 53.00N 132.30W
Queen Charlotte Str. Canada **54** 51.00N 129.00W
Queen Elizabeth Is. Canada **55** 78.30N 99.00W
Queen Maud G. Canada **55** 68.30N 99.00W
Queen Maud Land Antarctica **64** 74.00S 10.00E
Queensberry *mtn.* Scotland **15** 55.16N 3.36W
Queensferry Scotland **15** 56.01N 3.24W
Queensland *d.* Australia **49** 23.30S 144.00E
Queenstown New Zealand **50** 45.03S 168.41E
Queenstown R.S.A. **48** 31.54S 26.53E
Quela Angola **46** 9.18S 17.05E
Quelimane Moçambique **47** 17.53S 36.57E
Quelpart *i.* S. Korea **41** 33.20N 126.30E
Que Que Rhodesia **48** 18.55S 29.51E
Querétaro Mexico **58** 20.38N 100.23W
Querétaro *d.* Mexico **58** 21.03N 100.00W
Quesnel Canada **54** 53.03N 122.31W
Quetta Pakistan **36** 30.15N 67.00E
Quezaltenango Guatemala **58** 14.50N 91.30W
Quezon City Phil. **39** 14.59N 121.01E
Qufa *des.* U.A.E. **35** 23.30N 53.30E
Quibala Angola **46** 10.48S 14.56E
Quibaxi Angola **46** 8.34S 14.37E
Quiberon France **22** 47.29N 3.07W
Quicama Nat. Park Angola **46** 9.40S 13.30E
Quilengues Angola **46** 14.09S 14.04E
Quill Lakes Canada **52** 51.50N 104.10W
Quimbele Angola **46** 6.29S 16.25E
Quimilí Argentina **61** 27.35S 62.25W
Quimper France **22** 48.00N 4.06W
Quimperlé France **22** 47.52N 3.33W
Quincy Ill. U.S.A. **56** 39.55N 91.22W
Quincy Mass. U.S.A. **57** 42.14N 71.00W
Quintana Roo *d.* Mexico **58** 19.00N 88.00W
Quinto Spain **23** 41.25N 0.30W
Quirigua *ruins* Guatemala **58** 15.20N 89.25W
Quissanga Moçambique **47** 12.24S 40.33E
Quissico Moçambique **48** 24.42S 34.44E
Quito Ecuador **62** 0.14S 78.30W
Quoich, Loch Scotland **16** 57.04N 5.15W
Quoyness Scotland **17** 58.54N 3.17W
Quseir Egypt **34** 26.04N 34.15E
Qutur Iran **35** 38.28N 44.25E

R

Raalte Neth. **27** 52.22N 6.17E
Raasay *i.* Scotland **16** 57.25N 6.05W
Raasay, Sd. of Scotland **16** 57.25N 6.05W
Raba Indonesia **38** 8.27S 118.45E
Rabat Morocco **44** 34.02N 6.51W
Racine U.S.A. **56** 42.42N 87.50W
Radcliffe England **12** 53.35N 2.19W
Radhwa, Jebel *mtn.* Saudi Arabia **34** 24.36N 38.18E
Radlett England **7** 51.42N 0.20W
Radom Poland **29** 51.26N 21.10E
Radomir Bulgaria **25** 42.32N 22.56E
Radstock England **8** 51.17N 2.25W
Rafaela Argentina **61** 31.16S 61.44W
Rafai C.A.R. **46** 4.56N 23.55E
Rafsanjan Iran **35** 30.24N 56.00E
Raglan Wales **11** 51.46N 2.51W
Ragusa Italy **24** 36.56N 14.44E
Rahbur Iran **35** 29.18N 56.56E
Raichur India **36** 16.15N 77.20E
Raigarh India **37** 21.53N 83.28E
Rainford England **12** 53.30N 2.48W
Rainham G.L. England **7** 51.31N 0.12E
Rainham Kent England **7** 51.23N 0.36E
Rainier, Mt. U.S.A. **52** 46.52N 121.45W
Rainy L. Canada **56** 48.40N 93.15W
Raipur India **37** 21.16N 81.42E
Raja *mtn.* Indonesia **38** 0.45S 112.45E
Rajahmundry India **37** 17.01N 81.52E
Rajang *r.* Malaysia **38** 2.10N 112.45E
Rajapalaiyam India **36** 9.26N 77.36E
Rajasthan *d.* India **36** 27.00N 74.00E
Rajkot India **36** 22.18N 70.53E
Rakaia *r.* New Zealand **50** 43.52S 172.13E
Rakvere U.S.S.R. **28** 59.22N 26.28E
Raleigh U.S.A. **53** 35.46N 78.39W
Rama Nicaragua **58** 12.09N 84.15W
Ramah Saudi Arabia **35** 25.33N 47.08E
Rambler Channel Hong Kong **33** 22.21N 114.06E
Rame Head England **11** 50.18N 4.13W
Ramelton Rep. of Ire. **18** 55.02N 7.40W
Ramhormoz Iran **35** 31.14N 49.37E
Ramillies Belgium **27** 50.39N 4.56E
Ramishk Iran **35** 26.52N 58.46E
Râmnicu Sarat Romania **25** 45.24N 27.06E
Ramor, Lough Rep. of Ire. **18** 53.49N 7.05W
Rampur India **37** 28.48N 79.03E
Ramree I. Burma **37** 19.10N 93.40E
Ramsar Iran **35** 36.54N 50.41E
Ramsbottom England **12** 53.38N 2.20W
Ramsey England **9** 52.27N 0.06W
Ramsey I.o.M. **12** 54.19N 4.23W
Ramsey *i.* Wales **10** 51.53N 5.21W
Ramsey B. I.o.M. **12** 54.20N 4.20W
Ramsgate England **9** 51.20N 1.25E
Ranchi India **37** 23.22N 85.20E
Randalstown N. Ireland **14** 54.45N 6.20W
Randers Denmark **28** 56.28N 10.03E
Ranfurly New Zealand **50** 45.08S 170.08E
Rangiora New Zealand **50** 43.18S 172.38E
Rangitaiki *r.* New Zealand **50** 37.55S 176.50E
Rangoon Burma **37** 16.45N 96.20E
Rannoch, Loch Scotland **17** 56.41N 4.20W
Rannoch Moor *f.* Scotland **17** 56.38N 4.40W
Rann of Kutch *f.* India **36** 23.50N 69.50E
Ranobe *r.* Malagasy Rep. **47** 17.20S 44.05E
Rantauparapat Indonesia **38** 2.05N 99.46E
Rantekombola *mtn.* Indonesia **38** 3.30S 119.58E
Rapallo Italy **22** 44.20N 9.14E
Rapid City U.S.A. **52** 44.06N 103.14W
Raqqa Syria **34** 35.57N 39.03E
Ras al Hadd *c.* Oman **35** 22.32N 59.49E
Ras Banas *c.* Egypt **34** 23.54N 35.48E
Ras Dashan *mtn.* Ethiopia **45** 13.20N 38.10E
Rasht Iran **35** 37.18N 49.38E
Ras Madraka *c.* Oman **36** 19.00N 57.55E
Ras Muhammad *c.* Egypt **34** 27.42N 34.13E
Rass Saudi Arabia **34** 25.54N 43.30E
Ras Tanura *c.* Saudi Arabia **35** 26.40N 50.10E
Rathangan Rep. of Ire. **19** 53.13N 7.00W
Rathcoole Rep. of Ire. **18** 53.17N 6.30W
Rathcormack Rep. of Ire. **19** 52.05N 8.18W
Rathdowney Rep. of Ire. **19** 52.51N 7.36W
Rathdrum Rep. of Ire. **19** 52.56N 6.15W
Rathfriland N. Ireland **18** 54.14N 6.10W
Rathkeale Rep. of Ire. **19** 52.30N 8.57W
Rathlin I. N. Ireland **14** 55.17N 6.15W
Rathlin Sd. N. Ireland **14** 55.15N 6.15W
Rath Luirc Rep. of Ire. **19** 52.21N 8.41W
Rathmore Rep. of Ire. **19** 52.05N 9.12W
Rathmullen Rep. of Ire. **18** 55.06N 7.32W
Rathnew Rep. of Ire. **19** 53.01N 6.07W
Rathvilly Rep. of Ire. **19** 52.52N 6.43W
Ratlam India **36** 23.18N 75.06E
Raton U.S.A. **52** 36.54N 104.27W
Rattray Head Scotland **17** 57.37N 1.50W
Rättvik Sweden **28** 60.56N 15.10E
Rauch Argentina **61** 36.45S 59.05W
Raukumara Range *mts.* New Zealand **50** 38.00S 177.45E
Rauma Finland **28** 61.09N 21.30E
Raunds England **9** 52.21N 0.33W
Ravar Iran **35** 31.14N 56.51E
Ravenna Italy **24** 44.25N 12.12E
Ravi *r.* Pakistan **36** 30.30N 72.13E
Rawalpindi Pakistan **36** 33.40N 73.08E
Rawlinna Australia **49** 31.00S 125.21E
Rawlins U.S.A. **52** 41.46N 107.16W
Rawmarsh England **13** 53.27N 1.20W
Rawtenstall England **12** 53.42N 2.18W
Rayen Iran **35** 29.34N 57.26E
Rayleigh England **7** 51.36N 0.36E
Razan Iran **35** 35.22N 49.02E
Razgrad Bulgaria **25** 43.32N 26.30E
Ré, Ile de *i.* France **22** 46.10N 1.26W
Reading England **8** 51.27N 0.57W
Reading U.S.A. **57** 40.20N 75.55W
Reay Forest *f.* Scotland **17** 58.17N 4.48W
Rebun jima *i.* Japan **42** 45.25N 141.04E
Recife Brazil **62** 8.06S 34.53W
Recklinghausen W. Germany **27** 51.36N 7.11E
Reconquista Argentina **61** 29.08S 59.38W
Recreo Argentina **61** 29.18S 65.05W
Red *r.* Canada **53** 50.30N 96.50W
Red *r.* N. Vietnam **40** 20.15N 106.25E
Red *r.* U.S.A. **53** 31.10N 92.00W
Red B. N. Ireland **14** 55.04N 6.02W
Red Bluff U.S.A. **52** 40.11N 122.16W
Redbourn England **7** 51.48N 0.24W
Redbridge England **7** 51.35N 0.06E
Redcar England **13** 54.37N 1.04W
Red Deer Canada **54** 52.15N 113.48W
Red Deer *r.* Canada **52** 50.55N 110.00W
Redding U.S.A. **52** 40.35N 122.24W
Redditch England **8** 52.18N 1.57W
Rede *r.* England **15** 55.08N 2.13W
Redhill England **7** 51.14N 0.11W
Red L. U.S.A. **53** 48.00N 95.00W
Red Lake *town* Canada **53** 50.59N 93.40W
Redpoint Scotland **16** 57.39N 5.49W
Redruth England **11** 50.14N 5.14W
Red Sea Africa/Asia **45** 20.00N 39.00E
Red Tower Pass Romania **25** 45.37N 24.17E
Red Wharf B. Wales **10** 53.20N 4.10W
Ree, Lough Rep. of Ire. **18** 53.31N 7.58W
Reedham England **9** 52.34N 1.33E
Reefton New Zealand **50** 42.05S 171.51E
Regen *r.* W. Germany **26** 49.02N 12.03E
Regensburg W. Germany **26** 49.01N 12.07E
Reggan Algeria **44** 26.30N 0.30E
Reggio Calabria Italy **24** 38.07N 15.38E
Reggio Emilia-Romagnaltaly **24** 44.40N 10.37E
Regina Canada **52** 50.30N 104.38W
Rehoboth S.W. Africa **48** 23.18S 17.03E
Reigate England **7** 51.14N 0.13W
Reims France **22** 49.15N 4.02E
Reindeer L. Canada **54** 57.00N 102.20W
Reinosa Mexico **58** 26.09N 97.10W
Reinosa Spain **23** 43.01N 4.09W
Reiss Scotland **17** 58.28N 3.09W
Rembang Indonesia **38** 6.45S 111.22E
Remich Lux. **27** 49.34N 6.23E
Remscheid W. Germany **27** 51.10N 7.11E
Renaix Belgium **27** 50.45N 3.36E
Renfrew Canada **57** 45.28N 76.44W
Renfrew Scotland **14** 55.52N 4.23W
Rengat Indonesia **38** 0.26S 102.35E
Reni U.S.S.R. **25** 45.28N 28.17E
Renish Pt. Scotland **16** 57.43N 6.58W
Renkum Neth. **27** 51.59N 5.46E
Rennes France **22** 48.06N 1.40W
Reno *r.* Italy **24** 44.36N 12.17E
Reno U.S.A. **52** 39.32N 119.49W
Renvyle Pt. Rep. of Ire. **18** 53.37N 10.04W
Republican *r.* U.S.A. **53** 39.05N 94.50W
Republic of Ireland Europe **19** 53.00N 8.00W
Republic of South Africa Africa **48** 28.30S 24.50E
Repulse B. Hong Kong **33** 22.14N 114.11E
Requena Spain **23** 39.29N 1.08W
Resistencia Argentina **61** 27.28S 59.00W
Resolute Canada **55** 74.40N 95.00W
Resolution I. New Zealand **50** 45.40S 166.30E
Resort, Loch Scotland **16** 58.03N 6.56W
Rethel France **27** 49.31N 4.22E
Réthimnon Greece **25** 35.22N 24.29E
Réunion *i.* Indian Oc. **3** 22.00S 55.00E
Reus Spain **23** 41.10N 1.06E
Reutlingen W. Germany **26** 48.30N 9.13E
Revelstoke Canada **52** 51.00N 118.12W
Revilla Gigedo Is. Mexico **51** 19.00N 111.00W
Revue *r.* Moçambique **48** 19.58S 34.40E
Reykjavik Iceland **28** 64.09N 21.58W
Rezaiyeh Iran **35** 37.32N 45.02E
Rêzekne U.S.S.R. **28** 56.30N 27.22E
Rhayader Wales **10** 52.19N 3.30W
Rheden Neth. **27** 52.01N 6.02E
Rheine W. Germany **27** 52.17N 7.26E
Rhenen Neth. **27** 51.58N 5.34E
Rheydt W. Germany **27** 51.10N 6.25E
Rhine *r.* Europe **27** 51.53N 6.03E
Rhinelander U.S.A. **56** 45.39N 89.23W
Rhinns of Kells *hills* Scotland **14** 55.08N 4.21W
Rhinns Pt. Scotland **14** 55.40N 6.29W
Rhino Camp *town* Uganda **47** 2.58N 31.20E
Rhode Island *d.* U.S.A. **57** 43.30N 71.35W
Rhodes Greece **25** 36.24N 28.15E
Rhodes *i.* Greece **25** 36.12N 28.00E
Rhodesia Africa **48** 18.55S 30.00E
Rhodope Mts. Bulgaria **25** 41.35N 24.35E
Rhondda Wales **11** 51.39N 3.30W
Rhondda Valley *f.* Wales **11** 51.38N 3.29W
Rhône *r.* France **22** 43.25N 4.45E
Rhosllanerchrugog Wales **10** 53.03N 3.04W
Rhosneigr Wales **10** 53.14N 4.31W
Rhum *i.* Scotland **16** 57.00N 6.20W
Rhum, Sd. of *str.* Scotland **16** 56.57N 6.15W
Rhyddhywel *mtn.* Wales **10** 52.25N 3.27W
Rhyl Wales **10** 53.19N 3.29W
Riau Is. Indonesia **38** 0.50N 104.00E
Rib *r.* England **7** 51.48N 0.04W
Ribadeo Spain **23** 43.32N 7.04W
Ribauè Moçambique **47** 14.57S 38.27E
Ribble *r.* England **12** 53.45N 2.44W
Ribblesdale *f.* England **12** 54.03N 2.17W
Ribeirão Prêto Brazil **61** 21.09S 47.48W
Riberac France **22** 45.14N 0.22E
Riccall England **13** 53.50N 1.04W
Richelieu *r.* Canada **57** 46.02N 73.03W
Richland U.S.A. **52** 46.20N 119.17W
Richmond England **12** 54.24N 1.43W
Richmond Cape Province R.S.A. **48** 31.25S 23.57E
Richmond Ind. U.S.A. **56** 39.50N 84.51W
Richmond Va. U.S.A. **53** 37.34N 77.27W
Richmond Park *f.* England **7** 51.26N 0.13W
Richmond-upon-Thames England **7** 51.26N 0.17W
Rickmansworth England **7** 51.39N 0.29W
Ridderkirk Neth. **27** 51.53N 4.39E
Rieti Italy **24** 42.24N 12.53E
Rift Valley *d.* Kenya **47** 1.00N 36.00E
Riga U.S.S.R. **28** 56.53N 24.08E
Riga, G. of U.S.S.R. **28** 57.30N 23.50E
Rigan Iran **35** 28.40N 58.58E
Rigmati Iran **35** 27.40N 58.11E
Riihimaki Finland **28** 60.45N 24.45E

Rijeka Yugo. 24 45.20N 14.25E
Rijswijk Neth. 27 52.03N 4.22E
Rima, Wadi *r.* Saudi Arabia 34 26.10N 44.00E
Rimini Italy 24 44.01N 12.34E
Rimouski Canada 57 48.27N 68.32W
Ringköbing Denmark 28 56.06N 8.15E
Ringvassöy *i.* Norway 28 70.00N 19.00E
Ringwood England 8 50.50N 1.48W
Rinrawros Pt. Rep. of Ire. 18 55.01N 8.34W
Riobamba Ecuador 62 1.44S 78.40W
Rio Branco *town* Brazil 62 10.00S 67.49W
Rio Claro *town* Brazil 61 22.19S 47.35W
Rio de Janeiro *town* Brazil 61 22.53S 43.17W
Rio Gallegos *town* Argentina 63 51.35S 69.15W
Rio Grande *town* Brazil 61 32.03S 52.08W
Rio Grande *r.* Mexico/U.S.A. 58 25.55N 97.08W
Río Grande *r.* Nicaragua 58 12.48N 83.30W
Rio Grande do Sul *d.* Brazil 61 30.15S 53.30W
Riohacha Colombia 59 11.34N 72.58W
Rio Negro *d.* Argentina 61 41.15S 67.15W
Riosucio Colombia 59 7.25N 77.05W
Rio Verde *town* Brazil 61 17.50S 50.55W
Ripley Derbys. England 13 53.03N 1.24W
Ripley Surrey England 7 51.18N 0.29W
Ripon England 13 54.08N 1.31W
Risca Wales 11 51.36N 3.06W
Risha, Wadi *r.* Saudi Arabia 35 25.40N 44.08E
Rishiri jima *i.* Japan 42 45.11N 141.15E
Risor Norway 28 58.44N 9.15E
Ristikent U.S.S.R. 28 68.40N 31.47E
Rivas Nicaragua 58 11.26N 85.50W
Riverhead England 7 51.17N 0.11E
Riversdale R.S.A. 48 34.05S 21.14E
Rivière-du-Loup *town* Canada 57 47.49N 69.32W
Riyadh Saudi Arabia 35 24.39N 46.44E
Rize Turkey 34 41.03N 40.31E
Rizzuto, C. Italy 25 38.53N 17.06E
Rjukan Norway 28 59.54N 8.33E
Roanne France 22 46.02N 4.05E
Roanoke *r.* U.S.A. 53 36.00N 76.35W
Roaringwater B. Rep. of Ire. 19 51.32N 9.26W
Robertson R.S.A. 48 33.48S 19.53E
Roberval Canada 57 48.31N 72.16W
Robin Hood's Bay *town* England 13 54.26N 0.31W
Roboré Bolivia 61 18.20S 59.45W
Robson, Mt. Canada 54 53.00N 121.00W
Roca, Cabo de Portugal 23 38.40N 9.31W
Roccella Italy 25 38.19N 16.24E
Rocha Uruguay 61 34.30S 54.22W
Rochdale England 12 53.36N 2.10W
Rochechouart France 22 45.49N 0.50E
Rochefort Belgium 27 50.10N 5.13E
Rochefort France 22 45.57N 0.58W
Rochester Kent England 7 51.22N 0.30E
Rochester Northum. England 15 55.16N 2.16W
Rochester U.S.A. 57 43.12N 77.37W
Rochfort Bridge Rep. of Ire. 18 53.25N 7.19W
Rock *r.* U.S.A. 56 41.30N 90.35W
Rockford U.S.A. 56 42.16N 89.06W
Rockhampton Australia 49 23.22S 150.32E
Rockingham Forest *f.* England 8 52.30N 0.35W
Rock Island *town* U.S.A. 56 41.30N 90.34W
Rockland U.S.A. 57 44.06N 69.08W
Rock Springs *town* U.S.A. 52 41.35N 109.13W
Rocky Harbour *b.* Hong Kong 33 22.20N 114.20E
Rocky Mts. N. America 54 50.00N 114.00W
Rocroi France 27 49.56N 4.31E
Rodel Scotland 16 57.44N 6.58W
Roden *r.* England 12 52.42N 2.36W
Rodez France 22 44.21N 2.34E
Roding *r.* England 7 51.31N 0.05E
Rodonit, C. Albania 25 41.34N 19.25E
Roe *r.* N. Ireland 14 55.06N 7.00W
Roermond Neth. 27 51.12N 6.00E
Rogan's Seat *mtn.* England 12 54.25N 2.05W
Rogers City U.S.A. 56 45.24N 83.50W
Rokan *r.* Indonesia 38 2.00N 101.00E
Rolla U.S.A. 53 37.56N 91.55W
Roma *i.* Indonesia 39 7.45S 127.20E
Romain, C. U.S.A. 53 33.01N 71.23W
Romaine *r.* Canada 55 50.20N 63.45W
Romania Europe 29 46.30N 24.00E
Romano, C. U.S.A. 53 25.50N 81.42W
Romans France 22 45.03N 5.03E
Rome Italy 24 41.54N 12.29E
Rome U.S.A. 57 43.13N 75.28W
Romford England 7 51.35N 0.11E
Romilly France 22 48.31N 3.44E
Romney Marsh *f.* England 9 51.03N 0.55E
Romorantin France 22 47.22N 1.44E
Romsey England 8 51.00N 1.29W
Rona *i.* Scotland 16 57.33N 5.58W
Ronas Hill Scotland 16 60.32N 1.26W
Ronas Voe *b.* Scotland 16 60.31N 1.29W
Ronay *i.* Scotland 16 57.29N 7.10W
Ronda Spain 23 36.45N 5.10W
Rönne Denmark 28 55.07N 14.43E
Roof Butte *mtn.* U.S.A. 52 36.29N 109.05W
Roosendaal Neth. 27 51.32N 4.28E
Roosevelt *r.* Brazil 62 5.00S 60.30W
Roper *r.* Australia 49 14.40S 135.30E
Roque Sáenz Peña Argentina 61 26.50S 60.28W
Rora Head Scotland 17 58.52N 3.26W
Roraima *mtn.* Venezuela 62 5.45N 61.00W
Röros Norway 28 62.35N 11.23E
Rosa, Monte Italy/Switz. 22 45.56N 7.51E
Rosario Argentina 61 33.00S 60.40W
Rosario Paraguay 61 24.28S 57.13W
Rosario Uruguay 61 34.20S 57.26W
Roscommon Rep. of Ire. 18 53.38N 8.13W
Roscommon *d.* Rep. of Ire. 18 53.38N 8.11W
Roscrea Rep. of Ire. 20 52.57N 7.49W
Roseau Dominica 59 15.18N 61.23W
Roseburg U.S.A. 52 43.13N 123.21W
Rosehearty Scotland 17 57.42N 2.07W
Rosenheim W. Germany 26 47.51N 12.09E
Rosetown Canada 54 51.34N 107.59W
Rosetta Egypt 34 31.25N 30.25E
Rosières France 27 49.49N 2.43E
Roskilde Denmark 28 55.39N 12.07E
Roslags-Näsby Sweden 28 59.01N 18.02E
Roslavl U.S.S.R. 29 53.55N 32.53E
Ross New Zealand 50 42.54S 170.48E
Rossall Pt. England 12 53.55N 3.03W
Ross Dependency Antarctica 64 75.00S 170.00W
Rosses B. Rep. of Ire. 18 55.01N 8.29W
Rosskeeragh Pt. Rep. of Ire. 18 54.21N 8.41W
Rosslare Rep. of Ire. 19 52.17N 6.23W
Rosslea N. Ireland 18 54.15N 7.12W
Ross of Mull *pen.* Scotland 14 56.19N 6.10W
Ross-on-Wye England 8 51.55N 2.36W
Ross Sea Antarctica 3 73.00S 179.00E
Rostock E. Germany 26 54.06N 12.09E
Rostov R.S.F.S.R. U.S.S.R. 29 47.15N 39.45E
Rostov R.S.F.S.R. U.S.S.R. 29 57.11N 39.23E
Rösvatn *l.* Norway 28 65.50N 14.00E
Rosyth Scotland 15 56.03N 3.26W
Rota *i.* Asia 39 14.10N 145.15E
Rothbury England 15 55.19N 1.54W
Rothbury Forest *f.* England 15 55.18N 1.52W
Rother *r.* E. Sussex England 9 50.56N 0.46E
Rother *r.* W. Sussex England 9 50.57N 0.32W
Rotherham England 13 53.26N 1.21W
Rothes Scotland 17 57.31N 3.13W
Rothesay Scotland 14 55.50N 5.03W
Rothwell Northants. England 8 52.25N 0.48W
Rothwell W. Yorks. England 13 53.46N 1.29W
Roti *i.* Indonesia 39 10.30S 123.10E
Rotorua New Zealand 50 38.07S 176.17E
Rotorua, L. New Zealand 50 38.00S 176.00E
Rotterdam Neth. 27 51.55N 4.29E
Roubaix France 27 50.42N 3.10E
Rouen France 22 49.26N 1.05E
Roulers Belgium 27 50.57N 3.06E
Roundup U.S.A. 52 46.27N 108.34W
Rousay *i.* Scotland 17 59.10N 3.02W
Rouyn Canada 57 48.15N 79.00W
Rovaniemi Finland 28 66.29N 25.40E
Rovinj Yugo. 24 45.06N 13.39E
Roxburgh New Zealand 50 45.34S 169.21E
Roxburgh Scotland 15 55.34N 2.23W
Royale, I. U.S.A. 56 48.00N 88.45W
Royal Leamington Spa England 8 52.18N 1.32W
Royal Tunbridge Wells England 9 51.07N 0.16E
Roydon England 7 51.46N 0.03E
Roye France 27 49.42N 2.48E
Royston Herts. England 9 52.03N 0.01W
Royston S. Yorks. England 13 53.37N 1.27W
Rozel Channel Is. 11 49.19N 2.03W
Rtishchevo U.S.S.R. 29 52.16N 43.45E
Ruabon Wales 10 53.00N 3.03W
Ruahine Range *mts.* New Zealand 50 40.00S 176.00E
Ruapehu *mtn.* New Zealand 50 39.20S 175.30E
Ruapuke I. New Zealand 50 46.45S 168.30E
Rub al Khali *des.* Saudi Arabia 36 20.20N 52.30E
Rubha A'Mhàil *c.* Scotland 14 55.57N 6.08W
Rubha Ardvule *c.* Scotland 16 57.15N 7.28W
Rubha Coigeach *c.* Scotland 16 58.06N 5.25W
Rubha Hunish *c.* Scotland 16 57.42N 6.21W
Rubh'an Dunain *c.* Scotland 16 57.09N 6.19W
Rubha Réidh *c.* Scotland 16 57.51N 5.49W
Rubi *r.* Zaïre 46 2.50N 24.06E
Rudan *r.* Iran 35 27.02N 56.53E
Rudbar Afghan. 35 30.10N 62.38E
Rud-i-Pusht *r.* Iran 35 29.09N 58.09E
Rud-i-Shur *r.* Kermān Iran 35 31.14N 55.29E
Rud-i-Shur *r.* Khorāsān Iran 35 34.05N 60.22E
Rudok China 40 33.30N 79.40E
Rudolf, L. Kenya 47 4.00N 36.00E
Ruenya *r.* Moçambique 48 16.29S 33.40E
Ruffec France 22 46.02N 0.12E
Rufford England 12 53.38N 2.50W
Rufiji *r.* Tanzania 47 8.02S 39.19E
Rufino Argentina 61 34.16S 62.45W
Rugby England 8 52.23N 1.16W
Rugby U.S.A. 52 48.24N 99.59W
Rugeley England 12 52.47N 1.56W
Rügen *i.* E. Germany 26 54.30N 13.30E
Ruhr *f.* W. Germany 27 51.22N 7.26E
Ruhr *r.* W. Germany 27 51.27N 6.41E
Ruislip England 7 51.35N 0.25W
Rukwa, L. Tanzania 47 8.00S 32.20E
Ruma Yugo. 25 44.59N 19.51E
Rum Cay *i.* Bahamas 59 23.41N 74.53W
Rumney Wales 11 51.32N 3.07W
Runabay Head N. Ireland 14 55.09N 6.02W
Runcorn England 12 53.20N 2.44W
Rungwa Singida Tanzania 47 6.57S 33.35E
Rungwa *r.* Tanzania 47 7.38S 31.55E
Rungwe Mt. Tanzania 47 9.10S 33.40E
Rupert *r.* Canada 53 51.25N 78.45W
Rur *r.* Neth. 27 51.12N 5.58E
Rusape Rhodesia 48 18.35S 32.08E
Ruse Bulgaria 25 43.50N 25.59E
Rush Rep. of Ire. 18 53.32N 6.06W
Rushden England 8 52.17N 0.37W
Russian Soviet Federal Socialist Republic *d.* U.S.S.R. 30 62.00N 80.00E
Rustenburg R.S.A. 48 25.40S 27.15E
Rutana Burundi 47 3.58S 30.00E
Rütenbrock W. Germany 27 52.51N 7.06E
Ruteng Indonesia 39 8.35S 120.28E
Rutherglen Scotland 14 55.49N 4.12W
Ruthin Wales 10 53.07N 3.18W
Rutland U.S.A. 57 43.37N 72.59W
Rutshuru Zaïre 47 1.10S 29.26E
Ruvu Coast Tanzania 47 6.50S 38.42E
Ruvuma *r.* Moçambique/Tanzania 47 10.30S 40.30E
Ruvuma *d.* Tanzania 47 10.45S 36.15E
Ruwandiz Iraq 35 36.38N 44.32E
Ruwenzori Range *mts.* Uganda/Zaïre 47 0.30N 30.00E
Ruyigi Burundi 47 3.26S 30.14E
Ruzayevka U.S.S.R. 29 54.04N 44.55E
Rwanda Africa 47 2.00S 30.00E
Ryan, Loch Scotland 14 54.56N 5.02W
Ryazan U.S.S.R. 29 54.37N 39.43E
Ryazhsk U.S.S.R. 29 53.40N 40.07E
Rybachi Pen. U.S.S.R. 28 69.45N 32.30E
Rybinsk U.S.S.R. 29 58.01N 38.52E
Rybinsk Resr. U.S.S.R. 29 58.30N 38.25E
Ryde England 8 50.44N 1.09W
Ryder's Hill England 11 50.31N 3.53W
Rye England 9 50.57N 0.46E
Rye *r.* England 13 54.10N 0.44W
Rye B. England 9 50.53N 0.48E
Ryton England 15 54.59N 1.47W
Ryukyu Is. Japan 41 26.30N 125.00E
Rzeszów Poland 29 50.04N 22.00E
Rzhev U.S.S.R. 29 56.15N 34.18E

S

Saale *r.* E. Germany 26 51.58N 11.53E
Saar *r.* W. Germany 27 49.43N 6.34E
Saarbrücken W. Germany 26 49.15N 6.58E
Saarburg W. Germany 27 49.36N 6.33E
Saaremaa *i.* U.S.S.R. 28 58.30N 22.30E
Saarijärvi Finland 28 62.44N 25.15E
Saba *i.* Neth. Antilles 58 17.42N 63.26W
Šabac Yugo. 25 44.45N 19.41E
Sabadell Spain 23 41.33N 2.07E
Sabana, Archipelago de Cuba 59 23.30N 80.00W
Sabi *r.* Rhodesia 48 21.16S 32.20E
Sabinas Mexico 52 26.33N 101.10W
Sabinas *r.* Mexico 58 27.31N 100.40W
Sabine *r.* U.S.A. 53 29.40N 93.50W
Sable, C. Canada 55 43.30N 65.50W
Sable, C. U.S.A. 58 25.05N 81.10W
Sable I. Canada 55 44.00N 60.00W
Sabzawar Afghan. 35 33.18N 62.05E
Sabzawar Iran 35 36.13N 57.38E
Sacedón Spain 23 40.29N 2.44W
Sacquoy Head Scotland 17 59.12N 3.05W
Sacramento U.S.A. 52 38.32N 121.30W
Sacramento *r.* U.S.A. 52 38.05N 122.00W
Sádaba Spain 23 42.19N 1.10W
Sá da Bandeira Angola 46 14.52S 13.30E
Sadani Tanzania 47 6.00S 38.40E
Saddle Head Rep. of Ire. 18 54.02N 10.12W
Saddleworth Moor *hills* England 12 53.32N 1.55W
Sadiya India 37 27.49N 95.38E
Sado *i.* Japan 42 38.00N 138.20E
Safaha *des.* Saudi Arabia 34 26.30N 39.30E
Safaniya Saudi Arabia 35 28.00N 48.48E
Safed Koh *mtn.* Afghan. 35 34.15N 63.30E
Säffle Sweden 28 59.08N 12.55E
Saffron Walden England 9 52.02N 0.15E
Safi Morocco 44 32.20N 9.17W
Safonovo U.S.S.R. 29 55.08N 33.16E
Saga Japan 42 33.08N 130.30E
Sagaing Burma 37 22.00N 96.00E
Sagar India 37 23.50N 78.44E
Saginaw U.S.A. 56 43.25N 83.54W
Saginaw B. U.S.A. 56 44.00N 83.30W
Sagua la Grande Cuba 59 22.55N 80.05W
Saguenay *r.* Canada 57 48.10N 69.43W
Sagunto Spain 23 39.40N 0.17W
Sahagún Spain 23 42.23N 5.02W
Sahara *des.* Africa 44 18.00N 12.00E
Saharan Atlas *mts.* Algeria 44 34.20N 2.00E
Saharanpur India 36 29.58N 77.33E
Sahba, Wadi *r.* Saudi Arabia 35 23.48N 49.50E
Saida Algeria 23 34.50N 0.10E
Saidabad Iran 35 29.28N 55.43E
Saidpur Bangla. 37 25.48N 89.00E
Saigon S. Vietnam 38 10.46N 106.43E
Sai Kung Hong Kong 33 22.22N 114.15E
Saimaa *l.* Finland 28 61.20N 28.00E
Saimbeyli Turkey 34 38.07N 36.08E
Saindak Pakistan 35 29.16N 61.36E
St. Abb's Head Scotland 15 55.54N 2.07W
St. Agnes England 11 50.18N 5.13W
St. Agnes *i.* England 11 49.53N 6.20W
St. Albans England 7 51.46N 0.21W
St. Alban's Head England 8 50.35N 2.04W
St. Aldhelm's Head England 8 50.35N 2.04W
St. Amand France 27 50.27N 3.26E
St. Amand-Mt. Rond *town* France 22 46.43N 2.29E
St. André, Cap Malagasy Rep. 47 16.10S 44.27E
St. Andrews Canada 57 45.05N 67.04W
St. Andrews Scotland 15 56.20N 2.48W
St. Andrews B. Scotland 15 56.23N 2.43W
St. Ann's Bay *town* Jamaica 59 18.26N 77.12W
St. Ann's Head Wales 11 51.41N 5.11W
St. Anthony Canada 55 51.24N 55.37W
St. Aubin Channel Is. 11 49.12N 2.10W
St. Augustine U.S.A. 53 29.54N 81.19W
St. Austell England 11 50.20N 4.48W
St. Austell B. England 11 50.16N 4.43W
St. Barthélemy C. America 59 17.55N 62.50W
St. Bees England 12 54.29N 3.36W
St. Bees Head England 12 54.31N 3.39W
St. Blazey England 11 50.22N 4.48W
St. Boniface Canada 53 49.58N 97.07W
St. Boswells Scotland 15 55.35N 2.40W
St. Brides B. Wales 10 51.48N 5.03W
St. Brieuc France 22 48.31N 2.45W
St. Catherines Canada 57 43.10N 79.15W
St. Catherine's Pt. England 8 50.34N 1.18W
St. Céré France 22 44.52N 1.53E
St. Christophe *i.* Malagasy Rep. 47 17.06S 42.53E
St. Clair, L. Canada 56 42.25N 82.35W
St. Clears Wales 10 51.48N 4.30W
St. Cloud U.S.A. 53 45.34N 94.10W
St. Columb Major England 11 50.26N 4.56W
St. Croix *r.* U.S.A. 56 44.43N 92.47W
St. Croix *i.* Virgin Is. 59 17.45N 64.35W
St. David's Wales 10 51.54N 5.16W
St. David's Head Wales 10 51.55N 5.19W
St. Denis France 22 48.56N 2.21E
St. Dié France 26 48.17N 6.57E
St. Dizier France 22 48.38N 4.58E
St. Elias, Mt. U.S.A. 54 60.20N 139.00W
Saintes France 22 45.44N 0.38W
St. Etienne France 22 45.26N 4.26E
Saintfield N. Ireland 18 54.28N 5.50W
St. Fillans Scotland 14 56.24N 4.07W
St. Finan's B. Rep. of Ire. 19 51.49N 10.21W
St. Flour France 22 45.02N 3.05E
St. Gallen Switz. 26 47.25N 9.23E
St. Gaudens France 22 43.07N 0.44E
St. George's Grenada 59 12.04N 61.44W
St. George's Channel U.K./Rep. of Ire. 20 52.00N 5.50W
St. Germain France 22 48.53N 2.04E
St. Gheorghe's Mouth *est.* Romania 25 44.51N 29.37E
St. Gilles-sur-Vie France 22 46.42N 1.56W
St. Girons France 22 42.59N 1.08E
St. Gotthard Pass Switz. 26 46.30N 8.55E
St. Govan's Head Wales 11 51.36N 4.55W
St. Helena *i.* Atlantic Oc. 4 16.00S 6.00W
St. Helena B. R.S.A. 48 32.35S 18.00E
St. Helens England 10 53.28N 2.43W
St. Helier Channel Is. 11 49.12N 2.07W
St. Hubert Belgium 27 50.02N 5.22E
St. Hyacinthe Canada 57 45.38N 72.57W
St. Ives Cambs. England 9 52.20N 0.05W
St. Ives Cornwall England 11 50.13N 5.29W
St. Ives B. England 11 50.14N 5.26W
St. Jean Pied de Port France 22 43.10N 1.14W
St. Jérôme Canada 57 45.47N 74.01W
St. John Canada 53 45.16N 66.03W
St. John *r.* Canada 55 45.30N 66.05W
St. John, L. Canada 57 48.40N 72.00W
St. John's Antigua 59 17.07N 61.51W
St. John's Canada 55 47.34N 52.41W
St. John's Pt. N. Ireland 18 54.14N 5.39W
St. John's Pt. Rep. of Ire. 18 54.34N 8.28W
St. Joseph U.S.A. 53 39.45N 94.51W
St. Joseph, L. Canada 53 51.00N 91.05W
St. Just England 11 50.07N 5.41W
St. Keverne England 11 50.03N 5.05W
St. Kilda *i.* U.K. 20 57.49N 8.34W
St. Kitts *i.* C. America 59 17.25N 62.45W
St. Lawrence *r.* Canada 57 48.45N 68.30W
St. Lawrence, G. of Canada 55 48.00N 62.00W
St. Lawrence I. U.S.A. 54 63.00N 170.00W
St. Leonard Canada 57 47.10N 67.55W
St. Lô France 22 49.07N 1.05W
St. Louis Senegal 44 16.01N 16.30W
St. Louis U.S.A. 56 38.40N 90.15W
St. Lucia C. America 59 14.05N 61.00W
St. Magnus B. Scotland 16 60.25N 1.35W
St. Maixent France 22 46.25N 0.12W
St. Malo France 22 48.39N 2.00W
St. Malo, Golfe de France 22 49.20N 2.00W
St. Marc Haiti 59 19.08N 72.41W
St. Margaret's at Cliffe England 9 51.10N 1.23E
St. Margaret's Hope Scotland 17 58.49N 2.57W
St. Martin Channel Is. 11 49.27N 2.34W
St. Martin C. America 59 18.05N 63.05W
St. Martin's *i.* England 11 49.57N 6.16W
St. Mary Channel Is. 11 49.14N 2.10W
St. Mary's *i.* England 11 49.55N 6.16W
St. Mary's Scotland 17 58.54N 2.55W
St. Mary's Loch Scotland 15 55.29N 3.12W
St. Maurice *r.* Canada 57 46.20N 72.30W
St. Mawes England 11 50.10N 5.01W
St. Moritz Switz. 26 46.30N 9.51E
St. Nazaire France 22 47.17N 2.12W
St. Neots England 9 52.14N 0.16W
St. Nicolas Belgium 27 51.10N 4.09E
St. Ninian's I. Scotland 16 59.58N 1.21W
St. Omer France 9 50.45N 2.15E
St. Pancras England 7 51.32N 0.08W
St. Paul France 22 42.49N 2.29E
St. Paul *i.* Indian Oc. 5 38.44S 77.30E
St. Paul U.S.A. 56 45.00N 93.10W
St. Paul's Cray England 7 51.24N 0.06E
St. Peter Port Channel Is. 11 49.27N 2.32W
St. Petersburg U.S.A. 53 27.45N 82.40W
St. Pierre-Miquelon *i.* N. America 55 47.00N 56.15W
St. Pölten Austria 26 48.13N 15.37E
St. Quentin France 27 49.51N 3.17E
St. Sampson Channel Is. 11 49.29N 2.31W
St. Stephen Canada 57 45.12N 67.18W
St. Thomas Canada 56 42.46N 81.12W
St. Thomas *i.* Virgin Is. 59 18.22N 64.57W
St. Trond Belgium 27 50.49N 5.11E
St. Tropez France 22 43.16N 6.39E
St. Vallier France 22 45.11N 4.49E
St. Vincent C. America 59 13.10N 61.15W
St. Vincent, C. Portugal 23 37.01N 8.59W
St. Vith Belgium 27 50.15N 6.08E
St. Wendel W. Germany 27 49.27N 7.10E
St. Yrieix France 22 45.31N 1.12E
Saipan *i.* Asia 39 15.12N 145.43E
Sai Wan Hong Kong 33 22.24N 114.21E
Sai Wan Ho Hong Kong 33 22.17N 114.13E
Sai Wan Shan *mtn.* Hong Kong 33 22.23N 114.22E

Sakai Japan **42** 34.37N 135.28E
Sakaka Saudi Arabia **34** 29.59N 40.12E
Sakania Zaire **47** 12.44S 28.34E
Sakarya r. Turkey **34** 41.08N 30.36E
Sakata Japan **42** 38.55N 139.51E
Sakhalin i. U.S.S.R. **41** 50.00N 143.00E
Sakrivier R.S.A. **48** 30.50S 20.26E
Sal r. U.S.S.R. **29** 47.33N 40.40E
Sala Sweden **28** 59.55N 16.38E
Salado r. La Pampa Argentina **61** 36.15S 66.45W
Salado r. Santa Fé Argentina **63** 32.30S 61.00W
Salado r. Mexico **58** 26.46N 98.55W
Salala Oman **36** 17.00N 54.04E
Salamanca Spain **23** 40.58N 5.40W
Salar de Uyuni l. Bolivia **63** 20.30S 67.45W
Salbris France **22** 47.26N 2.03E
Salcombe England **11** 50.14N 3.47W
Saldanha B. R.S.A. **48** 33.00S 17.56E
Sale England **12** 53.26N 2.19W
Salekhard U.S.S.R. **30** 66.33N 66.35E
Salem India **37** 11.38N 78.08E
Salem U.S.A. **56** 38.37N 88.58W
Salen Highland Scotland **14** 56.43N 5.46W
Salen Strath. Scotland **14** 56.31N 5.56W
Salerno Italy **24** 40.41N 14.45E
Salerno, G. of Med. Sea **24** 40.30N 14.45E
Salford England **12** 53.30N 2.17W
Salfords England **7** 51.12N 0.12W
Salima Malawi **47** 13.45S 34.29E
Salina Cruz Mexico **58** 16.11N 95.12W
Salins France **22** 46.56N 4.53E
Salisbury Rhodesia **48** 17.43S 31.05E
Salisbury England **8** 51.04N 1.48W
Salisbury U.S.A. **53** 38.22N 75.37W
Salisbury, L. Uganda **47** 1.35N 34.08E
Salisbury Plain f. England **8** 51.15N 1.55W
Salmon r. U.S.A. **52** 45.50N 116.50W
Salmon River Mts. U.S.A. **52** 44.30N 114.30W
Salo Finland **28** 60.23N 23.10E
Salobreña Spain **23** 36.45N 3.35W
Salon France **22** 43.38N 5.06E
Salonga r. Zaire **46** 0.09S 19.52E
Salop d. England **8** 52.35N 2.40W
Salsk U.S.S.R. **29** 46.30N 41.33E
Salso r. Italy **24** 37.07N 13.57E
Salt Jordan **34** 32.03N 35.44E
Salta Argentina **61** 24.46S 65.28W
Salta d. Argentina **61** 25.05S 65.00W
Saltash England **11** 50.25N 4.13W
Saltburn-by-the-Sea England **13** 54.35N 0.58W
Saltcoats Scotland **14** 55.37N 4.47W
Saltee Is. Rep. of Ire. **19** 52.08N 6.36W
Saltfleet England **13** 53.25N 0.11E
Saltillo Mexico **58** 25.30N 101.00W
Salt Lake City U.S.A. **52** 40.45N 111.55W
Salto Uruguay **61** 31.27S 57.50W
Salton Sea l. U.S.A. **52** 33.25N 115.45W
Salûm Egypt **34** 31.31N 25.09E
Salvador Brazil **62** 12.58S 38.20W
Salwa Qatar **35** 24.44N 50.50E
Salween r. Burma **37** 16.30N 97.33E
Salyany U.S.S.R. **35** 39.36N 48.59E
Salzach r. Austria **26** 48.35N 13.30E
Salzburg Austria **26** 47.54N 13.03E
Salzgitter W. Germany **26** 52.02N 10.22E
Samana Dom. Rep. **59** 19.14N 69.20W
Samana Cay i. Bahamas **59** 23.05N 73.45W
Samar i. Phil. **39** 11.45N 125.15E
Samarinda Indonesia **38** 0.30S 117.09E
Samarkand U.S.S.R. **30** 39.40N 66.57E
Samarra Iraq **35** 34.13N 43.52E
Samawa Iraq **35** 31.18N 45.18E
Sambalpur India **37** 21.28N 84.04E
Samborombon Bay Argentina **61** 36.00S 56.50W
Sambre r. Belgium **27** 50.29N 4.52E
Same Tanzania **47** 4.10S 37.43E
Samer France **9** 50.38N 1.45E
Samirum Iran **35** 31.31N 52.10E
Sam Neua Laos **38** 20.25N 104.04E
Samoa Is. Pacific Oc. **3** 13.00S 171.00W
Sámos i. Greece **25** 37.44N 26.45E
Samothráki i. Greece **25** 40.26N 25.35E
Sampit Indonesia **38** 2.34S 112.59E
Sam Shing Hui Hong Kong **33** 22.23N 113.58E
Samsun Turkey **34** 41.17N 36.22E
San Mali **44** 13.21N 4.57W
Sana Yemen **45** 16.02N 49.44E
Sana r. Yugo. **24** 45.03N 16.22E
Sanaga r. Cameroon **46** 3.35N 9.40E
San Ambrosio i. Pacific Oc. **63** 26.28S 79.53W
Sanandaj Iran **35** 35.18N 47.01E
San Antonio U.S.A. **52** 29.25N 98.30W
San Antonio, C. Cuba **58** 21.50N 84.57W
San Antonio, Punta c. Mexico **52** 29.45N 115.41W
San Antonio Oeste Argentina **61** 40.45S 65.05W
San Bernardino U.S.A. **52** 34.07N 117.18W
San Blas, C. U.S.A. **53** 29.40N 85.25W
San Carlos Argentina **63** 41.11S 71.23W
San Carlos Phil. **39** 15.59N 120.22E
San Cristóbal Argentina **61** 30.20S 61.14W
San Cristóbal Dom. Rep. **59** 18.27N 70.07W
San Cristóbal Venezuela **59** 7.46N 72.15W
Sancti Spíritus Cuba **59** 21.55N 79.28W
Sanda i. Scotland **14** 55.17N 5.34W
Sandakan Malaysia **38** 5.52N 118.04E
Sanday i. Scotland **17** 59.15N 2.33W
Sanday Sd. Scotland **17** 59.11N 2.35W
Sandbach England **12** 53.09N 2.23W
Sandbank Scotland **14** 55.59N 4.58W
Sanderstead England **7** 51.21N 0.05W
Sandgate England **9** 51.05N 1.09E
San Diego U.S.A. **52** 32.45N 117.10W
Sandling England **7** 51.18N 0.33E
Sandnes Norway **28** 58.51N 5.45E
Sandness Scotland **16** 60.18N 1.38W
Sandö i. Faroe Is. **28** 61.50N 6.45W
Sandoa Zaire **46** 9.41S 22.56E
Sandoway Burma **37** 18.28N 94.20E
Sandown England **8** 50.39N 1.09W
Sandpoint U.S.A. **52** 48.17N 116.34W
Sandray i. Scotland **16** 56.53N 7.31W
Sandringham England **13** 52.50N 0.30E
Sandusky U.S.A. **56** 41.27N 82.42W
Sandviken Sweden **28** 60.38N 16.50E
Sandwich England **9** 51.16N 1.21E
Sandwick Scotland **16** 60.00N 1.14W
Sandy England **9** 52.08N 0.18W
Sandy B. Hong Kong **33** 22.16N 114.07E
Sandy L. Canada **53** 53.00N 93.00W
San Felipe Mexico **52** 31.03N 114.52W
San Felipe Venezuela **59** 10.25N 68.40W
San Feliu de Guixols Spain **23** 41.47N 3.02E
San Felix i. Pacific Oc. **63** 26.23S 80.05W
San Félix Venezuela **59** 8.22N 62.37W
San Fernando Phil. **39** 16.39N 120.19E
San Fernando Spain **23** 36.28N 6.12W
San Fernando Trinidad **59** 10.16N 61.28W
San Fernando Venezuela **59** 7.53N 67.15W
San Francisco Argentina **61** 31.29S 62.06W
San Francisco U.S.A. **52** 37.45N 122.27W
San Francisco, C. Ecuador **62** 0.38N 80.08W
San Francisco de Macorís Dom. Rep. **59** 19.19N 70.15W
Sangha r. Congo **46** 1.10S 16.47E
Sangi i. Indonesia **39** 3.30N 125.30E
Sangihe Is. Indonesia **39** 2.45N 125.20E
Sangkan Ho r. China **41** 40.23N 115.18E
Sangonera r. Spain **23** 37.58N 1.04W
San Javier Bolivia **61** 16.22S 62.38W
San Jorge r. Colombia **59** 9.10N 74.40W
San Jorge, G. of Argentina **63** 46.00S 66.00W
San Jorge, G. of Spain **23** 40.50N 1.10E
San José Costa Rica **58** 9.59N 84.04W
San José Guatemala **58** 13.58N 90.50W
San José Uruguay **61** 34.20S 56.42W
San Jose U.S.A. **52** 37.20N 121.55W
San José de Chiquitos Bolivia **61** 17.53S 60.45W
San Juan Argentina **63** 31.33S 68.31W
San Juan r. Costa Rica **58** 10.50N 83.40W
San Juan Puerto Rico **59** 18.29N 66.08W
San Juan r. U.S.A. **52** 37.20N 110.05W
San Juan del Norte Nicaragua **58** 10.58N 83.40W
San Juan de los Morros Venezuela **59** 9.53N 67.23W
San Juan Mts. U.S.A. **52** 37.30N 107.00W
Sankuru r. Zaire **46** 4.20S 20.27E
San Leonardo Spain **23** 41.49N 3.04W
Sanlúcar de Barrameda Spain **23** 36.46N 6.21W
San Lucas, C. N. America **2** 22.50N 110.00W
San Luis Argentina **61** 33.20S 66.23W
San Luis d. Argentina **61** 33.00S 66.10W
San Luis Cuba **59** 20.13N 75.50W
San Luis Obispo U.S.A. **52** 35.16N 120.40W
San Luis Potosí Mexico **58** 22.10N 101.00W
San Luis Potosí d. Mexico **58** 23.00N 100.00W
San Marino Europe **24** 43.55N 12.27E
San Marino town San Marino **24** 43.55N 12.27E
San Matias, G. of Argentina **61** 41.30S 64.00W
San Miguel El Salvador **58** 13.28N 88.10W
San Miguel de Tucumán Argentina **61** 26.47S 65.15W
San Nicolás Argentina **61** 33.25S 60.15W
San Pablo Phil. **39** 13.58N 121.10E
San Pedro Argentina **61** 24.30S 65.00W
San Pedro Dom. Rep. **59** 18.30N 69.18W
San Pedro Mexico **58** 24.50N 102.59W
San Pedro Paraguay **61** 24.08S 57.08W
San Pedro, Punta c. Costa Rica **58** 8.30N 83.30W
San Pedro, Sierra de mts. Spain **23** 39.20N 6.20W
San Pedro Sula Honduras **58** 15.26N 88.01W
San Pietro i. Italy **24** 39.09N 8.16E
San Po Kong Hong Kong **33** 22.20N 114.12E
Sanquhar Scotland **15** 55.22N 3.56W
San Remo Italy **22** 43.48N 7.46E
San Salvador i. Bahamas **59** 24.00N 74.32W
San Salvador El Salvador **58** 13.40N 89.10W
San Salvador de Jujuy Argentina **61** 24.10S 65.18W
Sansanné-Mango Togo **44** 10.23N 0.30E
San Sebastián Spain **23** 43.19N 1.59W
San Severo Italy **24** 41.40N 15.24E
Santa Ana El Salvador **58** 14.00N 79.31W
Santa Barbara U.S.A. **52** 34.25N 119.41W
Santa Catarina d. Brazil **61** 27.00S 52.00W
Santa Clara Cuba **59** 22.25N 79.58W
Santa Cruz Bolivia **61** 17.45S 63.14W
Santa Cruz d. Bolivia **61** 17.45S 62.00W
Santa Elena, C. Costa Rica **58** 10.54N 85.56W
Santa Fé Argentina **61** 31.38S 60.43W
Santa Fé d. Argentina **61** 31.00S 61.00W
Santa Fe U.S.A. **52** 35.41N 105.57W
Santa Maria Brazil **61** 29.40S 53.47W
Santa Maria U.S.A. **52** 34.56N 120.25W
Santa Maria di Leuca, C. Italy **25** 39.47N 18.24E
Santa Marta Colombia **59** 11.18N 74.10W
Santander Spain **23** 43.28N 3.48W
Santañy Spain **23** 39.20N 3.07E
Santarém Brazil **62** 2.26S 54.41W
Santarém Portugal **23** 39.14N 8.40W
Santa Rosa Argentina **63** 36.00S 64.40W
Santa Rosa Honduras **58** 14.47N 88.46W
Santa Rosa de Toay Argentina **61** 36.36S 64.15W
Santa Rosalía Mexico **52** 27.20N 112.20W
Santiago Chile **63** 33.30S 70.40W
Santiago Dom. Rep. **59** 19.30N 70.42W
Santiago Panamá **58** 8.08N 80.59W
Santiago de Compostela Spain **23** 42.52N 8.33W
Santiago de Cuba Cuba **59** 20.00N 75.49W
Santiago del Estero Argentina **61** 27.48S 64.15W
Santiago del Estero d. Argentina **61** 28.00S 63.50W
Santo André Brazil **61** 23.39S 46.29W
Santo Antonio do Zaire Angola **46** 6.12S 12.25E
Santo Domingo Dom. Rep. **59** 18.30N 69.57W
Santoña Spain **23** 43.27N 3.26W
Santos Brazil **61** 23.56S 46.22W
Santo Tomé Argentina **61** 28.31S 56.03W
San Valentín, Cerro mtn. Chile **63** 46.33S 73.20W
San Vicente El Salvador **58** 13.38N 88.42W
Sanza Pombo Angola **46** 7.20S 16.12E
São Borja Brazil **61** 28.35S 56.01W
São Carlos Brazil **61** 22.02S 47.53W
São Francisco r. Brazil **62** 10.10S 36.40W
São Francisco do Sul Brazil **61** 26.17S 48.39W
São Luís Brazil **62** 2.34S 44.16W
Saona i. Dom. Rep. **59** 18.09N 68.42W
Saône r. France **22** 45.46N 4.52E
São Paulo Brazil **61** 23.33S 46.39W
São Paulo d. Brazil **61** 22.05S 48.00W
São Paulo de Olivença Brazil **62** 3.34S 68.55W
São Roque, C. Brazil **62** 5.00S 35.00W
São Salvador do Congo Angola **46** 6.18S 14.16E
São Sebastião I. Brazil **61** 24.00S 45.25W
São Tomé i. Africa **46** 0.20N 6.30E
Sapporo Japan **42** 43.05N 141.21E
Sapri Italy **24** 40.04N 15.38E
Saqqiz Iran **35** 36.14N 46.15E
Sarab Iran **35** 37.56N 47.35E
Sara Buri Thailand **38** 14.32N 100.53E
Sarajevo Yugo. **25** 43.52N 18.26E
Sarangarh India **37** 21.38N 83.09E
Saransk U.S.S.R. **29** 54.12N 45.10E
Saratov U.S.S.R. **29** 51.30N 45.55E
Saratov Resr. U.S.S.R. **29** 51.00N 46.00E
Sarbaz Iran **35** 26.39N 61.20E
Sardinia i. Italy **24** 40.00N 9.00E
Sarek mtn. Sweden **28** 67.10N 17.45E
Sarh Chad **44** 9.08N 18.22E
Sari Iran **35** 36.33N 53.06E
Sarigan i. Asia **39** 16.43N 145.47E
Sark i. Channel Is. **11** 49.26N 2.22W
Sarmi Asia **39** 1.51S 138.45E
Sarmiento Argentina **63** 45.38S 69.08W
Särna Sweden **28** 61.40N 13.10E
Sarnia Canada **56** 42.57N 82.24W
Sarny U.S.S.R. **29** 51.21N 26.31E
Saros, G. of Turkey **25** 40.32N 26.25E
Sarpsborg Norway **28** 59.17N 11.06E
Sarre r. see Saar France **26**
Sarrebourg France **26** 48.43N 7.03E
Sarria Spain **23** 42.47N 7.25W
Sartène France **24** 41.38N 8.48E
Sarthe r. France **22** 47.29N 0.30W
Sarur Oman **35** 23.25N 58.10E
Sasebo Japan **42** 33.10N 129.42E
Saskatchewan d. Canada **54** 55.00N 105.00W
Saskatchewan r. Canada **55** 53.25N 100.15W
Saskatoon Canada **52** 52.10N 106.40W
Sasovo U.S.S.R. **29** 54.21N 41.58E
Sassandra Ivory Coast **44** 4.58N 6.08W
Sássari Italy **24** 40.43N 8.33E
Sassnitz E. Germany **26** 54.32N 13.40E
Sasyk, L. U.S.S.R. **25** 45.38N 29.38E
Satara India **36** 17.43N 74.05E
Satpura Range mts. India **36** 21.50N 76.00E
Satu Mare Romania **29** 47.48N 22.52E
Sauda Norway **28** 59.38N 6.23E
Saudi Arabia Asia **34** 26.00N 44.00E
Saulieu France **22** 47.17N 4.14E
Sault Sainte Marie Canada **56** 46.32N 84.20W
Sault Sainte Marie U.S.A. **56** 46.29N 84.22W
Saumur France **22** 47.16N 0.05W
Saundersfoot Wales **11** 51.43N 4.42W
Sava r. Yugo. **25** 44.50N 20.26E
Savannah U.S.A. **53** 32.09N 81.01W
Savannah r. U.S.A. **53** 32.10N 81.00W
Savannakhet Laos **38** 16.34N 104.55E
Savé Dahomey **44** 8.04N 2.37E
Save r. France **23** 43.30N 0.55E
Save r. Moçambique **48** 21.00S 35.01E
Saveh Iran **35** 35.00N 50.25E
Savona Italy **22** 44.18N 8.28E
Savonlinna Finland **28** 61.52N 28.51E
Savu Sea Pacific Oc. **39** 9.30S 122.30E
Sawbridgeworth England **7** 51.50N 0.09E
Sawston England **9** 52.07N 0.11E
Sawu i. Indonesia **39** 10.30S 121.50E
Saxmundham England **9** 52.13N 1.29E
Saxthorpe England **9** 52.50N 1.09E
Sayan Mts. U.S.S.R. **40** 51.30N 102.00E
Sayn Shand Mongolia **41** 44.58N 110.10E
Sayula Mexico **58** 19.52N 103.36W
Sázava r. Czech. **26** 49.53N 14.21E
Sbeitla Tunisia **24** 35.16N 9.10E
Scafell Pike mtn. England **12** 54.27N 3.12W
Scalasaig Scotland **14** 56.04N 6.12W
Scalby England **13** 54.18N 0.26W
Scalloway Scotland **16** 60.08N 1.17W
Scalpay i. Highland Scotland **16** 57.18N 5.58W
Scalpay i. W. Isles Scotland **16** 57.52N 6.40W
Scammon Bay town U.S.A. **54** 61.50N 165.35W
Scandinavia f. Europe **3** 65.00N 18.00E
Scapa Flow str. Scotland **17** 58.53N 3.05W
Scarba i. Scotland **14** 56.11N 5.42W
Scarborough England **13** 54.17N 0.24W
Scariff I. Rep. of Ire. **19** 51.43N 10.16W
Scarinish Scotland **14** 56.30N 6.48W
Scarp i. Scotland **16** 58.02N 7.07W
Scavaig, Loch Scotland **16** 57.10N 6.08W
Schaffhausen Switz. **26** 47.42N 8.38E
Schagen Neth. **27** 52.47N 4.47E
Schefferville Canada **55** 54.50N 67.00W
Schelde r. Belgium **27** 51.13N 4.25E
Schenectady U.S.A. **57** 42.28N 73.57W
Scheveningen Neth. **27** 52.07N 4.16E
Schiedam Neth. **27** 51.55N 4.25E
Schiehallion mtn. Scotland **15** 56.40N 4.08W
Schiermonnikoog i. Neth. **27** 53.28N 6.15E
Schleiden W. Germany **27** 50.32N 6.29E
Schleswig W. Germany **26** 54.32N 9.34E
Schouten Is. Indonesia **39** 0.45S 135.50E
Schouwen i. Neth. **27** 51.42N 3.45E
Schwandorf W. Germany **26** 49.20N 12.07E
Schwaner Mts. Indonesia **38** 0.45S 113.20E
Schwecht E. Germany **26** 53.04N 14.17E
Schweinfurt W. Germany **26** 50.03N 10.16E
Schwelm W. Germany **27** 51.17N 7.18E
Schwerin E. Germany **26** 53.38N 11.25E
Sciacca Italy **24** 37.31N 13.05E
Scilly, Isles of England **11** 49.55N 6.20W
Scioto r. U.S.A. **56** 38.43N 83.00W
Scotland U.K. **20** 56.30N 4.00W
Scottsbluff U.S.A. **52** 41.52N 103.40W
Scourie Scotland **16** 58.20N 5.08W
Scranton U.S.A. **57** 41.25N 75.40W
Scridain, Loch Scotland **14** 56.22N 6.06W
Scunthorpe England **13** 53.35N 0.38W
Seaford England **9** 50.46N 0.08E
Seaham England **13** 54.52N 1.21W
Seahouses England **15** 55.35N 1.38W
Seal r. Canada **55** 59.00N 95.00W
Seamill Scotland **14** 55.41N 4.52W
Seascale England **12** 54.24N 3.29W
Seaton Cumbria England **12** 54.41N 3.31W
Seaton Devon England **8** 50.43N 3.05W
Seaton Delaval England **15** 55.05N 1.31W
Seattle U.S.A. **52** 47.35N 122.20W
Sebago L. U.S.A. **57** 43.37N 71.20W
Sebastian Vizcaino B. Mexico **52** 28.20N 114.45W
Sebha Libya **44** 27.04N 14.25E
Sebinkarahisar Turkey **34** 40.19N 38.25E
Séda r. Portugal **23** 38.55N 7.30W
Sedan France **27** 49.42N 4.57E
Sedbergh England **12** 54.20N 2.31W
Sedgefield England **13** 54.40N 1.27W
Segovia Spain **23** 40.57N 4.07W
Segre r. Spain **23** 41.25N 0.21E
Segura r. Spain **23** 38.07N 0.14W
Segura, Sierra de mts. Spain **23** 38.00N 2.50W
Sehkuheh Iran **35** 30.45N 61.29E
Seil i. Scotland **14** 56.18N 5.33W
Seiland Norway **28** 70.30N 23.00E
Seinäjoki Finland **28** 62.45N 22.55E
Seine r. France **22** 49.28N 0.25E
Seistan f. Iran **35** 31.00N 61.15E
Sekondi-Takoradi Ghana **44** 4.59N 1.43W
Selaru i. Asia **39** 8.15S 131.00E
Selby England **13** 53.47N 1.05W
Sele r. Italy **24** 40.30N 14.50E
Selenga r. U.S.S.R. **40** 52.20N 106.20E
Sélestat France **26** 48.16N 7.28E
Selkirk Scotland **15** 55.33N 2.51W
Selkirk Mts. Canada/U.S.A. **52** 50.00N 116.30W
Selsdon England **7** 51.21N 0.03W
Selsey England **8** 50.44N 0.47W
Selsey Bill c. England **8** 50.44N 0.47W
Selukwe Rhodesia **48** 19.40S 30.00E
Selvas f. Brazil **62** 9.00S 68.00W
Selwyn Mts. Canada **54** 63.00N 130.00W
Seman r. Albania **25** 40.53N 19.25E
Semarang Indonesia **38** 6.58S 110.29E
Seminoe Resr. U.S.A. **52** 42.05N 106.50W
Semipalatinsk U.S.S.R. **30** 50.26N 80.16E
Semliki r. Zaire **47** 1.12N 30.27E
Semmering Pass Austria **26** 47.40N 16.00E
Semnan Iran **35** 35.31N 53.24E
Semois r. France **27** 49.53N 4.45E
Semu r. Tanzania **47** 3.57S 34.20E
Senanga Zambia **46** 15.52S 23.19E
Send England **7** 51.17N 0.33W
Sendai Japan **42** 38.20N 140.50E
Seneca L. U.S.A. **57** 42.35N 77.07W
Senegal Africa **44** 14.15N 14.15W
Sénégal r. Senegal/Mauritania **44** 16.00N 16.28W
Senekal R.S.A. **48** 28.19S 27.38E
Senigallia Italy **24** 43.42N 13.14E
Senja i. Norway **28** 69.20N 17.30E
Senlis France **22** 49.12N 2.35E
Sennar Sudan **45** 13.31N 33.38E
Sennen England **11** 50.04N 5.42W
Senneterre Canada **57** 48.24N 77.16W
Sennybridge Wales **10** 51.57N 3.35W
Sens France **22** 48.12N 3.18E
Sentery Zaire **46** 5.19S 25.43E
Seoul S. Korea **41** 37.30N 127.00E
Sepik r. P.N.G. **39** 3.54S 144.30E
Sept Iles town Canada **55** 50.13N 66.22W
Seraing Belgium **27** 50.37N 5.33E
Serengeti Nat. Park Tanzania **47** 2.30S 35.00E
Serengeti Plain f. Tanzania **47** 3.00S 35.00E
Serenje Zambia **47** 13.12S 30.50E
Sérevac France **24** 44.20N 3.05E
Sergach U.S.S.R. **29** 55.32N 45.27E
Sermate i. Indonesia **39** 8.30S 129.00E
Serov U.S.S.R. **30** 59.22N 60.32E
Serowe Botswana **48** 22.25S 26.44E
Serpa Portugal **23** 37.56N 7.36W
Serpent's Mouth str. Venezuela **59** 9.50N 61.00W
Serpukhov U.S.S.R. **29** 54.53N 37.25E
Sérrai Greece **25** 41.04N 23.32E
Serrat, C. Tunisia **24** 37.15N 9.12E
Serre r. France **27** 49.40N 3.22E
Sese Is. Uganda **47** 0.20S 32.30E
Sesheke Zambia **46** 17.14S 24.22E
Sesimbra Portugal **23** 38.26N 9.06W
Sète France **22** 43.25N 3.43E
Sete Lagoas Brazil **61** 19.29S 44.15W
Sétif Algeria **24** 36.10N 5.26E

Sollefteå Sweden 28 63.09N 17.15E
Soller Spain 23 39.47N 2.41E
Solling mtn. W. Germany 26 51.45N 9.30E
Solomon Is. Austa. 5 10.00S 160.00E
Solomon Sea Austa. 49 7.00S 150.00E
Solta i. Yugo. 24 43.23N 16.17E
Solway Firth est. England/Scotland 12 54.50N 3.30W
Solwezi Zambia 47 12.11S 26.23E
Soma Turkey 25 39.11N 27.36E
Somabula Rhodesia 48 19.40S 29.38E
Somali Republic Africa 45 5.30N 47.00E
Sombor Yugo. 25 45.48N 19.08E
Somerset d. England 8 51.09N 3.00W
Somerset East R.S.A. 48 32.44S 25.35E
Somerset I. Canada 55 73.00N 93.30W
Somerton England 8 51.03N 2.44W
Somes r. Hungary 29 48.40N 22.30E
Somme r. France 22 50.01N 1.40E
Son r. India 37 25.55N 84.55E
Sönderborg Denmark 26 54.55N 9.48E
Sondrio Italy 26 46.11N 9.52E
Songea Tanzania 47 10.42S 35.39E
Songkhla Thailand 37 7.13N 100.37E
Songololo Zaire 46 5.40S 14.05E
Sonora r. Mexico 52 28.45N 111.55W
Sonsorol i. Asia 39 5.20N 132.13E
Soochow China 41 31.21N 120.40E
Sorel Canada 57 46.03N 73.06W
Soria Spain 23 41.46N 2.28W
Sorisdale Scotland 14 56.40N 6.28W
Sor Kvalöy i. Norway 28 69.45N 18.20E
Sorocaba Brazil 61 23.30S 47.32W
Sorol i. Asia 39 8.09N 140.25E
Sorong Asia 39 0.50S 131.17E
Soroti Uganda 47 1.40N 33.37E
Söröya i. Norway 28 70.30N 22.30E
Sorraia r. Portugal 23 39.00N 8.51W
Sorsele Sweden 28 65.32N 17.34E
Sortavala U.S.S.R. 28 61.40N 30.40E
Sotik Kenya 47 0.40S 35.08E
Sotra i. Norway 28 60.20N 5.00E
Souk Ahras Algeria 24 36.14N 7.59E
Soure Portugal 23 40.04N 8.38W
Souris r. U.S.A. 52 49.38N 99.35W
Sousse Tunisia 24 35.48N 10.38E
Soustons France 22 43.45N 1.19W
Southall England 7 51.31N 0.23W
Southam England 8 52.16N 1.24W
South America 62
Southampton England 8 50.54N 1.23W
Southampton I. Canada 55 64.30N 84.00W
Southampton Water est. England 8 50.52N 1.21W
South Atlantic Ocean 63
South Australia d. Australia 49 29.00S 135.00E
South Barrule mtn. I.o.M. 12 54.09N 4.41W
South Bend U.S.A. 56 41.40N 86.15W
South Benfleet England 7 51.33N 0.34E
South Beveland f. Neth. 27 51.30N 3.50E
Southborough England 9 51.10N 0.15E
South Brent England 11 50.26N 3.50W
South Carolina d. U.S.A. 53 34.00N 81.00W
South Cave England 13 53.46N 0.37W
South Cerney England 8 51.40N 1.55W
South China Sea Asia 38 12.30N 115.00E
South Dakota d. U.S.A. 52 44.30N 100.00W
South Dorset Downs hills England 8 50.40N 2.25W
South Downs hills England 8 50.04N 0.34W
South East C. Australia 49 43.38S 146.48E
Southend Scotland 14 55.19N 5.38W
Southend-on-Sea England 9 51.32N 0.43E
Southern Alps mts. New Zealand 50 43.20S 170.45E
Southern Uplands hills Scotland 15 55.30N 3.30W
Southern Yemen Asia 45 16.00N 49.30E
South Esk r. Scotland 15 56.43N 2.32W
South Flevoland f. Neth. 27 52.22N 5.22E
South Foreland c. England 9 51.08N 1.24E
Southgate England 7 51.38N 0.07W
South Georgia i. Atlantic Oc. 63 54.00S 37.00W
South Glamorgan d. Wales 11 51.27N 3.22W
South-haa Scotland 16 60.34N 1.17W
South Harris f. Scotland 16 57.49N 6.55W
South Haven U.S.A. 56 42.25N 86.16W
South Hayling England 8 50.47N 0.56W
South Holland d. Neth. 27 52.00N 4.30E
South Hornchurch England 7 51.32N 0.13E
South Horr Kenya 47 2.10N 36.45E
South I. New Zealand 50 43.00S 171.00E
South Kirby England 13 53.35N 1.25W
South Korea Asia 41 36.00N 128.00E
Southland f. New Zealand 50 45.40S 167.15E
Southminster England 9 51.40N 0.51E
South Molton England 11 51.01N 3.50W
South Nahanni r. Canada 54 61.00N 123.20W
South Norwood England 7 51.24N 0.04W
South Nutfield England 7 51.14N 0.06W
South Ockendon England 7 51.32N 0.18E
South Orkney Is. Atlantic Oc. 63 63.00S 45.00W
South Oxhey England 7 51.38N 0.24W
Southport England 12 53.38N 3.01W
South Ronaldsay i. Scotland 17 58.47N 2.56W
South Sandwich Is. Atlantic Oc. 63 58.00S 27.00W
South Sandwich Trench Atlantic Oc. 63 57.00S 25.00W
South Saskatchewan r. Canada 52 50.45N 108.30W
South Sd. Rep. of Ire. 19 53.03N 9.28W
South Shetland Is. Antarctica 2 62.00S 60.00W
South Shields England 13 55.00N 1.24W
South Tyne r. England 15 54.59N 2.08W
South Uist i. Scotland 16 57.15N 7.20W
South Vietnam Asia 38 12.00N 108.00E
South Walls i. Scotland 17 58.45N 3.07W
Southwark d. England 7 51.30N 0.06W
Southwell England 13 53.05N 0.58W
South West Africa Africa 48 22.30S 17.00E
Southwest C. New Zealand 50 47.15S 167.30E
Southwick England 9 50.50N 0.14W
Southwold England 9 52.19N 1.41E
South Woodham Ferrers England 7 51.39N 0.36E
South Yorkshire d. England 13 53.28N 1.25W
Sovetsk U.S.S.R. 28 55.02N 21.50E
Sovetskaya Gavan U.S.S.R. 31 48.57N 140.16E
Spa Belgium 27 50.29N 5.52E
Spain Europe 23 40.00N 4.00W
Spalding England 13 52.47N 0.09W
Spandau W. Germany 26 52.32N 13.13E
Spanish Sahara Africa 44 25.00N 13.30W
Sparta U.S.A. 56 43.57N 90.50W
Spárti Greece 25 37.04N 22.28E
Spartivento, C. Calabria Italy 24 37.55N 16.04E
Spartivento, C. Sardinia Italy 24 38.53N 8.51E
Spassk Dal'niy U.S.S.R. 42 44.37N 132.37E
Spátha, C. Greece 25 35.42N 23.43E
Spean Bridge town Scotland 17 56.53N 4.54W
Speke G. Tanzania 47 2.20S 33.30E
Spence Bay town Canada 55 69.30N 93.20W
Spencer G. Australia 49 34.30S 136.10E
Spennymoor town England 13 54.43N 1.35W
Spenser Mts. New Zealand 50 42.15S 172.45E
Sperrin Mts. N. Ireland 14 54.49N 7.06W
Spey r. Scotland 17 57.40N 3.06W
Spey B. Scotland 17 57.42N 3.04W
Speyer W. Germany 26 49.18N 8.26E
Spiekeroog i. W. Germany 27 53.48N 7.45E
Spilsby England 13 53.10N 0.06E
Spithead str. England 8 50.45N 1.05W
Spitsbergen is. Europe 32 78.00N 17.00E
Spittal Austria 26 46.48N 13.30E
Split Yugo. 25 43.32N 16.27E
Spokane U.S.A. 52 47.40N 117.25W
Spooner U.S.A. 56 45.50N 91.53W
Spratly I. Asia 38 8.45N 111.54E
Spree r. W. Germany 26 52.32N 13.15E
Springbok R.S.A. 48 29.43S 17.55E
Springfield Ill. U.S.A. 56 39.49N 89.39W
Springfield Mass. U.S.A. 57 42.07N 72.35W
Springfield Miss. U.S.A. 53 37.11N 93.19W
Springfield Ohio U.S.A. 56 39.55N 83.48W
Springfontein R.S.A. 48 30.16S 25.42E
Springs town R.S.A. 48 26.15S 28.26E
Spungabera Moçambique 48 20.28S 32.47E
Spurn Head England 13 53.35N 0.08E
Sredne Kolymskaya U.S.S.R. 31 67.27N 153.35E
Sri Lanka Asia 37 7.30N 80.50E
Srinagar Jammu and Kashmir 36 34.08N 74.50E
Stack's Mts. Rep. of Ire. 19 52.18N 9.36W
Stadskanaal Neth. 27 53.02N 6.55E
Stadtkyll W. Germany 27 50.21N 6.32E
Staffa i. Scotland 14 56.26N 6.21W
Staffin Scotland 16 57.38N 6.13W
Stafford England 12 52.49N 2.09W
Staffordshire d. England 8 52.40N 1.57W
Staines England 7 51.26N 0.31W
Stainforth England 13 53.37N 1.01W
Stalbridge England 8 50.57N 2.22W
Stalham England 9 52.46N 1.31E
Stamford England 9 52.39N 0.29W
Stamford U.S.A. 57 41.03N 73.32W
Stamford Bridge town England 13 53.59N 0.53W
Standerton R.S.A. 48 26.57S 29.14E
Standon England 7 51.53N 0.02E
Stanford le Hope England 7 51.31N 0.26E
Stanger R.S.A. 48 29.20S 31.18E
Stanhope England 12 54.45N 2.00W
Stanley England 12 54.53N 1.42W
Stanley Falkland Is. 63 51.45S 57.56W
Stanley Hong Kong 33 22.13N 114.12E
Stanley Scotland 15 56.29N 3.28W
Stanley B. Hong Kong 33 22.13N 114.12E
Stanley Pen. Hong Kong 33 22.12N 114.13E
Stanmore England 7 51.38N 0.19W
Stanovoy Range mts. U.S.S.R. 31 56.00N 125.40E
Stanstead Abbots England 7 51.47N 0.01E
Stansted Mountfitchet England 7 51.55N 0.12E
Stapleford England 13 52.56N 1.16W
Staraya Russa U.S.S.R. 29 58.00N 31.22E
Stara Zagora Bulgaria 25 42.26N 25.37E
Stargard Poland 26 53.21N 15.01E
Start B. England 11 50.17N 3.35W
Start Pt. England 11 50.13N 3.38W
Start Pt. Scotland 17 59.17N 2.24W
Staunton England 8 51.58N 2.19W
Stavanger Norway 28 58.58N 5.45E
Staveley England 13 53.16N 1.20W
Stavelot Belgium 27 50.23N 5.54E
Staveren Neth. 27 52.53N 5.21E
Stavropol' U.S.S.R. 29 45.03N 41.59E
Stavropol Highlands U.S.S.R. 29 45.00N 42.30E
Staxton England 13 54.11N 0.26W
Steelpoort R.S.A. 48 24.48S 30.11E
Steenbergen Neth. 27 51.36N 4.19E
Steenvorde France 27 50.49N 2.35E
Steenwijk Neth. 27 52.47N 6.07E
Steep Holm i. England 8 51.20N 3.06W
Steep I. Hong Kong 33 22.16N 114.18E
Steeping r. England 13 53.06N 0.19E
Steinkjer Norway 28 64.00N 11.30E
Stellenbosch R.S.A. 48 33.56S 18.51E
Stenay France 27 49.29N 5.12E
Stepanakert U.S.S.R. 35 39.48N 46.45E
Stepney England 7 51.31N 0.04W
Sterling U.S.A. 52 40.37N 103.13W
Steubenville U.S.A. 56 40.22N 80.39W
Stevenage England 9 51.54N 0.11W
Stevenston Scotland 14 55.39N 4.45W
Stewart Canada 54 55.56N 130.01W
Stewart I. New Zealand 50 47.00S 168.00E
Stewarton Scotland 14 55.41N 4.31W
Stewartstown N. Ireland 14 54.35N 6.42W
Steyning England 9 50.54N 0.19W
Steyr Austria 26 48.04N 14.25E
Stikine r. Canada 54 56.45N 132.30W
Stikine Mts. Canada 54 59.00N 129.00W
Stilton England 9 52.29N 0.17W
Stinchar r. Scotland 14 55.06N 5.00W
Stirling Scotland 15 56.07N 3.57W
Stjördalshalsen Norway 28 63.30N 10.59E
Stock England 7 51.40N 0.26E
Stockbridge England 8 51.07N 1.30W
Stockholm Sweden 28 59.20N 18.05E
Stockport England 12 53.25N 2.11W
Stocksbridge England 13 53.30N 1.36W
Stockton U.S.A. 52 37.59N 121.20W
Stockton-on-Tees England 13 54.34N 1.20W
Stoer Scotland 16 58.12N 5.20W
Stoer, Pt. of Scotland 16 58.16N 5.23W
Stoke D'Abernon England 7 51.19N 0.22W
Stoke Newington England 7 51.34N 0.04W
Stoke-on-Trent England 12 53.01N 2.11W
Stokesley England 13 54.27N 1.12W
Stone Kent England 7 51.27N 0.17E
Stone Staffs. England 12 52.55N 2.10W
Stonecutters I. Hong Kong 33 22.19N 114.08E
Stonehaven Scotland 17 56.58N 2.13W
Stony Stratford England 8 52.04N 0.51W
Stony Tunguska r. U.S.S.R. 31 61.40N 90.00E
Stopsley England 7 51.54N 0.24W
Stora Lule r. Sweden 28 65.40N 21.48E
Stora Lulevatten l. Sweden 28 67.00N 19.30E
Storavan l. Sweden 28 65.45N 18.10E
Storby Finland 28 60.14N 19.36E
Stord i. Norway 28 59.50N 5.25E
Store Baelt str. Denmark 28 55.30N 11.00E
Stören Norway 28 63.03N 10.16E
Stornoway Scotland 16 58.12N 6.23W
Storsjön l. Sweden 28 63.10N 14.20E
Storuman Sweden 28 65.05N 17.10E
Storuman l. Sweden 28 65.14N 16.50E
Stotfold England 9 52.02N 0.13W
Stoughton England 7 51.15N 0.36W
Stour r. Dorset England 8 50.43N 1.47W
Stour r. Kent England 9 51.19N 1.22E
Stour r. Suffolk England 9 51.56N 1.03E
Stourbridge England 8 52.28N 2.08W
Stourport-on-Severn England 8 52.21N 2.16W
Stow Scotland 15 55.42N 2.52W
Stowmarket England 9 52.11N 1.00E
Stow on the Wold England 8 51.55N 1.42W
Strabane N. Ireland 18 54.50N 7.30W
Strachur Scotland 14 56.10N 5.04W
Stradbally Laois Rep. of Ire. 19 53.01N 7.09W
Stradbally Waterford Rep. of Ire. 19 52.08N 7.29W
Stralsund E. Germany 26 54.18N 13.06E
Strangford Lough N. Ireland 18 54.28N 5.35W
Stranorlar Rep. of Ire. 18 54.48N 7.48W
Stranraer Scotland 14 54.54N 5.02W
Strasbourg France 26 48.35N 7.45E
Stratford Canada 56 43.22N 81.00W
Stratford New Zealand 50 39.20S 174.18E
Stratford-upon-Avon England 8 52.12N 1.42W
Strathallan f. Scotland 15 56.14N 3.52W
Strathardle f. Scotland 15 56.42N 3.28W
Strathaven town Scotland 15 55.41N 4.05W
Strath Avon f. Scotland 17 57.21N 3.21W
Strathbogie f. Scotland 17 57.25N 2.55W
Strathclyde d. Scotland 14 55.45N 4.45W
Strathdearn f. Scotland 17 57.17N 4.00W
Strathearn f. Scotland 15 56.20N 3.45W
Strathglass f. Scotland 17 57.25N 4.38W
Strath Halladale f. Scotland 17 58.27N 3.53W
Strathmore f. Tayside Scotland 17 56.44N 2.45W
Strath More f. Highland Scotland 17 58.25N 4.38W
Strathnairn f. Scotland 17 57.23N 4.10W
Strathnaver f. Scotland 17 58.24N 4.12W
Strath of Kildonan f. Scotland 17 58.09N 3.50W
Strathpeffer town Scotland 17 57.34N 4.33W
Strathspey f. Scotland 17 57.25N 3.25W
Strath Tay f. Scotland 15 56.38N 3.41W
Strathy Pt. Scotland 17 58.35N 4.01W
Stratton England 11 50.49N 4.31W
Straumnes c. Iceland 28 66.30N 23.05W
Streatham England 7 51.26N 0.07W
Streek Head Rep. of Ire. 19 51.29N 9.43W
Street England 8 51.07N 2.43W
Strichen Scotland 17 57.35N 2.05W
Striven, Loch Scotland 14 55.57N 5.05W
Strokestown Rep. of Ire. 18 53.46N 8.08W
Stroma i. Scotland 17 58.41N 3.09W
Stromboli i. Italy 24 38.48N 15.14E
Stromeferry Scotland 16 57.21N 5.34W
Stromness Scotland 17 58.57N 3.18W
Strömö i. Faroe Is. 28 62.08N 7.00W
Strömstad Sweden 28 58.56N 11.11E
Ströms Vattudal l. Sweden 28 63.55N 15.30E
Stronsay i. Scotland 17 59.07N 2.36W
Stronsay Firth est. Scotland 17 59.05N 2.45W
Strontian Scotland 14 56.42N 5.33W
Strood England 7 51.24N 0.28E
Stroud England 8 51.44N 2.12W
Struma r. Greece 25 40.45N 23.51E
Strumble Head Wales 10 52.03N 5.05W
Strumica Yugo. 25 41.26N 22.39E
Stryn Norway 28 61.55N 6.47E
Stryy U.S.S.R. 29 49.16N 23.51E
Stura r. Italy 22 44.53N 8.38E
Sturgeon Falls town Canada 56 46.22N 79.57W
Sturminster Newton England 8 50.56N 2.18W
Stuttgart W. Germany 26 48.47N 9.12E
Styr r. U.S.S.R. 29 52.07N 26.35E
Suakin Sudan 45 19.04N 37.22E
Subotica Yugo. 25 46.04N 19.41E
Suchan r. U.S.S.R. 42 42.53N 132.54E
Suchow China 41 34.17N 117.18E
Suck r. Rep. of Ire. 18 53.16N 8.04W
Sucre Bolivia 61 19.05S 65.15W
Sudan Africa 45 14.00N 30.00E
Sudbury Canada 56 46.30N 81.01W
Sudbury England 9 52.03N 0.45E
Sudd f. Sudan 45 7.50N 30.00E
Sudeten Mts. Czech./Poland 26 50.30N 16.30E
Sudirman Mts. Asia 39 3.50S 136.30E
Suez Egypt 34 29.59N 32.33E
Suez, G. of Egypt 34 28.48N 33.00E
Suez Canal Egypt 34 30.40N 32.20E
Suffolk d. England 9 52.16N 1.00E
Sugar Hill Rep. of Ire. 19 52.26N 9.11W
Sugluk Canada 55 62.10N 75.40W
Sui Lam Hong Kong 33 22.22N 114.00E
Sui Lang Shui Hong Kong 33 22.22N 113.56E
Sui Lek Yuen Hong Kong 33 22.22N 114.12E
Suir r. Rep. of Ire. 19 52.17N 7.00W
Sukabumi Indonesia 38 6.55S 106.50E
Sukadana Indonesia 38 1.15S 110.00E
Sukaradja Indonesia 38 2.23S 110.35E
Sukhinichi U.S.S.R. 29 54.07N 35.21E
Sukhona r. U.S.S.R. 6 61.30N 46.28E
Sukhumi U.S.S.R. 29 43.01N 41.01E
Sukkertoppen Greenland 55 65.40N 53.00W
Sukkur Pakistan 36 27.42N 68.54E
Sulaimaniya Iraq 35 35.32N 45.27E
Sulaiman Range mts. Pakistan 36 30.50N 70.20E
Sulaimiya Saudi Arabia 35 24.10N 47.20E
Sula Is. Indonesia 39 1.50S 125.10E
Sulawesi d. Indonesia 39 2.00S 120.30E
Sulina Romania 25 45.08N 29.40E
Sullana Peru 62 4.52S 80.39W
Sullane r. Rep. of Ire. 19 51.53N 8.56W
Sullom Voe b. Scotland 16 60.29N 1.16W
Sulmona Italy 24 42.04N 13.57E
Sultanabad Iran 35 36.25N 58.02E
Sulu Archipelago Phil. 39 5.30N 121.00E
Sulu Sea Pacific Oc. 39 8.00N 120.00E
Sumatra i. Indonesia 38 2.00S 102.00E
Sumba i. Indonesia 38 9.30S 119.55E
Sumbar r. U.S.S.R. 35 38.00N 55.20E
Sumbawa i. Indonesia 38 8.45S 117.50E
Sumbawanga Tanzania 47 7.58S 31.36E
Sumburgh Head Scotland 16 59.51N 1.16W
Sumgait U.S.S.R. 35 40.35N 49.38E
Sumisu jima i. Japan 42 31.29N 140.02E
Summan f. Saudi Arabia 35 27.00N 47.00E
Summer Is. Scotland 16 58.01N 5.26W
Sumy U.S.S.R. 29 50.55N 34.49E
Sunagawa Japan 42 43.30N 141.55E
Sunart f. Scotland 16 56.44N 5.35W
Sunart, Loch Scotland 16 56.43N 5.45W
Sunbury England 7 51.24N 0.25W
Sunbury U.S.A. 57 40.52N 76.47W
Sundarbans f. India/Bangla. 37 22.00N 89.00E
Sunda Str. Indonesia 38 6.00S 105.50E
Sundays r. R.S.A. 48 33.49S 25.46E
Sunderland England 15 54.55N 1.22W
Sundsvall Sweden 28 62.22N 17.20E
Sungari r. China 41 47.46N 132.30E
Sungurlu Turkey 34 40.10N 34.23E
Sunninghill town England 7 51.24N 0.39W
Sunset Peak Hong Kong 33 22.15N 113.57E
Sunyani Ghana 44 7.22N 2.18W
Suomussalmi Finland 28 64.52N 29.10E
Suo nada str. Japan 42 33.45N 131.30E
Suonenjoki Finland 28 62.40N 27.06E
Superior U.S.A. 56 46.42N 92.05W
Superior, L. N. America 56 48.00N 88.00W
Süphan Dağlari mtn. Turkey 34 38.55N 42.55E
Sur Oman 35 22.23N 59.32E
Sura U.S.S.R. 29 53.52N 45.45E
Sura r. U.S.S.R. 29 56.13N 46.00E
Surabaya Indonesia 38 7.14S 112.45E
Surakarta Indonesia 38 7.32S 110.50E
Surat India 36 21.10N 72.54E
Surat Thani Thailand 37 9.03N 99.28E
Surbiton England 7 51.24N 0.19W
Sûre r. Lux. 27 49.43N 6.31E
Surigao Phil. 39 9.47N 125.29E
Surin Thailand 37 14.50N 103.34E
Surinam S. America 62 4.30N 56.00W
Surrey d. England 9 51.16N 0.30W
Surrey Hill England 7 51.23N 0.43W
Surtsey i. Iceland 28 63.18N 20.37W
Susquehanna r. U.S.A. 57 39.33N 76.05W
Sutherland R.S.A. 48 32.24S 20.40E
Sutlej r. Pakistan 36 29.26N 71.09E
Sutton G.L. England 7 51.22N 0.12W
Sutton Surrey England 7 51.12N 0.26W
Sutton Bridge England 13 52.46N 0.12E
Sutton Coldfield England 8 52.33N 1.50W
Sutton in Ashfield England 13 53.08N 1.16W
Sutton on Sea England 13 53.18N 0.18E
Suwanee r. U.S.A. 58 29.15N 82.50W
Suzu misaki c. Japan 42 37.30N 137.21E
Svartisen mtn. Norway 28 66.30N 14.00E
Sveg Sweden 28 62.02N 14.20E
Svendborg Denmark 28 55.04N 10.38E
Sverdlovsk U.S.S.R. 30 56.52N 60.35E
Svetogorsk U.S.S.R. 28 61.07N 28.50E
Svishtov Bulgaria 25 43.36N 25.23E
Svobodnyy U.S.S.R. 41 51.24N 128.05E
Svolvaer Norway 28 68.15N 14.40E
Swabian Jura mts. W. Germany 26 48.20N 9.20E
Swadlincote England 13 52.47N 1.34W
Swaffham England 9 52.38N 0.42E
Swakop r. S.W. Africa 48 22.38S 14.30E
Swakopmund S.W. Africa 48 22.40S 14.34E
Swale r. England 13 54.05N 1.20W
Swanage England 8 50.36N 1.59W

Swanley England **7** 51.24N 0.12E
Swanlinbar Rep. of Ire. **18** 54.12N 7.44W
Swan River *town* Canada **52** 52.06N 101.17W
Swanscombe England **7** 51.26N 0.19E
Swansea Wales **11** 51.37N 3.57W
Swansea B. Wales **11** 51.33N 3.50W
Swarbacks Minn *str.* Scotland **16** 60.22N 1.21W
Swatow China **38** 23.23N 116.39E
Swaziland Africa **48** 26.30S 32.00E
Sweden Europe **28** 63.00N 16.00E
Sweetwater U.S.A. **52** 32.37N 100.25W
Swidnica Poland **26** 50.51N 16.29E
Swift Current *town* Canada **52** 50.17N 107.49W
Swilly *r.* Rep. of Ire. **18** 54.57N 7.42W
Swilly, Lough Rep. of Ire. **18** 55.10N 7.32W
Swindon England **8** 51.33N 1.47W
Swinford Rep. of Ire. **18** 53.56N 8.57W
Swinoujscie Poland **26** 53.55N 14.18E
Switzerland Europe **26** 47.00N 8.15E
Swords Rep. of Ire. **18** 53.27N 6.15W
Syderö *i.* Faroe Is. **28** 61.30N 6.50W
Sydney Australia **49** 33.55S 151.10E
Sydney Canada **55** 46.10N 60.10W
Syktyvkar U.S.S.R. **30** 61.42N 50.45E
Sylhet Bangla. **37** 24.53N 91.51E
Sylt *i.* W. Germany **26** 54.50N 8.20E
Syracuse U.S.A. **57** 43.03N 76.10W
Syr Darya *r.* U.S.S.R. **30** 46.00N 61.12E
Syria Asia **34** 35.00N 38.00E
Syrian Desert Asia **34** 32.00N 39.00E
Syzran U.S.S.R. **29** 53.10N 48.29E
Szczecin Poland **26** 53.25N 14.32E
Szczecinek Poland **26** 53.42N 16.41E
Szechwan *d.* China **40** 30.30N 103.00E
Szeged Hungary **25** 46.16N 20.08E
Szekszárd Hungary **25** 46.22N 18.44E
Szemao China **37** 22.50N 101.00E
Szenan China **41** 27.56N 108.22E
Szombathely Hungary **29** 47.12N 16.38E

T

Tabarka Tunisia **24** 36.56N 8.43E
Tabas Khorāsān Iran **35** 32.48N 60.14E
Tabas Khorāsān Iran **35** 33.36N 56.55E
Tabasco *d.* Mexico **58** 18.30N 93.00W
Table B. R.S.A. **48** 33.30S 18.05E
Tabór Czech. **26** 49.25N 14.41E
Tabora Tanzania **47** 5.02S 32.50E
Tabora *d.* Tanzania **47** 5.30S 32.00E
Tabriz Iran **35** 38.05N 46.18E
Tacloban Phil. **39** 11.15N 124.59E
Tacoma U.S.A. **52** 47.16N 122.30W
Taconic Mts. U.S.A. **57** 42.00N 73.45W
Tacuarembó Uruguay **61** 31.42S 56.00W
Tadcaster England **13** 53.53N 1.16W
Tademait Plateau Algeria **44** 28.45N 2.10E
Tadoussac Canada **57** 48.09N 69.43W
Tadzhikistan Soviet Socialist Republic *d.* U.S.S.R. **40** 39.00N 70.30E
Taegu S. Korea **41** 35.52N 128.36E
Taejon S. Korea **41** 36.20N 127.26E
Tafersit Morocco **23** 35.01N 3.33W
Taganrog U.S.S.R. **29** 47.14N 38.55E
Taganrog, G. of U.S.S.R. **29** 47.00N 38.30E
Taghmon Rep. of Ire. **19** 52.20N 6.40W
Tagus *r.* Portugal **23** 39.00N 8.57W
Tahat, Mt. Algeria **44** 23.20N 5.40E
Taichow China **41** 32.30N 119.50E
Taichung Taiwan **41** 24.09N 120.40E
Tai Hang Hong Kong **33** 22.16N 114.11E
Taihape New Zealand **50** 39.40S 175.48E
Tai Lam Camp *town* Hong Kong **33** 22.22N 113.59E
Tai Lam Chung Resr. Hong Kong **33** 22.22N 114.01E
Tai Lam Chung Wu Uk Hong Kong **33** 22.21N 114.01E
Tai Lin Pai Hong Kong **33** 22.21N 114.07E
Tai Long Hong Kong **33** 22.25N 114.22E
Tai Long B. Hong Kong **33** 22.24N 114.23E
Taima Saudi Arabia **34** 27.37N 38.30E
Tai Miu Wan *b.* Hong Kong **33** 22.15N 114.17E
Tai Mong Tsai Hong Kong **33** 22.23N 114.18E
Tai Mo Shan *mtn.* Hong Kong **33** 22.24N 114.07E
Tai Mun Shan *mtn.* Hong Kong **33** 22.25N 114.21E
Tain Scotland **17** 57.48N 4.04W
Tainan Taiwan **39** 23.01N 120.14E
Taipei Taiwan **41** 25.05N 121.32E
Taiping Malaysia **38** 4.54N 100.42E
Tai Po Tsai Hong Kong **33** 22.20N 114.15E
Tai Shui Hang Hong Kong **33** 22.24N 114.13E
Tai Tam B. Hong Kong **33** 22.13N 114.13E
Tai Tam Tuk Resr. Hong Kong **33** 22.15N 114.13E
Tai Tau Chau *i.* Hong Kong **33** 22.22N 114.19E
Tai Tong Hong Kong **33** 22.25N 114.01E
Taivalkoski Finland **28** 65.35N 28.20E
Tai Wai Hong Kong **33** 22.22N 114.10E
Taiwan Asia **41** 23.30N 121.00E
Tai Wan Tau Hong Kong **33** 22.17N 114.17E
Tai Wong Ha Hong Kong **33** 22.21N 114.06E
Tai Wo Ping Hong Kong **33** 22.20N 114.09E
Taiyuan China **41** 37.50N 112.30E
Taizz Yemen **45** 13.35N 44.02E
Tajan Indonesia **38** 0.02S 110.05E
Tajrish Iran **35** 35.48N 51.20E
Tajuna *r.* Spain **23** 40.10N 3.35W
Tak Thailand **37** 16.47N 99.10E
Takamatsu Japan **42** 34.28N 134.05E
Takaoka Japan **42** 36.47N 137.00E
Takeley England **7** 51.52N 0.15E
Takestan Iran **35** 36.02N 49.40E
Takht-i-Suleiman *mtn.* Iran **35** 36.23N 50.59E
Takla Makan *des.* China **40** 38.10N 82.00E
Talasskiy Ala Tau *mts.* U.S.S.R. **40** 42.20N 73.20E
Talaud Is. Indonesia **39** 4.20N 126.50E
Talavera de la Reina Spain **23** 39.58N 4.50W
Talca Chile **63** 35.28S 71.40W
Talcahuano Chile **63** 36.40S 73.10W
Taldom U.S.S.R. **29** 56.49N 37.30E
Talgarth Wales **10** 51.59N 3.15W
Taliabu *i.* Indonesia **39** 1.50S 124.55E
Talkeetna U.S.A. **54** 62.20N 150.09W
Tallahassee U.S.A. **53** 30.28N 84.19W
Tallinn U.S.S.R. **28** 59.22N 24.48E
Tallow Rep. of Ire. **19** 52.06N 8.01W
Talsi U.S.S.R. **29** 57.18N 22.39E
Tamale Ghana **44** 9.26N 0.49W
Tamanrasset Algeria **44** 22.50N 5.31E
Tamar *r.* England **11** 50.28N 4.13W
Tamatave Malagasy Rep. **43** 18.10S 49.23E
Tamaulipas *d.* Mexico **58** 24.00N 98.20W
Tambacounda Senegal **44** 13.45N 13.40W
Tambohorano Malagasy Rep. **47** 17.40S 43.59E
Tambov U.S.S.R. **29** 52.44N 41.28E
Tambre *r.* Spain **23** 42.50N 8.55W
Tamega *r.* Portugal **23** 41.04N 8.17W
Tamil Nadu *d.* India **37** 11.15N 79.00E
Tampa U.S.A. **53** 27.58N 82.38W
Tampa B. U.S.A. **58** 27.48N 82.15W
Tampere Finland **28** 61.32N 23.45E
Tampico Mexico **58** 22.18N 97.52W
Tamsag Bulag Mongolia **41** 47.10N 117.21E
Tamworth England **12** 52.38N 1.42W
Tana *r.* Kenya **47** 2.32S 40.32E
Tana Norway **28** 70.26N 28.14E
Tana *r.* Norway **28** 69.45N 28.15E
Tana, L. Ethiopia **45** 12.00N 37.20E
Tanacross U.S.A. **54** 63.12N 143.30W
Tanana U.S.A. **54** 65.11N 152.10W
Tananarive Malagasy Rep. **43** 18.52S 47.30E
Tanaro *r.* Italy **24** 45.01N 8.46E
Tanat *r.* Wales **10** 52.46N 3.07W
Tanderagee N. Ireland **18** 54.22N 6.27W
Tandil Argentina **61** 37.18S 59.10W
Tandjungpandan Indonesia **38** 2.44S 107.36E
Tandjungredeb Indonesia **38** 2.09N 117.29E
Tanega shima *i.* Japan **42** 30.32N 131.00E
Tanga Tanzania **47** 5.07S 39.05E
Tanga *d.* Tanzania **47** 5.20S 38.30E
Tanganyika, L. Africa **47** 6.00S 29.30E
Tanger *see* Tangier Morocco **23**
Tangier Morocco **23** 35.48N 5.45W
Tanglha Range *mts.* China **40** 32.40N 92.30E
Tang Lung Chau *i.* Hong Kong **33** 22.20N 114.03E
Tangra Yum *l.* China **37** 31.00N 86.30E
Tangshan China **41** 39.37N 118.05E
Tanimbar Is. Indonesia **39** 7.50S 131.30E
Tanjung Datu *c.* Malaysia **38** 2.00N 109.30E
Tanjung Puting *c.* Indonesia **38** 3.35S 111.52E
Tanjung Selatan *c.* Indonesia **38** 4.20S 114.45E
Tannu Ola Range *mts.* U.S.S.R. **31** 51.00N 93.30E
Tanta Egypt **34** 30.48N 31.00E
Tanzania Africa **47** 5.00S 35.00E
Taonan China **41** 45.25N 122.46E
Tapachula Mexico **58** 14.54N 92.15W
Tapai Shan *mtn.* China **37** 34.00N 107.40E
Tapajós *r.* Brazil **62** 2.40S 55.30W
Tapti *r.* India **36** 21.05N 72.45E
Taquari *r.* Brazil **61** 19.00S 57.22W
Tara *r.* U.S.S.R. **30** 56.30N 74.40E
Tara *r.* Yugo. **25** 43.23N 18.47E
Tarakan Indonesia **38** 3.20N 117.38E
Tarancón Spain **23** 40.01N 3.01W
Taransay *i.* Scotland **16** 57.53N 7.03W
Taranto Italy **25** 40.28N 17.14E
Taranto, G. of Italy **25** 40.00N 17.20E
Tararua Range *mts.* New Zealand **50** 40.45S 175.30E
Tarbagatay Range *mts.* U.S.S.R. **40** 47.00N 83.00E
Tarbat Ness *c.* Scotland **17** 57.52N 3.46W
Tarbert Rep. of Ire. **19** 52.34N 9.24W
Tarbert Strath. Scotland **14** 55.51N 5.25W
Tarbert W. Isles Scotland **16** 57.54N 6.49W
Tarbert, Loch Scotland **14** 55.48N 5.31W
Tarbes France **22** 43.14N 0.05E
Tarbolton Scotland **14** 55.31N 4.29W
Tardoire *r.* France **22** 45.57N 1.00W
Taree Australia **49** 31.54S 152.26E
Tarfa, Wadi *r.* Egypt **34** 28.36N 30.50E
Tarifa Spain **23** 36.01N 5.36W
Tarija Bolivia **61** 21.33S 64.45W
Tarija *d.* Bolivia **61** 21.30S 64.00W
Tarim *r.* China **40** 41.00N 83.30E
Tarim Basin *f.* Asia **3** 40.00N 83.00E
Tarlac Phil. **39** 15.29N 120.35E
Tarland Scotland **17** 57.08N 2.52W
Tarleton England **12** 53.41N 2.50W
Tarn *r.* France **22** 44.15N 1.15E
Tarnow Poland **29** 50.01N 20.59E
Tarporley England **12** 53.10N 2.42W
Tarragona Spain **23** 41.07N 1.15E
Tarrasa Spain **23** 41.34N 2.00E
Tarsus Turkey **34** 36.52N 34.52E
Tartary, G. of U.S.S.R. **31** 47.40N 141.00E
Tartu U.S.S.R. **28** 58.20N 26.44E
Tashkent U.S.S.R. **40** 41.16N 69.13E
Tasman B. New Zealand **50** 41.00S 173.15E
Tasmania *d.* Australia **49** 42.30S 147.00E
Tasman Mts. New Zealand **50** 41.00S 172.40E
Tasman Sea Pacific Oc. **3** 38.00S 163.00E
Tatarsk U.S.S.R. **30** 55.14N 76.00E
Tates Cairn *mtn.* Hong Kong **33** 22.21N 114.13E
Tathong Channel Hong Kong **33** 22.14N 114.16E
Tatnam, C. Canada **55** 57.00N 91.00W
Tatsaitan China **40** 37.44N 95.08E
Tatsfield England **7** 51.18N 0.02E
Tatu *r.* China **37** 28.47N 104.40E
Tatvan Turkey **34** 38.31N 42.15E
Taubaté Brazil **61** 23.00S 45.36W
Taumarunui New Zealand **50** 38.53S 175.16E
Taung R.S.A. **48** 27.32S 24.48E
Taung-gyi Burma **37** 20.49N 97.01E
Taunton England **11** 51.01N 3.07W
Taunus *mts.* W. Germany **26** 50.07N 7.48E
Taupo New Zealand **50** 38.42S 176.06E
Taupo, L. New Zealand **50** 38.45S 175.30E
Tauranga New Zealand **50** 37.42S 176.11E
Taurus Mts. Turkey **34** 37.15N 34.15E
Taveta Kenya **47** 3.23S 37.42E
Tavira Portugal **23** 37.07N 7.39W
Tavistock England **11** 50.33N 4.09W
Tavoy Burma **37** 14.07N 98.18E
Tavy *r.* England **11** 50.27N 4.10W
Taw *r.* England **11** 51.05N 4.05W
Tawau Malaysia **38** 4.16N 117.54E
Tawe *r.* Wales **11** 51.38N 3.56W
Tay *r.* Scotland **15** 56.21N 3.18W
Tay, Loch Scotland **14** 56.32N 4.08W
Taylor, Mt. U.S.A. **52** 35.14N 107.36W
Taymyr, L. U.S.S.R. **31** 74.20N 101.00E
Taymyr Pen. U.S.S.R. **31** 75.30N 99.00E
Taynuilt Scotland **14** 56.26N 5.14W
Tayport Scotland **15** 56.27N 2.53W
Tayshet U.S.S.R. **31** 55.56N 98.01E
Tayside *d.* Scotland **15** 56.35N 3.28W
Taytay Phil. **38** 10.47N 119.32E
Taz *r.* U.S.S.R. **30** 67.30N 78.50E
Tbilisi U.S.S.R. **35** 41.43N 44.48E
Tchibanga Gabon **46** 2.52S 11.07E
Te Anau, L. New Zealand **50** 45.10S 167.15E
Te Araroa New Zealand **50** 37.38S 178.25E
Te Awamutu New Zealand **50** 38.00S 175.20E
Tebessa Algeria **24** 35.22N 8.08E
Tebuk Saudi Arabia **34** 28.25N 36.35E
Tecuci Romania **25** 45.49N 27.27E
Teddington England **7** 51.25N 0.20W
Tees *r.* England **13** 54.35N 1.11W
Tees B. England **13** 54.40N 1.07W
Teesdale *f.* England **12** 54.38N 2.08W
Tegucigalpa Honduras **58** 14.05N 87.14W
Tehran Iran **35** 35.40N 51.26E
Tehtsin China **37** 28.45N 98.58E
Tehuacán Mexico **58** 18.30N 97.26W
Tehuantepec Mexico **58** 16.21N 95.13W
Tehuantepec, G. of Mexico **58** 16.00N 95.00W
Tehuantepec, Isthmus of Mexico **58** 17.00N 94.00W
Teifi *r.* Wales **10** 52.05N 4.41W
Teign *r.* England **11** 50.32N 3.46W
Teignmouth England **11** 50.33N 3.30W
Teith *r.* Scotland **15** 56.09N 4.00W
Teixeira de Sousa Angola **46** 10.41S 22.09E
Tekapo, L. New Zealand **50** 43.35S 170.30E
Tekirdağ Turkey **25** 40.59N 27.30E
Te Kuiti New Zealand **50** 38.20S 175.10E
Tela Honduras **58** 15.56N 87.25W
Telavi U.S.S.R. **35** 41.56N 45.30E
Tel Aviv-Jaffa Israel **34** 32.05N 34.46E
Tele *r.* Zaïre **46** 2.48N 24.00E
Telford England **8** 52.42N 2.30W
Telgte W. Germany **27** 51.59N 7.46E
Tel Kotchek Syria **34** 36.48N 42.04E
Tell Atlas *mts.* Algeria **44** 36.10N 4.00E
Telok Anson Malaysia **38** 4.00N 101.00E
Teluk Berau *b.* Asia **39** 2.20S 133.00E
Telukbetung Indonesia **38** 5.28S 105.16E
Teluk Irian *b.* Asia **39** 2.30S 135.20E
Tembo Aluma Angola **46** 7.42S 17.15E
Teme *r.* England **8** 52.10N 2.13W
Tempio Italy **24** 40.54N 9.06E
Temple U.S.A. **53** 31.06N 97.22W
Temple Ewell England **9** 51.09N 1.16E
Temple Hill Hong Kong **33** 22.21N 114.11E
Templemore Rep. of Ire. **19** 52.48N 7.51W
Temuco Chile **63** 38.45S 72.40W
Tenasserim Burma **38** 12.05N 99.00E
Tenasserim *d.* Burma **37** 13.00N 99.00E
Tenbury Wells England **8** 52.18N 2.35W
Tenby Wales **11** 51.40N 4.42W
Ten Degree Channel Indian Oc. **38** 10.00N 92.30E
Tenerife *i.* Africa **44** 28.10N 16.30W
Tengchung China **37** 25.02N 98.28E
Tenghsien China **41** 35.10N 117.14E
Tengiz, L. U.S.S.R. **30** 50.30N 69.00E
Tenke Zaïre **46** 10.34S 26.07E
Tennant Creek *town* Australia **49** 19.31S 134.15E
Tennessee *d.* U.S.A. **53** 36.00N 86.00W
Tennessee *r.* U.S.A. **53** 37.10N 88.25W
Tenterden England **9** 51.04N 0.42E
Teófilo Otoni Brazil **63** 17.52S 41.31W
Ter *r.* England **7** 51.45N 0.36E
Ter *r.* Spain **23** 42.02N 3.10E
Tera *r.* Portugal **23** 38.55N 8.01W
Téramo Italy **24** 42.40N 13.43E
Teresina Brazil **62** 4.50S 42.50W
Termez U.S.S.R. **30** 37.15N 67.15E
Termini Italy **24** 37.59N 13.42E
Terminos Lagoon Mexico **58** 18.30N 91.30W
Termoli Italy **24** 41.58N 14.59E
Ternate Indonesia **39** 0.48N 127.23E
Terneuzen Neth. **27** 51.20N 3.50E
Terni Italy **24** 42.34N 12.44E
Ternopol U.S.S.R. **29** 49.35N 25.39E
Terre Haute U.S.A. **56** 39.27N 87.24W
Terschelling *i.* Neth. **27** 53.25N 5.25E
Teruel Spain **23** 40.21N 1.06W
Teslin *r.* Canada **54** 62.00N 135.00W
Test *r.* England **8** 50.55N 1.29W
Tet *r.* France **22** 42.43N 3.00E
Tetbury England **8** 51.37N 2.09W
Tete Moçambique **47** 16.10S 33.30E
Tete *d.* Moçambique **47** 15.30S 33.00E
Teterev *r.* U.S.S.R. **29** 51.03N 30.30E
Tetney England **13** 53.30N 0.01W
Tetuan Morocco **23** 35.34N 5.22W
Tetyukhe Pristan U.S.S.R. **42** 44.17N 135.52E
Teuco *r.* Argentina **61** 25.37S 60.10W
Teviot *r.* Scotland **15** 55.36N 2.27W
Teviotdale *f.* Scotland **15** 55.26N 2.46W
Teviothead Scotland **15** 55.20N 2.56W
Tewkesbury England **8** 51.59N 2.09W
Texarkana U.S.A. **53** 33.28N 94.02W
Texas *d.* U.S.A. **52** 32.00N 100.00W
Texel *i.* Neth. **27** 53.05N 4.47E
Texoma, L. U.S.A. **53** 34.00N 96.40W
Tezpur India **37** 26.38N 92.49E
Thabana Ntlenyana *mtn.* Lesotho **48** 29.30S 29.10E
Thabazimbi R.S.A. **48** 24.41S 27.21E
Thailand Asia **37** 16.00N 102.00E
Thakhek Laos **37** 17.25N 104.45E
Thala Tunisia **24** 35.35N 8.38E
Thale Luang *l.* Thailand **38** 7.30N 100.20E
Thame England **8** 51.44N 0.58W
Thame *r.* England **8** 51.38N 1.10W
Thames *r.* Canada **56** 42.20N 82.25W
Thames *r.* England **7** 51.30N 0.05E
Thames New Zealand **50** 37.08S 175.35E
Thames Haven England **7** 51.31N 0.31E
Thana India **36** 19.14N 73.02E
Thanh Hoa N. Vietnam **38** 19.50N 105.48E
Thar Desert India **36** 28.00N 72.00E
Tharrawaddy Burma **40** 17.37N 95.48E
Tharthar, Wadi *r.* Iraq **34** 34.18N 43.07E
Tharthar Basin *f.* Iraq **34** 33.56N 43.16E
Thásos *i.* Greece **25** 40.40N 24.39E
Thaton Burma **37** 17.00N 97.39E
Thaungdut Burma **37** 24.26N 94.45E
Thaxted England **9** 51.57N 0.20E
Thayetmyo Burma **37** 19.20N 95.18E
The Aird *f.* Scotland **17** 57.26N 4.23W
Thebes *ruins* Egypt **34** 25.41N 32.40E
The Brothers *is.* Hong Kong **33** 22.20N 113.58E
The Buck *mtn.* Scotland **17** 57.18N 2.59W
The Cherokees, L. O' U.S.A. **53** 36.45N 94.50W
The Cheviot *mtn.* England **15** 55.29N 2.10W
The Cheviot Hills England/Scotland **15** 55.22N 2.24W
The Everglades *f.* U.S.A. **53** 26.00N 80.30W
The Fens *f.* England **9** 52.32N 0.13E
The Glenkens *f.* Scotland **14** 55.10N 4.13W
The Grenadines *is.* St. Vincent **59** 13.00N 61.20W
The Hague Neth. **27** 52.05N 4.16E
The Hebrides, Sea of Scotland **16** 57.05N 7.05W
The Hunch Backs *mts.* Hong Kong **33** 22.25N 114.15E
The Little Minch *str.* Scotland **16** 57.40N 6.45W
Thelon *r.* Canada **55** 64.23N 96.15W
The Long Mynd *hill* England **8** 52.33N 2.50W
The Machers *f.* Scotland **14** 54.45N 4.28W
The Marsh *f.* England **13** 52.50N 0.10E
The Minch *str.* Scotland **16** 58.10N 5.50W
The Mumbles Wales **11** 51.34N 4.00W
The Naze *c.* England **9** 51.53N 1.17E
The Needles *c.* England **8** 50.39N 1.35W
The North Sd. Scotland **17** 59.18N 2.45W
Theodore Roosevelt L. U.S.A. **52** 33.30N 111.10W
The Ox Mts. Rep. of Ire. **18** 54.06N 8.52W
The Paps *mts.* Rep. of Ire. **19** 52.01N 9.14W
The Pas Canada **55** 53.50N 101.15W
The Pennines *hills* England **12** 55.40N 2.20W
The Potteries *f.* England **12** 53.00N 2.10W
The Rhinns *f.* Scotland **14** 54.50N 5.02W
The Six Towns *town* N. Ireland **14** 54.45N 6.53W
The Skerries *is.* Wales **10** 53.27N 4.35W
The Solent *str.* England **8** 50.45N 1.20W
The Solent *str.* U.K. **20** 50.45N 1.20W
Thessaloniki Greece **25** 40.38N 22.56E
Thessaloniki, G. of Med. Sea **25** 40.10N 23.00E
The Storr *mtn.* Scotland **16** 57.30N 6.11W
The Swale *str.* England **9** 51.22N 0.58E
Thetford England **9** 52.25N 0.44E
Thetford Mines *town* Canada **57** 46.06N 71.18W
The Trossachs *f.* Scotland **14** 56.15N 4.25W
The Twelve Pins *mts.* Rep. of Ire. **18** 53.30N 9.49W
The Wash *b.* England **13** 52.55N 0.15E
The Weald *f.* England **9** 51.05N 0.20E
The Woods, L. of N. America **53** 49.46N 94.30W
The Wrekin *hill* England **8** 52.40N 2.33W
Theydon Bois England **7** 51.40N 0.05E
Thiers France **22** 45.51N 3.33E
Thimphu Bhutan **37** 27.29N 89.40E
Thionville France **26** 49.22N 6.11E
Thíra *i.* Greece **25** 36.24N 25.27E
Thirsk England **13** 54.15N 1.20W
Thisted Denmark **28** 56.58N 8.42E
Thitu Is. Asia **38** 10.50N 114.20E
Thjórsá *r.* Iceland **28** 63.53N 20.38W
Thok-Jalung China **37** 32.26N 81.37E
Tholen *i.* Neth. **27** 51.34N 4.07E
Thomastown Rep. of Ire. **19** 52.32N 7.08W
Thomasville U.S.A. **53** 30.50N 83.59W
Thomson's Falls *town* Kenya **47** 0.04N 36.22E
Thornaby-on-Tees England **13** 54.34N 1.18W
Thornbury England **8** 51.36N 2.31W
Thorne England **13** 53.30N 0.56W
Thorney England **9** 52.37N 0.08W
Thornhill Scotland **15** 55.15N 3.46W
Thornton England **12** 53.53N 3.00W
Thornwood Common *town* England **7** 51.43N 0.08E
Thorpe England **7** 51.25N 0.31W
Thorpe-le-Soken England **9** 51.50N 1.11E
Thorshavn Faroe Is. **28** 62.02N 6.47W
Thouars France **22** 46.59N 0.13W
Thrapston England **9** 52.24N 0.32W

Three Fathoms Cove *b.* Hong Kong **33** 22.25N 114.16E
Thrushel *r.* England **11** 50.38N 4.19W
Thuin Belgium **27** 50.21N 4.20E
Thule Greenland **55** 77.40N 69.00W
Thun Switz. **26** 46.46N 7.38E
Thunder Bay *town* Canada **56** 48.25N 89.14W
Thuringian Forest *f.* E. Germany **26** 50.40N 10.50E
Thurles Rep. of Ire. **19** 52.41N 7.50W
Thurnscoe England **13** 53.31N 1.19W
Thursby England **15** 54.40N 3.03W
Thursday I. Australia **39** 10.45S 142.00E
Thurso Scotland **17** 58.35N 3.32W
Thurso *r.* Scotland **17** 58.35N 3.32W
Tiaret Algeria **23** 35.20N 1.20E
Tibati Cameroon **44** 6.25N 12.33E
Tiber *r.* Italy **24** 41.45N 12.16E
Tiberias, L. Israel **34** 32.49N 35.36E
Tibesti Mts. Chad **44** 21.00N 17.30E
Tibet *d.* China **37** 32.20N 86.00E
Tibetan Plateau *f.* China **37** 34.00N 84.30E
Tiburon I. Mexico **52** 29.00N 112.25W
Ticehurst England **9** 51.02N 0.23E
Ticino *r.* Italy **22** 45.09N 9.12E
Tickhill England **13** 53.25N 1.08W
Tide Cove *b.* Hong Kong **33** 22.23N 114.12E
Tidjikja Mauritania **44** 18.29N 11.31W
Tiel Neth. **27** 51.53N 5.26E
Tielt Belgium **27** 51.00N 3.20E
Tien Shan *mts.* Asia **40** 42.00N 80.30E
Tienshui China **40** 34.25N 105.58E
Tientsin China **41** 39.08N 117.12E
Tierra Blanca Mexico **58** 18.28N 96.12W
Tierra del Fuego *i.* S. America **63** 54.00S 68.30W
Tiétar *r.* Spain **23** 39.50N 6.00W
Tietê *r.* Brazil **61** 20.43S 51.30W
Tighnabruaich Scotland **14** 55.56N 5.14W
Tigris *r.* Asia **35** 31.00N 47.27E
Tihama *f.* Saudi Arabia **45** 20.30N 40.30E
Tihwa China **40** 43.43N 87.38E
Tijuana Mexico **52** 32.29N 117.10W
Tikhoretsk U.S.S.R. **29** 45.52N 40.07E
Tikhvin U.S.S.R. **29** 59.35N 33.29E
Tiko Cameroon **46** 4.09N 9.19E
Tiksi U.S.S.R. **31** 71.40N 128.45E
Tilburg Neth. **27** 51.34N 5.05E
Tilbury England **7** 51.28N 0.23E
Till *r.* England **15** 55.41N 2.12W
Tillicoultry Scotland **15** 56.09N 3.45W
Tilt *r.* Scotland **17** 56.46N 3.50W
Timagami L. Canada **56** 46.55N 80.03W
Timaru New Zealand **50** 44.23S 171.41E
Timbuktu Mali **44** 16.49N 2.59W
Timişoara Romania **25** 45.47N 21.15E
Timişul *r.* Yugo. **25** 44.49N 20.28E
Timmins Canada **56** 48.30N 81.20W
Timok *r.* Yugo. **25** 44.13N 22.40E
Timoleague Rep. of Ire. **19** 51.38N 8.46W
Timor *i.* Austa. **39** 9.30S 125.00E
Timor Sea Austa. **49** 13.00S 122.00E
Tinahely Rep. of Ire. **19** 52.48N 6.19W
Tin Chung Chau *i.* Hong Kong **33** 22.20N 114.19E
Tin Fu Tsai Hong Kong **33** 22.23N 114.03E
Ting Kau Hong Kong **33** 22.22N 114.04E
Tinglev Denmark **26** 54.57N 9.15E
Tingsryd Sweden **28** 56.31N 15.00E
Tinian *i.* Asia **39** 14.58N 145.38E
Tinne *r.* Norway **28** 59.05N 9.43E
Tínos *i.* Greece **25** 37.36N 25.08E
Tintagel Head England **11** 50.40N 4.45W
Tinto Hills Scotland **15** 55.36N 3.40W
Tin Tsai Hong Kong **33** 22.22N 114.18E
Tioman *i.* Malaysia **38** 2.45N 104.10E
Tipperary Rep. of Ire. **19** 52.29N 8.10W
Tipperary *d.* Rep. of Ire. **19** 52.37N 7.55W
Tiptree England **9** 51.48N 0.46E
Tiranë Albania **25** 41.20N 19.48E
Tirano Italy **24** 46.12N 10.10E
Tiraspol U.S.S.R. **29** 46.50N 29.38E
Tirebolu Turkey **34** 41.02N 38.49E
Tiree *i.* Scotland **14** 56.30N 6.50W
Tirga Mor *mtn.* Scotland **16** 58.00N 6.59W
Tirgu-Jiu Romania **25** 45.03N 23.17E
Tirgu Mures Romania **29** 46.33N 24.34E
Tirlemont Belgium **27** 50.49N 4.56E
Tirso *r.* Italy **24** 39.52N 8.33E
Tiruchirapalli India **37** 10.50N 78.43E
Tiruppur India **36** 11.05N 77.20E
Tisza *r.* Yugo. **25** 45.09N 20.16E
Titicaca, L. Bolivia/Peru **62** 16.00S 69.00W
Titograd Yugo. **25** 42.30N 19.16E
Titovo Užice Yugo. **25** 43.52N 19.51E
Titov Veles Yugo. **25** 41.43N 21.49E
Tiu Keng Leng Hong Kong **33** 22.18N 114.15E
Tiumpan Head Scotland **16** 58.15N 6.10W
Tiverton England **11** 50.54N 3.30W
Tizimín Mexico **58** 21.10N 88.09W
Tizi Ouzou Algeria **23** 36.44N 4.05E
Tjirebon Indonesia **38** 6.46S 108.33E
Tlaxcala *d.* Mexico **58** 19.45N 98.20W
Tlemcen Algeria **23** 34.53N 1.21W
Tletat ed Douair Algeria **23** 36.15N 3.40E
Toba, L. Indonesia **38** 2.45N 98.50E
Tobago S. America **59** 11.15N 60.40W
Tobelo Indonesia **39** 1.45N 127.59E
Tobermory Scotland **14** 56.37N 6.04W
Tobi *i.* Asia **39** 3.01N 131.10E
Tobi shima *i.* Japan **42** 39.12N 139.32E
Toboali Indonesia **38** 3.00S 106.30E
Tobol *r.* U.S.S.R. **30** 58.15N 68.12E
Tobolsk U.S.S.R. **30** 58.15N 68.12E
Tobruk Libya **45** 32.06N 23.58E
Tocantins *r.* Brazil **62** 2.40S 49.20W
Tocorpuri *mtn.* Bolivia **63** 22.26S 67.53W
Todmorden England **12** 53.43N 2.07W
Toe Head Rep. of Ire. **19** 51.29N 9.15W
Toe Head Scotland **16** 57.50N 7.07W
Tofuku *d.* Japan **42** 39.00N 139.50E
Togian Is. Indonesia **39** 0.20S 122.00E
Togo Africa **44** 8.30N 1.00E
Tokai *d.* Japan **42** 35.00N 137.00E
Tokat Turkey **34** 40.20N 36.35E
Tokoroa New Zealand **50** 38.13S 175.53E
Tokuno *i.* Japan **41** 27.40N 129.00E
Tokushima Japan **42** 34.03N 134.34E
Tokyo Japan **42** 35.40N 139.45E
Tolbukhin Bulgaria **25** 43.34N 27.52E
Toledo Spain **23** 39.52N 4.02W
Toledo U.S.A. **56** 41.40N 83.35W
Toledo, Montes de *mts.* Spain **23** 39.35N 4.30W
Tolo, G. of Indonesia **39** 2.00S 122.30E
Tolob Scotland **16** 59.53N 1.16W
Tolosa Spain **23** 43.09N 2.04W
Tolsta Head Scotland **16** 58.20N 6.10W
Toluca Mexico **58** 19.20N 99.40W
Toluca *mtn.* Mexico **58** 19.10N 99.40W
Tomatin Scotland **17** 57.20N 3.59W
Tombigbee *r.* U.S.A. **53** 31.05N 87.55W
Tomelloso Spain **23** 39.09N 3.01W
Tomini Indonesia **39** 0.31N 120.30E
Tomini G. Indonesia **39** 0.30S 120.45E
Tomintoul Scotland **17** 57.15N 3.24W
Tomsk U.S.S.R. **30** 56.30N 85.05E
Tona, G. of U.S.S.R. **31** 72.00N 136.10E
Tonalá Mexico **58** 16.08N 93.41W
Tonbridge England **7** 51.12N 0.16E
Tönder Denmark **26** 54.57N 8.53E
Tone *r.* England **11** 50.59N 3.15W
Tonga Is. Pacific Oc. **3** 21.00S 175.00W
Tonga Trench Pacific Oc. **3** 20.00S 172.00W
Tongking, G. of Asia **38** 20.00N 107.50E
Tongland Scotland **15** 54.52N 4.02W
Tongres Belgium **27** 50.47N 5.28E
Tongue Scotland **17** 58.28N 4.25W
Tonk India **36** 26.10N 75.50E
Tonle Sap *l.* Cambodia **38** 12.50N 104.00E
Tonnerre France **22** 47.51N 3.59E
Tönsberg Norway **28** 59.16N 10.25E
Toowoomba Australia **49** 27.35S 151.54E
Top, L. U.S.S.R. **28** 65.45N 32.00E
Topeka U.S.A. **53** 39.03N 95.41W
Topko, Mt. U.S.S.R. **31** 57.20N 138.10E
Topsham England **11** 50.40N 3.27W
Tor Egypt **34** 28.14N 33.37E
Tor B. England **11** 50.25N 3.30W
Torbat-i-Shaikh Jam Iran **35** 35.15N 60.37E
Torbay *town* England **11** 50.27N 3.31W
Tordesillas Spain **23** 41.30N 5.00W
Töre Sweden **28** 65.55N 22.40E
Torhout Belgium **27** 51.04N 3.06E
Tori shima *i.* Japan **42** 30.28N 140.20E
Torit Sudan **47** 4.27N 32.31E
Torksey England **13** 53.18N 0.45W
Tormes *r.* Spain **23** 41.18N 6.29W
Torne *r.* Sweden **28** 67.13N 23.30E
Torne Träsk *l.* Sweden **28** 68.15N 19.20E
Tornio Finland **28** 65.52N 24.10E
Tornio *r.* Finland **28** 65.53N 24.07E
Toro Spain **23** 41.31N 5.24W
Toronaios, G. of Med. Sea **25** 40.05N 23.38E
Toronto Canada **57** 43.42N 79.25W
Tororo Uganda **47** 0.42N 34.13E
Torpoint England **11** 50.23N 4.12W
Torquato Severo Brazil **61** 31.04S 54.10W
Torran Rocks *is.* Scotland **14** 56.15N 6.20W
Tôrre de Moncorvo Portugal **23** 41.10N 7.03W
Torrelavega Spain **23** 43.21N 4.00W
Torrens, L. Australia **49** 31.00S 137.50E
Torreón Mexico **58** 25.34N 103.25W
Torres Str. Pacific Oc. **39** 10.30S 142.20E
Tôrres Vedras Portugal **23** 39.05N 9.15W
Torrevieja Spain **23** 37.59N 0.40W
Torridge *r.* England **11** 51.01N 4.12W
Torridon Scotland **16** 57.23N 5.31W
Torridon, Loch Scotland **16** 57.35N 5.45W
Tortola *i.* Virgin Is. **59** 18.28N 64.40W
Tortosa Spain **23** 40.49N 0.31E
Tortue *i.* Haiti **59** 20.05N 72.57W
Tortuga *i.* Venezuela **59** 11.00N 65.20W
Toruń Poland **29** 53.01N 18.35E
Tory I. Rep. of Ire. **18** 55.16N 8.13W
Tory Sd. Rep. of Ire. **18** 55.14N 8.15W
Torzhok U.S.S.R. **29** 57.02N 34.51E
Tosan *d.* Japan **42** 36.00N 138.00E
Tosa wan *b.* Japan **42** 33.10N 133.40E
Tosno U.S.S.R. **29** 59.38N 30.46E
Tosson Hill England **15** 55.16N 2.00W
Tostado Argentina **61** 29.15S 61.45W
Totana Spain **23** 37.46N 1.30W
Totland England **8** 50.40N 1.32W
Totley England **13** 53.19N 1.32W
Totma U.S.S.R. **29** 59.59N 42.44E
Totnes England **11** 50.26N 3.41W
Totora Bolivia **61** 17.40S 65.10W
Tottenham England **7** 51.35N 0.05W
Totton England **8** 50.55N 1.29W
Tottori Japan **42** 35.32N 134.12E
Toubkal *mtn.* Morocco **44** 31.03N 7.57W
Touggourt Algeria **44** 33.08N 6.04E
Toul France **26** 48.41N 5.54E
Toulon France **22** 43.07N 5.53E
Toulouse France **22** 43.33N 1.24E
Toungoo Burma **37** 19.00N 96.30E
Tourcoing France **27** 50.44N 3.09E
Tournai Belgium **27** 50.36N 3.23E
Tournus France **22** 46.33N 4.55E
Tours France **22** 47.23N 0.42E
Tovada *r.* U.S.S.R. **30** 57.40N 67.00E
Tovil England **7** 51.18N 0.31E
Towcester England **8** 52.07N 0.56W
Tower Hamlets *d.* England **7** 51.32N 0.03W
Tow Law *town* England **15** 54.45N 1.49W
Townsville Australia **49** 19.13S 146.48E
Towyn Wales **10** 52.37N 4.08W
Toyama Japan **42** 36.42N 137.14E
Toyohashi Japan **42** 34.46N 137.22E
To Yuen Wai Hong Kong **33** 22.25N 113.59E
Trabzon Turkey **34** 41.00N 39.43E
Trafalgar, C. Spain **23** 36.10N 6.02W
Trail Canada **52** 49.04N 117.29W
Trajan's Gate *f.* Bulgaria **25** 42.13N 23.58E
Tralee Rep. of Ire. **19** 52.16N 9.42W
Tralee B. Rep. of Ire. **19** 52.18N 9.55W
Tramore Rep. of Ire. **19** 52.10N 7.10W
Tramore B. Rep. of Ire. **19** 52.09N 7.07W
Tranås Sweden **28** 58.03N 15.00E
Tranent Scotland **15** 55.57N 2.57W
Trang Thailand **38** 7.35N 99.35E
Trangan *i.* Asia **39** 6.30S 134.15E
Transkei *f.* R.S.A. **48** 32.00S 28.00E
Transvaal *d.* R.S.A. **48** 24.30S 29.00E
Transylvanian Alps *mts.* Romania **25** 45.35N 24.40E
Trápani Italy **24** 38.02N 12.30E
Trasimeno, Lago *l.* Italy **24** 43.09N 12.07E
Travers, Mt. New Zealand **50** 42.05S 172.45E
Traverse City U.S.A. **56** 44.46N 85.38W
Travnik Yugo. **25** 44.14N 17.40E
Třeboň Czech. **26** 49.01N 14.50E
Tredegar Wales **8** 51.47N 3.16W
Tregaron Wales **10** 52.14N 3.56W
Tregony England **11** 50.16N 4.55W
Treig, Loch Scotland **17** 56.48N 4.49W
Treinta-y-Tres Uruguay **61** 33.16S 54.17W
Trelew Argentina **63** 43.13S 65.15W
Trelleborg Sweden **28** 55.10N 13.15E
Tremadoc B. Wales **10** 52.52N 4.14W
Trenque Lauquén Argentina **61** 35.56S 62.43W
Trent *r.* England **13** 53.41N 0.41W
Trentham England **12** 52.59N 2.12W
Trento Italy **26** 46.04N 11.08E
Trenton U.S.A. **57** 40.15N 74.43W
Tres Arroyos Argentina **61** 38.26S 60.17W
Tres Forcas, Cap Morocco **23** 35.26N 2.57W
Treshnish Is. Scotland **14** 56.29N 6.26W
Treshnish Pt. Scotland **14** 56.32N 6.21W
Três Lagoas Brazil **61** 20.46S 51.43W
Três Marias Dam Brazil **63** 18.15S 45.15W
Treuchtlingen W. Germany **26** 48.57N 10.55E
Treviso Italy **24** 45.40N 12.14E
Trevose Head *c.* England **11** 50.33N 5.05W
Trier W. Germany **27** 49.45N 6.39E
Trieste Italy **24** 45.40N 13.47E
Triglav *mtn.* Yugo. **24** 46.21N 13.50E
Trikkala Greece **25** 39.34N 21.46E
Trim Rep. of Ire. **18** 53.33N 6.50W
Trincomalee Sri Lanka **37** 8.34N 81.13E
Tring England **7** 51.48N 0.40W
Trinidad Bolivia **62** 15.00S 64.50W
Trinidad Cuba **59** 21.48N 80.00W
Trinidad S. America **59** 10.30N 61.20W
Trinidad U.S.A. **52** 37.11N 104.31W
Trinity *r.* U.S.A. **53** 29.55N 94.45W
Tripoli Lebanon **34** 34.27N 35.50E
Tripoli Libya **44** 32.58N 13.12E
Tripolitania *f.* Libya **44** 29.45N 14.30E
Tripura *d.* India **37** 23.45N 91.45E
Tristan da Cunha *i.* Atlantic Oc. **4** 38.00S 12.00W
Trivandrum India **36** 8.41N 76.57E
Troisdorf W. Germany **27** 50.50N 7.07E
Trois-Rivières *town* Canada **57** 46.21N 72.34W
Troitsko Pechorsk U.S.S.R. **30** 62.40N 56.08E
Trollhättan Sweden **28** 58.17N 12.20E
Tromsö Norway **28** 69.42N 19.00E
Trondheim Norway **28** 63.36N 10.23E
Trondheim Fjord *est.* Norway **28** 63.40N 10.30E
Troon Scotland **14** 55.33N 4.40W
Trostan *mtn.* N. Ireland **14** 55.03N 6.10W
Trotternish *f.* Scotland **16** 57.33N 6.15W
Troup Head Scotland **17** 57.41N 2.18W
Trout L. Canada **53** 51.10N 93.20W
Trowbridge England **8** 51.18N 2.12W
Troy U.S.A. **57** 42.43N 73.43W
Troyes France **22** 48.18N 4.05E
Trujillo Peru **62** 8.06S 79.00W
Trujillo Spain **23** 39.28N 5.53W
Trujillo Venezuela **59** 9.20N 70.38W
Truro Canada **53** 45.54N 64.00W
Truro England **11** 50.17N 5.02W
Trysil *r.* Norway **28** 61.03N 12.30E
Tsangpo *r.* see Brahmaputra China **37**
Tsavo Nat. Park Kenya **47** 2.45S 38.45E
Tselinograd U.S.S.R. **30** 51.10N 71.28E
Tseng Tau Hong Kong **33** 22.25N 114.16E
Tsetang China **37** 29.05N 91.50E
Tshane Botswana **48** 24.05S 21.54E
Tshela Zaïre **46** 4.57S 12.57E
Tshikapa Zaïre **46** 6.28S 20.48E
Tshofa Zaïre **46** 5.13S 25.20E
Tshopo *r.* Zaïre **46** 0.30N 25.07E
Tshuapa *r.* Zaïre **46** 0.14S 20.45E
Tsim Sha Tsui Hong Kong **33** 22.18N 114.10E
Tsinan China **41** 36.50N 117.00E
Tsing Chau Wan Hong Kong **33** 22.20N 114.02E
Tsinghai *d.* China **40** 36.15N 96.00E
Tsingtao China **41** 36.04N 120.22E
Tsing Yi *i.* Hong Kong **33** 22.21N 114.06E
Tsining Shantung China **41** 35.25N 116.40E
Tsitsihar China **41** 47.23N 124.00E
Tskhinvali U.S.S.R. **29** 42.14N 43.58E
Tsna *r.* U.S.S.R. **29** 54.45N 41.54E
Tsu Japan **42** 34.43N 136.35E
Tsuen Wan Hong Kong **33** 22.22N 114.07E
Tsugaru kaikyo *str.* Japan **42** 41.30N 140.50E
Tsumeb S.W. Africa **48** 19.13S 17.42E
Tsuruga Japan **42** 35.40N 136.05E
Tsushima *i.* Japan **42** 34.30N 129.20E
Tsuyama Japan **42** 35.04N 134.01E
Tsuyung China **37** 25.03N 101.33E
Tsz Wai Hong Kong **33** 22.25N 113.58E
Tuam Rep. of Ire. **18** 53.32N 8.52W
Tuamgrenay Rep. of Ire. **19** 52.54N 8.32W
Tuamotu Archipelago *is.* Pacific Oc. **2** 16.00S 145.00W
Tuapse U.S.S.R. **29** 44.06N 39.05E
Tuatapere New Zealand **50** 46.09S 167.42E
Tuath, Loch Scotland **14** 56.30N 6.13W
Tubbercurry Rep. of Ire. **18** 54.03N 8.45W
Tübingen W. Germany **26** 48.32N 9.04E
Tubja, Wadi *r.* Saudi Arabia **34** 25.35N 38.22E
Tucacas Venezuela **59** 10.46N 68.20W
Tucson U.S.A. **52** 32.15N 110.57W
Tucumán Argentina **61** 26.55S 65.15W
Tucumcari U.S.A. **52** 35.11N 103.44W
Tudela Spain **23** 42.04N 1.37W
Tudweiliog Wales **10** 52.54N 4.37W
Tuen Mun San Hui Hong Kong **33** 22.23N 113.58E
Tuguegarao Phil. **39** 17.36N 121.44E
Tukangbesi Is. Indonesia **39** 5.30S 124.00E
Tukums U.S.S.R. **28** 56.58N 23.10E
Tukuyu Tanzania **47** 9.20S 33.37E
Tula *r.* Mongolia **40** 48.53N 104.35E
Tula U.S.S.R. **29** 54.11N 37.38E
Tulcea Romania **25** 45.10N 28.50E
Tuléar Malagasy Rep. **43** 23.20S 43.41E
Tuli Indonesia **39** 1.25S 122.23E
Tuli Rhodesia **48** 21.50S 29.15E
Tuli *r.* Rhodesia **48** 21.49S 29.00E
Tulkarm Jordan **34** 32.19N 35.02E
Tulla Rep. of Ire. **19** 52.52N 8.48W
Tullamore Rep. of Ire. **19** 53.17N 7.31W
Tulle France **22** 45.16N 1.46E
Tullins France **22** 45.18N 5.29E
Tullow Rep. of Ire. **19** 52.49N 6.45W
Tuloma *r.* U.S.S.R. **28** 68.56N 33.00E
Tulsa U.S.A. **53** 36.07N 95.58W
Tulun U.S.S.R. **31** 54.32N 100.35E
Tumaco Colombia **62** 1.51N 78.46W
Tumba, L. Zaïre **46** 0.45S 18.00E
Tumen *r.* China **42** 43.00N 130.00E
Tummel *r.* Scotland **17** 56.39N 3.40W
Tummel, Loch Scotland **17** 56.43N 3.55W
Tummo Libya **44** 22.45N 14.08E
Tump Pakistan **36** 26.06N 62.24E
Tumpat Malaysia **37** 6.11N 102.10E
Tunceli Turkey **34** 39.07N 39.34E
Tunchwang China **40** 40.00N 94.40E
Tunduru Tanzania **47** 11.08S 37.21E
Tundzha *r.* Bulgaria **25** 41.40N 26.34E
Tungabhadra *r.* India **36** 16.00N 78.15E
Tungkwan China **41** 34.36N 110.21E
Tung Lo Wan Hong Kong **33** 22.22N 114.10E
Tung Lung I. Hong Kong **33** 22.15N 114.17E
Tung Ting Hu *l.* China **41** 29.40N 113.00E
Tunis Tunisia **24** 36.47N 10.10E
Tunis, G. of Med. Sea **24** 37.00N 10.30E
Tunisia Africa **44** 34.00N 9.00E
Tunja Colombia **62** 5.33N 73.23W
Tupelo U.S.A. **53** 34.15N 88.43W
Tupiza Bolivia **61** 21.27S 65.45W
Tura Tanzania **47** 5.30S 33.50E
Tura U.S.S.R. **31** 64.05N 100.00E
Turbo Colombia **59** 8.06N 76.44W
Turfan China **40** 42.55N 89.06E
Turfan Depression *f.* China **40** 43.40N 89.00E
Turgutlu Turkey **25** 38.30N 27.43E
Turi U.S.S.R. **28** 58.48N 25.28E
Turia *r.* Spain **23** 39.27N 0.19W
Turin Italy **22** 45.04N 7.40E
Turkestan *f.* Asia **35** 40.00N 79.30E
Turkestan U.S.S.R. **30** 43.17N 68.16E
Turkey Asia **34** 39.00N 35.00E
Turkey *r.* U.S.A. **56** 42.58N 91.03W
Turkmenistan Soviet Socialist Republic *d.* U.S.S.R. **30** 40.00N 60.00E
Turks I. C. America **59** 21.30N 71.10W
Turku Finland **28** 60.27N 22.15E
Turneffe I. Belize **58** 17.30N 87.45W
Turnhout Belgium **27** 51.19N 4.57E
Tŭrnovo Bulgaria **25** 43.04N 25.39E
Turnu Măgurele Romania **25** 43.43N 24.53E
Turnu Severin Romania **25** 44.37N 22.39E
Turquino *mtn.* Cuba **59** 20.05N 76.50W
Turret Hill Hong Kong **33** 22.23N 114.13E
Turriff Scotland **17** 57.32N 2.28W
Turtkul U.S.S.R. **35** 41.30N 61.00E
Tuscaloosa U.S.A. **53** 33.12N 87.33W
Tuscola U.S.A. **56** 39.49N 88.18W
Tuskar Rock *i.* Rep. of Ire. **19** 52.12N 6.13W
Tuticorin India **37** 8.48N 78.10E
Tuttlingen W. Germany **26** 47.59N 8.49E
Tutubu Tanzania **47** 5.28S 32.43E
Tuxpan Mexico **58** 21.00N 97.23W
Tuxtla Gutiérrez Mexico **58** 16.45N 93.09W
Tuz, L. Turkey **34** 38.45N 33.24E
Tuzla Yugo. **25** 44.33N 18.41E
Tweed *r.* Scotland **15** 55.46N 2.00W
Twickenham England **7** 51.27N 0.20W
Twin Falls *town* U.S.A. **52** 42.34N 114.30W
Two Harbors *town* U.S.A. **56** 47.02N 91.40W
Twyford Berks. England **8** 51.29N 0.51W
Twyford Hants. England **8** 51.01N 1.19W
Tyler U.S.A. **53** 32.22N 95.18W
Tyndrum Scotland **14** 56.27N 4.43W
Tyne *r.* England **15** 55.00N 1.25W
Tyne *r.* Scotland **15** 56.00N 2.36W
Tyne and Wear *d.* England **15** 54.57N 1.35W

Tynemouth England 15 55.01N 1.24W
Tyre Lebanon 34 33.16N 35.12E
Tyrone d. N. Ireland 18 54.35N 7.15W
Tyrrellspass town Rep. of Ire. 18 53.23N 7.24W
Tyrrhenian Sea Med. Sea 24 40.00N 12.00E
Tyumen U.S.S.R. 30 57.11N 65.29E
Tywi r. Wales 11 51.46N 4.22W
Tywyn Wales 10 53.14N 3.49W
Tzaneen R.S.A. 48 23.50S 30.09E
Tzekung China 40 29.20N 104.42E
Tzepo China 41 36.32N 117.47E

U

Ubaiyidh, Wadi r. Iraq 34 32.04N 42.17E
Ubangi r. Congo/Zaïre 46 0.25S 17.40E
Ube Japan 42 34.00N 131.16E
Ubeda Spain 23 38.01N 3.22W
Uberaba Brazil 61 19.47S 47.57W
Uberlândia Brazil 61 18.57S 48.17W
Ubombo R.S.A. 48 27.35S 32.05E
Ubon Ratchathani Thailand 37 15.15N 104.50E
Ubsa Nur l. Mongolia 40 50.30N 92.30E
Ubundu Zaïre 46 0.24S 25.28E
Ucayali r. Peru 62 4.00S 73.30W
Uchiura wan b. Japan 42 42.20N 140.40E
Uckfield England 9 50.58N 0.06E
Udaipur India 36 24.36N 73.47E
Uddevalla Sweden 28 58.20N 11.56E
Uddjaur l. Sweden 28 65.55N 17.50E
Udine Italy 24 46.03N 13.15E
Udon Thani Thailand 37 17.29N 102.46E
Uele r. Zaïre 46 4.08N 22.25E
Uelen U.S.S.R. 54 66.13N 169.48W
Uelzen W. Germany 26 52.58N 10.34E
Uere r. Zaïre 46 3.30N 25.15E
Ufa U.S.S.R. 30 54.45N 55.58E
Uffculme England 8 50.45N 3.19W
Ugalla r. Tanzania 47 5.15S 29.45E
Uganda Africa 47 2.00N 33.00E
Ugie r. Scotland 17 57.31N 1.48W
Uglegorsk U.S.S.R. 31 49.01N 142.04E
Ugra r. U.S.S.R. 29 54.30N 36.10E
Uig Scotland 16 57.35N 6.22W
Uige Angola 46 7.40S 15.09E
Uige d. Angola 46 7.00S 15.30E
Uinta Mts. U.S.A. 52 40.45N 110.30W
Uitenhage R.S.A. 48 33.46S 25.25E
Uithuizen Neth. 27 53.24N 6.41E
Ujiji Tanzania 47 4.55S 29.39E
Ujjain India 36 23.11N 75.50E
Ujpest Hungary 29 47.33N 19.05E
Uka U.S.S.R. 31 57.50N 162.02E
Ukerewe I. Tanzania 47 2.00S 33.00E
Ukiah U.S.A. 52 39.09N 123.12W
Ukraine Soviet Socialist Republic d. U.S.S.R. 29 49.30N 32.04E
Ulan Bator Mongolia 40 47.54N 106.52E
Ulan Göm Mongolia 40 49.59N 92.00E
Ulan-Ude U.S.S.R. 40 51.55N 107.40E
Uliastaj Mongolia 40 47.42N 96.52E
Ulindi r. Zaïre 46 1.38S 25.55E
Ulla r. Spain 23 42.38N 8.45W
Ullapool Scotland 16 57.54N 5.10W
Ullswater l. England 12 54.34N 2.52W
Ullung do i. S. Korea 42 37.40N 130.55E
Ulm W. Germany 26 48.24N 10.00E
Ulsberg Norway 28 62.45N 10.00E
Ulsta Scotland 16 60.30N 1.08W
Ulster d. N. Ireland/Rep. of Ire. 18 54.40N 6.45W
Ulua r. Honduras 58 15.50N 87.38W
Uluguru Mts. Tanzania 47 7.05S 37.40E
Ulva i. Scotland 14 56.29N 6.12W
Ulverston England 12 54.13N 3.07W
Ul'yanovsk U.S.S.R. 29 54.19N 48.22E
Uman U.S.S.R. 29 48.45N 30.10E
Ume r. Sweden 28 63.43N 20.20E
Umfuli r. Rhodesia 48 17.32S 29.14E
Umiat U.S.A. 54 69.25N 152.20W
Umm-al-Gawein U.A.E. 35 25.32N 55.34E
Umm-al-Hamir Saudi Arabia 35 29.07N 46.35E
Umm Lajj Saudi Arabia 34 25.03N 37.17E
Umm Sa'id Qatar 35 24.47N 51.36E
Umniati r. Rhodesia 48 17.28S 29.20E
Umtali Rhodesia 48 18.58S 32.38E
Umtata R.S.A. 48 31.35S 28.47E
Umvukwe Range mts. Rhodesia 48 16.30S 30.50E
Umvuma Rhodesia 48 19.16S 30.30E
Una r. Yugo. 24 45.03N 16.22E
Unapool Scotland 16 58.14N 5.01W
Uncompahgre Peak U.S.A. 52 38.04N 107.28W
Underberg R.S.A. 48 29.47S 29.30E
Undur Khan Mongolia 31 47.20N 110.40E
Ungava B. Canada 55 59.00N 67.30W
Unggi N. Korea 42 42.19N 130.24E
Uniondale R.S.A. 48 33.40S 23.07E
Union of Arab Emirates Asia 35 24.00N 54.00E
Union of Soviet Socialist Republics Europe/Asia 30 60.00N 80.00E
United Kingdom Europe 20 54.00N 3.00W
United States of America N. America 52 39.00N 100.00W
Unna W. Germany 27 51.32N 7.41E
Unshin r. Rep. of Ire. 18 54.13N 8.31W
Unst i. Scotland 16 60.45N 0.55W
Unye Turkey 34 41.09N 37.15E
Upavon England 8 51.17N 1.49W
Upemba, L. Zaïre 47 8.35S 26.28E
Upemba Nat. Park Zaïre 47 9.00S 26.30E
Upernavik Greenland 55 72.50N 56.00W
Upington R.S.A. 48 28.28S 21.14E
Upminster England 7 51.34N 0.15E
Upper Egypt f. Egypt 34 26.00N 32.00E
Upper Lough Erne N. Ireland 18 54.13N 7.32W
Upper Taymyr r. U.S.S.R. 31 74.10N 99.50E
Upper Tean England 12 52.57N 1.59W
Upper Tooting England 7 51.26N 0.10W
Upper Volta Africa 44 12.15N 1.30W
Uppingham England 8 52.36N 0.43W
Uppsala Sweden 28 59.55N 17.38E
Upton upon Severn England 8 52.04N 2.12W
Ur ruins Iraq 35 30.55N 46.07E
Uraba, G. of Colombia 59 8.30N 77.00W
Ural r. U.S.S.R. 30 47.00N 52.00E
Ural Mts. U.S.S.R. 30 55.00N 59.00E
Ural'sk U.S.S.R. 30 51.09N 51.20E
Uranium City Canada 54 59.32N 108.43W
Urbana U.S.A. 56 40.07N 88.12W
Urbino Italy 24 43.43N 12.38E
Ure r. England 13 54.05N 1.20W
Uren U.S.S.R. 29 57.30N 45.50E
Urfa Turkey 34 37.08N 38.45E
Urgüp Turkey 34 38.39N 34.55E
Urlingford Rep. of Ire. 19 52.44N 7.35W
Urmia, L. Iran 35 37.40N 45.28E
Urmston England 12 53.28N 2.22W
Urr Water r. Scotland 15 54.54N 3.50W
Uruapan Mexico 58 19.26N 102.04W
Uruguaiana Brazil 61 29.45S 57.05W
Uruguay S. America 61 33.15S 56.00W
Uruguay r. Argentina/Uruguay 61 34.00S 58.30W
Uryu Ko l. Japan 42 44.22N 142.15E
Uşak Turkey 34 38.42N 29.25E
Usambara Mts. Tanzania 47 4.45S 38.25E
Ushant i. see Ouessant, Ile d' France 22
Ushnuiyeh Iran 35 37.03N 45.05E
Usk Wales 11 51.42N 2.53W
Usk r. Wales 11 51.34N 2.59W
Usküdar Turkey 25 41.00N 29.03E
Ussuriysk U.S.S.R. 42 43.50N 132.00E
Ustica i. Italy 24 38.42N 13.11E
Usti nad Labem Czech. 26 50.41N 14.00E
Ust'kamchatsk U.S.S.R. 31 56.14N 162.28E
Ust Kut U.S.S.R. 31 56.40N 105.50E
Ust'Maya U.S.S.R. 31 60.25N 134.28E
Ust Olenek U.S.S.R. 31 72.59N 120.00E
Ust'Tsilma U.S.S.R. 30 65.28N 53.09E
Ust Urt Plateau f. U.S.S.R. 30 43.30N 55.20E
Usumacinta r. Mexico 58 18.48N 92.40W
Utah d. U.S.A. 52 39.00N 112.00W
Utembo r. Angola 48 17.03S 22.00E
Utete Tanzania 47 8.00S 38.49E
Utica U.S.A. 57 43.06N 75.15W
Utiel Spain 23 39.33N 1.13W
Utrecht Neth. 27 52.04N 5.07E
Utrecht d. Neth. 27 52.04N 5.10E
Utrecht R.S.A. 48 27.40S 30.20E
Utrera Spain 23 37.10N 5.47W
Utsunomiya Japan 42 36.40N 139.52E
Uttaradit Thailand 37 17.38N 100.05E
Uttar Pradesh d. India 37 27.40N 80.00E
Uttoxeter England 12 52.53N 1.50W
Uusikaupunki Finland 28 60.48N 21.30E
Uvinza Tanzania 47 5.08S 30.23E
Uvira Zaïre 47 3.22S 29.06E
'Uwaina Saudi Arabia 35 26.46N 48.13E
Uwajima Japan 42 33.13N 132.32E
Uxbridge England 7 51.33N 0.30W
'Uyun Saudi Arabia 35 26.32N 43.41E
Uyuni Bolivia 63 20.28S 66.47W
Uzbekistan Soviet Socialist Republic d. U.S.S.R. 30 42.00N 63.00E
Uzhgorod U.S.S.R. 29 48.38N 22.15E

V

Vaago i. Faroe Is. 28 62.03N 7.14W
Vaal r. R.S.A. 48 29.03S 23.42E
Vaalbank Dam R.S.A. 48 27.00S 28.15E
Vaasa Finland 28 63.06N 21.36E
Vaduz Liech. 26 47.08N 9.32E
Vaggeryd Sweden 28 57.30N 14.10E
Váh r. Czech. 29 47.40N 17.50E
Vaila i. Scotland 16 60.12N 1.34W
Valdai Hills U.S.S.R. 29 57.10N 33.00E
Valday U.S.S.R. 29 57.59N 33.10E
Valdemarsvik Sweden 28 58.13N 16.35E
Valdepeñas Spain 23 38.46N 3.24W
Valdez U.S.A. 54 61.07N 146.17W
Valdivia Chile 63 39.46S 73.15W
Val-d'Or town Canada 57 48.07N 77.47W
Valença Portugal 23 42.02N 8.38W
Valence France 22 44.56N 4.54E
Valencia Spain 23 39.29N 0.24W
Valencia Venezuela 59 10.14N 67.59W
Valencia, G. of Spain 23 39.38N 0.20W
Valencia, L. Venezuela 59 10.09N 67.30W
Valencia de Alcántara Spain 23 39.25N 7.14
Valenciennes France 27 50.22N 3.32E
Valentia I. Rep. of Ire. 19 51.54N 10.21W
Vale of Berkeley f. England 8 51.42N 2.25W
Vale of Evesham f. England 8 52.05N 1.55W
Vale of Gloucester f. England 8 51.54N 2.15W
Vale of Kent f. England 9 51.08N 0.38E
Vale of Pewsey f. England 8 51.21N 1.45W
Vale of Pickering f. England 13 54.11N 0.45W
Vale of White Horse f. England 8 51.38N 1.32W
Vale of York f. England 13 54.12N 1.25W
Valga U.S.S.R. 28 57.44N 26.00E
Valinco, G. of Med. Sea 22 41.40N 8.50E
Valjevo Yugo. 25 44.16N 19.56E
Valkeakoski Finland 28 61.17N 24.05E
Valkenswaard Neth. 27 51.21N 5.27E
Valladolid Spain 23 41.39N 4.45W
Valle Venezuela 59 9.15N 66.00W
Valledupar Colombia 62 10.10N 73.16W
Valletta Malta 24 35.53N 14.31E
Valley City U.S.A. 52 46.57N 97.58W
Valleyfield Canada 57 45.15N 74.08W
Valmiera U.S.S.R. 28 57.32N 25.29E
Valnera mtn. Spain 23 43.10N 3.40W
Valognes France 22 49.31N 1.28W
Valparaíso Chile 63 33.05S 71.40W
Vals, C. Indonesia 39 8.30S 137.30E
Valverde Dom. Rep. 59 19.37N 71.04W
Valverde del Camino Spain 23 37.35N 6.45W
Van Turkey 34 38.28N 43.20E
Van, L. Turkey 34 38.35N 42.52E
Vancouver Canada 52 49.13N 123.06W
Vancouver I. Canada 54 50.00N 126.00W
Vänern l. Sweden 28 59.00N 13.15E
Vänersborg Sweden 28 58.23N 12.19E
Vanga Kenya 47 4.37S 39.13E
Vanka Järvi l. Finland 28 61.30N 23.50E
Vännäs Sweden 28 63.56N 19.50E
Vannes France 22 47.40N 2.44W
Vanrhynsdorp R.S.A. 48 31.36S 18.45E
Var r. France 22 43.39N 7.11E
Varanasi India 37 25.20N 83.00E
Varangerenfjord est. Norway 28 70.00N 29.30E
Varaždin Yugo. 24 46.18N 16.20E
Varberg Sweden 28 57.06N 12.15E
Vardar r. Greece 25 40.31N 22.43E
Varel W. Germany 27 53.24N 8.08E
Varennes France 22 46.19N 3.24E
Varginha Brazil 61 21.33S 45.25W
Varkaus Finland 28 62.15N 27.45E
Varna Bulgaria 25 43.13N 27.57E
Värnamo Sweden 28 57.11N 14.03E
Vasilkov U.S.S.R. 29 50.12N 30.15E
Västerås Sweden 28 59.36N 16.32E
Västerdal r. Sweden 28 60.32N 15.02E
Västervik Sweden 28 57.45N 16.40E
Vaternish Pt. Scotland 16 57.37N 6.39W
Vatersay i. Scotland 16 56.56N 7.32W
Vatnajökull mts. Iceland 28 64.20N 17.00W
Vättern l. Sweden 28 58.30N 14.30E
Vaughn U.S.A. 52 34.35N 105.14W
Vavuniya Sri Lanka 37 8.45N 80.30E
Växjö Sweden 28 56.52N 14.50E
Vaygach i. U.S.S.R. 30 70.00N 59.00E
Vecht r. Neth. 27 52.39N 6.01E
Vega i. Norway 28 65.40N 11.55E
Vejle Denmark 28 55.43N 9.33E
Vélez Málaga Spain 23 36.48N 4.05W
Velikaya r. U.S.S.R. 28 57.54N 28.06E
Velikiye-Luki U.S.S.R. 29 56.19N 30.31E
Velletri Italy 24 41.41N 12.47E
Vellore India 37 12.56N 79.09E
Velsen Neth. 27 52.28N 4.39E
Veluwe f. Neth. 27 52.17N 5.45E
Venachar, Loch Scotland 14 56.13N 4.19W
Venado Tuerto Argentina 61 33.45S 61.56W
Vendas Novas Portugal 23 38.41N 8.27W
Vendôme France 22 47.48N 1.04E
Venezuela S. America 62 7.00N 66.00W
Venezuela, G. of Venezuela 59 11.30N 71.00W
Veniaminof Mtn. U.S.A. 54 56.05N 159.20W
Venice Italy 24 45.26N 12.20E
Venice, G. of Med. Sea 24 45.20N 13.00E
Venlo Neth. 27 51.22N 6.10E
Venraij Neth. 27 51.32N 5.58E
Venta r. U.S.S.R. 28 57.22N 21.31E
Ventnor England 8 50.35N 1.12W
Ventspils U.S.S.R. 28 57.22N 21.31E
Ver r. England 7 51.42N 0.20W
Vera Argentina 63 29.31S 60.30W
Vera Spain 23 37.15N 1.51W
Veracruz Mexico 58 19.11N 96.10W
Veracruz d. Mexico 58 18.00N 95.00W
Veraval India 36 20.53N 70.28E
Vercelli Italy 22 45.19N 8.26E
Verde r. Paraguay 61 23.10S 57.45W
Verde, C. Senegal 44 14.45N 17.25W
Verdon r. France 22 43.42N 5.39E
Verdun France 22 49.10N 5.24E
Vereeniging R.S.A. 48 26.41S 27.56E
Verin Spain 23 41.55N 7.26W
Verkhoyansk U.S.S.R. 31 67.25N 133.25E
Verkhoyansk Range mts. U.S.S.R. 31 66.00N 130.00E
Vermont d. U.S.A. 57 43.50N 72.50W
Verona Italy 24 45.27N 10.59E
Versailles France 22 48.48N 2.08E
Verviers Belgium 27 50.36N 5.52E
Vervins France 27 49.50N 3.55E
Verwood England 8 50.53N 1.53W
Vesoul France 26 47.38N 6.09E
Vesterålen is. Norway 28 68.55N 15.00E
Vest Fjorden est. Norway 28 68.10N 15.00E
Vestmanna Is. Iceland 28 63.30N 20.20W
Vesuvius mtn. Italy 24 40.48N 14.25E
Vetlanda Sweden 28 57.26N 15.05E
Vetluga r. U.S.S.R. 29 56.18N 46.19E
Vettore, Monte mtn. Italy 24 42.50N 13.18E
Vézere r. France 22 44.53N 0.55E
Viana do Castelo Portugal 23 41.41N 8.50W
Viborg Denmark 28 56.28N 9.25E
Vicenza Italy 24 45.33N 11.32E
Vich Spain 23 41.56N 2.16E
Vichuga U.S.S.R. 29 57.12N 41.50E
Vichy France 22 46.07N 3.25E
Victoria d. Australia 49 37.00S 145.00E
Victoria Cameroon 46 4.03N 9.12E
Victoria Canada 52 48.26N 123.20W
Victoria Hong Kong 33 22.17N 114.10E
Victoria U.S.A. 58 28.49N 97.01W
Victoria, L. Africa 47 1.00S 33.00E
Victoria, Mt. P.N.G. 49 8.10S 147.20E
Victoria de las Tunas Cuba 59 20.58N 76.59W
Victoria Falls f. Rhodesia/Zambia 48 17.58S 25.45E
Victoria Harbour str. Hong Kong 33 22.17N 114.10E
Victoria I. Canada 54 71.00N 110.00W
Victoria Nile r. Uganda 47 2.14N 31.20E
Victoria Peak Hong Kong 33 22.16N 114.08E
Victoria West R.S.A. 48 31.25S 23.08E
Vidin Bulgaria 25 43.58N 22.51E
Viedma Argentina 61 40.45S 63.00W
Vienna Austria 26 48.13N 16.22E
Vienne France 22 45.32N 4.54E
Vienne r. France 22 47.13N 0.05W
Vientiane Laos 38 18.01N 102.48E
Vieques i. Puerto Rico 59 18.08N 65.30W
Vierwaldstätter See l. Switz. 22 47.00N 8.35E
Vierzon France 22 47.14N 2.03E
Vignemale, Pic de mtn. France 22 42.46N 0.08W
Vigo Spain 23 42.15N 8.44W
Vijayawada India 37 16.34N 80.40E
Vijose r. Albania 25 40.39N 19.20E
Vikna i. Norway 28 64.59N 11.00E
Vila Cabral Moçambique 47 13.09S 35.17E
Vila Coutinho Moçambique 47 14.34S 34.21E
Vila da Ponte Angola 46 14.28S 16.25E
Vila de João Belo Moçambique 48 25.05S 33.38E
Vila de Manica Moçambique 48 19.00S 33.00E
Vila de Mocuba Moçambique 47 16.52S 37.02E
Vila de Sena Moçambique 47 17.36S 35.00E
Vila Franca Portugal 23 38.57N 8.59W
Vila General Machado Angola 46 12.01S 17.22E
Vilaine r. France 22 47.30N 2.25W
Vila Luso Angola 46 11.46S 19.55E
Vila Maganja Moçambique 47 17.25S 37.32E
Vila Mariano Machado Angola 46 12.58S 14.39E
Vilanculos Moçambique 48 22.01S 35.19E
Vila Nova do Seles Angola 46 11.24S 14.15E
Vila Pereira de Eça Angola 48 17.03S 15.41E
Vila Pery Moçambique 48 19.04S 33.29E
Vila Real Portugal 23 41.17N 7.45W
Vila Real de Santo Antonio Portugal 23 37.12N 7.25W
Vila Salazar Angola 46 9.12S 14.54E
Vila Serpa Pinto Angola 46 14.40S 17.41E
Vila Silva Porto Angola 46 12.25S 16.58E
Vila Teixeira da Silva Angola 46 12.13S 15.46E
Vila Vasco da Gama Moçambique 47 14.55S 32.12E
Vila Verissimo Sarmento Angola 46 8.08S 20.38E
Vilhelmina Sweden 28 64.38N 16.40E
Viljandi U.S.S.R. 28 58.22N 25.30E
Villa Angela Argentina 61 27.34S 60.45W
Villablino Spain 23 42.57N 6.19W
Villacañas Spain 23 39.38N 3.20W
Villach Austria 26 46.37N 13.51E
Villa Cisneros Span. Sahara 44 23.43N 15.57W
Villa Constitución Argentina 61 33.15S 60.20W
Villagarcia Spain 23 42.35N 8.45W
Villaguay Argentina 61 31.55S 59.01W
Villahermosa Mexico 58 18.00N 92.53W
Villa Huidobro Argentina 61 34.50S 64.34W
Villajoyosa Spain 23 38.31N 0.14W
Villa María Argentina 61 32.25S 63.15W
Villa Montes Bolivia 61 21.15S 63.30W
Villanueva de la Serena Spain 23 38.58N 5.48W
Villanueva-y-Geltru Spain 23 41.13N 1.43E
Villaputzu Italy 24 39.28N 9.35E
Villarrica Paraguay 61 25.45S 56.28W
Villarrobledo Spain 23 39.16N 2.36W
Villa Sanjurjo Morocco 23 35.14N 3.56W
Villefranche France 22 46.00N 4.43E
Villena Spain 23 38.39N 0.52W
Villeneuve France 22 44.25N 0.43E
Villeurbanne France 22 45.46N 4.54E
Vilnius U.S.S.R. 28 54.40N 25.19E
Vilvoorde Belgium 27 50.56N 4.25E
Vilyuy r. U.S.S.R. 31 64.20N 126.55E
Vilyuysk U.S.S.R. 31 63.46N 121.35E
Vimmerby Sweden 28 57.40N 15.50E
Viña del Mar Chile 63 33.02S 71.35W
Vincennes U.S.A. 56 38.42N 87.30W
Vindel r. Sweden 28 63.56N 19.54E
Vindhya Range mts. India 36 22.55N 76.00E
Vineland U.S.A. 57 39.29N 75.02W
Vinh N. Vietnam 37 18.42N 105.41E
Vinnitsa U.S.S.R. 29 49.11N 28.30E
Vire France 22 48.50N 0.53W
Vire r. France 22 49.20N 0.53W
Virgin Gorda i. Virgin Is. 59 18.30N 64.26W
Virginia Rep. of Ire. 18 53.50N 7.06W
Virginia U.S.A. 56 47.30N 92.28W
Virginia d. U.S.A. 53 37.30N 79.00W
Virginia Water town England 7 51.24N 0.36W
Virgin Is. C. America 59 18.30N 65.00W
Virovitica Yugo. 25 45.51N 17.23E
Virton Belgium 27 49.35N 5.32E
Virunga Nat. Park Zaïre 47 0.30S 29.15E
Vis i. Yugo. 24 43.03N 16.10E
Visby Sweden 28 57.37N 18.20E
Viscount Melville Sd. Canada 54 74.30N 104.00W
Visé Belgium 27 50.44N 5.42E
Višegrad Yugo. 25 43.47N 19.20E
Viseu Portugal 23 40.40N 7.55W
Vishakhapatnam India 37 17.42N 83.24E
Viso, Monte mtn. Italy 22 44.38N 7.05E
Vistula r. Poland 29 54.23N 18.52E
Vitebsk U.S.S.R. 29 55.10N 30.14E
Viterbo Italy 24 42.26N 12.07E
Vitim r. U.S.S.R. 31 59.30N 112.36E
Vitória Espírito Santo Brazil 63 20.19S 40.21W
Vitória Bahia Brazil 62 14.53S 40.52W
Vitoria Spain 23 42.51N 2.40W
Vittória Italy 24 36.57N 14.21E
Vizianagaram India 37 18.07N 83.30E
Vlaardingen Neth. 27 51.55N 4.20E

Vladimir U.S.S.R. **29** 56.08N 40.25E
Vladivostok U.S.S.R. **42** 43.06N 131.50E
Vlieland *i.* Neth. **27** 53.15N 5.00E
Vlorë Albania **25** 40.28N 19.27E
Vltava *r.* Czech. **26** 50.22N 14.28E
Voe Scotland **16** 60.21N 1.15W
Vogelkop *f.* Asia **39** 1.10S 132.30E
Vogelsberg *mtn.* W. Germany **26** 50.30N 9.15E
Voghera Italy **24** 44.59N 9.01E
Voi Kenya **47** 3.23S 38.35E
Voil, Loch Scotland **14** 56.21N 4.26W
Voiron France **22** 45.22N 5.35E
Volga *r.* U.S.S.R. **30** 45.45N 47.50E
Volga Uplands *hills* U.S.S.R. **29** 53.15N 45.45E
Volgograd U.S.S.R. **29** 48.45N 44.30E
Volkhov *r.* U.S.S.R. **29** 60.15N 32.15E
Vologda U.S.S.R. **29** 59.10N 39.55E
Vólos Greece **25** 39.22N 22.57E
Volsk U.S.S.R. **29** 52.04N 47.22E
Volta *r.* Ghana **43** 5.50N 0.41E
Volta, L. Ghana **44** 7.00N 0.00
Volta Redonda Brazil **63** 22.31S 44.05W
Volterra Italy **24** 43.24N 10.51E
Volturno *r.* Italy **24** 41.02N 13.56E
Volzhskiy U.S.S.R. **29** 48.48N 44.45E
Voorburg Neth. **27** 52.05N 4.22E
Vopna Fjördhur *est.* Iceland **28** 65.50N 14.30W
Vordingborg Denmark **26** 55.01N 11.55E
Vorkuta U.S.S.R. **30** 67.27N 64.00E
Voronezh U.S.S.R. **29** 51.40N 39.13E
Voroshilovgrad U.S.S.R. **29** 48.35N 39.20E
Vosges *mts.* France **26** 48.10N 7.00E
Voss Norway **28** 60.38N 6.25E
Votuporanga Brazil **61** 20.26S 49.53W
Vouga *r.* Portugal **23** 40.41N 8.38W
Voves France **22** 48.16N 1.37E
Voznesensk U.S.S.R. **29** 47.34N 31.21E
Vranje Yugo. **25** 42.34N 21.52E
Vratsa Bulgaria **25** 43.12N 23.33E
Vrbas *r.* Yugo. **25** 45.06N 17.29E
Vršac Yugo. **25** 45.08N 21.18E
Vryburg R.S.A. **48** 26.57S 24.44E
Vyatka *r.* U.S.S.R. **29** 55.45N 51.30E
Vyatskiye Polyany U.S.S.R. **29** 56.14N 51.08E
Vyazma U.S.S.R. **29** 55.12N 34.17E
Vyazniki U.S.S.R. **29** 56.14N 42.08E
Vyborg U.S.S.R. **28** 60.45N 28.41E
Vyrnwy *r.* Wales **10** 52.45N 3.01W
Vyrnwy, L. Wales **10** 52.46N 3.30W
Vyshka U.S.S.R. **35** 39.19N 49.12E
Vyshniy-Volochek U.S.S.R. **29** 57.34N 34.23E

W

Waal *r.* Neth. **27** 51.45N 4.40E
Waalwijk Neth. **27** 51.42N 5.04E
Wabash *r.* U.S.A. **56** 38.25N 87.45W
Wabush City Canada **55** 53.00N 66.50W
Waco U.S.A. **53** 31.33N 97.10W
Wad Pakistan **36** 27.21N 66.30E
Wadden Sea Neth. **27** 53.15N 5.05E
Waddesdon England **8** 51.50N 0.54W
Waddington, Mt. Canada **54** 51.30N 125.00W
Wadebridge England **11** 50.31N 4.51W
Wadesmill England **7** 51.51N 0.03W
Wadhurst England **9** 51.03N 0.21E
Wadi Halfa Sudan **45** 21.55N 31.20E
Wad Medani Sudan **45** 14.24N 33.30E
Wafra Kuwait **35** 28.39N 47.56E
Wageningen Neth. **27** 51.58N 5.39E
Wager Bay *town* Canada **55** 65.55N 90.40W
Wahpeton U.S.A. **53** 46.16N 96.36W
Waiau New Zealand **50** 42.39S 173.02E
Waiau *r.* New Zealand **50** 42.47S 173.23E
Waigeo *i.* Indonesia **39** 0.05S 130.30E
Waihou *r.* New Zealand **50** 37.12S 175.33E
Waikato *r.* New Zealand **50** 37.19S 174.50E
Waimakariri *r.* New Zealand **50** 43.23S 172.40E
Waimarie New Zealand **50** 41.33S 171.58E
Wainfleet All Saints England **13** 53.07N 0.16E
Waingapu Indonesia **39** 9.30S 120.10E
Wainwright U.S.A. **54** 70.39N 160.00W
Waipara New Zealand **50** 43.03S 172.47E
Waipukurau New Zealand **50** 40.00S 176.33E
Wairau *r.* New Zealand **50** 41.32S 174.08E
Wairoa New Zealand **50** 39.03S 177.25E
Wairoa *r.* New Zealand **50** 36.07S 173.59E
Waitaki *r.* New Zealand **50** 44.56S 171.10E
Waitara New Zealand **50** 38.59S 174.13E
Wajir Kenya **47** 1.46N 40.05E
Wakasa wan *b.* Japan **42** 35.50N 135.40E
Wakatipu, L. New Zealand **50** 45.10S 168.30E
Wakayama Japan **42** 34.12N 135.10E
Wakefield England **13** 53.41N 1.31W
Wakeham Canada **55** 61.30N 72.00W
Wakkanai Japan **42** 45.26N 141.43E
Walachian Plain *f.* Romania **29** 44.30N 26.30E
Walbrzych Poland **26** 50.48N 16.19E
Walbury Hill England **8** 51.21N 1.30W
Walcheren *f.* Neth. **27** 51.32N 3.35E
Walderslade England **7** 51.21N 0.33E
Wales U.K. **10** 52.30N 3.45W
Wallasey England **12** 53.26N 3.02W
Wallingford England **8** 51.36N 1.07W
Wallington England **7** 51.22N 0.09W
Walls Scotland **16** 60.14N 1.34W
Wallsend England **15** 55.00N 1.31W
Walmer England **9** 51.12N 1.23E
Walney, Isle of England **12** 54.05N 3.12W
Walsall England **8** 52.36N 1.59W
Waltham Abbey England **7** 51.42N 0.01E
Waltham Forest *d.* England **7** 51.36N 0.02W
Waltham on the Wolds England **13** 52.49N 0.49W
Walthamstow England **7** 51.34N 0.01W
Walton-on-Thames England **7** 51.23N 0.23W
Walton on the Hill England **7** 51.17N 0.02W
Walton on the Naze England **9** 51.52N 1.17E
Walvis B. R.S.A. **48** 22.48S 14.29E
Walvis Bay *d.* R.S.A. **48** 22.55S 14.35E
Walvis Bay *town* R.S.A. **48** 22.50S 14.31E
Wamba Kenya **47** 0.58N 37.19E
Wamba Zaïre **47** 2.10N 27.59E
Wamba *r.* Zaïre **46** 4.35S 17.15E
Wami *r.* Tanzania **47** 6.10S 38.50E
Wanaka, L. New Zealand **50** 44.30S 169.10E
Wan Chai Hong Kong **33** 22.17N 114.10E
Wandsworth *d.* England **7** 51.27N 0.11W
Wanganui New Zealand **50** 39.56S 175.00E
Wang Chau *i.* Hong Kong **33** 22.20N 114.22E
Wangeroog *i.* W. Germany **27** 53.50N 7.50E
Wangford Fen *f.* England **9** 52.25N 0.31E
Wanhsien China **41** 30.54N 108.20E
Wankie Rhodesia **48** 18.18S 26.30E
Wankie Nat. Park Rhodesia **48** 19.00S 26.30E
Wansbeck *r.* England **15** 55.10N 1.33W
Wanstead England **7** 51.34N 0.02E
Wantage England **8** 51.35N 1.25W
Wan Tuk Hong Kong **33** 22.19N 114.02E
Warangal India **37** 18.00N 79.35E
Ward Rep. of Ire. **18** 53.26N 6.20W
Warden R.S.A. **48** 27.50S 28.58E
Wardha India **37** 20.41N 78.40E
Ward Hill Orkney Is. Scotland **17** 58.54N 3.20W
Ward Hill Orkney Is. Scotland **17** 58.58N 3.09W
Ward's Stone *mtn.* England **12** 54.03N 2.36W
Ware England **7** 51.49N 0.02W
Wareham England **8** 50.41N 2.08W
Warendorf W. Germany **27** 51.57N 8.00E
Wark Forest *hills* England **15** 55.06N 2.24W
Warley England **8** 52.29N 2.02W
Warlingham England **7** 51.19N 0.04W
Warmbad S.W. Africa **48** 28.29S 18.41E
Warminster England **8** 51.12N 2.11W
Warren U.S.A. **56** 41.15N 80.49W
Warri Nigeria **44** 5.36N 5.46E
Warrington England **12** 53.25N 2.38W
Warsaw Poland **29** 52.15N 21.00E
Warsop England **13** 53.13N 1.08W
Warta *r.* Poland **29** 52.45N 15.09E
Warwick Australia **49** 28.12S 152.00E
Warwick England **8** 52.17N 1.36W
Warwickshire *d.* England **8** 52.13N 1.30W
Washington England **15** 54.55N 1.30W
Washington U.S.A. **57** 38.55N 77.00W
Washington *d.* U.S.A. **52** 47.00N 120.00W
Washington, Mt. U.S.A. **57** 44.17N 71.19W
Wasior Asia **39** 2.38S 134.27E
Wassy France **22** 48.30N 4.59E
Wast Water *l.* England **12** 54.25N 3.18W
Waswanipi L. Canada **57** 49.30N 76.20W
Watampone Indonesia **39** 4.33S 120.20E
Watchet England **11** 51.10N 3.20W
Waterbury U.S.A. **57** 41.33N 73.03W
Waterford Rep. of Ire. **19** 52.16N 7.08W
Waterford *d.* Rep. of Ire. **19** 52.10N 7.40W
Waterford Harbour *est.* Rep. of Ire. **19** 52.12N 6.56W
Watergate B. England **11** 50.28N 5.06W
Waterloo Belgium **27** 50.44N 4.24E
Waterloo Canada **56** 43.28N 80.32W
Waterloo U.S.A. **56** 42.30N 92.20W
Waterlooville England **8** 50.53N 1.02W
Watertown Wisc. U.S.A. **56** 43.12N 88.46W
Watertown N.Y. U.S.A. **57** 43.57N 75.56W
Watertown S.Dak. U.S.A **53** 44.54N 97.08W
Waterville Rep. of Ire. **19** 51.50N 10.11W
Waterville U.S.A. **57** 44.34N 69.41W
Watford England **7** 51.40N 0.25W
Watlington England **8** 51.38N 1.00W
Watson Lake *town* Canada **54** 60.07N 128.49W
Watten, Loch Scotland **17** 58.29N 3.20W
Watton England **9** 52.35N 0.50E
Wau P.N.G. **39** 7.22S 146.40E
Wau Sudan **45** 7.40N 28.04E
Waukegan U.S.A. **56** 42.21N 87.52W
Waukesha U.S.A. **56** 43.01N 88.14W
Wausau U.S.A. **56** 44.58N 89.40W
Waveney *r.* England **9** 52.29N 1.46E
Wavre Belgium **27** 50.43N 4.37E
Waxham England **9** 52.47N 1.38E
Waycross U.S.A. **53** 31.08N 82.22W
Wealdstone England **7** 51.36N 0.20W
Wear *r.* England **15** 54.55N 1.21W
Weardale *f.* England **15** 54.45N 2.05W
Weaver *r.* England **12** 53.19N 2.44W
Weda Indonesia **39** 0.30N 127.52E
Weddell Sea Antarctica **2** 73.00S 42.00W
Wedmore England **8** 51.14N 2.50W
Weert Neth. **27** 51.14N 5.40E
Weifang China **41** 36.44N 119.10E
Weihai China **41** 37.30N 122.04E
Weimar E. Germany **26** 50.59N 11.20E
Weirton U.S.A. **56** 40.24N 80.37W
Welhamgreen England **7** 51.44N 0.11W
Welkom R.S.A. **48** 27.59S 26.44E
Welland Canada **57** 45.59N 79.14W
Welland *r.* England **13** 52.53N 0.00
Welling England **7** 51.28N 0.08E
Wellingborough England **8** 52.18N 0.41W
Wellington Salop England **10** 52.42N 2.31W
Wellington Somerset England **11** 50.58N 3.13W
Wellington New Zealand **50** 41.17S 174.47E
Wellingtonbridge Rep. of Ire. **19** 52.16N 6.45W
Wellington I. Chile **63** 49.30S 75.00W
Wells England **8** 51.12N 2.39W
Wellsford New Zealand **50** 36.16S 174.32E
Wells-next-the-Sea England **13** 52.57N 0.51E
Welshpool Wales **10** 52.40N 3.09W
Welwyn England **7** 51.50N 0.13W
Welwyn Garden City England **7** 51.48N 0.13W
Wem England **12** 52.52N 2.45W
Wembere *r.* Tanzania **47** 4.07S 34.15E
Wembley England **7** 51.34N 0.18W
Wemyss Bay *town* Scotland **14** 55.52N 4.52W
Wenatchee U.S.A. **52** 47.26N 120.20W
Wenchow China **41** 28.02N 120.40E
Wendover England **7** 51.46N 0.46W
Wenlock Edge *hill* England **8** 52.33N 2.40W
Wenshan China **37** 23.25N 104.15E
Wensleydale *f.* England **12** 54.19N 2.04W
Wensum *r.* England **9** 52.37N 1.20E
Wepener R.S.A. **48** 29.44S 27.03E
Werne W. Germany **27** 51.39N 7.36E
Wesel W. Germany **27** 51.39N 6.37E
Weser *r.* W. Germany **26** 53.15N 8.30E
Wessel, C. Australia **49** 11.00S 136.58E
West Bridgford England **13** 52.56N 1.08W
West Bromwich England **8** 52.32N 2.01W
West Brother *i.* Hong Kong **33** 22.20N 113.57E
West Buffalo Hill Hong Kong **33** 22.22N 114.14E
West Burra *i.* Scotland **16** 60.05N 1.21W
Westbury England **8** 51.16N 2.11W
West Calder Scotland **15** 55.51N 3.34W
West Clandon England **7** 51.16N 0.30W
Westcott England **7** 51.13N 0.20W
Westerham England **7** 51.16N 0.05E
Western *d.* Kenya **47** 0.30N 34.30E
Western Australia *d.* Australia **49** 25.00S 123.00E
Western Cleddau *r.* Wales **11** 51.47N 4.56W
Western Cordillera *mts.* N. America **2** 46.00N 120.00W
Western Germany Europe **26** 51.00N 8.00E
Western Ghats *mts.* India **36** 15.30N 74.30E
Western Hajar *mts.* Oman **35** 24.00N 56.30E
Western Isles *d.* Scotland **16** 57.40N 7.10W
Western Sayan *mts.* U.S.S.R. **31** 53.00N 92.00E
Wester Ross *f.* Scotland **16** 57.37N 5.20W
Westerstede W. Germany **27** 53.15N 7.56E
Westerwald *f.* W. Germany **27** 50.40N 8.00E
West Felton England **10** 52.49N 2.58W
West Frisian Is. Neth. **27** 53.20N 5.00E
West Glamorgan *d.* Wales **11** 51.42N 3.47W
West Haddon England **8** 52.21N 1.05W
West Ham England **7** 51.32N 0.01E
West Hanningfield England **7** 51.41N 0.31E
West Horsley England **7** 51.17N 0.27W
West Indies C. America **59** 21.00N 74.00W
West Irian *d.* Indonesia **39** 4.00S 138.00E
West Kilbride Scotland **14** 55.42N 4.51W
West Kingsdown England **7** 51.21N 0.14E
West Kirby England **12** 53.22N 3.11W
West Lake *d.* Tanzania **47** 2.00S 31.20E
West Lamma Channel Hong Kong **33** 22.14N 114.05E
Westland Bight *b.* New Zealand **50** 43.30S 169.30E
West Linton Scotland **15** 55.45N 3.21W
West Loch Roag Scotland **16** 58.14N 6.53W
West Loch Tarbert Scotland **16** 57.55N 6.53W
West Malaysia *d.* Malaysia **38** 4.00N 102.00E
Westmeath *d.* Rep. of Ire. **18** 53.30N 7.30W
West Mersea England **9** 51.46N 0.55E
West Midlands *d.* England **8** 52.28N 1.50W
West Nicholson Rhodesia **48** 21.06S 29.25E
Weston Malaysia **38** 5.14N 115.35E
Weston-super-Mare England **8** 51.20N 2.59W
West Palm Beach *town* U.S.A. **53** 26.42N 80.05W
Westport New Zealand **50** 41.46S 171.38E
Westport Rep. of Ire. **18** 53.48N 9.32W
Westray *i.* Scotland **17** 59.18N 2.58W
Westray Firth *est.* Scotland **17** 59.13N 3.00W
West Schelde *est.* Neth. **27** 51.25N 3.40E
West Siberian Plain *f.* U.S.S.R. **30** 60.00N 75.00E
West Sussex *d.* England **9** 50.58N 0.30W
West Terschelling Neth. **27** 53.22N 5.13E
West Thurrock England **7** 51.29N 0.17E
West Virginia *d.* U.S.A. **53** 39.00N 80.30W
West Water *r.* Scotland **17** 56.47N 2.35W
West Wickham England **7** 51.22N 0.02W
West Wittering England **8** 50.42N 0.54W
West Yorkshire *d.* England **12** 53.45N 1.40W
Wetar *i.* Indonesia **39** 7.45S 126.00E
Wetheral England **15** 54.53N 2.50W
Wetherby England **13** 53.56N 1.23W
Wewak P.N.G. **39** 3.35S 143.35E
Wexford Rep. of Ire. **19** 52.20N 6.28W
Wexford *d.* Rep. of Ire. **19** 52.20N 6.25W
Wexford B. Rep. of Ire. **19** 52.27N 6.18W
Wey *r.* England **7** 51.23N 0.28W
Weybridge England **7** 51.23N 0.28W
Weyburn Canada **52** 49.39N 103.51W
Weymouth England **8** 50.36N 2.28W
Whakatane New Zealand **50** 37.56S 177.00E
Whale *r.* Canada **55** 58.00N 57.50W
Whaley Bridge *town* England **12** 53.20N 2.00W
Whalley England **12** 53.49N 2.25W
Whalsay *i.* Scotland **16** 60.22N 0.59W
Whangarei New Zealand **50** 35.43S 174.20E
Wharfe *r.* England **12** 53.50N 1.07W
Wharfedale *f.* England **12** 54.00N 1.55W
Wheathampstead England **7** 51.49N 0.17W
Wheeler Peak *mtn.* Nev. U.S.A. **52** 38.59N 114.29W
Wheeler Peak *mtn.* N. Mex. U.S.A. **52** 36.34N 105.25W
Wheeling U.S.A. **56** 40.05N 80.43W
Whernside *mtn.* England **12** 54.14N 2.25W
Whickham England **15** 54.57N 1.40W
Whipsnade England **7** 51.52N 0.33W
Whitburn Scotland **15** 55.52N 3.41W
Whitby England **13** 54.29N 0.37W
Whitchurch Bucks. England **8** 51.53N 0.51W
Whitchurch Hants. England **8** 51.14N 1.20W
Whitchurch Salop England **12** 52.58N 2.42W
White *r.* Ark. U.S.A. **53** 35.30N 91.20W
White *r.* Ind. U.S.A. **56** 38.25N 87.45W
White *r.* S. Dak. U.S.A. **52** 43.40N 99.30W
Whiteabbey N. Ireland **14** 54.42N 5.53W
Whiteadder Water *r.* Scotland **15** 55.46N 2.00W
White Coomb *mtn.* Scotland **15** 55.26N 3.20W
Whitefish Pt. U.S.A. **56** 46.46N 84.58W
Whitehaven England **12** 54.33N 3.35W
Whitehead N. Ireland **14** 54.45N 5.43W
Whitehorse Canada **54** 60.41N 135.08W
Whitehorse Hill England **8** 51.35N 1.35W
White Mountain Peak U.S.A. **52** 37.40N 118.15W
White Mts. U.S.A. **57** 44.15N 71.10W
Whiten Head Scotland **17** 58.34N 4.32W
White Nile *r.* Sudan **45** 15.45N 32.25E
White Parish England **8** 51.01N 1.39W
White Russia Soviet Socialist Republic *d.* U.S.S.R. **29** 53.30N 28.00E
Whitesand B. England **11** 50.20N 4.20W
White Sea U.S.S.R. **30** 65.30N 38.00E
White Volta *r.* Ghana **44** 9.13N 1.15W
Whithorn Scotland **14** 54.44N 4.25W
Whitland Wales **10** 51.49N 4.38W
Whitley Bay *town* England **15** 55.03N 1.25W
Whitney Canada **57** 45.29N 78.15W
Whitney, Mt. U.S.A. **52** 36.35N 118.17W
Whitstable England **9** 51.21N 1.02E
Whittington England **10** 52.53N 3.00W
Whittlesey England **9** 52.34N 0.08W
Whitton England **13** 53.42N 0.39W
Whitwell England **7** 51.53N 0.18W
Whyalla Australia **49** 33.04S 137.34E
Wiay *i.* Scotland **16** 57.24N 7.13W
Wichita U.S.A. **53** 37.43N 97.20W
Wichita Falls *town* U.S.A. **52** 33.55N 98.30W
Wick Scotland **17** 58.26N 3.06W
Wick *r.* Scotland **17** 58.26N 3.06W
Wickford England **7** 51.38N 0.31E
Wickham England **8** 50.54N 1.11W
Wickham Market England **9** 52.09N 1.21E
Wicklow Rep. of Ire. **19** 52.59N 6.03W
Wicklow *d.* Rep. of Ire. **19** 52.59N 6.25W
Wicklow Head Rep. of Ire. **19** 52.58N 6.00W
Wicklow Mts. Rep. of Ire. **19** 53.06N 6.20W
Wick of Gruting *b.* Scotland **16** 60.37N 0.49W
Widford England **7** 51.50N 0.04E
Widnes England **12** 53.22N 2.44W
Wien *see* Vienna Austria **26**
Wiener Neustadt Austria **26** 47.49N 16.15E
Wiesbaden W. Germany **26** 50.05N 8.15E
Wigan England **12** 53.33N 2.38W
Wight, Isle of England **8** 50.40N 1.17W
Wigmore England **7** 51.21N 0.36E
Wigston Magna England **8** 52.35N 1.06W
Wigton England **15** 54.50N 3.09W
Wigtown Scotland **14** 54.47N 4.26W
Wigtown B. Scotland **14** 54.47N 4.15W
Wilberfoss England **13** 53.57N 0.53W
Wildhorn *mtn.* Switz. **26** 46.22N 7.22E
Wildspitze *mtn.* Austria **26** 46.55N 10.55E
Wildwood U.S.A. **57** 38.59N 74.49W
Wilhelm, Mt. P.N.G. **39** 6.00S 144.55E
Wilhelmshaven W. Germany **27** 53.32N 8.07E
Wilkes-Barre U.S.A. **57** 41.15N 75.50W
Willemstad Neth. Antilles **59** 12.12N 68.56W
Willersley England **10** 52.07N 3.00W
Willesden England **7** 51.33N 0.14W
Williamsport U.S.A. **57** 41.16N 77.03W
Willington England **15** 54.43N 1.41W
Williston R.S.A. **48** 31.20S 20.52E
Williston U.S.A. **52** 48.09N 103.39W
Williton England **11** 51.09N 3.20W
Willmar U.S.A. **53** 45.06N 95.00W
Willowmore R.S.A. **48** 33.18S 23.30E
Wilmington Del. U.S.A. **57** 39.46N 75.31W
Wilmington N.C. U.S.A. **53** 34.14N 77.55W
Wilmslow England **12** 53.19N 2.14W
Wilrijk Belgium **27** 51.11N 4.25E
Wilson, Mt. U.S.A. **52** 37.51N 107.51W
Wilstone Resr. England **7** 51.48N 0.40W
Wilton England **8** 51.05N 1.52W
Wiltshire *d.* England **8** 51.20N 2.00W
Wimbledon England **7** 51.26N 0.12W
Wimbledon Park England **7** 51.26N 0.17W
Wimborne Minster England **8** 50.48N 2.00W
Winburg R.S.A. **48** 28.31S 27.01E
Wincanton England **8** 51.03N 2.24W
Winchester England **8** 51.04N 1.19W
Windermere England **12** 54.24N 2.56W
Windermere *l.* England **12** 54.20N 2.56W
Windhoek S.W. Africa **48** 22.34S 17.06E
Windlesham England **7** 51.22N 0.39W
Windrush *r.* England **8** 51.42N 1.25W
Windsor Canada **56** 42.18N 83.00W
Windsor England **7** 51.29N 0.38W
Windsor Great Park *f.* England **7** 51.27N 0.37W
Windward Is. C. America **59** 13.00N 60.00W
Windward Passage *str.* Carib. Sea **59** 20.00N 74.00W
Wingate England **15** 54.44N 1.23W
Wingrave England **7** 51.52N 0.44W
Winisk *r.* Canada **55** 55.20N 85.20W
Winkleigh England **11** 50.49N 3.57W
Winnebago, L. U.S.A. **56** 44.00N 88.25W
Winnipeg Canada **53** 49.59N 97.10W
Winnipeg, L. Canada **55** 52.45N 98.00W
Winnipegosis, L. Canada **52** 52.00N 100.00W
Winnipesaukee, L. U.S.A. **57** 43.40N 71.20W
Winona U.S.A. **56** 44.02N 91.37W
Winschoten Neth. **27** 53.07N 7.02E
Winscombe England **8** 51.19N 2.50W
Winsford England **12** 53.12N 2.31W